Did you know that...?

- 100% of College Students are internet users
- 50% are online more than 6 hours every week
- Community College Students are even more likely than those at 4 year institutions to use mobile devices
- 71% of student would prefer to use digital learning materials over print

Zou, J.J. (2011, July 19). Gadgets, study finds. *Chronicle of Higher Education*

Challenge:

6 of 10 college language programs either have completed or are planning to complete an Introductory Spanish Course Redesign, which will likely result in less face-to-face class time and greater numbers of hybrid or fully online classes.

Solution:

- Pearson Education is the undisputed leader in Higher Education Course Redesign.
- Pearson is an **experienced partner** with over 1150 faculty selecting Pearson to implement a Course Redesign.
- **Evidence-based ongoing Case Studies and Success Stories** demonstrate improved student performance in Course Redesigns that implemented **MyLanguageLabs**.
- **MyLanguageLabs** offers the most extensive opportunities for course personalization that enables instructors to modify instruction according to individual needs, teaching style, grading philosophies, and more, which results in a more **engaging experience** for students.

Redesigning courses around MyLanguageLabs has been a success. The curriculum and course requirements are uniform across all sections so students receive a consistent learning experience. Because MyLanguageLabs automates the grading process, instructors report that they have more time to offer students one-on-one assistance. When I examine the data from before and after MyLanguageLabs it is clear to me what a great success MyLanguageLabs is and how useful it is for our students.

—Jason Fetters, Purdue University

MyLanguageLabs
in Action:
Proven Performance

ALWAYS LEARNING · PEARSON

A GUIDE TO UNIDOS ICONS

 Readiness Check
This icon, located at the beginning of the first *Gramática en contexto* section online, reminds students to take the Readiness Check to test their understanding of the English grammar related to the Spanish grammar concepts in the chapter.

 Answers for *Piénsalo*
This icon accompanies the *Piénsalo* activities. Students click on the icon to get answers.

Online

 Text Audio Program
This icon indicates that recorded material to accompany *Unidos* is available online. In addition, audio for all in-class listening activities and *En directo* dialogues is available on CD.

 Pair Activity
This icon indicates that the activity is designed to be done by students working in pairs.

 Group Activity
This icon indicates that the activity is designed to be done by students working in small groups or as a whole class.

Classroom Manual

 Interactive Globe
This icon indicates that additional cultural resources in the form of videos, web links, interactive maps, and more, relating to a particular country, are organized on an interactive globe online.

Art Tour
This icon accompanies the works of art highlighted in each chapter opener. It links to a virtual art tour and interactive activity about the work of art.

 MediaShare
This icon, presented with all *Situaciones* activities, refers to the video-posting feature available online.

UNIDOS

An Interactive Approach

Annotated Instructor's Edition

ELIZABETH E. GUZMÁN

University of Iowa

PALOMA LAPUERTA

Central Connecticut State University

JUDITH E. LISKIN-GASPARRO

University of Iowa

Boston   Columbus   Indianapolis   New York   San Francisco   Upper Saddle River
Amsterdam   Cape Town   Dubai   London   Madrid   Milan   Munich   Paris   Montréal   Toronto
Delhi   Mexico City   São Paulo   Sydney   Hong Kong   Seoul   Singapore   Taipei   Tokyo

Executive Editor, Content Creation and Development:
   Julia Caballero
Senior Acquisitions Editor: Tiziana Aime
Senior Digital Product Manager: Samantha Alducin
Development Editor: Celia Meana
Development Editor: Meriel Martínez
Digital Product Managers: María Felicidad García, Bill Bliss
Media Coordinator: Regina Rivera
Senior Production Project Manager: Nancy Stevenson
Project Manager: Melissa Sacco, PreMediaGlobal
Senior Art Director: Maria Lange
Operations Manager: Mary Fischer
Operations Specialist: Alan Fischer
Editorial Assistant: Jonathan Ortiz
Editorial Assistant: Andrew Culbreth
Editorial Intern: Patricia Wu

For Pearson World Languages
Senior Vice President: Steve Debow
Editor in Chief: Bob Hemmer
Director of Market Development: Kristine Suárez
Senior Marketing Manager: Denise Miller
Marketing Associate: Benjamin Zachs
Marketing Assistant: Millie Chapman
Customer Experience Program Manager: Mary Reynolds
Director of Program Management: Lisa Iarkowski
Director of Project Management: Paula Soloway
Senior Managing Editor: Mary Rottino
Associate Managing Editor: Janice Stangel
World Languages Consultants: Yesha Brill, Silvana Falconi, Jessica
   Garcia, Amy Hughes Maxwell, Mellissa Yokell

This book was set in Serifa Std 45 Light 10/12.

Credits and acknowledgments borrowed from other sources and reproduced, with permission, in this textbook appear on appropriate page within text (or on page A-31).

10 9 8 7 6 5 4 3 2 1

Student Edition, ISBN-10:   0-205-95033-7
Student Edition, ISBN-13:   978-0-205-95033-1
Annotated Instructor's Edition, ISBN-10:   0-205-95046-9
Annotated Instructor's Edition, ISBN-13: 978-0-205-95046-1

■

For her vision, ingenuity, and dedication to this project, we thank Julia Caballero,

Executive Editor for Content Creation and Development, and her team.

■

BRIEF CONTENTS

Unidos, powered by the award-winning MySpanishLab™, effectively **prepares your students to communicate with confidence.** *It's time to talk!*

Instructors and coordinators of Elementary Spanish tell us in survey after survey that their primary goal is to increase the communicative nature of their classrooms and their courses. For many reasons, creating a communicative course is also a challenge for instructors. There's so little time to talk! With a unique online environment that offers a guided approach to instruction and practice, **Unidos** prepares students to come to class and communicate with confidence. The Classroom Manual offers a wide variety of communicative activities for students to put into practice the skills they learned in the online component.

At the heart of the **Unidos** program are the carefully sequenced online learning modules. These offer guided instruction and practice accompanied by individualized learning support and assessment to ensure students master concepts and come to class ready to communicate.

▼

Vocabulario en contexto 03: Las diversiones LEARNING MODULE

Vocabulario en contexto 03: Los planes LEARNING MODULE

Vocabulario en contexto 03: La comida LEARNING MODULE

READINESS CHECK

Gramática en contexto 03: Present tense of hacer, poner, salir, traer.

Gramática en contexto 03: Present tense of ir and ir + a infinitive LEA

Gramática en contexto 03: Numbers 100 to 2,000,000 LEARNING MODU

Students follow a guided lesson plan that begins with an interactive presentation and continues with tutorials and adaptive lessons, and culminates in a set of *Apply* activities. The *Apply* section offers both machine-gradable, discrete-point activities, and more complex instructor-graded activities in which the students write sentences or paragraphs or verbally record their responses. Students have multiple opportunities to practice, and a wealth of individualized, point-of-need support.

▼

☐ Interactive Presentation 03-01: Las diversiones
Viewed

☐ Vocabulary Tutorial 03: Las diversiones A
Viewed ⏰ Due: Due on 6/10/2012 at 11:59:00 PM

☐ Vocabulary Tutorials 03: Las diversiones B
Not viewed

☐ Apply 03-01 Diversiones.
Started

☐ Apply 03-02 ¿Dónde?
Started

☐ Apply 03-03 Las rutinas.

The activities in the Classroom Manual, which are intended to be completed in class, build on the learning that takes place out of class and foster a highly engaging and effective social environment in which participants achieve meaningful communication and interaction.

▼

" I like the idea of individualized online learning and assessment and freeing time for more communication activities so students can **'use' the language more and not just 'talk' about it**… The student is given ample activities to practice vocabulary, grammar, and learn about Hispanic culture. "

LUIS LATOJA
Columbus State Community College

"Unidos is a truly comprehensive program that best integrates the technology-supported online practices with in-class communicative and theme-based activities with culture-rich content to **develop students' abilities to communicate in the target language. "**

AN CHUNG CHENG
University of Toledo

Vocabulario en contexto

LEARN Read the following conversation between Liliana and Manuel at a restaurant. **What do you like to have for dinner?** Click on the highlighted words to see images that will help you learn the vocabulary.

La comida

En el restaurante. Ahora Liliana y Manuel están en el restaurante El Jardín Limeño para **celebrar** el cumpleaños de Liliana. Hablan con el **camarero.**

CAMARERO: Buenas noches. ¿Qué desean los señores?

MANUEL: Liliana, ¿qué vas a comer?

LILIANA: Para mí, primero una **ensalada** y después **pollo** con

Unidos, powered by MySpanishLab, gives you the flexibility and powerful tools to easily manage your course.

Instructors are faced with more demands for their time and expertise than ever before. They want a better way to manage all aspects of their courses and an online program that saves them time, not one that takes more time. The **Unidos** online component offers the most powerful instructor tools to help instructors efficiently manage their courses.

By completing open-ended activities in which they write sentences or paragraphs, students demonstrate that they understand how to use the language. Instructors want to ensure that comments they entered while grading open-ended activities are reviewed by their students. The student dashboard alerts students when they have comments from their instructor and they can easily review to assimilate corrections and suggestions.

To make assigning easier than ever, the online component offers a **drag-and-drop Assignment Calendar.** Instructors simply choose what they would like to assign to any given day, check the box, and drag it to the due date. They can choose one or multiple items, making course creation quick and easy.

Instructors tell us in that they want a flexible program that allows them to grade as if they were grading by hand. The intuitive grading palette in the online component gives instructors a host of options to **efficiently grade open-ended activities,** and the preferences in the online component offer a **wealth of customization options for grading student work.** Instructors concerned with students using accent marks properly can set the percentage that the system deducts from the student grade if accent marks are used incorrectly. The online component also offers a Grace Period preference that allows instructors to set automatic deductions for late work. Preferences in the online component give instructors tools to tailor the course to individual teaching styles.

> MySpanishLab is the most robust and dependable program I have ever used with my introductory courses. The program can be **completely tailored to your course needs and teaching style** as well as to your colleagues' different needs/styles. With regard to learning, students are completely and clearly in control of their success and progress with the program. **99**
>
> **KRISTY BRITT**
> *University of South Alabama*

66 MySpanishLab provides a consistent teaching environment throughout all sections of a course and **makes it easy to manage changes and updates in one central location.** With over 3,000 students enrolled in first-year Spanish classes, it is vital that we provide the same learning experience to all, and MySpanishLab helps us accomplish this. **99**

MÓNICA MONTALVO
University of Central Florida

The individualized support of the online component to Unidos maximizes learning by students at all skill levels.

Students studying Spanish for the first time are often sitting next to students who have taken Spanish in high school or students who speak Spanish at home. With its array of adaptive learning tools and individualized tutorials, the online component for **Unidos** tailors learning to every student's individual needs and provides the support they need to come to class prepared to engage and to communicate.

Apply activities promote student success by providing **students with the immediate support they need to understand** why they may not have been successful when completing a machine-graded activity. If a response is incorrect, students receive feedback hints that help them think critically. With the student's second attempt, a "Need help with this activity?" feature appears that **brings additional resources specific to the activity directly to the student.** Resources include links to the exact page in the Interactive Presentations where the activity topic is explained, as well as tutorials and additional practice exercises. **Each question becomes a true learning opportunity** via this layered feedback, and students are better prepared for the in-class communicative environment!

By understanding English grammar, students can more quickly grasp concepts in Spanish grammar. Not all students have a strong grasp of English grammar, but explaining it in class takes time away from using the target language. Online, students complete a **Readiness Check that tests whether they understand the English grammar** that correlates with the Spanish grammar that they will learn in the chapter. If the Readiness Check results indicate that students need help with a specific topic, an **individual study plan is generated, linking students to animated English grammar tutorials** for the instruction they need.

Since language learning is a process that builds upon previous knowledge, students need support to help them retain the information. *amplifire™* adaptive vocabulary and grammar lessons in the online component are based on the latest research in neuroscience on how we learn best. The unique "game-like" application makes learning fun and effective. Students can quickly ascertain what they know, what they aren't sure of, and what they need to review in-depth. *amplifire's* patented methodology **helps students increase their long-term retention and master concepts before coming to class.** The results lead to class time focused on using the language instead of taking time for instruction of vocabulary and grammar.

> " The benefits are tremendous. **It caters to all learning styles.** No student would be left out. Students will be able to take advantage in their learning through this approach. "
>
> **FRANCES ALPREN**
> *Vanderbilt University*

> " The interactive nature of the exercises makes the learning experience outside the classroom **more individualized,** more interesting, and, therefore, **more effective.** "
>
> **LEA RAMSDELL**
> *Towson University*

The **consistent, explicit focus on learning objectives** in Unidos will help you **achieve consistent learning outcomes** across all course models.

Spanish classes take many forms now: fully online, hybrid, and face-to-face. Achieving consistent learning outcomes for all these models is increasingly difficult. Instructors want their students in an online course to have the same skills as their face-to-face or hybrid students at the end of the course. The **Unidos** program reinforces learning objectives and gives instructors the tools to prove outcomes are achieved.

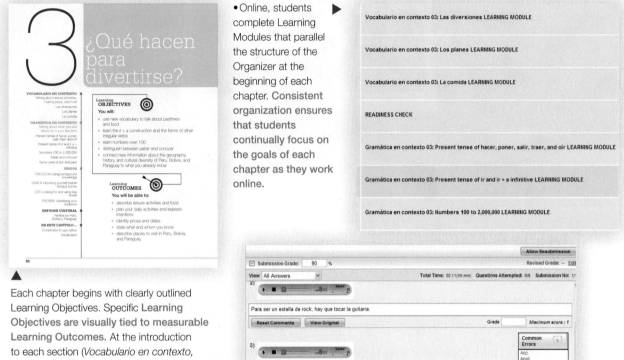

- Online, students complete Learning Modules that parallel the structure of the Organizer at the beginning of each chapter. **Consistent organization ensures that students continually focus on the goals of each chapter as they work online.**

Each chapter begins with clearly outlined Learning Objectives. Specific **Learning Objectives are visually tied to measurable Learning Outcomes.** At the introduction to each section (*Vocabulario en contexto*, *Gramática en contexto*, *Enfoque cultural*), each Learning Objective is repeated to remind students what they will be able to achieve at the end of the section.

> "This is a GREAT part of the chapter. It isn't in the margin. It isn't an aside. It is front and center, and clearly stated: **here is what you'll be doing and this is how you will know if you 'got it.'**"
>
> **ELIZABETH CALVERA**
> *Virginia Tech University*

> "I like that there is a distinction between objectives, which are what a student will 'learn' with his or her brain as they memorize vocabulary and grammar points, **but the outcomes describe the meaningful contexts in which the student can actually 'acquire'** the ability to communicate without thinking through the various grammar points and vocabulary."
>
> **JANIE MCNUTT**
> *Texas Tech University*

▲ The Unidos instructor online dashboard offers at-a-glance views of class performance for each Learning Module. The Course Performance functionality quickly shows instructors how students are progressing with each learning objective. Instructors can tailor their face-to-face time based on student results and can assess whether or not students are achieving the desired learning outcomes for the course.

Unidos is a first. Incorporating the **flip teaching model** into its highly flexible approach, it capitalizes on using technology so that valuable class time is focused on applying knowledge rather than on instruction—it literally flips the nature of what typically takes place in class and out of class. Instead of first learning in the classroom and then practicing learned material out of class, students will, with **Unidos**, learn outside of class and then apply what they have learned in the communicative environment of the classroom.

Without question, instructors and coordinators of Elementary Spanish tell us that their number one goal is to increase the communicative nature of their classrooms and their courses. They also describe this among their greatest challenges. Limited contact hours, increasing class size, and varied levels of student preparedness make it difficult for students to learn vocabulary, grammar, and culture in class. At the same time, instructors want ample time for students to communicate. In short, there's little time to talk!

The creators of **Unidos** seek to embrace the goal and confront the challenge of increasing the communicative nature of the Elementary Spanish course head-on. This innovative communicative language program offers a unique online environment where students receive guided instruction and practice accompanied by individualized learning support and assessment. Students encounter continuous formative and summative assessment opportunities, all of which

prepares them for communicative practice in the classroom. **Unidos** frees the classroom to be what instructors and students have always wanted it to be: a space for social interaction—in Spanish.

Whether learning in a face-to-face traditional classroom or in a hybrid program where, by necessity, significant learning must take place outside the classroom, **Unidos** offers an array of resources to help instructors and students achieve their goals.

CHAPTER ORGANIZATION
HOW THE UNIDOS PROGRAM WORKS

Through its highly articulated and individualized **online learning and assessment system, Unidos** meets students at their point of need. Its personalized learning and practice modules provide learners with continuous formative and cumulative assessment opportunities. The activities in the **Classroom Manual** build on the learning that takes place outside of class and make for a highly engaging and effective social environment in which participants achieve meaningful communication and interaction.

Unidos provides a seamless integration of out-of-class work and in-class communication. Here we show you how the pieces fit together.

Unidos *gives you the time to create a truly communicative classroom—It's time to talk!*

Sequential Walkthrough of Chapter 3
Unidos Online Component
Unidos Classroom Manual

 CHAPTER OPENING ORGANIZER ▶

Prepares students visually with clear goals for the chapter. Specific Learning Objectives are tied to measurable Learning Outcomes. For example, the learning objective "distinguish between **saber** and **conocer**" is expected to result in students' ability to "state what and whom they know (the outcome)."

Both the online component and the Classroom Manual use consistent language to describe learning objectives and outcomes so that the goals of every chapter are clear and accessible to students.

Reporting features in the online component provide instructors with at-a-glance views of student performance for each learning objective.

3 ¿Qué hacen para divertirse?

VOCABULARIO EN CONTEXTO
Talking about leisure activities, making plans, and food
Las diversiones
Los planes
La comida

GRAMÁTICA EN CONTEXTO
Talking about what you and others do in your free time
Present tense of *hacer, poner, salir, traer,* and *oir*
Present tense of *ir* and *ir a + infinitive*
Numbers 100 to 2,000,000
Saber and *conocer*
Some uses of *por* and *para*

UNIDOS
ESCUCHA Using background knowledge
HABLA Informing yourself before doing a survey
LEE Looking for and using key words
ESCRIBE Identifying your audience

ENFOQUE CULTURAL
Perfiles de Perú, Bolivia y Paraguay

EN ESTE CAPÍTULO...
Comprueba lo que sabes
Vocabulario

Learning **OBJECTIVES**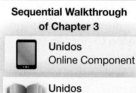

You will:

- use new vocabulary to talk about pastimes and food
- learn the *ir + a* construction and the forms of other irregular verbs
- learn numbers over 100
- distinguish between *saber* and *conocer*
- connect new information about the geography, history, and cultural diversity of Peru, Bolivia, and Paraguay to what you already know

Learning **OUTCOMES**

You will be able to:

- describe leisure activities and food
- plan your daily activities and express intentions
- identify prices and dates
- state what and whom you know
- describe places to visit in Peru, Bolivia, and Paraguay

82

CULTURE

Unidos fosters awareness of the diversity of the Spanish-speaking world by deeply integrating culture throughout the entire program.

 CULTURA EN LÍNEA

Experience online interactive introductions to the cultural theme and countries of focus through videos, art, and an array of resources in the *Cultura en línea.* These can be assigned either before class or after completing the in-class *Cultura interactiva* sections.

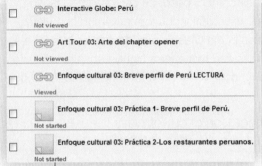

		Interactive Globe: Perú
☐	🔗	Not viewed
☐	🔗	Art Tour 03: Arte del chapter opener
		Not viewed
☐	🔗	Enfoque cultural 03: Breve perfil de Perú LECTURA
		Viewed
☐		Enfoque cultural 03: Práctica 1- Breve perfil de Perú.
		Not started
☐		Enfoque cultural 03: Práctica 2-Los restaurantes peruanos.
		Not started

Vistas culturales videos present cultural artifacts of the country or countries of focus. With native speakers from each country providing the narration for each clip, students are introduced to the variations of the Spanish language throughout the Hispanic world.

Art of the Hispanic world comes to life through interactive Art Tours. These tours, featuring Spanish narrations, offer an in-depth look at key works of art, enabling students to zoom in on details they couldn't otherwise see.

 **CULTURA INTERACTIVA**

The *Cultura interactiva* activity provides an immediate orientation to the target culture(s) of the chapter. As many students have insufficient prior knowledge about the countries of the Hispanic world (including their location), **Unidos** includes a map with visual clues about important cultural aspects of each country.

A warm-up activity activates background knowledge and prepares students to learn more about the culture(s) throughout the chapter.

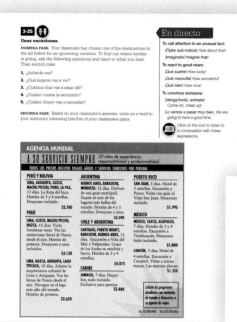

INTEGRATED CULTURE

Culture is **integrated throughout the chapter in rich realia pieces, photos, activities, and maps**. The first *Cultura* box in Chapter 3 highlights the unique regional cuisine in Peru, Bolivia, and Paraguay. Other boxes describe cultural products, practices, and perspectives, making the cultural contexts of the vocabulary and grammar activities meaningful and accessible to students.

Cultura

Fast food (*La comida rápida*) is popular among young Hispanics, and American-style hamburger places may be found in Hispanic countries. They often adapt to local tastes, and it is not unusual to have hamburgers served with rice and black beans instead of fries. Beer and wine may also be sold in addition to soft drinks.

Compara: Do you know of any fast food places in your community that are not American style? What types of foods do they serve?

90   Capítulo 3

VOCABULARY

Vocabulary is presented in communicative and cultural contexts to help students truly learn how to use words in oral and written communication.

VOCABULARIO EN CONTEXTO

Study begins with the *Vocabulario en contexto* section in the **Unidos** online component. **Vocabulary instruction and mechanical practice are completed online, freeing up valuable class time for communication.** All learning is divided into a series of carefully sequenced learning modules. Each module contains two components: *Learn* and *Apply*. Students complete each learning module before coming to class and are guided throughout the process with point-of-need support.

La comida

Go to the *Capítulo 3* folder online to complete the Learning Module for *Vocabulario en contexto: La comida*.

PLAN DE ESTUDIO

LEARN
- Interactive presentation: *La comida*
- Vocabulary tutorials
- *Entrevistas* video

APPLY
- Activities
- *Entrevistas* video activities

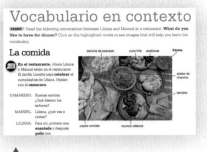

Vocabulario en contexto

LEARN ▶ Read the following conversation between Liliana and Manuel at a restaurant. **What do you like to have for dinner?** Click on the highlighted words to see images that will help you learn the vocabulary.

La comida

En el restaurante. Ahora Liliana y Manuel están en el restaurante El Jardín Limeño para **celebrar** el cumpleaños de Liliana. Hablan con el **camarero**.

CAMARERO: Buenas noches. ¿Qué desean los señores?

MANUEL: Liliana, ¿qué vas a comer?

LILIANA: Para mí, primero una **ensalada** y después **pollo** con

▲

STEP 1 Interactive Presentation.

The interactive presentation introduces new words in appropriate linguistic and cultural contexts. Language samples, photos, line drawings, and realia present new materials, rather than word lists and translations. Boldface type highlights new words and phrases that students will use actively. Clickable audio offers recorded versions of the language samples.

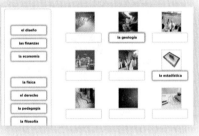

▲

STEP 2 Tutorials.

With the guided vocabulary tutorials, **students work through a series of word recognition activities that help them tie words to images.** Each tutorial culminates with a pronunciation activity where students compare their pronunciation to that of a native speaker.

APPLY 03-08 La comida

You are thinking about going out to dinner and the food you might like to order. Complete the sentences with the most appropriate words from the word bank. Be sure not to repeat any answers.

cerveza   helado   refresco   vino
ensalada   pollo   té

1) Una buena cena incluye el _____ y los vegetales.

2) El _____ es una bebida caliente que me fascina.

STEP 3 Application Activities.

Students put new vocabulary to use with the *Apply* activities. Both machine-gradable, discrete-point activities and more complex instructor-graded activities appear in the activity set. Students have multiple opportunities to respond and a wealth of individualized, point-of-need support. Machine-graded *Apply* activities offer **layered feedback to help students successfully complete the activity**:

- In the first attempt, the **Resource Toolbar** within the activity window offers several help options: the full array of vocabulary and grammar tutorials, a glossary, verb charts, and the full eText (with both interactive presentations and a digital version of the Classroom Manual).

- After the first attempt, **critical thinking hints** appear for answers that are incorrect. Hints help students think about what they got wrong instead of showing them the correct answer. Students can then try again.

  Your Score 83.33%
  1) Una buena cena incluye el ✗ cerveza 💬 y los vegetales.
  Score: 0 out of 1
  Feedback: This is a kind of poultry

- With the second attempt, the **"Need help with this activity?"** button offers help based on the vocabulary the student is practicing. Links to the exact section of the interactive presentation where the vocabulary is presented and links to the vocabulary tutorials are listed to provide point-of-need support.

  Need help with this activity? Click the following links.
  eBook
  Extra Practice 03-02: La comida
  Vocabulario

- As a default, students see the **correct answer** after the third attempt, but instructors can easily decide and change when students see the correct answers. Students can easily review activities from their student dashboard.

  3) Un postre delicioso es el ✗ pollo 💬.
  Score: 0 out of 1
  Correct Answer: helado
  Feedback: This is frozen dessert.

Entrevistas **video.** After the final vocabulary chunk in each chapter, the *Entrevistas* video and accompanying assessment activities **further model vocabulary in context** and introduce students to the thematic content of the chapter through a series of authentic interviews.

VOCABULARIO EN CONTEXTO (PRÁCTICA COMUNICATIVA)

It's time to talk!

Students are ready to communicate. The *Práctica comunicativa* activities foster active use of new and previously learned vocabulary in natural, thematically relevant contexts.

In this example, students recycle vocabulary within a cultural context and are asked to plan a trip to Machu Picchu and to pack a lunch for the trip. All activities in the **Classroom Manual** move from controlled to open-ended production.

3-13

Un viaje (*trip*). You and your partner are in Peru and are planning a day trip to Machu Picchu. Arrange to take some food and beverages with you.

1. Make a list of the food and beverages that you need to take.

2. Talk in detail about at least five activities that you are going to do.

GRAMMAR

Grammar is presented as a means to effective communication. Students focus on the functions, not just the structures, they will need to express themselves in Spanish.

GRAMÁTICA EN CONTEXTO

Similar to the *Vocabulario en contexto* modules, the *Gramática en contexto* modules make it possible for students to learn and master grammatical concepts out of class and come to class ready to communicate.

Stating what you know:
Saber and *conocer*

Go to the *Capítulo 3* [folder] online to complete the Learning Module for *Gramática en contexto: Saber* and *conocer*

PLAN DE ESTUDIO

◉ LEARN
- Interactive presentation: *Saber* and *conocer*
- Grammar tutorials

APPLY ◉
- Activities
- Extra Practice

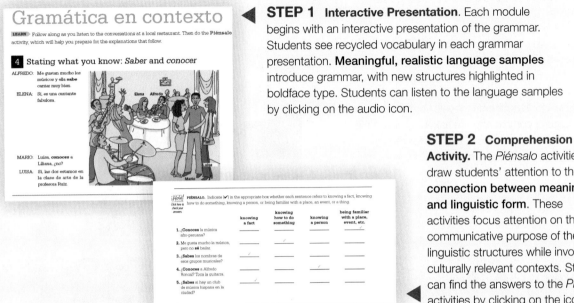

Gramática en contexto

LEARN Follow along as you listen to the conversations at a local restaurant. Then do the **Piénsalo** activity, which will help you prepare for the explanations that follow.

4 Stating what you know: *Saber* and *conocer*

ALFREDO: Me gustan mucho los músicos y ella **sabe** cantar muy bien.

ELENA: Sí, es una cantante fabulosa.

MARIO: Luisa, **conoces** a Liliana, ¿no?

LUISA: Sí, las dos estamos en la clase de arte de la profesora Ruiz.

PIÉNSALO. Indicate (✔) in the appropriate box whether each sentence refers to knowing a fact, knowing how to do something, knowing a person, or being familiar with a place, an event, or a thing.

	knowing a fact	knowing how to do something	knowing a person	being familiar with a place, event, etc.
1. ¿**Conoces** la música afro-peruana?				
2. Me gusta mucho la música, pero no **sé** bailar.		✔		
3. ¿**Sabes** los nombres de esos grupos musicales?	✔			
4. ¿**Conoces** a Alfredo Roncal? Toca la guitarra.			✔	
5. ¿**Sabes** si hay un club de música hispana en la ciudad?	✔			

Both **saber** and **conocer** mean *to know*, but they are not used interchangeably.

	SABER	CONOCER
yo	**sé**	conozco
tú	**sabes**	conoces
Ud., él, ella	**sabe**	conoce
nosotros/as	**sabemos**	conocemos
vosotros/as	**sabéis**	conocéis
Uds., ellos/as	**saben**	conocen

Use **saber** to express knowledge of facts or pieces of information.

Él **sabe** dónde está el club. *He knows where the club is.*

Use **saber** + *infinitive* to express knowing how to do something.

Yo **sé** tocar la guitarra. *I know how to play the guitar.*

Use **conocer** to express familiarity with someone or something. **Conocer** also means *to meet*. Remember to use the *personal* **a** when referring to people.

Conozco a los músicos. *I know the musicians.*
Conozco bien ese club. *I am very familiar with that club.*
Ella va a **conocer a** Luis. *She is going to meet (be introduced to) Luis.*

APPLY Now you are ready to move on to the next *Learn* or *Apply* Learning Module in the Online Component.

LENGUA **Sé**, the *yo* form of the verb **saber**, has a written accent to distinguish it from the pronoun **se**.

Yo que sé automáticamente **se** llama José.

Saber and Conocer   Spanish Tutorial

Saber and Conocer
- mean "to know"
- used in different contexts

Saber
- to know a fact
- to know a language
- to know information

¿Sabes cuánto cuesta?
information

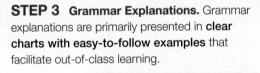

Apply 07-11 tú menú de la música. (Saber y conocer)

Rosario and her friends are very talented and would like to start a rock band. Complete the paragraph using the correct forms of **saber** or **conocer**.

Todos mis amigos y yo tenemos muchos ____ hacer muchas cosas. Fernando ____ tocar el piano, mi amigo ____ ____ tocar la guitarra, Sara (4) ____ tocar la batería (drums), y nuestros amigos Mario y Teresa (5) ____ cantar (to sing) muy bien. Nosotros queremos tener un grupo de música rock. ¿Quieres ser parte de nuestro grupo? ¿(6) ____ tú tocar el bajo (bass guitar)? Nosotros tenemos gustos (tastes) musicales muy diversos y eso puede ser muy interesante para nuestro grupo Yo (7) ____ mucha música latina. Pablo y Teresa (8) ____ mucha música jazz y Mario (9) ____ mucha música rock de los años setenta. Susana trabaja para una compañía discográfica y por eso, (10) ____ a muchos agentes que nos pueden ayudar.

STEP 1 **Interactive Presentation**. Each module begins with an interactive presentation of the grammar. Students see recycled vocabulary in each grammar presentation. **Meaningful, realistic language samples** introduce grammar, with new structures highlighted in boldface type. Students can listen to the language samples by clicking on the audio icon.

STEP 2 **Comprehension Activity.** The *Piénsalo* activities draw students' attention to the **connection between meaning and linguistic form**. These activities focus attention on the communicative purpose of the linguistic structures while invoking culturally relevant contexts. Students can find the answers to the *Piénsalo* activities by clicking on the icon.

STEP 3 **Grammar Explanations.** Grammar explanations are primarily presented in **clear charts with easy-to-follow examples** that facilitate out-of-class learning.

STEP 4 **Tutorials.** The interactive grammar tutorials offer **narrated explanations and illustrated examples to help students further comprehend the concepts** they are learning.

STEP 5 **Application Activities.** The *Apply* section offers a series of machine-gradable and open-ended practice activities that prepare students for communicating in class. Students receive the valuable point-of-need support within the online component as they did with vocabulary. (See pg. xii to review the focused, multilayered support for students.)

GRAMÁTICA EN CONTEXTO

It's time to talk!
Having ample opportunities to learn, apply, and practice new grammar structures online, out of class, students complete a series of engaging *Práctica comunicativa* exercises. **Activities require students to process meaning as well as form so that they develop confidence in speaking** and skill in using their linguistic knowledge to gather information, answer questions, and resolve problems. ▶

3-27

¿Sabes quién es...? Ask your classmate if he/she knows who is being referred to and say what you know about the person. Take turns asking questions.

Modelo

❝ la actriz principal de *Los juegos del hambre* ❞

¿Sabes quién es la actriz principal de *Los juegos del hambre*?

Sí, sé quién es; es Jennifer Lawrence.

¿Conoces a Jennifer Lawrence en persona?

No, no conozco a Jennifer Lawrence pero sé que es muy guapa.

1. el/la representante de la Cámara de Representantes (*Congress*) de tu distrito
2. el decano/la decana de la Facultad de Humanidades/Ciencias
3. tu profesor/a de español
4. el rey de España
5. el gobernador de tu estado
6. el vicepresidente de Estados Unidos

Situaciones

1

ROLE A. Make a list of five people whom you think your partner knows personally. Choose three of them and ask: a) if your partner knows them and b) what your partner knows about each one of them. Be ready to answer similar questions.

ROLE B. Make a list of five people whom you think your partner knows personally. Your partner will tell you the names of three people on his/her list and will ask: a) if you know each one of them and b) what you know about them. Answer and then ask your partner the same questions about three of the people on your list.

2

ROLE A. You are looking for a third roommate for your apartment. Your partner knows a student from Bolivia who is looking for a place to live. Ask your partner: a) the Peruvian student's name; b) where in Peru he/she is from; and c) if your partner knows the Peruvian student well. Also find out if the Peruvian student knows how to cook Peruvian dishes and how to play soccer (**fútbol**).

ROLE B. Your partner is looking for a third roommate for his/her apartment. Mention that you know a student from Peru who is looking for a place to live. Answer your partner's questions about that person.

◀ *Situaciones* are cumulative activities that prompt students to integrate relevant grammatical structures within contexts drawn from the chapter theme. These role-plays offer students an exciting way to **put together everything they've learned in realistic contexts**.

When assigned online instead of in class, students can use the MediaShare tool within the **Unidos** online component to **post videos of the role-plays** completed with a partner. Instructors can choose to have other class members review and grade the assignments, or review them on their own.

SKILLS DEVELOPMENT

The **Unidos** skills development section provides students with a unique opportunity to bring together the chapter's thematic content and vocabulary with its linguistic structures and cultural focus.

UNIDOS

Each *Unidos* section begins with *Escucha*, followed by *Habla, Lee*, and *Escribe* sections. **Specific strategies are presented for each of the four skills**. The strategies build on each other within and across chapters. Activities are designed so that students **systematically** practice implementing the strategies presented.

Escribe (and the other skills) begins with *Preparación,* which **introduces the writing topic and a offers series of steps to prepare.** In this example, students are writing an e-mail about their vacation.

A series of pre- and post-writing activities guide students through the critical steps in the writing process. In *Escribe,* students will actually write their e-mail. Before they write, students can listen to the *En directo* colloquial expressions in context. Following the listening step, students will write their email. A quick check, *Comprueba,* ensures they have covered the important points with accuracy.

In the last step, *Un paso más,* students review a classmate's work, take notes, and report back to the class about the classmate's vacation. **Even in the writing step, students practice listening, speaking, and writing, a true four-skills synthesis.**

Estrategia is directly related to *Preparación* and **gives a specific focus to help approach the writing activity.** This strategy is focused on *Identifying your audience.* For this activity, students are writing to their friend so they will need to use the familiar *tú* form. This strategy will direct them as they write their e-mail.

ESCRIBE

3-45 | Interpretive |

Preparación. Choose a vacation spot that you know well (or find information online) and that you like a lot. Then make a list of words (adjectives) that describe the place, write some enjoyable activities (verbs) that people do there.

3-46

Escribe. | Presentational |

Now write the e-mail to your friend, telling about your vacation. Use the information you prepared in *Preparación* and any other that you think may be of interest to your friend.

En directo

Salutations for casual correspondence:

Querido/a...:

Hola...,

Closings for casual correspondence:

Tu amigo/a,

Hasta pronto,

 Click on the icon to listen to a conversation with these expressions.

3-47

Un paso más. | Interpersonal |

After completing your e-mail, exchange it with a classmate, read his/hers and take notes to answer the following questions: a) where your classmate is spending vacation; b) what he/she does during the vacation. Inform the class.

ESTRATEGIA

Identify your audience

When you write an e-mail to your friend it is essential to identify the parts of the e-mail (To, From, Subject, the salutation or greeting, the body, and the closing farewell). You are expected to address your friend with the **tú** form.

Comprueba:
I was able to...

____ **present main ideas clearly, with some details.**

____ **use a wide range of learned vocabulary.**

____ **conjugate verbs appropriately and make the right agreements.**

____ **use accurate spelling, capitalization, and punctuation.**

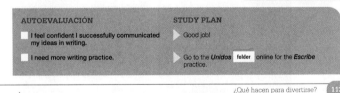

AUTOEVALUACIÓN

☐ I feel confident I successfully communicated my ideas in writing.

☐ I need more writing practice.

STUDY PLAN

▶ Good job!

▶ Go to the *Unidos* folder online for the *Escribe* practice.

Finally, **students complete a self-assessment.** If they determine that they need more practice writing, students can go to the *Unidos* folder in the online component for additional practice.

ADDITIONAL CULTURAL EXPLORATION

The *Enfoque cultural* provides an understanding of the relationship between culture and language throughout the Hispanic world.

 ## ENFOQUE CULTURAL

After honing their communicative skills in the *Unidos* section in class, students complete the *Enfoque cultural* reading in the *Cultura* online learning module that **delves deeper into the culture(s) of focus.**

In Chapter 3, students learn more about the cultures of Peru, Bolivia, and Paraguay.

En otras palabras introduces students to **regional variations** in the Spanish language.

EN OTRAS PALABRAS

Expresiones peruanas

Me conseguí una **chamba.**
I found a job.

José y yo somos **patas.**
José and I are buddies.

¡Juanita es una **chancona!**
Juanita is a nerd!

Expresiones bolivianas

Es tan desconfiado/a como **gallo tuerto.**
He/She mistrusts everyone.

Te voy a dar una **samba canuta.**
I am going to spank you.

Expresiones paraguayas

No seas **caigue.**
Don't be lazy.

ENFOQUE *cultural* Perú, Bolivia y Paraguay

LEARN Read and listen to the following passage to learn more about Perú, Bolivia y Paraguay. Then do the **Comprensión** activities.

Perfiles de Perú, Bolivia y Paraguay

Perú, Bolivia y Paraguay forman lo que se puede llamar la región central de América del Sur, junto con Brasil. Los tres países, aunque muy diferentes entre sí, tienen algunas características comunes.

Perú es un país extraordinario por su diversidad histórica, geográfica y cultural. Antes de la llegada de los españoles, fue el centro del gran imperio inca. Durante la colonia, fue una de las regiones más ricas y desarrolladas. La geografía de Perú tiene tres regiones muy diferentes y variadas: la costa, los Andes y la selva del Amazonas. Y, finalmente, en Perú encontramos ruinas espectaculares de las culturas indígenas y de la época colonial, y también ciudades modernas con una diversidad étnica muy grande.

En Perú se conservan monumentos maravillosos que muestran la historia del país. La misteriosa ciudad de Machu Picchu revela la riqueza de la arquitectura indígena. En otras ciudades, como en Cusco, conviven la arquitectura indígena y la tradicional española.

Similar to the online vocabulary and grammar sections, the students engage in a variety of activities online to provide ample practice of the material presented.

ENFOQUE CULTURAL

It's time to talk!
Students now are ready to complete the highly applied and engaging *Práctica comunicativa* activities centered on cultural content and exchange. **All activities synthesize chapter vocabulary and grammar within a cultural context.**

SELF-ASSESSMENT

The self-assessment section, *Comprueba lo que sabes*, asks students to demonstrate mastery of chapter content through further practice in a variety of activities and games that reinforce chapter vocabulary, grammar, and culture in different ways.

COMPRUEBA LO QUE SABES

The **Practice Test with Study Plan** is a machine-graded full-length test that reviews chapter vocabulary and grammar. Students are given a study plan based on their performance. The study plan refers them to explanations in the interactive presentations, extra practice activities, and tutorials to help them review concepts where they need additional practice.

Vocabulary Flashcards help students review words and quiz themselves on the active vocabulary.

Flashcards can also be downloaded to mobile devices for practice on the go.

Games are an engaging way to practice new skills. Games vary from *Concentration* (flip cards to match words to visuals), to *Soccer* (provide the appropriate word in a context), to a *Quiz Show* game during which students choose the appropriate response in a multiple-choice format. Questions are contextualized and move beyond simple form-based exercises to more meaningful, engaging activities.

VOCABULARIO

The chapter ends with the audio-enhanced comprehensive list of vocabulary words. Students can click on the each word to hear its pronunciation. Additional pronunciation practice is available in the online component. ▼

Vocabulario

Las diversiones y las celebraciones
la boda
la canción
el cumpleaños
la fiesta
la guitarra
la música
la película
la reunión
el tiempo libre
las vacaciones

Las personas
el camarero/la camarera
el hombre
el/la joven
la mujer

En un café o restaurante
el agua
el almuerzo
el arroz
la bebida
el bistec
el café
la cena
el cereal
la cerveza
el ceviche
la comida
el desayuno
la ensalada
los espaguetis

el frijol
la fruta
la hamburguesa
el helado
el huevo
el jamón
el jugo
la leche
la lechuga
la naranja
el pan
el pan tostado/
   la tostada
la papa
las papas fritas
el pescado
el pollo
el queso
el refresco
el sándwich
la sopa
el té
el tomate
el vegetal/la verdura
el vino

La comunicación
el periódico
la revista
el teléfono

Los lugares
el cine
la ciudad
el mar
el país

Las descripciones
caliente
fabuloso/a
frío/a
frito/a
rápido/a
típico/a

Verbos
alquilar
cantar
celebrar
cenar
descansar
hacer la cama
nadar
poner la mesa
tocar (un instrumento)
tomar el sol

Palabras y expresiones útiles
¿adónde?
al
al aire libre
cerca de
¡claro!
después, luego
durante
¡estupendo!
felicidades
mientras
otro/a
¿qué te parece?
si

Los números de 100 a 2.000.000
cien/ciento
doscientos/as
trescientos/as
cuatrocientos/as
quinientos/as
seiscientos/as
setecientos/as
ochocientos/as
novecientos/as
mi
mil cien
dos mil
diez mil
cien mil
ciento cincuenta mil
quinientos mil
un millón (de)
dos millones (de)

Expresiones con por
por ciento
por ejemplo
por eso
por fin
por lo menos
por supuesto

SCOPE & SEQUENCE

Capítulo	Learning Outcomes	Vocabulario en contexto
Preliminar Bienvenidos a Unidos 2	• introduce yourself, greet others, and say good-bye • identify people and classroom objects and tell where they are in the classroom • listen to and respond to classroom expressions and requests • spell names and addresses and express phone numbers • express dates and tell time • comment on the weather	*Las presentaciones* *Los saludos y las despedidas* *¿Qué hay en el salón de clase?* *Los meses del año y los días de la semana* *El tiempo* *Expresiones útiles en la clase* *El alfabeto*
1 ¿Qué estudias? 22	• talk about studies, campus, and academic life • describe daily routines and activities • specify gender and number • express location and states of being • ask and answer questions • compare the educational system of Spain to that of your own country	*Los estudiantes y los cursos* *La universidad* *Las actividades de los estudiantes*
2 ¿Quiénes son tus amigos? 52	• describe people, places, and things • express origin and possession • talk about where and when events take place • describe what someone or something is like and express changeable conditions • identify what belongs to you and others • discuss the people, things, and activities you and others like and dislike • present information about Hispanic influences on state flags and other U.S. symbols	*Mis amigos y yo* *Las descripciones* *El origen*
3 ¿Qué hacen para divertirse? 82	• describe leisure activities and food • plan your daily activities and express intentions • identify prices and dates • state what and whom you know • describe places to visit in Peru, Bolivia, and Paraguay	*Las diversiones* *Los planes* *La comida*

Gramática en contexto	Unidos	Enfoque cultural
Identifying and describing people: **Singular forms of *ser*** Locating people and things: ***¿Dónde está?*** Using numbers: ***Los números de 0 a 99*** Telling time: ***La hora***		
Talking about academic life and daily occurrences: **Present tense of regular *-ar* verbs** Talking about academic life and daily occurrences: **Present tense of regular *-er* and *-ir* verbs** Specifying gender and number: **Articles and nouns** Expressing location and states of being: **Present tense of the verb *estar*** Asking and answering questions: **Interrogative words**	**Escucha** • Listen for the gist **Habla** • Ask questions to gather information **Lee** • Identify the format of a text **Escribe** • Brainstorm key ideas before writing	**Cultural focus:** España *Escuelas y universidades en España*
Describing people, places, and things: **Adjectives** Identifying and describing, expressing origin, possession, location of events, and time: **Present tense of *ser*** Expressing inherent qualities and changeable conditions: ***Ser* and *estar* with adjectives** Expressing ownership: **Possessive adjectives** Expressing likes and dislikes: ***Gustar***	**Escucha** • Listen for specific information **Habla** • Describe a person **Lee** • Scan a text for specific information **Escribe** • Consider audience and purpose	**Cultural focus:** Estados Unidos *Los hispanos y la expansión de Estados Unidos*
Talking about daily activities: **Present tense of *hacer*, *poner*, *salir*, *traer*, and *oír*** Expressing movement and plans: **Present tense of *ir* and *ir a* + infinitive** Talking about quantity: **Numbers 100 to 2,000,000** Stating what you know: ***Saber* and *conocer*** Expressing intention, means, movement, and duration: **Some uses of *por* and *para***	**Escucha** • Use background knowledge **Habla** • Inform yourself before you do a survey **Lee** • Look for and use key words **Escribe** • Identify your audience	**Cultural focus:** Perú, Bolivia y Paraguay *Perfiles de Perú, Bolivia y Paraguay*

Capítulo	Learning Outcomes	Vocabulario en contexto
4 ¿Cómo es tu familia? 116	• talk about families and their daily routines • express opinions, plans, preferences, and feelings • express obligation • express when, where, or how an action occurs • express how long something has been going on • talk about daily routines • relay information you have researched about famous Colombians from a variety of fields	*Los miembros de la familia* *¿Qué hacen los parientes?* *Las rutinas familiares*
5 ¿Dónde vives? 146	• talk about housing, the home, and household activities • express ongoing actions • describe physical and emotional states • avoid repetition in speaking and writing • point out and identify people and things • compare cultural and geographic information of Nicaragua, El Salvador, and Honduras	*En casa* *La casa, los muebles y los electrodomésticos* *Las tareas domésticas*
6 ¿Qué te gusta comprar? 178	• talk about shopping and clothes • talk about events in the past • indicate to whom or for whom an action takes place • express likes and dislikes • describe people, objects, and events • compare Simón Bolívar and Venezuela with leaders in the history of your own country	*Las compras* *La ropa* *¿Qué debo llevar?*
7 ¿Cuál es tu deporte favorito? 208	• talk about sports • emphasize and clarify information • talk about past events • compare ranching and fishing industries in Argentina, Uruguay, and Chile with those in your own country	*Los deportes* *El tiempo y las estaciones* *¿Qué pasó ayer?*

Gramática en contexto	Unidos	Enfoque cultural
Expressing opinions, plans, preferences, and feelings: **Present tense of stem-changing verbs: *e → ie, o → ue, e → i*** Expressing obligation: ***Tener que* + infinitive** Expressing when, where, or how an action occurs: **Adverbs** Expressing how long something has been going on: ***Hace* with expressions of time** Talking about daily routine: **Reflexive verbs and pronouns**	**Escucha** • Listen for a purpose **Habla** • Organize information to make comparisons **Lee** • Use title and illustrations to anticipate content **Escribe** • Choose between informal and formal language to express the desired tone	**Cultural focus:** Colombia *La riqueza de Colombia*
Expressing ongoing actions: **Present progressive** Describing physical and emotional states: **Expressions with *tener*** Avoiding repetition in speaking and writing: **Direct object nouns and pronouns** Pointing out and identifying people and things: **Demonstrative adjectives and pronouns**	**Escucha** • Create mental images **Habla** • Plan what you want to say **Lee** • Inform yourself about a topic before you start to read **Escribe** • Select the appropriate content and tone for a formal description	**Cultural focus:** Nicaragua, El Salvador y Honduras *La geografía espectacular de Nicaragua, El Salvador y Honduras*
Talking about the past: **Preterit tense of regular verbs** Talking about the past: **Preterit of *ir* and *ser*** Indicating to whom or for whom an action takes place: **Indirect object nouns and pronouns** Expressing likes and dislikes: ***Gustar* and similar verbs** Describing people, objects, and events: **More about *ser* and *estar***	**Escucha** • Take notes to recall information **Habla** • Negotiate a price **Lee** • Use context to figure out the meaning of unfamiliar words **Escribe** • Recounting events in sequence	**Cultural focus:** Venezuela *El mundo fascinante de Simón Bolívar*
Talking about the past: **Preterit of reflexive verbs** Talking about the past: **Preterit of *-er* and *-ir* verbs whose stem ends in a vowel** Talking about the past: **Preterit of stem-changing *-ir* verbs (*e → i*) (*o → u*)** Emphasizing or clarifying information: **Pronouns after prepositions** Talking about the past: **Some irregular preterits**	**Escucha** • Differentiate fact from opinion **Habla** • Focus on key information to report what was said **Lee** • Predict and guess content **Escribe** • Use supporting details	**Cultural focus:** Argentina, Uruguay y Chile *El ganado y el pescado en la vida de Argentina, Uruguay y Chile*

Capítulo	Learning Outcomes	Vocabulario en contexto
8 ¿Cuáles son sus tradiciones? 240	• discuss situations and celebrations • describe conditions and express ongoing actions in the past • tell stories about past events • compare people and things • talk about a Mexican celebration	*Las fiestas y las tradiciones* *Otras celebraciones* *Las invitaciones*
9 ¿Dónde trabajas? 274	• talk about careers and employment • avoid repetition • describe past events in more detail • give instructions and suggestions • compare demographic and economic changes in Guatemala and in the United States	*El trabajo* *Los oficios y las profesiones* *Buscando trabajo*
10 ¿Cuál es tu comida preferida? 306	• talk about ingredients, recipes, and meals • state impersonal information • talk about the recent past • give instructions in informal settings • talk about the future • present information, concepts, and ideas about food and public health in Ecuador and other Latin American countries	*Los productos y las recetas* *En el supermercado* *La mesa*

Gramática en contexto	Unidos	Enfoque cultural
Expressing ongoing actions and describing in the past: **The imperfect** Narrating in the past: **The preterit and the imperfect** Comparing people and things: **Comparisons of inequality** Comparing people and things: **Comparisons of equality** Comparing people and things: **The superlative**	**Escucha** • Draw conclusions based on what you know **Habla** • Conduct an interview **Lee** • Make inferences **Escribe** • Select and sequence details to write effective narratives	**Cultural focus:** México *Cultura y tradiciones mexicanas*
Avoiding repetition: **Review of direct and indirect object pronouns** Avoiding repetition: **Use of direct and indirect object pronouns together** Talking about the past: **More on the imperfect and the preterit** Giving instructions or suggestions: **Formal commands**	**Escucha** • Use contextual guessing **Habla** • Gather information strategically to express a decision **Lee** • Organize textual information into categories **Escribe** • Focus on purpose, content, and audience	**Cultural focus:** Guatemala *Historia y trabajo en Guatemala*
Stating impersonal information: *Se* + **verb constructions** Talking about the recent past: **Present perfect and participles used as adjectives** Giving instructions in informal settings: **Informal commands** Talking about the future: **The future tense**	**Escucha** • Record relevant detail **Habla** • Give and defend reasons for a decision **Lee** • Learn new words by analyzing their connections with known words **Escribe** • Summarize information	**Cultural focus:** Ecuador *Ecuador: alimentación y salud pública*

Capítulo	Learning Outcomes	Vocabulario en contexto
11 ¿Cómo es tu salud? 338	• discuss health and medical treatments • express expectations and hopes • describe emotions, opinions, and wishes • express goals, purposes, and means • present information about music and dance traditions in Cuba, the Dominican Republic, and Puerto Rico	*Médicos, farmacias y hospitales* *Las partes del cuerpo* *La salud* 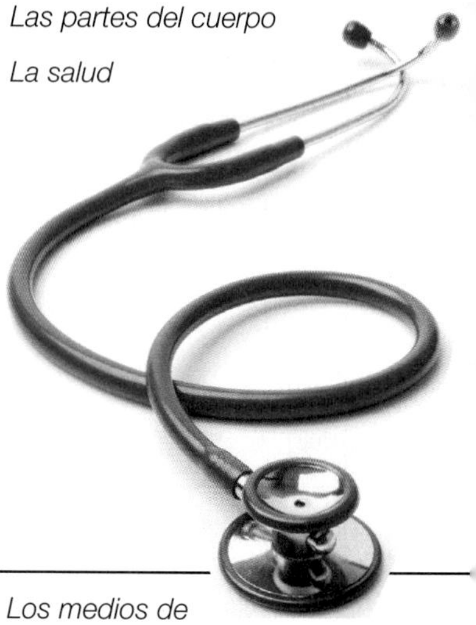
12 Buen viaje 368	• talk about travel arrangements and preferences • express possession and clarify what belongs to you and others • express affirmation and negation • express doubt and uncertainty • talk about past travel experiences • talk about the social and economic impact of the Panama Canal	*Los medios de transporte* *El alojamiento y las reservaciones* *Viajando en coche* 

Gramática en contexto	Unidos	Enfoque cultural
Expressing expectations and hopes: **Introduction to the present subjunctive** Expressing emotions, opinions, and attitudes: **The Subjunctive with expressions of emotion** Expressing goals, purposes, and means: **Uses of *por* and *para***	**Escucha** • Listen for the main idea **Habla** • Select appropriate phrases to offer opinions **Lee** • Focus on relevant information **Escribe** • Persuade through suggestions and advice	**Cultural focus:** Cuba, República Dominicana y Puerto Rico *Cuba, República Dominicana y Puerto Rico: la música y el baile*
Expressing possession: **Possessive pronouns** Expressing affirmation and negation: **Affirmative and negative expressions** Expressing doubt and uncertainty: **Subjunctive with expressions of doubt** Talking about the past: **Review of the preterit and imperfect**	**Escucha** • Use background knowledge to support comprehension **Habla** • Engage and maintain the interest of your listeners **Lee** • Focus on logical relationships **Escribe** • Use facts to support a point of view	**Cultural focus:** Panamá y Costa Rica *Centroamérica: un puente entre dos océanos* 

The **Unidos** Program

With a unique online environment that offers a guided approach to instruction and practice, **Unidos** prepares students to come to class and communicate with confidence. The Classroom Manual (available in print or digital format) offers a wide variety of communicative activities for students put into practice the skills they learned in the online component.

FOR STUDENTS

Students have the option to purchase **Unidos** in a completely digital format (online component which includes a digital version the classroom manual) or with a printed classroom manual for a nominal fee. Access to **Unidos** is available in one-semester or multi-semester duration.

- **Classroom Manual** contains a wide variety of communicative practice activities to use in a face-to-face, hybrid, or fully online classroom. If students choose the print version, the three-hole-punched, loose-leaf format offers them the flexibility to bring to class only what they need.

FOR INSTRUCTORS

Annotated Instructor's Edition (AIE)

Available in a convenient, three-hole-punched, loose-leaf version, the **Unidos** AIE gives instructors the flexibility to bring to class only the chapters they need. They can add worksheets, notes, or other materials to the chapter needed for the day. The extensive, clearly labeled annotations make the AIE an indispensable handbook for both novice and experienced instructors. Notes offer technology

tips and ideas for implementation of activities, for expansion, alternative practice, and review. They also highlight the integration of the National Standards and Integrated Performance Assessment throughout the program. Other notes provide in-depth linguistic and cultural information that the instructor may find useful.

Instructor's Resource Manual (Download Only)

The Instructor's Resource Manual (IRM) offers integrated syllabi for traditional and hybrid classroom settings at different paces. The IRM is available in the **Unidos** online component.

Testing Program (Download Only)

A highly flexible testing program allows instructors to customize tests by selecting the modules they wish to use or by changing individual items in the pre-built chapter exams, midterms, and finals. The assessment goal, content area, and response type are identified for each module. The full testing program is available in the **Unidos** online component. Also available in the online component is a user-friendly test-generating program known as **MyTest** that allows instructors to select, arrange, and customize testing modules to meet the needs of their courses. Once created, tests can be administered online.

Testing Audio CD

This CD contains the recordings to accompany the listening comprehension activities in the **Testing Program**. These recordings are also available within the online component.

Situaciones adicionales (Download Only)

Situaciones adicionales offer alternative *Situaciones* to use with the *Práctica comunicativa* sections of the Classroom Manual.

PowerPoint Presentations (Download Only)

PowerPoint presentations are offered for each chapter. They can help readdress key concepts before communicative practice. **Unidos** Powerpoints are available in the online component.

About the Authors

Elizabeth with her husband in Petra, Jordan

ELIZABETH E. GUZMÁN

I did my graduate studies in Spanish Applied Linguistics at the University of Pittsburgh.

One of my proudest teaching moments was... when my former students have shown me what a difference I can make in my students through my love of teaching.

My favorite vacation spots in the Hispanic world are... the lake regions of my native Chile and Peru.

I can't live without... my laptop and Pandora radio.

My favorite feature in Unidos is... that it opens the doors to the fascinating Spanish-speaking world, its people, and its diverse cultures.

My favorite activities are... traveling, gardening, and listening to music.

The people closest to my heart are... my family, my friends, and the people who value freedom and justice as much as I do.

What makes me happy is... knowing that my work transcends me.

The people I admire are... those from whom I can learn something.

My favorite classroom is... one in which students and I become part of one community working toward common goals.

Judy with student Jia and her first apple pie

JUDITH E. LISKIN-GASPARRO

My Ph.D. is from... the University of Texas–Austin

My research area is... classroom-based second language acquisition.

One of my proudest teaching moments was... when my doctoral student won the ACTFL-MLJ Birkmaier Award for Doctoral Dissertation Research. There have been four proudest moments, because four of my SLA students have won this award since 2007.

My favorite vacation spot in the Hispanic world is... For its mystery and sheer beauty, Machu Picchu. For the lifestyle and amazing *tortillas de patatas*, San Sebastián.

I can't live without my... laptop.

My favorite feature in Unidos is... its clickability (my made-up word). It invites students and instructors to challenge linear patterns of learning.

My public talent is... baking cookies—all kinds, and for all occasions. I also give pie workshops.

My secret talent is... making up cool games to play with toddlers.

I am thrilled when... people think I am a native speaker of Spanish.

PALOMA LAPUERTA

My Ph.D. is from... Université de Genève, Switzerland, but I did my "licenciatura" in Universidad de Salamanca, Spain.

My research area is... Spanish Language and Peninsular Literature.

One of my proudest teaching moments was... when I noticed that everybody was having a good time... and learning!

My favorite vacation spot in the Hispanic world is... I have two: Castellón, Spain, which is by the sea, and Pereira, Colombia, which is near the Andes.

I can't live without my... Moleskine®.

My favorite feature in Unidos is... that it takes you to places beyond the textbook.

The movie I have seen most often is... *Volver*, by Pedro Almodóvar.

My favorite activity is... to travel.

The site that I found most beautiful was... Machu Picchu.

The landscape I found most impressive was... Namibia.

Paloma in Istanbul, Turkey

Acknowledgments

We created **Unidos** so that students will learn important vocabulary, grammar, and culture concepts online on their own, making it possible for instructors to organize face-to-face classroom meetings in any way they wish and ultimately to provide for a meaningful, culturally rich communicative environment in which their students and their students' language skills flourish. We identified the need for a program like this first by observing one another in our own classes and in those taught at our own institutions. We then began to ask our students and colleagues about the issues and challenges they were facing and soon found out that the issues and challenges they expressed seemed to match those that we were experiencing in our own institutions and impeding the goals of language study that were being articulated by the many students enrolling in face-to-face, hybrid, and fully online courses at our colleges and those of our friends and colleagues. As a result, we traveled around the country conducting workshops on how to infuse active learning into beginning language courses, including even those taught online with upwards of 100 students. In every visit, we asked instructors to list the goals of their beginning language course, and, specifically what they were doing to motivate students to continue to move through the intermediate and even to advanced levels of study. At every institution we visited, the critical course outcomes were similar and are consistent with those expressed by proponents of Course Redesign around the country.

When we asked instructors to rank goals in order of importance to them and to estimate the ratio between "student talk" and "teacher talk" (or how much valuable class time students were using to put language and culture into meaningful practice) in a typical class period or online session, it became crystal clear that instructors were doing all the talking—teaching, explaining, and drilling discrete grammar points—and that they were desperately seeking ideas about ways to increase "student talk." Many spoke quite eloquently about how their lives and the lives of their students would change if there were a program developed to take advantage of what's possible for students to achieve outside of class, so that they could put language concepts learned, mastered, and assessed outside of class to good use in meaningful, engaging contexts in class. Many instructors observed that beginning language textbooks dedicate the vast majority of their pages to vocabulary and grammar explanations and just don't offer enough opportunities for personalized practice and progression to open-ended, inspiring situations. At the same time, learners told us their textbooks included so much material that they were unable to distinguish the important from the exceptional, which resulted in their becoming discouraged and electing not to continue with their studies.

We wish to thank the many contributors who created content and activities to the program, in some cases working under tremendous speed and impossible deadlines: Angela Carlson-Lombardi, Juliet Falce-Robinson, Rob Martinsen, Maggie Snyder, and Marta Tecedor Cabrero, thank you. We could not have developed the program without you!

Developing a new kind of approach would not have been possible without the critical analysis, questioning, and encouragement we received from students, fellow instructors, friends, and professionals from across the country and around the world. We are deeply indebted to the members of the **Unidos Content and User Experience Advisory Board** who responded to the concepts, words, illustrations, and online tutorials and adaptive learning and assessment components that comprise **Unidos** with open minds. We also thank the many professional colleagues who collaborated with us by carefully reading and assessing selected portions of the **Unidos** materials. You have all made this program what it is today and we're humbled by your colleagueship, patience, and generosity.

It is rare for a learning company to reach out to students enrolled in beginning language courses to elicit their feedback and response to new materials in development. Our Student Advisory Board's comments have been indispensable to us as we sought to develop a program that would speak to today's and tomorrow's learners. Thank you!

CONTENT AND USER EXPERIENCE ADVISORY BOARD

Rose Marie Brougham
University of Akron

Robert D. Cameron
College of Charleston

Maritza Chinea-Thornberry
University of South Florida

An Chung Cheng
University of Toledo

Jorge Cubillos
University of Delaware

Elizabeth V. Dowdy
State College of Florida

Héctor Fabio Espitia
Grand Valley State University

Ana Menendez-Collera
Suffolk Community College

María Mercedes Freeman
University of North Carolina, Greensboro

Heidi Herron-Johnson
Ivy Tech Community College of Indiana

Margarita Jácome
Loyola University of Maryland

Yun Sil Jeon
Coastal Carolina University

Rob Martinsen
Brigham Young University

Janie B. McNutt
Texas Tech University

Ana Menendez Collera
Suffolk Community College

Ivan Mino
Tarrant County College, Southeast Campus

Alicia Muñoz Sánchez
University of California, San Diego

Jaime Palmer
Tarrant County College, Northeast Campus

Teresa Pérez-Gamboa
University of Georgia

Lee J. Rincón
Moraine Valley Community College

Lilia Delfina Ruiz-Debbe
Stonybrook University

Toni Trives
Santa Monica College

Griselle Vargas
Virginia Tech

Matt Wyszynski
University of Akron

STUDENT ADVISORY BOARD

Emily Bronaugh,
College of Charleston

Senandina Dedovic,
Central Connecticut State University

Caroline Fox,
University of Iowa

Evan Holleran,
University of Iowa

Sarah Jestel,
University of Georgia

Cieara Juliano,
Central Connecticut State University

Elizabeth Kelley,
College of Charleston

Justin Lyons,
College of Charleston

Monica Murray,
College of Charleston

Kathryn Nasenbenny,
University of Iowa

Bryan Oakley,
University of Georgia

Magdalena Petecka,
Central Connecticut State University

Katrina Rego,
Central Connecticut State University

Fiona Szepanski,
Central Connecticut State University

Maura Warner,
University of Iowa

Victoria Watson,
University of Iowa

Patricia Wu,
Princeton University

PEDAGOGICAL CONSULTANTS AND REVIEWERS

Frances Alpren
Vanderbilt University

Fleming L. Bell
Valdosta State University

Flavia Belpoliti
University of Houston

Yadira Berigan
University of Arizona

Encarna Bermejo
Houston Baptist University

Bruce A. Boggs
University of Oklahoma

Elizabeth Calvera
Virginia Tech University

Amy Carbajal
Western Washington University

Alyce Cook
Columbus State University

Lisa DeWaard
Clemson University

Isabel Dulfano
University of Utah

Jennifer Ewald
Saint Joseph's University

Lorenzo García-Amaya
Northern Illinois University

Margarita Garcia-Notario
State University of New York, Plattsburgh

Kenneth Gordon
Winthrop University

Marie Guiribitey
Florida International University

Florencia Henshaw
University of Illinois at Urbana-Champaign

Dawn Heston
University of Missouri, Georgia

Laura Hortal
Forsyth Technical Community College

Yun Sil Jeon
Coastal Carolina University

Cheryl Johnson
Denison University

Michelle Kopuz
Burlington County College

Paul Larson
Baylor University

Luis E Latoja
Columbus State Community College

Kajsa Larson
Northern Kentucky University

James J. López
University of Tampa

Joanne Lucena
Arcadia University

Ellen McArdle
Raritan Valley Community College

Mandy R. Menke
Grand Valley State University

Lori Mesrobian
University of Southern California

Daniel J. Nappo
University of Tennessee at Martin

Lea Ramsdell
Towson University

Donna Boston Ross
Catawba Valley Community College

Kathryn Quinn Sanchez
Georgian Court University

Michael Sawyer
University of Central Missouri

Victor Slesinger
Palm Beach State College

Chin-Sook Pak
Ball State University

Shannah Steel
Bob Jones University

Julie Szucs
Miami University

Mark K. Warford
Buffalo State College (SUNY)

U. Theresa Zmurkewycz
Saint Joseph's University

There could not be a more fitting title for a program that has engaged us in so much creativity, coordination, and teamwork. We thank our colleagues and the many members of the Pearson product creation and development team for working "unidos" to bring this cutting-edge program to instructors and students worldwide. To Samantha Alducin, Celia Meana, Meriel Martínez, Nancy Stevenson, Mary Rottino, Melissa Sacco, Kristine Suárez, Denise Miller, and the incomparable Julia Caballero, our deepest gratitude and, of course *abrazos fuertes*. Finally, to our friends and families, you continue to be our source of inspiration and support.

Thank you!

Preliminar

Bienvenidos a Unidos

VOCABULARIO EN CONTEXTO

Making introductions and talking about the classroom

Las presentaciones

Los saludos y las despedidas

¿Qué hay en el salón de clase?

Los meses del año y los días de la semana

El tiempo

Expresiones útiles en la clase

El alfabeto

GRAMÁTICA EN CONTEXTO

Describing people and things, and sharing information related to the classroom

Singular forms of *ser*

¿Dónde está?

Los números de 0 a 99

La hora

EN ESTE CAPÍTULO...

Comprueba lo que sabes

Vocabulario

Learning OBJECTIVES

You will:

- learn expressions used in introductions, greetings, introductions, leave taking, and the classroom
- learn vocabulary for the numbers from 0 to 99, the days, and the months
- learn expressions to describe the weather
- learn the letters of the Spanish alphabet
- use the verb *ser* to identify people and things
- use the verb *estar* to locate people and classroom objects

Learning OUTCOMES

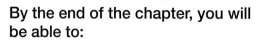

By the end of the chapter, you will be able to:

- introduce yourself, greet others, and say good-bye
- identify people and classroom objects and tell where they are in the classroom
- listen to and respond to classroom expressions and requests
- spell names and addresses and express phone numbers
- express dates and tell time
- comment on the weather

online learning **tip**

Before you begin

Be self-motivated and self-disciplined. With the freedom and flexibility of the online environment comes responsibility. The online process takes commitment and discipline to keep up with the flow of the content and online assignments.

Use critical thinking in your learning process. All learning involves integrating new information into what you already know. When you read explanations and do homework, you have to use your critical thinking skills to make use of the new information and practice opportunities. Just doing the activities is not enough; you have to think actively in order to learn.

Have regular access to a computer and a high-speed Internet connection. Key parts of the course content and interaction are engaged by computer through the Internet. You must have access to the necessary equipment and meet the system requirements to successfully engage with the online materials.

Take advantage of learning opportunities online and in class. Take responsibility for your learning by familiarizing yourself with all aspects of the technology, completing assignments on time, and participating actively in class.

CULTURA INTERACTIVA

Personas que
hablan español
(en millones)

Estados Unidos 44,4
Cuba 11,2
República Dominicana 10,1
México 103,5
Puerto Rico 3,8
Guatemala 9,2
El Salvador 6,1
Honduras 7,9
Nicaragua 5
Venezuela 28
Costa Rica 4,3
Colombia 43,3
Panamá 2,6
Ecuador 13,2
Perú 23,7
Bolivia 4,3
Paraguay 4
Chile 15,5
Uruguay 3,2
Argentina 39,6
España 41,8
Guinea
Ecuatorial 1
Filipinas 3

¿Cuánto sabes?

Relying on your knowledge of
the world, look at the map and
determine whether each statement
is true (**Cierto**) or false (**Falso**).

1. _Cierto_ Más de (*More than*) 350
   millones de personas
   hablan español en el
   mundo.

2. _Falso_ En Filipinas no se habla
   español.

3. _Cierto_ En Estados Unidos
   hablan español más
   personas que (*more …
   than*) en Chile.

4. _Cierto_ En Guinea Ecuatorial se
   habla español.

5. _Falso_ En Brasil se habla español.

6. _Cierto_ El español se habla en
   23 países.

Bienvenidos al mundo hispano.

LEARN

Hispanic Cultures

In the *Unidos* online component you will find a variety of
engaging cultural materials. Browse on your own through
videos, interactive art tours, and readings to learn more about
the Spanish-speaking world.

Cultura en línea
To learn more about the Spanish-speaking
world, go to the *Cultura en línea* folder in
the *Unidos* online component to view the
Vistas culturales video.

Online prep for students
Students will have completed each Learning Module for *Vocabulario en contexto* online before coming to class. This includes the interactive presentations plus all corresponding Apply activities. View content for learning modules online. You will find additional in-class activities in the Supplementary Activities folder under Instructor's Resources online.

Suggestions
Review *Me llamo* by pointing to yourself and saying your name. Then write *Me llamo* and repeat the sentence. Now ask individual students for their names. Accept answers if they say only their names, but encourage them to use *Me llamo…*, pointing to the board to guide them. Introduce yourself to a student, asking his/her name; answer with *Mucho gusto*. Write *Mucho gusto*, and encourage the same response from the student. You can shake the student's hand to make the introduction more realistic. Repeat with another student. Again, encourage the student to say *Mucho gusto* after his or her name; this time respond with *Igualmente*. Repeat it again before asking students to introduce themselves to a classmate. You may replay the audio from the online component for the dialogue if needed.
    You may wish to spend a few minutes having students introduce themselves to several students sitting near them.

Tech tip for *Las presentaciones*
Project pictures of people of various ages to quickly compare the uses of *tú* and *usted*. Tell students to use *tú* when addressing each other. Model *encantado/a* by acting out a short dialogue with a female and a male to show the change.

Expansion
You may introduce the phrase *Tu nombre, por favor*. For further practice, have a student ask you your name or the names of two classmates.

Vocabulario en contexto

Making introductions and talking about the classroom

LEARN

Vocabulary in context

Unidos is designed to put learning in your own hands. A complete study plan, *Plan de estudio*, will appear before each *Vocabulario en contexto* section to guide you through the online vocabulary learning modules and application activities. In the *Unidos* program, you will complete learning modules online to prepare for engaging speaking activities you will do in class in *Práctica comunicativa*.

Las presentaciones

Go to the *Capítulo preliminar* [folder] in the online component to complete the Learning Module for *Vocabulario en contexto: Las presentaciones*.

PLAN DE ESTUDIO

◎ LEARN	APPLY ◎
• Interactive presentation: *Las presentaciones*	• Activities
• Vocabulary tutorials	

PRÁCTICA COMUNICATIVA

P-1 👥

Presentaciones.

PRIMERA FASE. With a partner complete the following conversation with the appropriate expressions from the list.

Encantado	Igualmente	mi amigo Pedro	Mucho gusto

ALICIA: Me llamo Alicia. Y tú, ¿cómo te llamas?

ISABEL: Isabel Pérez. _____Mucho gusto_____.

ALICIA: _____Igualmente_____.

ALICIA: Isabel, _____mi amigo Pedro_____.

ISABEL: Mucho gusto.

PEDRO: _____Encantado_____.

Suggestion for P-2
Primera fase
When doing the pre-listening activity explain that in some Spanish-speaking countries children are brought up to address their parents as *usted*.

Note for P-2 *Primera fase*
Unidos differentiates between *Vocabulario en contexto* audio, found in the online component and Listening activities, which are to be done in class. The online audio is input based; it provides students with models of pronunciation as they read the accompanying text. The Listening activities provide opportunities to interpret texts and produce language in response.

Note for P-2 *Segunda fase*
The listening activity audioscripts appear in the margins for instructors.
You may wish to use the following procedure: 1) Play the conversations; students mark their answers; 2) have students check their answers with a partner; and 3) play the conversations again, repeating difficult parts.

Audioscript for P-2
Conversación 1
—*Buenos días, señora Gómez.*
—*Buenos días. ¿Cómo está usted, señor Jiménez?*
—*Bastante bien, gracias. ¿Y usted?*
—*Bien, gracias.*

Conversación 2
—*¡Hola, Felipe! ¿Qué tal? ¿Cómo estás?*
—*Regular, ¿y tú?*
—*Bien, gracias.*

Conversación 3
—*Buenas tardes, señora Mena. ¿Cómo está usted?*
—*Bastante bien, gracias. Y usted, ¿cómo está, señora?*
—*Regular, regular.*
—*Lo siento.*

Conversación 4
—*Me llamo Carlos Martínez. Y tú, ¿cómo te llamas?*
—*Me llamo Cristina Camacho.*
—*Mucho gusto.*
—*Igualmente.*

SEGUNDA FASE. Move around the classroom, introducing yourself to several classmates and introducing classmates to each other.

Conversaciones.

PRIMERA FASE. Before you listen to four brief conversations in which people greet each other, complete the following chart with the pronoun you think you would use in each case. Compare your answers with those of a classmate and explain why you chose *tú* or *usted*.

LENGUA When you talk to different people, you address them with various degrees of formality, depending on how well you know the person and the context of the exchange. For example, when you talk to a professor, you probably use more formal language than when you talk to classmates or friends. In Spanish, one way to mark this difference is by using **tú** (informal) and **usted** (formal).

 SEGUNDA FASE. As you listen to the four conversations, mark (✓) the appropriate column to indicate whether the greetings are formal (with **usted**) or informal (with **tú**).

WHEN TALKING TO YOUR...	TÚ	USTED
1. brother or sister		
2. doctor		
3. coach		
4. parent		

	FORMAL	INFORMAL
1.	✓	
2.		✓
3.	✓	✓
4.		✓

Los saludos y las despedidas

Go to the *Capítulo preliminar* folder in the online component to complete the Learning Module for *Vocabulario en contexto: Los saludos y las despedidas.*

PLAN DE ESTUDIO

◎ LEARN
- Interactive presentation: *Los saludos y las despedidas*
- Vocabulary tutorials

APPLY ◎
- Activities

PRÁCTICA COMUNICATIVA

Saludos.

Which greeting (**buenos días, buenas tardes, buenas noches**) is appropriate at the following times? Compare your answers with a classmate. For the last item, give your partner a new time to which he/she will respond with an appropriate greeting.

1. 9:00 A.M.
Buenos días

2. 11:00 P.M.
Buenas noches

3. 4:00 P.M.
Buenas tardes

4. 8:00 A.M.
Buenos días

5. 1:00 P.M.
Buenas tardes o buenos días

6. 10:00 P.M.
Buenas noches

7. …

Cultura

When saying *hello* or *good-bye* and when being introduced, Spanish-speaking men and women almost always shake hands. When greeting each other, young girls and women often kiss each other on one cheek. This is also the custom for men and women who are close friends. In Spain they kiss on both cheeks. Men who are close friends normally embrace and pat each other on the back.

Native Spanish speakers also tend to stand physically closer to the person with whom they are talking than do English speakers.

Compara: What are common greetings in your culture? Do you greet your family and your friends in the same way?

P-4

Despedidas. What would you say and respond to your partner in the following situations?

Modelo **"** You run into a good friend on campus. **"**

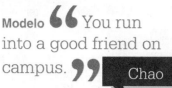

Chao

Adiós

1. You'll see your friend tomorrow. Hasta mañana.

2. You arrange to meet your classmate at the library in ten minutes. Hasta pronto.

3. Your roommate is leaving for a semester abroad. Adiós.

P-6

Despedidas y expresiones de cortesía. Which expression(s) would you use in the following situations? Compare your answers with a classmate and then provide a new situation for him/her to respond to.

Adiós.	Gracias.
Por favor.	De nada.
Hasta luego.	¡Qué pena!

1. Someone thanks you. De nada.

2. You say good-bye to a friend you will see later this evening. Hasta luego.

3. You ask if you can borrow a classmate's notes. Por favor.

4. You hear that your friend is sick. ¡Qué pena!

5. You receive a present from your cousin. Gracias.

6. ...

P-5

¿Perdón o con permiso? Would you use **perdón** or **con permiso** in these situations? Compare your answers with those of a classmate. Then create a similar situation to act out for the class.

1. Perdón.

2. Perdón, con permiso.

3. Perdón.

4. Perdón.

5. Con permiso.

P-7

Encuentros (*Encounters*). You meet the following people on the street. Greet them, ask how they are, and then say good-bye. Switch roles and role-play the encounters again.

1. tu (*your*) amigo Miguel
2. tu profesor/a
3. tu amiga Isabel
4. tu doctor/a

Warm-up for P-4
Model the *despedidas*, using hand gestures while speaking. Point out that some Spanish speakers use a different hand gesture when saying good-bye: palm facing out, fingers moving up and down. With a student, model the use of *adiós* meaning "hello" when two people pass each other, but do not stop to talk.

Suggestion for P-4 and P-6
Model correct pronunciation of the *d* in *adiós*: Students should place the tip of the tongue against the back of the upper front teeth. (English **d** is pronounced with the tip of the tongue on the ridge behind the upper teeth.) Explain that the word has only two syllables: *a-diós*.

Suggestion for P-5
Model the difference between *con permiso* and *perdón* by walking in front of a student and saying *con permiso*, and by lightly stepping on a student's toe or bumping into him/her and saying *perdón*. For additional modeling of *con permiso* or *perdón*, bump into chairs and so forth, as you pass through the classroom.

Warm-up for P-7
Model the exchange with a student before beginning the activity.

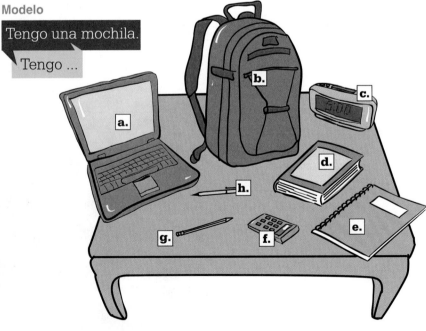

¿Qué hay en el salón de clase?

Go to the *Capítulo preliminar* folder in the online component to complete the Learning Module for *Vocabulario en contexto: ¿Qué hay en el salón de clase?*

PLAN DE ESTUDIO

◎ **LEARN**
- Interactive presentation: *¿Qué hay en el salón de clase?*
- Vocabulary tutorials

APPLY ◎
- Activities

PRÁCTICA COMUNICATIVA

P-8 👥

Identificación. With a partner, identify the items on this table and then tell him/her which of the items you have.

Modelo

Tengo una mochila.
Tengo ...

a. un/a computador/a; una computadora portátil; un ordenador
b. una mochila
c. un reloj
d. un libro
e. un cuaderno
f. una calculadora
g. un lápiz
h. un bolígrafo

P-9

Para la clase de español.
Write down a list of the things you need for this class. Compare your list with that of your partner.

P-10

¿Qué hay en el salón de clase?
There are eight hidden classroom objects in the following word puzzle. Work with a partner to name them in Spanish. Then look around your classroom and take turns telling your partner what objects you see.

Suggestion for P-9
Provide additional vocabulary if needed (e.g., *un diccionario*).

Note
Whenever possible, students should take turns answering. This provides additional opportunities to communicate in Spanish. Then the whole class reviews the activity.

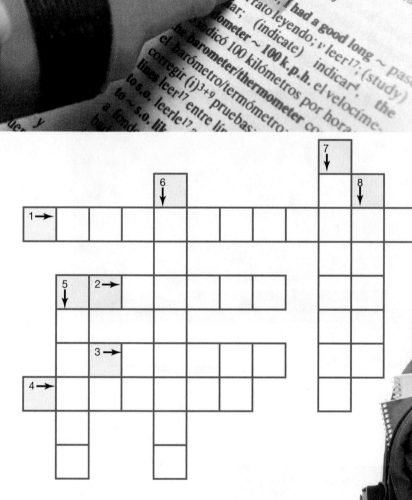

1. It is essential for your math problems. calculadora
2. Without it, you cannot write lápiz
3. Old papers and waste go here. cesto
4. You need them to study. libros
5. You sit on it. silla
6. You write your notes on it. cuaderno
7. You pack and carry your books in it every morning. mochila
8. It tells the time. reloj

Los meses del año y los días de la semana

Go to the *Capítulo preliminar* **folder** in the online component to complete the Learning Module for *Vocabulario en contexto: Los meses del año y los días de la semana*.

PLAN DE ESTUDIO

◎ LEARN
- Interactive presentation: *Los meses del año y los días de la semana*
- Vocabulary tutorials

◎ APPLY
- Activities

ENERO CALENDARIO

lunes	martes	miércoles	jueves	viernes	sábado	domingo
		1 AÑO NUEVO	2	3	4	5
6 LOS SANTOS REYES	7	8	9	10	11	12
13	14	15	16	17	18	19
20	21	22	23	24	25	26
27	28	29	30	31		

PRÁCTICA COMUNICATIVA

P-11 👥

¿Qué día de la semana es?

Using the calendar, take turns asking, **¿Qué día de la semana es… ?** Then tell your partner your favorite day of the week.

ENERO CALENDARIO

lunes	martes	miércoles	jueves	viernes	sábado	domingo
		1 AÑO NUEVO	2	3	4	5
6 LOS SANTOS REYES	7	8	9	10	11	12
13	14	15	16	17	18	19
20	21	22	23	24	25	26
27	28	29	30	31		

1. el 2
2. el 5
3. el 22
4. el 18
5. el 10
6. el 13
7. el 28
8. el…

LENGUA Here are the numbers you need to give the date:

1	uno	17	diecisiete
2	dos	18	dieciocho
3	tres	19	diecinueve
4	cuatro	20	veinte
5	cinco	21	veintiuno
6	seis	22	veintidós
7	siete	23	veintitrés
8	ocho	24	veinticuatro
9	nueve	25	veinticinco
10	diez	26	veintiséis
11	once	27	veintisiete
12	doce	28	veintiocho
13	trece	29	veintinueve
14	catorce	30	treinta
15	quince	31	treinta y uno
16	dieciséis		

P-12

Preguntas. Take turns asking and answering these questions.

1. ¿Qué día es hoy?

2. Hoy es… ¿Qué día es mañana?

3. Hoy es… de… ¿Qué fecha es mañana?

4. ¿Hay clase de español los domingos? ¿Y los sábados?

5. ¿Qué días hay clase de español?

P-13

Fechas importantes. Take turns asking your partner the dates on which these events take place. Then add your own important event. Your partner will ask you for the date.

Modelo **" la reunión de estudiantes (10/9) "**

¿Cuándo es la reunión de estudiantes?

(Es) el 10 de septiembre.

1. el concierto de Juanes (12/11)
(Es) el 12 de noviembre.

2. el aniversario de Carlos y María (14/4) (Es) el 14 de abril

3. el banquete (1/3)
(Es) el primero/el uno de marzo.

4. la graduación (22/5)
(Es) el 22 de mayo.

5. la fiesta de bienvenida (24/8)
(Es) el 24 de agosto.

6. (your own event)

P-14

El cumpleaños (birthday). Find out when your classmates' birthdays are. Write their names and birthdays in the appropriate space in the chart.

Modelo

¿Cuándo es tu cumpleaños?

(Es) el 3 de mayo.

LENGUA You may have noticed that the word **tú** (meaning *you*) has a written accent mark, and that the word **tu** (meaning *your*) does not. In this book, boxes similar to this one will help you focus on when to use accent marks. You will find all of the rules for accentuation in the online component.

CUMPLEAÑOS			
enero	febrero	marzo	abril
mayo	junio	julio	agosto
septiembre	octubre	noviembre	diciembre

Warm-up for P-12
Ask *¿Hoy es… ?* using the wrong day; students will answer *no.* Then say *¡Ah! Hoy es…* using another wrong day. Students answer *no.* Then ask *¿Qué día es hoy?*

Note for P-12
Although less common, some people use the article in this expression: *Hoy es el 15 de agosto.*

Note for P-13
Both, *el primero de marzo* and *el uno de marzo* are used.

Suggestion for P-13
Provide additional vocabulary or suggestions for other events in Spanish if needed (e.g., *el último día de clase, el Día de la Independencia, el cumpleaños de…*, etc.)

El tiempo

Go to the *Capítulo preliminar* folder in the online component to complete the Learning Module for *Vocabulario en contexto: El tiempo*.

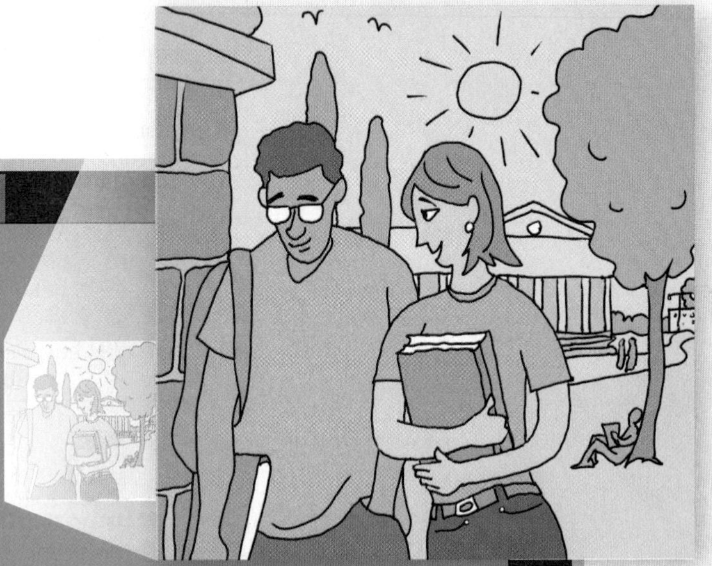

PLAN DE ESTUDIO

◎ **LEARN**
- Interactive presentation: *El tiempo*
- Vocabulary tutorials

APPLY ◎
- Activities

PRÁCTICA COMUNICATIVA

P-15 👥

¿Qué tiempo hace hoy? Take turns with your partner asking about the weather in these cities. Then ask about the weather in your city.

Modelo Miami: ☀️

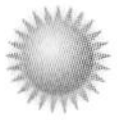

1. Madrid: ☀️

2. Quito: 🌧️

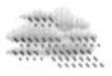

3. Lima: 🌧️

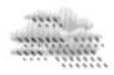

4. Ciudad de México: ☀️

5. Bogotá: 🌧️

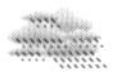

6. Nueva York: ☀️

7. (your city today)

¿Qué tiempo hace en Miami?

En Miami hace buen tiempo. Hace sol.

Expresiones útiles en la clase

Go to the *Capítulo preliminar* [folder] in the online component to complete the Learning Module for *Vocabulario en contexto: Expresiones útiles en la clase.*

PLAN DE ESTUDIO

◎ **LEARN**
- Interactive presentation: *Expresiones útiles en la clase*
- Vocabulary tutorials

◎ **APPLY**
- Activities

Online prep for students
Students will have completed the Learning Module for *Expresiones útiles en la clase* online. You will find additional in-class activities in the Supplementary Activities folder under Instructor's Resources.

Suggestions
Use Total Physical Response (TPR) procedures to review the expressions in this section: *escuchen* (cup hand behind ear); *contesten* (make motion of talking); *abran el libro* (open a book); *vayan a la pizarra* (go to the board).

Point to several students, give a command, and have them do it. Write the command. Then point to one student, give the *tú* command so students can hear and understand the difference between plural and singular commands.

PRÁCTICA COMUNICATIVA

P-16

Las expresiones útiles. Match the following expressions with their pictures and compare your answers with a classmate. Then take turns telling your partner three things he/she needs to do and your partner will act them out.

1. Ve a la pizarra. e   **3.** Pregúntale a tu compañero. c   **5.** Siéntate. b

2. Abre el libro. a   **4.** Repite. d   **6.** Lean. f

a.

b.

c.

d.

e.

f.

Spelling in Spanish:
El alfabeto

Go to the *Capítulo preliminar* in the online component to complete the Learning Module for *Vocabulario en contexto: El alfabeto*.

PLAN DE ESTUDIO

◎ LEARN
- Interactive presentation: *El alfabeto*
- Vocabulary tutorials
- Pronunciation

APPLY ◎
- Activities
- Pronunciation activities

PRÁCTICA COMUNICATIVA

EN OTRAS PALABRAS
Like English speakers, Spanish speakers have different accents that reflect their region or country of origin. For example, the letter **c** before vowels **e** and **i** and the letter **z** are pronounced like **s,** except in certain regions of Spain, where they are similar to the English *th.*

P-17 👥
¿Cómo se escribe?
Spell out in Spanish to your partner the name of the street where you live. Then check if he/she wrote it correctly.

P-18 👥
Los nombres. You are at the admissions office of a university in a Spanish-speaking country. Spell out your first or last name for the clerk. Take turns.
Modelo

¿Cómo se llama usted?

Me llamo David Robinson.

¿Cómo se escribe Robinson?

ere-o-be-i-ene-ese-o-ene.

Gramática en contexto

Describing people and things and sharing information related to the classroom

LEARN

Grammar in context

Remember that *Unidos* is designed to put learning in your own hands. A complete study plan, *Plan de estudio,* will appear before each *Gramática en contexto* section to guide you through the online grammar learning modules and application activities. In the *Unidos* program, you will complete learning modules online to prepare for engaging speaking activities that you will do in class in *Práctica comunicativa.*

Identifying and describing people:
Singular forms of *ser*

Go to the *Capítulo preliminar* **folder** in the online component to complete the Learning Module for *Gramática en contexto:* Singular forms of *ser*.

LEARN

Piénsalo activities

Learning Modules in the online grammar presentations are accompanied by an introductory activity, ***Piénsalo*** (Think about it). Here you will be asked to read a short dialogue or text and do a comphension-based activity before reading the grammar explanation. The activity will get you to think about the grammar point before you read the explanation, which will help you to understand it better.

PLAN DE ESTUDIO

◎ **LEARN**
- Interactive presentation: Singular forms of *ser*
- Grammar tutorials

APPLY ◎
- Activities
- Extra Practice

PRÁCTICA COMUNICATIVA

 P-19 👥

Yo soy... Ask your partner about his/her personality. Use the cognates provided or others that you know.

Modelo

¿Eres pesimista?

No, no soy pesimista.

generoso/a
independiente
inteligente
optimista
nervioso/a
responsable
tímido/a

¿Cómo eres?

Soy activo, optimista y creativo.

 P-20 👥

Descripciones. Ask each other about your classmates. Describe them by using cognates.

Modelo

¿Cómo es... ?

Es...

Online prep for students
Students will have completed the Learning Module including Apply activities for Singular forms of *ser* online. View content for learning modules online. Additional in-class activities are available for download in the Supplementary Activities folder online.

Note
The goal of this section is to introduce forms of the verb *ser* needed for communication at this stage and to preview the notion of gender and its relationship to adjective endings.

Tech Tip for Singular forms of *ser*
Project images from the Internet of well-known people, to practice *¿Quién es?* Use the pictures again to ask: *¿Cómo es X, serio/a o cómico/a? ¿Es sentimental? ¿Es optimista o pesimista?* Point to a male or a female student using the appropriate adjective. Model and personalize short dialogues by pointing to individual students and having classmates respond.

Suggestion
Review *soy* by pointing to yourself as you describe yourself. *Yo soy activo/a y serio/a. Soy optimista. No soy pesimista.*
Introduce *eres* and *es* by substituting names of students in similar exchanges.

Suggestion for P-19
Ask students to come up with other words they know in Spanish that have English cognates. Focus attention on adjectives by providing examples such as: a secretary *es responsable, es muy eficiente;* a poet *es idealista y sentimental, es creativo/a;* a musician *es rebelde y romántico/a.* Ask yes/no questions to check understanding.

Warm-up for P-19
Give a photo of a well-known person to each pair of students, and have them describe his/her personality.

Follow-up for P-20
Have students get together in groups of 4 to exchange information.

Online prep for students
Students will have completed the Learning Module for *Gramática en contexto* online before coming to class. Additional in-class activities are available for download in the Supplementary Activities folder online.

Note
Spanish has 2 words for "in front of." *Marta está delante de Pedro* means that Marta is in front of (ahead of) Pedro when they are facing in the same direction. *Marta está enfrente de Pedro* means that they are facing each other. Also use *enfrente* to express "in front of" with objects or a building. *Los turistas están enfrente de la catedral.* (The tourists are in front of the cathedral.)

Standard 1.2
Students understand and interpret written and spoken language on a variety of topics.

In P-21 the pre-listening activity and the drawing aid comprehension of the spoken word at this early learning stage. Students can understand more than they can say, so instructors should focus on comprehension, rather than limit input to only the words and structures that students can produce orally.

Audioscript for P-21
1. *El televisor está detrás de la profesora.*
2. *El libro está sobre el escritorio.*
3. *María está al lado de Juan.*
4. *La pizarra está al lado de la puerta.*
5. *El cuaderno está debajo del pupitre.*
6. *El cesto está entre la ventana y el escritorio.*

Locating people and things:
¿Dónde está?

Go to the *Capítulo preliminar* `folder` in the online component to complete the Learning Module for *Gramática en contexto: ¿Dónde está?*

PLAN DE ESTUDIO

◎ LEARN
- Interactive presentation: *¿Dónde está?*
- Grammar tutorials

APPLY ◎
- Activities
- Extra Practice

PRÁCTICA COMUNICATIVA

P-21

Personas y lugares.

 PRIMERA FASE. Take turns telling your partner the location of three people or objects in the classroom scene.

SEGUNDA FASE. Listen to the statements about the location of people and objects in the classroom scene. Indicate (✓) whether each statement is true (**Cierto**) or false (**Falso**). Compare your answers with those of a classmate.

	CIERTO	FALSO
1.	✓	
2.	✓	
3.		✓
4.	✓	
5.		✓
6.		✓

P-22 👥

En la clase. Look at the student name tags in Professor Gallegos's class. Ask your partner where Juan, Pedro, Cristina, Mercedes, and Roberto are sitting and he/she will ask you about María, Susana, Carlos, and Profesor Gallegos.

Modelo

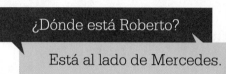

¿Dónde está Roberto?

Está al lado de Mercedes.

El profesor Gallegos

María | Pablo | Mercedes | Roberto

Susana | Juan | Cristina | Pedro | Carlos

P-23 👥

¿Dónde está? Take turns asking where several items in your classroom are. Answer by giving their position in relation to a person or another object.

Modelo

¿Dónde está el libro?

Está sobre el escritorio.

P-24 👥

¿Quién es? Based on what your partner says regarding the location of another student, guess who he/she is.

Modelo

Está al lado de Juan. ¿Quién es?

Es María.

Suggestions for P-22
Review the contrasting pair *enfrente de/detrás de* by standing in front of a student. Say *¿Dónde está el profesor/la profesora? Está enfrente de…* Then move behind a student and ask the same question. *Está detrás de…* Reinforce understanding by asking three students to form a line in front of the class. Make statements about their positions. The remaining students respond with *sí* or *no*, depending on whether your statements are correct or incorrect.
    Ask either/or questions about students and objects: *¿Está Manuel enfrente de Carolina o detrás de ella?*
    Ask questions using *¿Dónde está… ?* You may want to introduce other expressions such as *la derecha (de), a la izquierda (de).*

Suggestion for P-22
Start by saying where some of the students are seated (e.g., *Pedro está al lado de Carlos*). Students answer *sí* or *no.* Point out that several statements are possible for each name. Then students do the activity.

Alternative for P-22
You may create an information gap activity by preparing 2 partially filled seating charts (in which version A includes the information missing in version B and vice versa). Pairs of students ask each other questions to fill in their respective charts, e.g., *¿Quién está delante de Ester?*

Warm-up for P-24
Model the activity with students before they pair up. You may wish to introduce the expressions *cerca (de)* and *lejos (de)* and use them in this guessing game: *Está lejos de Susana. Está lejos de Arturo. Está muy cerca de Amelia. ¿Quién es?* Students take turns providing information and guessing.

Using numbers:
Los números de 0 a 99

Go to the *Capítulo preliminar* [folder] in the online component to complete the Learning Module for *Gramática en contexto: Los números de 0 a 99.*

PLAN DE ESTUDIO

◎ LEARN
- Interactive presentation: *Los números de 0 a 99*
- Grammar tutorials

APPLY ◎
- Activities
- Extra Practice

PRÁCTICA COMUNICATIVA

P-25

¿Qué número es? Your instructor will read a number from each group. Circle the number you hear. Then compare your responses with those of your partner and tell him/her your favorite number.

a. 8   4   3   5

b. 12   9   16   6

c. 37   59   41   26

d. 54   38   76   95

e. 83   62   72   49

f. 47   14   91   56

P-26

Para la oficina. You and your partner have to check a shipment of equipment and supplies delivered to the Spanish department. Take turns asking your partner how many of each there are. Then ask each other about the items without a number and respond with your own amount.

Modelo

4 relojes

¿Cuántos relojes hay?

Hay 4 relojes.

- 10 teléfonos
- 12 escritorios
- 20 cestos
- 95 bolígrafos
- 70 rotuladores
- 34 libros
- ... diccionarios
- ... cuadernos

P-27

Problemas. Take turns solving the following arithmetic problems. Use **y (+)**, **menos (–)**, and **son (=)**. Then create a new arithmetic problem and ask your partner to solve it.

Modelo
"$12 - 5 =$"
"Doce menos cinco son siete"

a. $11 + 4 =$ _____15_____
b. $8 + 2 =$ _____10_____
c. $13 + 3 =$ _____16_____
d. $20 - 6 =$ _____14_____
e. $39 + 50 =$ _____89_____
f. $80 - 1 =$ _____79_____
g. $50 - 25 =$ _____25_____
h. $26 + 40 =$ _____66_____
i. ...

P-28

Los números de teléfono y las direcciones (addresses). Take turns asking each other the phone numbers and addresses of the people listed in the following directory. Then ask your partner for his/her address and phone number (real or imaginary).

Cárdenas Alfaro, Joaquín	General Páez 40	423–4837
Cárdenas Villanueva, Sara	Avenida Bolívar 7	956–1709
Castelar Torres, Adelaida	Paseo del Prado 85	218–3642
Castellanos Rey, Carlos	Colón 62	654–6416
Castelli Rivero, Victoria	Chamberí 3	615–7359
Castillo Montoya, Rafael	Santa Cruz 73	956–3382

Modelo **"Castellanos Rey, Carlos"**

¿Cuál es la dirección de Carlos Castellanos Rey?

Calle Colón, número 62.

¿Cuál es su número de teléfono?

(Es el) 6-54-64-16

Cultura

In Spanish-speaking countries, the name of the street precedes the house or building number. Sometimes a comma is placed before the number.

Calle (Street) Bolívar 132   **Avenida (Avenue) de Gracia, 18**

Telephone numbers are generally not stated as individual numbers, but in groups of two, depending on how the numbers are written or on the number of digits, which varies from country to country.

12-24-67: **doce, veinticuatro, sesenta y siete**
243-89-07: **dos cuarenta y tres, ochenta y nueve, cero siete**

Compara: How do you say or write a street address in your language? How do you say a phone number?

Note for P-26 and P-27
An ellipsis (…) next to an item number in an activity signals an opportunity for students to provide their own cue or response.

Suggestion for P-28
Introduce the word *calle*. Explain that in addresses, the word *calle* may be understood if *calle*, *avenida* or *paseo* is not specified.

Suggestion for P-28
Clarify the meaning of *dirección* by giving addresses of places with which students are familiar. You may want to explain the use of both paternal and maternal surnames in most Spanish-speaking countries (Argentina is an exception). Say *La dirección de… es…* Write the numbers as you say them.

Telling time:

La hora

Go to the *Capítulo preliminar* **folder** in the online component to complete the Learning Module for *Gramática en contexto: La hora.*

PLAN DE ESTUDIO

◎ LEARN
• Interactive presentation: *La hora*
• Grammar tutorials

APPLY ◎
• Activities
• Extra Practice

PRÁCTICA COMUNICATIVA

P-29 **¿Qué hora es en… ?** Take turns telling your partner what time it is in the following cities. Then draw another time clock and ask your partner to give you the time.

México, P.M.   San Juan, P.M.   Buenos Aires, P.M.   Madrid, P.M.

P-30

El horario de María. Take turns asking and answering questions about María's schedule. Then write down your own Monday schedule, omitting the time each class meets. Exchange schedules with your partner, and find out what time each of his/her classes starts.

Modelo

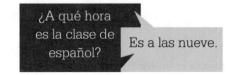

¿A qué hora es la clase de español?

Es a las nueve.

LUNES	
9:00	la clase de español
10:00	la clase de matemáticas
11:00	la clase de psicología
12:00	el laboratorio
12:30	el almuerzo
1:00	la clase de física
5:00	la clase de tenis

Cultura

In Spanish-speaking countries, events such as concerts, shows, classes, and professional meetings generally begin on time. Medical appointments are also kept at the scheduled hour. However, informal social functions, such as parties and private gatherings, do not usually begin on time. In fact, guests are expected to arrive at least a half hour after the appointed time. When in doubt, you may ask **¿En punto?** to find out whether you should be punctual.

Compara: What is the convention in your culture regarding the time you should get to someone's house? Is it polite to arrive right on time? In what situations are you expected to be punctual?

LENGUA To ask the time at which an event takes place or something happens, use **¿A qué hora es…?** To answer, use **Es a la(s)…** or simply **A la(s)…**
¿A qué hora es la clase de español? *At what time is Spanish class?*
(Es) a las nueve y media. *It is at 9:30.*

En este capítulo...

Comprueba lo que sabes

Go to the *Comprueba lo que sabes* folder online to review what you have learned in this chapter. Practice with the following:

Flashcards | **Games** | **Oral Practice** | **Practice Test/Study Plan**

LEARN **Assess yourself at the end of the chapter**

At the end of each chapter MySpanishLab features ample opportunity for you to assess if you have achieved the learning outcomes presented at the beginning of each chapter. Visit the *Comprueba lo que sabes* folder in MySpanishLab to access different practice resources:

- An **Audio-enhanced Vocabulary Flashcard** tool that can be exported to your mobile phone.
- **Games:** *Concentración* (Concentration), *Un partido de fútbol* (soccer-inspired hangman), and *Un concurso* (Quiz Show), which test your knowledge of the chapter's vocabulary and structures.
- **Oral Practice:** Record your answers to the **Oral Practice** comprehensive speaking activities to practice the vocabulary and grammar from the chapter.
- A comprehensive **Practice Test** that generates a personalized Study Plan with support materials.

Note for *Vocabulario*
End of chapter vocabulary lists are designed for students to know which words are considered active for each chapter. The Spanish-English Glossary in the appendices provides English translations if students need them.

Vocabulario

Las presentaciones
¿Cómo se llama usted?
¿Cómo te llamas?
Encantado/a.
Igualmente.
Me llamo…
Mucho gusto.

Los saludos
bastante
bien
buenas tardes/buenas noches
buenos días
¿Cómo está?
¿Cómo estás?
hola
mal
muy
regular
¿Qué tal?

En el salón de clase
el bolígrafo
el borrador
la calculadora
el cesto
la computadora
la computadora portátil
el cuaderno
el DVD
el escritorio
el lápiz
el libro
el mapa
el marcador/el rotulador
la mesa
la mochila
la pantalla
la pizarra
la puerta
el reloj
la silla
la tableta
el televisor
la ventana

Las personas
el amigo/la amiga
el chico/la chica
él
ella

el/la estudiante
el profesor/la profesora
el señor (Sr.)
la señora (Sra.)
la señorita (Srta.)
tú
usted
yo

La posición
al lado (de)
debajo (de)
detrás (de)
enfrente (de)
entre
sobre

Verbos
eres
es
está
estás
hay
soy

Palabras y expresiones útiles
a
el año
¿Cómo es?
el día
¿Dónde está…?
en
ese/a
hoy
mañana
la mañana
más o menos
el mes
mi(s)
¿Quién es…?
la semana
sí
su(s)
tu(s)
un/una
y

Las despedidas
adiós
chao
hasta luego
hasta mañana
hasta pronto

Expresiones de cortesía
con permiso
de nada
gracias
lo siento
perdón
por favor

Cognados
activo/a
ambicioso/a
arrogante
atlético/a
atractivo/a
cómico/a
creativo/a
dinámico/a
eficiente
elegante
extrovertido/a
generoso/a
idealista
importante
impulsivo/a
independiente
inteligente
interesante
introvertido/a
moderno/a
nervioso/a
optimista
paciente
pasivo/a
perfeccionista
pesimista
popular
religioso/a
responsable
romántico/a
sentimental
serio/a
sincero/a
tímido/a
tradicional
tranquilo/a

Los números de 0 a 99
cero
uno
dos
tres
cuatro

cinco
seis
siete
ocho
nueve
diez
once
doce
trece
catorce
quince
dieciséis
diecisiete
dieciocho
diecinueve
veinte
veintiuno
veintidós
veintitrés
treinta
treinta y uno
cuarenta
cincuenta
sesenta
setenta
ochenta
noventa

Los meses del año
enero
febrero
marzo
abril
mayo
junio
julio
agosto
septiembre
octubre
noviembre
diciembre

Los días de la semana
lunes
martes
miércoles
jueves
viernes
sábado
domingo

La hora
de la mañana

de la noche
de la tarde
en punto
Es la…
menos…
Son las…
¿Qué hora es?
y cuarto / y quince
y media / y treinta

El tiempo
Hace buen/mal tiempo
Hace sol.
Llueve. / Está lloviendo.
¿Qué tiempo hace?

Expresiones útiles en la clase
¿Comprenden? / ¿Comprendes? / ¿Comprende?
Contesta.
Contesten, por favor. / Contesta, por favor. / Conteste, por favor.
Escribe.
Lee.
Levanta la mano.
Repite.
La tarea, por favor.
¿Tienen alguna pregunta? / ¿Tienes alguna pregunta? / ¿Tiene alguna pregunta?
Vayan a la pizarra. / Ve a la pizarra. / Vaya a la pizarra.

Otras expresiones útiles
¿Cómo se dice… en español?
¿En qué página?
Más alto, por favor.
Más despacio/lento, por favor.
Otra vez.
Presente.
No comprendo.
No sé.

1

¿Qué estudias?

Learning OBJECTIVES

You will:

- use new vocabulary to talk about your studies and daily activities

- learn the present tense forms of regular -ar, -er, and -ir verbs

- learn to indicate gender and number in articles and nouns

- learn the forms and some uses of the verb *estar*

- learn interrogative words

- connect new information about Spain and its universities to what you already know

Learning OUTCOMES

You will be able to:

- talk about studies, campus, and academic life

- describe daily routines and activities

- specify gender and number

- express location and states of being

- ask and answer questions

- compare the educational system of Spain to that of your own country

CULTURA INTERACTIVA

ESPAÑA

 Un fresco del siglo XVI en la Universidad de Salamanca

Museo Guggenheim

FRANCIA

Santiago de Compostela

Bilbao

OCÉANO ATLÁNTICO

Universidad de Salamanca

ESPAÑA

Barcelona

Salamanca

Segovia

Paella valenciana

PORTUGAL

Madrid ✪

Valencia

Plaza de toros

Mar Mediterráneo

Córdoba

Sevilla

Granada

La Alhambra

¿Cuánto sabes?

Look at the map and complete the following sentences based on what you know.

1. ___b___ España está en…
   a. América.   b. Europa.   c. Asia.

2. ___b___ La capital de España es…
   a. Barcelona.   b. Madrid.   c. Sevilla.

3. ___a___ La paella es típica de…
   a. Valencia.   b. Salamanca.   c. Madrid.

4. ___a___ En la universidad hay…
   a. estudiantes.   b. catedrales.   c. toros.

5. ___c___ En la plaza de toros hay espectáculos (shows)…
   a. religiosos.   b. cómicos.   c. populares.

Cultura en línea
To learn more about Spain and the chapter theme, go to the *Cultura en línea* folder online to view the *Vistas culturales* video and take a virtual art tour.

Note
Vocabulario en contexto provides a richly contextualized cultural framework for learning and practicing vocabulary online. View content for Learning Modules online. New material is presented in thematic groups, accompanied by photographs, illustrations, and authentic documents.

Active vocabulary appears in boldface. The vocabulary list at the end of the chapter contains that vocabulary, as well as other key words that are used in the chapter.

Online prep for students
Students will have completed the Learning Module for *Los estudiantes y los cursos* online before class. This includes the Interactive presentation and corresponding Apply activities. You will find additional in-class activities in the Supplementary Activities folder online under Instructor's Resources.

Tech tip for *Los estudiantes y los cursos*
You may want to project the images from the online Learning Module in class and begin by describing Rosa Pereda. Use gestures and cognates to facilitate comprehension: *Rosa Pereda es estudiante. Es inteligente, activa y muy popular entre los estudiantes. Estudia sociología en la Universidad de Salamanca.* Recycle some additional cognates from *Capítulo preliminar.* Use connectors such as *pero*, *entonces*, and *ahora*, as needed. Finally, ask yes/no and either/or questions to check comprehension: *¿Llega Rosa a la universidad a las once? ¿Estudia economía? ¿Estudia psicología o matemáticas?* Follow a similar procedure to describe David.

Vocabulario en contexto

Talking about students, their studies, and their activities

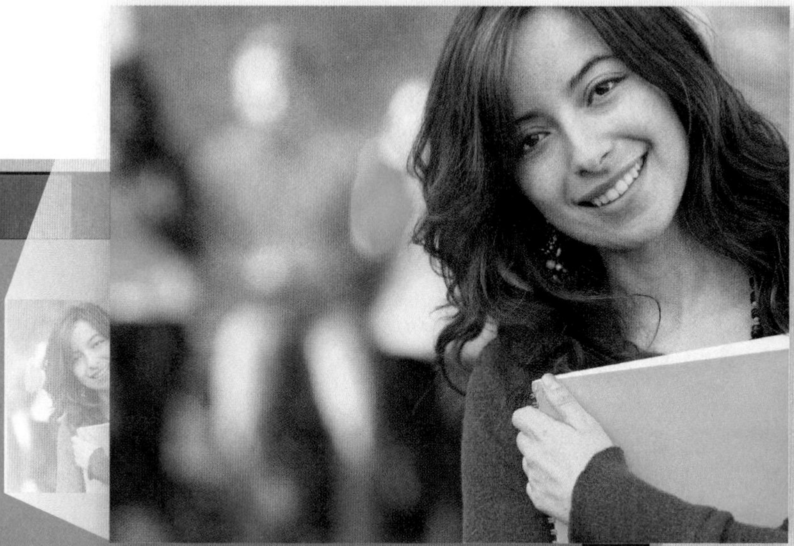

Los estudiantes y los cursos

Go to the *Capítulo 1* folder online to complete the Learning Module for *Vocabulario en contexto: Los estudiantes y los cursos*.

PLAN DE ESTUDIO

LEARN
- Interactive presentation: *Los estudiantes y los cursos*
- Vocabulary tutorials
- Pronunciation

APPLY
- Activities
- Pronunciation activities

PRÁCTICA COMUNICATIVA

1-1

¿Qué sabes de tu compañero/a?
Take turns asking you partner the following information.

Modelo

¿Cuál es tu ...?

Es...

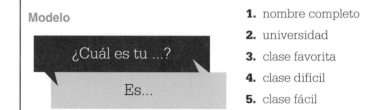

1. nombre completo
2. universidad
3. clase favorita
4. clase difícil
5. clase fácil

1-2

Más información. To learn more about your partner, take turns asking him/her the following questions.

1. ¿De dónde eres?
2. ¿Qué estudias?
3. ¿A qué hora llegas a la universidad?
4. ¿Qué clase es divertida ?

Cultura

Some of Spain's public universities, such as the Universidad de Salamanca, the Universidad de Santiago, and the Universidad Complutense de Madrid, are among the oldest in Europe, dating back hundreds of years. Most private universities in Spain, which are much newer, have higher tuition. To be accepted to a university, students take a competitive comprehensive exam, known as **Selectividad.** Many universities offer Spanish language and culture courses for foreign students.

Compara: What is the oldest university in your country? Is there a difference in tuition between public and private universities in your country, as there is in Spain?

El arzobispo Alonso de Fonseca III fundó la Universidad de Santiago en 1526.

Suggestions for 1-2
Ask additional questions using cognates: ¿Tu compañero/a habla portugués? ¿Estudia álgebra/física?

Expansion
Introduce additional courses (informática, química). Use the verb estudiar to preview introduction of names of courses. You can talk about yourself by saying Yo no estudio economía. Yo no estudio español. Yo soy profesor(a) de español. Yo enseño español. Ustedes estudian español. Ask yes/no questions and either/or questions: ¿Estudias informática? ¿Español? ¿Estudias mucho o poco?

Note for Cultura
The first universities in Latin America were founded by the Spaniards in the 16th century: the Universidad de Santo Tomás de Aquino in Santo Domingo, Dominican Republic; the Universidad de San Marcos in Lima, Peru; and the Universidad Nacional Autónoma de México (UNAM) in Mexico City.

La universidad

Go to the *Capítulo 1* folder online to complete the Learning Module for *Vocabulario en contexto: La universidad.*

PLAN DE ESTUDIO

◎ LEARN
- Interactive presentation: *La universidad*
- Vocabulary tutorials

APPLY ◎
- Activities

PRÁCTICA COMUNICATIVA

1-3

¿En qué clase...? Match the words with the appropriate class. Compare answers with a partner. Then give your partner two other key words for him/her to identify the appropriate class.

1. ___c___ *Don Quijote* (Cervantes)   **a.** geografía

2. ___e___ números   **b.** biología

3. ___a___ mapa digital   **c.** literatura

4. ___b___ animales   **d.** historia

5. ___f___ Freud   **e.** matemáticas

6. ___d___ Napoleón   **f.** psicología

7. . . .

8. . . .

Cultura

Miguel de Cervantes Saavedra (1547–1616) was a Spanish novelist and playwright. He was born in Alcalá de Henares, a town near Madrid. His famous novel *Don Quijote de la Mancha* is one of the most important books in the history of world literature. It is a parody of the romances of chivalry, which were very popular at that time. The main character is Alonso Quijano, an older man who has read too many of those romances and has come to believe that he is a heroic knight. He dubs himself "Don Quijote de la Mancha" and sets off to fight injustice.

Compara: Name a famous literary character in your culture. Who, in your opinion, is the most famous writer in your language?

Estatua de Don Quijote y Sancho Panza

1-4

¿En qué facultad estudian?

PRIMERA FASE. Match the names of the university students pictured with where they study.

1. ___b___ Juan
2. ___a___ Carmen
3. ___d___ Lorena
4. ___c___ Álvaro

a. Facultad de Medicina
b. Facultad de Arquitectura
c. Facultad de Humanidades
d. Facultad de Ciencias

Suggestion for 1-4
Bring in copies of your school's campus map, and have students label buildings in Spanish and have students work with a partner and ask each other questions to locate places.

CARMEN

LORENA

JUAN

ÁLVARO

LITERATURA

SEGUNDA FASE. Exchange information with a classmate and indicate two classes that each student is probably taking.

Modelo

¿Dónde estudia Carmen?

Carmen estudia en la Facultad de… Probablemente tiene clase de…y de…

Note
An ellipsis (…) signals that students need to provide their own response.

1-5

Mis clases.

PRIMERA FASE. Make a list of your classes. Indicate the days and time each class meets and whether it is easy or difficult, interesting or boring.

economía	comunicaciones	negocios
bioquímica	sociología	historia del arte
física	cálculo	informática
artes plásticas	estadística	seminario de…
contabilidad	astronomía	filosofía

CLASE	DÍAS	HORA	¿CÓMO ES?

SEGUNDA FASE. Tell your partner about your classes. Take turns completing the following ideas.

1. Mis clases comienzan (*start*) a la(s)…
2. Mi clase favorita es…
3. El profesor/La profesora se llama…
4. La clase es muy…
5. Practico español en…
6. En mi clase de español hay…

EN OTRAS PALABRAS

Words related to computers and computing are often borrowed from English (e.g., **software**, **e-mail**), and they vary from country to country. As you have already learned, one word for computer is **la computadora**, used mainly in Latin America, along with **el computador**. Computer is **el ordenador** in Spain. *Computer science* is **la informática** in Spain and **la computación** in some countries in Latin America.

 1-6

Las clases de mis compañeros/as.

PRIMERA FASE. Use the following questions to interview your partner. Then switch roles.

1. ¿Qué estudias este semestre?
2. ¿Cuántas clases tienes?
3. ¿Cuál es tu clase favorita?
4. ¿Qué día y a qué hora es tu clase favorita?
5. Tu clase de español, ¿cómo es? ¿Es fácil o difícil? ¿Es interesante o aburrida?
6. ¿Sacas buenas notas?
7. ¿Tienes muchos exámenes?

SEGUNDA FASE. Introduce your partner to another classmate and state one piece of interesting information about him/her. Your classmate will ask your partner about his/her classes.

Modelo

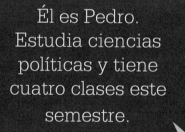

Él es Pedro. Estudia ciencias políticas y tiene cuatro clases este semestre.

Mucho gusto. ¿. . .?

Las actividades de los estudiantes

Go to the *Capítulo 1* [folder] online to complete the Learning Module for *Vocabulario en contexto: Las actividades de los estudiantes*.

PLAN DE ESTUDIO

◎ LEARN
- Interactive presentation: *Las actividades de los estudiantes*
- Vocabulary tutorials
- *Entrevistas* video

APPLY ◎
- Activities
- *Entrevistas* video activities

PRÁCTICA COMUNICATIVA

1-7

Para escoger. Take turns with your partner telling him/her what the students do by filling in the blanks. Then ask your partner about his/her activities.

Modelo

> Los estudiantes buscan palabras en el diccionario. ¿Y tú?
>
> Yo, en Internet.

1. Los estudiantes ___b___ en la biblioteca.
   - **a.** toman café
   - **b.** estudian
   - **c.** hablan

2. Miran televisión en ___c___.
   - **a.** la biblioteca
   - **b.** la playa
   - **c.** casa

3. Montan en bicicleta ___a___.
   - **a.** los fines de semana
   - **b.** en el café
   - **c.** en una discoteca

1-8

Otra conversación. With a partner, read the conversation between a student and a clerk. Then, change the conversation to role play a similar situation.

ESTUDIANTE: Necesito comprar un diccionario para mi clase de literatura española.

DEPENDIENTE: Aquí hay un diccionario muy bueno.

ESTUDIANTE: ¿Cuánto cuesta?

DEPENDIENTE: Cuarenta y ocho euros.

1-9

¿Cuánto cuesta? During your semester in Spain, you go to the university bookstore. Take turns with a partner asking how much the following items cost and responding as the salesclerk.

Modelo

ESTUDIANTE: *¿Cuánto cuesta el mapa?*

DEPENDIENTE/A: *Cuesta cincuenta euros.*

Suggestion for 1-10
Make sure that students understand *dónde* and *cuándo*. You may ask: *¿Cuándo es la clase de español, el lunes o el martes? ¿Dónde es?*

1-10

Entrevista (*Interview*). Ask where and when your classmate does each of the following activities. Then share your findings with the class.

Modelo 66 practicar baloncesto (*basketball*) 99

¿Dónde practicas baloncesto? ¿Y cuándo?

Practico baloncesto en el gimnasio por la tarde.

Cultura

Since 2002, the euro has been the official monetary unit of the Eurozone, which includes (as of 2012) Austria, Belgium, Cyprus, Estonia, Finland, France, Germany, Greece, Ireland, Italy, Luxembourg, Malta, the Netherlands, Portugal, Slovakia, Slovenia, and Spain. In some other European countries and the United Kingdom, the euro, although not official, is accepted in stores. The euro currency sign is € and the banking code is EUR.

Compara: What is the currency in your country? When did it become the official monetary unit?

ACTIVIDAD	DÓNDE	CUÁNDO
1. estudiar para un examen difícil		
2. mirar televisión		
3. tomar café		
4. conversar con tus amigos		
5. escuchar música		
6. comprar unos cuadernos para tus clases		

1-11

Las actividades de tus compañeros.

PRIMERA FASE. Go around the classroom and interview three people. Take notes to report back to the class.

1. ¿Qué haces (*do you do*) los fines de semana?
2. ¿Dónde miras tu programa de televisión favorito?
3. ¿Qué compras en la librería?
4. ¿Dónde estudias normalmente?
5. ¿Trabajas los fines de semana? ¿Dónde trabajas?

SEGUNDA FASE. Now share your classmates' answers with the rest of the class.

Modelo

> **"** *María estudia normalmente en casa.*
> *No trabaja los fines de semana.* **"**

1-12

¿Qué hacen? (*What do they do?*)

PRIMERA FASE. You will hear three people talking about their activities during the week and on weekends. Before you listen, list your own activities in the chart. Ask your partner if he/she does the same things. What do you have in common?

MIS ACTIVIDADES DIARIAS (*DAILY*)	MIS ACTIVIDADES DEL FIN DE SEMANA

SEGUNDA FASE. Now pay attention to the general idea of what is said in the conversation. Then write the number of the speaker (1, 2, 3) next to each topic.

___2___ los estudios

___3___ el tiempo libre (*free time*)

___1___ el trabajo

Discoteca Tropical House en Madrid

Note for 1-11
Students have already practiced conjugating -*ar* verbs. You may go over them before starting **1-11** or ask students to review verb endings in *Gramática en contexto*.

Suggestion for 1-11
Segunda fase
You may wish to ask students to compare the routine of one of the classmates with their own. *María estudia normalmente en casa. Yo estudio en la biblioteca.*

Note for Listening activity
Listening activities provide many learning opportunities when done in the classroom and they can be used to enhance communication. You may, for example, play the audio once and ask students to communicate in pairs about what they have understood. Then, play it again and change the pairs successively until the main ideas have been completely understood by most.

Suggestion for 1-12
Mention that students will hear the word *fútbol* and that in Spanish this word usually refers to soccer.

Audioscript for 1-12
1. *Por las mañanas camino a la oficina. Trabajo en el departamento de informática de una compañía muy importante. Llego a la oficina a las nueve menos diez, y a las nueve ya estoy frente al ordenador. Mi trabajo es muy interesante.*
2. *Estudio biología, química e italiano. Mis clases son por la mañana y por la tarde. La clase de biología es difícil, pero no es aburrida. Hay muchos alumnos en mis clases de biología y de química, pero hay menos alumnos en las prácticas de laboratorio.*
3. *Los sábados por la mañana, practico fútbol con mis amigos. Por la tarde, miro televisión y hablo con mi amiga Alicia. Por la noche, Alicia y unos amigos toman algo en un café y yo bailo en una discoteca.*

Gramática en contexto

Note
The structures in the *Gramática en contexto* online Learning Module are presented in context to stress their functions in communication. Each structure is presented first as meaningful input through a visual and a short dialogue or text, and is accompanied by a comprehension-based activity, *Piénsalo,* designed to highlight function/form connections. Brief grammar explanations come next and are followed by practice within a focused, contextualized framework. View content for Learning Module online. In class, students will practice the communicative/task-oriented activities.

Online prep for students
Students will have completed the Learning Module for Present tense of regular -*ar* verbs online before class. This includes the Interactive presentation and corresponding Apply activities. You will find additional in-class activities in the Supplementary Activities folder online under Instructor's Resources.

Suggestion
Review subject pronouns (*Capítulo preliminar*) by pointing to a student or students and having classmates provide the appropriate pronouns.

Tech tip for Present tense of regular -*ar* verbs
Use visuals and comprehensible input to review the verb forms with students, say: *Yo hablo español.* Point to a student (or project an image of a well-know Hispanic person) and say: *Él/Ella habla español.* Point to the student (or image) and to yourself and say: *Nosotros hablamos español. También hablamos inglés. No hablamos italiano.* Point to another student and to yourself, and give another example: *Nosotros miramos televisión.* Point to one student and say: *Él/Ella habla inglés.* Point to another student and repeat the same sentence. Then point to both students and say: *Ellos/Ellas hablan inglés, pero no hablan portugués.*

Talking about academic life and daily occurrences:
Present tense of regular -*ar* verbs

Go to the *Capítulo 1* [folder] online to complete the Learning Module for *Gramática en contexto:* Present tense of regular -*ar* verbs.

PLAN DE ESTUDIO

◎ LEARN
- Interactive presentation: Present tense of regular -*ar* verbs
- Grammar tutorials

APPLY ◎
- Activities
- Extra Practice

PRÁCTICA COMUNICATIVA

1-13

Preferencias. **PRIMERA FASE.** Rank these activities from 1 to 9, according to your preferences (1 = most interesting, 9 = least interesting).

_____ bailar en una discoteca

_____ mirar televisión en casa

_____ estudiar otras culturas

_____ comprar DVD y CD

_____ caminar en la playa

_____ montar en bicicleta cuando hace sol

_____ escuchar música rock

_____ conversar con los amigos con mensajes de texto

_____ bajar (*download*) música de Internet

SEGUNDA FASE. Now compare your answers with those of a classmate. Follow the model.

Modelo

Para mí, bailar en una discoteca es número 1. ¿Y para ti?

Para mí, caminar en la playa es número 1.

1-14

Mi rutina.

PRIMERA FASE. Indicate the activities that are part of your routine at school.

1. _____ Llego a la universidad a las nueve de la mañana.
2. _____ Llamo a mis amigos por teléfono.
3. _____ Tomo notas en todas las clases.
4. _____ Hablo con mis compañeros en la cafetería.
5. _____ Estudio en la biblioteca por la mañana.
6. _____ Trabajo en mis tareas todas las noches.
7. _____ Miro dramas policíacos en la televisión.
8. _____ A veces practico un deporte con mis amigos/as.

 SEGUNDA FASE. Now compare your answers with those of a classmate. Report your findings to the class.

Modelo

> Daniel y yo somos parecidos (*similar*). Miramos dramas policiacos en la televisión.

> Ben y yo somos diferentes. Yo estudio por la mañana; él estudia por la tarde.

1-15

A preguntar.

PRIMERA FASE. Find four different classmates, each of whom does one of the following activities. Write each name on the appropriate line. The *En directo* expressions will help you.

Modelo  **" mirar televisión por la tarde "**

> ¡Oye! ¿Miras televisión por la tarde?

> No, no miro televisión por la tarde. Miro televisión por la noche.

PERSONA	ACTIVIDAD
_____	estudiar español todos los días
_____	llegar a clase a las 9:30 A.M.
_____	escuchar música clásica en casa por la noche
_____	trabajar en una oficina por la tarde

En directo

To get someone's attention:

¡Oye! (to someone your age or younger)

Oiga, por favor. (to someone unknown to you)

To interrupt to ask a question:

Perdón, tengo una pregunta.

To agree to answer:

Con mucho gusto.

 Click on the icon to listen to a conversation with these expressions.

SEGUNDA FASE. Now report to the class your findings about your classmates' activities.

Suggestion for 1-14
Students can work in small groups to determine the group's most and least interesting activity. The whole class can then tally the responses.

Warm-up for 1-15
Model the activity by asking one student *¿Practicas español con tus amigos?* If he/she responds *sí*, say: *Yo escribo el nombre de… en el libro.* If he/she says *no*, ask another student. Then say: *Ahora ustedes preguntan a sus compañeros. Levántense, por favor.* Signal for them to get up and move around to ask their classmates.

Follow-up for 1-15
After students complete the activity, have them report their results to the class. To practice plural verb forms, students can work in groups and pull together their findings: *David y Amanda llegan a la universidad a las 9:30.*

Audioscript for *En directo*
Jill: *¡Oye! ¡Profesora Enríquez!*
Jake: *Jill, tienes que ser más formal con la profesora. Dile, "Oiga, por favor" o "Perdón, tengo una pregunta."*
Jill: *Está bien… ¡Profesora Enríquez! Tengo una pregunta para usted.*
Profesora Enríquez: *Con mucho gusto.*

1-16

Mis actividades. PRIMERA FASE. Indicate how often you do the following activities:

ACTIVIDADES	A VECES	MUCHAS VECES	SIEMPRE	NUNCA
estudiar con amigos				
hacer/ejercicio				
montar en bicicleta los fines de semana				
mirar televisión por la tarde				
bailar los sábados				
tomar café				

 SEGUNDA FASE. Now tell each other how often you do these activities, and then ask your partner where he/she does them.

Modelo

Yo estudio con mis amigos a veces. ¿Y tú?

¿Dónde estudian ustedes?

Yo siempre estudio con amigos.

Estudiamos en la biblioteca.

1-17

Un día típico en la vida de Luisa.

Take turns describing what Luisa does on a typical day. Then select two of the times to tell your partner what you do at those times.

Modelo

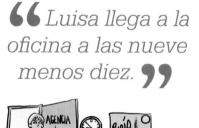
66 *Luisa llega a la oficina a las nueve menos diez.* 99

1.

2.

3.

4.

Cultura

A popular social activity in Spain is **ir de tapas** (to go out for **tapas**). **Tapas** are small portions of different dishes that are served in most bars with wine or beer. They range from a piece of bread with an anchovy to elaborate appetizers.

Compara: Do you know of other cultures in which small portions are shared among friends or family in restaurants or bars?

Este bar de Madrid tiene una selección de tapas deliciosas.

Situaciones

1

ROLE A. Your friend works in the afternoon. Ask: a) where he/she works; b) the days of the week and the hours that he/she works; and c) if the job (**trabajo**) is interesting/boring/difficult/easy. Then answer your friend's questions about your job.

ROLE B. Tell your friend that you work in the afternoon. Answer your friend's questions about your job. Then ask three questions about his/her job (**trabajo**).

2

ROLE A. There is a new international student in your class. He/she is interested in learning about your routines as a student. Explain to him/her what time you get to campus, what classes you are taking, if you study in the library, if you do (**practicar**) any sports at the gym, etc.

ROLE B. You are a new international student. You meet another student and you ask him/her questions about his/her routine and that of other students.

Online prep for students
Students will have completed the Learning Module for Present tense of regular *-er* and *-ir* verbs online before class. See content online. Additional in-class activities are available for download in the Supplementary Activities folder.

Tech Tip for Present tense of regular *-er* and *-ir* verbs
Project the image from the online *Piénsalo* activity in the Learning Module to review *-er* and *-ir* verbs and person markers (*-s, -mos, -n*). Contextualize your language as you review the verbs: *Antonio asiste a sus clases todos los días. Y tú, ¿asistes a tus clases todos los días? Antonio aprende mucho con el profesor. Y tú, ¿aprendes mucho? Antonio y Pedro escriben muchos trabajos de investigación. Y ustedes, ¿escriben mucho también?* Point out the similarities and differences between *-er* and *-ir* verbs. *¿Lees mucho? ¿Qué libros lees? Y tus amigos, ¿leen mucho también? ¿Lees el periódico por la mañana? ¿Lees el periódico en Internet o en papel? ¿Dónde vives? ¿Vives en una casa o en un apartamento?*

Talking about academic life and daily occurrences:

Present tense of regular *-er* and *-ir* verbs

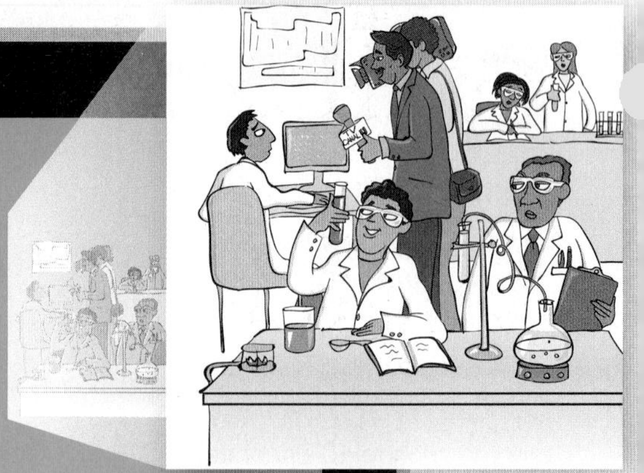

Go to the *Capítulo 1* **folder** online to complete the Learning Module for *Gramática en contexto:* Present tense of regular *-er* and *-ir* verbs.

PLAN DE ESTUDIO

LEARN
- Interactive presentation: Present tense of regular *-er* and *-ir* verbs
- Grammar tutorials

APPLY
- Activities
- Extra Practice

PRÁCTICA COMUNICATIVA

1-18

Mi profesor/a modelo. **PRIMERA FASE.** Indicate which of the following activities are part of the routine of an ideal instructor inside and outside the classroom.

	SÍ	NO
1. Lee el periódico (*newspaper*) en clase.	______	______
2. Escucha los problemas de los estudiantes.	______	______
3. Bebe café y come en la clase.	______	______
4. Escribe buenos ejemplos en la pizarra.	______	______
5. Nunca prepara sus clases.	______	______
6. Siempre asiste a clase.	______	______
7. Responde a las preguntas de los estudiantes.	______	______
8. Habla con los estudiantes en su oficina.	______	______

SEGUNDA FASE. Compare your answers with those of a classmate. Together write two more activities typical of an ideal instructor and ask your instructor if they are part of his/her academic routine.

1-19

Para pasarlo bien (*To have a good time*).

PRIMERA FASE. Indicate (✓) which of the following activities you do to have a good time.

1. _____ Leo libros en español todas las semanas.
2. _____ Escribo mensajes de texto.
3. _____ Practico deportes con los amigos.
4. _____ Asisto a clase a las ocho de la mañana.
5. _____ Corro en el gimnasio y en el parque.
6. _____ Veo películas y programas de televisión en casa.
7. _____ Charlo con mis amigos y con mi familia por Skype.
8. _____ Bebo solo Coca-Cola en las fiestas.

SEGUNDA FASE. Compare your answers with those of a classmate. Then exchange information with another pair about the activities you all do to have a good time. Use the expressions in *En directo*.

Modelo

Nosotros bailamos en discotecas para pasarlo bien. ¿Y ustedes?

Bebemos café y conversamos con los amigos.

En directo

To react to what someone has said:

¡Qué interesante!

¡Qué increíble!

¡Qué casualidad! *What a coincidence!*

¡Qué divertido! *How funny!*

¡Qué aburrido! *How boring!*

Click on the icon to listen to a conversation with these expressions.

1-20

Lugares y actividades.

Ask what your classmate does in the following places. He/She will respond with one of the activities listed. Then ask what your classmate does not do in those places.

Modelo

❝ en la clase ❞

¿Qué haces en la clase?

Veo películas en español.

¿Qué no haces en la clase?

No leo mensajes de texto.

LUGARES	ACTIVIDADES
en la playa	beber cerveza
en un café	tomar el sol
en una discoteca	bailar salsa
en una fiesta	mirar televisión
en el cine	leer el periódico
en la casa	ver películas de horror
en un restaurante	escribir mensajes de texto
en la biblioteca	comer un sándwich y tomar un café

Un café con leche en el Café Gijón de Madrid.

Suggestion for 1-19
Pasarlo bien is introduced as a lexical item. Before the activity, expand on the meaning by giving examples: *Hay muchas maneras de pasarlo bien. Yo, por ejemplo, para pasarlo bien, escucho música, corro en el parque cuando hace buen tiempo, preparo comida mexicana en casa, etc. Y tú, ¿lees o bailas para pasarlo bien? ¿Cuáles son tus actividades los fines de semana para pasarlo bien?*

Note for *solo*
According to the RAE, *solo* (without an accent) can be both an adjective and an adverb. Adjective: *Mi tío vive solo en su apartamento.* (My uncle lives alone in his apartment.) Adverb: *Solo tengo una hermana.* (I have only one sister.) Alternatively, *solamente* can replace the adverb *solo/sólo* in all cases.

Audioscript for *En directo*
Ruby: *Cristián y yo tomamos una clase para aprender a hacer tapas.*
Zuli: *¡Qué interesante! Yo tengo clase de cocina francesa.*
Ruby: *¡Qué divertido!*
Zuli: *Al contrario, ¡qué aburrido! No me gusta la comida francesa.*
Ruby: *¡Qué increíble! Y ¿por qué tomas la clase?*

Note for 1-20
In this activity students use *¿Qué (no) haces?* as a fixed phrase. Using the phrase gives students broader opportunities for communication, but they do not use *hacer* in their responses.

Suggestion for 1-20
Encourage students to expand on their answers (e.g., *En la playa tomo el sol y también bebo agua cuando hace mucho calor*).

Expansion for 1-20
Additional places: *la librería, el laboratorio, el trabajo, el gimnasio, el parque.* You can also ask questions with *dónde*; students answer by giving the appropriate place: *¿Dónde come(s) los sábados? ¿Dónde escribes?*

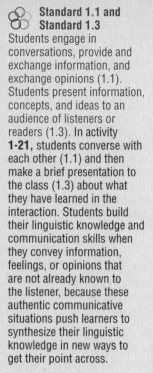

A preguntar.

PRIMERA FASE. Find four different classmates, each of whom does one of the following activities. Write each name in the chart below.

Modelo **" ver películas en casa "**

> ¿Ves películas en casa?

> Sí, veo películas en casa.

PERSONA	ACTIVIDAD
_____	asistir a conciertos de música rock
_____	beber café todos los días
_____	vivir en casa con tu familia
_____	escribir mensajes de texto por la noche

SEGUNDA FASE. Now report to the class your findings about your classmates' activities.

 Situaciones

¿Qué deben hacer? Take turns giving advice to the people in the following situations. Then create your own situation and your partner will give you advice.

Modelo

> Maricela desea sacar buenas notas

> Debe estudiar todos los días.

1. Carlos desea aprender sobre cine español.
2. Luisa y Jorge beben muchos refrescos.
3. Los estudiantes desean comer tapas.
4. Oscar desea aprender a bailar.
5. Carolina desea preparar tacos y enchiladas.
6. . . .

1

ROLE A. You see a classmate at a coffee shop with laptop and books spread out on the table. Ask if he/she: a) drinks coffee every day; b) how often he/she studies in the coffee shop; c) whether he/she does homework there; and d) whether he/she writes papers there.

ROLE B. You are sitting at a table with your laptop and books at your favorite coffee shop. A classmate comes in and walks over. Answer your classmate's questions about what you usually do there.

2

ROLE A. On the way to Spanish class you run into a classmate and ask how he/she is. Your classmate confides that he/she isn't getting good grades in Spanish. Suggest that he/she: a) should always attend class; b) must read the chapter every week; c) should study in the library; and d) ought to look for a good dictionary.

ROLE B. In the hallway you run into the person who sits next to you in Spanish class. When he/she asks how you are, say you're so-so. Explain that you are not getting good grades in Spanish and that you are not learning the vocabulary. Listen to your classmate's advice and thank him/her.

Specifying gender and number:
Articles and nouns

Go to the *Capítulo 1* [folder] online to complete the Learning Module for *Gramática en contexto:* Articles and nouns.

PLAN DE ESTUDIO

◎ **LEARN**
- Interactive presentation: Articles and nouns
- Grammar tutorials

APPLY ◎
- Activities
- Extra Practice

Online prep for students
Students will have completed the Learning Module for Articles and nouns online before class. Additional in-class activities are available for download in the Supplementary Activities folder online.

Suggestions
Write *el/un* on the board or on a visual next to the word *libro*, circling or underlining the *o*. Write *la/una* and the word *tarea*, circling the *a*. Give other examples of vocabulary presented in the chapter. Write *el mapa* and say *excepción;* do the same thing with *el día* and *la mano*. Continue with *la actividad, la lección,* and *la televisión*, underlining the endings *-dad, -ción,* and *-sión*, pointing out that words with these endings use the articles *la/una*.

As a mnemonic device, write the following words in a vertical column on the board, *el cereal, el libro, el salón, el café, el borrador, el tenis.* Circle the final letters of each word to spell "loners"; point out that words ending in these letters are usually masculine.

Suggestion for 1-23
Students may do this activity individually and then check answers with a partner, noting discrepancies that they cannot resolve on their own.

PRÁCTICA COMUNICATIVA

1-23

Conversaciones incompletas.

PRIMERA FASE. Complete the dialogues. Compare answers with a classmate.

1. Supply the definite articles (**el, la, los, las**).

En la universidad

E1: ¿Dónde está María?

E2: Está en ___la___ clase de ___la___ profesora Sánchez.

E1: ¡Qué lástima! Necesito hablar con ella. Es urgente. ¿A qué hora llega?

E2: Llega a ___las___ dos, más o menos.

2. Supply the indefinite articles (**un, una, unos, unas**).

En la librería

E1: Necesito comprar ___unos___ lápices.

E2: Y yo necesito ___un___ cuaderno. ¿Qué más compro?

E1: Para el curso de español, ___unos___ profesores usan ___un___ diccionario electrónico.

SEGUNDA FASE. With a partner select one of the conversations and role play a similar situation.

¿Qué necesitan? Take turns saying what these classmates need. Then tell your partner what you should do and he/she will tell you what you need.

Modelo

Alicia debe buscar unas palabras.

Necesita un diccionario.

1. Mónica debe tomar apuntes en la clase de historia.
2. Carlos y Ana deben hacer la tarea de matemáticas.
3. Alfredo debe estudiar para el examen de geografía.
4. Isabel debe escribir una composición para su clase de inglés.
5. Blanca y Lucía deben buscar las capitales de Sudamérica.
6. David debe marcar las partes importantes del libro de texto.
7. Yo debo...

Situaciones

Suggestions for *Situaciones*
You may wish to have students review the phrases in the *En directo* boxes in this chapter to increase the amount of language they produce and to make their exchanges sound more natural.

For the second *Situación*, student A interviews two classmates. Afterward, groups may share information with the class.

1

ROLE A. You have missed the first day of class. Ask a classmate a) what time the class meets; b) who the professor is; and c) what you need for the class.

ROLE B. Tell your classmate a) the time the class meets; b) the name of the professor and what he/she is like; and c) at least three items that your classmate needs for the class.

2

ROLE A. You work for the student newspaper at your college and have been asked to interview two students to find out how they typically spend their weekends. After introducing yourself, find out a) if they work and, if so, where; b) what they study; and c) what they do (**hacen**) on Saturdays and Sundays.

ROLES B, C. Tell the interviewer a) if you work and, if so, where; b) the classes you take; and c) what you do on weekends, where, and with whom.

Expressing location and states of being:
Present tense of *estar*

Go to the *Capítulo 1* [folder] online to complete the Learning Module for *Gramática en contexto:* Present tense of *estar*.

PLAN DE ESTUDIO

◎ LEARN
- Interactive presentation: Present tense of *estar*
- Grammar tutorials

APPLY ◎
- Activities
- Extra Practice

PRÁCTICA COMUNICATIVA

1-25

En la cafetería. In the cafeteria, Roberto runs across a former classmate. Complete the conversation, using the correct forms of **estar**. Then indicate in parentheses if **estar** signals location (**L**) or a state of being (**S**). Compare answers with a classmate and role play a similar conversation.

ROBERTO: Hola, Carlos. ¿Qué tal? ¿Cómo ___estás (S)___?

CARLOS: ___Estoy (S)___ muy bien. ¿Y tú?

ROBERTO: Muy bien, muy bien. ¿Y cómo ___está (S)___ tu hermana (*sister*) Ana?

CARLOS: Bien, gracias. Ella y mamá ___están (L)___ en España ahora.

ROBERTO: ¡Qué suerte! Y nosotros ___estamos (L)___ en la universidad, ¡y en la semana de exámenes!

Online prep for students
Students will have completed the Learning Module for Present tense of *estar* online before class. See content online and Instructor's Resources for Supplementary Activities.

Note
Remind students that they have already used two verbs that translate as "to be" in English. Write *ser* and *estar* on the board. Ask students basic questions they practiced in the previous chapter (¿*Cómo estás?* ¿*Dónde está…?* ¿*Cómo es…?*) while pointing to the appropriate verb.

Tech Tip for Present tense of *estar*
Use images from the online component or illustrations of people in various places to practice forms of *estar*, some of which students have already seen: *Ellos están en un café, y estas chicas están en una oficina* (write *están* on the board). *Pero ustedes están en la clase de español. Yo estoy aquí también. Nosotros* (use gesture) *estamos en la clase de español.*

Cross-reference
The uses of *ser* and *estar* are contrasted in *Capítulo 2*. You have already been using some forms of *estar*. All the present tense forms are presented here.

Note for 1-25
Activity 1-25 engages students in active learning. Rather than memorize a set of rules, they articulate to themselves and to their partners how a rule applies to a particular statement. This metalinguistic approach –thinking and talking about the language –pushes students to take their understanding of a grammatical concept to a deeper level. Metalinguistic talk, termed "languaging" by researchers (e.g., Swain, 2006) in second language acquisition, has been shown to contribute to language learning.

1-26

Horas y lugares favoritos.

PRIMERA FASE. Choose two different times of day and ask your partner where he/she usually is at that time.

Modelo

> ¿Dónde estás generalmente a las 10:00 de la mañana?
>
> Estoy en…
>
> ¿Y dónde estás a la 1:00 de la tarde?

SEGUNDA FASE. Compare your responses with those of your partner. Identify any similarities and/or differences in your schedules.

1-27

Conversación. Ask a classmate where any of the people in these drawings are and what they are doing. Then draw where you would like to be and your partner will say where you are and what you do there.

Modelo "María Luisa"

> ¿Dónde está María Luisa?
>
> Está en la biblioteca.
>
> ¿Qué hace?
>
> Estudia.

María Luisa

Berta   Lorena

Carlos   El Dr. Núñez

Marcelo   Eduardo

Yo

Situaciones

1

ROLE A. You call a friend you haven't had contact with for a long time. Ask him/her: a) how he/she is doing, and b) how his/her family is. Tell him/her: c) that you are well and d) that you are in town.

ROLE B. An old friend calls you. Greet him/her and ask him/her: a) how he/she is, b) where he/she is, and c) how his/her family is.

2

ROLE A. You are a new student at the university and you do not know where some of these buildings are located. Introduce yourself to a classmate and ask where they are.

la biblioteca
la cafetería
la Facultad de Ciencias
la Facultad de Humanidades

ROLE B. You meet a new student on campus. Answer his/her questions about the location of certain places.

Asking and answering questions:
Interrogative words

Go to the *Capítulo 1* [folder] online to complete the Learning Module for *Gramática en contexto:* Interrogative words.

PLAN DE ESTUDIO

◎ LEARN
- Interactive presentation: Interrogative words
- Grammar tutorials

APPLY ◎
- Activities
- Extra Practice

PRÁCTICA COMUNICATIVA

 1-28

Preguntas. First look at the cues after each question and then complete each question with **quién, cuándo, cuántos/as, cuál,** or **por qué** as logical. Use your questions to interview two people as you walk around the room.

1. ¿ __Cuántas/Qué__ clases tomas? Tomo…

2. ¿ __Cuándo__ son tus clases? Por la…

3. ¿ __Cuál__ es tu clase favorita? La clase de…

4. ¿ __Quién__ es tu profesor/a favorito/a? El profesor/La profesora…

5. ¿ __Por qué__ estudias español? Porque…

6. ¿ __Cuántos__ estudiantes hay en tu clase de español? Hay…

Online prep for students
Students will have completed the Learning Module for Interrogative words online before class. See content online and Instructor's Resources for Supplementary Activities.

Suggestions
Ask questions such as the following: *¿Dónde está la pizarra? ¿Y quién(es) está(n) al lado de la pizarra? ¿Cuántos alumnos hay en esta fila? ¿Quiénes son? ¿Cómo es…?* Point out the difference in stress and meaning between *¿por qué?* and *porque.*

To practice asking for definitions, provide students with words such as *lugar* and *objeto: ¿Qué es una librería? Es un lugar donde compramos libros. ¿Qué es un lápiz? Es un objeto que usamos para escribir.* In small groups, have students practice giving simple definitions (e.g., *oficina, tiza*).

Ask questions using *cuál(es): ¿Cuál es la mochila de Alberto? ¿Y cuáles son los libros de Ana y Pedro?*

Point out that intonation rises at the end of yes/no questions. Lift your hand as you raise intonation asking yes/no questions with subjects before and after the verb.

To practice interrogative tags ask several questions of the same student: *Tú eres David, ¿verdad? Y eres norteamericano, ¿no?*

Practice *¿cómo?* to request repetition or clarification.

Some speakers accept *cuál + adjective,* as in *¿Cuál mochila es tuya?,* whereas others do not. *Unidos* uses *cuál(es) + ser* (or phrase, as in *¿Cuál de las mochilas es tuya?*).

Follow-up for 1-28
Have students create more questions using the interrogative words in the directions.

Entrevista. Take turns asking each other questions to find out the following information. Use appropriate phrases to express disbelief, interest, etc.

1. número de clases que toma este semestre

2. su clase favorita y razón (por qué)

3. número de alumnos en la clase favorita

4. nombre del profesor favorito/de la profesora favorita

5. lugar donde estudia generalmente y cuántas horas estudia por (*per*) día

6. lugar donde trabaja

Situaciones

1

ROLE A. You have just run across a friend you have not seen all year. Inquire about your friend's life in college including: a) the location and size of his/her college/university; b) his/her courses this semester; and c) his/her activities.

ROLE B. You are talking with a friend you have not seen in a long time. Answer your friend's questions about your life in college. Then ask your friend some questions to get the same information.

2

ROLE A. It is the beginning of the term, and you need to add a history class. One of your friends is in a class that looks promising. Ask: a) who the professor is; b) if there is a lot of homework; c) when the class meets; and d) if there is an exam soon. Then ask if you should know (**saber**) anything else (**algo más**) about the class.

ROLE B. Your friend wants some information about your history class. Reply as specifically as possible to all of his/her questions. Then offer some additional information about the class.

Unidos

ESCUCHA

Note for *Unidos*

The design of the activities in this section follows some of the principles that inform the Integrated Performance Assessment model (IPA): a) students "do something with the language" (complete a task), b) tasks assess knowledge and skills within realistic contexts, and c) tasks reflect a sequence that integrates the three modes of communication: interpretive, interpersonal, and presentational. When completing these tasks, students monitor their progress through a simplified standards box that will focus on some aspects of a given task.

1-30 [Presentational]

Preparación. You will hear two college students talking about their classes. Before listening, think about the topics they may talk about and make a list of the things you may expect to hear, based on your experience as a student.

1-31  [Interpretive]

Escucha. Listen to the conversation between Ana and Mario and indicate whether each statement is true (**Cierto**) or false (**Falso**).

1. ___C___ Mario y Ana estudian en la misma (*same*) universidad este semestre.

2. ___C___ Mario toma clases de ciencias y humanidades.

3. ___C___ Ana lee en la biblioteca para sus clases.

4. ___C___ Ana toma clases por la tarde.

5. ___F___ Mario realmente visita otros países en una de sus clases.

ESTRATEGIA

Listen for the gist

You can get the gist of what others are saying by relying on what you do understand, your knowledge of the topic, and your expectations of what happens in different types of conversations. You will find these techniques helpful when listening to Spanish.

Comprueba

I was able to…

_____ recognize academic subjects.

_____ recognize places within the university context.

_____ identify actions that refer to students' routines.

Audioscript for *Escucha*

Ana: *Hola, Mario, ¿qué tal? ¿Cómo estás?*
Mario: *Muy bien, ¿y tú?*
Ana: *Bien, gracias. ¿Estudias aquí este año?*
Mario: *Sí, solo este semestre.*
Ana: *¿Y qué clases tomas?*
Mario: *Matemáticas, inglés, historia y geografía. ¿Y tú?*
Ana: *Yo tomo cinco clases: física, química, matemáticas, biología…*
Mario: *¿Todas de ciencias? ¿No tomas clases de humanidades?*
Ana: *¡Oh, sí! También estudio literatura. Es una clase muy interesante, pero necesitamos leer mucho. Pasamos horas y horas en la biblioteca.*
Mario: *¿Y quién es tu profesor?*
Ana: *Es una profesora que se llama Catalina Gómez. Es excelente. Pero mi clase favorita es la de biología. Trabajamos mucho en el laboratorio. ¿Y cuál es tu clase favorita, Mario?*
Mario: *Pues, la clase de geografía.*
Ana: *¿Geografía?*
Mario: *Sí, es excelente. Es una clase con computadoras. Visitamos un país diferente en cada clase: España, México, Colombia, Chile, Perú… Es una clase muy popular entre los estudiantes.*
Ana: *¡Qué interesante! ¡Uy! Son las tres menos diez. Mi clase de física es a las tres. Hablamos otro día.*

1-32 **Un paso más.** [Interpersonal]

PRIMERA FASE.

Tell your classmate what you usually do on the following days and times. Ask each other questions.

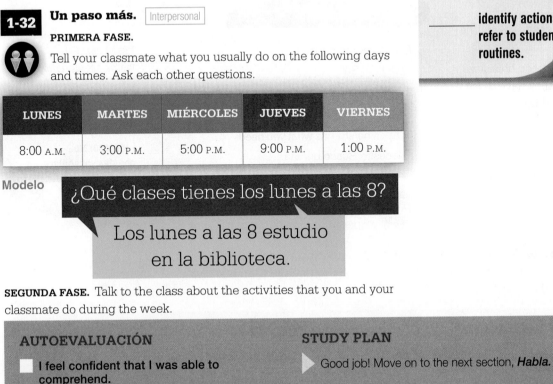

LUNES	MARTES	MIÉRCOLES	JUEVES	VIERNES
8:00 A.M.	3:00 P.M.	5:00 P.M.	9:00 P.M.	1:00 P.M.

Modelo

¿Qué clases tienes los lunes a las 8?

Los lunes a las 8 estudio en la biblioteca.

SEGUNDA FASE. Talk to the class about the activities that you and your classmate do during the week.

AUTOEVALUACIÓN

☐ I feel confident that I was able to comprehend.

☐ I need more listening practice.

STUDY PLAN

▶ Good job! Move on to the next section, *Habla.*

▶ Go to the *Unidos* [folder] online for the *Escucha* practice.

HABLA

1-33 [Interpretive]

Preparación. Write the questions answered by the clerk at your campus bookstore.

1. _____ La dirección de la librería es Calle Mayor, número 50.
2. _____ Sí, tengo libros de historia de España en español.
3. _____ Sí, tengo diccionarios en español.
4. _____ El diccionario bilingüe cuesta 40 euros.

1-34 [Interpersonal]

Habla.

PRIMERA FASE. Read the ad and make a list of five items that you need for your classes, and that you may be able to buy in this bookstore.

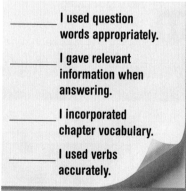

LIBRERÍA CERVANTES

Papelería • Fotocopias • Accesorios para computadora
Libros de texto • Revistas
Casa especializada en cartuchos y toners

Plaza Constitución, 3
29005   Málaga
Teléfono 221 19 99

SEGUNDA FASE. Take turns playing the following roles.

Role A. Call the bookstore and ask if they have those articles, and how much they cost.

Role B. You are the bookstore clerk. Answer your client's questions. Ask for details.

1-35 [Presentational]

Un paso más. Write an e-mail to your best friend explaining the things that you need to buy for your classes, where to find them, and how much they cost.

En directo

To answer the phone in Spain:
    ¿Diga?/¿Sí?

To greet someone formally:
    Buenos días./Buenas tardes.

To ask if he/she has what you need:
    Necesito/Busco un/una…
        /¿Tiene(n)…?

 Click on the icon to listen to a conversation with these expressions.

Comprueba
In my conversation…

_____ I used question words appropriately.

_____ I gave relevant information when answering.

_____ I incorporated chapter vocabulary.

_____ I used verbs accurately.

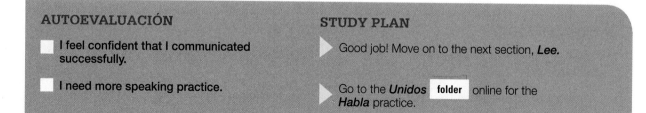

AUTOEVALUACIÓN

☐ I feel confident that I communicated successfully.

☐ I need more speaking practice.

STUDY PLAN

▶ Good job! Move on to the next section, *Lee.*

▶ Go to the *Unidos* [folder] online for the *Habla* practice.

LEE

1-36 Interpersonal

Preparación

Discuss with a classmate which courses from the list students in the following majors (**carreras**) should take.

MEDICINA	BELLAS ARTES	FARMACIA	PSICOLOGÍA	FILOLOGÍA
fisiología, anatomía	diseño gráfico, muralistas mexicanos	drogas tóxicas, medicinas alternativas	conflictos sociales, depresión	estructura del español; historia de la lengua

anatomía

conflictos sociales

depresión

diseño gráfico

drogas tóxicas

estructura del español

fisiología

historia de la lengua

medicinas alternativas

muralistas mexicanos

1-37 Interpretive

Lee.

PRIMERA FASE. Choose the word or phrase that best completes each statement, based on the information of the text below.

1. Esta es una…
   a. página de un libro.
   b. página web.
2. El logo indica que esta institución es…
   a. muy nueva.
   b. muy antigua.

3. Esta página web presenta una lista de…
   a. carreras.
   b. clases.
4. La información de esta página web es…
   a. muy específica.
   b. muy general.
5. Esta institución tiene…
   a. un campus.
   b. más de un campus.

ESTRATEGIA

Identify the format of a text

You have lots of reading experience in your first language with different types of texts. Before you start to read a text in Spanish, look at the illustrations, headings, and layout to help you make educated guesses about the content of the text.

Comprueba

I was able to..

_____ make informed guesses.

_____ recognize important words.

_____ recognize contexts.

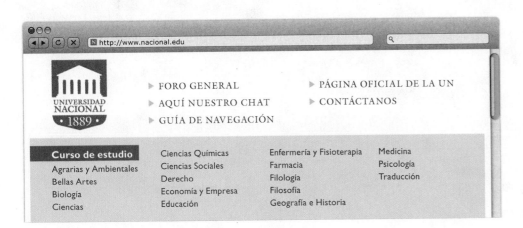

SEGUNDA FASE. Answer the following questions, according to the information in the text.

1. En esta página web hay varios enlaces *(links)*. ¿En qué enlace hacen clic los estudiantes para conversar…?

Aquí Nuestro Chat

2. Imagina que necesitas información sobre tu carrera en esta universidad. ¿Qué facultad tiene la información que necesitas? Answers may vary.

1-38 Presentational

Un paso más. Use the Internet to access the Universidad de Salamanca website and explore the **Servicio Central de Idiomas** page. Explain to your classmates: a) what languages you can study in Salamanca; b) what the address of this office is; and c) why you would or wouldn't like to study at this university in Spain. Your classmates should ask you questions.

AUTOEVALUACIÓN

☐ I feel confident I understood the reading and was able to use the information.

☐ I need more reading practice.

STUDY PLAN

▶ Good job! Move on to the next section, *Escribe.*

▶ Go to the *Unidos* folder online for the *Lee* practice.

ESCRIBE

1-39 [Interpretive]

Preparación. As part of course work in your Spanish class, you have been asked to respond to an e-mail written by a university student in Spain. Read the e-mail and write down four questions you may want to ask the student about his college life in Spain.

Hola, me llamo Pedro. Estudio historia en la Universidad. Tengo cuatro clases. Por las tardes practico deportes en el gimnasio.

¡Hasta pronto!
Pedro

1-40 [Presentational]

Escribe. Now write the Spanish student an e-mail about life at your college or university. Use the information you gathered in 1-39. Consider including the following points:

- introduce yourself
- describe your school and your classes
- describe your daily routine at school, what you do after classes and on weekends, etc.
- ask some questions about college life in Spain

Comprueba

I was able to..

_____ present main ideas clearly with adequate details.

_____ use a wide range of vocabulary words.

_____ use correct gender and number agreement with nouns and adjectives.

_____ conjugate verbs correctly and make them agree with their subjects.

_____ use accurate spelling, capitalization, and punctuation.

ESTRATEGIA

Brainstorm key ideas before writing

Brainstorming helps you come up with good ideas for your writing. To brainstorm, write down a topic or a concept that you want to write about. Then list words and phrases that come to mind. Once you see your ideas laid out on paper, you can start to organize them for your writing.

1-41

Un paso más. [Interpersonal]

Exchange your e-mail with a classmate. Then, respond with a brief note and ask two additional related questions.

Suggestions for 1-39
You may wish to have students do *Preparación* in pairs. You may also want to model the brainstorming process. Keep input (teacher-talk) as natural and spontaneous as possible so students become comfortable with discussing the writing process. Accept any complete or partial response. Keep in mind that this is probably the students' first formal experience writing in Spanish. Elicit information from them rather than give it yourself. If you decide to have students do the task in pairs, have them approach it as if they were one writer, using the first-person singular.

Suggestion for *Un paso más*
Have students check the following after they've written their e-mail:

1. They have provided the information their Spanish friend may need or any other they deem necessary.
2. They have checked any errors in language use, spelling, punctuation, accentuation, and so on.
3. They have used the nosotros form when talking about activities they share.

AUTOEVALUACIÓN

☐ I feel confident I successfully communicated my ideas in writing.

☐ I need more writing practice

STUDY PLAN

▶ Good job!

▶ Go to the *Unidos* [folder] online for the *Escribe* practice.

ENFOQUE *cultural*

CULTURA INTERACTIVA–ESPAÑA

La monarquía constitucional española es una de las más antiguas de Europa. El rey Juan Carlos I y la reina Sofía tienen tres hijos: Elena, Cristina y Felipe, príncipe de Asturias y heredero del trono. En el 2004, el príncipe Felipe se casó con la periodista Letizia Ortiz. En la actualidad tienen dos hijas, Leonor y Sofía.

La Mezquita Catedral de Córdoba es uno de los monumentos más importantes de la arquitectura hispano-musulmana. Es conocida mundialmente por su grandiosidad y su historia.

Escuelas y universidades en España

Go to the *Enfoque cultural* folder in *Capítulo 1* online to learn more about this country.

◎ LEARN
- Interactive presentation: *Escuelas y universidades en España*

APPLY ◎
- Activities

La Casa Batlló representa la arquitectura de la Barcelona modernista. Una de las obras más conocidas de Antoni Gaudí, la casa fue restaurada por él en 1904–1906.

PRÁCTICA COMUNICATIVA

1-42 **Usa la información.** Prepare a poster to present to the class comparing what you have learned about the educational system of Spain to that of your own country. Use visuals to illustrate the different stages of the educational system, a few of the oldest and most important universities, and some of the activities that are popular with students in their free time.

En este capítulo...

Comprueba lo que sabes

Go to the *Comprueba lo que sabes* folder online to review what you have learned in this chapter. Practice with the following:

| Vocabulary Flashcards | Games | Oral Practice | Practice Test/ Study Plan | Video en contexto |

Vocabulario

Note for *Vocabulario*
End of chapter vocabulary lists are designed for students to know which words are considered active for each chapter. The Spanish-English Glossary in the appendices provides English translations if students need them.

Las materias o asignaturas
la antropología
las ciencias políticas
la economía
el español
la estadística
la geografía
la historia
la informática/
la computación
la literatura
la psicología
la sociología

Los lugares
la biblioteca
el café
la cafetería
la casa
la discoteca
el gimnasio
el laboratorio
la librería
la oficina
la playa
la plaza
la universidad

Las Facultades
de Arquitectura
de Ciencias
de Humanidades

de Informática
de Medicina

Las personas
el alumno/la alumna
el compañero/
la compañera
el dependiente/la
dependienta
ellos/ellas
nosotros/nosotras
ustedes

Las descripciones
aburrido/a
antiguo/a
bueno/a
difícil
estudioso/a
excelente
fácil
favorito/a
grande
interesante
malo/a
norteamericano/a
pequeño/a

Verbos
aprender
asistir
bailar
beber

buscar
caminar
comer
comprar
comprender
conversar
correr
deber
escribir
escuchar
estar
estudiar
hablar
leer
llegar
mirar
montar (en bicicleta)
necesitar
participar
practicar
sacar buenas/malas notas
tomar
tomar apuntes/notas
trabajar
ver
vivir

Palabras y expresiones útiles
ahora
algo
¡Buena suerte!
¿Cómo te va?

con
¿Cuánto cuesta?
el diccionario
este/a
el examen
el fin de semana
para
pero
¡Qué lástima!
solo
también
la tarea
tengo/tienes
¿verdad?

Expresiones de frecuencia
a veces
muchas veces
nunca
siempre
todos los días / meses
todas las semanas

Palabras interrogativas
¿cómo?
¿cuándo?
¿cuál(es)?¿qué?
¿cuánto/a? / ¿cuántos/as?
¿dónde?
¿para qué?
¿por qué?
¿quién(es)?

Introduction to chapter
Introduce the chapter theme about how we identify and talk about ourselves and others. Ask questions to recycle content from the previous chapter. Help students access meaning by making frequent use of gestures or visuals.

¿Cómo eres? ¿Eres independiente? ¿Eres optimista? ¿Eres paciente o impulsivo? ¿Estudias mucho? ¿Eres muy estudioso o solo un poco? ¿Cómo son tus amigos? ¿Son generosos? ¿Son atléticos? ¿Son inteligentes? ¿Sacan buenas notas? ¿Hablan español tus amigos? ¿Viven todos en Estados Unidos? ¿Dónde están tus amigos ahora?

Integrated Performance Assessment: Three Modes of Communication

Presentational: See activities 2-5, 2-6, 2-10, 2-21, 2-24, 2-25, 2-27, 2-28, 2-33, 2-36, 2-38, and 2-40.

Interpretive: See activities 2-3, 2-4, 2-7, 2-8, 2-11, 2-12, 2-14, 2-15, 2-19, 2-20, 2-21, 2-26, 2-29, 2-31, 2-35, and 2-37

Interpersonal: See activities 2-1, 2-2, 2-3, 2-4, 2-5, 2-6, 2-8, 2-9, 2-10, 2-11, 2-12, 2-13, 2-14, 2-15, 2-16, 2-17, 2-18, 2-19, 2-20, 2-21, 2-22, 2-23, 2-24, 2-25, 2-26, 2-27, 2-30, 2-32, 2-34, 2-39, and all *Situaciones*.

2 ¿Quiénes son tus amigos?

Learning OBJECTIVES

You will:

- learn vocabulary to describe your friends and say what you like to do
- learn the forms and uses of the verb *ser*
- learn to distinguish meaning when using *ser* and *estar* with adjectives
- use possessive adjectives to express ownership
- discuss likes and dislikes using the verb *gustar*
- connect new information about Hispanic presence and influences in the United States to what you already know

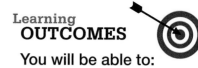

Learning OUTCOMES

You will be able to:

- describe people, places, and things
- express origin and possession
- talk about where and when events take place
- describe what someone or something is like and express changeable conditions
- identify what belongs to you and others
- discuss the people, things, and activities you and others like and dislike
- present information about Hispanic influences on state flags and other U.S. symbols

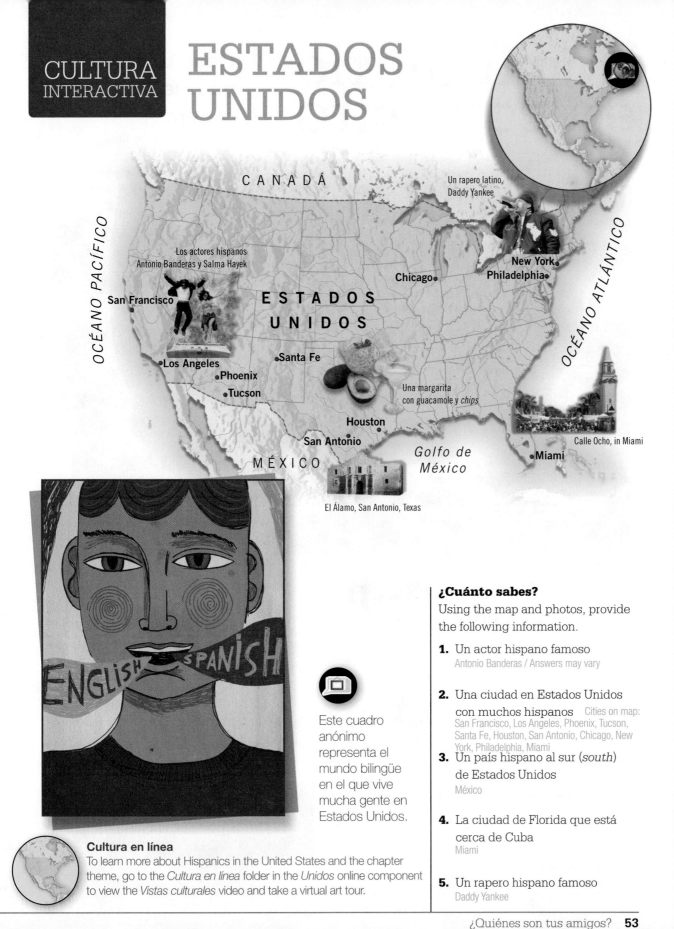

CULTURA INTERACTIVA

ESTADOS UNIDOS

CANADÁ

OCÉANO PACÍFICO

OCÉANO ATLÁNTICO

Un rapero latino, Daddy Yankee

New York
Philadelphia

Los actores hispanos
Antonio Banderas y Salma Hayek

Chicago

San Francisco

E S T A D O S
U N I D O S

Los Angeles

Santa Fe

Phoenix

Tucson

Una margarita
con guacamole y *chips*

Houston

San Antonio

MÉXICO

Golfo de
México

Miami

Calle Ocho, in Miami

El Álamo, San Antonio, Texas

Este cuadro
anónimo
representa el
mundo bilingüe
en el que vive
mucha gente en
Estados Unidos.

Cultura en línea
To learn more about Hispanics in the United States and the chapter
theme, go to the *Cultura en línea* folder in the *Unidos* online component
to view the *Vistas culturales* video and take a virtual art tour.

¿Cuánto sabes?

Using the map and photos, provide
the following information.

1. Un actor hispano famoso
   Antonio Banderas / Answers may vary

2. Una ciudad en Estados Unidos
   con muchos hispanos   Cities on map:
   San Francisco, Los Angeles, Phoenix, Tucson,
   Santa Fe, Houston, San Antonio, Chicago, New
   York, Philadelphia, Miami

3. Un país hispano al sur (*south*)
   de Estados Unidos
   México

4. La ciudad de Florida que está
   cerca de Cuba
   Miami

5. Un rapero hispano famoso
   Daddy Yankee

Vocabulario en contexto

Describing yourself and others

Mis amigos y yo

Go to the *Capítulo 2* [folder] online to complete the Learning Module for *Vocabulario en contexto: Mis amigos y yo.*

PLAN DE ESTUDIO

◎ LEARN
- Interactive presentation: *Mis amigos y yo*
- Vocabulary tutorials
- Pronunciation

APPLY ◎
- Activities
- Pronunciation activities

PRÁCTICA COMUNICATIVA

2-1

¿Quién es?

PRIMERA FASE. With a partner, write a list of eight expressions that you may use to describe people, including physical appearance such as height, hair and eye color, etc. and personality traits such as shy, fun, etc.

SEGUNDA FASE. Without mentioning his/her name, describe a classmate. The rest of the group will try to guess who this person is.

Modelo

Es delgado y de estatura mediana. Tiene el pelo negro. Es fuerte y callado.

¿Es… ?

LENGUA Depending on the region or country, **moreno/a** or **negro/a** may be used to refer to African ancestry and skin color or to hair color. The word **trigueño/a** (from **trigo,** wheat) is used to describe light brown skin color. **Corto/a** generally refers to length (**pelo corto**), while **bajo/a** refers to height (**Ella es baja**).

Cultura

Puerto Rico was a Spanish colony for almost four centuries until it was ceded to the United States following the Spanish–American War in 1898. Puerto Rico is a commonwealth (*estado libre asociado*) of the United States, and its people have been U.S. citizens since 1917. However, Puerto Rico remains geographically and culturally part of Latin America and almost all of its residents speak Spanish as their primary language. English is also widely spoken. Being bilingual opens doors to better economic opportunities in Puerto Rico and on the mainland.

COMPARA: What other Hispanic groups have an important presence in the United States? Where is that presence evident—in business, music, art, food?

2-2 👥

¿Qué me gusta? Tell your classmate if you like each of the following activities. Then compare your responses.

Modelo

❝estar en casa por la noche❞

¿Te gusta estar en casa por la noche?

Sí, me gusta.

- bailar los sábados por la noche
- comer en restaurantes italianos
- escribir correos electrónicos
- estudiar español
- practicar tenis/fútbol/béisbol
- tener animales en casa
- tomar café por la noche
- trabajar los fines de semana

2-3 👥

Mi ídolo Select a well-known person or celebrity and describe him/her to your partner. Your partner will ask questions until he/she guesses the name.

Note for 2-2
The *gustar* construction is presented in *Gramática en contexto* of this chapter and in *Capítulo 6*. Here students should use phrases with *gustar* as set expressions.

Warm-up for 2-2
Say what you like/do not like to do: *Me gusta caminar. Por las noches me gusta mirar televisión.* Ask students: *¿Te gusta estudiar español? ¿Te gusta estudiar en la biblioteca/caminar/mirar televisión por las noches/bailar en las discotecas?* Have students take turns asking and answering.

Suggestion for 2-2
Ask students to describe the type of people their classmates are according to their answers.

Online prep for students
Students will have completed the Learning Module for *Las descripciones* online before class. Additional in-class activities are available for download in the Supplementary Activities folder online.

Warm-up for *Las descripciones*
Describe yourself and/or students using adjectives and expressions introduced in this chapter, or describe people in photos that you and/or students bring in. For words such as *alto/bajo, rubio/moreno,* and *tengo* or *tiene el pelo negro castaño/corto/largo,* point to students who fit those descriptions. To recycle *¿quién?,* ask questions using adjectives: *¿Quién es alto y moreno? ¿Quién tiene el pelo castaño?* Students can answer using names of classmates. Recycle numbers: *¿Cuántos son altos? ¿morenos?,* etc.

Suggestion
Describe famous people using adjectives from this chapter. Ask students to do the same.

Expansion
Tape the name and photo of a famous person to the back of each student. Students move around the room asking yes/no questions to discover who they are. You may demonstrate by having them choose a name for you and answering your yes/no questions.

Alternate
Have students complete the following sentences with an adjective: *Me gusta mucho trabajar. Soy... ; Berta tiene quince años. Es muy... ; Manuela y Marcos siempre están en el laboratorio. Son muy...*

Note
Explain that some Spanish speakers consider *viejo/a* impolite when describing people and prefer to use *mayor.*

Suggestion
Bring photos of people and animals to class. Have students work in groups to describe them by giving physical characteristics or other traits.

Las descripciones

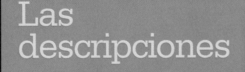

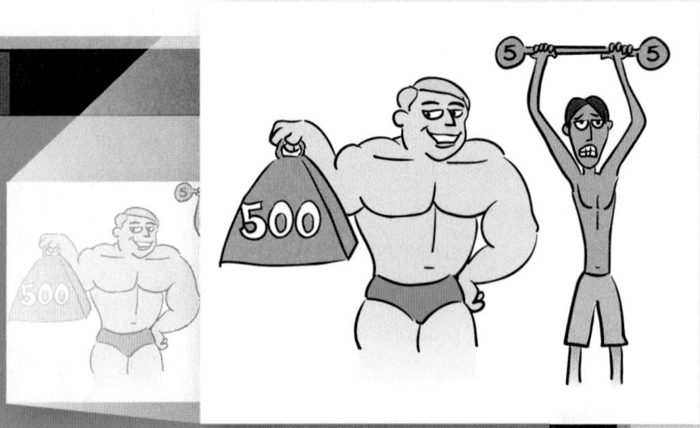

Go to the *Capítulo 2* **folder** online to complete the Learning Module for *Vocabulario en contexto: Las descripciones.*

PLAN DE ESTUDIO

LEARN
- Interactive presentation: *Las descripciones*
- Vocabulary tutorials

APPLY
- Activities

PRÁCTICA COMUNICATIVA

EN OTRAS PALABRAS

Depending on the region, Spanish speakers may use **bonita, linda,** or **guapa** to refer to a female. **Bien parecido, buen mozo,** and **guapo** usually refer to a male.

2-4

Opuestos. Complete the following statements about these famous people. Then describe yourself to your partner in two affirmative and two negative statements.

Modelo "Shakira no es mayor, es *joven*."

1. __c__ Penélope Cruz no es gorda, es...	**a.** trabajadora
2. __a__ Sofía Vergara no es perezosa, es...	**b.** lista
3. __f__ Jennifer López no es antipática, es...	**c.** delgada
4. __b__ Madonna no es tonta, es...	**d.** rico
5. __d__ Bill Gates no es pobre, es...	**e.** guapo
6. __e__ Enrique Iglesias no es feo, es...	**f.** simpática

7. Yo soy..., yo no soy...

2-5

¿De qué color son estas banderas (*flags*)?

PRIMERA FASE. Read each description and then write the name of the country under its flag. Check your answers with a partner.

1. La bandera de Bolivia es roja, amarilla y verde.

2. La bandera de Estados Unidos es roja, blanca y azul.

3. La bandera de España es roja y amarilla.

4. La bandera de México es verde, blanca y roja.

5. La bandera de Colombia es amarilla, azul y roja.

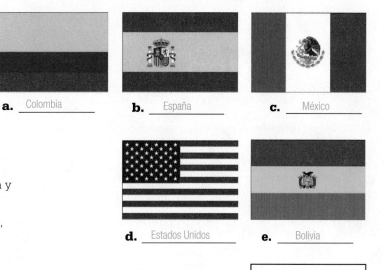

a. Colombia   b. España   c. México

d. Estados Unidos   e. Bolivia

SEGUNDA FASE. Invent a flag and describe it to your partner using colors. He/She will recreate it based on your description. Write the name of the colors on the flag if necessary.

Mi bandera

2-6   **Vamos a describir.** Take turns describing the people in these photos. Then describe your best friend to your partner.

Eva

Alicia y Raquel

Alejandro

José Luis

2-7

¿Quién soy? Write a brief description of yourself including at least three physical traits, two personality traits, and two activities you like to do. Do not include your name on the paper.

El origen

Go to the *Capítulo 2* [folder] online to complete the Learning Module for *Vocabulario en contexto: El origen.*

PLAN DE ESTUDIO

◎ LEARN
- Interactive presentation: *El origen*
- Vocabulary tutorials
- *Entrevistas* video

APPLY ◎
- Activities
- *Entrevistas* video activities

PRÁCTICA COMUNICATIVA

2-8 👥 **Países.**

PRIMERA FASE. Indicate the origin of the following people. Check your answers with a partner.

Modelo
❝ Carolina Herrera es una diseñadora famosa de Venezuela.
Es *venezolana*. ❞

1. Hanley Ramírez es un jugador de béisbol de República Dominicana. Es ___dominicano___.

2. Sofía Vergara es una modelo y actriz de Colombia, protagonista de la serie *Modern Family.* Es ___colombiana___.

3. Rigoberta Menchú es una activista de Guatemala, Premio Nobel de la Paz, 1992. Es ___guatemalteca___.

4. El doctor José Manuel Pérez, de Puerto Rico, investiga el uso de la nanotecnología para detectar el cólera. Es ___puertorriqueño___.

5. Isabel Allende es escritora, originaria de Chile, autora de *La casa de los espíritus.* Es ___chilena___.

6. Jorge Ramos es un presentador de noticias (*news*) de México. Es ___mexicano___.

7. Gabriel García Márquez es un escritor de Colombia, autor de *Cien años de soledad,* Premio Nobel, 1982. Es ___colombiano___.

8. Enrique Iglesias es un cantante de España. Es ___español___.

SEGUNDA FASE. Discuss with your partner which of the personalities in *Primera fase* is interesting to you. Why?

Modelo

> ❝Para mí, <u>Enrique Iglesias</u> es interesante. Es un cantante famoso.❞

Audioscript for *En directo*
Ana: *Dime, Celia, ¿por qué te gusta tanto Isabel Allende?*
Celia: *Bueno, me gustan mucho sus libros.*
Ana: *Es cierto. Escribe novelas fascinantes.*
Celia: *Exactamente. Y, también es muy elegante.*

En directo

To explain why a person might interest you:

Me gustan sus libros.

Escribe novelas fascinantes.

Trabaja por los pobres.

Es muy guapo/bonita/elegante.

Baila muy bien.

 Click on the icon to listen to a conversation with these expressions.

Cultura

Hispanics in the United States come from countries all over the world. According to the 2010 census, one of every seven people in the United States is of Hispanic origin. With a population of 50.5 million, Hispanics account for 16% of the country's inhabitants. Some are recent immigrants, but others have roots here that go back centuries. For example, Mexicans were living in what is now Texas, New Mexico, Arizona, Colorado, Nevada, and California, among other places, long before those territories became part of the United States after the Mexican War (1846–1848).

Zonas con alta concentración de hispanos

Más de 50.000 · De 10.000 a 49.999 · De 1.000 a 9.999 · Menos de 999

COMPARA: Are there any Hispanics in your community? Where are they from? Does your community have a Hispanic area or neighborhood, or businesses with a predominantly Hispanic clientele?

2-9

Adivinanzas (*Guesses*). Think of a well-known person. A classmate will try to guess the identity by asking you questions.

Modelo

¿De dónde es?

Es de Estados Unidos.

¿Cómo es?

Es bajo, moreno y muy cómico.

¿Qué es?/ ¿En qué trabaja?

Es actor.

¿Es Jack Black?

¡Sí!

Note for 2-10
This activity guides students to use a maximum of the vocabulary and resources learned in this and the two previous chapters. Students can practice questions and develop interpersonal skills in *Primera fase.* The information they gather will allow them to write a description in *Segunda fase,* which they will then share. Encourage them to use as many details as possible in this description.

Alternate for 2-10
Have students interview a Hispanic person on campus or in the community. Alternatively, have them read online (in English or Spanish) about a prominent Hispanic figure in the United States and then answer the questions in the activity. Finally, have them report findings to the class. You may wish to provide a list of names to choose from. Have students write their questions individually before interviewing. To check for accuracy, have them read their questions aloud.

Warm-up for 2-11
As a pre-listening activity, divide the class into pairs or small groups and have them draw three columns: Hispanic names, physical descriptions, areas of study. Ask them to write—in 3 minutes—as many words as possible that they can associate with each column. Or, you may provide words and have students sort them to the appropriate columns.

Audioscript for 2-11
¡Hola! Me llamo Miguel Jiménez. Soy de Buenos Aires, Argentina, y tengo 26 años. Estudio medicina en la Universidad de Virginia. Estoy en el tercer año de la carrera. Soy alto, delgado y muy trabajador.

Entrevista.

PRIMERA FASE. Interview a classmate to find out the following information. Include some other information you would like to know about him/her.

1. his/her name
2. his/her age
3. what he/she is like
4. the things he/she likes to do
5. where he/she is from
6. …

SEGUNDA FASE. Write an introduction to the interview and a description of this person, including physical traits. Then share it with the class.

¡Hola! **PRIMERA FASE.** You will hear a student describe himself. Before you listen, mark (✓) in the *Antes de escuchar* column the information you think he may provide. Then tell your partner what other information not listed you would provide about yourself.

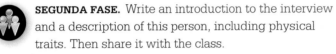

	ANTES DE ESCUCHAR	DESPUÉS DE ESCUCHAR
1. name		✓
2. age		✓
3. parents' names	Answers will vary	
4. physical description		✓
5. country where he was born		✓
6. place where he intends to work	Answers will vary	

SEGUNDA FASE. Now, listen and pay attention to the general idea of what is said. Then, in the *Después de escuchar* column, indicate which information the speaker provided.

Gramática en contexto

Talking about people and places you know and things you like

Describing people, places, and things:

Adjectives

Go to the *Capítulo 2* **folder** online to complete the Learning Module for *Gramática en contexto: Adjectives.*

PLAN DE ESTUDIO

◎ **LEARN**
- Interactive presentation: Adjectives
- Grammar tutorials

APPLY ◎
- Activities
- Extra Practice

PRÁCTICA COMUNICATIVA

2-12

¿Cómo son estas personas? Choose the correct completion to describe the following people. Check your answers with a partner and then share your own opinion about a classmate.

1. Muchos estudiantes de mi universidad son…

   a. latinoamericano.
   c. norteamericanas.

   (b.) hispanos.
   d. mexicana.

2. Mi profesora favorita es muy…

   a. jóvenes.
   (c.) inteligente.

   b. activo.
   d. delgado.

3. Mi amigo Nicolás es muy…

   a. tonta.
   (c.) callado.

   b. lista.
   d. antipática.

4. Las dos chicas más inteligentes de la clase son…

   a. activos y sociables.
   c. altos y morenos.

   (b.) trabajadoras y estudiosas.
   d. interesante y optimista.

5. Para mí, el/la estudiante más…es…

Expansion for 2-13
Remind students to pay attention to whether they are describing males or females, or one or more persons.

Encourage them to provide additional adjectives. Model or brainstorm adjectives they can use for variety. They may also use the negative with the opposite quality: *La directora de relaciones públicas no es antipática. Por el contrario, es muy simpática.*

Also encourage students to ask questions, such as: *¿Es joven/Son jóvenes? ¿Habla(n) español bien? ¿Cómo se llama(n)?*

2-13

Cualidades necesarias. Your school is hiring recent graduates who were language majors. Mark (✓) the qualities these new employees should have and describe them to your partner. Your partner will mention additional qualities.

Modelo

" dos empleados bilingües en inglés y español **"**

> Los empleados bilingües hablan bien inglés y español. Son activos y extrovertidos.

1. dos especialistas en computadoras para el laboratorio de lenguas

_____ activo   _____ pasivo   _____ extrovertido

_____ bilingüe   _____ agradable   _____ trabajador

_____ competente   _____ callado   _____ listo

> Sí. Son simpáticos, no son antipáticos. Hablan con los estudiantes y los padres de los estudiantes.

2. una recepcionista para la Oficina de Admisiones

_____ imparcial   _____ habladora

_____ perezosa   _____ interesante

_____ simpática   _____ perfeccionista

2-14

Personas importantes.

PRIMERA FASE. Take turns describing the people in the photos.

Jimmy Smits es un actor famoso de cine (*movies*) y televisión.

Tish Hinojosa es una cantante mexicano-americana. Canta y escribe canciones también.

Alex Rodríguez es un jugador de béisbol muy bueno.

Julia Álvarez es una novelista y poeta dominicana. También es profesora.

SEGUNDA FASE. Now, take turns describing someone important in your life. Your classmates will ask questions to get more information about that person.

Expansion for 2-14
Ask students to describe other well-known people, such as actors or people prominent in public affairs. Introduce *¿Estás de acuerdo?* to ask students if they agree with the descriptions given.

Have students use one adjective to describe two people *Salma Hayek y Julia Roberts son creativas y simpáticas.*

Suggestion for 2-14
Segunda fase
Since asking questions is a difficult skill for beginners, you may wish to have students write down some questions before they do *Segunda fase* to make the most of this activity. Remind them to listen attentively and ask follow-up questions. Provide vocabulary as needed.

En directo

To address someone on the phone about an ad:

Hola, buenos días, llamo por el anuncio…

To respond:

¡Ah, sí, hola! Buenos días…

To greet someone you know on the phone:

Hola, ¿qué tal?

Soy María… /Habla María…

To respond:

Ah, ¡hola!

¿Qué tal, María?/¿Cómo estás?

 Click on the icon to listen to a conversation with these expressions.

Situaciones

1

ROLE A. You have just rented an apartment near campus and are looking for a roommate (**compañero/a de apartamento**). An interested student calls you. Verify the student's name and ask a) where he/she is from; b) what his/her personality traits are; c) if he/she works and, if so, where; and d) what he/she likes to do in his/her free time (**tiempo libre**).

ROLE B. Through an ad (**anuncio**) on a campus bulletin board, you see that someone is looking for a roommate (**compañero/a de apartamento**). Call that person, answer his/her questions in detail, and ask any questions you may have.

2

ROLE A. Your friend calls to tell you that he/she has been dating someone new. Ask a) where your friend's new boyfriend/girlfriend (**novio/a**) is from; b) what he/she is like; c) what he/she studies; d) if he/she has a car and, if so, what it looks like (color, size); and e) at least one other question of your own invention.

ROLE B. You call your friend to talk about your new boyfriend/girlfriend. Your friend asks a lot of questions. Answer in as much detail as possible.

Suggestion for *Situaciones*
Before students begin, review the expressions in *En directo*.

Audioscript for *En directo*
Fernando: *Hola, buenos días, llamo por el anuncio del apartamento en la Avenida Campos.*
Sr. Rivera: *¡Ah, sí, hola! Buenos días. Yo soy el señor Rivera. ¿Te interesa mi apartamento?*
Fernando: *Sí, mi amigo y yo necesitamos un apartamento.*
Sr. Rivera: *Muy bien. ¿Desean verlo esta tarde a las 3?*
Fernando: *¡Sí! A las 3.*
[*un minuto más tarde…*]
Fernando: *Soy Fernando.*
Amigo: *Hola, ¿qué tal, Fernando?*
Fernando: *Bien. Mira, hay un apartamento muy interesante. Necesitamos verlo hoy a las 3.*
Amigo: *¡Perfecto!*

Tech tip for *Situaciones*
You may want to assign partners and have pairs create a mini-skit using the video-posting feature, MediaShare online.

Identifying and describing; expressing origin, possession, location of events, and time:
Present tense of *ser*

Go to the *Capítulo 2* [folder] online to complete the Learning Module for *Gramática en contexto:* Adjectives.

PLAN DE ESTUDIO

◎ LEARN
- Interactive presentation: Adjectives
- Grammar tutorials

APPLY ◎
- Activities
- Extra Practice

PRÁCTICA COMUNICATIVA

2-15

¿Cómo somos?

PRIMERA FASE. Look at the following statements and indicate if the descriptions are true for you.

	Sí	No
1. Yo soy muy estudioso/a y trabajador/a.		
2. A veces soy callado/a.		
3. Soy norteamericano/a.		
4. Mis abuelos son de otro (*another*) país.		
5. Mi familia es muy religiosa y tradicional.		
6. Mi mejor amigo/a es extrovertido/a y conversador/a.		
7. Mis amigos y yo somos sociables y activos.		
8. Mis clases este semestre son interesantes.		

SEGUNDA FASE. Now compare your answers with your partner. Ask questions to get additional information.

¿Cómo es? Ask what the following people, places, and objects are like.

Modelo   **"tu profesor/a de inglés "**

¿Cómo es tu profesor de inglés?

Es alto, moreno y muy simpático.

1. tus amigos
2. tu cuarto (*bedroom*)
3. tu compañero/a de cuarto (*roommate*)
4. el auto de tu mejor amigo/a
5. la biblioteca de la universidad

2-17

¿Qué es esto? Take turns describing an object and its location in the classroom. Your partner will ask you questions and guess what it is.

Modelo

E1: Es grande, es de plástico, está al lado de la ventana.
E2: ¿De qué color es?
E1: Es roja.
E2: ¿Es la mochila de Juan?

> **LENGUA**   **Madera** (*wood*), **plástico, tela** (*fabric*), **metal, oro** (*gold*), and **vidrio** (*glass*) are some words used to describe what material something is made of.

Follow-up for 2-16
Students change partners. Each new partner should tell the other the information he/she gathered. To facilitate the reporting of information, you may wish to teach and model the following: *X dice que el laboratorio de computadoras es grande. Tiene muchas computadoras.*

Expansion for 2-16
You may ask students to give additional information, using *estar* for location (*Capítulo 1*): *El laboratorio de computadoras está en la biblioteca.*

Warm-up for 2-17
Ask students questions about classroom objects with *¿De quién es/son… ?* and *¿De qué es?* Before students begin the activity, encourage variety by brainstorming questions they may ask their partners.

2-18

Eventos y lugares. You are working at the university's information booth, and a visitor (your classmate) stops by. Answer his/her questions. Then switch roles.

Modelo   **❝ la exposición del club de fotografía ❞**

> Perdón, ¿dónde es la exposición del club de fotografía?

> Es en la biblioteca.

> ¿Dónde está la biblioteca?

> Está en la calle Madison, enfrente de la Facultad de Ciencias.

1. el concierto de música
2. la conferencia (*lecture*) sobre el arte mexicano
3. la fiesta para los estudiantes internacionales
4. la reunión de profesores
5. la ceremonia de graduación

Situaciones

1

ROLE A. You meet a student from a Spanish-speaking country in one of your classes. Introduce yourself and find out a) the student's name; b) his/her city and country of origin; and c) characteristics of his/her city.

ROLE B. You are an international student from a Spanish-speaking country. Answer your classmate's questions and then ask questions to get the same information from him/her.

2

ROLE A. A friend has invited you to a party at his/her house on Saturday. Ask a) where the house is located; b) what it looks like (so you can find it easily); and c) the time of the party.

ROLE B. You have invited a friend to a party at your house on Saturday. Answer your friend's questions. Then explain that the house belongs to your parents (**padres**), and tell your friend why your parents are not at home that weekend.

Expressing inherent qualities and changeable conditions:

Ser and *estar* with adjectives

Go to the *Capítulo 2* **folder** online to complete the Learning Module for *Gramática en contexto: Ser* and *estar* with adjectives.

PLAN DE ESTUDIO

LEARN
- Interactive presentation: *Ser* and *estar* with adjectives
- Grammar tutorials

APPLY
- Activities
- Extra Practice

PRÁCTICA COMUNICATIVA

2-19

¿Qué pasa aquí? Look at the drawing and then complete the description in each paragraph with the appropriate form of **ser** or **estar.** Check your answers with a partner. Take turns explaining why you chose *ser* or *estar* in each case.

1. Esteban (1) __es__ un joven listo y estudioso. Este semestre saca buenas notas, excepto en la clase de economía. (2) __Es__ una clase muy difícil. Esteban (3) __está__ nervioso porque mañana hay un examen sobre la Unión Europea, pero él no (4) __está__ listo. Debe estudiar toda la noche.

¿Quiénes son tus amigos? **67**

Online prep for students
Students will have completed the Learning Module for *Ser* and *estar* with adjectives online. This includes the Interactive presentation and corresponding Apply activities. See content online. Additional in-class activities are available for download in the Supplementary Activities folder online.

Warm-up for *Ser* and *estar* with adjectives
Use questions with *ser* to ask for descriptions of people and objects in photos and in the classroom: *¿De qué color es la mochila de Nancy? ¿Cómo es este señor? ¿Es alto o bajo? ¿Es joven o mayor?* Make statements using *estar* and adjectives (*cansado/a, contento/a, furioso/a, triste*) to convey emotional or physical states. Use gestures or visuals to explain meaning as needed.

Suggestion
To help students develop their metalinguistic awareness, you may wish to ask why *estar* is always used with *contento/a, cansado/a,* and *enojado/a.*

Suggestions for 2-19
You may wish to remind students to focus on adjective agreement. Have partners exchange roles. Encourage them to use as many adjectives as possible.

Standard 4.1
Students demonstrate an understanding of the nature of language through comparisons of the language studied and their own.
Students encounter many opportunities to reflect on the different ways that languages accomplish the same function. The existence *ser* and *estar* in Spanish—two verbs with different meanings, but both are expressed as "to be" in English—can serve as the starting point for reflection on the fact that languages express meanings in different ways.

2. ¡Pobres niños! (*Poor children!*) La fruta
(5) _____es_____ buena y saludable (*healthful*),
pero estas manzanas (6) _____están_____ verdes,
no (7) _____están_____ buenas. Ahora los niños
no (8) _____están_____ contentos. Una niña (9)
_____está_____ mala porque le duele el estómago
(*her stomach hurts*).

¡Qué ácida!

¡Horrible!

You may wish to remind students to focus on adjective agreement. Have partners exchange roles. Encourage them to use as many adjectives as possible.

Follow-up for 2-20
Brainstorm with the class the conditions that might have prompted the changes in the persons listed by asking questions such as *¿Por qué está delgado ahora Arturo?* (e.g., *dieta*). Focus on the concept that a change of state/condition prompts the switch from *ser* to *estar*.

Suggestion for 2-21
Segunda fase
First introduce *tienes razón* and *estás equivocado/a.* Provide several examples. As students report to the class, you may wish to ask each student alluded to in the report to agree or disagree with what was said about him/her by responding: *Tienes razón* or *Estás equivocado/a.*

2-20

Cambios (*Changes*). You and your partner know the people mentioned in the chart. One of you will describe a person, using an adjective from the list. The other explains how the person has changed and why. Then switch roles.

Modelo **"Arturo, fuerte/por su enfermedad (*illness*)"**

Arturo es fuerte.

Pero por su enfermedad, ahora está muy débil.

PERSONAS	CARACTERÍSTICAS	RAZONES
1. Ramón	alegre	por sus problemas
2. Laura y Gustavo	callado/a	por la dieta
3. Cristina	conversador/a	por el ejercicio
4. Andrés	débil	por el exceso de estudio
5. Ana y Sofía	extrovertido/a	por la falta (*lack*) de motivación
6. Teresa	feliz	por su depresión
	fuerte	por sus buenas notas
	introvertido/a	
	optimista	
	perezoso/a	
	pesimista	
	trabajador/a	
	triste	

2-21

Termómetro emocional.

PRIMERA FASE. Indicate (✓) how you feel in each situation.

LUGARES	ABURRIDO/A	CONTENTO/A	TRANQUILO/A	TRISTE	RELAJADO/A	NERVIOSO/A
en la cafetería con mis compañeros						
en los exámenes finales						
en la oficina de un profesor/una profesora						
en un concierto con mis amigos						
en una fiesta formal						
en mi casa por la noche						

SEGUNDA FASE. Write a text message to your classmate telling him/her how you feel in one of the situations in *Primera fase*. Then, reply to his/her text.

Modelo **❝** *Yo estoy nerviosa en un concierto, pero mi compañero está tranquilo.* **❞**

Situaciones

1 **ROLE A.** You have traveled to another city for a job interview. A friend of a friend who lives in that city has offered to show you around. Make arrangements over the phone to meet this person, whom you do not know. Find out what the person looks like, so you will be able to spot him/her at your meeting place.

ROLE B. You have offered to get together with a friend of a friend who has a job interview in your city. You do not know this person, so when you arrange over the phone to meet, you have to find out what the person looks like and something about his/her personality, in order to decide what to show him/her.

2 **ROLE A.** Show your classmate a photo. Identify the people and explain what they are like. Then respond to your friend's questions and react to his/her comments about them.

ROLE B. After your classmate tells you about the people in the photo, ask and comment about a) how they seem to be feeling, based on their facial expressions or what they are doing, and b) where they appear to be.

Suggestions for *Situaciones*
Before students begin the first *Situación*, brainstorm with them about the questions they will need to ask.

For the second *Situación*, students will need a photo of two or more people (family, friends, or a magazine photo). If they use a magazine photo, they can invent the information. Students should do this *Situación* twice so that everyone plays both roles.

Online prep for students
Students will have completed the Learning Module for Possessive adjectives online. This includes the Interactive presentation and corresponding Apply activities. See content online. Additional in-class activities are available for download in the Supplementary Activities folder in Instructor's Resources.

Suggestions
Students were introduced to *mi(s), tu(s), su(s)* as lexical items in the *Capítulo preliminar*. You may wish to go over these forms by pointing to objects: *mi libro, mi escritorio, mis lápices, mis bolígrafos*. Use *tu(s)* and *su(s)* by pointing to objects and asking questions to check comprehension. You may also wish to explain to students that *vuestro(s)* and *vuestra(s)* are used only in Spain, whereas *su(s)* is used in Latin American varieties of Spanish.

Expressing ownership:
Possessive adjectives

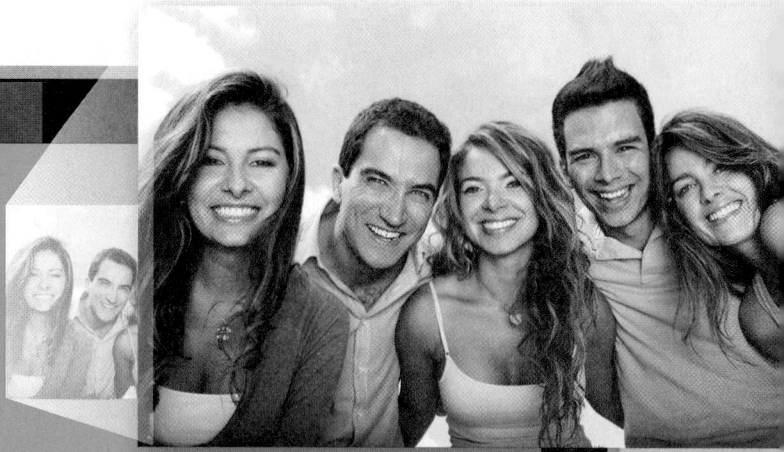

Go to the *Capítulo 2* **folder** online to complete the Learning Module for *Gramática en contexto:* Possessive adjectives.

PLAN DE ESTUDIO

LEARN
- Interactive presentation: Possessive adjectives
- Grammar tutorials

APPLY
- Activities
- Extra Practice

PRÁCTICA COMUNICATIVA

2-22

Mi mundo (*world*).

PRIMERA FASE. Write down two things you own (**pertenencias**) and two people you value very much. You may use the words in the box or choose others.

Pertenencias:	**Personas:**
un carro	un amigo/una amiga
una computadora portátil	un profesor ideal/una profesora ideal
un iPod	un actor/una actriz

PERTENENCIAS	PERSONAS
1. ______________	**1.** ______________
2. ______________	**2.** ______________

SEGUNDA FASE. Take turns describing your selections. Take notes so that you can share with the class the similarities and differences between you and your classmate.

Pertenencias

E1: *Yo tengo un auto. Es rápido y moderno. Y tú, tienes un auto?*

E2: *Sí.*

E1: *¿Y cómo es tu auto?*

E2: *Mi auto es rojo y muy viejo.*

Personas

E1: *Mi madre es importante en mi vida* (life). *Es muy alegre. Y tu mamá, ¿cómo es?*

E2: *Mi madre es tranquila y muy inteligente.*

EN OTRAS PALABRAS

The word for car in Spanish varies, depending on the country or region. The most widely accepted word is **el auto**, commonly used in the southern half of South America. In Mexico, Central America, the Caribbean, and the northern countries of South America, **el carro** is frequently used. **El coche** is used in Spain, Cuba or Chile.

2-23

¿Cómo es/son...? Which of these statements apply to your friends? Mark (✓) your answers in the spaces under **Yo.** Then interview a classmate.

	Yo	Mi compañero/a
1. Mis amigos son aburridos.	_____	_____
2. Mi compañero/a de cuarto es colombiano/a.	_____	_____
3. Mis amigos hablan español.	_____	_____
4. Nuestro deporte favorito es el tenis.	_____	_____
5. Nuestra ciudad es muy grande.	_____	_____
6. El carro de mi mejor amiga es rojo.	_____	_____

Suggestions for 2-23
After interviewing each other, students should compare answers, and then write one similarity and one difference between them. Students can share their findings with the class.

Nuestra universidad.

PRIMERA FASE. With a partner, list some words that generally describe the following aspects of your university: **los profesores, las clases, los estudiantes, el campus, los equipos (*teams*) de fútbol, baloncesto, béisbol, etc**.

SEGUNDA FASE. Now write 1 or 2 sentences about each topic in *Primera fase*. Present your sentences to the class. The class will decide which sentences a) describe the school most accurately and b) present an appealing view of the school for prospective students.

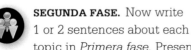 **Situaciones**

1

ROLE A. Show a photo of your friends to one of your classmates. Describe them and answer your classmate's questions.

ROLE B. Show a photo of your friends to one of your classmates. Describe them and answer your classmate's questions.

2

ROLE A. Call your cousin and tell him/her about your new friends on campus. Describe each of them, including their ages, appearance, personalities, the things you do together and your favorite places.

ROLE B. Your cousin calls you to tell you about his/her new friends in college. Ask questions about them and about their favorite activities and places.

Expressing likes and dislikes:
Gustar

Go to the *Capítulo 2* [folder] online to complete the Learning Module for *Gramática en contexto: Gustar.*

PLAN DE ESTUDIO

◎ LEARN
- Interactive presentation: *Gustar*
- Grammar tutorials

APPLY ◎
- Activities
- Extra Practice

PRÁCTICA COMUNICATIVA

2-25

Mis preferencias.

PRIMERA FASE. Indicate (✓) your preferences in the following chart.

ACTIVIDAD	ME GUSTA MUCHO	ME GUSTA UN POCO	NO ME GUSTA
escribir correos electrónicos en español			
comer en restaurantes de comida mexicana			
bailar salsa			
escuchar música rock en español			
aprender sobre la cultura de otros países			
visitar lugares históricos			

 SEGUNDA FASE. Now, compare your answers with those of a classmate. Share with the class one similarity and one difference in your preferences.

Online prep for students
Students will have completed the Learning Module for *Gustar* online before class. This includes the Interactive presentation and corresponding Apply activities.

Note
In *Vocabulario en contexto*, students used *me gusta, te gusta,* and *le gusta* as lexical terms. Here they will find a brief explanation of the forms that they will need for communication at this stage. A detailed grammar explanation is not necessary at this point.

Suggestions
Be sure to point out that the singular *gusta* is always used with infinitives, even when there is more than one infinitive in the sentence.
   Explain that the expression *me cae bien* is often used to refer to people because in some contexts *gustar* may have a sexual connotation.

Suggestion for 2-25
Tell students about the kind of music you like. Ask about their preferences. Play some traditional music from the Spanish-speaking world (*pasodoble* from Spain, *ranchera* from Mexico, *tango* from Argentina, *son* and *chachachá* from *Cuba,* hip-hop from Puerto Rico/ Dominican Republic, Andean music, etc.). Mention that in areas with large Hispanic populations local radio stations play music from Spanish-speaking countries.

2-26

¿Te gusta...?

PRIMERA FASE. Ask a classmate if he/she likes the following. Be sure to ask follow-up questions as appropriate.

1. el gimnasio de la universidad
2. la informática
3. los autos de este año
4. los animales
5. los conciertos de música clásica
6. la clase de español

SEGUNDA FASE. Write a brief note to another classmate in which you share two pieces of information about yourself and two pieces of information you discovered about your partner.

2-27

¿Qué te gusta hacer?

PRIMERA FASE. Write down some questions that you would ask a classmate to find out the following:

1. what he/she likes to do in his/her free time
2. in what restaurants he/she likes to eat with his/her friends

SEGUNDA FASE. Interview two classmates and ask each of them the questions you prepared in the *Primera fase*. Compare their responses and share your conclusions with the class.

Tech tip for *Situaciones*
You may assign partners and have pairs create a mini-skit using the video-posting feature, MediaShare online.

Suggestion for *Situaciones*
Additional situations are available in the Instructor's Resource folder.

Situaciones

1

ROLE A. You are at a park where you hear someone giving commands to a dog in Spanish. Break the ice and introduce yourself. Ask a) the person's name; b) the dog's name and age; and c) if the dog is friendly (**manso**). Compliment the dog (smart, strong, very pretty, etc.). Tell the person that you like dogs very much and that you also like cats. Answer the questions this person asks.

ROLE B. You are in the park training your dog and someone approaches. Answer this person's questions and ask if he/she has a dog, and if so, what it looks like. Say that you don't like cats and say why you don't like them. Finally, ask where this person is from and where he/she is studying Spanish.

2

ROLE A. You are at Panchero's, a Mexican restaurant. You see one of your friends speaking Spanish to a child. Greet your friend and ask the child's name and age. Find out where the child is from, what he/she likes to eat, and what things he/she likes to do.

ROLE B. You have taken the child you are babysitting to Panchero's, a Mexican restaurant. You see one of your friends, who asks you about the child. Greet your friend and answer his/her questions.

Unidos

ESCUCHA

2-28 | Presentational |

Preparación. You will listen to a student tell her mother about how different her two roommates are. Before listening to their conversation, write the name(s) of your two best friends and a sentence that describes each one.

2-29  | Interpretive |

Escucha. Listen to the conversation between a student and her mother. Mark (✓) the appropriate column(s) to indicate whether the following statements describe Rita or Marcela.

	RITA	MARCELA
1. Estudia economía.	✓	
2. Le gusta bailar.		✓
3. Es alta, morena y tiene los ojos negros.		✓
4. Es muy seria, baja y delgada.	✓	
5. Estudia arte moderno.		✓

2-30  | Interpersonal |

Un paso más.

PRIMERA FASE. Ask a classmate what his/her friends are like, what they like to do, and what they study.

SEGUNDA FASE. Complete the following sentences with the information you gathered from your classmate.

1. Sus mejores amigos son…

2. A ellos les gusta…

3. Sus amigos y yo somos semejantes/diferentes porque…

ESTRATEGIA

Listen for specific information

When you ask someone questions, he/she may provide not only the answers you need, but also additional information. To listen effectively, focus on the information you requested. This will help you remember it afterwards.

Comprueba

I was able to…

_____ classify information as general or specific.

_____ recognize the names of people.

_____ associate specific information to each person.

_____ hear and remember descriptive words.

_____ recognize words that refer to actions.

AUTOEVALUACIÓN

☐ I feel confident that I was able to listen for the information I needed.

☐ I need more listening practice.

STUDY PLAN

▶ Good job! Move on to the next section, *Habla.*

▶ Go to the *Unidos* [folder] online for the *Escucha* practice.

Integrated Performance Assessment (IPA)

The activities in each *Unidos* section correspond to the three modes of communication as indicated by the tag next to each activity.

Suggestion for audio
Listening activities provide many learning opportunities when done in the classroom. Instructors are encouraged to guide students' attention to certain passages, and to vary the ways in which the listening activity is presented. For example, you may choose to have students listen to the audio three times or less depending on how well they develop the listening skills.

Audioscript for *Escucha*
Estudiante: *¡Hola, mamá! ¿Cómo estás?*
Mamá: *Bien, muy bien. Y tú, ¿cómo estás, hija?*
Estudiante: *Aquí muy contenta con mis nuevas compañeras de la universidad. Son muy agradables, pero muy diferentes.*
Mamá: *¿Sí? ¿Por qué?*
Estudiante: *Bueno, Rita es mexicana y estudia economía. Es muy seria y trabajadora. Ella es baja, delgada y tiene el pelo rubio. Es callada y muy tranquila. No le gusta salir mucho. Marcela es de Honduras. Es alta, morena, tiene el pelo largo y los ojos negros. Ella es muy activa y le gustan la música moderna, el rock y la salsa. Le gusta bailar y salir con sus amigos todos los fines de semana.*
Mamá: *¿Y qué estudia Marcela?*
Estudiante: *Estudia arte moderno.*
Mamá: *Bueno, veo que son diferentes, pero las dos son agradables, ¿no?*
Estudiante: *Sí, y las dos me caen muy bien.*
Mamá: *Bueno, me alegro, hija.*

HABLA

2-31 [Interpretive]

Preparación.
Find photos and research information online about one of the following Hispanic people.

1. Shakira
2. Eva Longoria
3. Selena Gómez
4. Marco Rubio
5. William Levy
6. Sonia Sotomayor

2-32  [Interpersonal]

Habla. Share information with your partner about the person you researched. Then switch roles. Describe the physical characteristics and personality traits of this person. Be prepared to respond to your partner's questions and comments.

Comprueba
In my conversation…

_____ my description was well organized.

_____ I used a variety of descriptive words.

_____ I made nouns and adjectives agree in gender and number.

_____ I asked questions that were clear and easy to answer.

_____ I gave clear information in response to questions.

2-33 [Presentational]

Un paso más. Write a paragraph describing the person that your classmate has described to you.

ESTRATEGIA

Describe a person

Descriptions are most effective when they are well organized. When describing a person, you may want to include demographic information (e.g., age, nationality/origin), physical characteristics, and personality traits. A well-organized description presents information by category, beginning with an introductory statement to orient your listener.

En directo

To introduce information about physical characteristics:

En cuanto a lo físico,… / Físicamente, es…

To introduce information about personality:

Es una persona…/Tiene un carácter…

 Click on the icon to listen to a conversation with these expressions.

Cultura

Many Hispanics who emigrate to other countries maintain connections to their culture by reading and listening to music in Spanish. In areas with large Hispanic populations, Spanish-language newspapers and magazines are widely available.

COMPARA: What food, music, and cultural practices from your culture would you miss if you lived in another country? What things would you most want to have available to you?

AUTOEVALUACIÓN

☐ I feel confident that I communicated successfully.

☐ I need more speaking practice.

STUDY PLAN

▶ Good job! Move on to the next section, *Lee.*

▶ Go to the *Unidos* [folder] online for the *Habla* practice.

LEE

2-34  [Interpersonal]

Preparación.

PRIMERA FASE. Read the title of the text and examine its format. What type of text is it: a series of e-mail messages, personal ads, or ads for items for sale? Compare your answers with your partner.

SEGUNDA FASE. What qualities do you appreciate in a partner/friend? Why? With a classmate, mark the qualities that you appreciate most and say why.

a. _____ sociable

b. _____ simpático/a

c. _____ divertido/a

d. _____ perfeccionista

e. _____ mayor

f. _____ flexible

g. _____ trabajador/a

h. _____ ocupado/a

2-35 [Interpretive]

Lee. Read the personal ads on the next page and scan them for the information needed in the form below. In some cases, it may not be possible to provide all of the information requested.

	PERSONA 1	PERSONA 2	PERSONA 3	PERSONA 4
nombre				
edad				
nacionalidad				
estado civil				
personalidad (1 o 2 adjetivos)				
le gusta…				

ESTRATEGIA

Scan a text for specific information

When you read in Spanish, you can search for particular pieces of information you think will be in the text. Often the comprehension questions after the text will help you decide what information to search for as you read. This approach to reading, called *scanning,* works best if you a) focus on the information you are seeking, and b) read the text through quickly at least twice, looking for specific information each time.

Comprueba

I was able to…

____ identify the type of text.

____ find the information I was looking for in each text.

____ recognize important words.

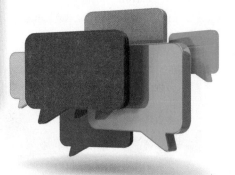

Suggestion for 2-35
Before the activity, make sure students have deduced that the text is a series of personal ads. Explain that they will now scan the ads for specific information about each person and that they should not worry about words they do not understand.

You may wish to explain the meaning of the following words before students read the ads: *fronteras, compromiso,* and *viajo* as follows: *Mi familia y yo viajamos por carro entre…* [your state] *y…* [a neighboring state] *para visitar a mis padres. Siempre cruzamos la frontera entre… y…* [the two states] *durante el día. No nos gusta viajar por la noche.*

Follow-up for 2-35
To check comprehension, students can compare their forms with a partner and report discrepancies. You may wish to teach phrases such as *En su anuncio, Susana dice que…* Make the activity as communicative as possible by having students answer *No sé* or *No se dice* when the information is not provided.

> Amigos sin fronteras

Soltera, sin hijos y sin compromiso. Me llamo Susana y tengo 24 años. Soy guatemalteca. Busco amigos extranjeros, solteros, separados o divorciados, jóvenes o mayores. Soy amable, cariñosa y muy trabajadora. Por mi trabajo, viajo mucho, pero me gusta la compañía de otras personas. Soy bilingüe. Hablo español e inglés. Escriban a sincompromiso@yahoo.net

Soy Ricardo Brown. 21 años, sincero, dedicado. Me gustan las fiestas. Soy soltero. Deseo conocer a una chica de unos 23 años, preferiblemente venezolana como yo. Prefiero una mujer activa e independiente. Me gusta practicar deportes y explorar lugares nuevos. Escríbanme a amigosincero@hotmail.org

Me llamo Pablo Sosa, tengo 31 años, y soy chileno. Soy agradable y muy trabajador. Me gusta hacer mi trabajo a la perfección, pero soy tolerante. Los autos convertibles son mi pasión. Deseo mantener correspondencia por correo electrónico con jóvenes del extranjero para intercambiar información sobre los convertibles europeos o americanos. Mi dirección electrónica es locoporlosautos@yahoo.com

Soy Xiomara Stravinsky, decoradora y fotógrafa argentina. Me gusta el arte, especialmente el impresionismo. Tengo 27 años y soy divorciada. Soy dinámica, agradable y generosa, pero tengo pocos amigos porque tengo dos trabajos y paso muchas horas con mis clientes. Necesito un cambio en mi vida. ¿Deseas ser mi amigo/a? Por favor, escríbeme a xiomarastravinsky@hotmail.com

2-36   Presentational

Un paso más.

PRIMERA FASE. Find the best match for Susana, Ricardo, Pablo, and Xiomara from the following responses received.

1. Tengo 22 años y me gustan todos los deportes. Mis padres viven en Caracas pero yo vivo en Miami.

2. Enseño arte en la escuela secundaria. Tengo tiempo para mis amigos los fines de semana.

3. Soy de Nicaragua. Soy muy sociable y deseo perfeccionar mi inglés.

4. Trabajo para *Autos de hoy,* una revista de Internet.

SEGUNDA FASE. Write your own personal ad including a description of your personality and the things you like to do. Share your ad with the class.

LENGUA The letter **y** changes to **e** when it precedes a word beginning with **i** or **h inglés y español,** but **español e inglés; inteligente y agradable,** but **agradable e inteligente.**

AUTOEVALUACIÓN

☐ I feel confident I understood the readings and was able to use the information.

☐ I need more reading practice.

STUDY PLAN

▷ Good job! Move on to the next section, *Escribe.*

▷ Go to the *Unidos* [folder] online for the *Lee* practice.

ESCRIBE

2-37 [Interpretive]

Preparación. Read the following ad written by a movie fan in your local Spanish-language newspaper and identify the purpose that fanaticodelcine has in mind:

a. _____ to find a girlfriend

b. ___✓___ to find someone (male or female) to talk with about movies

> Soy un fanático del cine y necesito amigos para conversar sobre películas los fines de semana. Tengo 24 años y estudio cinematografía. Me fascinan las películas de acción y también las románticas. Soy fuerte, activo, atlético y aventurero. Me gusta practicar deportes, especialmente el tenis y el esquí. Siempre estoy muy ocupado, pero tengo unas horas todas las semanas para conversar sobre películas. Interesados, favor de enviar correo electrónico a **fanaticodelcine@yahoo.com**

ESTRATEGIA

Consider audience and purpose

Writing is an act of communication between the writer and the reader. Writers usually have a purpose in mind, such as presenting information, describing a person or place, or expressing an opinion. As you write, keep your purpose in mind. Organize your text so that your message is clear to your readers.

2-38 [Presentational]

Escribe. Write an e-mail to fanaticodelcine in response to the ad.

Before starting your e-mail, identify your purpose:

a. _____ to share your interest in movies

b. _____ to date fanaticodelcine

Comprueba

I was able to…

____ introduce myself.

____ explain the purpose of my e-mail.

____ give details about myself.

____ share my taste in movies.

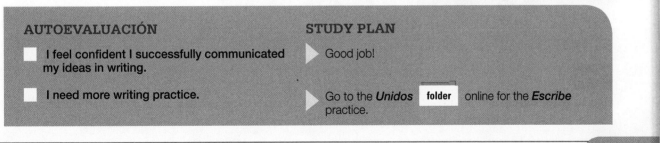

Suggestion for 2-38
Students who prefer not to talk about themselves can assume a different identity for this activity.

Suggestion for 2-38
Encourage students to include in their e-mail a description of themselves. Have them proofread to correct spelling and grammatical errors.

2-39  [Interpersonal]

Un paso más. Exchange e-mails with your partner and write a possible response from fanaticodelcine. Include the following and follow up with other information:

1. a greeting

2. the description of a film you would like to discuss

3. whether you like the film or not, and why

AUTOEVALUACIÓN

☐ **I feel confident I successfully communicated my ideas in writing.**

☐ **I need more writing practice.**

STUDY PLAN

▶ Good job!

▶ Go to the *Unidos* [folder] online for the *Escribe* practice.

ENFOQUE *cultural*

Note for *El barrio Pilsen*
Like so many neighborhoods throughout the United States, Pilsen has been home to an array of immigrant populations. People from what is known today as the Czech Republic named the area after a city in their native land. Immigrant populations from places like Croatia and Poland have also called Pilsen home. The Hispanic presence began to establish itself in the 1950s and, by the 1970s, had grown to become the majority population in this vibrant area of Chicago.

Note for *Mes de la Hispanidad*
National Hispanic Heritage Month is not only a time for celebrating Hispanic culture and heritage, but it is also a period when the contributions of Hispanics are highlighted. September 15 was selected as the opening date of these celebrations, because it coincides with the independence days of five Latin American countries. Other Latin American countries also celebrate their independence days during the course of this 30-day period.

Note for *La misión de San Diego de Alcalá*
Mission San Diego de Alcalá is the first of California's missions, and is therefore known as the "Mother of the missions." Founded by Father Junípero Serra, the Mission has been relocated, rebuilt and renovated multiple times during its long history. Today it is an active Catholic Parish as well as a cultural center where all are welcome.

El barrio Pilsen de Chicago cuenta con numerosos murales inspirados por el movimiento muralista mexicano. Los murales coloridos de Francisco Mendoza representan escenas de la vida diaria de esta comunidad hispana.

En 1988 el presidente Reagan declaró el periodo entre el 15 de septiembre y el 15 de octubre el Mes de la Hispanidad, días dedicados a celebrar la herencia y cultura hispana en Estados Unidos.

La Misión de San Diego de Alcalá, establecida en 1769 por los españoles, forma parte del famoso Camino Real en California. Hay 21 misiones desde San Francisco hasta San Diego.

Los hispanos y la expansión de Estados Unidos

Go to the *Enfoque cultural* [folder] in *Capítulo 2* online to learn more about this topic.

PLAN DE ESTUDIO

◎ LEARN
- Interactive presentation: *Los hispanos y la expansión de Estados Unidos*

APPLY ◎
- Activities

PRÁCTICA COMUNICATIVA

2-40

Usa la información. Prepare an oral presentation describing the current flag or a historic flag of one of the states that has a Hispanic heritage.

En este capítulo...

Comprueba lo que sabes

Go to the *Comprueba lo que sabes* folder online to review what you have learned in this chapter. Practice with the following:

Vocabulary Flashcards	Games	Oral Practice	Practice Test/ Study Plan	Video en contexto

Vocabulario

Las descripciones
agradable
alegre
alto/a
antipático/a
bajo/a
bilingüe
bonito/a
callado/a
cansado/a
casado/a
contento/a
conversador/a
corto/a
de estatura mediana
débil
delgado/a
divertido/a
enojado/a
feo/a
fuerte
gordo/a
guapo/a
joven
largo/a
listo/a
mayor
moreno/a
nervioso/a
nuevo/a
oscuro/a

pelirrojo/a
perezoso/a
pobre
rico/a
rubio/a
simpático/a
soltero/a
tonto/a
trabajador/a
triste
viejo/a

Las nacionalidades
alemán/alemana
argentino/a
boliviano/a
canadiense
chileno/a
colombiano/a
costarricense
cubano/a
dominicano/a
ecuatoriano/a
español/a
estadounidense
francés/francesa
guatemalteco/a
hispano/a
hondureño/a
japonés/japonesa

marroquí
mexicano/a
nicaragüense
nigeriano/a
panameño/a
paraguayo/a
peruano/a
polaco/a
portugués/portuguesa
puertorriqueño/a
salvadoreño/a
uruguayo/a
venezolano/a

Los colores
amarillo/a
anaranjado/a
azul
blanco/a
gris
marrón
morado/a
negro/a
rojo/a
rosado/a, rosa
verde

Verbos
desear
ser
usar

Palabras y expresiones útiles
el auto, el coche, el carro
de
¿de quién?
del
la flor
le gusta(n)
los lentes de contacto
me gusta(n)
mucho (*adv.*)
mucho/a (*adj.*)
el ojo
el pelo
te gusta(n)
Tengo... años.
tiene
todos/as

Adjetivos posesivos
mi(s)
tu(s)
su(s)
nuestro(s), nuestra(s)
vuestro(s), vuestra(s)El origen

Notas

3 ¿Qué hacen para divertirse?

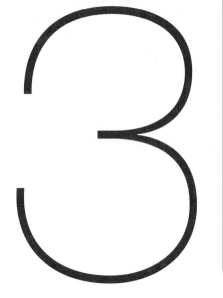

VOCABULARIO EN CONTEXTO

Talking about leisure activities, making plans, and food

Las diversiones

Los planes

La comida

GRAMÁTICA EN CONTEXTO

Talking about what you and others do in your free time

Present tense of *hacer, poner, salir, traer,* and *oír*

Present tense of *ir* and *ir a + infinitive*

Numbers 100 to 2,000,000

Saber and *conocer*

Some uses of *por* and *para*

UNIDOS

ESCUCHA Using background knowledge

HABLA Informing yourself before doing a survey

LEE Looking for and using key words

ESCRIBE Identifying your audience

ENFOQUE CULTURAL

Perfiles de Perú, Bolivia y Paraguay

EN ESTE CAPÍTULO...

Comprueba lo que sabes

Vocabulario

Learning OBJECTIVES

You will:

- use new vocabulary to talk about pastimes and food
- learn the *ir + a* construction and the forms of other irregular verbs
- learn numbers over 100
- distinguish between *saber* and *conocer*
- connect new information about the geography, history, and cultural diversity of Peru, Bolivia, and Paraguay to what you already know

Learning OUTCOMES

You will be able to:

- describe leisure activities and food
- plan your daily activities and express intentions
- identify prices and dates
- state what and whom you know
- describe places to visit in Peru, Bolivia, and Paraguay

PERÚ, BOLIVIA Y PARAGUAY

En este detalle de un cuadro anónimo del siglo XVIII, vemos a unos invitados a la boda entre la princesa inca Ñusta Beatriz y un noble español, D. Martín de Loyola.

Cultura en línea

To learn more about Peru, Bolivia, and Paraguay, and the chapter theme, go to the *Cultura en línea* folder in the *Unidos* online component to view the *Vistas culturales* video and take a virtual art tour.

¿Cuánto sabes?

Using the map and photos, indicate whether each statement is true (**Cierto**) or false (**Falso**).

1. _Falso_ La capital de Perú está en la costa del Atlántico.

2. _Falso_ Perú está al sur de Bolivia.

3. _Cierto_ El río Paraná está en la frontera entre Paraguay y Argentina.

4. _Cierto_ Bolivia es más grande que Paraguay.

5. _Cierto_ El Lago Titicaca está entre Perú y Bolivia.

6. _Falso_ La cordillera de los Andes pasa por los tres países.

the cursor. *¿Qué países están al norte de Perú? ¿Cuáles están al sur? ¿Y al oeste?* Also ask: *¿Cómo se llama el océano que está al lado de Perú? ¿Qué países no tienen costa? ¿Cómo se llaman las montañas que hay en Perú y Bolivia?* Explain *cordillera* by drawing a chain of mountains or by pointing to them on the map. *¿Cuál es la capital de Bolivia? ¿Qué países rodean Paraguay?*

Tech tip for *Cultura en línea*
You can view the *Vistas culturales* videos in class or assign them for homework. Each clip has corresponding before, during, and after viewing video activities in the *Cultura en línea* folder online.

Note for art
The detail shown here is from the painting depicting the wedding between people from different cultures. Represented here are Túpac Amaru y Sayri Túpac, whose presence at the wedding validates the union. The marriage documents the ties between Incan nobility and European bloodlines. Several copies of this painting exist and served to spread news of these events. Introduce the word *boda* by pointing to the couple in the painting and the word *casarse*. Ask questions to elicit vocabulary:
¿Cómo es el hombre del cuadro? ¿Cómo es la mujer? ¿Qué hacen las personas en una boda normalmente? ¿Comen mucho o poco? ¿Beben? ¿Bailan?

Standard 2.1
Students demonstrate an understanding of the relationship between the practices and perspectives of the culture studied. This painting depicts a wedding between people from different cultures. Have students reflect on how practices of both cultures are combined (or not) when members of one culture are the conquerors and members of the other culture have been conquered.

Tech tip for Virtual Art Tour
You can launch the Virtual Art Tour from the eText to view together in class. You can also assign it for homework.

Vocabulario en contexto

Talking about leisure activities, making plans, and food.

Las diversiones

Go to the *Capítulo 3* **folder** online to complete the Learning Module for *Vocabulario en contexto: Las diversiones.*

PLAN DE ESTUDIO

◎ LEARN
- Interactive presentation: *Las diversiones*
- Vocabulary tutorials
- Pronunciation

APPLY ◎
- Activities
- Pronunciation activities

PRÁCTICA COMUNICATIVA

3-1

Asociaciones. Which leisure activities do you associate with the following places? Then, ask your partner if he/she does the same things in these places.

1. ___c___ la playa
2. ___e___ la fiesta
3. ___a___ el cine
4. ___b___ la biblioteca
5. _a, b, d, e_ la casa

a. ver una película
b. leer el periódico
c. tomar el sol
d. mirar televisión
e. bailar y conversar

Nuestro tiempo libre. What do you do in the following places? Take turns asking one another, and take notes on the responses.

Modelo

"las vacaciones"

¿Qué haces en tus vacaciones?

En mis vacaciones generalmente voy a la playa. ¿Y tú?

Suggestion for 3-2
The expression ¿Qué hacen los estudiantes? was introduced in Capítulo 1. Remind students what hacer means by writing on the board ¿Qué haces los fines de semana? Ask questions to review the verb and recycle vocabulary: ¿Qué haces en la universidad? ¿Qué hace Elisa en el gimnasio? ¿Qué hacemos en la clase de español?

Expansión for 3-2
7. en una reunión; 8. en el cine; 9. en un restaurante elegante; 10. en el auto; 11. en el centro de la ciudad; 12. en el gimnasio.

	COMPAÑERO/A 1	COMPAÑERO/A 2	COMPAÑERO/A 3	YO
1. en la universidad después de clase				
2. en la biblioteca pública de tu ciudad				
3. en casa el fin de semana				
4. en un parque de tu ciudad				
5. en la playa durante las vacaciones				
6. en la discoteca con tus amigos				

3-3

¿Qué hacen Pedro y Carmen?

PRIMERA FASE. Look at the drawings and take turns explaining what your friends Pedro and Carmen do on weekends.

SEGUNDA FASE. Each of you write an e-mail to Pedro explaining what you and your friends do on weekends.

Pedro

Carmen

Suggestion for 3-3
This is a good opportunity to recycle vocabulary from previous chapters and to use new vocabulary. Before the Segunda fase, brainstorm with students the vocabulary related to activities that they have learned (mirar televisión, practicar básquetbol/baloncesto, montar en bicicleta). You may introduce new words, such as piano, trompeta, violín.

Los planes

Go to the *Capítulo 3* [folder] oline to complete the Learning Module for *Vocabulario en contexto: Los planes.*

PLAN DE ESTUDIO

◎ LEARN
- Interactive presentation: *Los planes*
- Vocabulary tutorials

APPLY ◎
- Activities

PRÁCTICA COMUNICATIVA

3-4

Otra conversación.

With a partner, read the telephone conversation between Liliana and Manuel. Then together change the conversation to make your own plans.

LILIANA: ¿Aló?

MANUEL: Hola, ¡felicidades por tu cumpleaños!

LILIANA: Ay, gracias, Manuel.

MANUEL: ¿Vamos al cine esta tarde y después a un restaurante?

LILIANA: Me parece fabuloso. ¿Dónde ponen la película?

MANUEL: Cerca de El Jardín Limeño, tu restaurante favorito.

LILIANA: Estupendo.

MANUEL: ¡Hasta luego!

EN OTRAS PALABRAS

Telephone greetings vary from country to country.

¿Diga? and **¿Dígame?** are used to answer the phone in Spain;

¡Bueno! in Mexico;

¿Aló? in Argentina, Peru, and Chile;

¡Oigo! and **¿Qué hay?** in Cuba.

Terms of endearment such as **mi amor, corazón, mi vida, querido/a,** and **mi cielo** also reflect regional preferences.

3-5

Una invitación.

PRIMERA FASE. Think of an activity you would like to do this weekend. Then call two classmates and invite them to join you in a weekend activity. Your classmates will accept or decline the invitation. Use the expressions in *En directo* for ideas.

SEGUNDA FASE. Explain your weekend plans to the class and how many people are joining you.

Modelo

> *El sábado por la tarde Juan, Verónica y yo vamos al gimnasio para ver un partido de básquetbol a las 6:00.*

En directo

To extend an invitation:

Te llamo para + *infinitive...*

Te escribo para invitarte a + *infinitive...*

To accept an invitation:

¡Estupendo! ¿Dónde quedamos? *Where do we meet?*

Sí, gracias/¡Ah, qué bien!/¡Qué buena idea! Me parece muy bien.

¡Qué bueno!

¡Fabuloso!

To decline an invitation:

Lo siento, pero no tengo tiempo/ tengo mucho trabajo/tengo mucha tarea...

Ese día no puedo (*I can't*), tengo un examen.

Click on the icon to listen to a conversation with these expressions.

3-6

Un plan para el sábado. Write a text message to a classmate inviting him/her to go to the movies on Saturday. Exchange texts and respond to your classmate's.

Cultura

Traditionally, Mexico, Spain, and Argentina have had important film industries, but films are made in other Spanish-speaking countries as well. Outstanding Spanish-language film directors like Pedro Almodóvar and Icíar Bollaín in Spain, Alfonso Cuarón and Alejandro González in Mexico, Sergio Cabrera in Colombia, and Juan Carlos Tabío in Cuba, among others, are internationally known.

Compara: What other famous directors (American or foreign-born) can you name? What do you like best about their style?

Tech tip for 3-5
Before doing the activity you may review the expressions in *En directo* and listen to the sample conversation by clicking on the audio icon from the eText. Provide other ways to accept or reject an invitation. For example, *Aceptar: ¡Cómo no! ¡Estupendo! Me gustaría mucho. No aceptar: No puedo. Es que debo estudiar.* You may also brainstorm with students about their plans for the weekend: *¿Qué planes tienen este fin de semana? ¿Van al cine? ¿Van a un concierto? ¿A un partido de béisbol? ¿Van a escuchar música en su casa?*

Audioscript for *En directo*
Inés: *Hola, Roberto. Te llamo para ver si quieres ir al cine el jueves.*
Roberto: *Ese día no puedo, tengo un examen el viernes y tengo que estudiar mucho.*
Inés: *Está bien. ¿Por qué no vamos el viernes?*
Roberto: *Sí, el viernes sí puedo. ¿Cenamos primero y luego vamos al cine?*
Inés: *¡Qué buena idea! ¿Dónde quedamos?*
Roberto: *En la biblioteca a las siete. ¿De acuerdo?*
Inés: *¡Sí, estupendo!*

3-7

¿Adónde vamos? Identify three activities on this page from a newspaper in Lima that you and your classmate find interesting. Then fill in the chart, including the day and time for each activity. Be prepared to share this information with the class.

¿Adónde vamos?	¿Qué vamos a hacer?	¿Cuándo?

AGENDA CULTURAL

La guía de Lima

Cine

El amor en los tiempos del cólera. Dir. Mike Newell. C.C. Británico. Calle Bellavista 531. Miraflores. 7:30 pm. Libre.

Teatro

La casa de Bernarda Alba. Grupo de Teatro Lorca. C.C. Británico. Av. La Marina 2554. San Miguel. 7:30 pm. Libre.
Entre visillos. Basada en "La cantante calva", de Eugenio Ionesco. Auditorio Municipalidad de San Isidro. La República 455. El Olivar. 8 pm. Boletería.

Música

Los andinos en concierto. Huainos, yaravíes, mulizas. ICPNA. Jr. Cuzco 446. Lima. 7 pm. S/. 10.00.
Noche flamenca. Ballet La flor de Sevilla. ICPNA. Av. Angamos Oeste 120. Miraflores. 7:30 p.m. S/. 25.00.
Amalia Sánchez en concierto. A beneficio del C.C. de Rehabilitación de Ciegos. C.C. Ricardo Palma. Larco 770. Miraflores. 8 pm. S/. 10.00.

Exposición

Maestros en acción. Asociación de Docentes de la ENSABAP. Bellas Artes de La Molina. Av. Rinconada del Lago 1515. 7 pm.

Libro

Lectura de poemas de Óscar Liria. Av. La Paz 646. 7:30 pm. Libre.

Conferencia

La mujer en el arte. Con Lola Reyes. C. C. San Marcos. Parque Universitario. Lima. 6:30 pm. Libre.

Literatura

Perú en la literatura francesa. Con Pierre Brillat. Alianza Francesa. Av. Arequipa 4595. Miraflores. 8 pm. S/.15.00, S/.10.00.

Cultura

Huaynos, *yaravíes*, and *mulizas* are Peruvian songs of pre-Columbian origin that are popular in the Andean region of the country. They are often performed and danced in the *peñas*, music clubs that promote traditional (Afro-Andean and Creole) music. In the *peñas* people dance all night long and enjoy excellent regional food. Search the Internet to listen to examples of these popular songs.

Compara: Are these songs similar to any other style of music you know? What type of music in your culture would you most closely associate with it?

La comida

Go to the *Capítulo 3* [folder] online to complete the Learning Module for *Vocabulario en contexto: La comida.*

PLAN DE ESTUDIO

◎ LEARN
- Interactive presentation: *La comida*
- Vocabulary tutorials
- *Entrevistas* video

APPLY ◎
- Activities
- *Entrevistas* video activities

PRÁCTICA COMUNICATIVA

3-8

Calorías. Which item in each group contains the most calories? Check to see if your partner agrees and then ask him/her which of the items in each group he/she likes best.

1. la sopa de tomate, la hamburguesa, la sopa de pollo   la hamburguesa

2. el pollo frito, el pescado, la ensalada
el pollo frito

3. las verduras, las frutas, las papas fritas
las papas fritas

4. la cerveza, la leche desnatada (*skim*), el café   la cerveza

5. el helado de chocolate, el cereal, el arroz   el helado de chocolate

---

3-9

Las comidas.

PRIMERA FASE. Discuss with your classmate what you usually have for breakfast, lunch, and dinner.

Modelo   **❝** *En el desayuno, como tostadas y bebo café. ¿Y tú?* **❞**

SEGUNDA FASE. Write a paragraph explaining what you and your classmate eat frequently for breakfast, lunch, and dinner.

Modelo   **❝** *Yo, para desayunar frecuentemente como cereal y bebo café con leche. Mi compañero…* **❞**

¿Qué hacen para divertirse?   **89**

Online prep for students
Students will have completed the Learning Module for *La comida* online before class. See content online and Instructor's Resources for Supplementary Activities.

Tech tip for *Vocabulario en contexto*
You may want to review the dialogue from the Learning Module in class by playing the audio and projecting the text image of the menu. Begin with *El camarero les pregunta a Liliana y a Manuel qué desean comer y qué van a beber* (make gestures). *Ellos van a beber vino para celebrar el cumpleaños de Liliana.* Explain the sections of the menu: *entradas, platos principales, postres* and that *entradas* is a false cognate, meaning "appetizers," not "entrées." Introduce food vocabulary as you talk about some of the dishes (*queso, huevos, atún, aguacate, pollo, nuez, arroz, leche*) and some methods of cooking (*frito, cocido, estofado*). Explain *relleno*.

Tech tip for *Vocabulario en contexto*
Use online images of the meals to review food vocabulary and ask questions such as: *¿Tomas café o té en el desayuno? ¿Comes cereal? ¿Qué comes a la hora del almuerzo? ¿Qué comida no te gusta? ¿Cuál es tu bebida/comida favorita? ¿Qué comida es rica en vitaminas?* Introduce *caliente* and *frío/a*: *La sopa está caliente. La cerveza está fría. Y el café, ¿está frío o caliente?* Explain that in several countries of Latin America the word *comida* is also used to mean the late afternoon/evening meal.

Suggestion for 3-8
Ask if students know which item in each group has the fewest calories.

Follow-up for 3-9
Ask additional questions: *¿A qué hora es el desayuno? ¿El almuerzo? ¿La cena? ¿Cuándo tomamos vino? ¿Leche? ¿Jugo de naranja? ¿Cerveza?…*

¿Qué debe comer? Take turns asking each other which items from the menu are the best options for the following people.

1. Tu amiga Luisa está un poco delgada y desea subir de peso (*gain weight*).
2. Tu mamá es alérgica a los mariscos (*seafood*).
3. Tu amigo José está un poco gordo y quiere bajar de peso (*lose weight*).
4. El profesor/La profesora de español está enfermo/a (*sick*) del estómago hoy.

MENÚ

SOPAS
Sopa de pollo	S/. 9
Sopa de tomate	S/. 7
Sopa de vegetales	S/. 7
Sopa de pescado	S/. 12

ENSALADAS
Ensalada de lechuga y tomate	S/. 8
Ensalada de pollo	S/. 14
Ensalada de atún	S/. 12

PLATOS PRINCIPALES
Bistec con papas y vegetales	S/. 20
Hamburguesa con papas fritas	S/. 16
Pescado con papas fritas	S/. 18
Arroz con vegetales	S/. 15

3-11

¿Qué te gusta más? Using the words below, discuss with your partner what you each prefer to drink **por la mañana, para el almuerzo, por la noche.** Then explain your partner's preferences to the class.

Modelo

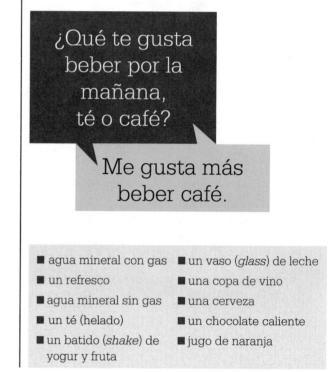

¿Qué te gusta beber por la mañana, té o café?

Me gusta más beber café.

- agua mineral con gas
- un refresco
- agua mineral sin gas
- un té (helado)
- un batido (*shake*) de yogur y fruta
- un vaso (*glass*) de leche
- una copa de vino
- una cerveza
- un chocolate caliente
- jugo de naranja

Cultura

Fast food (*La comida rápida*) is popular among young Hispanics, and American-style hamburger places may be found in Hispanic countries. They often adapt to local tastes, and it is not unusual to have hamburgers served with rice and black beans instead of fries. Beer and wine may also be sold in addition to soft drinks.

Compara: Do you know of any fast food places in your community that are not American style? What types of foods do they serve?

3-12

En el café. It is 9:00 on Saturday morning, and you and a friend are in a café in Lima. Ask what your friend wants to order. Then say what you are going to order.

Modelo

E1: *El desayuno es muy bueno aquí. ¿Qué deseas comer?*

E2: _____ *¿Y tú?*

E1: *Yo _____ ¿Y qué vas a tomar?*

DESAYUNOS

café	S/.3
té	S/.3
café con leche	S/.5
jugo de naranja	S/.5
chocolate	S/.6
tostadas	S/.5
pan con mantequilla	S/.5
pan dulce	S/.6
cereal	S/.8
huevos fritos	S/.10

En directo

Expressions to order food:

Para mí, unas tostadas, café…

Me gustaría/Quisiera comer/ tomar… *I would like to eat/ drink…*

Yo quiero/deseo…

Click on the icon to listen to a conversation with these expressions.

3-13

Un viaje (*trip*). You and your partner are in Peru and are planning a day trip to Machu Picchu. Arrange to take some food and beverages with you.

1. Make a list of the food and beverages that you need to take.

2. Talk in detail about at least five activities that you are going to do.

3-14

¿Qué hacen estos estudiantes?

PRIMERA FASE.

Rafael and Miguel talk about their activities and weekend plans. Before you listen to their conversation, write down three activities you normally do during the week, and three that you plan for this weekend. Then, ask your partner if he/she is going to do the same things.

 SEGUNDA FASE. Now, listen to Rafael and Miguel's conversation. Check (✔) the activities they mention they will do during the weekend.

1. ____ estudiar para los exámenes
2. _✔_ comer en un restaurante
3. _✔_ descansar y tomar el sol
4. ____ trabajar en la librería
5. ____ celebrar el cumpleaños de Rafael

Cultura

Peruvian cooking mostly uses regional ingredients and follows preparation methods inherited from indigenous cultures. *Ceviche* is a typical dish of Peru and other countries in Latin America. It is generally made with seafood and fish that is not cooked but rather marinated in lime juice and spices.

With 200 varieties, potatoes are a common staple in Bolivian cooking along with meats such as pork, goat, llama or *cuy* (guinea pig). Hearty soups laden with chicken, pork, potatoes, and other ingredients accompany most meals.

In Paraguay, cassava, corn, and beef are the main ingredients used in cooking. Typical corn-based dishes include *locro*, *sopa paraguaya*, and *mbaipy-so-ó*.

Compara: What similarities do you see between the food described here and the food of your culture? What are some differences?

Audioscript for *En directo*
Camarero: *Buenas noches. ¿Qué desean los señores?*
Luisa: *Para mí, unas tostadas y un café con leche.*
Esteban: *Yo quiero una ensalada de pollo. También quisiera tomar agua bien fría.*
Camarero: *Muy bien. Regreso pronto con sus bebidas.*

Suggestions for 3-12
Bring menus to class. Have pairs of students play the roles of diner and server in a restaurant.

Suggestion for 3-13
Review ir + a + infinitive to help students talk about their plans. Prepare for this activity by showing photos of Machu Picchu or ask them to read the text in *Enfoque cultural*.

Audioscript for 3-14
Rafael: *Hola, Miguel, ¿cómo estás?*
Miguel: *Muy bien, Rafael. ¿Y tú?*
Rafael: *Bien, pero cansado. Tomo muchas clases este semestre y estudio mucho porque mi clase de economía es muy difícil. Además trabajo en una librería los martes y jueves por la tarde. Esta semana tenemos exámenes y voy a la biblioteca todos los días.*
Miguel: *¿Y qué vas a hacer este fin de semana?*
Rafael: *No sé. Me gustaría descansar.*
Miguel: *Perfecto. Mira, Rafael, mi familia tiene una casa en la playa. El viernes vamos un grupo de amigos, después del último examen. Vamos a descansar, nadar y tomar el sol. Por la noche vamos a comer en un restaurante. La comida es excelente, especialmente el pescado, y los camareros son muy amables. ¿Por qué no vienes con nosotros? Te va a gustar.*
Rafael: *¡Ah! ¡Qué bien! Me gusta mucho descansar en la playa. ¡Y también me gusta la buena comida!*
Miguel: *¡Estupendo! Nos vemos el viernes, entonces.*
Rafael: *Sí, y gracias, ¿eh?*

Gramática en contexto

Talking about what you and others do in your free time

Talking about daily activities:
Present tense of *hacer, poner, salir, traer,* and *oír*

Go to the *Capítulo 3* **folder** online to complete the Learning Module for *Gramática en contexto*: Present tense of *hacer, poner, salir, traer,* and *oír*.

PLAN DE ESTUDIO

◎ LEARN
- Interactive presentation: Present tense of *hacer, poner, salir, traer,* and *oír*
- Grammar tutorials

APPLY ◎
- Activities
- Extra Practice

PRÁCTICA COMUNICATIVA

3-15

La perfección andante (*Perfection in motion*).

PRIMERA FASE. Are you organized, considerate, studious, and punctual? Check (✔) the statements that refer to things you do or don't do regularly.

1. ____ Yo **hago** mi cama temprano por la mañana.

2. ____ Cuando **oigo** que un amigo está triste, lo invito a salir.

3. ____ Siempre **pongo** música rock cuando estudio.

4. ____ Generalmente, **traigo** mi iPad a clase para tomar apuntes.

5. ____ En general, no **traigo** mi iPod porque necesito escuchar al profesor.

6. ____ Por las mañanas, **hago** ejercicio y luego **salgo** para la universidad.

SEGUNDA FASE. Take turns talking about the activities you both do that show off your best qualities.

Modelo

Yo soy organizada. Siempre hago mi cama temprano. ¿Y tú?

Pues, yo también…

3-16

¿Usas bien tu tiempo libre?

PRIMERA FASE. Check (✔) the version of each pair of activities that fits you.

1. ____ Pongo la mesa para cenar.
   ____ Como en cualquier lugar de la casa.

2. ____ Hago el desayuno.
   ____ Salgo a desayunar fuera de casa.

3. ____ Hago la cama todos los días.
   ____ Hago la cama una vez por semana.

4. ____ Siempre oigo mi teléfono celular.
   ____ No oigo mi teléfono cuando vibra.

5. ____ Traigo el periódico a la casa.
   ____ Leo el periódico en Internet.

6. ____ Pongo la televisión para ver películas.
   ____ Salgo al cine para ver películas.

SEGUNDA FASE. Share your answers with a classmate. Explain why you like your way of doing things.

3-17

Mi rutina.

PRIMERA FASE. Talk about the activities that you routinely do. Then ask your classmate about his/her activities.

Modelo **❝** *tener clases (por la mañana / por la tarde)* **❞**

> Yo tengo clases por la mañana. ¿Y tú?

> Yo tengo clases por la mañana y por la tarde.

1. salir de casa (temprano/tarde) por la mañana
2. poner (el iPod/la computadora) para escuchar música por la mañana
3. hacer la tarea (en casa/en la biblioteca)
4. salir a (comer/ver películas) con amigos por la noche
5. traer muchos (libros/amigos) a casa después de las clases

SEGUNDA FASE. Write a brief paragraph comparing your routine with that of your classmate. In your opinion, who has a more interesting routine, and why? Provide a few reasons.

3-18

Para pasarlo bien.

PRIMERA FASE. Indicate (✔) the activities that, in your opinion, your classmates probably do to have fun. Compare answers with a partner.

1. ____ Alquilan películas los fines de semana.
2. ____ Oyen música y bailan mientras estudian para los exámenes.
3. ____ Frecuentemente hacen fiestas con sus amigos.
4. ____ Asisten a conciertos y exposiciones de arte.
5. ____ Hacen ejercicio en el gimnasio o en el parque.
6. ____ Escuchan programas en la Radio Pública Nacional (NPR).
7. ____ Salen a comer en grupo.
8. ____ Hablan por Skype constantemente.

Alternate for 3-18
Students may ask partners if and when they do some of the activities listed. Then they switch partners and tell each other the information they gathered.

Suggestion for 3-18
Para pasarlo bien appeared earlier in the chapter. You may wish to reinforce its meaning: *Hay muchas maneras de pasarlo bien. Yo, por ejemplo, para pasarlo bien, escucho música, voy al cine con amigos, tengo/hago fiestas en mi casa y otras actividades similares. ¿Y tú, lees o bailas para pasarlo bien? ¿Qué haces para pasarlo bien los fines de semana/durante las vacaciones?*

SEGUNDA FASE. Using the activities you marked in the *Primera fase*, ask your instructor if he/she does these activities to have fun.

Modelo

> Para pasarlo bien, nosotros asistimos a conciertos de música rock. ¿Usted asiste a conciertos de música rock para pasarlo bien?

> No, no asisto a conciertos de música rock. Para pasarlo bien escucho conciertos de música jazz en la radio pública.

> ¡Qué interesante!

En directo

To react to what someone has said:

¡Qué interesante! *How interesting!*

¡Qué divertido! *How fun!*

¡Qué aburrido! *How boring!*

¡Qué lata! *What a nuisance!*

 Click on the icon to listen to a conversation with these expressions.

Situaciones

1

ROLE A. You have made a new friend, and you are asking him/her about the things he/she likes to do in his/her free time. Ask him/her: a) if he/she goes out a lot and where; b) if he/she does any sports; c) if he/she goes to parties and what does he/she bring; and d) if he/she likes to listen to music and what music he/she listens to.

ROLE B. You are new in town, and you have just met someone who is interested in knowing more about you. Answer the questions in as much detail as possible and ask some questions of your own.

2

ROLE A. You have just been hired to take care of a five-year-old boy for the summer. Ask the following: a) what time the parent leaves the house in the morning; b) what his favorite activities are; and c) if you may turn on the television or not.

ROLE B. You have just hired a college student to take care of your five-year-old son for the summer. Answer his/her questions. To get to know him/her better, ask: a) what he/she studies at school and b) what he/she likes to do in his/her free time.

Suggestion for 3-18 *Segunda fase*
Encourage students to be creative in their questions about your activities, and use humor to exaggerate similarities and/or differences between students' leisure activities and your own.

Audioscript for *En directo*
Verónica: *Hay una exposición de las primeras obras de Picasso.*
Chela: *¡Qué interesante! A mí me encanta Picasso.*
Verónica: *Después ponen una película sobre la vida de Picasso. ¿Vamos esta tarde?*
Chela: *Lo siento. Tengo mucho trabajo.*
Verónica: *¡Qué lata!*

Suggestion for *Situaciones*
Encourage students to make their conversations sound natural and realistic. To help them compensate for possible lack of vocabulary, review greetings and communication strategies, such as asking for repetition, asking questions, and using synonyms/opposite (*Repite, por favor*; *No comprendo*; *Más despacio, por favor*; *¿Qué significa?*).

Tech tip for *Situaciones*
You may want to assign partners and have pairs create a mini-skit using the video-posting feature, *MediaShare*, online.

Suggestion for *Situaciones*
Additional situations are available in the Instructor's Resource folder online.

Expressing movement and plans:
Present tense of *ir* and *ir a* + infinitive

Go to the *Capítulo 3* [folder] online to complete the Learning Module for *Gramática en contexto*: Present tense of *ir* and *ir a* + *infinitive*.

PLAN DE ESTUDIO

◎ LEARN
- Interactive presentation: Present tense of *ir* and *ir a* + *infinitive*.
- Grammar tutorials

APPLY ◎
- Activities
- Extra Practice

PRÁCTICA COMUNICATIVA

 3-19

¿Adónde van?

PRIMERA FASE. Josh and Steve are North American students visiting Peru for their summer vacation. Match the descriptions with the places they plan to see.

a. Machu Picchu   **b.** las líneas de Nazca   **c.** la Universidad de San Marcos   **d.** una peña

1. _c_ Steve estudia historia. Por eso, busca una institución prestigiosa. Está en Lima. Él va a…

2. _b_ Los dos amigos van a visitar uno de los lugares más misteriosos del planeta. Allí hay enormes figuras geométricas trazadas (*drawn*) en la tierra que son visibles solamente desde el aire. Ellos van a…

3. _d_ Josh conoce (*meets*) a Susana en Perú. Ella lo invita a un evento folclórico donde las personas oyen poesía, música tradicional y comen y bailan también. Josh y Susana van a…

4. _a_ Steve y Josh van a un lugar histórico imposible de ignorar. Es considerado el símbolo del imperio inca. Está cerca de Cuzco. Steve y Josh van a…

SEGUNDA FASE. Now take turns asking your partner where you two will go to do the following in Peru.

1. ¿Adónde vamos para hacer amigos, conversar y bailar ritmos peruanos? una peña

2. ¿Adónde vamos para tomar fotos de los alumnos y el edificio de una universidad muy antigua? la Universidad de San Marcos

3. ¿Adónde vamos para escalar unas montañas altas de mucha importancia histórica?
Machu Picchu

Expansion for 3-20
You may wish to have groups of students create schedules and repeat the activity using the real-life information they learn from their partners.

Intercambio.

PRIMERA FASE. Your classmate's friends Bob, Juan, Alicia, and Sofía are busy today. Ask your classmate when each friend is leaving the place listed and where he/she is going afterward.

Modelo

¿A qué hora sale del trabajo tu amigo Bob?

(Sale) a las seis de la tarde.

¿Adónde va después?

Va al cine.

NOMBRE	HORA	LUGAR	DESTINO
Juan	8:00 A.M.	gimnasio	clase
Alicia	9:30 A.M.	laboratorio de computadoras	biblioteca
Sofía	8:30 P.M.	oficina	cafetería
Tú	…	…	…

SEGUNDA FASE. Exchange information with your partner about what each of you does at the times listed in the *Primera fase*.

Modelo

¿Qué haces a las 8:00 de la mañana?

Salgo de mi casa para la universidad.

¿Adónde vas después

Voy al gimnasio ¿Qué haces tú a las 8:00 de la mañana?

Suggestion for 3-21 *Segunda fase*
You may wish to ask students to support their responses. Model as follows: *Los padres van a conversar seriamente con Cristina sobre las fiestas secretas. Creen que no es correcto hacer fiestas secretas, etc.*

3-21

¡Qué desorden! (*What a mess!*)

PRIMERA FASE. Cristina had a party at her house, and now her friends are helping her clean up. Match each situation with its probable solution. Compare answers with a partner.

1. __b__ Hay muchos platos sucios.

2. __c__ Cristina ve mucha comida en la mesa.

3. __a__ La casa está desordenada.

4. __d__ Cristina y sus amigos necesitan energía para limpiar la casa.

5. __e__ Los amigos de Cristina están cansados después de la fiesta.

a. Dos chicos van a ordenar todo.

b. Algunos amigos van a recoger (*pick up*) los platos.

c. Una amiga va a refrigerar la comida.

d. Una amiga va a preparar café.

e. Van a descansar.

SEGUNDA FASE. Brainstorm how Cristina's parents are going to react when they find out about her party. Some reactions may include: *cancelar su tarjeta de crédito/su teléfono celular, prohibir fiestas/amigos, estar enojados, ...*

Modelo

Sus padres no van a estar contentos.

Sí, y van a conversar muy seriamente con Cristina.

Suggestion for 3-22
Before students do the activity, model with a few of them how to issue, accept, and reject invitations. Refer students to the *En directo* box on p. 87.

Expansion for 3-22
Have students prepare their agenda for the upcoming week and then take turns asking questions to find out what their classmates are going to do. Model as follows: *¿Qué vas a hacer la próxima semana? ¿Adónde vas a ir?*

3-22

Mi agenda para la semana. Invite six classmates individually to do the following activities with you. They are going to accept or reject your invitation.

Modelo

❝ estudiar en la biblioteca el lunes por la noche ❞

¿Vamos a estudiar en la biblioteca el lunes por la noche?

Lo siento, Miguel, el lunes por la noche voy a ir al cine con David. Pero, ¿por qué no estudiamos el martes por la mañana?

Buena idea. Vamos a estudiar el martes temprano por la mañana.

1. ir a un concierto el viernes por la noche

2. mirar una buena película en casa el lunes a mediodía

3. tomar algo en un café el sábado por la mañana

4. estudiar para un examen difícil el miércoles por la tarde

5. bailar en la discoteca el jueves por la noche

6. hacer ejercicio el domingo a mediodía

3-23

Los planes de Maribel.

PRIMERA FASE. Take turns telling each other what Maribel is going to do at the times indicated.

SEGUNDA FASE. Chat with your classmate about what you are going to do at those times on Friday.

Situaciones

1

ROLE A. Your friend has invited you to a concert. Call him/her to find out: a) where and when the concert is going to be; b) who is going to sing; c) who is going to introduce (**presentar**) the group; and d) how much the ticket (**el boleto/el billete/ la entrada**) costs.

ROLE B. Your friend calls to find out about a concert you invited him/her to. Answer all the questions with as much information as possible.

2

ROLE A. You call to invite a friend to a café tonight where a mutual friend is going to sing. After your friend responds, ask about his/her plans for later in the evening: a) where he/she is going; b) with whom; and c) what time, etc.

ROLE B. A friend calls to invite you to a café tonight where a mutual friend is going to sing. Inquire about the event to find out a) what time and where it will be and b) if other friends are going to go. Accept the invitation and mention your plans for later in the evening.

Warm-up for 3-23
Use posters of people engaged in a variety of activities to solicit spontaneous descriptions of what each person is going to do. Then ask students to compare their activities with those shown in the drawings.

Tech tip for *Situaciones*
Some students may want to film themselves and post their conversations using the MediaShare feature online.

Talking about quantity:
Numbers 100 to 2,000,000

Go to the *Capítulo 3* **folder** online to complete the Learning Module for *Gramática en contexto:* Numbers 100 to 2,000,000.

PLAN DE ESTUDIO

◎ LEARN
- Interactive presentation: Numbers 100 to 2,000,000
- Grammar tutorials

APPLY ◎
- Activities
- Extra Practice

PRÁCTICA COMUNICATIVA

3-24

¿Cuándo va a ocurrir? Exchange opinions with a classmate about when each of the following events will (or will not) occur. Then create one of your own to share.

Modelo   **" Todos los libros van a ser electrónicos. "**

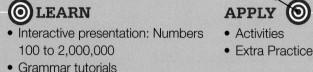
En el año 2020.

No estoy de acuerdo. Todos los libros van a ser electrónicos en 2050.

1. Los adultos van a trabajar solo 20 horas por semana.
2. Los estudiantes no van a ir a clases. Van a estudiar en universidades virtuales.
3. Todos los autos van a ser eléctricos y van a ser muy rápidos.
4. Muchos turistas van a viajar (*travel*) al espacio interplanetario.
5. Los viajes en avión van a ser más rápidos y van a costar poco.
6. Las personas. . .

3-25

Unas vacaciones.

PRIMERA FASE. Your classmate has chosen one of the destinations in the ad below for an upcoming vacation. To find out where he/she is going, ask the following questions and react to what you hear. Then switch roles.

1. ¿Adónde vas?

2. ¿Qué lugares vas a ver?

3. ¿Cuántos días vas a estar allí?

4. ¿Cuánto cuesta la excursión?

5. ¿Cuánto dinero vas a necesitar?

SEGUNDA FASE. Based on your classmate's answers, write an e-mail to your instructor informing him/her of your classmates plans.

En directo

To call attention to an unusual fact:

¡Fíjate qué noticia! *How about that!*

¡Imagínate! *Imagine that!*

To react to good news:

¡Qué suerte! *How lucky!*

¡Qué maravilla! *How wonderful!*

¡Qué bien! *How nice!*

To convince someone:

¡Venga/Anda, anímate!
Come on, cheer up!

Lo vamos a pasar muy bien. *We are going to have a good time.*

 Click on the icon to listen to a conversation with these expressions.

AGENCIA MUNDIAL

A SU SERVICIO SIEMPRE
20 años de experiencia, responsabilidad y profesionalidad.

TODOS LOS PRECIOS INCLUYEN PASAJES AÉREOS Y SERVICIOS TERRESTRES POR PERSONA

PERÚ Y BOLIVIA

LIMA, AREQUIPA, CUZCO, MACHU PICCHU, PUNO, LA PAZ, 15 días. La Ruta del Inca. Hoteles de 3 y 4 estrellas. Desayuno incluido.
$2.760

PERÚ

LIMA, CUZCO, MACHU PICCHU, NAZCA, 12 días. Visite fortalezas incas. Vea las misteriosas líneas de Nazca desde el aire. Hoteles de primera. Desayuno y cena incluidos.
$3.150

LIMA, NAZCA, AREQUIPA, LAGO TITICACA, 10 días. Admire la arquitectura colonial de Lima y Arequipa. Vea las líneas de Nazca desde el aire. Navegue en el lago más alto del mundo. Hoteles de primera.
$2.620

ARGENTINA

BUENOS AIRES, BARILOCHE, MENDOZA, 12 días. Disfrute de una gran metrópoli. Esquíe en uno de los lugares más bellos del mundo. Hoteles de 4 y 5 estrellas. Desayuno y cena.
$3.590

CHILE Y ARGENTINA

SANTIAGO, PUERTO MONTT, BARILOCHE, BUENOS AIRES, 12 días. Excursión a Viña del Mar y Valparaíso. Cruce de los Andes en minibús y barco. Hoteles de 3 y 4 estrellas.
$4.075

CARIBE

JAMAICA, 7 días. Happy Inn, todo incluido. Exclusivo para parejas.
$2.480

PUERTO RICO

SAN JUAN, 5 días. Hotel de 5 estrellas. Excursión a Ponce. Visita con guía al Viejo San Juan. Desayuno incluido.
$1.995

MÉXICO

MÉXICO, TAXCO, ACAPULCO, 7 días. Hoteles de 3 y 4 estrellas. Excursión a Teotihuacán. Desayuno bufet incluido.
$1.800

CANCÚN, 5 días. Hotel de 4 estrellas. Excursión a Cozumel. Visita a ruinas mayas. Las mejores playas.
$1.510

Solicite los programas detallados con variantes de hoteles e itinerarios a su agente de viajes.

Tel. 312-785-4455   Fax: 312-785-4456

Suggestion for *Tercera fase* Pass out a card to each student with a number ranging from 100 to 2,000,000. After the students have written out their numbers on separate pieces of paper, collect their original cards and place them in a bag. Have a student draw a number and read it aloud. The student whose number was called must show written proof of the number. Check that it is correct. If it's not written correctly, then have a different student call a new number and continue until the number called has been written out correctly by the student. Time permitting, have the student write the number out on the board just as it appears on his/her paper, and ask the class if it's written correctly.

Note for *Situaciones* Now that students have been doing *Situaciones* for several chapters, you may wish to give them guidance on how to maximize the communicative potential of this activity. Each student should read the instructions for his/her role only, not the partner's instructions. Give them 2 to 3 minutes to prepare for the task. As an oral assessment, you may wish to have students practice the role-play with a partner, and then ask several pairs to perform for the class. (Other pairs may perform for a different role-play in the chapter.) Pay close attention to the use of register (*usted* or *tú*), vocabulary, and negotiation strategies (to clarify meaning, to agree, disagree, refuse politely, etc.) between students.

TERCERA FASE. La Agencia Mundial is offering a free trip and it's up to your instructor to select the winner. Your instructor will hand out raffle ticket numbers. On a separate piece of paper, write out the number your instructor gives you. Keep what you have written and return the original number to your instructor. You win when your number is called and you have written it correctly.

Modelo 1.315
mil trescientos quince

Situaciones

1

ROLE A. You have been saving up for a special trip (**viaje**) during the next school vacation, and you are now making plans. Call a friend to explain: a) where you plan to go; b) who will travel with you; and c) what you plan to do during this trip.

ROLE B. Your friend calls to tell you about his/her travel plans for the next school break. Ask a) with whom he/she is planning to go; and b) what places he/she is going to visit. You are curious about the cost of the trip (**viaje**), so you inquire about the cost of the ticket (**el billete**), the hotel, and the activities your friend plans to do.

2

ROLE A. You have been working hard, and you would like to splurge on a weekend trip to do some special (but expensive) activities, like rent a car, go to a professional sports event or rock concert, eat in good restaurants, and shop (**ir de compras**). Call and invite your friend to go. Explain your plan and be prepared to answer questions about the cost of this weekend adventure.

ROLE B. Your friend calls to invite you on an exciting (but expensive) weekend trip. Accept or reject your friend's invitation and ask questions to get an idea of the cost. Decide whether you can afford it, and either accept or decline the invitation. Thank your friend for the invitation.

Stating what you know:
Saber and *conocer*

Go to the *Capítulo 3* [folder] online to complete the Learning Module for *Gramática en contexto: Saber* and *conocer*

PLAN DE ESTUDIO

◎ **LEARN**
- Interactive presentation: *Saber* and *conocer*
- Grammar tutorials

◎ **APPLY**
- Activities
- Extra Practice

Online prep for students
Students will have completed the Learning Module for *Saber* and *conocer* online before class. See content online and Instructor's Resources for Supplementary Activities.

Tech Tip for *Gramática en contexto*
Use visuals of well-known people to practice *saber* and *conocer*. For example, use a picture of Sofia Vergara: *Yo sé quién es esta persona. Es Sofia Vergara. Sé que es una actriz famosa y que es de Colombia. Sé que vive en Hollywood. Sé quién es, pero no la conozco.*
   Point out that *saber* can be followed by *que*, but not *conocer*.
   Remind students that both verbs are irregular in first person and that *conozco* has a *z* because *c* is pronounced *k* before *o*.

PRÁCTICA COMUNICATIVA

3-26

Un encuentro entre dos estudiantes. Raúl just arrived on campus, and he asks Sergio some questions. Select the correct words to complete their conversation. Then practice the dialogue with a partner to compare your answers and then take turns telling each other what you know about your own university. Who knows more?

RAÚL: Soy un nuevo estudiante y no (1) __a__ dónde está la biblioteca.
    a. sé   b. conozco

SERGIO: Es muy fácil. Tú (2) __a__ dónde está la cafetería, ¿no? Pues, está al lado.
    a. sabes   b. conoces

RAÚL: Gracias. ¿Y (3) __a__ si hay un club de español?
    a. sabes   b. conoces

SERGIO: Sí, claro, y (4) __a__ que esta noche tiene una reunión.
    a. sé   b. conozco

RAÚL: Magnífico. Solo (5) __b__ a dos o tres personas en la universidad.
    a. sé   b. conozco

SERGIO: Pues allí vas a (6) __b__ a muchos estudiantes.
    a. saber   b. conocer

Note for 3-27
Students should have no difficulty in understanding cognates (e.g., *representante*, *gobernador*). Other words may need some explanation, for example, *rey. En España hay un rey, Juan Carlos I. Su esposa es la reina Sofía. Su hijo es el príncipe Felipe.* (Bring in pictures if possible.)

3-27

¿Sabes quién es...? Ask your classmate if he/she knows who is being referred to and say what you know about the person. Take turns asking questions.

Modelo

❝ la actriz principal de *Los juegos del hambre* ❞

> ¿Sabes quién es la actriz principal de *Los juegos del hambre*?

> Sí, sé quién es; es Jennifer Lawrence.

> ¿Conoces a Jennifer Lawrence en persona?

> No, no conozco a Jennifer Lawrence pero sé que es muy guapa.

1. el/la representante de la Cámara de Representantes (*Congress*) de tu distrito
2. el decano/la decana de la Facultad de Humanidades/Ciencias
3. tu profesor/a de español
4. el rey de España
5. el gobernador de tu estado
6. el vicepresidente de Estados Unidos

Note for 3-28
Gigante is not glossed since it is a near cognate. Context will help students guess meaning.

Expansion for 3-28
Use gestures as needed to clarify the following:
• *Es un animal de los dibujos animados. Es gris, corre muy rápido y tiene orejas muy largas* (Bugs Bunny).
• *Es una chica muy bonita y buena que vive en el bosque con siete enanitos. Tiene una madrastra muy mala* (Blancanieves).

3-28

Adivina, adivinador. In small groups, take turns reading the descriptions and guessing who is being described. Then, create your own description and ask another group to guess.

Modelo

> Es una chica muy pobre que va a un baile. Allí conoce a un príncipe, pero a las 12:00 de la noche ella debe volver a su casa.

> Sé quién es. Es Cenicienta (*Cinderella*).

1. Es un gorila gigante con sentimientos (*feelings*) humanos. En una película aparece en el edificio Empire State de Nueva York. King Kong
2. Es una cantante muy famosa. Tiene el pelo largo y rubio. Canta, baila, compone canciones y también participa en organizaciones benéficas. Es de Colombia. Shakira
3. Es una película de ciencia-ficción. Los personajes son altos y azules y viven en los árboles. Es impresionante ver la película en 3 dimensiones. Avatar
4. Es...

3-29

¿Qué sabes hacer? Ask your classmate if he/she knows how to do the following things. If your classmate says yes, ask more questions to get additional information.

Modelo **" preparar platos peruanos "**

¿Sabes preparar platos peruanos?

No, no sé preparar platos peruanos. ¿Y tú?

1. tocar un instrumento musical
2. cantar karaoke
3. bailar salsa y merengue
4. hablar otras lenguas
5. …

Suggestion for 3-29
Use visuals and personalized questions to elicit the use of *saber + infinitive*: *¿Sabe bailar esta persona? Y tú, ¿sabes bailar? ¿Sabes bailar muy bien?* Ask some students to name one thing they can do.

3-30

Bingo. To win this game, you have to fill in three boxes (horizontal, vertical, or diagonal) with the names of classmates who answer the questions correctly.

¿Quién sabe dónde está la ciudad de La Paz?	¿Quién sabe cuál es la capital de Paraguay?	¿Quién sabe qué es Machu Picchu?
¿Quién conoce al presidente de Bolivia?	¿Quién sabe cuál es la unidad monetaria de Perú?	¿Quién sabe el nombre de un lago importante que está entre Perú y Bolivia?
¿Quién conoce unos platos típicos de la cocina (*cuisine*) peruana?	¿Quién conoce algún país hispanoamericano?	¿Quién sabe cómo se llaman las montañas de Perú?

Suggestion for 3-30
Students may consult the *Enfoque cultural* reading online or read about these countries on the Internet prior to doing this activity so they will be able to answer the questions. Options for doing this activity: 1. Students close their books, and the instructor asks the questions, calling on the first student to raise his/her hand. 2. In groups of 4 or 5, students spend 5 minutes preparing answers to the questions. Then they close their books and the game proceeds as above, but groups take turns giving the first response to the question.

Answers for 3-30
Top row: *En Bolivia*; *Asunción*; *las ruinas de los incas*
    Middle row: *Evo Morales (2005)*; *Nuevo Sol*; *el lago Titicaca*
    Bottom row: Possible answers: *ceviche de pescado, yuca frita, adobo de chancho, chupe de camarones*; answers may vary; *los Andes*.

3-31

Saber y conocer. Complete the conversation with the correct forms of **saber** and **conocer.** Then practice the dialogue with your partner to review your answers. Be sure to explain why you selected **saber** or **conocer** in each case.

PACO: ¿ _Conoces_ (1) a esa chica?

AUGUSTO: Sí, yo _conozco_ (2) a todas las chicas aquí.

PACO: Entonces, ¿ _sabes_ (3) dónde vive?

AUGUSTO: No, no _sé_ (4) dónde vive.

PACO: ¿ _Sabes_ (5) cómo se llama?

AUGUSTO: Lo siento, pero no _sé_ (6).

PACO: Pero ¿cómo dices que _conoces_ (7) a la chica? Tú no _sabes_ (8) dónde vive ni además (*in addition*), no _sabes_ (9) su nombre.

Situaciones

1

ROLE A. Make a list of five people whom you think your partner knows personally. Choose three of them and ask: a) if your partner knows them and b) what your partner knows about each one of them. Be ready to answer similar questions.

ROLE B. Make a list of five people whom you think your partner knows personally. Your partner will tell you the names of three people on his/her list and will ask: a) if you know each one of them and b) what you know about them. Answer and then ask your partner the same questions about three of the people on your list.

2

ROLE A. You are looking for a third roommate for your apartment. Your partner knows a student from Bolivia who is looking for a place to live. Ask your partner: a) the Peruvian student's name; b) where in Peru he/she is from; and c) if your partner knows the Peruvian student well. Also find out if the Peruvian student knows how to cook Peruvian dishes and how to play soccer (**fútbol**).

ROLE B. Your partner is looking for a third roommate for his/her apartment. Mention that you know a student from Peru who is looking for a place to live. Answer your partner's questions about that person.

Expressing intention, means, movement, and duration:
Some uses of *por* and *para*

Go to the *Capítulo 3* **folder** online to complete the Learning Module for *Gramática en contexto: Some uses of por and para.*

PLAN DE ESTUDIO

◎ **LEARN**
- Interactive presentation: Some uses of *por* and *para*
- Grammar tutorials

APPLY ◎
- Activities
- Extra Practice

Online prep for students
Students will have completed the Learning Module for *Gramática en contexto* online before coming to class. Additional in-class activities are available for download in the Supplementary Activities folder online.

Note
Since the uses of *por* and *para* are not easy for students to master, these prepositions are presented more than once in *Unidos*. This first presentation gives only those uses necessary for communication about the theme of the chapter. *Capítulo 11* has a complete presentation of *por* and *para*, including uses that students are familiar with.

Tech Tip for *Gramática en contexto*
Use visuals to contrast the use of *por* and *para* to express movement: *Josefina está en su casa ahora. Ella va para la playa* (show visual of a beach) *después. Ella camina con su amiga por la playa* (show online image of young women walking on the beach).

PRÁCTICA COMUNICATIVA

3-32

¿Por o para? With a partner, choose the use of **por** and **para** in the following text with its appropriate meaning from the list. Then ask your partner what he/she does on Friday nights and what he/she does to celebrate a birthday.

> Mis amigos y yo siempre estamos ocupados los fines de semana. Los viernes **por**[1] la noche, siempre vamos a un cine cerca de nuestro barrio. Cuando vamos **para**[2] el cine, caminamos **por**[3] el parque. Después del cine, a veces hacemos fiestas en casa. Si es una fiesta de cumpleaños, compro un regalo especial **para**[4] mi amigo. **Para**[5] celebrar, también invito a todos nuestros amigos.

1. __c__   **a.** intended for (person)

2. __d__   **b.** in order to

3. __e__   **c.** length of time

4. __a__   **d.** movement toward a destination

5. __b__   **e.** movement through or by a place

Suggestion for 3-32 Have students explain their answers to a partner as a way to develop a metalinguistic awareness of language and meaning.

3-33

¿Para dónde van? Take turns guessing where these people are going. Then find out where your classmate is going after class, and why.

Modelo　**❝Jorge tiene su guitarra.❞**

❝*Va para la fiesta.*❞

1. Es la una de la tarde y Pedro desea comer.
2. Sebastián lleva una mochila con sus libros de química.
3. Lola y Pepe van a consultar unos libros porque tienen un examen.
4. Gregorio va a comprar un libro para su clase de español.
5. Ana María va a ver una película de su actor favorito.
6. Amanda y Clara están muy elegantes y contentas.

3-34

Caminante. Your classmate likes to walk. Ask him/her the following questions. Then switch roles.

1. ¿Te gusta caminar con amigos o solo/a? ¿Por qué?
2. ¿Por dónde caminas cuando quieres estar solo/a?
3. ¿Te gusta caminar por la playa o por un parque?
4. ¿Caminas por la mañana o por la tarde?
5. Cuando sales a caminar, ¿caminas por media hora o por más tiempo?

Suggestions for 3-35
You may wish to provide words for some family members, so students can use them for gift recipients: *hermano/a*, *primo/a*, *tío/a*, etc. This will serve as a warm-up for the presentation of kinship terms in *Capítulo 4*. Have students alternate roles or change roles halfway through. Ask them to elaborate on their responses by identifying the recipient as well as the purpose of the gift.

Tech tip for *Situaciones*
Students may use the video-posting feature, MediaShare, available online, to share videos of their presentations with the class.

3-35

¿Para quiénes son los regalos (*gifts*)? You are very generous and have bought the following gifts. Your partner asks for whom they are.

Modelo　**❝una revista❞**

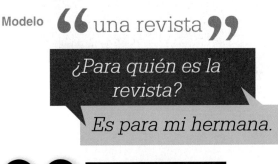

¿Para quién es la revista?

Es para mi hermana.

1. tres libros de español
2. dos billetes de avión
3. un teléfono celular
4. iPad
5. una computadora portátil
6. un buen vino chileno

Situaciones

1

ROLE A. You run into a friend who is carrying a gift box. You ask what it is and whom it is for.

ROLE B. You are walking out of a store carrying a gift. You run into a friend who asks you about the gift. Answer and explain why you are giving the gift.

2

ROLE A. You see your neighbor leaving with a big suitcase. You ask: a) where he/she is going; b) if the plane leaves in the afternoon or evening; c) how long he/she will be there; and d) why he/she is going.

ROLE B. You are about to go on a long trip, and as you are leaving with your suitcase you see your neighbor. He/She asks a lot of questions. Answer in detail.

Unidos

ESCUCHA

3-36 Presentational

Preparación. Before you listen to an ad for the travel agency *ViajaMás*, use what you already know about Latin America to write down the name of one large city in Peru, Argentina, and Venezuela, and the likely cost of each ticket. Compare answers with the class.

3-37

Escucha. Interpretive

Now listen to the ad and complete the chart with the information you hear.

CIUDAD	VUELO #	DÍAS	PRECIO DEL BOLETO
Lima	#881	sábados y domingos	$730
Buenos Aires	#479	todos los días	$980
Caracas	#963	todos los días	$250
Bogotá	#1247	lunes, martes y sábado	$455

ESTRATEGIA

Use background knowledge

When you listen to a conversation, you can use your experiences and your knowledge of the situation to enhance your comprehension.

Comprueba:

I was able to…

___ recognize names of places.

___ identify numbers.

___ recognize days of the week.

3-38

Un paso más. Interpersonal

PRIMERA FASE.

ROLE A. You are interested in one of the trips that you heard in the ad. Call the airline help service to ask further details: a) at what time the flight leaves, and b) at what time it arrives at its destination.

ROLE B. You are the airline agent. Provide the information requested by your client and add further details: a) approximate duration of the flight, and b) if the flights are direct or not.

SEGUNDA FASE. Exchange an e-mail to your best friend explaining your travel plans. Include destination, date, time and cost of your flight.

Suggestion for 3-36
In *Preparación* students use their background knowledge to help them focus on key words and phrases that they will need to identify in the interpretive phase of the task. Help students think in numbers by asking them to guess prices and read them aloud after they write them down.

Audioscript for 3-37
Agencia ViajaMás anuncia sus precios especiales de ida y vuelta para las siguientes ciudades desde Miami: Lima, vuelo número 881, solo sábados y domingos, precio especial: $730. Buenos Aires, vuelo número 479, todos los días, precio: $980. Caracas, vuelo número 963, todos los días, precio especial: $250. Bogotá, vuelo 1247, lunes, martes y sábados, precio: $455. ¡Gracias por llamar a la Agencia ViajaMás y buen viaje!

Suggestion for 3-37
Make sure that the students use the information gathered from the previous task and that they attempt to create with language by adding some information of their own.

AUTOEVALUACIÓN

☐ I feel confident that I was able to comprehend.

☐ I need more listening practice.

STUDY PLAN

▶ Good job! Move on to the next section, *Habla*.

▶ Go to the **Unidos** folder online for the *Escucha* practice.

HABLA

3-39 Interpretive

Preparación. Read the following recommendations provided by an organization that wants to promote healthy habits in the schools, and prepare five related questions to ask students in your university about their own eating habits.

ESTRATEGIA

Inform yourself before you do a survey.

When preparing to do a survey, it is helpful to gather as much information as you can about the topic in order to ask questions.

Tabla 1 Frecuencia de consumo recomendada en alimentación

Frutas, verduras, ensaladas, lácteos y pan	**Todos los días**
Legumbres	**2 a 4 veces por semana** (2 como primer plato, y 2 de acompañamiento)
Arroz, pasta, patatas	**2 a 4 veces por semana.** Alternar su consumo
Pescados y carnes	**3 a 4 veces por semana.** Alternar su consumo
Huevos	**4 unidades a la semana** (alternando con carnes y pescados)
Dulces, refrescos, comida rápida	**Ocasionalmente.** Sin abusar

SOURCE: Eroski Consumer, Fundación Eroski

3-40

Habla. Interpersonal

Use your questions to find out what your classmates normally eat and drink and how many times a week.

Modelo

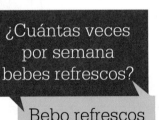

¿Cuántas veces por semana bebes refrescos?

Bebo refrescos todos los días.

En directo

To express frequency

Todos los días *every day*

Dos veces por semana *twice a week*

Una vez al mes *once a month*

Cada día *each day*

 Click on the icon to listen to a conversation with these expressions.

Comprueba:
In my conversation…

____ **my questions were easily understood.**

____ **I mentioned lots of foods in my responses.**

____ **I used expressions of frequency.**

3-41 Presentational

Un paso más. Presentational

Compare the recommendations with the answers you gathered and present the findings to the class. Include in your report answers to the following questions.

1. ¿Tienen los estudiantes una dieta equilibrada? ¿Por qué? ¿Por qué no?

2. ¿Qué productos comen en exceso? ¿Qué productos no consumen bastante (*enough*)?

AUTOEVALUACIÓN

☐ I feel confident that I communicated successfully.

☐ I need more speaking practice.

STUDY PLAN

▶ Good job! Move on to the next section, *Lee.*

▶ Go to the *Unidos* folder online for the *Habla* practice.

LEE

3-42

Preparación. [Interpretive]

PRIMERA FASE. The three ads below come from a newspaper in Lima, Peru. Look them over quickly without reading them. Then mark which ad goes with each of the following descriptions.

1. __3__ un restaurante de comida china

2. __1__ actividades para niños

3. __2__ un restaurante de comida tradicional peruana

SEGUNDA FASE. What word(s) in each ad helped you answer the questions in the *Primera fase*?

ESTRATEGIA

Look for and use key words

Even though you may not know all the words when you read a text in Spanish, identifying and focusing on key words can help you understand the main ideas. Look the text over before starting to read to get a sense of what type of text it is and what it may be about.

3-43

Lee. [Presentational]

PRIMERA FASE. Read the ads below to get a sense of what each is about.

NIÑOS

CORPORACIÓN CULTURAL DE LIMA. Santa María y Gálvez. 2209451. A las 12 y 16 horas. Bagdhadas. S/. 12.

TEATRO INFANTIL A DOMICILIO. 2390176. El patito feo. Adaptación del cuento de Andersen. Compañía Arcoiris.

CENTRO LIMA. Av. Grau y Velásquez. A las 12, show especial de Navidad.

FANTASÍA DISNEY. Desde las 15. Niños, S/. 8; adultos, S/. 14. Parque de entretenimientos.

EL MUNDO FANTÁSTICO DE MAFALDA. Desde las 10. Entrada general a todos los juegos. Niños, S/. 12. Calle Domingo Sarmiento 358.

PLANETARIO DEL MORRO SOLAR. A las 12, 17 y 19. Gratis para niños; adultos, S/. 15. Circunvalación, Nuevo Perú. Tel. 5620841.

PARQUE DE LAS LEYENDAS (ZOO). De 9 a 19 hrs. Niños y 3ra edad, S/. 5; S/. 10, otro público. Cerro Tongoy, 3701725.

Costa Verde

Sabrosa comida tradicional peruana
Menú especial los fines de semana

■ Aperitivo
■ Entrada
■ Segundo
■ Postre
■ Café y plus café (crema de café, crema de menta, anisado)

Valor: S/. 75

Carnes, pescados y mariscos preparados por los mejores cocineros del país

Avenida Arequipa 357
Reservas: 428 9654
Fax: 428 9655

B.

El Chifa Lungfung

La más exquisita, variada y exótica carta de comida cantonesa-peruana: finas carnes, pescados y todo tipo de mariscos.

SÁBADOS Y DOMINGOS:

Almuerzos y cenas familiares

...los esperamos

AIRE ACONDICIONADO
MÚSICA AMBIENTAL
CAMAREROS PROFESIONALES
AV. REPÚBLICA DE PANAMÁ 8720
RESERVAS 3817543, 3816532, 3814241

C.

Suggestion for 3-43 *Segunda fase*
You may wish to have each pair of students present a solution to the class, including key words that helped them make their decision. Pairs who have a different solution to the one presented should be encouraged to present their alternative.

SEGUNDA FASE. Now offer a solution for the following choices that have to be made. Explain your solutions to the class.

1. Los señores Molina tienen cuatro hijos entre tres y ocho años. A los niños les fascinan los animales. ¿Adónde van a ir probablemente? ¿Por qué?

2. Carlos está triste porque se fracturó una pierna y no puede (*he can't*) salir de la casa. Su mamá tiene una sorpresa para él. ¿Qué es?

3. Cuatro médicos franceses visitan el Hospital Central. El Dr. Moreira, director del hospital, desea invitar a sus colegas a cenar en un restaurante cómodo con comida tradicional peruana. ¿A qué restaurante va a invitarlos? ¿Por qué?

Comprueba:
I was able to . . .

____ recognize important words.

____ identify the main ideas.

____ recognize contexts.

3-44  Interpersonal

Un paso más.
With a classmate, answer the following questions about the four ads from Peru.

1. ¿Cuál de las siguientes actividades desean hacer ustedes en Lima: ir a un parque de entretenimiento (*amusement park*), comer comida tradicional peruana, ver teatro o comer comida china? ¿Por qué?

2. ¿Cuál de los dos restaurantes sirve comida que a ustedes les gusta más, Costa Verde o Chifa Lungfung? ¿Por qué?

AUTOEVALUACIÓN

☐ I feel confident I understood the reading and was able to use the information.

☐ I need more reading practice.

STUDY PLAN

▶ Good job! Move on to the next section, *Escribe*.

▶ Go to the *Unidos* folder online for the *Lee* practice.

ESCRIBE

3-45 [Interpretive]

Preparación. Choose a vacation spot that you know well (or find information online) and that you like a lot. Then make a list of words (adjectives) that describe the place, write some enjoyable activities (verbs) that people do there.

3-46

Escribe. [Presentational]

Now write the e-mail to your friend, telling about your vacation. Use the information you prepared in *Preparación* and any other that you think may be of interest to your friend.

En directo

Salutations for casual correspondence:

Querido/a...:

Hola...,

Closings for casual correspondence:

Tu amigo/a,

Hasta pronto,

Click on the icon to listen to a conversation with these expressions.

3-47 [Interpersonal]

Un paso más.

After completing your e-mail, exchange it with a classmate, read his/hers and take notes to answer the following questions: a) where your classmate is spending vacation; b) what he/she does during the vacation. Inform the class.

ESTRATEGIA

Identify your audience

When you write an e-mail to your friend it is essential to identify the parts of the e-mail (To, From, Subject, the salutation or greeting, the body, and the closing farewell). You are expected to address your friend with the **tú** form.

Comprueba:
I was able to...

_____ **present main ideas clearly, with some details.**

_____ **use a wide range of learned vocabulary.**

_____ **conjugate verbs appropriately and make the right agreements.**

_____ **use accurate spelling, capitalization, and punctuation.**

AUTOEVALUACIÓN

☐ I feel confident I successfully communicated my ideas in writing.

☐ I need more writing practice.

STUDY PLAN

▶ Good job!

▶ Go to the *Unidos* [folder] online for the *Escribe* practice.

ENFOQUE *cultural*

PERÚ

Las islas flotantes del lago Titicaca son islas artificiales construidas por sus habitantes, los Uros de Perú. Además de las islas, los Uros contruyen barcos de totora (*reed*) llamados caballitos de totora.

BOLIVIA

El Salar de Uyuni es el desierto de sal más grande del mundo. Tiene también grandes reservas de litio al igual que de potasio, boro y magnesio.

PARAGUAY

Vista de Asunción, la capital y el centro de actividad nacional del país. Bordea la bahía de Asunción, donde convergen los ríos Paraguay y Pilcomayo.

Perfiles de Perú, Bolivia y Paraguay

Go to the *Enfoque cultural* [folder] in *Capítulo 3* online to learn more about this region.

PLAN DE ESTUDIO

LEARN
- Interactive presentation: *Perfiles de Perú, Bolivia y Paraguay*

APPLY
- Activities

PRÁCTICA COMUNICATIVA

3-48

Usa la información. You are visiting one of these three countries: Peru, Bolivia, or Paraguay, and you will spend tomorrow visiting one of the big cities and its surroundings. Although it is late and you are tired, you take a few minutes to write an e-mail to someone you really care about. Explain your plans for tomorrow: mention a) the city you plan to visit; b) how you are going to get there; c) what you are going to see; and d) some information that you have researched about the place. Use the Internet to research some information on the city to include in your e-mail.

En este capítulo...

Comprueba lo que sabes

Go to the *Comprueba lo que sabes* folder online to review what you have learned in this chapter. Practice with the following:

Vocabulary Flashcards | Games | Oral Practice | Practice Test / Study Plan | Video en contexto

Vocabulario

Las diversiones y las celebraciones
la boda
la canción
el cumpleaños
la fiesta
la guitarra
la música
la película
la reunión
el tiempo libre
las vacaciones

Las personas
el camarero/la camarera
el hombre
el/la joven
la mujer

En un café o restaurante
el agua
el almuerzo
el arroz
la bebida
el bistec
el café
la cena
el cereal
la cerveza
el ceviche
la comida
el desayuno
la ensalada
los espaguetis

el frijol
la fruta
la hamburguesa
el helado
el huevo
el jamón
el jugo
la leche
la lechuga
la naranja
el pan
el pan tostado/
    la tostada
la papa
las papas fritas
el pescado
el pollo
el queso
el refresco
el sándwich
la sopa
el té
el tomate
el vegetal/la verdura
el vino

La comunicación
el periódico
la revista
el teléfono

Los lugares
el cine
la ciudad
el mar
el país

Las descripciones
caliente
fabuloso/a
frío/a
frito/a
rápido/a
típico/a

Verbos
alquilar
cantar
celebrar
cenar
descansar
hacer la cama
nadar
poner la mesa
tocar (un instrumento)
tomar el sol

Palabras y expresiones útiles
¿adónde?
al
al aire libre
cerca de
¡claro!
después, luego
durante
¡estupendo!
felicidades
mientras
otro/a
¿qué te parece?
si

Los números de 100 a 2.000.000
cien/ciento
doscientos/as
trescientos/as
cuatrocientos/as
quinientos/as
seiscientos/as
setecientos/as
ochocientos/as
novecientos/as
mi
mil cien
dos mil
diez mil
cien mil
ciento cincuenta mil
quinientos mil
un millón (de)
dos millones (de)

Expresiones con por
por ciento
por ejemplo
por eso
por fin
por lo menos
por supuesto

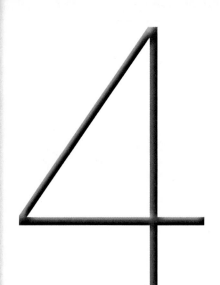

4 ¿Cómo es tu familia?

Learning OBJECTIVES

You will:

- learn vocabulary to describe family members, relationships, and daily routines
- learn the forms of stem-changing verbs
- use *tener que* + infinitive to talk about what you and others have to do
- learn how to form adverbs in Spanish
- describe lengths of time using *hace*
- learn the forms and uses of reflexive verbs and pronouns
- connect new information about Colombia, its people, landscape, and culture to what you already know

Learning OUTCOMES

You will be able to:

- talk about families and their daily routines
- express opinions, plans, preferences, and feelings
- express obligation
- express when, where, or how an action occurs
- express how long something has been going on
- talk about daily routines
- relay information you have researched about famous Colombians from a variety of fields

COLOMBIA

Las calles
de Cartagena de Indias

Mar Caribe

Barranquilla
Cartagena de Indias

PANAMÁ

VENEZUELA

Medellín

Bucaramanga

Pereira

⊕ Bogotá

Pieza antigua del Museo
del Oro de Bogotá

El Parque de café
Departamento El Quindío

Cali

COLOMBIA

CORDILLERA DE LOS ANDES

Río Magdalena

Popayán

OCÉANO
PACÍFICO

BRASIL

ECUADOR

Arepas de queso

PERÚ

Cordillera de Los Andes

Cultura en línea

To learn more about Colombia and the chapter theme, go to the *Cultura en línea* folder in the *Unidos* online component to view the *Vistas culturales* video and take a virtual art tour.

¿Cuánto sabes?

Completa estas oraciones (*sentences*) con la información correcta.

1. Ecuador, _____Perú_____ y Brasil están al sur de Colombia.

2. _____Bogotá_____ es la capital de Colombia.

3. Las casas pintadas de diferentes colores son típicas en la ciudad de _____Cartagena de Indias_____.

4. Fernando Botero es un _____pintor/artista_____ colombiano.

Fernando Botero, uno de los pintores contemporáneos más famosos de Colombia, pinta a unos padres con sus hijos en este cuadro titulado *En familia*.

Tech tip for interactive map
Brainstorm with students information they already may know about Colombia. Project the map, found in the Interactive Globe folder online or click on the icon in the eText. Zoom in and out as desired. You may point out the locations of *Bogotá* (official name *Santafé de Bogotá*) and *Cartagena* (official name *Cartagena de Indias*). Ask: *¿Qué país está al noroeste de Colombia? ¿Y al noreste? ¿Con qué mares limita Colombia? (el Mar del Caribe y el Océano Pacífico) ¿Qué río desemboca (flows into) en Barranquilla? (el Magdalena) ¿Cómo se llaman las montañas que cruzan Colombia? (Cordillera de Los Andes)*

Tech tip for art
Present *familia, padre, madre, hijo/a, hijos* and project the text image of the painting. Ask questions about the family in the painting: *¿Cómo es el padre? ¿Cómo es la madre? ¿Y el hijo mayor?* Show other paintings by Botero that you may find online. Write his name on the board and explain that he features mostly rotund people in his paintings. Compare this painting with *La familia presidencial* and others in which he depicts families. Use cognates to talk about the themes of some of his other paintings: *la injusticia social, la violencia, la tortura, el abuso de poder,* etc.

Warm-up for *¿Cuánto sabes?*
This activity can be done in pairs or as a class warm-up. Tell students not to worry if they cannot answer some of these questions. *¿Quién es un escritor colombiano muy importante que recibió el premio Nobel? (Gabriel García Márquez) ¿Conocen algún producto que exporta Colombia? (el café, las flores)*

Vocabulario en contexto

Talking about family members and their daily routines

Los miembros de la familia

Go to the *Capítulo 4* [folder] online to complete the Learning Module for *Vocabulario en contexto: Los miembros de la familia.*

PLAN DE ESTUDIO

◎ LEARN
- Interactive presentation: *Los miembros de la familia*
- Vocabulary tutorials
- Pronunciation

APPLY ◎
- Activities
- Pronunciation activities

PRÁCTICA COMUNICATIVA

4-1 👥

Asociación. Asocia (*Match*) las dos columnas. Después selecciona a dos personas de la columna derecha y dile (*tell*) a tu compañero/a cómo se llaman estos miembros de tu familia.

1. ___c___ la esposa de mi padre
2. ___a___ el hermano de mi prima
3. ___d___ los padres de mi padre
4. ___b___ el hijo de mi hijo
5. ___e___ el hermano de mi madre

a. mi primo
b. mi nieto
c. mi madre
d. mis abuelos
e. mi tío

Cultura

The ending **-ito/a** (**Jorge** → **Jorgito**) is very common in Hispanic countries. It is frequently used to differentiate parents from children of the same name. It also expresses smallness (**hermanito/a, sillita**), affection, and intimacy (**mi primita**). Names that end in a consonant use the ending **-cito/a** (**Carmen** → **Carmencita**).

Hispanics are often given more than one name (**Carlos Alberto, María del Carmen**). These names are often combined (**Mariví,** from **María Victoria**). **María** may also be part of a man's name: **José María**.

Compara: Are diminutives common in your family or community? How are they formed? Does your family call you by a special name or nickname?

Note for *Cultura*
Introduce the terms of endearment *abuelito/a; mamá, papá; mami, papi,* etc. You may mention that little children are often called *mami/mamita* or *papi/papito* as terms of endearment.

Suggestions
To help students build confidence in discussing families 1) ask questions to identify different members in Pablo's family; 2) using the board, describe your own family tree and ask *¿Es mi nieto o mi abuelo? ¿Es mi hermana o mi madre?*; 3) ask questions about magazine pictures of people of different ages; 4) have students bring pictures of their families and explain them to the class.

Note
Point out that *novio/a* means "fiancé/e," as well as "groom/bride," and in many places, "boy/girlfriend."

4-2

La familia de Pablo.

PRIMERA FASE. Con tu compañero/a, completa las oraciones de acuerdo con (*according to*) la información que tienen sobre la familia de Pablo.

1. La hermana de Pablo se llama ____Inés____.

2. Don José y doña Olga son los ____abuelos____ de Pablo.

3. Pablo es el ____hijo____ de Jaime.

4. Jaime es el ____padre____ de Pablo, y Elena es su ____madre____.

5. Inés y Ana son ____primas____. Elenita y Ana son ____hermanas gemelas____.

6. Elena es la ____tía____ de Jorgito, Elenita y Ana.

7. Lola es la ____hermana____ de Jorge y Elena.

SEGUNDA FASE. Tu compañero/a selecciona a un miembro de la familia de Pablo y tú debes describir la relación con otros dos miembros.

Modelo

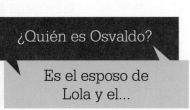

¿Quién es Osvaldo?

Es el esposo de Lola y el...

4-3

¿Quién es y cómo es? PRIMERA FASE.
Escojan (*Choose*) un miembro de una familia famosa (la familia real [*royal*] española, los Jackson, los Kennedy, los Kardashian, etc.). Preparen su árbol familiar.

SEGUNDA FASE. Túrnense (*Take turns*) para describir el árbol familiar de esta persona.

Modelo ❝Malia❞

Su padre es el presidente de Estados Unidos. Su madre es Michelle. Malia tiene una hermana. Ella se llama Sasha.

Su perro se llama Bo y vive en la Casa Blanca con la familia.

 **4-4**

El arte de preguntar. PRIMERA FASE. Túrnense y preparen las preguntas necesarias para obtener las siguientes respuestas.

Modelo ❝Mi madre se llama Dolores.❞
❝*¿Cómo se llama tu madre?*❞

1. Tengo cuatro abuelos vivos (*alive*).
2. No, no soy hijo único/hija única.
3. Tengo dos hermanos.
4. Vivo con mi madre y mi padrastro.
5. Mis abuelos no viven con nosotros.
6. Tengo muchos primos.
7. Tengo una media hermana, pero no vive con nosotros.
8. Mi media hermana vive con su madre.

SEGUNDA FASE. Ahora háganse (*ask each other*) preguntas para obtener información sobre la familia de su compañero/a. Después, compartan (*share*) esta información con la clase.

4-5

Mi familia.

PRIMERA FASE. Preparen su árbol familiar individualmente. Luego, intercambien (*exchange*) su árbol.

SEGUNDA FASE. Háganse preguntas sobre su familia para obtener la siguiente información.

1. nombre de los abuelos vivos
2. nombre de los padres (padrastro/madrastra)
3. número y nombre de los hermanos (medios hermanos, hermanastros)
4. número y nombre de los primos
5. descripción de dos parientes (*relatives*)

¿Qué hacen los parientes?

Go to the *Capítulo 4* **folder** online to complete the Learning Module for *Vocabulario en contexto: ¿Qué hacen los parientes?*

PLAN DE ESTUDIO

LEARN
- Interactive presentation: *¿Qué hacen los parientes?*
- Vocabulary tutorials

APPLY
- Activities

PRÁCTICA COMUNICATIVA

4-6

Otra conversación. Con un compañero/a lee la conversación entre Meriel y Paloma. Después cambia la conversación para hablar de tu propia (*own*) familia.

MERIEL: Mis abuelos viven en una casa al lado del parque. Normalmente, ellos pasean por las mañanas y almuerzan muy temprano.

PALOMA: Pues los míos, duermen la siesta todos los días y por la tarde visitan a sus parientes.

4-7

¿Y qué hace tu familia? Pídele (*Ask for*) la siguiente información a tu compañero/a sobre su familia.

1. número de personas en la casa, edad (*age*) y relación de parentesco (*kinship*)

2. ocupación y descripción (física y de personalidad) de dos miembros de la familia

3. actividades de estas personas en su tiempo libre

4. nombre del pariente favorito, relación familiar y razón (*reason*) de su preferencia

Online prep for students
Students will have completed the Learning Module for *¿Qué hacen los parientes?* online before class. See Instructor's Resources for Supplementary Activities.

Suggestion
You may want to point out that *pariente* is a false cognate. Use visuals to practice *pasear* and *almorzar*. Personalize: *Me gusta pasear por el parque por las tardes. ¿Y a ti te gusta pasear? ¿Paseas por las calles o por el parque? ¿Duermes la siesta alguna vez? Yo duermo la siesta en las vacaciones. ¿Visitas a tus parientes frecuentemente?* Recycle *correr* and *jugar*. Personalize. You may also use additional visual aids.

You may want to review the *Lengua* box, presented online in the Learning Module, regarding the use of the preposition *a* before a direct object that is a person or a specific animal.

Suggestion for 4-7
Tell students that if they don't feel comfortable talking about their real families they can talk about their ideal or an imaginary family. To ensure students will ask questions accurately, give them a minute or two to write down the questions first. Ask for volunteers to read their questions out loud. Have students work in small groups to list the advantages/disadvantages (*ventajas/desventajas*) of a large family. Have them compare lists.

Follow-up for 4-7
Have students report to the class what a classmate has said about his/her family, reinforcing *él/ella* verb forms.

Online prep for students
Students will have completed the Learning Module for *Las rutinas familiares* online before class. See content online and Instructor's Resources for Supplementary Activities.

Tech tip for *Las rutinas familiares*
The vocabulary of daily routines associated with reflexive verbs is presented here for recognition in the context of family life. Students do not conjugate reflexive verbs at this point. To review this vocabulary, project the images from the online Learning Module and model the activity by talking about your daily routine with the help of gestures: *Me despierto a las 6:30, me levanto, me ducho, me visto, me lavo los dientes,* etc. comparing them to the times Pablo and his family do them. Use *temprano* and *tarde: No me acuesto tarde porque me levanto temprano; a las 6:00 de la mañana.* Also ask yes/no questions or questions that do not require students to produce structures they have not studied, such as *¿A qué hora te levantas? ¿Te levantas temprano? ¿Te duchas por las mañanas o por las noches?*

Tech tip for *Las rutinas familiares*
The online images present an opportunity to preview some vocabulary related to housing that students will learn in *Capítulo 5.* Introduce *cocina* and *cuarto de baño,* then ask: *¿Dónde desayuna la familia?,* etc.

Introduce the expression *Poco después* by comparing it to *luego* and *más tarde.*

Warm-up for 4-8
Before doing this activity, explain the expression *Cada cosa a su tiempo* and review the *Lengua* box with students.

Las rutinas familiares

Go to the *Capítulo 4* **folder** online to complete the Learning Module for *Vocabulario en contexto: Las rutinas familiares.*

PLAN DE ESTUDIO

◎ LEARN
- Interactive presentation: *Las rutinas familiares*
- Vocabulary tutorials
- *Entrevistas* video

APPLY ◎
- Activities
- *Entrevistas* video activities

PRÁCTICA COMUNICATIVA

4-8

Cada cosa a su tiempo. Ordena las oraciones según (*according to*) crees que ocurren en la casa de tu compañero/a. Tu compañero/a va a confirmar el orden correcto.

_____ Se levanta.

_____ Se baña y luego se pone la ropa.

_____ Se ducha.

_____ Sale de casa.

_____ Desayuna.

LENGUA Use the following expressions to organize time sequentially: **Primero, luego, poco después, más tarde,** and **por último.**

4-9

Las rutinas diarias. Túrnense y contesten las siguientes preguntas.

1. ¿Quién en tu familia se despierta primero los domingos?
2. ¿Con quién desayunas?
3. ¿Quién sale de tu casa primero por la mañana?
4. ¿Quién se afeita por la mañana?
5. ¿Quién se maquilla?

4-10

Mañanas ocupadas (busy). Marca (✓) las acciones diarias de los miembros de tu familia. Después, compara las rutinas de tu familia con las de tu compañero/a.

	SE DESPIERTA TEMPRANO	SE DUCHA POR LA MAÑANA	SE PONE ROPA ELEGANTE	DESAYUNA CON LA FAMILIA
Mi padre (padrastro)				
Mi madre (madrastra)				
Mi hermano/a				
Mi abuelo/a				
Mi tío/a				

4-11

¿Y tú? Completa el siguiente párrafo con las expresiones de la lista para describir tu rutina. Compara tus respuestas con tu compañero/a para ver lo que tienen en común.

> me ducho
> salgo para la universidad
> me despierto
> me levanto
> desayuno

Primero ___me despierto___, luego ___me levanto___.
Poco después ___me ducho___, más tarde ___desayuno___.
Por último ___salgo para la universidad___.

4-12

¿A qué hora? Túrnense para hacerse las siguientes preguntas sobre la rutina diaria.

1. ¿Te duchas por la mañana o por la noche?
2. ¿Quién se levanta temprano en tu familia?
3. ¿Te vistes antes o después de desayunar?
4. ¿Te pones ropa elegante o informal para ir a clase?
5. ¿A qué hora te acuestas durante la semana?
6. ¿A qué hora te acuestas durante los fines de semana?
7. ¿A qué hora te levantas durante los fines de semana?
8. ¿A qué hora tienes la clase de español?

4-13

Algunas familias hispanas.

PRIMERA FASE. Before listening to the descriptions of four Hispanic families, take turns asking the following questions: Is your family large or small? How many brothers and sisters, cousins, aunts, and uncles do you have?

 SEGUNDA FASE. Now listen to the descriptions of four Hispanic families. Pay attention to the general idea of what is said. As you hear each description, write a check mark (✓) in the corresponding column. Then compare your answers with those of a classmate.

	TIENE UNA FAMILIA GRANDE	TIENE HERMANOS	TIENE MUCHOS TÍOS	TIENE PRIMOS
Pedro	X	X	X	
Alicia	X	X		
Magdalena	X	X	X	X
Alberto		X		

Suggestions for 4-12
Students will learn the conjugation of reflexives in *Gramática en contexto*. Students may respond to questions with information words only, rather than with complete sentences, e.g., ¿A qué hora se levanta tu madre? Answer: *A las siete.*

Suggestions for 4-12
Although students do not have to produce conjugated verbs in this activity, you may wish to preview the infinitives and the first, second, and third persons of the conjugation to help them understand the questions.

Note for 4-13
Directions for listening activities are in English to ensure that students understand what they have to do.

Warm-up for 4-13
As a pre-listening activity, have students work in groups of four to describe their families. Then, each student writes a description of his/her family.

Audioscript for 4-13
1. *Pedro tiene diez hermanos y seis tíos.* 2. *Alicia tiene cuatro hermanos, pero no tiene tíos ni primos.* 3. *Magdalena tiene cuatro hermanos. Además, tiene varios tíos y muchos primos.* 4. *Alberto vive solo. Él tiene un hermano, pero no tiene tíos.*

Standard 4.2
Students demonstrate understanding of the concept of culture through comparisons of the cultures studied and their own. Students' image of a park and what activities people do there are formed by their experience. Activity **4-13**, which asks them to anticipate the context of the listening activity by referring to their experience, offers instructors the opportunity to help students reflect on their often-unconscious assumptions about what life is like in Spanish-speaking cultures.

Online prep for students
Students will have completed the Learning Module for Present tense of stem-changing verbs online before class. This includes the Interactive presentation and corresponding Apply activities. See content online. You will find additional in-class activities in the Instructor's Resources folder.

Tech tip for *Present tense of stem-changing verbs*
Use visuals and comprehensible input to review some of the verbs: *Este chico almuerza con sus amigos en una cafetería. Ellos almuerzan a la una. Yo no almuerzo a la una, almuerzo a las doce y media. También almuerzas a las doce y media, ¿verdad? Ah, entonces nosotros (no) almorzamos a la misma hora. ¿Quién (más) almuerza temprano/tarde?*

Gramática en contexto

Talking about family members, their activities, and their routines

Expressing opinions, plans, preferences, and feelings:

Present tense of stem-changing verbs: *e → ie, o → ue,* and *e → i*

Go to the *Capítulo 4* **folder** online to complete the Learning Module for *Gramática en contexto:* Present tense of stem-changing verbs: *e → ie, o → ue,* and *e → i.*

PLAN DE ESTUDIO

◉LEARN
- Interactive presentation: Present tense of stem-changing verbs: *e → ie, o → ue,* and *e → i*
- Grammar tutorials

APPLY ◉
- Activities
- Extra Practice

PRÁCTICA COMUNICATIVA

4-14

Los planes. Haz preguntas a tu compañero/a sobre sus planes y preferencias.

1. ¿Prefieres tener una familia grande o pequeña? ¿Por qué?
2. ¿Quieres tomar cursos en el verano o prefieres trabajar? ¿Por qué?
3. ¿Sigues las tradiciones de tu familia o quieres ser más independiente? ¿Por qué?
4. Cuando tienes amigos en casa, ¿sirves vino, cerveza o refrescos? ¿Por qué?
5. Cuando terminas las vacaciones, ¿vuelves a casa deprimido/a, contento/a o cansado/a?

4-15

¿Qué piensan hacer? Túrnense para decir qué piensa hacer cada (*each*) miembro de la familia en las situaciones siguientes.

Modelo

66 Mi hermano quiere estar delgado. 99

Tu hermano probablemente piensa correr mucho.

Probablemente piensa empezar una dieta.

Y probablemente piensa ir al gimnasio todos los días.

1. Mi hermana tiene un examen de matemáticas mañana.
2. Mi hermana estudia bastante, pero no entiende muchos de los problemas.
3. Mi tía está enferma, por eso se siente muy débil y cansada.
4. Mis abuelos están de vacaciones en Colombia.
5. Mis primos quieren ir a Cartagena para visitar a los abuelos.
6. Mi tío lee y escucha las noticias sobre Colombia porque quiere aprender más sobre el país.

LENGUA

- **Pensar en** is the Spanish equivalent of *to think about someone or something*.

  ¿**Piensas en** tu familia cuando estás fuera de casa?
  Do you think of/about your family when you are away from home?

  Sí, **pienso** mucho **en** ellos.
  Yes, I think of/about them a lot.

- **Pensar de** is used to ask for an opinion. **Pensar que** is normally used in the answer.

  ¿Qué **piensas de** los planes de ayuda familiar?
  What do you think of the plans to help families?

  Pienso que son excelentes.
  I think they are excellent.

Follow-up for 4-15
Each group chooses the best reply for each item and shares them with the class. You may wish to stage a competition for replies that are the most sensible, the most creative, etc.

Suggestion for 4-16
Encourage students to give their partners as much information as possible so they can identify the similarities and differences between the gatherings in their respective families.

Follow-up for 4-16
Segunda fase
You may wish to have the pairs share their similarity/difference with the class, and then find out which activities, roles, or customs are the most prevalent among your students.

4-16

¿Qué pasa en las reuniones familiares? PRIMERA FASE. Descríbele las reuniones de tu familia a tu compañero/a. Ambos (*Both*) deben tomar nota de las semejanzas y las diferencias.

Modelo

❝preparar la comida❞

En las reuniones de mi familia, mi abuela prepara mucha comida.

En las reuniones de mi familia, tenemos mucha comida también. Pero mi madre y mi tía preparan la comida.

1. servir la comida

2. jugar con los niños

3. venir de muy lejos

4. dormir en el sofá

5. preferir hablar de temas políticos

6. volver a casa todos los años

 SEGUNDA FASE. Hablen de una semejanza y una diferencia entre las reuniones de sus familias. Compartan la información con la clase.

Suggestion for 4-17
Provide time for students to prepare the questions they are going to ask.

Follow-up for 4-18
Primera fase
Encourage students to get as much information as possible from their partners.

4-17

Entrevista. Túrnense para entrevistarse (*interview each other*). Hablen sobre los siguientes temas (*topics*) y después compartan la información con otro compañero/otra compañera.

1. la hora del almuerzo, qué prefiere comer y dónde

2. los deportes que prefiere practicar o mirar en la televisión

3. a qué hora empieza a hacer la tarea generalmente

4. si duerme una siesta durante el día

5. si vuelve a la casa de sus padres para las vacaciones

6. qué piensa hacer después de la universidad

4-18

¿Cuándo y con quién? PRIMERA FASE. Pregúntale a tu compañero/a para obtener la siguiente información.

1. qué actividades hace generalmente con miembros de su familia y cuándo

2. qué actividades hace con sus amigos los fines de semana

3. qué actividades hace con sus amigos durante la semana

SEGUNDA FASE. Preparen una lista de sus actividades semejantes o diferentes. Comparen su lista con la de otra pareja (*pair*).

Modelo ❝*Durante la semana, almorzamos en la cafetería de la universidad. ¿Y ustedes?*❞

4-19

Una reunión. En tu universidad hay un fin de semana cuando los padres visitan a sus hijos en el campus. Ustedes quieren organizar una reunión para las familias de los miembros de su grupo. Decidan lo siguiente:

1. lugar y hora de la reunión
2. número de niños y adultos que van a participar (especifiquen la relación familiar)
3. comida y bebida que piensan servir
4. actividades y diversiones para los niños y para los adultos

En directo

These expressions help maintain the flow of conversation:

¡Cuánto me alegro!
I am so happy for you!

Claro, claro…
Of course …

¡Qué bien/bueno!
That's great!

 Click on the icon to listen to a conversation with these expressions.

Suggestions for *En directo*
Model the pronunciation and intonation patterns of the expressions in the box to help students sound more natural. You may also play the audio to listen to the sample conversation in class.

Audioscript for *En directo*
David: *¿Qué tal, Paula? ¿Cómo estás?*
Paula: *Muy bien. Empiezo a trabajar en la librería esta semana, así que estoy muy contenta.*
David: *¡Cuánto me alegro!*
Paula: *Voy a trabajar muchas horas, porque necesito dinero para comprar un carro.*
David: *Claro, claro… Bueno, tengo que irme porque hoy es la graduación de mi hermano.*
Paula: *¡Qué bien!*

Situaciones

1

ROLE A. You and a member of your family are planning to visit Latin America. Your friend has heard about your plans and calls with some questions. Answer your friend's questions in detail.

ROLE B. Your friend is planning to go to Latin America with a relative. Call to find out a) when he/she is planning to go; b) with whom; c) what country and cities he/she wants to visit and why; d) if his/her relative prefers to go to other places; and e) when they are returning.

2

ROLE A. Your family has gathered at a party for the holidays. A relative is very curious about your life in college. After commenting on the party and several family members, answer her/his questions politely.

ROLE B. You are at a family holiday gathering and are very happy to see your relative who is in college. After commenting on the party and several family members, ask about these aspects of college life: a) his/her classes; b) which class(es) he/she prefers; c) if the food is good; and d) when vacation (**las vacaciones**) starts.

Tech tip for *Situaciones*
Additional situations are available in the Instructor's Resource folder.

Expressing obligation:
Tener que + infinitive

Go to the *Capítulo 4* folder online to complete the Learning Module for *Gramática en contexto: Tener que + infinitive.*

PLAN DE ESTUDIO

◎ **LEARN**
- Interactive presentation: *Tener que* + infinitive
- Grammar tutorials

APPLY ◎
- Activities
- Extra Practice

PRÁCTICA COMUNICATIVA

Mis obligaciones. **PRIMERA FASE.** Marca (✓) las tareas que tienes que hacer regularmente. Con tu compañero/a comparen sus obligaciones diarias.

_____ sacar a caminar al perro

_____ hacer ejercicio

_____ comprar comida

_____ hacer la tarea para mis clases

_____ revisar el aceite (*oil*) del carro

_____ poner los platos sucios en el lavaplatos (*dishwasher*)

_____ leer y contestar el correo electrónico

_____ ir a la universidad

_____ trabajar por las tardes

_____ visitar a mis parientes

SEGUNDA FASE. Ahora dile (*tell*) a tu compañero/a cuándo tienes que hacer cada tarea doméstica. Luego comparen sus obligaciones.

Modelo

Tengo que poner la mesa todos los días. ¿Y tú?

Yo no tengo que poner la mesa, pero tengo que preparar la comida los domingos.

4-21

Un viaje (*trip*) a Colombia. PRIMERA FASE. Tu familia va a viajar a Colombia. Escoge la mejor recomendación para cada persona. Después añade (*add*) algo que quieres hacer tú y por qué.

1. __b__ Mi hermana quiere visitar un lugar religioso muy original.

2. __c__ A mis padres les gustaría ver joyas (*jewels*) precolombinas.

3. __a__ Mi prima quiere escuchar música colombiana.

4. __d__ Mis abuelos prefieren las actividades al aire libre.

5. Yo quiero/prefiero... porque...

a. Tiene que asistir a un concierto de Los Príncipes del Vallenato.

b. Tiene que ir a la Catedral de Sal.

c. Tienen que ir al Museo del Oro.

d. Tienen que conocer el Parque Ecológico El Portal.

Cultura

El Portal is an ecological park near Bucaramanga, in the northeastern part of Colombia. With its natural springs and wooded trails, it is a well-known destination for ecotourism. Guests may visit a working sugar mill, and they may also enjoy activities such as horseback riding and mountain biking.

Compara: Are there any areas in your city or state dedicated to ecotourism? Where are they? What do people do there?

La Catedral de Sal

SEGUNDA FASE. Busca información en Internet y prepara una breve descripción de uno de los lugares, grupos o eventos siguientes. Incluye la localización y las actividades que las personas hacen allí. Luego, comparte la información con la clase y explica tu selección.

1. los Príncipes del Vallenato

2. la Catedral de Sal

3. el Museo del Oro

4. el Parque Ecológico El Portal

Suggestion for 4-22
To model, do one of the scenes partially with the class and then assign the scenes to individual groups.

Tech tip for *Situaciones*
Some students may want to film themselves and post their interaction using the MediaShare feature online.

 4-22

Sugerencias. **PRIMERA FASE.** ¿Qué tienen que hacer (o no) las personas en estas circunstancias?

Modelo **"Luis no tiene dinero (*money*)."**

> Tiene que buscar trabajo en Internet.

> No tiene que mirar Facebook.

1. Mi amigo Juan tiene un examen el lunes.
2. Francisco siempre está cansado.
3. Manuel y Victoria no tienen una buena relación de pareja (*couple*).
4. Mi hermana Marta ve televisión todos los días y saca malas notas en sus clases.
5. Luis y Emilia quieren aprender español.
6. Isabel y Lucía desean visitar un país hispano, pero no hablan español.

 SEGUNDA FASE. Escribe tres circunstancias personales. Explícale tus circunstancias a tu compañero/a y dile qué tienes que hacer.

Modelo **"*Vivo en un apartamento muy feo. Tengo que buscar un apartamento bonito.*"**

Situaciones

1

ROLE A. You run into your cousin downtown. Exchange greetings and explain that today is your father's birthday and that you have to buy a gift (**regalo**). You don't have much time because you have to return home by 5:00. Say that you are thinking of buying a DVD and ask what he/she thinks of the idea. Thank your cousin for the advice (**gracias por los consejos**).

ROLE B. You run into your cousin downtown. Exchange greetings. Your cousin needs some advice. Listen to his/her concerns and ask pertinent questions. Offer your opinion about whether a DVD is a good idea and, if so, what kind of DVD and where your cousin can find it.

2

ROLE A. You are worried about your bad relationship with your parents. They are angry because a) when you go out, you frequently come home late; b) you do not study enough; c) you prefer to spend a lot of time with your friends, but not with your family; d) you never play with your little sister; and e) when you are home you watch a lot of TV. Call a friend for advice. Answer your friend's questions in as much detail as possible.

ROLE B. A friend calls you to discuss family problems. Listen and ask appropriate questions. Say that he/she a) must return home early in the evenings; b) has to spend more time with family and play with his/her little sister; c) has to study every day to get good grades; and d) must not watch TV before studying.

Expressing when, where, or how an action occurs:
Adverbs

Go to the *Capítulo 4* **folder** online to complete the Learning Module for *Gramática en contexto:* Adverbs.

PLAN DE ESTUDIO

◎ LEARN
- Interactive presentation: Adverbs
- Grammar tutorials

APPLY ◎
- Activities
- Extra Practice

Online prep for students
Students will have completed the Learning Module for Adverbs online before class. See content online and Instructor's Resources for Supplementary Activities.

Suggestions
Point out secondary stress on *-mente*. Provide practice by saying an adjective and asking for the corresponding adverb. Ask questions to elicit adverbs: *¿Cómo caminas a clase? ¿Cómo juegas al tenis? ¿Cómo hablas español?*
You may present the expressions *con frecuencia* and *por lo general* as equivalents of *frecuentemente* and *generalmente*, respectively.

PRÁCTICA COMUNICATIVA

4-23

¿Estás de acuerdo o no? PRIMERA FASE. Las características de la familia pueden variar de una comunidad a otra. Indica si estás de acuerdo (**Sí** o **No**) con las siguientes afirmaciones.

En mi comunidad...

1. ____ los padres frecuentemente hablan con los hijos adolescentes sobre temas importantes.

2. ____ los nietos regularmente visitan a sus abuelos.

3. ____ generalmente los hijos solteros viven con sus padres.

4. ____ el padre trabaja fuera de casa y la madre trabaja en casa.

5. ____ los hijos adolescentes siempre tratan a sus padres cortésmente.

Follow-up for 4-23
Segunda fase
You may wish to have students write on index cards some traits they consider characteristic of families. Then you can shuffle the cards and read them aloud one at a time. Volunteers can agree or disagree with the statements.

Note for 4-24
You may want to point out the activity title and mention again how to form adverbs that are used in a series.

Alternate for 4-24
Students can work in pairs and then share with the class what they do *lenta o rápidamente* in: 1. *la casa*; 2. *la biblioteca*; 3. *el gimnasio*; 4. *un restaurante*.

SEGUNDA FASE. Comparen sus respuestas y digan por qué están de acuerdo o no.

Modelo

Estoy de acuerdo con el número uno. Generalmente los padres hablan sobre temas importantes con sus hijos.

No estoy de acuerdo. Los padres generalmente hablan sobre educación o dinero, pero no hablan de otras cosas importantes.

4-24

¿Lenta o rápidamente? Escribe tres actividades de la siguiente lista que haces rápidamente y tres que haces lentamente. Indica el lugar y/o las circunstancias. Comparte tus respuestas con tu compañero/a.

almorzar	escribir composiciones	hablar español	pasear
beber	estudiar	leer el periódico	tomar apuntes

Modelo

❝ Como rápidamente cuando tengo poco tiempo. ❞

4-25

¿Cómo lo haces? Escribe cómo o cuándo haces las siguientes actividades. Forma adverbios con las palabras de la lista para describir tus actividades. Luego, comparen sus actividades para ver si son parecidas o no.

difícil	frecuente	lógico	perfecto
fácil	lento	ocasional	rápido

1. caminar cuando tú estás muy cansado/a
2. pensar en la clase de matemáticas
3. respirar (*breathe*) después de una hora de ejercicio en el gimnasio
4. responder en un examen fácil

4-26

Actividades frecuentes. PRIMERA FASE. Háganse estas preguntas y tomen apuntes sobre las respuestas.

1. ¿Qué haces normalmente con tu familia?

2. ¿A qué lugares vas regularmente con tu familia? ¿Y con tus amigos?

3. Generalmente, ¿sales por las noches? ¿Adónde vas y con quién?

4. ¿A quiénes llamas por teléfono más frecuentemente, a tus amigos o a tu familia?

SEGUNDA FASE. Escribe una breve comparación, basada en las respuestas de tu compañero/a a las preguntas en la *Primera fase*. ¿Hacen ustedes actividades semejantes o diferentes?

En directo

To express surprise at what you hear:

¡Qué increíble! *Incredible!*

¡No me diga(s)! *Really!*

Click on the icon to listen to a conversation with these expressions.

Situaciones

1

ROLE A. Your class is conducting a survey regarding students' movie-viewing practices. Ask a classmate a) when and with whom he/she generally goes to the movies; b) the type of movies he/she normally prefers (**románticas, dramáticas, de ciencia ficción,** etc.); c) what he/she often eats or drinks at the movies; and d) the name of his/her favorite movie.

ROLE B. Answer the questions your classmate will ask about your movie preferences.

2

ROLE A. You are helping to conduct a survey about family traditions and activities. Ask a classmate a) if the members of his/her immediate family generally eat together; b) if they visit other family members frequently; and c) which family member normally organizes family gatherings.

ROLE B. First answer your classmate's questions about your family. Then ask him/her these questions for the survey: a) Who is generally more organized (**organizado/a**) at home, men or women?; b) Do family members frequently do activities together?; c) Who in the family cooks well?; d) Who talks calmly when angry, your father or your mother?

Audioscript for *En directo*
Lisa: [*very excited*] Joanna, tengo buenas noticias de mamá…
Laura: [*interrupting*] ¿Qué, qué?
Lisa: Escucha… dice que vamos a ir de vacaciones a El Portal, el parque ecológico cerca de Bucaramanga. ¡Vamos toda la familia!
Joanna: ¡No me digas! ¡Qué increíble!

Note for 4-26
Although comparatives are presented in *Capítulo 8*, students can use them in this activity since the structures are similar in both languages. Model the use of *y* and *pero* to compare and contrast by talking about yourself: *Mi esposo/a y yo hacemos actividades semejantes por la tarde. Él y yo trabajamos. Pero hacemos algunas actividades diferentes. Regularmente él va a los partidos de fútbol con sus amigos, pero yo voy a los centros comerciales con mis amigas. Mi esposo/a es más sociable y le gusta salir con amigos y hablar por teléfono. Yo prefiero estar en casa y escuchar música.*

Tech tip for *Situaciones*
You may want to assign partners and have pairs create a mini-skit using the video-posting feature, MediaShare, online.

Expressing how long something has been going on:
Hace with expressions of time

Go to the *Capítulo 4* online to complete the Learning Module for *Gramática en contexto: Hace* with expressions of time.

PLAN DE ESTUDIO

◎ LEARN
- Interactive presentation: *Hace* with expressions of time
- Grammar tutorials

APPLY ◎
- Activities
- Extra Practice

PRÁCTICA COMUNICATIVA

4-27

Este soy yo. **PRIMERA FASE.** Lee esta descripción y contesta las preguntas. Compara tus respuestas con las de tu compañero/a.

Me llamo Jaime Caicedo y soy de Cali, Colombia. Quiero aprender inglés para poder trabajar en una compañía internacional. Estudio inglés hace dos años, pero tengo que estudiar más para hablar correctamente. Siempre miro programas de televisión en inglés. Mis favoritos son *NCIS* y *Grey's Anatomy*. Hace dos años que miro estos programas y me gustan mucho. Tengo un auto hace un año, y salgo en él con mis amigos y también con mi novia. Hace seis meses que somos novios. Somos muy felices.

1. Jaime Caicedo es de…
    a. Estados Unidos.   **b.** Cali.   **c.** *Grey's Anatomy.*

2. Hace dos años que Jaime…
    a. tiene novia.   **b.** va al cine.   **c.** mira televisión en inglés.

3. Hace seis meses que Jaime…
    a. va a fiestas.   **b.** estudia inglés.   **c.** tiene novia.

SEGUNDA FASE. Escribe tu propia descripción, siguiendo el modelo en la *Primera fase*. Luego, comparte tu descripción con tu compañero/a.

¿Cuánto tiempo hace que… ? Túrnense para hacerse las siguientes preguntas. Después compartan la información con otra pareja.

1. ¿Dónde vive tu familia? ¿Cuánto tiempo hace que viven allí?

2. ¿Dónde trabajas? ¿Cuánto tiempo hace que trabajas allí?

3. ¿Cuánto tiempo hace que estudias en esta universidad? ¿Y por qué estudias español?

4. ¿Practicas algún deporte? ¿Cuánto tiempo hace que juegas al… ? ¿Juegas bien?

Suggestion for 4-31
Tell students that those who do not have a job may respond to question 2 with information about a friend or family member: *Yo no trabajo, pero mi amiga Susana trabaja en…*

Situaciones

Suggestion for *Situaciones*
For the second *Situación*, you may offer a short list of possible problems students can discuss, e.g., *un compañero/una compañera de cuarto muy desordenado/a, problemas con un curso, falta de amigos/actividades sociales.*

1

ROLE A. A friend has come to visit you in your hometown. Give him/her a tour and take him/her to your local Colombian restaurant for dinner. Give details about the places you visit and answer your friend's questions.

ROLE B. You are visiting a friend in his/her hometown and s/he is giving you a tour. Ask your friend questions: a) how long he/she has lived here; and b) how long he/she has known the places he/she shows you on the tour.

2

ROLE A. You go to see your counselor (**consejero/a**) to talk about a personal problem (**un problema**). Greet the counselor and explain your problem. Answer the counselor's questions in as much detail as possible. When the session is over, thank the counselor.

ROLE B. You are a university counselor (**consejero/a**). A student comes to you with a problem (**un problema**). Exchange greetings and ask a) how long the student has been at the university; b) how long he/she has been having the problem; and c) what he/she is doing to solve (**resolver**) the problem and for how long. Finally, suggest several things he/she has to do to improve (**mejorar**) the situation.

Talking about daily routine:
Reflexive verbs and pronouns

Go to the *Capítulo 4* **folder** online to complete the Learning Module for *Gramática en contexto:* Reflexive verbs and pronouns.

PLAN DE ESTUDIO

◎ LEARN
- Interactive presentation: Reflexive verbs and pronouns
- Grammar tutorials

APPLY ◎
- Activities
- Extra Practice

PRÁCTICA COMUNICATIVA

4-29

¿Qué hacemos todos los días? Pon estas actividades en el orden más lógico (1 = primero; 6 = finalmente). Luego, comparte tus respuestas con tu compañero/a. ¿Hace tu compañero/a las actividades en el mismo orden? ¿En qué se difieren?

_____6_____ Me duermo.

_____1_____ Me levanto.

_____4_____ Salgo para mis clases.

_____5_____ Me acuesto.

_____2_____ Me ducho y me lavo la cara (*face*).

_____3_____ Desayuno.

4-30

¿Tenemos las mismas rutinas? Hablen sobre sus actividades diarias.

Modelo 66 despertarse 99

Yo me despierto a las siete. ¿Y tú?

Generalmente, me despierto a las ocho.

1. levantarse   4. desayunar
2. ducharse   5. acostarse
3. vestirse   6. dormirse

4-31

Los horarios. Usen la información de la actividad 4-30. Completen la tabla y escriban un párrafo sobre sus horarios. ¿Qué tienen en común? ¿En qué son diferentes?

	Yo	Mi compañero/a
despertarse		
levantarse		
bañarse		
vestirse		

Situaciones

1

ROLE A. Your young cousin has to do a report based on an interview of a family member. You have offered to be interviewed. Exchange greetings and answer his/her questions as completely as possible.

ROLE B. You have to write a report based on an interview with a family member. Your college-age cousin has agreed to be interviewed. Greet him/her and explain the purpose of the interview. Then find out a) where he/she lives and for how long he/she has lived there; b) what his/her daily routine is; and c) some differences between your routine and his/her routine.

2

ROLE A. You are applying for a summer language program (**programa de verano**) to practice your Spanish in Bogotá. Call the organizers to get information about the daily routine at the residence where you will be staying: a) where the students sleep; b) what time they go to bed; c) when they get up; and d) where they eat.

ROLE B. You are the director of a summer language school (**programa de verano**) in Bogotá. Answer the questions of a prospective student, giving as much information as possible.

Follow-up for 4-31
Have students write portions of their paragraphs on the board to provide input for conversation about the activities of the characters/reflexive forms. Students can question each other to find out who wakes up the earliest/gets up immediately after awakening/gets dressed before eating breakfast, etc.

Audioscript for 4-33

¡Hola, Julio! Habla Pedro. Te llamo porque mi prima Josefina llega hoy de Colombia y mi hermano y yo queremos darle una fiesta sorpresa. Mi hermana y mi madre van a preparar la comida, así que te va a gustar. Yo solo me ocupo de las bebidas. La fiesta va a ser el domingo, en mi casa. Debes llegar temprano, a las ocho y media, más o menos, porque Josefina va a venir a las nueve y, como es una sorpresa, todos tenemos que estar aquí antes que ella. Dice mi hermano que tienes unos CD de vallenatos y otra música típica de Colombia. ¿Puedes traer algunos? Bueno, recuerda, la hora: ocho y media, en mi casa: calle 12, número 127. Te esperamos el domingo. Chao.

Note for 4-33

As mentioned in *Vocabulario en contexto*, directions for listening activities are given in English to ensure that students understand what they have to do.

ESCUCHA [Presentational]

4-32

Preparación. Antes de escuchar el mensaje de Pedro para Julio sobre una fiesta sorpresa (*surprise*), escribe el posible propósito (*purpose*) de este mensaje y la información específica que puede ser importante. Presenta tus notas a la clase y comparen sus ideas.

ESTRATEGIA

Listen for a purpose

Listening with a purpose in mind will help you focus your attention on the most relevant information. As you focus your attention, you screen what you hear and select only the information you need.

4-33  [Interpretive]

Escucha. First read the information you will need to attend the party Pedro is organizing. Then, as you listen, complete the sentences with the rest of the information. Don't worry if you do not understand every word.

1. La fiesta es para… Josefina

2. La fiesta va a ser en la casa de… Pedro

3. El día de la fiesta es… domingo

4. Julio debe llevar (*take*)… música típica de Colombia

5. Julio tiene que llegar a la casa a las… ocho y media

6. La dirección es… calle 12, número 127

Comprueba

I was able to…

____ **recognize the names of people.**

____ **identify specific information about an event.**

4-34  [Interpersonal]

Un paso más. Vas a organizar una fiesta sorpresa para tu profesor/a de español y deseas invitar a tu compañero/a. Llámalo por teléfono y explícale lo siguiente:

1. cuándo y dónde va a ser la fiesta

2. qué van a comer y beber

3. qué música van a escuchar

4. otros planes

AUTOEVALUACIÓN

☐ I feel confident that I understood most of the message.

☐ I need more listening practice.

STUDY PLAN

▶ Good job! Move on to the *Habla* section.

▶ Go to the *Unidos* [folder] online for the *Escucha* practice.

HABLA

4-35 [Interpretive]

Preparación. Completa las siguientes afirmaciones con los nombres de tus parientes, la relación de parentesco y sus actividades.

Modelo *"Mi primo David come en restaurantes los fines de semana."*

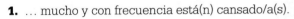

1. … mucho y con frecuencia está(n) cansado/a(s).
2. … en casa los fines de semana. Descansan, leen, escuchan música, etc.
3. … ejercicio físico tres o cuatro veces por semana.
4. … con amigos o con la familia en casa el día de su cumpleaños.
5. … por el teléfono celular. Llama(n) a sus amigos día y noche.

ESTRATEGIA

Organize information to make comparisons

In *Capítulo 3*, you practiced organizing information for a presentation. Now you will focus on organizing information for a conversation about a specific topic. Follow these steps in organizing your information.

- List the names of family members you are going to talk about.
- Indicate the family relationships.
- Decide on possible categories for your comparisons (*aburridos, divertidos; extrovertidos, tímidos; trabajadores, perezosos*).

4-36 [Interpersonal]

Habla. En grupos pequeños, háganse las siguientes preguntas y comparen la información.

1. ¿Quiénes son las personas más artísticas en tu familia? ¿Por qué?
2. ¿Quiénes son las personas más activas en tu familia? ¿Por qué?
3. ¿Qué miembros de la familia pasan mucho tiempo en casa? ¿Por qué?

Comprueba

In my conversation…

____ I used question words appropriately.

____ I described and compared family members.

____ I gave relevant information when answering.

____ I used adjectives accurately.

En directo

To make comparisons and contrasts:

Por un lado…
On the one hand …

Por otro lado…
On the other hand …

En cambio…
On the other hand …

En contraste… *In contrast …*

Click on the icon to listen to a conversation with these expressions.

4-37 [Presentational]

Un paso más. En los mismos grupos, comparen sus respuestas y completen un pequeño informe (*report*) con la información anterior. Luego compartan la información con el resto de la clase.

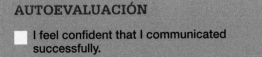

AUTOEVALUACIÓN

☐ I feel confident that I communicated successfully.

☐ I need more speaking practice.

STUDY PLAN

▶ Good job! Move on to the next section, *Lee*.

▶ Go to the *Unidos* [folder] online for the *Habla* practice.

Note for *Estrategia*
The focus here is on organizing information for a purpose. You may wish to introduce as lexical items *más… que, menos… que,* if you think the phrases will help students converse more naturally. (Comparisons are presented in *Capítulo 8*.)

Preparation for 4-35
Make sure students notice that the sample response in the model includes three pieces of information: name (*David*), relationship (*primo*), and activity (*come*). Encourage them to include more than one family member in each response.

Warm-up for 4-36
Ask questions about students' families: *¿Cuántos hermanos tienes? ¿Dónde viven?* Ask other students to recall information given by their classmates.

Audioscript for *En directo*
Roberto: *Oye, Jaime. Tengo un problema con mi hermano y necesito tu opinión.*
Jaime: *Por supuesto. Dime, ¿qué pasa?*
Roberto: *Pues, mi hermano quiere usar mi carro. Por un lado, no me importa porque ahora estoy en la universidad. Por otro lado, mi hermano no es cuidadoso.*
Jaime: *Entiendo lo que dices. En cambio, pienso que en esta ocasión tu hermano va a tener mucho cuidado y comprende que es un gran favor.*
Roberto: *Tienes razón, Jaime.*

Suggestion for 4-37
Have students discuss their responses and draw conclusions with the class as a whole.

Suggestion for 4-37
To help students write their reports you may give them a few sentences to complete: 1. *En nuestras familias…*

Have students present their
responses to the class
or exchange them with a
classmate. Question 3 lends
itself to discussion, since the
concept of communication
may be interpreted differently
in different families. To help
students compare responses
to question 3, you may write
on the board: *Es necesario… ;
No es necesario…* and give an
example: *Es necesario estar
en contacto con la familia.
No es necesario hablar por
teléfono todos los días.*

LEE

ESTRATEGIA

4-38 | Presentational

Preparación. Lee el título y los subtítulos del artículo en la página siguiente y observa las fotos. Luego, usa la información del título, los subtítulos y las fotos para contestar las siguientes preguntas. Comparte tus respuestas con la clase.

1. ¿Cuál es el tema del artículo?
   a. la comunicación entre amigos
   (b.) la comunicación entre los miembros de una familia
   c. la comunicación con los colegas en el trabajo

2. En tu opinión, ¿cuáles de las siguientes ideas va a incluir el artículo? (Hay más de una respuesta correcta.)
   a. Hoy en día la comunicación entre padres e hijos es mejor que (*better than*) en el pasado.
   b. Los jóvenes no hablan con sus padres sobre sus problemas porque los padres siempre están ocupados.
   c. La vida moderna afecta la comunicación entre padres e hijos.
   d. La tecnología tiende a reducir la comunicación sobre temas importantes.

3. Marca (✓) las actividades de la siguiente lista que asocias con una buena relación entre padres e hijos.
   a. ___✓___ conversar
   b. ___✓___ pasar tiempo juntos
   c. ___✓___ hablar por teléfono
   d. _____ pelear (*argue*)
   e. ___✓___ escribir correos electrónicos a un miembro de la familia que vive lejos (*far*)
   f. ___✓___ comprar regalos con frecuencia
   g. ___✓___ expresar cariño (*affection*) verbalmente
   h. _____ no hablar de sus problemas con los padres

Use title and illustrations to anticipate content

Before you start to read, it is important to gather as much information about the text as possible. The title, section headings, and illustrations can help you anticipate content, so pay special attention to them before you start to read. Take notes on what you think the text is about, and refer to your notes as you are reading, correcting them as necessary. This will help you focus on understanding each section of the text as you read it.

Suggestion for 4-39
Remember that students
may comprehend more than
they can verbalize or write.
Therefore, it is advisable not
to force them to respond to
questions in their own words
or paraphrase at this stage.
Let them quote their answers
directly from the text if they
prefer.

Answers for 4-39
1. *tecnología;* 2. *el uso
excesivo;* 3. *Internet/el correo
electrónico, el teléfono
celular;* 4. *breve, superficial;*
5. *para pasar tiempo con sus
familiares y para expresar el
amor y el cariño que siente
por ellos.*

4-39 | Interpretive

Lee. Lee el artículo e indica…

1. una palabra asociada con los problemas de comunicación familiares.

2. por qué la tecnología probablemente afecta las relaciones de la familia.

3. dos ejemplos de cómo la tecnología puede causar problemas en la familia.

4. dos palabras que indican la calidad de la comunicación cuando usamos el correo electrónico o los mensajes de texto.

5. dos formas de usar la tecnología positivamente en la comunicación con la familia.

Comprueba

I was able to…

___ **use headings and photos to identify the main idea.**

___ **focus on one piece of information at a time.**

___ **write effective notes.**

LA IMPORTANCIA DE LA COMUNICACIÓN FAMILIAR

La tecnología puede facilitar la comunicación familiar.

LA FAMILIA EN CRISIS

Los expertos afirman que la familia de hoy está en crisis por la falta[1] de comunicación entre sus miembros o por la mala comunicación que existe entre ellos. También dicen que la comunicación es vital en todas las relaciones, especialmente en las relaciones familiares.

La comunicación entre padres e hijos sobre temas importantes crea (*creates*) relaciones familiares fuertes y cariñosas.

AUSENCIA DE LOS PADRES

¿Por qué hay problemas de comunicación en las familias? Hay varias razones. Una razón es que la madre y el padre trabajan largas horas fuera de casa y los hijos están solos mucho tiempo, sin la compañía y la supervisión de sus mayores. La ausencia casi todos los días de los padres puede crear cierta independencia en los hijos y una distancia emocional que causa dificultades en la comunicación entre padres e hijos.

LA TECNOLOGÍA

Un segundo factor es la tecnología. Nuestro mundo está controlado por la tecnología en casa, en el trabajo, etc. Evidentemente la tecnología facilita muchas cosas, pero su uso excesivo puede complicar la vida. Un gran número de hogares[2] están conectados a Internet, así que muchos jóvenes tienen acceso ilimitado al correo electrónico y a la Red, sobre todo a los sitios web de comunicación social y entretenimiento, como Facebook y YouTube. Idealmente, el bajo costo de la conexión debería afectar positivamente la comunicación en la familia, pero la realidad indica que la comunicación moderna (e.g., correo electrónico, mensajes de texto) tiende a ser más breve y más superficial. Los hijos prefieren no discutir sus problemas por correo electrónico o mensajes de texto. Prefieren hablar directamente con sus padres, si es que sus padres tienen el tiempo. Lo mismo ocurre con el teléfono celular. Es cierto que muchos jóvenes usan celulares para llamar a sus padres, pero muy pocos usan el celular para conversar largamente con sus padres sobre temas personales importantes.

CONCLUSIÓN

En conclusión, el tiempo limitado que los padres pueden dar a sus hijos y la tendencia a usar la tecnología para comunicaciones muy breves pueden afectar negativamente las relaciones familiares. Por eso es importante crear oportunidades para una comunicación real y profunda dentro de la familia. Si usas la tecnología de manera positiva para pasar tiempo con tus familiares y para expresar el amor y el cariño que sientes por ellos, tu familia va a ser más fuerte y unida.

[1]*lack*   [2]*homes*

4-40  [Interpersonal]

Un paso más. Habla con tu compañero/a sobre el impacto de la tecnología en la comunicación familiar entre los estudiantes universitarios y sus padres. Fíjate (*Focus*) en los dos temas principales del artículo:

- la separación física entre los padres y los hijos
- el uso de la tecnología como medio de comunicación

Follow-up for 4-40
Students may share their ideas with another pair. Or you may wish to have a class discussion that focuses on making connections between the content of the article and the reality of students' lives: the process of establishing and maintaining communication with family when they are no longer living at home.

AUTOEVALUACIÓN

☐ I feel confident I understood the reading and was able to use the information.

☐ I need more reading practice.

STUDY PLAN

▶ Good job! Move on to the next section, *Escribe*.

▶ Go to the *Unidos* folder online for the *Lee* practice.

ESCRIBE

Preparación.

PRIMERA FASE. Tu madre está triste y preocupada porque estudias en una universidad lejos de casa y te escribe el siguiente correo electrónico.

Querido hijo:

¿Qué tal estás? ¿Cómo van tus clases? Hace un mes que no tenemos información sobre ti. ¡No escribes correos electrónicos, no llamas por teléfono! ¿Qué ocurre?

Bueno, es el fin del semestre y debes tener mucho trabajo. ¿Tienes mucho estrés? ¿Duermes suficiente? ¿Comes bien en la universidad? En tu próxima visita, pienso preparar tus platos favoritos.

Tu padre y yo pensamos mucho en ti. ¿Por qué no escribes? ¿Tienes problemas en tus clases? ¿Trabajas mucho? ¿Estás desconectado de Internet? Por favor, escribe o llama pronto.

Un beso de papá y mamá,

Tu madre

SEGUNDA FASE. Prepárate para responder a la carta de tu madre. Identifica las preguntas de tu madre que quieres contestar y escribe algunas ideas.

ESTRATEGIA

Choose between informal and formal language to express the desired tone

Choosing the appropriate level of formality when you write to someone depends on your relationship to that person. When writing to older people in your family it might be best to avoid the abbreviated format and casual language of computer-based communication. Instead, choose your language more carefully and write about issues more seriously than you would when corresponding with friends.

The salutation, closing, and forms of address used in letter writing also reflect your degree of closeness and formality. The expressions in *En directo* include some common salutations and forms of address that are appropriate to use when you write to elders in your family.

En directo

To write a salutation:

Querido papá/abuelo:
Dear ...,

Querida mamá/abuelita:
Dear ...,

To close correspondence:

Con cariño, *Affectionately,*

Con mucho cariño,
With much love,

Abrazos y besos,
Hugs and kisses,

Te recuerdo con cariño,
I remember you (familiar) with affection,

 Click on the icon to listen to an e-mail with these expressions.

Escribe. Ahora responde a la carta de tu madre.

Querida mamá:

Comprueba

I was able to…

____ present main ideas clearly with adequate details.

____ use a wide range of vocabulary words.

____ use correct gender and number agreement with nouns and adjectives.

____ conjugate verbs correctly and make them agree with their subjects.

____ use accurate spelling, capitalization, and punctuation.

____ close the message properly.

Un paso más. Lee la respuesta de tu compañero/a a su madre. Escríbanse (*Write to each other*) un correo electrónico en el que hacen una lista de las semejanzas (*similarities*) y diferencias entre tu carta y la de tu compañero/a.

AUTOEVALUACIÓN

☐ I feel confident I successfully communicated my ideas in writing.

☐ I need more writing practice.

STUDY PLAN

▶ Good job!

▶ Go to the *Unidos* folder online for the *Escribe* practice.

ENFOQUE *cultural*

COLOMBIA

Note for *Barranquilla*

Barranquilla hosts other significant cultural events as well. Among the most important is *Barranquijazz*, a music festival held in September that highlights top jazz musicians. The *Carnaval de las Artes* is another noteworthy event that draws artists and thinkers of both national and international renown. Yet another event rooted in Barranquilla is the *Festival Internacional de Cuenteros*, which celebrates the whimsy and talent of storytellers.

Note for *Bogotá*

Bogotá is the largest city in Colombia and has the largest population of any city in the country. It is also the primary industrial and economic center of Colombia, thanks in great part to its central location.

Note for *Gabriel García Márquez*

García Márquez is by far the most celebrated Colombian writer. Author of novels, short stories and screenplays, he began his career as a law student and journalist. His works have been embraced not only by fellow Colombians, but also by people throughout Latin American and the world.

El carnaval de Barranquilla es una celebración importante de la cultura y folclor colombiano. Se celebra cada año cuatro días antes de la Cuaresma (*Lent*). Atrae a gente de todas partes del país y del mundo para disfrutar de la música, el baile y las tradiciones colombianas.

Bogota, la capital, está situada en el centro del país en el altiplano se la Cordillera Oriental. Es una ciudad moderna y a la vez tradicional donde todavía se celebran corridas de toros (*bullfights*) en la Plaza de Santamaría.

El escritor y Premio Nobel de Literatura colombiano, Gabriel García Márquez cuenta con grandes éxitos literarios entre ellos, su obra maestra, "Cien años de Soledad" (*One Hundred Years of Solitude*). El uso del realismo mágico es una característica de su estilo literario.

La riqueza de Colombia

Go to the *Enfoque cultural* folder in Capítulo 4 online to learn more about Colombia.

⊙ LEARN
- Interactive presentation: *La riqueza de Colombia*

APPLY ◎
- Activities

PRÁCTICA COMUNICATIVA

4-44

Usa la información. Prepara un afiche (*poster*) para hacer una presentación sobre dos colombianos famosos. Ve a Internet y elige personas que representen áreas diferentes de la vida colombiana, como la política, las artes, la música, los deportes, etc. Incluye fotos y la siguiente información: lugar donde viven, el trabajo que hacen y otra información de interés.

En este capítulo...

Comprueba lo que sabes

Go to the *Comprueba lo que sabes* folder online to review what you have learned in this chapter.

| Flashcards | Games | Oral Practice | Practice Test / Study Plan | Video en contexto |

Vocabulario

La familia
la abuela
el abuelo
el ahijado/la ahijada
la esposa
el esposo
la hermana
el hermano
el hermanastro
la hermanastra
la hija
el hijo
el hijo único/la hija única
la madrastra
la madre
la madrina
la mamá
la media hermana
el medio hermano
la nieta
el nieto
el niño/la niña
la novia
el novio

el padrastro
el padre
los padres
el padrino
el papá
el pariente
el primo/la prima
la sobrina
el sobrino
la tía
el tío

Verbos
acostar(se) (ue)
afeitar(se)
almorzar (ue)
bañar(se)
casar(se)
cerrar(ie)
costar (ue)
decir (g, i)
desayunar
despertar(se) (ie)
dormir(se) (ue)

dormir (ue) la siesta
duchar(se)
empezar (ie)
entender (ie)
jugar (ue)
lavar(se)
levantar(se)
maquillar(se)
pasar
pasear
pedir (i)
peinar(se)
pensar (ie)
pensar (ie) + infinitive
poder (ue)
poner(se) (g) la ropa
preferir (ie)
querer (ie)
quitar(se)
secar(se)
seguir (i)
sentarse (ie)
sentir(se) (ie)
servir (i)

tener (g, ie)
venir (g, ie)
vestir(se) (i)
visitar
volver (ue)

Las descripciones
divorciado/a
gemelo/a
ocupado/a

Palabras y
el bautizo
la derecha
la foto(grafía)
la izquierda
juntos/as
el/la mayor
el/la menor
la noticia
tarde
temprano
un poco

Notas

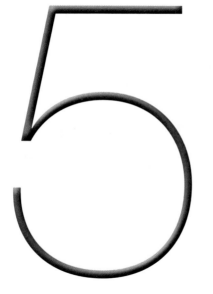

5 ¿Dónde vives?

Introduction to chapter
Introduce the chapter theme. Help students access meaning by making frequent use of gestures or visuals.

Related questions: *¿Dónde vives? ¿Vives en una casa o en un apartamento? ¿O alquilas un cuarto en una casa? ¿Vives con tu familia o con otros estudiantes? ¿Te gusta el lugar en donde vives ahora? Después de graduarte, ¿dónde quieres vivir? ¿En la ciudad o en el campo?*

Presentational: See activities 5-5, 5-12, 5-28, 5-31, 5-34, 5-38, and 5-40.

Interpretive: See activities 5-1, 5-2, 5-3, 5-4, 5-8, 5-9, 5-10, 5-13, 5-15, 5-16, 5-17, 5-18,4, 5-19, 5-20, 5-21, 5-22, 5-24, 5-25, 5-26, 5-5-29, 5-32, 5-35, and 5-37.

Interpersonal: See activities 5-1, 5-2, 5-3, 5-4, 5-5, 5-6, 5-7, 5-8, 5-9, 5-10, 5-11, 5-12, 5-13, 5-14, 5-15, 5-16, 5-17, 5-18, 5-19, 5-20, 5-21, 5-22, 5-23, 5-24, 5-25, 5-26, 5-27, 5-30, 5-32, 5-33, 5-36, 5-39, and all *Situaciones*.

Learning OBJECTIVES

You will:

- use new vocabulary to talk about housing, furnishings, and daily chores
- learn the forms of the present progressive
- learn expressions with *tener*
- learn to refer to people and objects with direct object pronouns
- learn to use demonstrative adjectives and pronouns
- connect new information about Nicaragua, El Salvador, Honduras, and the architecture of this region to what you already know

Learning OUTCOMES

You will be able to:

- talk about housing, the home, and household activities
- express ongoing actions
- describe physical and emotional states
- avoid repetition in speaking and writing
- point out and identify people and things
- compare cultural and geographic information of Nicaragua, El Salvador, and Honduras

Mar Caribe

BELICE

MÉXICO

Ruinas mayas

HONDURAS

GUATEMALA

Copán   Tegucigalpa

El café

EL SALVADOR

San Salvador

NICARAGUA

Cuadro de Fernando Llort,
pintor de El Salvador

Mango verde
con limón y sal

León

Managua

Un edificio de arquitectura colonial

Granada

El Volcán de Izalco

OCÉANO PACÍFICO

COSTA
RICA

NICARAGUA, EL SALVADOR Y HONDURAS

¿Cuánto sabes?

Mira el mapa y después asocia la información de las dos columnas.

1. __c__ Tegucigalpa…

2. __a__ El mango verde con limón y sal…

3. __f__ Al oeste de El Salvador…

4. __e__ Las ruinas de Copán…

5. __b__ El café…

6. __d__ Granada y otras ciudades de Nicaragua…

a. es un aperitivo típico de El Salvador.

b. es un producto de exportación importante.

c. es la capital de Honduras.

d. tienen arquitectura colonial.

e. son de la civilización maya.

f. está el volcán de Izalco.

Cultura en línea
To learn more about Nicaragua, El Salvador, and Honduras, and the chapter theme, go to the *Cultura en línea* folder online to view the *Vistas culturales* video and take a virtual art tour.

Online prep for students
Students will have completed the Learning Module for *En casa* online before coming to class. This includes the Interactive presentation and corresponding Apply activities. See content online and Instructor's Resources for Supplementary Activities.

Tech tip for *En casa*
You may want to project the images from the Learning Module in class and ask questions to review the vocabulary.

For image of Granada, ask questions so that students describe the street and the houses in the photo. *¿Qué hay en esta foto? ¿Les gusta esta calle? ¿Cómo son las casas?* Point to the street arcades, which are typical of Granada in Nicaragua. Explain: *Estos corredores son típicos de Granada, son para pasear. Las casas en esta ciudad son antiguas. En la capital, Managua, hay edificios modernos y rascacielos* (write word on board).

Then personalize by asking: *Y tú, ¿vives en el centro o en las afueras de la ciudad? ¿Vives en un apartamento o en una casa? ¿Tu casa tiene arcos/puertas/ ventanas grandes?*

Suggestion for 5-1
Encourage students to adapt the communicative situation modeled in *Otra conversación* to talk about another apartment they might be visiting.

Note
The monetary unit of Honduras is *el lempira*, named in honor of Lempira (1497–1537), a Lenca chieftain who fought against the Spanish. House prices are often given in dollars as well as in *lempiras* (Lps). As of July, 2012 1 $US = 19 Lps, approximately. You may ask students to find the current rate of exchange.

Vocabulario en contexto

Talking about housing, the home, and household activities

En casa

Go to the *Capítulo 5* **folder** online to complete the Learning Module for *Vocabulario en contexto: En casa*.

PLAN DE ESTUDIO

◎ LEARN
- Interactive presentation: *En casa*
- Vocabulary tutorials
- Pronunciation

APPLY ◎
- Activities
- Pronunciation activities

PRÁCTICA COMUNICATIVA

5-1 👥

Otra conversación. Con tu compañero/a lee la conversación entre Marta y el Sr. López. Después cambien la conversación para hablar de un apartamento que le interesa a uno de ustedes.

MARTA:	Hola, buenos días. Me gustaría ver el apartamento.
SR. LÓPEZ:	Sí, claro. Pase, pase. Esta es la sala. Es muy grande. Junto a la sala hay un comedor pequeño y al lado está la cocina.
MARTA:	¡El refrigerador es lindísimo!
SR. LÓPEZ:	A la izquierda del pasillo hay dos habitaciones y un baño.
MARTA:	¿Cuánto es el alquiler?
SR. LÓPEZ:	12.000 lempiras al mes.
MARTA:	Me encanta el apartamento y el precio es muy bueno. Voy a decidir esta noche.
SR. LÓPEZ:	Perfecto. Hasta mañana.

5-2 👥

¿En qué piso viven? Túrnense y pregúntense dónde viven las diferentes personas. Tu compañero/a debe contestar de acuerdo con el dibujo (*drawing*).

Modelo

> ¿Dónde viven los Girondo?

> Viven en el cuarto piso, en el apartamento 4-A.

5-A López	5-B Alemán
4-A Girondo	4-B Mujica
3-A Ozollo	3-B Ponce
2-A Cárdenas	2-B García-Gil
1-A Jiménez	1-B Valbuena
PB-A Martínez	PB-B Casal

décimo
noveno
octavo
séptimo
sexto
quinto
cuarto
tercero
segundo
primer piso
planta baja

LENGUA Ordinal numbers are adjectives and agree in gender and number with the noun they modify (e.g., **la segunda casa, el cuarto edificio**). **Primero** and **tercero** drop the final -o when used before a masculine singular noun.

el **primer** apartamento   el **tercer** piso

Cultura

Notice that the first floor is normally called **la planta baja** in most Hispanic countries. The second floor is called **el primer piso**.

Compara. ¿Cómo se le llama a la planta baja en tu lengua?

```
6 ◯
5 ◯
4 ◯
3 ◯
2 ◯
1 ◯
0 ◯  PLANTA BAJA
STOP ◯
▢ ◯
```

5-3 👥

Un hotel de lujo.

Tu amigo (tu compañero/a) es un arquitecto que va a construir un hotel de lujo en la Bahía de Jiquilisco, cerca de San Salvador, y te pide consejo sobre cómo distribuir los siguientes espacios del hotel.

Modelo

> ❝ el restaurante ❞

> ¿En qué piso vamos a poner el restaurante?

> Debe estar en la planta baja.

1. la discoteca
2. la recepción
3. el gimnasio
4. la oficina de seguridad
5. las habitaciones
6. la piscina
7. la cafetería con vista a la playa
8. el salón de computadoras

Tech tip for 5-2
You may want to project the text image to review ordinal numbers before students complete the activity. Ask questions about the drawing to check comprehension: *¿Es este un edificio moderno o antiguo? ¿Tiene piscina/pileta/ alberca? ¿En qué planta/piso está la piscina probablemente: en la planta baja o en el piso décimo?¿Hay terrazas en este edificio? ¿Dónde están? En este edificio hay una oficina de administración. ¿En qué piso está probablemente?*

Suggestion for 5-2
Before doing this activity, ask questions to personalize: *¿Quién vive en un edificio de apartamentos? ¿En qué piso vives?¿Te gusta vivir en un edificio de apartamentos muy alto? ¿Por qué?*

Suggestion for 5-3
Before doing this activity you may brainstorm with students a list of rooms or spaces that you may find in a big hotel: *salas de conferencias, terraza, baños, cocina, lavandería, tiendas, bar.* These may be added to the ones listed in the activity.

Suggestion for 5-4
You may want to have students compare their housing with the drawing by asking them about these features: *tipo de vivienda, número de baños, número de habitaciones, ubicación*, etc.

Suggestion for 5-4
Explain the word *anuncio* by projecting the ad from the Learning Module online. Ask questions to check comprehension: *¿Qué hacemos en el comedor? ¿Y en la cocina?*

Suggestion for 5-5
You may wish to have students prepare their advantages and disadvantages as lists of simple sentences to facilitate the exchange of views; e.g., *Las casas son grandes. Hay más espacio; Preferimos los apartamentos porque no tenemos que cortar el césped.*

5-4

La casa de alquiler.

PRIMERA FASE. Ustedes van a mudarse (*move*) a un apartamento porque la casa donde viven es muy grande y la quieren alquilar. Escriban un anuncio para alquilar su casa.

Incluyan la siguiente información: número de habitaciones y de baños, distribución (*layout*) de los cuartos, color de la sala, otras características (garaje, jardín, sótano [*basement*], ático, etc.), ubicación (*location*) de la casa en relación al centro de la ciudad, de la universidad, precio, etc.

SEGUNDA FASE. Presenten su anuncio a la clase y contesten las preguntas de sus compañeros sobre la casa que quieren alquilar.

Exterior de la casa

Interior de la casa

5-5

Ventajas y desventajas. Hablen de las ventajas y desventajas de los temas relacionados con las viviendas. Escriban las más importantes y luego compartan sus opiniones con la clase.

	VENTAJAS	DESVENTAJAS
1. vivir en un apartamento		
2. vivir en una casa		
3. tener una piscina		
4. compartir una casa con 3 o 4 compañeros/as		

La casa, los muebles y los electrodomésticos

Go to the *Capítulo 5* [folder] online to complete the Learning Module for *Vocabulario en contexto: La casa, los muebles y los electrodomésticos.*

PLAN DE ESTUDIO

◎ LEARN
- Interactive presentation: *La casa, los muebles y los electrodomésticos*
- Vocabulary tutorials

APPLY
- Activities

PRÁCTICA COMUNICATIVA

EN OTRAS PALABRAS

Words for household items often vary from one region to another, for example:

manta, cobija, frazada

armario, clóset

bañera, bañadera, tina

refrigerador, nevera

estufa, cocina

5-6

¿Aparatos eléctricos, muebles o accesorios?

PRIMERA FASE. Escribe las siguientes palabras en la columna apropiada.

la alfombra	las cortinas	el/la radio
el armario	el cuadro	el refrigerador
la butaca	el horno	las sábanas
la cómoda	el lavaplatos	la silla

APARATOS ELÉCTRICOS	MUEBLES	ACCESORIOS
el refrigerador	el armario	el cuadro
el/la radio	la cómoda	las cortinas
el horno	la silla	la alfombra
el lavaplatos	la butaca	las sábanas

Suggestion for *La casa, los muebles y los electrodomésticos*
Tell students to imagine that the classroom is a house. Walk around and "identify" the different "rooms." First, whisper to individual students what activities they will act out in pantomime in each part of the house. Later, you may ask the rest of the class questions: *Mark y Susan están en la cocina. ¿Qué hacen? (Preparan la comida.) Esta es la sala y aquí están María y Carlota. ¿Qué hacen en la sala? (Miran televisión.)* Encourage students to include items from each room in their responses. You may also review colors using the illustration, and/or by having students give the color of rooms in their own house or apartment.

Suggestion
You may introduce some additional vocabulary, such as *pared, congelador, ventilador.*

Note
When referring to a microwave oven, people usually shorten it to *el microondas,* instead of saying *el horno microondas.*

Note for 5-6
Point out that some Spanish speakers prefer to say *el radio.* In Spain, *la radio* is more common.

Standard 4.1
Students demonstrate understanding of the nature of language through the language studied and their own. The information in the *En otras palabras* box shows students that different words are used for the same entity in different parts of the Spanish-speaking world. Instructors may wish to have students brainstorm words they know for apartment in English (flat, rooms) as well as other items (e.g., soda = soft drink, pop; long sandwich with meat, lettuce, etc. = sub, hero, hoagie, grinder, po' boy).

1. Según ustedes, ¿qué aparato eléctrico cuesta más dinero?
2. ¿Qué muebles necesitan todos los días los estudiantes?
3. ¿Qué accesorios tienen ustedes en su cuarto?
4. ¿En qué parte de la casa generalmente están estos objetos?

Follow-up for 5-7
You may wish to have students report the most interesting feature of their partners' house/apartment. This type of follow-up makes students accountable for focusing on the pair work.

El curioso. Intercambien preguntas para describir los cuartos de la casa/del apartamento de cada uno/a. Traten (*Try*) de obtener la mayor información posible.

Modelo

> ¿Cómo es la sala de tu casa?

> Es pequeña. Hay una alfombra verde y un sofá blanco grande. También hay una mesa de cristal. ¿Y cómo es tu dormitorio?

LENGUA Here are some electronics that you may have in your house:

la impresora	*printer*
la consola de videojuegos	*games console*
el cargador del móvil/celular	*cell phone charger*

5-8

Preparativos.

PRIMERA FASE. Vas a mudarte (*move*) a una casa muy grande y tienes que comprar muchas cosas. Organiza tu lista de compras según las siguientes categorías.

SEGUNDA FASE. Comparte tu lista de compras con tu compañero/a. Él/Ella te va a recordar (*remind you about*) otras cosas que probablemente vas a necesitar.

Modelo

Voy a comprar una cama nueva para el dormitorio.

¿No vas a comprar sábanas y mantas?¿Y no necesitas un sofá?

	MUEBLES	ACCESORIOS	ELECTRODOMÉSTICOS/ APARATOS ELECTRÓNICOS
para el dormitorio			
para la sala			
para el comedor			
para la cocina			

5-9

Por catálogo. Miren los objetos del catálogo y elijan (*choose*) un producto de cada categoría. Intercambien sus preferencias y expliquen dónde van a poner estos accesorios.

barato/a	caro/a	de buena calidad
grande	pequeño/a	bonito/a
cómodo	de color…	lindo/a

Modelo

Me gusta la toalla gris porque no es cara y es muy linda. Es para el cuarto de baño.

Yo prefiero la azul porque es más grande.

Las tareas domésticas

Go to the *Capítulo 5* folder online to complete the Learning Module for *Vocabulario en contexto: Las tareas domésticas.*

PLAN DE ESTUDIO

◎ LEARN

- Interactive presentation: *Las tareas domésticas*
- Vocabulary tutorials
- *Entrevistas* video

APPLY ◎

- Activities
- *Entrevistas* video activities

PRÁCTICA COMUNICATIVA

5-10

Por la mañana. ¿En qué orden haces estas actividades por la mañana? Usa las siguientes expresiones para indicar el orden: **primero, luego, más tarde, después, finalmente.** Compara tus respuestas con las de tu compañero/a. ¿Hacen las mismas cosas y en el mismo orden?

Modelo

> Yo primero preparo el café. ¿Y tú?
>
> Yo primero hago la cama.

_____ lavar los platos

_____ preparar el café

_____ salir para la universidad

_____ desayunar

_____ secar los platos

_____ hacer la cama

5-11

Actividades en la casa. Pregúntale a tu compañero/a dónde hace estas cosas normalmente cuando está en casa.

Modelo

¿Dónde lavas la ropa?

Lavo la ropa en la lavandería. ¿Y tú?

1. dormir la siesta
2. escuchar música
3. ver la televisión
4. pasar la aspiradora
5. estudiar para un examen
6. hablar por teléfono con amigos/as

5-12

¡A compartir las tareas!

PRIMERA FASE. Ustedes van a compartir una casa el próximo año académico. Preparen una lista de todas las tareas domésticas que van a hacer.

SEGUNDA FASE. Discutan qué tareas va a hacer cada uno/a de ustedes según sus gustos. Finalmente, hagan un calendario de tareas y compártanlo con el resto de la clase.

Modelo

66 A mí me gusta lavar la ropa pero a mi compañera no le gusta. Por eso, yo voy a lavar la ropa los sábados por la tarde. 99

5-13

El agente de bienes raíces.

PRIMERA FASE. Mr. and Mrs. Mena and their two children live in San Salvador. They have decided to move to a larger place and they are talking to a real estate agent. Before listening, write down with your partner the kind of dwelling and the characteristics of the neighborhood they may be looking for.

SEGUNDA FASE. Now, as you listen, circle the letter next to the correct information and compare your answers with those of your classmate.

1. Los señores Mena quieren comprar…
   a. una casa.
   b. un apartamento.

2. El señor y la señora Mena prefieren vivir…
   a. en una buena zona.
   b. lejos de un parque.

3. El agente de bienes raíces…
   a. no sabe cómo ayudarlos.
   b. tiene una casa buena para ellos.

4. El agente dice que la casa del barrio La Mascota…
   a. cuesta mucho.
   b. tiene un buen precio.

5. El señor Mena dice que…
   a. los niños necesitan estar al aire libre para jugar.
   b. los niños no necesitan jugar al aire libre.

Warm-up for 5-11
Have students name rooms of a house associated with the following activities: *preparar la comida, pasar tiempo con los amigos, almorzar, cultivar vegetales, leer el periódico, ver televisión.*

Suggestion for 5-12
This activity provides a good opportunity to recycle *ir + a + infinitive.* Students work together on their lists and then role-play their conversation on the distribution of chores you may ask questions to elicit some ideas: *¿Quién va a preparar la comida? ¿Quién va a pasar la aspiradora?,* etc.

Audioscript for 5-13
Agente: *Señor Mena, creo que esta casa es una buena compra. Además, está cerca de su trabajo.*
Sra. Mena: *Sí, pero no me gusta la zona donde está. Nosotros preferimos comprar algo más pequeño, pero en una buena zona, especialmente por los niños.*
Agente: *Es que una casa con tres habitaciones, dos baños, sala, comedor y garaje para dos autos en un barrio bueno cuesta bastante… ¿Y un apartamento? Hay unos apartamentos nuevos, muy buenos, en la calle Sol.*
Sr. Mena: *Mire, preferimos una casa. Los niños necesitan estar al aire libre para jugar. Por eso queremos una casa con un jardín pequeño.*
Agente: *Pues hay una casa en la Colonia La Mascota que no es muy grande, 200 metros cuadrados, pero que tiene dos habitaciones grandes, una tercera habitación más pequeña y dos baños.*
Sr. Mena: *La Mascota es un barrio muy bueno. ¿La casa tiene jardín?*
Agente: *Sí, uno pequeño.*
Sra. Mena: *¿Y cuánto piden?*
Agente: *Déjeme ver… 1.200.000 colones, un buen precio para esa zona.*
Sr. Mena: *Pues, creo que debemos verla.*

Gramática en contexto

Talking about what you and others are doing and about how you and others feel

Expressing ongoing actions:
Present progressive

Go to the *Capítulo 5* **folder** online to complete the Learning Module for *Gramática en contexto:* Present progressive.

PLAN DE ESTUDIO

◎ LEARN
- Interactive presentation: Present progressive
- Grammar tutorials

APPLY ◎
- Activities
- Extra Practice

PRÁCTICA COMUNICATIVA

5-14

Un día ocupado.
Hoy es un día muy ocupado para la familia. Imagina lo que están haciendo ahora algunos miembros de tu familia.

Modelo

Creo que mi madre está trabajando en su oficina y mi padre está jugando al tenis.

Pues yo creo que mi...

5-15

La vida activa.

Túrnense para describir lo que está haciendo cada persona en estas escenas. Indiquen en qué lugar de la casa está cada uno de ellos. Luego hablen de lo que cada persona va a hacer más tarde. Finalmente, miren a sus compañeros de la clase y túrnense para describir lo que están haciendo algunos de ellos.

Modelo

> Rodrigo y Soledad están cantando en una fiesta. Están en la terraza.
>
> Después van a bailar y conversar con sus amigos.

Rodrigo   Soledad

Arturo

Pepe

Catalina

Carlos

Gonzalo

Standard 3.1
Students reinforce and further their knowledge of other disciplines through the foreign language. In activity **5-16**, students use the information in the photos and their knowledge of Hispanic cultures to figure out which cultural activity each photo depicts. Instructors will provide additional cultural information. The information they gain through this activity, as well as the skill of focusing on cultural information in visual material, may be useful to them in their courses in art, history, and other disciplines.

Suggestion for 5-16
You may divide the class into groups of 3 or 4 and assign one photo to each group. To make the activity more communicative, students should interact with classmates in other groups.

Follow-up for 5-16
You may wish to have students repeat this activity with photos of places and celebrations they bring from home, or with culturally relevant photos that you bring to class or that are in the chapter. They can find information in the *Enfoque cultural*.

Tech tip for *Situaciones*
You may want to assign partners and have pairs create mini-skits using MediaShare, the video-posting feature online.

Lugares y actividades.

Mira las siguientes fotografías de celebraciones y descríbele a tu compañero/a dos o tres actividades que las personas están haciendo en una de las fotos. Tu compañero/a va a hacer lo mismo (*the same*) con otra fotografía.

Situaciones

1

ROLE A. Your best friend calls to invite you to go out. Respond that you and your housemates are busy cleaning the apartment. Say what chores each of you is doing.

ROLE B. Call your best friend to invite her/him to go out with you. Ask what your friend and her/his roommates are doing. Ask if your friend can go out later (**más tarde**).

2

ROLE A. There is a big family gathering at your aunt's house today, but you are away at school. Call and greet the family member who answers the phone. Explain that you cannot attend, and express your regret for not being there. Ask how everyone is and what each family member is doing at the moment.

ROLE B. You are at a big family gathering today. A family member calls to say he/she cannot attend. Answer the phone. Greet the caller and answer his/her questions. Finally, tell the caller that everyone says hello (**todos te mandan saludos**) and say good-bye.

Describing physical and emotional states:
Expressions with *tener*

Go to the *Capítulo 5* [folder] online to complete the Learning Module for *Gramática en contexto:* Expressions with *tener*.

PLAN DE ESTUDIO

 LEARN
- Interactive presentation: Expressions with *tener*
- Grammar tutorials

APPLY
- Activities
- Extra Practice

PRÁCTICA COMUNICATIVA

5-17

Asociaciones.

Pregúntale a tu compañero/a lo que hace cuando tiene:

1. sed.
2. prisa.
3. suerte.
4. mucho frío.
5. hambre.

Modelo

¿Qué haces cuando tienes sueño?

Cuando tengo sueño siempre duermo.

Online prep for students
Students will have completed the Learning Module for Expressions with *tener* before coming to class. This includes the Interactive presentation and corresponding Apply activities.

Suggestion for Expressions with *tener*
Personalize these expressions as follows: *¿Tienes calor en este momento? ¿Tienes sed? ¿Qué tomas cuando tienes sed? ¿A qué hora tienes sueño generalmente?* Ask other students about their classmates' answers.

Suggestion
You may wish to explain that *mucha prisa* is the Spanish equivalent of being in a rush/great hurry. Provide an example: *Son las ocho menos cinco y Emilio está corriendo por el pasillo para llegar a su clase de español. Hay un examen a las ocho y no quiere llegar tarde. Emilio tiene mucha prisa.*
Review *ser* and *estar* with *frío* and *caliente* versus *tener frío/calor.* Visuals will be helpful.

5-18

¿Qué están haciendo, dónde están y cómo se sienten?

PRIMERA FASE. Túrnense y describan qué están haciendo las personas en los dibujos, dónde está(n) y cómo se sienten cada una de ellas.

Modelo   **" *El padre y su hijo están durmiendo en el sofá. Tienen sueño.* "**

1. La familia está comiendo en un restaurante. Tienen hambre y sed.

2. Estos niños están en casa solos por la noche. Escuchan un ruido. Tienen mucho miedo.

3. Esta mujer está esperando el autobús. Es invierno. Tiene mucho frío.

4. Estos hombres están trabajando en la calle. Tienen calor y probablemente tienen sed.

SEGUNDA FASE. Respondan a las siguientes preguntas sobre las escenas de la *Primera fase*.

1. ¿Cuál de los dibujos describe mejor cómo se sienten ustedes en este momento?

2. ¿Qué dibujo refleja (*reflects*) el clima de su región en diciembre?

3. ¿A qué hora se sienten ustedes como las personas del dibujo del modelo?

Suggestion for 5-19
Segunda fase
You may wish to have pairs present their most striking difference to the class to serve as the starting point for additional interaction using expressions with *tener*.

5-19

Estados físicos y estados de ánimo (moods).

PRIMERA FASE. Termina las siguientes ideas y, luego, compara tus respuestas con las de tu compañero/a para ver si tienen muchas en común. Usa expresiones con **tener.**

1. Generalmente, cuando mis hermanos y yo hacemos una barbacoa, nosotros...

2. Cuando mi madre pasa mucho tiempo limpiando nuestra casa, ella. . .

3. En las mañanas de invierno, yo siempre...

4. Cuando yo leo un libro aburrido, siempre...

5. Inmediatamente yo... cuando llego a casa y mi esposo está preparando mi plato favorito.

SEGUNDA FASE. Usando tus apuntes de la *Primera fase,* escribe una semejanza y una diferencia entre tu compañero/a y tú.

Situaciones

Tech tip for *Situaciones*
You may want to film themselves and post their presentations using the MediaShare feature online.

1

ROLE A. You share an apartment with a messy friend. Complain to him/her that: a) his/her books, backpack, etc., are always all over the living room; b) he/she uses a lot of dishes, but never washes them; c) soft drinks bottles (**botellas para refrescos**) are always on the table; and d) he/she makes a lot of noise (**ruido**) during the night and you can't sleep.

ROLE B. The friend with whom you share an apartment has some complaints about you. Apologize and explain that you: a) don't pick up your books or wash the dishes because you are always in a rush to do homework; b) drink a lot of soft drinks because you are always thirsty; and c) go to bed late because you're not sleepy before midnight or later and also because you're scared at night. Say as convincingly as you can that you are going to be more careful in the future.

2

ROLE A. You are staying at a hotel. You call the front desk and say the following: a) You are very tired, but you cannot sleep because the people in the next room are making a lot of noise (**ruido**); you are cold and need more blankets (**mantas**); and c) you want to know what time the dining room opens because you are always hungry in the morning.

ROLE B. You work at the front desk in a hotel. A guest calls you with two complaints and a question. Be as sympathetic and helpful as possible in responding to the guest.

Online prep for students
Students will have completed the Learning Module for Direct object nouns and pronouns online. This includes the Interactive presentation and Apply activities. See Instructor's Resources for Supplementary Activities.

Tech Tip for Direct object nouns and pronouns
You may want to project the images from the Learning Module in class and have students identify the direct object nouns in the photos by asking questions using *¿Qué?;* e.g., *El padre lava los platos. ¿Qué lava el padre? (Lava) los platos. Los niños secan los platos. ¿Qué secan los niños? (Secan) los platos. Ellas preparan la comida. ¿Qué preparan? (Preparan) la comida.* Ask questions using *¿Quién?* and *¿A quién?* with the photo of the grandmother and child, e.g., *La abuela cuida a la niña. ¿Quién cuida a la niña? ¿A quién cuida la abuela? (Cuida) a la niña.* For additional practice with *¿A quién?*, have one student look at another and ask questions, e.g., *Juan, mira a María. ¿A quién mira Juan? (Mira) a María.*

Suggestion
To practice direct object pronouns, distribute some of your classroom items among the students and then ask questions: *¿Tienes mi lápiz? Sí, lo tengo./No, no lo tengo. Y tú, ¿tienes mi libro?* Ask students if they use certain household items, e.g., *¿Usas la aspiradora en tu casa? Sí, la uso./No, no la uso. ¿Y el horno microondas?* Help them if necessary. You may also ask if they eat certain items, e.g., *¿Comes cereal en el desayuno… ? Sí, lo como. ¿Y, frutas? Si tienes frío, ¿bebes chocolate caliente?* Introduce *me* afterwards by asking *¿Me ves? ¿Me escuchas?*, and then guide students to ask each other the same questions to practice both *me* and *te*. During the rest of the course be sure to integrate direct object pronouns into regular speech.

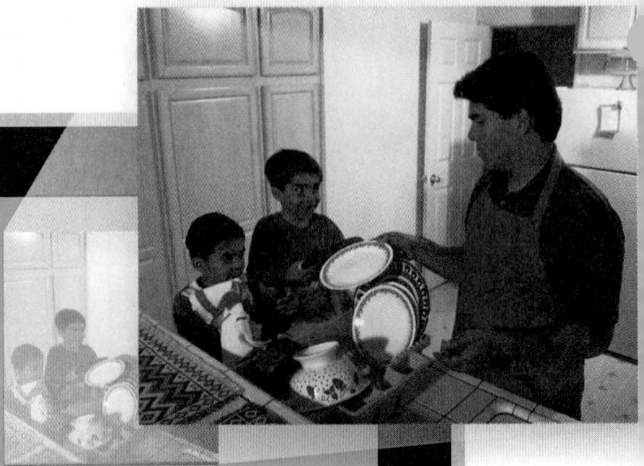

Avoiding repetition in speaking and writing:
Direct object nouns and pronouns

Go to the *Capítulo 5* folder online to complete the Learning Module for *Gramática en contexto:* Direct object nouns and pronouns.

PLAN DE ESTUDIO

LEARN
- Interactive presentation: Direct object nouns and pronouns
- Grammar tutorials

APPLY
- Activities
- Extra Practice

PRÁCTICA COMUNICATIVA

5-20

¿Qué es lógico?

PRIMERA FASE. Mira el dibujo en la página siguiente y asocia las situaciones con las acciones más lógicas.

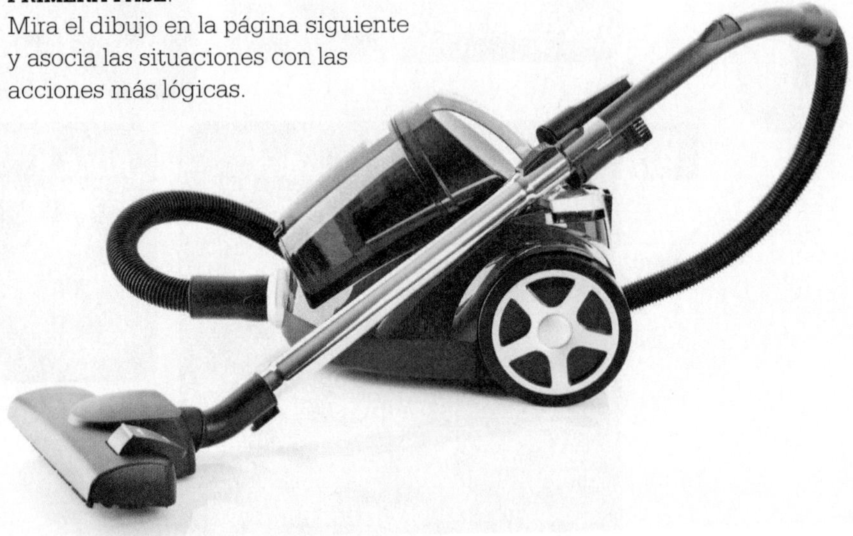

SITUACIÓN	ACCIÓN
1. _b_ Las camas están sin hacer.	**a.** Los hijos los van a ordenar.
2. _d_ La ropa está seca.	**b.** La madre las hace después de leer el periódico.
3. _a_ Los dormitorios están desordenados.	**c.** El padre las va a limpiar.
4. _f_ El aire acondicionado no funciona.	**d.** La hija va a plancharla.
5. _c_ Las ventanas están sucias.	**e.** Los hijos lo van a organizar y limpiar.
6. _e_ No pueden poner el auto en el garaje porque hay muchos muebles viejos y cajas con libros.	**f.** El hijo mayor lo va a reparar (*fix*).

 SEGUNDA FASE. Dile a tu compañero/a cuáles de las afirmaciones de la *Primera fase* describen mejor tu apartamento o tu casa en este momento.

Suggestion for 5-20
Segunda fase
Encourage students to expand on their descriptions to each other. You may wish to have them share them with the class or with another pair.

5-21

Mis responsabilidades en casa.

PRIMERA FASE. Averigua (*Find out*) si tu compañero/a es responsable de las siguientes tareas domésticas en su casa. Añade una más.

Modelo   ❝ lavar los platos ❞

> Lavas los platos

> Sí, los lavo. ¿Y tú?

1. sacar la basura   **4.** lavar las sábanas

2. ordenar el garaje   **5.** cortar el césped (*grass*)

3. limpiar la bañera   **6.** ...

SEGUNDA FASE. Comparen sus respuestas. Después díganle a otra pareja cuáles son las tareas domésticas que ustedes dos hacen y averigüen si ellos las hacen también.

Modelo

> Nosotros no lavamos los platos en casa porque tenemos lavaplatos. ¿Y ustedes los lavan?

> Sí, los lavamos y los secamos también.

5-22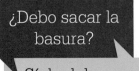

El apartamento de mi compañero/a. Vas a cuidar el apartamento de tu compañero/a por una semana, y quieres saber lo que debes y lo que puedes hacer allí.

Modelo

> ¿Debo sacar la basura?

> Sí, la debes sacar todos los días.

¿DEBO O NO DEBO?	SÍ	NO	¿PUEDO O NO PUEDO?	SÍ	NO
regar (*water*) las plantas	___	___	leer los libros	___	___
pasear al perro	___	___	usar los electrodomésticos	___	___
limpiar el apartamento	___	___	invitar a un amigo/una amiga	___	___
poner la alarma	___	___	hacer la tarea en la computadora	___	___
...	___	___	...	___	___

5-23

Los preparativos para la visita.

La familia Granados está muy ocupada porque espera la visita de unos parientes. Túrnense y contesten las preguntas de su compañero/a sobre lo que está haciendo cada miembro de la familia.

Modelo

¿Quién está preparando la comida?

La abuela está preparándola.

Suggestion for 5-23
You may wish to have students take turns asking the questions. To expand the activity, you may have pairs of students come up with additional questions (to ask other pairs) whose answers cannot be found in the drawing; e.g., *¿Qué plato está preparando el señor Granados? ¿Qué parientes vienen de visita?*, etc.

 5-24

Una mano amiga.

PRIMERA FASE. Tu compañero/a te va a hacer preguntas sobre tus relaciones con otras personas. Contesta, escogiendo a una de las personas de la lista.

mi madre	mi novio/a	mis abuelos
mi mejor amigo/a	mi padre	¿…?

Modelo

" ayudar económicamente "

¿Quién te ayuda económicamente?

Mis padres me ayudan económicamente.

1. querer mucho
2. escuchar en todo momento
3. llamar por teléfono con frecuencia
4. ayudar con los problemas
5. aconsejar (*advise*) cuando estás indeciso/a
6. entender siempre

Suggestions for 5-24
Have students do *Primera fase* in pairs, taking note of similarities and differences. As a follow-up, pairs can get together in small groups and share their answers to both parts of the activity.

SEGUNDA FASE. Dile a tu compañero/a lo que haces por las siguientes personas. Indica en qué circunstancias lo haces.

Modelo ❝ tu amigo/a ❞

> Lo/La ayudo cuando está cansado/a.

> Y yo lo/la escucho cuando tiene problemas en el trabajo.

1. tu papá
2. tu mamá
3. tu novio/a
4. tus vecinos (_neighbors_)
5. tu compañero/a de cuarto
6. tu mejor amigo/a

To assist a customer in a store:

¿Qué desea? _What would you like?_ (lit., _What do you desire?_)

¿En qué puedo ayudarlo/la? _How can I help you?_

To request a product:

Quisiera… _I would like …_

¿Podría ver…? _Could I see …?_

¿Podría mostrarme…? _Could you show me …?_

 Click on the icon to listen to a conversation with these expressions.

En directo

Situaciones

1

ROLE A. You have to buy a bed for your new apartment. You have picked one out, but you need the store to deliver (**entregar**) it. Arrange a day and time with the salesperson.

ROLE B. You are a salesperson at a mattress store. A customer has bought a bed and needs to have it delivered (**entregar**). The delivery service is not available on the day and time the customer suggests, so negotiate a more suitable time.

2

ROLE A. You and your brother/sister have to do some chores at home. Since you are older, you tell your sibling three or four things that he/she has to do. Be prepared to respond to complaints and questions.

ROLE B. You and your older brother/sister have to do some chores at home. Because you are younger, you get some orders from your sibling about what you have to do. You do not feel like working, and you especially do not like being bossed around, so respond to everything you hear with a complaint or a question.

Pointing out and identifying people and things:

Demonstrative adjectives and pronouns

Go to the *Capítulo 5* [folder] online to complete the Learning Module for *Gramática en contexto:* Demonstrative adjectives and pronouns.

PLAN DE ESTUDIO

◎ LEARN
- Interactive presentation: Demonstrative adjectives and pronouns
- Grammar tutorials

APPLY ◎
- Activities
- Extra Practice

PRÁCTICA COMUNICATIVA

5-25

Cerca, relativamente cerca o lejos. Decide cuál de las opciones debes usar según el lugar donde se encuentran los siguientes objetos. Compara tus respuestas con las de tu compañero/y explica la razón de tu preferencia.

Cerca de ustedes

1. __a__ mesa es de Honduras.   **a.** Esta   **b.** Esa   **c.** Aquella

2. __a__ cuadros también son de Honduras.   **a.** Estos   **b.** Esos   **c.** Aquellos

Relativamente cerca de ustedes

3. __b__ sofá es muy grande.   **a.** Este   **b.** Ese   **c.** Aquel

4. __b__ alfombra tiene unos colores muy alegres.   **a.** Esta   **b.** Esa   **c.** Aquella

Lejos de ustedes

5. __c__ espejo es nuevo.   **a.** Este   **b.** Ese   **c.** Aquel

6. __c__ lámparas son antiguas.   **a.** Estas   **b.** Esas   **c.** Aquellas

Online prep for students
Students will have completed the Learning Module for Demonstrative adjectives and pronouns online. See content online and Instructor's Resources for Supplementary Activities.

Suggestion
To introduce demonstratives, point to objects in class, relating demonstrative adjectives to their location and stressing the demonstrative adjectives as you speak: *Este libro es mi libro de español. Ese cuaderno es su cuaderno de ejercicios, ¿no? Aquellas mochilas son de los estudiantes.* Walk around the room to show how demonstratives change in relation to the speaker and the person spoken to.

Suggestion
As you walk around the classroom pointing to different objects, you may introduce the words *aquí, acá, allí,* and *allá* along with the corresponding demonstrative adjective.

Note
Since the use of accent marks with demonstrative pronouns is optional (see *Real Academia de la Lengua Española,* 1999), they are not used in *Unidos.* You may wish to tell students that they may see demonstrative pronouns with written accent marks in pre-1999 publications.

Note for 5-25
This activity heightens students' metalinguistic awareness by having them think and talk about the language and not just memorize rules. Metalinguistic talk, termed "languaging" by researchers (e.g., Swain, 2006) in second language acquisition, has been shown to contribute to language learning.

5-26

En una mueblería en Managua. Tu compañero/a y tú deciden vivir juntos/as en Nicaragua y van a una mueblería para comprar muebles y accesorios. Usen las palabras y frases siguientes para hablar sobre lo que ven. Sigan el modelo.

bonito/a

feo/a

(no) me gusta(n)

cómodo/a

caro/a

me encanta(n)

Modelo

¿Te gusta el sofá?

¿Cuál? ¿Aquel sofá verde?

No, ese sofá azul.

Sí, me encanta.

5-27

Descripciones. Piensa en tres objetos o muebles y el lugar de la casa dónde están. Tu compañero/a va a hacerte preguntas para adivinar qué mueble u objeto es.

Modelo

Este mueble está generalmente en el comedor.

¿Es grande?

Puede ser grande o pequeño.

¿Lo usamos para comer?

Sí.

Es la mesa.

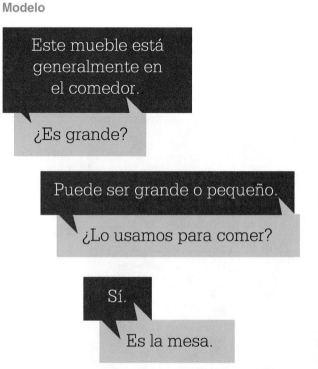

Situaciones

Suggestion for first *Situación*
Students should use *ese apartamento* to refer to the first apartment (the one they saw before) and *este apartamento* or *este* to refer to the pictures of the apartment they are looking at now.

1

ROLE A. You want to rent a nice apartment. The assistant to the property manager of several apartment complexes has already shown you pictures of one apartment (**ese apartamento**) and is now showing you pictures of a second one (**este apartamento**). Discuss with the assistant a) the rent (**el alquiler**); b) the number of rooms; and c) the facilities of both apartments, such as the laundry room (**lavandería**), garage, and pool. Say which of the two apartments you want to see and explain why.

ROLE B. You work in the property management office for several apartment complexes. You have already shown a customer pictures of one apartment (**ese apartamento**) and now are showing pictures of a second one (**este apartamento**). Answer his/her questions by saying that a) the rent of the first apartment is $900 per month and the second one is $1,100; b) both apartments have two bedrooms; and c) the first apartment comes with a one-car garage, while this one has a two-car garage. Also tell him/her the advantages of each of the two apartments.

2

ROLE A. Your parents have just moved to a house in a different neighborhood. You are visiting them and you ask your younger brother/sister to tell you about the people who live next to you (**esta casa**), the people in the house across the street (**esa casa**), and the ones in the big house at the end of the block (**aquella casa**).

ROLE B. Your older brother/sister is home for a visit and wants to know about the people in your new neighborhood. Answer your sibling's questions.

ESCUCHA

 5-28 👥 [Presentational]

Preparación. Vas a escuchar la descripción de una casa. Antes de escuchar, piensa en las casas que conoces y prepara una lista de cuatro cuartos y de tres objetos (muebles, aparatos eléctricos o accesorios) que esperas encontrar en cada uno de los cuartos. Compártela con la clase.

5-29 🔊 [Interpretive]

Escucha. Listen to the different statements about the location of pieces of furniture and objects. Indicate whether each statement is true (**Cierto**) or false (**Falso**) according to the drawing.

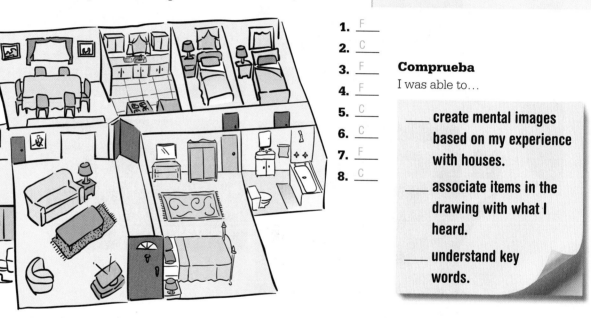

1. F
2. C
3. F
4. F
5. C
6. C
7. F
8. C

ESTRATEGIA

Create mental images

You have already learned that visual cues can increase your listening comprehension. For example, seeing the pictures or objects that a speaker refers to can help you understand what is being said. You can also create mental pictures by using your imagination or by making associations with familiar things or experiences. As you listen, practice creating mental images to help you develop your listening skills in Spanish.

Comprueba

I was able to…

____ create mental images based on my experience with houses.

____ associate items in the drawing with what I heard.

____ understand key words.

 **5-30** 👥 [Interpersonal]

Un paso más. Descríbele tu vivienda (número de cuartos, colores, muebles, etc.) a un compañero/una compañera. Él/Ella va a tomar notas para describirle tu vivienda a otra persona de la clase. Comprueba si la información es correcta. Luego, intercambien roles.

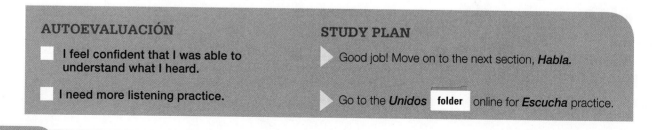

AUTOEVALUACIÓN

☐ I feel confident that I was able to understand what I heard.

☐ I need more listening practice.

STUDY PLAN

▶ Good job! Move on to the next section, *Habla*.

▶ Go to the *Unidos* [folder] online for *Escucha* practice.

HABLA

5-31 [Presentational]

Preparación. Necesitas alquilar un apartamento. Escribe algunas características esenciales y algunas secundarias del apartamento que necesitas. Compártelas con la clase.

5-32 [Interpretive/Interpersonal]

Habla.

Tu mejor amigo/a y tú estudian en San Salvador este año y quieren alquilar un apartamento. Lean los anuncios y decidan qué apartamento prefieren y por qué. Hablen sobre las ventajas y desventajas de uno u otro.

ALQUILERES

1. Se alquila condominio residencial privado, 3er nivel, 2 dormitorios, 1 baño, cuarto y baño, empleada, cocina con despensa, sala y comedor separados, garaje 2 carros, área recreación niños. SVC 4.500 vigilancia incluida. 22 24 46 30.

2. Alquilo apartamento cerca de centro comercial. Transporte público a la puerta. Ideal para profesionales. 1 dormitorio, 1 baño con jacuzzi, con muebles y electro-domésticos, terraza, sistema de seguridad, garaje doble. SVC 7.500. Tfno. 22 65 16 92.

3. Alquilo apartamento, cerca zona universitaria. 3 dormitorios. 1ra planta. Ideal para estudiantes. (SVC 1.800) Contactar al 22 35 37 83.

4. Alquilo preciosa habitación en casa particular. Semi-amueblada. Amplia, enorme clóset, cable gratis. Alimentación opcional. Información al teléfono 22 63 28 07.

5-33 [Interpersonal]

Un paso más. Ya que (*Since*) saben qué apartamento les gusta más, tienen que dar el próximo paso (*next step*). Conversen para decidir lo siguiente:

1. ¿Por qué es este apartamento el favorito de ustedes?

2. ¿Qué preguntas quieren hacerle al dueño del apartamento para obtener más información?

ESTRATEGIA

Plan what you want to say

Speaking consists of more than knowing the words and structures you need. You also have to know what you want to say. Planning what you want to say—both the information you want to ask for or convey and the language you will need to express yourself—before you start to speak will make your speech more accurate and also more coherent.

Comprueba

In my conversation…

___ **I was able to convey my preferences.**

___ **I asked appropriate questions.**

___ **I gave relevant responses.**

___ **I was able to come to an agreement with my partner.**

En directo

To find out who is answering your call:
¿Con quién hablo? *Who is this?*

To request to talk with someone specific:
¿Está… [nombre de la persona], por favor?
Is … [person's name] there, please?

Deseo hablar con… [nombre de la persona].
I would like to speak with … [person's name].

 Click on the icon to listen to a conversation with these expressions.

AUTOEVALUACIÓN

☐ I feel confident that I communicated successfully.

☐ I need more speaking practice.

STUDY PLAN

▶ Good job! Move on to the next section, *Lee.*

▶ Go to the *Unidos* [folder] online for *Habla* practice.

LEE

Suggestion for 5-34
You may wish to have students correct the false statements so that students articulate what they know about the topic.

5-34  [Presentational]

Preparación. ¿Qué sabes sobre el tema? Indica si las afirmaciones son ciertas (**C**) o falsas (**F**). Luego, escribe tu opinión sobre este tema en un párrafo y preséntalo a la clase.

1. ___C___ Hoy en día muchos jóvenes viven con sus padres después de graduarse de la universidad.

2. ___F___ Los jóvenes de hoy desean independizarse (*become independent*) de sus padres más que hace 10 o 15 años.

3. ___F___ Vivir en la casa de los padres es un fenómeno norteamericano solamente.

4. ___C___ El desempleo (*unemployment*) entre los jóvenes es una razón importante para vivir con los padres después de graduarse.

5. ___C___ Más hombres que mujeres viven con sus padres después de graduarse.

Answers for 5-35
1. Answers may vary.
2. *Es mucho más barato no tener que pagar un alquiler o comprar comida, los jóvenes disfrutan de la comodidad de la casa familiar, los padres hoy son más tolerantes.*
3. *basement dwellers, solteros parásitos, bamboccioni (bebés grandes)*
4. *Muchos padres están contentos de tener la compañía de los hijos. A veces los padres prefieren irse de la casa para independizarse de sus hijos.*

5-35 [Interpretive]

Lee.

El siguiente artículo describe un nuevo fenómeno social. Leélo y sigue las instrucciones.

1. En el primer párrafo, el autor del artículo presenta el nuevo fenómeno social. Explícalo con tus propias palabras.

2. El segundo párrafo presenta tres causas del fenómeno. ¿Cuáles son?

3. El tercer párrafo menciona los sobrenombres (*nicknames*) que se les dan a los adultos que viven con sus padres en varios países. ¿Cuáles son?

4. En el último párrafo se presenta la perspectiva de los padres. ¿Cuál es?

Estrategia

Inform yourself about a topic before you start to read

To get acquainted with a topic, you should think about what you already know, read something about it on the web (it is okay to read something in English), talk with people who know about the topic; a combination of these three approaches is the best preparation. The goal is to build your knowledge about the topic before you start to read. Then, when you read the text, try to apply that knowledge to support your comprehension.

Comprueba

I was able to…

___ **anticipate content related to the topic.**

___ **use the statistics to confirm my comprehension of the main ideas.**

___ **identify the two main reasons that adults live with their parents.**

___ **find other countries where the phenomenon is common.**

Un nuevo fenómeno social

No abandonar el nido (nest) familiar

Cada vez hay más adultos entre los 20 y los 34 años que viven en la casa de sus padres. En el pasado, esto era bastante normal en los países hispanos pero no en Estados Unidos donde, tradicionalmente, los jóvenes se independizaban más pronto. Según un estudio de la Oficina del Censo de Estados Unidos, en 2011 un 59% de los chicos entre 18 y 24 años y un 50% de las chicas vivían todavía en el domicilio familiar en comparación con el 53% y el 46%, respectivamente, en 2005.

Las causas principales de este fenómeno son variadas. Para algunos jóvenes es mucho más barato no tener que pagar un alquiler o comprar comida, sobre todo si no tienen un trabajo estable. Pero la razón para otros jóvenes es que disfrutan (enjoy) de la comodidad (comfort) de la casa familiar. Además, los padres hoy son más tolerantes que en el pasado, por eso los hijos no sienten la necesidad de irse.

Esta tendencia social no solo se limita a Estados Unidos, donde a estos jóvenes se les llama basement dwellers porque muchos tienen su habitación en el sótano de la casa, sino que se encuentra en todo el mundo. En América Latina los jóvenes solían vivir con los padres antes de casarse (get married), pero ahora hay muchos que después de casarse y de tener hijos continúan viviendo en la misma casa. En Japón a los hijos adultos que prefieren vivir en casa con sus padres les llaman solteros (unmarried) parásitos, y en Italia bamboccioni (bebés grandes).

Curiosamente, en Estados Unidos esta tendencia afecta más a los hombres que a las mujeres. El porcentaje de hombres de entre 25 y 34 años que viven con sus padres creció (grew) de un 14% en 2005 a un 19% en 2011 y de un 8% a un 10% para las mujeres en el mismo periodo.

¿Qué opinan los padres de esta situación? Muchos padres están contentos de tener la compañía de los hijos. Pero a veces la situación cambia y son los padres quienes tienen que irse de la casa para independizarse de sus hijos.

Suggestion for 5-36
To increase student
engagement with the activity,
you may wish to have the
groups share their results
with the class.

5-36   [Interpersonal]

Un paso más. Hablen sobre los temas siguientes y escriban sus respuestas en la tabla.

1. ¿Qué significa para ustedes independizarse de sus padres?

2. ¿Cuáles son las ventajas y desventajas de vivir con sus padres después de graduarse? ¿Bajo qué circunstancias es necesario vivir con ellos?

Ser independientes de los padres significa…	_____ no vivir con ellos _____ pagar todos nuestros gastos (teléfono, carro, apartamento, etc.) _____ hablar con ellos solamente 1–2 veces por semana _____ hablar con los amigos cuando necesitamos consejos (*advice*), no con ellos _____ (otro) _____
Ventajas de vivir con los padres	1. 2. 3.
Desventajas de vivir con los padres	1. 2. 3.

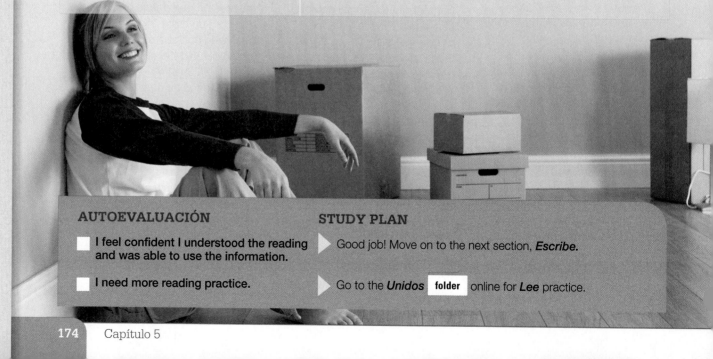

AUTOEVALUACIÓN

☐ I feel confident I understood the reading and was able to use the information.

☐ I need more reading practice.

STUDY PLAN

▶ Good job! Move on to the next section, *Escribe.*

▶ Go to the *Unidos* folder online for *Lee* practice.

ESCRIBE

5-37 Interpretive

Preparación. Lee los requisitos sobre el concurso (*contest*) *La casa ideal para las familias multigeneracionales* que apareció en el periódico *La Prensa* de Tegucigalpa, Honduras.

El diario *La Prensa* invita al público a participar en el concurso *La casa ideal para las familias multigeneracionales.*

Bases del concurso:

Los participantes deben enviar la siguiente información por correo electrónico al Comité de Selección de *La casa ideal para las familias multigeneracionales*:

1. información personal: nombre completo, dirección, teléfono y correo electrónico

2. un panfleto descriptivo de la casa para varias personas adultas y niños con la siguiente información: tamaño de la casa, número y nombre de las habitaciones, distribución del espacio, aparatos electrónicos y un dibujo o foto digital de la casa

Fecha límite: el 30 de marzo

Premio: Una computadora portátil de último modelo y alta resolución, con programas de alta capacidad y funcionalidad.

ESTRATEGIA

Select the appropriate content and tone for a formal description

To write a description using a formal tone, you will need to anticipate what your audience may know about the topic, including relevant details; adapt the language of your text to the level of your readership. If you wish to address your reader(s) directly, use **usted/ustedes**.

5-38 Presentational

Escribe. Decides participar en el concurso con un proyecto excepcional. Prepara un panfleto incluyendo toda la información que pide el concurso. Considera la cantidad de información necesaria y el tono apropiado para tus lectores, los miembros del Comité de Selección. ¡Buena suerte!

Comprueba

I was able to…

____ include relevant details about the topic.

____ provide the appropriate amount of information.

____ use the appropriate form to address the audience.

5-39 Interpersonal

Un paso más. Habla con tu compañero/a sobre tu panfleto. Descríbanse sus proyectos y averigüen lo siguiente:

1. Tamaño de la casa

2. Estilo de la decoración

3. Características originales

Suggestion for 5-38
Remind students that they are writing this pamphlet for a jury of experts. Depending on your students' skill, you may wish to have them do this writing task in pairs. If possible, students with artistic skills should be paired with those who may not be so artistic. As indicated in item 3 in the announcement, a drawing or digital picture of the house is optional. If some of your students are skilled in computer design, invite them to share their *La casa ideal para las familias multigeneracionales* with the class.

Suggestion for 5-39
Before doing *Un paso más* have students check their texts in relation to the following items that you may write on the board:

1. la claridad de ideas
2. la cantidad de la información
3. el tono apropiado para un comité de periodistas
4. la precisión gramatical

AUTOEVALUACIÓN

☐ I feel confident I successfully communicated my ideas in writing.

☐ I need more writing practice.

STUDY PLAN

▶ Good job!

▶ Go to the *Unidos* [folder] online *Escribe* practice.

ENFOQUE *cultural*

NICARAGUA

Masaya, Nicaragua es conocido como la cuna del folclore nicaragüense. Es el centro de la artesanía en Nicaragua.

EL SALVADOR

Las pupusas son la comida nacional de El Salvador. Hay pupuserías por todas partes del país donde se pueden saborear estas delicias.

HONDURAS

Los garífuna son un grupo étnico de origen africano con una gran presencia en el golfo de Honduras. Mantienen una cultura rica en ritmo, música y baile.

La geografía espectacular de Nicaragua, El Salvador y Honduras

Go to the *Enfoque cultural* [folder] in *Capítulo 5* of the online component to learn more about this region.

PLAN DE ESTUDIO

◎ **LEARN**
- Interactive presentation: *La geografía espectacular de Nicaragua, El Salvador y Honduras*

◎ **APPLY**
- Activities

PRÁCTICA COMUNICATIVA

5-40 **Usa la información.** Tienes $300.000 y quieres comprar una casa en Nicaragua, Honduras o El Salvador. Investiga en Internet y busca la mejor casa, apartamento o propiedad rural que puedes comprar con ese dinero. Prepara un afiche (*poster*) para mostrar en la clase. Debes incluir: localización, tipo de propiedad, características más importantes de la propiedad y su precio. Incluye también información adicional de interés.

En este capítulo...

Comprueba lo que sabes

Go to the *Comprueba lo que sabes* folder online to review what you have learned in this chapter. Practice with the following:

Vocabulary flashcards	Games	Oral Practice	Practice Test/ Study Plan	Video en contexto

Vocabulario

La arquitectura
el alquiler
el apartamento
el edificio
el estilo
las ruinas
la vivienda

En una casa
el aire acondicionado
el armario
el baño
la basura
la calefacción
la chimenea
la cocina
el comedor
el cuarto
la escalera
el garaje
la habitación
la lavandería
el pasillo
la piscina
el piso
la planta baja
la sala
la terraza

Los muebles y accesorios
la alfombra
la butaca
la cama
la cómoda
la cortina
el cuadro
el espejo
la lámpara
el sofá

Los electro- domésticos
la aspiradora
la lavadora

el lavaplatos
el (horno)
   microondas
el/la radio
el refrigerador
la secadora
el ventilador

Para la cama
la almohada
la manta
la sábana

En el baño
la bañera
la ducha
el inodoro
el jabón
el lavabo
la toalla

En la cocina
la estufa
el fregadero
el plato

En el jardín
la barbacoa
el césped
la hoja

Los lugares
las afueras
el barrio
la calle
el centro
cerca (de)
lejos (de)
el pueblo
la zona

Las descripciones
cómodo/a
limpio/a

ordenado/a
seco/a
sucio/a

Verbos
ayudar
barrer
cocinar
cortar
creer
doblar
limpiar
ordenar
pasar la aspiradora
planchar
preparar
recoger (j)
regar (ie)
sacar
tender (ie)

Palabras útiles
la desventaja
el trabajo
la ventaja
la vista

Los números ordinales
primero / primer
segundo
tercero / tercer
cuarto
quinto
sexto
séptimo
octavo
noveno
décimo

Expresiones con tener
tener... calor
cuidado
frío
hambre

miedo
prisa
razón
sed
sueño
suerte

Pronombres de objeto directo
me
te
lo
la
nos
os
los
las

Adjetivos demostrativos
este / estos
esta / estas
ese / esos
esa / esas
aquel / aquellos
aquella / aquellas

Pronombres desmostrativos
este / estos
esta / estas
ese / esos
esa / esas
aquel / aquellos
aquella / aquellas
esto
eso
aquello

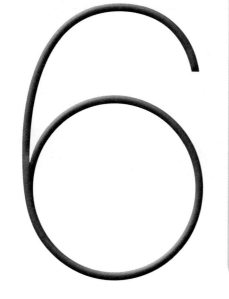

¿Qué te gusta comprar?

Learning OBJECTIVES

You will:

- learn new vocabulary related to clothing, prices, and shopping
- learn the preterit forms of regular verbs and *ir* and *ser*
- learn the forms of indirect object pronouns
- use *gustar* and similar verbs to express preferences
- learn more uses of *ser* and *estar*
- connect new information about Venezuela and Simón Bolívar to what you already know

Learning OUTCOMES

You will be able to:

- talk about shopping and clothes
- talk about events in the past
- indicate to whom or for whom an action takes place
- express likes and dislikes
- describe people, objects, and events
- compare Simón Bolívar and Venezuela with leaders in the history of your own country

---

VENEZUELA

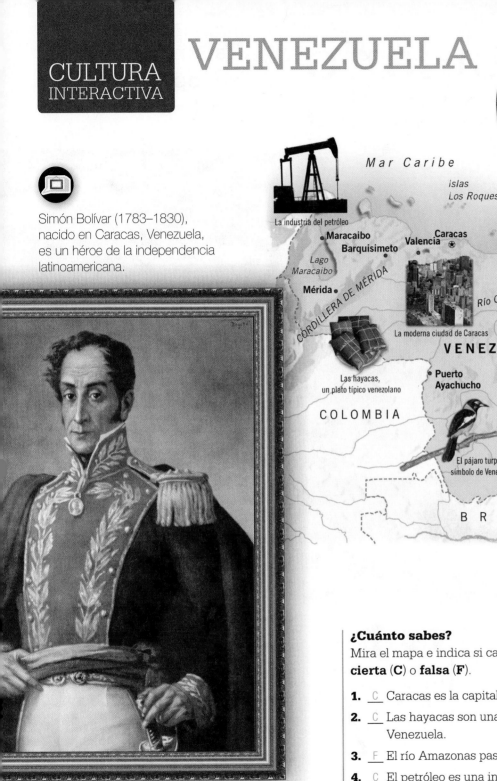

Simón Bolívar (1783–1830), nacido en Caracas, Venezuela, es un héroe de la independencia latinoamericana.

Mar Caribe

Islas Los Roques

OCÉANO ATLÁNTICO

Isla Margarita

La industria del petróleo

Maracaibo
Barquisimeto
Valencia
Caracas
Barcelona
Maturín

Lago Maracaibo

Mérida

CORDILLERA DE MÉRIDA

Río Orinoco

Ciudad Bolívar
Ciudad Guayana

La moderna ciudad de Caracas

VENEZUELA

Salto Ángel

GUYANA

Las hayacas, un plato típico venezolano

Puerto Ayachucho

COLOMBIA

El pájaro turpial, símbolo de Venezuela

Salto Ángel

BRASIL

¿Cuánto sabes?

Mira el mapa e indica si cada afirmación es **cierta (C)** o **falsa (F)**.

1. _C_ Caracas es la capital de Venezuela.

2. _C_ Las hayacas son una comida típica de Venezuela.

3. _F_ El río Amazonas pasa por Venezuela.

4. _C_ El petróleo es una industria importante de Venezuela.

5. _F_ Caracas está cerca del océano Pacífico.

6. _F_ Panamá está al sur de Venezuela.

Cultura en línea

To learn more about Venezuela and the chapter theme, go to the *Cultura en línea* folder in the *Unidos* online component to view the *Vistas culturales* video and take a virtual art tour.

Online prep for students
Students will have completed the Learning Module for *Las compras* online before class. This includes the Interactive presentation and the corresponding Apply activities. See content online. You will find additional in-class activities in the Supplementary Activities folder online.

Tech tip for *Las compras*
Project the images from the online Learning Module in class and ask the following to review new vocabulary: *Esta foto es de un centro comercial. En todas las capitales del mundo hispano hay grandes almacenes, como, por ejemplo, Macro en Venezuela y El Corte Inglés en España. Ir a estos almacenes es como ir a un centro comercial.*

Suggestion for *Lengua*
Introduce and compare *quisiera* and *me gustaría*. Use the *De compras* dialogue from the online Learning Module as a model for students to create new interactions. Have students select a different item, substituting *me gustaría* for *quisiera*, and paying with a credit card instead of cash.

Suggestion
Explain that the currency of Venezuela is called the bolívar. Call students' attention to the name. In 2007 the *bolívar* was revalued by the government at a ratio of 1 to 1,000, and was renamed the *bolívar fuerte* (BsF) in 2008. The equivalent is approximately $1.00 = BsF 4.30, but the rate varies widely. You may wish to ask students to find the current equivalent to BsF 500 in dollars.

Suggestion for 6-1
Students should have no problem guessing the meaning of *juguetería, joyería,* and *zapatería*. Call their attention to the ending. Ask what would be sold in *una carnicería, una pescadería, una papelería*, etc.

Vocabulario en contexto

Talking about shopping and clothes

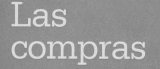

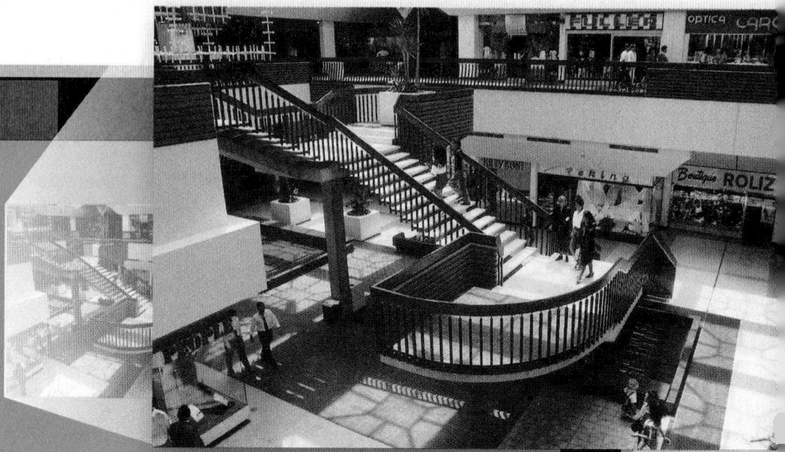

Las compras

Go to the *Capítulo 6* **folder** online to complete the Learning Module for *Vocabulario en contexto: Las compras.*

PLAN DE ESTUDIO

LEARN
- Interactive presentation: *Las compras*
- Vocabulary tutorials
- Pronunciation

APPLY
- Activities
- Pronunciation activities

PRÁCTICA COMUNICATIVA

6-1

¿Adónde van? Las siguientes personas necesitan comprar algunas cosas. Túrnense e indiquen a qué tienda deben ir. Después dile a tu compañero/a algo que necesitas comprar y pregúntale a qué tienda debes ir.

Modelo "Celia necesita un sofá para su nueva casa."
"*Pues tiene que ir a una mueblería.*"

1. María necesita unos libros para su clase de literatura.
2. Juan quisiera cocinar comida venezolana para sus amigos.
3. Rosa piensa comprar unos regalos para sus sobrinos.
4. Felipe necesita una cama para su cuarto.
5. Olga necesita unos zapatos nuevos para una entrevista de trabajo.
6. Catalina va a comprar un collar elegante para ir a una fiesta.

mueblería
juguetería
zapatería
supermercado
joyería
librería

LENGUA To soften requests, Spanish uses the forms **me gustaría** (instead of **me gusta**) and **quisiera** (instead of **quiero**). English does this with the phrase **would like.**
***Me gustaría/Quisiera* ir a ese almacén.**
I would like to go to that department store.

Suggestion for 6-2
Students saw the expression *Necesito comprar* in *Capítulo 1*. You may re-enter here *tener que* + *infinitive* to express obligation, which they have seen in *Capítulo 4*. This is also an opportunity to recycle *ir* + *a* + *infinitive/pensar* + *infinitive* that appeared in *Capítulos 3* and *4*.

6-2

¿Qué tienen que hacer? Ustedes tienen que hacer muchas cosas esta semana. Hablen de lo que necesitan comprar y decidan a qué tiendas van a ir.

Modelo **&&comprar zapatos para nuestro viaje 99**

> Necesitamos comprar unos zapatos elegantes para salir de noche.
> Podemos comprarlos en una zapatería en Venezuela.

1. preparar las maletas
2. comprar una guía turística
3. pagar el viaje
4. planear nuestras vacaciones en Isla de Margarita
5. leer blogs sobre Venezuela

Cultura

People in many cultures engage in some form of haggling (**regatear**), a business-like transaction between a customer and a vendor that has (usually unspoken) rules as to when, where, and how it is done. In Spanish-speaking countries, haggling is not expected or acceptable in a pharmacy, supermarket, restaurant, or governmental office, for example. However, people often haggle at outdoor markets.

Compara: ¿Se regatea en tu país? ¿En qué situaciones? ¿Alguna vez regateaste? ¿Cuánto te pedían por el producto? ¿Cuánto pagaste finalmente?

6-3

En el mercado tradicional.

PRIMERA FASE. Túrnense para comprar unos recuerdos (*souvenirs*) en un mercado tradicional en Caracas. Pregunten el precio de los siguientes productos. Regateen (*haggle*) para obtener un precio más barato.

Modelo

Quisiera comprar este collar. ¿Cuánto cuesta?

Cuesta 650 bolívares.

¡Uy, es muy caro! Lo compro por 600.

Pero, es muy bonito.

Sí, es muy bonito, pero no tengo suficiente dinero.

Bueno, está bien. Lo vendo por 600.

SEGUNDA FASE. Muestra tus compras a un compañero/a y explica qué es, para quién lo compras y cuánto cuesta.

Modelo ❝*Esto es un collar de plata para mi prima Isabel. Cuesta 400 bolívares.*❞

La ropa

Go to the *Capítulo 6* **folder** online to complete the Learning Module for *Vocabulario en contexto: La ropa.*

PLAN DE ESTUDIO

◎ LEARN
- Interactive presentation: *La ropa*
- Vocabulary tutorials

APPLY ◎
- Activities

PRÁCTICA COMUNICATIVA

6-4

¿Cuándo se usa? Túrnensey pregúntense qué prendas de vestir (*articles of clothing*) usan en cada situación.

Modelo ❝para venir a clase❞

¿Qué usas para venir a clase?

Uso unos vaqueros.

1. para ir a correr o al gimnasio
2. para ir a dormir
3. para ir a una fiesta
4. después de bañarte y antes de vestirte

Online prep for students
Students will have completed the Learning Module for *La ropa* online. This includes the Interactive presentation and corresponding Apply activities. See content online and Instructor's Resources for Supplementary Activities.

Suggestions for *La ropa*
You may use fashion magazines when introducing the vocabulary of clothing. Identify and describe each piece. Ask questions to check comprehension. Describe the clothes you're wearing and then comment on students' clothes: *¿De qué color es el vestido de… ? Es bonita la blusa de… , ¿no?* Use expressions such as *de lunares, de cuadros, de rayas,* and *de color entero/un solo color.*

Describe a student's clothing without mentioning his or her name. Other students guess who the person is.

You may introduce additional vocabulary such as: *ropa interior, de manga corta/ larga, bolsillo, de tacón alto, elegante.*

Suggestion for *La ropa*
Review vocabulary by commenting on clothing students are wearing: *Pedro lleva una camisa de cuadros. Es muy bonita. Y Juan, ¿lleva una camisa de cuadros? No, es de rayas. Le queda muy bien. No le queda ancha.* Introduce the word *vestido.*

Suggestion for *Las rebajas*
Explain *rebajas: A veces hay rebajas* (write word on the board) *muy buenas. ¿Saben ustedes qué es una rebaja? Pues si un reloj normalmente cuesta 50 dólares, en una rebaja pueden comprarlo por 40 dólares o menos.* Ask questions to check comprehension.

Use visuals and comprehensible input to review vocabulary. *¿Te pruebas la ropa en las tiendas? ¿Vas a las tiendas cuando hay rebajas? ¿Cuál es tu tienda favorita?* You may explain that the approximate equivalent of size 38 is an 8. Sizes 40, 42, and 44 are similar to sizes 10, 12, and 14, respectively.

Suggestion for 6-5
Encourage students to adapt the communicative situation modeled in *Otra conversación* to talk about other clothes-shopping scenarios.

Suggestion for 6-6
Before doing this activity, talk about the different parts of the body by pointing to yourself or to the people in the drawings. Call attention to the *Lengua* box. Then ask questions to relate clothing to parts of the body: *¿Qué lleva Marisa en la mano? ¿Cuántos aretes lleva Miguel en la oreja? ¿Qué tipo de zapatos lleva Sonia en los pies?*

Suggestion for 6-7
To help students' speech sound more natural, you may wish to review ways to express agreement/disagreement as they work together to solve the problems presented in the chart.

Encourage students to be creative and expand on their answers in this activity: *En el almacén El Encanto hay unos collares muy bonitos. ¿Por qué no miramos los collares allá?* Have them think of other gifts and come to a conclusion: *¿Le vamos a regalar una camisa? ¿Le interesan las zapatillas? ¿Qué le vamos a dar?* They can do this exercise in groups of 3 or 4.

6-5

Otra conversación. Con un compañero/a lee la conversación entre Marta y Ana. Después cambien la conversación para hablar de otra compra que hacen ustedes en una tienda de ropa.

> **LENGUA** The word **talla** is normally used when talking about clothing size; **número** refers to shoe size. **Tamaño** means size in all other contexts: **¿Cuál es tu número de zapatos?**
>
> The word **calzado** is used to express footwear in general. The verb **calzar** is also used to ask about someone's shoe size; **¿Qué número calzas? ¿Cuánto calzas?**

MARTA:	Las rebajas son magníficas. Mira esa falda de rayas. Está rebajada de 840 bolívares a 775.
ANA:	Las faldas de rayas no me quedan bien.
MARTA:	Bueno, si te queda mal, te pruebas otra.
	(Marta se prueba la falda.)
MARTA:	¿Qué piensas?
ANA:	Pienso que te queda ancha.
MARTA:	Es verdad. Voy a probarme una talla más pequeña.
	(Marta se prueba otra falda.)
ANA:	¡Esta te queda muy bien!

6-6

¿Qué ropa llevan?

PRIMERA FASE. Túrnense para describir la ropa que llevan algunas personas de la clase y adivinen (*guess*) quiénes son.

SEGUNDA FASE. Cuenten (*Count*) cuántas personas de la clase llevan los siguientes accesorios y prendas de vestir. Después comparen sus números.

1. aretes en las orejas _____

2. camisetas con el logotipo de la universidad _____

3. zapatillas de deporte _____

4. vaqueros rotos (*with holes*) _____

5. corbatas _____

6. collares de oro _____

> **LENGUA** Here is some useful vocabulary for the body (**el cuerpo**): **la cabeza** (*head*), **las orejas** (*ears*), **la nariz** (*nose*), **los brazos** (*arms*), **las manos** (*hands*), **las piernas** (*legs*), **los pies** (*feet*). You will learn more words related to parts of the body in *Capítulo 11*.

6-7

El cumpleaños de Nuria.
Ustedes van a una tienda para comprarle un regalo a una buena amiga, pero cada artículo que ven presenta un problema. Piensen en la solución.

ARTÍCULO	PROBLEMA	SOLUCIÓN
collar	Es muy caro.	*Debemos buscar uno más barato.*
impermeable	Le queda ancho.	
vaqueros	Son de poliéster.	
sudadera	Es pequeña.	
blusa	Las rayas son muy anchas.	
bolso	No es de cuero.	

¿Qué debo llevar?

Go to the *Capítulo 6* **folder** online to complete the Learning Module for *Vocabulario en contexto: ¿Qué debo llevar?*

PLAN DE ESTUDIO

◎LEARN
- Interactive presentation: *¿Qué debo llevar?*
- Vocabulary tutorials
- *Entrevistas* video

APPLY ◎
- Activities
- *Entrevistas* video activities

PRÁCTICA COMUNICATIVA

6-8

¿Frío o calor? Túrnense y pregunten qué ropa o accesorios de la lista usan en las siguientes situaciones. Añadan (*Add*) otras opciones en sus respuestas.

el sombrero	las botas
el traje de baño	los guantes
los pantalones cortos	el suéter

Modelo 66 cuando llueve 99

¿Qué usas cuando llueve?

Uso un paraguas. ¿Y tú?

Uso un impermeable

1. para protegerte del sol
2. para las manos cuando hace frío
3. hace buen tiempo
4. para ir a la playa
5. cuando hace frío
6. para los pies en invierno

Online prep for students.
Students will have completed the Learning Module for *¿Qué debo llevar?* online. See content online and Instructor's Resources for Supplementary Activities.

Suggestion for *¿Qué debo llevar?*
Use visuals to illustrate weather expressions and clothes. Tell students what you wear in winter: *En el invierno, yo llevo un suéter y pantalones largos. Cuando hace mucho frío, me pongo un abrigo y unos guantes. A veces llevo una bufanda.* Ask yes/no and either/or questions to check understanding. Personalize by asking what students wear and do in winter and in summer.

Note
More weather-related terms are introduced in *Capítulo 7.*

Suggestion for 6-8
Recycle vocabulary of body parts that was presented before. You may ask: *¿Dónde se pone el sombrero?* Or *Llevamos un sombrero en... ¿Qué llevamos en los pies, las botas o los guantes? En los pies nos ponemos...*

Suggestions for 6-9
Point out Isla de Margarita on a map and explain that it is an island in the Caribbean, north of Venezuela, and that Canaima is in western Venezuela. You may also mention that the highest waterfall in the world, Salto Ángel, is there.
Students can expand their lists by describing the items. Have students plan a trip in another season, focusing on the different clothing they will need. Point out that there are only two seasons in Venezuela, dry (December to April) and rainy (May to November).

6-9

Vacaciones en Venezuela.

Tu amigo/a y tú van a pasar unas vacaciones en Venezuela. Escojan el plan que más les interesa y preparen una lista de la ropa y accesorios que van a necesitar. Presenten su plan a la clase.

Plan A. Quince días en Isla de Margarita. Por el día: ir a la playa; por la noche: ir a las discotecas.

Plan B. Tomar un curso de verano en la Universidad Central de Venezuela en Caracas. Por la mañana: clases de español; por las tardes: lugares de interés turístico.

Plan C. Explorar la fauna y flora de la región de Canaima. Por el día: caminar mucho; por las noches: estar en un campamento.

Modelo

" Vamos a ir a Isla de Margarita. Yo necesito un traje de baño y mi compañera necesita unos pantalones cortos. "

  6-10

Ropa para todos.
Cada uno/a debe comprar ropa para hacer unos regalos a tres personas diferentes de la lista siguiente. Explícale a tu compañero/a qué vas a comprar, dónde y para quién son estos regalos.

1. tu sobrina de seis años
2. tu mamá para el Día de la Madre
3. un amigo/una amiga que necesita ropa informal
4. tu padre para su cumpleaños
5. tu novio/a para el Día de los Enamorados

La Elegante

Todo lo que está de moda este verano

Ave. Andrés Bello
con 3ª Transversal,
Local B, 576 38 21

BARCELÓ
Las mejores camisas y guayaberas a los mejores precios

Segunda Avenida / N° 40
271.88.20

Almacenes Carrasco

Llévate tus jeans ahora
a los mejores precios del año

30% menos

Ave. Teresa de la Parra
Edificio Codazzi
al lado del Banco Federal
661.45.81

LOS REYES MAGOS

Grandes rebajas

Ropa infantil de calidad

Plaza de las Américas
Local Q-15
985 13 31

 **6-11**

Ropa para cada ocasión.

PRIMERA FASE. Tell your classmate what you would wear on the following occasions: *una fiesta elegante* and *una fiesta informal.*

 **SEGUNDA FASE.** Listen to the conversation and indicate [✓] the clothes and the event mentioned.

ROPA	EVENTO
✓ ropa elegante	_____ entrevista de trabajo
_____ falda y chaqueta	_____ reunión de jóvenes
_____ traje pantalón y blusa	_____ excursión de fin de semana
_____ pantalones cortos y camiseta	✓ fiesta formal

Note for 6-10
A *guayabera* is a loose short- or long-sleeved man's shirt that is not tucked in. It is worn in place of a shirt or jacket and tie in areas where the weather is very hot.

Warm-up for 6-11
As a pre-listening activity, have students in groups of 4 describe the clothes they wear for parties, classes, family reunions, weddings, and graduations.

Audioscript for 6-11
Berta: *Alfredo, dime una cosa, ¿vas a la fiesta en la embajada esta noche?*
Alfredo: *Sí. Tú también vas, ¿verdad?*
Berta: *Sí, y no sé qué me voy a poner. Supongo que es formal.*
Alfredo: *Sí, es formal. Yo voy a ir con un traje azul y mi hermana va a llevar un traje de la diseñadora Carolina Herrera, sencillo pero elegante.*
Berta: *¡Qué bien! Yo no sé todavía qué me voy a poner. ¿Y a qué hora van a ir?*
Alfredo: *A las nueve más o menos.*
Berta: *Bueno, nos vemos entonces.*

Gramática en contexto

Talking about the past, personal preferences, and descriptions

Talking about the past:
Preterit tense of regular verbs

Go to the *Capítulo 6* **folder** online to complete the Learning Module for *Gramática en contexto:* Preterit tense of regular verbs.

PLAN DE ESTUDIO

◎ LEARN
- Interactive presentation: Preterit tense of regular verbs
- Grammar tutorials

APPLY ◎
- Activities
- Extra Practice

PRÁCTICA COMUNICATIVA

6-12

Ayer yo...

PRIMERA FASE. En el cuadro de la página siguiente, marca (✓) tus actividades de ayer y añade una actividad en cada columna.

Online prep for students
Students will have completed the Learning Module for Preterit tense of regular verbs online. This includes the Interactive presentation and corresponding Apply activities. See content online and Instructor's Resources for Supplementary Activities.

Note
This chapter presents the preterit tense of regular verbs and of *ser* and *ir*. The preterit of irregular and reflexive verbs is in *Capítulo 7*.

Suggestion
Describe what you generally do each morning and mention how today differed from the routine: *Normalmente desayuno en casa, pero hoy desayuné en la cafetería. Generalmente tomo té, pero hoy tomé un café y conversé con unos estudiantes* (write preterit forms on the board). *Después caminé a mi oficina y hablé por teléfono.* Ask questions to check understanding and then ask personal questions using the verb forms on the board: *¿Tomaste café en el desayuno? Y tú, ¿tomaste café o té? ¿Desayunaste en casa o en un café?* If necessary, write the verb forms on the board. Repeat information provided by students using the *él/ella* verb form: *Pedro tomó té, pero Arturo tomó café.*

POR LA MAÑANA	POR LA TARDE	POR LA NOCHE
_____ Desayuné.	_____ Almorcé en la cafetería.	_____ Preparé la cena.
_____ Llegué a tiempo a mis clases.	_____ Saqué libros de la biblioteca.	_____ Miré televisión.
_____ Estudié varias horas.	_____ Lavé la ropa.	_____ Planché mi ropa.
_____ Llamé por teléfono a un/a amigo/a.	_____ Compré comida para toda la semana.	_____ Salí con mis amigos.
. . .	. . .	. . .

 **SEGUNDA FASE.** Comparen sus respuestas. ¿Tienen actividades semejantes o diferentes? Expliquen.

Follow-up for 6-12 *Segunda fase*
After students compare their answers in pairs, they can exchange information with another pair about what they did yesterday.

Follow-up for 6-13
Assign students in pairs or small groups to write as many sentences as they can about the activities of Carmen and Rafael in one subset of the drawings. Encourage them to use as many different verbs in the preterit as possible. Then create a detailed story of the couple's day by combining the work of all. Copies of the story (with verbs removed) can be used as an activity for a future class.

6-13

El sábado pasado.

PRIMERA FASE. Miren las siguientes escenas. Túrnense y expliquen cómo pasaron el sábado Carmen y Rafael.

El sábado por la mañana

El sábado por la tarde

El sábado por la noche

SEGUNDA FASE. Escriban un párrafo para compartir oralmente con la clase sobre el sábado pasado de Carmen y Rafael.

6-14

¿Cómo pasaron el fin de semana?

PRIMERA FASE. Conversen sobre el fin de semana de ustedes.

1. ¿Cuáles fueron (*were*) las actividades de cada uno/a?

2. ¿Dónde y con quién?

3. ¿A qué hora?

4. ¿Gastó cada uno/a mucho dinero? ¿Cómo lo gastó cada uno de ustedes?

SEGUNDA FASE. Determinen quién de ustedes pasó el mejor fin de semana. Describan las actividades de esta persona en una presentación oral a la clase.

Situaciones

Suggestion for *Situaciones*
Additional situations are available in the Instructor's Resource folder.

1

ROLE A. You run into a classmate whose parents visited campus the previous weekend. Ask a) what day and time his/her parents arrived; b) where they ate breakfast and lunch; c) what places on campus they visited; and d) what time his/her parents left. React to the information you hear.

ROLE B. Your classmate wants to know about your parents' visit to campus last weekend. Answer his/her questions in as much detail as possible. Ask if your classmate's parents are going to visit soon.

2

ROLE A. Your classmate and his/her significant other (**pareja**) went on a shopping spree last weekend. Ask a) what store(s) they shopped in; b) what each of them bought; c) what time they returned home; and d) what his/her plans are for wearing or using the items.

ROLE B. Answer your classmate's questions about your shopping spree with your significant other (**pareja**) over the weekend. Then find out if your classmate went shopping over the weekend, played a sport, or watched a lot of TV.

Online prep for students
Students will have completed the Learning Module for Preterit of *ir* and *ser* online. This includes the Interactive presentation and corresponding Apply activities. See content online and Instructor's Resources for Supplementary Activities.

Additional practice with *ir* and *ser*
Ask: *¿Adónde fueron las siguientes personas?* 1. *Ayer fue el cumpleaños de Javier. Su novia le compró un traje de muy buena calidad. (una boutique)* 2. *Javier invitó a Paula a escoger su anillo de boda. (una joyería)* 3. *Marcela, la hermana de Javier, fue a comprar las últimas (the latest) fragancias de Óscar de la Renta y Paloma Picasso. (una perfumería)* 4. *Paula compró sus zapatos blancos. (una zapatería)*

Suggestion for 6-15
In the class before the one in which you do this activity, you may ask students to research the places mentioned so that they can contribute more in class. They should be ready to answer the following questions: *¿En qué región de Venezuela está este lugar? ¿Cuándo se fundó? ¿Qué hacen los turistas que visitan este lugar?*

Note
You may want to mention that *cataratas* (*Cataratas de Niágara*) in question #2 is another word for *salto* (*Salto Ángel*).

Follow-up for 6-15
Ask students to a) explain why they think each person chose that particular place and b) tell about 3 or 4 activities that each person probably did there.

Talking about the past:
Preterit of *ir* and *ser*

Go to the *Capítulo 6* **folder** online to complete the Learning Module for *Gramática en contexto:* Preterit of *ir* and *ser*.

PLAN DE ESTUDIO

◎ **LEARN**
- Interactive presentation: Preterit of *ir* and *ser*
- Grammar tutorials

APPLY ◎
- Activities
- Extra Practice

PRÁCTICA COMUNICATIVA

6-15

¿Quién fue a este lugar?

Estas personas fueron a Venezuela para conocer algunos lugares. Asocia cada situación con la foto correspondiente en la página siguiente. Compara tus respuestas con las de tu compañero/a y dile a cuál de estos lugares te gustaría ir (*would like to go*) y por qué.

1. __d__ Andrés visitó un lugar con agua para navegar. Le fascinan los deportes acuáticos, pero no le gusta el mar.

2. __a__ Alguien te habló sobre este lugar espectacular y único en el mundo. Es semejante a las cataratas de Niágara y tú decidiste ir para ver lo [verlo].

3. __b__ Los estudiantes del primer año de español de tu universidad fueron de viaje a una playa exótica. Allí conocieron a otros turistas de muchas partes del mundo.

4. __c__ Los ingenieros Roberto y Angélica decidieron ir a este lugar para investigar las últimas tecnologías en el procesamiento del petróleo.

a. Salto Ángel   **b.** Isla de Margarita   **c.** Maracaibo   **d.** El puente Angostura sobre el río Orinoco

Suggestion for 6-16
We suggest you limit the number of students per group to 3. You can assign this activity ahead of time or bring information to class about these people. Explain in advance the format and guidelines for presenting.

 6-16

¿Quiénes fueron? Elijan uno de estos personajes famosos y hagan una breve presentación en clase. Respondan a las siguientes preguntas.

1. ¿Quién fue esta persona?

2. ¿Dónde nació, vivió y murió (*died*)?

3. ¿Por qué fue famoso/a? Indiquen como mínimo dos o tres hechos (*facts*) sobre su vida.

Atahualpa	Roberto Clemente
Frida Kahlo	Simón Bolívar
Ernesto Guevara	Mario Molina
Pablo Casals	Nicolás Guillén

 Situaciones

1

ROLE A. A classmate tells you that he/she went to a concert last weekend. Ask a) where the concert was; b) what time it started; c) with whom he/she went; d) what time the concert ended; and e) where he/she went afterwards. React to the information you hear.

ROLE B. Your classmate wants to know about the concert you went to last weekend. Answer your classmate's questions to find out if he/she went to a party or concert over the weekend, if he/she went out with friends, and so on. Ask for details about where, when, and with whom he/she went.

2

ROLE A. You have been asked to interview a classmate about the roles some people have had in his/her life. Ask a) who was an important authority figure (**figura de autoridad**) in his/her childhood (**infancia**); b) who was his/her best childhood friend; and c) who was his/her favorite teacher in elementary school (**escuela primaria**). React to what you hear and ask additional questions.

ROLE B. Your classmate will interview you to find out about some important people in your childhood (**infancia**). Answer the questions in as much detail as possible.

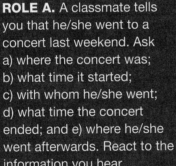

Indicating to whom or for whom an action takes place:

Indirect object nouns and pronouns

Go to the *Capítulo 6* [folder] online to complete the Learning Module for *Gramática en contexto:* Indirect object nouns and pronouns.

PLAN DE ESTUDIO

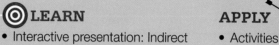

◎ LEARN
- Interactive presentation: Indirect object nouns and pronouns
- Grammar tutorials

APPLY ◎
- Activities
- Extra Practice

PRÁCTICA COMUNICATIVA

6-17 👥

Para estar a la última moda. Cada uno/a de ustedes desea o necesita lo que se indica en la lista siguiente. Explíquense (*Explain to each other*) la situación y después pidan y den una recomendación.

Modelo

Quiero llevar zapatos muy cómodos. ¿Qué me recomiendas?

Te recomiendo unas sandalias de la marca Teva.

1. Quiero llevar pantalones de moda (*in style*).
2. Deseo protegerme del sol.
3. Quiero ropa buena y barata.
4. Quiero verme (*look*) más delgado/a.
5. Me gustaría llevar ropa elegante y fina a la entrevista de trabajo.

6-18 👥

Afortunados. Ustedes ganaron la lotería ayer y quieren compartir su fortuna con su familia y sus compañeros de clase.

1. Hagan una lista de dos o tres personas a quienes desean regalarles algo.

2. Indiquen el regalo que piensan hacerle a cada uno/a y expliquen por qué.

Modelo

> A nuestros padres les vamos a regalar un crucero por el Caribe.

> A Sara vamos a comprarle una mochila.

6-19 👥

Entrevista.

PRIMERA FASE. Basándose en la siguiente lista, pregúntense sobre sus hábitos de compras y los regalos que ustedes hacen y reciben de otras personas.

1. ir de compras: ¿Qué? ¿Con qué frecuencia? ¿Tienda(s) favoritas?

2. comprar regalos caros: ¿A quién(es)? ¿Cuándo?

3. comprarte regalos: ¿Quién(es)?

SEGUNDA FASE. Escribe una comparación entre tus hábitos de compras y los de tu compañero/a en la *Primera fase*. Usa las siguientes preguntas como guía (*as a guide*).

1. ¿Tienen ustedes hábitos de compras semejantes o diferentes?

2. ¿Compran en las mismas tiendas? ¿Compran regalos semejantes o diferentes?

3. ¿A quién(es) le(s) dan regalos? ¿Quiénes les dan regalos a ustedes? ¿Qué tipos de regalos reciben?

Situaciones

1

ROLE A. You are a customer at a department store. Tell the salesperson a) you are looking for a present for a friend (specify male or female); b) you are not sure what you should buy for him/her; and c) the amount that you can spend.

ROLE B. You are a salesperson. A customer asks for your advice. Inquire about the friend's age, taste, size, favorite color, and any other pertinent information. Make suggestions and offer information about the quality of the products, prices, sales, and so forth.

2

ROLE A. You are shopping for clothes for your new job. Tell the salesperson that you like a garment (specify) in the window and inquire if they have your size. Answer the salesperson's questions and decide what you want to try on.

ROLE B. You work in a clothing store. First ask the customer for more details to identify the garment the customer is referring to. Then explain that: a) you have it in brown, blue, gray, and black; b) you also have some new items that you can show him/her (describe the styles); and c) ask if he/she would like to see them.

Suggestion for 6-18
As preparation, have students think of gifts for an elderly person, an athlete, a baby, a boyfriend/girlfriend.

Suggestion for 6-18
You may write down some gift ideas and have students decide in groups to whom in the class they will give them as awards and why: 1) *una invitación para un desfile de moda* (fashion show); 2) *una suscripción a una revista;* 3) *200 bolívares para gastar en el Centro Sambil en Caracas;* 4) *el libro más vendido* (bestseller) *del mes.*

Suggestion for 6-19
You may encourage students to talk about changes in their gift-giving practices and tastes. *¿Dónde les gusta comprar regalos, en los grandes almacenes, o por Internet? ¿Prefieren recibir regalos, o prefieren recibir tarjetas regalo* (gift cards), *para escoger su propio regalo?*

Tech tip for *Situaciones*
You may want to assign partners and have pairs create mini-skits using *MediaShare,* the video-posting feature online.

Expressing likes and dislikes:
Gustar and similar verbs

Go to the *Capítulo 6* **folder** online to complete the Learning Module for *Gramática en contexto: Gustar* and similar verbs.

PLAN DE ESTUDIO

◎ LEARN
- Interactive presentation: *Gustar* and similar verbs
- Grammar tutorials

APPLY ◎
- Activities
- Extra Practice

PRÁCTICA COMUNICATIVA

6-20
Preferencias en la ropa

PRIMERA FASE. Indiquen si les encanta, les gusta o no la ropa siguiente y comparen sus preferencias.

la ropa deportiva	los suéteres de lana	los vaqueros
las chaquetas de cuero	las gorras	los pantalones cortos

SEGUNDA FASE. Expliquen a la clase si coinciden en sus gustos.

Modelo

A nosotros nos gusta la ropa deportiva.

Y a mí me encantan los vaqueros.

6-21 👥

¿Cuánto dinero les queda? Túrnense y lean estas situaciones. Calculen cuánto dinero les queda a estas personas.

Modelo

> 66 Adriana tiene 500 bolívares. Paga 250 bolívares por un vestido y 200 por unos aretes. 99

> ¿Cuánto dinero le queda?

> Le quedan 50 bolívares.

1. Ernesto tiene 750 bolívares. Le da 150 a su hermano. ¿Cuánto dinero le queda?   600 bolívares

2. Érica tiene 550 bolívares. Va al cine con una amiga y luego cenan en un restaurante. El cine cuesta 55 y la cena 120. ¿Cuántos bolívares le quedan?   375 bolívares

3. Gilberto tiene 700 bolívares. Compra un suéter por 300. ¿Cuánto dinero le queda?   400 bolívares

4. Marco y Luisa tienen 300 bolívares. Van a la playa y almuerzan en un restaurante por 140 bolívares por persona. ¿Cuántos bolívares les quedan?   20 bolívares

Follow-up for 6-21
Play a game to see who can follow money transactions and answer quickly. 1. *Tienes $26. Compras un video por $21. ¿Cuánto dinero te queda?* 2. *Sales de casa con $75. Gastas $10 en el almuerzo, compras un suéter que cuesta $35 y pagas $20 por unas gafas de sol. ¿Cuánto dinero te queda?* 3. *Tengo $200 y quiero salir esta noche. Gasto $40 en el restaurante, las entradas al teatro cuestan $60 y le pago $15 al taxista. ¿Cuánto dinero me queda?* 4. *Tienes $150 en total, $50 en la cartera y $100 en la chaqueta. Alguien te roba la chaqueta. ¿Cuánto dinero te queda?*

6-22 👥

¿Qué les parece? Los siguientes famosos asisten a eventos públicos. Den su opinión sobre su ropa y sus accesorios.

Modelo

> No me gusta el vestido de Alejandra Guzmán porque no es apropiado llevar un traje transparente.

> Pues a mí me encanta.

La cantante de rock latino, Alejandra Guzmán.

Expansion for 6-22
You may extend this activity by providing additional photos of famous people or by having students bring photos to class.
    You may wish to introduce *no pega* and *no combina* as alternates for *no va.*

1. El cantante puertorriqueño Yandel, Jennifer López y Enrique Iglesias.

2. Las diseñadoras Carolina Herrera y su hija Carolina Adriana Herrera.

En directo

To state that doing something is appropriate or not:

(No) Es apropiado + *infinitivo*…

Es inapropiado + *infinitivo*…

To explain why some clothes are inappropriate:

… no es apropiado/a porque la ocasión es formal/informal.

En un/a… (*evento*) no es elegante/apropiado llevar…

(*Ropa*)… no va bien con… (*accesorio*)

 Click on the icon to listen to a conversation with these expressions.

Audioscript for *En directo*
Pedro: *Mamá, ¿que te parece si llevo esta camiseta para la boda de Marisa?*
Sra. Méndez: *Pedro, sabes que no es apropiado llevar ropa informal para una boda.*
Pedro: *Pero el único traje que tengo me queda muy estrecho.*
Sra. Méndez: *No te preocupes, hijo. Ahora mismo vamos a comprarte uno nuevo.*

Tech tip for *Situaciones*
You may want to assign partners and have pairs create mini-skits using *MediaShare*, the video-posting feature online.

Situaciones

1

ROLE A. You are shopping at a community crafts fair where haggling is the norm. You select an item that you plan to give as a gift. In your interaction with the vendor a) say how much you like what the vendor is selling; b) ask the price of the item you are interested in; c) react to what you hear and offer a lower price; d) comment on the item, saying whom you plan to give it to; and e) come to an agreement on the price.

ROLE B. You are selling your handicrafts and jewlery at a community crafts fair. A customer is interested in one of your items. In your interaction with the customer a) respond to his/her compliments; b) give the price of the item; c) explain why you cannot accept the customer's offer of a lower price; d) respond to his/her comments on the item; and e) come to an agreement on the price.

2

ROLE A. Your brother/sister sent you a leather jacket for your birthday. When you open the package, you are disappointed because a) it doesn't fit well; in addition, b) you were hoping for a black jacket and this one is brown. You call your sibling to talk about it.

ROLE B. Your brother/sister calls to tell you that he/she is not happy with the leather jacket you sent him/her as a birthday present. Ask questions to find out what the problem is. Suggest a solution: You have the receipt and can exchange the jacket for a different one.

Describing people, objects, and events:
More about *ser* and *estar*

Go to the *Capítulo 6* [folder] online to complete the Learning Module for *Gramática en contexto:* More about **ser** and **estar**.

PLAN DE ESTUDIO

◎ LEARN
- Interactive presentation: More about *ser* and *estar*
- Grammar tutorials

APPLY ◎
- Activities
- Extra Practice

PRÁCTICA COMUNICATIVA

6-23

Una familia va de compras. Esta familia venezolana sale de un centro comercial en Caracas. Túrnense y describan a las personas. Respondan a las preguntas y usen la imaginación para inventar detalles.

1. ¿Quiénes son estas personas? Expliquen su relación.
2. ¿Cómo son?
3. ¿Dónde están?
4. ¿Cómo están?
5. ¿Qué están haciendo?
6. ¿Qué ropa llevan?

Online prep for students
Students will have completed the Learning Module for More about *ser* and *estar* online. This includes the Interactive presentation and corresponding Apply activities.

Suggestion
Ask students which verb they use to talk about events, nationality, possession, and characteristics (*ser*) or location, perceptions, and appearance (*estar*).

Tech Tip for More about *ser* and *estar*
You may want to project images from the online Learning Module in class to help students understand the function of *ser* in sentences like *Es muy alta para su edad* and compare it to the use of *estar* in *La niña está muy grande.* Explain that the child is tall in comparison to others of her age (which is a characteristic of the child), whereas in the second sentence, *estar* is used because the comparison is not with others, but with the child herself at a different moment in time. Point out the contrast between *El café está caliente* and *La nieve en las montañas es fría.* In the first sentence the temperature of coffee varies according to circumstances (and therefore *estar* is used), but a cold temperature is an intrinsic characteristic of snow (and therefore *ser* is used).

Follow-up for 6-23
Have students work in pairs to compare their answers and figure out the function of each use of *ser* and *estar*.

6-24

De compras. Las personas en las fotos siguientes fueron de compras. Escojan una de las fotos y escriban una breve descripción usando la siguiente información. Después la clase va a adivinar qué foto describen.

1. Nombre de las personas y la relación entre ellas (usen su imaginación)
2. Probable lugar de origen de las personas
3. Lugar donde las personas están en esta foto y por qué están allí
4. Su estado de ánimo
5. Artículos que compraron y dos o tres actividades que hicieron en este lugar

6-25

¿Quiénes son y cómo están? Explica quiénes son estas personas, cómo son y cómo están en estas situaciones. Compara tus respuestas con las de tu compañero/a.

Situaciones

1

ROLE A. Your classmate asks about the photo of your family (or friends). Explain a) who the people are; b) where they are; c) what they are like; and d) how they are feeling in the photo.

ROLE B. Ask your classmate to see the photo he/she is holding. Ask as many questions as you can about the people in the photo, their activities, and the setting.

2

ROLE A. You lost (**perder**) your favorite sweater. You think you left it in your Spanish class, so you go to the department office, where they have a lost-and-found box (**una caja de objetos perdidos**). Explain to the receptionist a) what you lost; b) where your Spanish class is held; and c) what your sweater is made of and what it looks like. Answer the student helper's questions.

ROLE B. You are a student who works part-time in the Spanish department, and the lost-and-found box (**la caja de objetos perdidos**) is in your office. A student comes to ask about a lost sweater. Ask the student a) to identify himself/herself; b) what the sweater looks like; and c) where and when the student lost (**perdió**) it.

Unidos

ESCUCHA

6-26 [Presentational]

Preparación. En esta conversación, Andrea habla con sus padres sobre la ropa que necesita durante el año académico. Antes de escuchar, prepara una lista de la ropa y accesorios que tuviste que comprar antes de empezar las clases este año. Comparte esta lista con la clase.

6-27  [Interpretive]

Escucha. Listen to the conversation between Andrea and her parents. As you listen, take notes on what she needs. Write at least three items for each category that Andrea mentions.

1. Para ir a clases Andrea necesita…
botas, guantes, una chaqueta, una bufanda y un abrigo
2. Para practicar deportes Andrea tiene que comprar…
pantalones cortos, camisetas, una sudadera, medias
3. Para salir con sus amigos Andrea quiere…
pantalones vaqueros, blusas, zapatos y muchas cosas más

6-28  [Interpersonal]

Un paso más. Túrnense para responder oralmente a las siguientes preguntas y tomen notas de sus respuestas. Al final, háganse preguntas para verificar si tienen la información correcta.

1. ¿Qué accesorios, muebles para tu cuarto y/o aparatos electrónicos compraste antes de comenzar tus clases en la universidad este semestre?

2. ¿Qué libros o artículos compraste para estudiar? ¿Dónde los compraste?

3. ¿Fuiste a las rebajas? ¿Qué compraste? ¿Cuánto gastaste?

ESTRATEGIA

Take notes to recall information

When you want to remember something that you are listening to, like a class lecture, you benefit from taking notes. Taking notes can also be helpful when you want to remember the homework assignment or other instructions.

Comprueba

I was able to…

____ **recognize clothing vocabulary.**

____ **identify the correct categories.**

____ **take notes to remember the information.**

Integrated Performance Assessment (IPA) The activities in each *Unidos* section correspond to the three modes of communication as indicated by the tag next to each activity.

Audioscript for *Escucha*
Andrea: *Mamá, ustedes saben que necesito muchas cosas. Por ejemplo, para ir a mis clases ahora en invierno, necesito unas botas, guantes y una chaqueta. También necesito una bufanda y un abrigo.*
Mamá: *Pero, Andrea, si el año pasado te compramos ropa de invierno. Todavía la puedes usar.*
Andrea: *No, mamá. Quiero estar a la última moda, y mi ropa ya está vieja. Quiero ir a una boutique elegante y comprarme toda mi ropa allí.*
Papá: *Me parece muy bien, Andrea. Puedes comprar todo lo que quieras, pero dime, ¿de dónde vas a sacar dinero para pagar por esa ropa? Tú no trabajas.*
Andrea: *¡Papá, por favor! Tú me puedes prestar dinero o me puedes dar tu tarjeta de crédito. Además necesito ropa para practicar deportes. Quiero comprar pantalones cortos, camisetas, una sudadera, medias y…*
Mamá: *Andrea, ¿estás loca? Nosotros no tenemos tanto dinero. No podemos pagar todo eso ni prestarte dinero ni mucho menos darte la tarjeta de crédito.*
Andrea: *Mamá, escucha, para salir con mis amigos necesito pantalones vaqueros, blusas, zapatos y muchas cosas más.*
Papá: *Todo me parece muy bien, Andrea. Trabaja, ahorra y gasta tu dinero, pero yo no te voy a dar ni un solo bolívar.*
Andrea: *Pero, papá, comprende, por favor.*
Papá: *Ni una palabra más.*

AUTOEVALUACIÓN

☐ I feel confident that I was able to understand what my partner said.

☐ I need more listening practice.

STUDY PLAN

▶ Good job! Move on to the next section, *Habla.*

▶ Go to the *Unidos* [folder] online for *Escucha* practice.

HABLA

6-29 Interpretive

Preparación. Quieres comprar unos regalos o algunas cosas para tu cuarto/apartamento en un mercado al aire libre. Mira los productos que venden en este mercado y completa la tabla siguiente.

alfombra
43 BsF

cuadro
de arte
abstracto
86 BsF

figuras
decorativas
21 BsF

cuadro
de flores
64 BsF

manta roja
30 BsF

Audioscript for *En directo*
Vendedor: Buenas tardes, ¿en qué puedo servirle?
Clienta: Me gusta este bolso de cuero, pero no tengo tanto dinero. Solo puedo pagar la mitad.
Vendedor: ¡Imposible! El material es de primera calidad. Lo siento, pero no puedo darle el bolso por ese precio.
Clienta: Está bien. Le pago la cantidad completa si usted incluye este cinturón. ¿Qué le parece?
Vendedor: De acuerdo.

¿QUÉ QUIERES COMPRAR?	¿PARA QUIÉN(ES)?	DESCRIPCIÓN Y PRECIO DEL PRODUCTO

ESTRATEGIA

Negotiate a price

In Hispanic cultures, negotiating the price of an item in an outdoor market or other location in which the price is not fixed follows both linguistic and cultural rules. You should haggle over a price only if you intend to buy the item. Your initial offer, while lower than the selling price given by the vendor, should be reasonable, because an excessively low price may be insulting. In your negotiation, which may last several turns, you may include a brief comment about the desirability of the item and a reaction to the price suggested by the vendor.

En directo

To haggle:

CLIENTE/A

Me gusta este/a _____, pero no tengo tanto dinero.

Solo puedo pagar…

¡Es muy caro/a!

¿Qué le parece(n)… bolívares/ dólares (etc.)?

Le doy… bolívares/dólares (etc.).

VENDEDOR/A

¡Imposible!

Me cuesta(n) más…

El material es importado/de primera calidad.

Lo siento, pero no puedo darle… por ese precio.

 Click on the icon to listen to a conversation with these expressions.

6-30  [Interpersonal]

Habla. Estás en un mercado al aire libre. Pregúntale al vendedor/a la vendedora (tu compañero/a) el precio de los productos que deseas comprar. Regatea (*Haggle*) para obtener el mejor precio posible. Luego, cambien de papel.

Comprueba

In my conversation…

____ **I discussed the price.**

____ **I showed my desire to buy the item if we could agree on a price.**

____ **I gave clear information in response to questions.**

____ **I negotiated the price successfully.**

Suggestion for 6-30
Remind students about where haggling over a price is appropriate (see *Cultura* box on p. 181). Before starting the activity, you may wish to review haggling and phrases used when negotiating price.

6-31 [Presentational]

Un paso más. Comparte con la clase tu experiencia de regateo en el mercado al aire libre.

1. qué productos compraste y para quién los compraste
2. qué precio te dio el vendedor/la vendedora por cada producto
3. cuánto dinero ofreciste por cada producto
4. cuánto pagaste finalmente

30% de descuento

Suggestion for 6-31
Have students change partners so they can hear about each other's experiences.

AUTOEVALUACIÓN

☐ I feel confident that I communicated successfully.

☐ I need more speaking practice.

STUDY PLAN

▷ Good job! Move on to the next section, *Lee.*

▷ Go to the *Unidos* [folder] online for *Habla* practice.

LEE

6-32 [Interpersonal]

Preparación. Habla con tu compañero/a sobre lo siguiente:

1. ¿Te gusta comprar en Internet, o prefieres ir a las tiendas? ¿Por qué?
2. ¿Conoces algunas megatiendas por Internet? ¿Cuál(es)?
3. ¿Qué cosas compras en las megatiendas en Internet?
4. ¿Qué cosas no compras en Internet? ¿Por qué?

ESTRATEGIA

Use context to figure out the meaning of unfamiliar words

When you come across unfamiliar words and phrases while reading, use the context and what you understand about the text so far to figure out the meaning. When you come to a word you don't know, reread the last line or two, focusing on the overall meaning. In many cases, this strategy will help you understand the unknown word without using a dictionary.

6-33 [Interpretive]

Lee. PRIMERA FASE. Lee la página web de compreeninternet.net e indica si las siguientes afirmaciones son correctas (**C**) o incorrectas (**I**). Si son incorrectas, corrige la información.

1. ___I___ Los productos y servicios que compreeninternet.net ofrece son principalmente para personas que viven fuera de Venezuela.
2. ___C___ La sección **Nuestro proceso** de la página web indica las fases de una compra en Internet.
3. ___I___ Las tiendas que promociona (*advertises*) compreeninternet.net incluyen solo tiendas que están en Venezuela.
4. ___C___ compreeninternet.net tiene su oficina central en Venezuela.
5. ___I___ Los clientes pueden comprar solo ropa.
6. ___C___ Los clientes pueden ahorrar (*save*) dinero si compran en Internet.

Bienvenido a CompreenInternet.net

Menú	Nuestro Proceso	Beneficios
• Nuestra compañía	1. Hágase miembro	• Excelentes precios
• Nuestros servicios	2. Busque su producto	• Pagos en bolívares
• Cómo puede comprar	3. Calcule los gastos de su envío	• Entrega en todo el país
• Recomendaciones prácticas	4. Pague con tarjeta de crédito	• Nuestras filiales de Nueva York o Miami hacen los envíos
• Preguntas frecuentes	5. Espere su envío y disfrútelo	
• Nuestras filiales		

Servicios

Compra de una gran variedad de productos en Internet:

- • Póngase en contacto con nosotros
- • Recomiéndenos y gane puntos
- • Búsqueda

Dirección en EE.UU.
1438 Flagler Street
Miami, Florida (Fl)
Código Zip: 33166
Tel : 305-328-6289
Utilice esta dirección para su envío (shipping)

- • Asistencia para afiliados
- • Actualizar datos personales
- • Modificación de clave
- • Salida

- • Aparatos eléctricos/electrónicos
- • Muebles accesorios, ropa, juguetes, software, etc.
- • Asistencia de expertos durante y después de su compra
- • Envío gratis en Venezuela
- • Descuentos por recomendarnos a otras personas
- • Lista de las mejores tiendas en Internet
- • Ofertas y gangas de la semana

Comprueba

I was able to…

___ **use context to decipher meaning of unknown expressions.**

___ **identify specific information correctly.**

  6-34 [Presentational]

Un paso más.

PRIMERA FASE. Diseña una página web o un anuncio publicitario para vender ropa y objetos para una tienda de segunda mano (*secondhand*) por Internet. Incluye lo siguiente:

1. Un logotipo de publicidad
2. Los productos y sus precios
3. Instrucciones para comprarlos

SEGUNDA FASE. Presenta tu página a la clase. Tus compañeros/as van a hacerte preguntas sobre el logotipo, los productos que elegiste, etc.

AUTOEVALUACIÓN

☐ I feel confident I understood the reading and was able to use the information.

☐ I need more reading practice.

STUDY PLAN

▶ Good job! Move on to the next section, *Escribe.*

▶ Go to the *Unidos* folder online for *Lee* practice.

Note
Writing an e-mail is usually considered a presentational activity because it does not involve an immediate interaction between two or more speakers.

Audioscript for *En directo*
María: *Tomás, no puedes imaginar cómo me fue hoy en el centro commercial.*
Tomás: *Uf, cómo te encanta ir de compras. Dime, ¿qué pasó esta vez?*
María: *Bueno, fui a mi tienda favorita para comprar una blusa y unos jeans. Primero, vi una blusa preciosa, pero no tenían mi talla. Luego, encontré unos jeans baratos y bonitos, pero cuando me los probé, me quedaban anchos. Después, vi otra blusa espectacular, pero era muy cara. Finalmente, encontré unos zapatos divinos de rebaja y los compré. ¡Qué suerte!*
Tomás: *Ay María, ¡tú y tus aventuras en el centro comercial me fascinan!*

ESCRIBE

ESTRATEGIA

Recounting events in sequence

When we tell a story either orally or in writing, we almost always organize the events in chronological order. Using appropriate connectors to indicate the order of the events will make your writing clearer.

6-35 Interpretive

Preparación. Lee el siguiente correo electrónico de Laura a su amiga Cristina, contándole su última experiencia comprando ropa. Después pon en orden cronológico la secuencia de eventos.

Querida Cristina,
¿Recuerdas el vestido que compré el jueves pasado cuando fuimos con mi hermana al centro comercial? Cuando me lo probé ella pensó "le queda ancho", pero no me dijo (*said*) nada. Luego me escribió un correo electrónico y me explicó que tampoco le gustó el color ni la forma. Esto me enojó mucho, pero después volví a probarme el vestido y pensé que mi hermana tenía razón (*was right*). Y devolví el vestido.

En directo

To indicate the succession of events or temporal transitions, you may use the following connectors:

primero, luego, más tarde, antes de eso, después (de eso), finalmente

 Click on the icon to listen to a conversation with these expressions.

_5_ Laura devolvió el vestido.

_2_ Laura se probó el vestido.

_1_ Laura fue de compras con Cristina y su hermana.

_3_ Su hermana le explicó a Cristina por qué no le gustó el vestido.

_4_ A su hermana no le gustó la forma del vestido.

Cultura

Although big department stores are increasingly popular in Spanish-speaking countries, many people still prefer to shop at their small neighborhood stores or markets. For example, instead of buying bread from a large supermarket, they go to their neighborhood bakery (**panadería**), where they probably have a long-standing relationship with the owner and employees.

Compara: ¿Dónde prefieres hacer tus compras, en los almacenes grandes, o en tiendas pequeñas? ¿Hay una panadería o una carnicería en tu barrio? ¿Qué ventajas o desventajas tienen estas tiendas en comparación con los supermercados?

6-36 Presentational

Escribe. Cuéntale a tu mejor amigo/a en un correo electrónico tu última experiencia comprando un producto.

INCLUYE:

1. el nombre de la tienda donde compraste el producto.

2. el producto que compraste y una descripción del producto.

3. un recuento de lo que ocurrió en orden cronológico. ¿Cuándo hiciste (*did you make*) la compra? ¿Qué ocurrió después? ¿Cuánto costó y cómo pagaste?

4. la razón de tu satisfacción o no con el producto.

Comprueba

I was able to...

____ **describe the parts of the event in order.**

____ **use connectors to indicate the order.**

____ **open and close the message properly.**

Suggestion for 6-36
Ask students to re-read their e-mail and provide them with a checklist:

1. *¿Incluiste toda la información necesaria?*
2. *¿Organizaste los eventos cronológicamente para contar paso a paso lo que ocurrió? ¿Usaste expresiones que indican transición temporal?*
3. *¿Revisaste la gramática, el vocabulario, la concordancia (agreement), el tiempo (presente, pasado)?*
4. *¿Usaste la puntuación y ortografía correctas?*

6-37 Interpersonal

Un paso más. Comparte con un/a compañero/a la experiencia de una mala compra. Utilicen las siguientes preguntas como guía y añadan otras. Túrnense para hacerse preguntas y responder:

1. ¿Qué compraste? ¿Cuándo? ¿Dónde?

2. ¿Qué pasó primero? ¿Qué pasó después?

3. ¿Cómo resolviste la situación finalmente?

AUTOEVALUACIÓN

☐ I feel confident I successfully communicated my experience in writing.

☐ I need more writing practice.

STUDY PLAN

▶ Good job!

▶ Go to the *Unidos* **folder** online for *Escribe* practice.

ENFOQUE *cultural*

VENEZUELA

La Plaza Francia en Caracas es un ícono de la ciudad. Allí se realizan numerosas actividades como conciertos, ferias y otras actividades recreativas durante todo el año.

Turistas de todas partes del mundo se divierten en las bellas playas de Isla de Margarita. Es uno de los destinos preferidos entre los venezolanos para pasar sus vacaciones.

El mundo fascinante de Simón Bolívar

Go to the *Enfoque cultural* folder in *Capítulo 6* online to learn more about Venezuela.

⊚ LEARN
- Interactive presentation *El mundo fascinante de Simón Bolívar*

APPLY
- Activities

La diversidad de la flora y la fauna se aprecian en los múltiples parques nacionales. El parque Cachamay cuenta con majestuosas caídas de aguas y rápidos formados por el río Caroní.

Note for *Caracas*
Santiago de León de Caracas is the economic, commercial and cultural hub of Venezuela. Those born and/or residing there are proud to call themselves *caraqueños*.

Note for *Isla de Margarita*
With the longest Caribbean coastline of any South American country, Venezuela offers many options for beach lovers. *Isla de Margarita, Los Roques Archipelago*, and Henry Pittier National Park are popular beach destinations.

Note for *Parques nacionales*
Visitors to Venezuela's vast network of national parks can appreciate the natural landscape of the country's various regions, including its coasts, valleys, and mountain ranges.

Standard 4.2
Students demonstrate an understanding of the concept of culture through comparisons of the cultures studied and their own. Simón Bolívar is often compared to George Washington. What similarities and differences can students find between the two leaders with respect to a) their accomplishments and b) how they are memorialized (statues, cities and buildings named for them, etc.)?

PRÁCTICA COMUNICATIVA

6-38

Usa la información. Prepara una presentación oral sobre algo relacionado con el nombre de Bolívar. Puede ser un país, una región de un país, una ciudad, dinero, una universidad, etc. Explica cuál es el propósito de tu presentación, en qué país está y algunas características interesantes.

En este capítulo...

Comprueba lo que sabes

Go to the *Comprueba lo que sabes* folder online to review what you have learned in this chapter. Practice with the following:

| Vocabulary flashcards | Games | Oral Practice | Practice Test/ Study plan | Video en contexto |

Vocabulario

Los accesorios
el anillo
el arete
la billetera
la bolsa/el bolso
la bufanda
el cinturón
el collar
las gafas de sol
la gorra
el guante
la joya
el pañuelo
el paraguas
la pulsera
el sombrero

Las compras
el almacén
el centro comercial
el escaparate
el mercado
el precio
la rebaja
el regalo
el supermercado
la tarjeta de crédito
la tienda

La ropa
el abrigo
la bata
la blusa
las botas
los calcetines
los calzoncillos

la camisa
la camiseta
el camisón
la chaqueta
la corbata
la falda
el impermeable
las medias
los pantalones
los pantalones cortos
las pantimedias
el/la piyama
la ropa interior
el saco
las sandalias
el sostén
la sudadera
el suéter
el traje
el traje de baño
el traje de chaqueta
el traje pantalón
los vaqueros/los jeans
el vestido
las zapatillas
las zapatillas de deporte
los zapatos
los zapatos de tacón

Verbos
cambiar
dar
encantar
encontrar (ue)
entrar (en)
fascinar

gastar
gustar
interesar
llevar
mostrar (ue)
pagar
parecer (zc)
ponerse
probarse (ue)
quedar
regalar
valer
vender

Las descripciones
ancho/a
barato/a
caro/a
estrecho/a
ganga
magnífico/a
precioso/a
rebajado/a

Palabras y expresiones útiles
la artesanía
la cosa
el cuero
el dinero
en efectivo
¿En qué puedo servirle(s)?
enseguida
estar de moda
ir de compras
el juguete

Me gustaría...
el oro
Quisiera...
la plata
la talla

Telas
el algodón
la lana
el poliéster
la seda

Diseños
de color entero
de cuadros
de lunares
de rayas

Las estaciones del año
el invierno
el otoño
la primavera
el verano

Expresiones de tiempo
anoche
anteayer
ante(a)noche
el año/mes pasado
ayer
hace un día/mes/año (que)
una semana atrás
la semana pasada

Introduction to chapter

Introduce the chapter theme about sports and other physical activities. Ask questions to recycle content from the previous chapter. Related questions: *¿Te gusta más el béisbol o el básquetbol? ¿Prefieres jugar deportes o verlos en la televisión? ¿Qué otras actividades físicas haces? ¿Corres? ¿Montas en bicicleta? ¿Corriste ayer? ¿Montaste en bicicleta ayer? ¿Cuándo fue la última vez? ¿Caminas mucho por campus? ¿Eres atlético? ¿Crees que debes ser más activo/a?*

7

¿Cuál es tu deporte favorito?

Integrated Performance Assessment: Three Modes of Communication

Presentational: See activities 7-5, 7-9, 7-14, 7-31, 7-35, 7-39, 7-42, and 7-43.

Interpretive: See activities 7-1, 7-3, 7-4, 7-5, 7-6, 7-8, 7-9, 7-10, 7-11, 7-13, 7-14, 7-15, 7-18, 7-19, 7-20, 7-21, 7-24, 7-26, 7-28, 7-29, 7-30, 7-32, 7-34, 7-38, and 7-41

Interpersonal: See activities 7-1, 7-2, 7-3, 7-4, 7-5, 7-6, 7-7, 7-8, 7-9, 7-10, 7-11, 7-12, 7-13, 7-14, 7-15, 7-16, 7-17, 7-18, 7-19, 7-20, 7-21, 7-22, 7-23, 7-24, 7-25, 7-26, 7-27, 7-28, 7-29, 7-30, 7-33, 7-36, 7-37, 7-40, and all *Situaciones*.

Learning OBJECTIVES

You will:

- learn vocabulary related to sports, physical activities, and weather conditions

- learn the preterit forms of reflexive, stem-changing, and irregular verbs

- use pronouns *mi* and *ti* after prepositions

- connect new information about key industries in Argentina, Uruguay, and Chile to what you already know

Learning OUTCOMES

You will be able to:

- talk about sports

- emphasize and clarify information

- talk about past events

- compare the ranching and fishing industries in Argentina, Uruguay, and Chile with those in your own country

CULTURA INTERACTIVA

ARGENTINA, URUGUAY Y CHILE

Hamlet y Ophelia de
Juan Carlos Liberti,
pintor argentino (1930–)

Una parrillada de carne

PARAGUAY

BRASIL

OCÉANO PACÍFICO

CORDILLERA DE LOS ANDES

CHILE

Tucumán

ARGENTINA
Córdoba
Mendoza

Distrito de La Boca
Buenos Aires
LA PAMPA

URUGUAY
Paysandú
Colonia
Punta del Este
Montevideo

Las playas
de Punta del Este

Mar del Plata
Bahía Blanca

Bariloche

LA PATAGONIA

Un gaucho dirigiendo el ganado

OCÉANO
ATLÁNTICO

Río Gallegos

Glaciar Perito Moreno

Ushuaia

¿Cuánto sabes?

Piensa en lo que sabes de estos países y contesta las preguntas.

1. Argentina está en…
   a. Centroamérica.   **b.** el Cono Sur de América.   **c.** el Caribe.

2. La capital de Uruguay es…
   a. Montevideo.   **b.** Buenos Aires.   **c.** Santiago.

3. Punta del Este está en…
   a. Uruguay.   **b.** Argentina.   **c.** Chile.

4. Chile exporta pescado y…
   a. vino.   **b.** oro.   **c.** petróleo.

5. En la Patagonia hay…
   a. ruinas mayas.   **b.** glaciares.   **c.** un clima tropical.

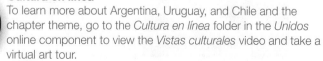

Cultura en línea

To learn more about Argentina, Uruguay, and Chile and the chapter theme, go to the *Cultura en línea* folder in the *Unidos* online component to view the *Vistas culturales* video and take a virtual art tour.

Tech tip for map
Brainstorm with students the information they may already know about Argentina, Uruguay, and Chile. Project the map from the *Unidos* online program, and point to the photos. Make comments as you ask what students know: *¿Cuál es la capital de Uruguay? ¿Y la de Argentina? ¿Qué países hay al norte de Argentina? ¿Y al oeste?* Introduce weather expressions: *Cuando en el hemisferio norte es verano, ¿qué estación tienen en el hemisferio sur? ¿Qué tiempo hace ahora probablemente allí?* Personalize questions: *¿Conocen a alguna persona famosa de estos países? ¿Saben cuál es la comida típica de Argentina y Uruguay?* Introduce some vocabulary of the chapter while pointing to Bariloche on the map. *¿Qué deportes practican los argentinos? En Argentina hay buenas pistas de esquí. ¿Les gusta esquiar a ustedes?*

Note for art
Juan Carlos Liberti was born in Buenos Aires, Argentina. A self-taught painter in the surrealist tradition, Liberti has exhibited in museums in Argentina, Spain, Puerto Rico, and the continental United States.

Suggestion for art
Ask students to interpret the meaning of the painting: *¿Es una obra realista o surrealista? ¿Qué elementos son más realistas? (el vestido de Ophelia y el traje de Hamlet, la barandilla [railing] ¿Y qué elementos son más irreales? (el pelo, no tienen caras) ¿Les gusta el cuadro? ¿No les gusta? ¿Por qué?*

Tech tip for Virtual Art Tour
You can view the Virtual Art Tour together in class or assign it for homework.

Tech tip for *Vistas culturales*
Each clip has corresponding before, during, and after viewing video activities.

Online prep for students
Students will have completed the Learning Module for *Los deportes* online before class. This includes the Interactive presentation plus corresponding Apply activities. See content online and Instructor's Resources for Supplementary Activities.

Tech tip for *Los deportes*
You may want to use the images from the online Learning Module to talk about the photos. Ask questions to emphasize the differences between *el fútbol americano* and *el fútbol* (soccer): *¿Cómo es el uniforme? ¿Cuántos jugadores hay en el equipo? ¿Cómo es el balón?* (Use gestures to explain *alargado, redondo.*) *¿Qué parte del cuerpo usan los jugadores para jugar al fútbol?*

Show news reports, photos, and video clips of Latin American and Spanish teams. Explain that the word *selección,* as used in the presentation, means team.

Talk about the photo of the ski slopes: *El esquí es un deporte popular en España. Hay centros de esquí importantes en los Pirineos, las montañas del norte. En Argentina y Chile el esquí también se practica mucho.* Check comprehension: *¿Dónde se puede esquiar en España? ¿Y dónde se puede esquiar en América del Sur?* Then personalize and review the seasons. *¿Esquías en el invierno? ¿Dónde esquías? Y a ti, ¿te gusta nadar? ¿Qué prefieres hacer: esquiar o nadar?*

En Estados Unidos hay muchos beisbolistas profesionales de República Dominicana, de Puerto Rico y de Cuba. ¿Conoces a algún beisbolista famoso? ¿Juegas al béisbol? ¿Y al baloncesto?

Suggestions for 7-1
Involve the entire class in an additional information-sharing activity. Ask: *¿Quién es un famoso ciclista norteamericano? ¿Sabes quién es Pau Gasol?* (a famous Spanish basketball player)

Vocabulario en contexto

Talking about sports, the weather, and the past

Los deportes

Go to the *Capítulo 7* online to complete the Learning Module for *Vocabulario en contexto: Los deportes.*

PLAN DE ESTUDIO

◎ **LEARN**
- Interactive presentation: *Los deportes*
- Vocabulary tutorials
- Pronunciation

APPLY ◎
- Activities
- Pronunciation activities

PRÁCTICA COMUNICATIVA

7-1

Deportes: ¿Quién es?

PRIMERA FASE. Asocia los deportes de la columna de la izquierda con los jugadores hispanos de la columna de la derecha. Compara tus respuestas con tu compañero/a.

1. _d_ ciclismo   **a.** Sergio García
2. _c_ tenis   **b.** Alex Rodríguez
3. _b_ béisbol   **c.** Rafael Nadal
4. _a_ golf   **d.** Alberto Contador

SEGUNDA FASE. Ahora hablen de dos de sus deportistas favoritos/as. Expliquen quiénes son y a qué deporte juegan, dónde juegan, qué campeonatos ganaron y por qué son sus deportistas favoritos/as.

7-2

¿Qué necesitamos para jugar?

PRIMERA FASE. Escribe el equipo que se necesita para practicar cada deporte.

DEPORTE	EQUIPO
béisbol	
golf	
vóleibol	
baloncesto	
tenis	

SEGUNDA FASE. Entrevista a tu compañero/a para conversar sobre el equipo que necesita para practicar deportes.

1. ¿Qué deporte(s) practicas? ¿Por qué?

2. ¿Qué equipo necesitas para practicarlo(s)?

3. ¿Dónde compras el equipo y la ropa que necesitas?

7-3

¿Qué deporte es? Túrnense para identificar los siguientes deportes. Después pregúntale a tu compañero/a cuál es su deporte favorito y por qué.

1. Hay nueve jugadores en cada equipo y usan un bate y una pelota.   béisbol

2. Es un juego para dos o cuatro jugadores; necesitan raquetas y una pelota.   tenis

3. En este deporte los jugadores no deben usar las manos.   fútbol

4. Para practicar este deporte necesitamos una bicicleta.   ciclismo

5. En cada equipo hay cinco jugadores que lanzan (*throw*) el balón a un cesto.   baloncesto

6. Para este deporte necesitamos una red y una pelota. Mucha gente lo juega en la playa.   vóleibol

EN OTRAS PALABRAS

Different words are used in Spanish for *ball*, depending on the context. The ball in basketball and volleyball is usually called **un balón**. Both **la pelota** and **el balón** are used for the soccer ball. **La pelota** is also used in golf and tennis. **La bola** is used in bowling.

Note for 7-2
Remind students that *equipo* means both "team" and "equipment." *El equipo es el grupo de jugadores, por ejemplo, el equipo de los Yankees de Nueva York, pero equipo también quiere decir lo que necesitan los jugadores para jugar. ¿Qué equipo necesitan los jugadores de béisbol? (bates, pelotas y guantes)*

Expansion for 7-3
You may wish to increase student-to-student talk by having the pairs give additional information about each sport after they identify it.

Follow-up for 7-3
Ask students to explain their partner's choice to the class: *¿Cuál es su deporte favorito? ¿Por qué?*

Follow-up for 7-4
Find out how many students attend sports events and how many watch them on TV: *¿Van ustedes a los partidos de… o prefieren verlos por televisión? ¿A qué partidos van?*

Suggestion for 7-5
You may introduce the words *asistencia* and *ninguno* to facilitate students' work.

Suggestion for 7-5
In this activity students will make connections with what they know. Many will be able to contribute a considerable amount of information about Tiger Woods, Lance Armstrong, and Serena Williams. To encourage competition, subtract points from teams whose members speak English. Alternatively, divide the class into groups and have them take turns answering the questions about the 3 athletes. If one group does not know an answer, the other group may respond. Record each group's points on the board.

Suggestion for 7-5
Ask students to research a Hispanic athlete of their choice. Ask them to bring in a photo of the athlete and do a short presentation that includes: 1. *quién es y de dónde es;* 2. *dónde juega;* 3. *qué campeonatos ganó.*

7-4

Tu deporte favorito. Háganse preguntas para averiguar lo siguiente.

Modelo

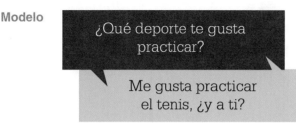

¿Qué deporte te gusta practicar?

Me gusta practicar el tenis, ¿y a ti?

1. el deporte que te gusta practicar
2. el lugar donde lo practicas, con quién y cuándo
3. el deporte que te gusta ver
4. el lugar y las personas con quienes lo ves
5. los nombres de tus equipos favoritos
6. la marca (*brand*) de ropa deportiva que más te gusta

7-5

Concurso. Van a organizar un concurso sobre deportes. En grupos de tres o cuatro, escojan a uno/a de los/las deportistas de las fotos.

1. Identifiquen al/a la atleta y su deporte. (5 pts)
2. Digan algún campeonato/torneo (*tournament*) que este/a atleta ganó. (5 pts)
3. Digan el equipo que necesita para practicar su deporte. (5 pts)
4. Cuenten algún dato personal o profesional de esta persona. (5 pts)

SEGUNDA FASE. Compartan con la clase la información sobre este/a atleta. El grupo con la información más completa gana el concurso.

El tiempo y las estaciones

Go to the *Capítulo 7* **folder** online to complete the Learning Module for *Vocabulario en contexto: El tiempo y las estaciones.*

PLAN DE ESTUDIO

◎ **LEARN**
- Interactive presentation: *El tiempo y las estaciones*
- Vocabulary tutorials

◎ **APPLY**
- Activities

Tech tip for *El tiempo y las estaciones*
You may want to project the images from the online Learning Module in class to review weather expressions including those they learned in *Capítulo preliminar* and in *Capítulo 6.* Ask when certain weather patterns are likely to occur and present additional weather vocabulary: *templado, cálido,* etc. Personalize: *¿Qué tiempo prefieres, el frío o el calor? ¿Te gusta la lluvia? ¿Y la nieve? ¿Qué deportes practicas cuando nieva?*

Suggestions
Recycle months by asking when the following occur; for each item ask what the weather is like both in your area and in the Southern Hemisphere: 1. *Termina el año escolar.* 2. *Empieza la temporada* (season) *de béisbol.* 3. *Celebras tu cumpleaños.* 4. *Sales de vacaciones.* 5. *Se juega al campeonato de fútbol americano "Super Bowl".* 6. *Se celebra el día de San Patricio.* 7. *Se celebra el cumpleaños de Martin Luther King Jr.* 8. *Es el cumpleaños de tu mejor amigo/a.* 9. *Este mes tiene el día más corto del año.*

Note
Some Spanish speakers use *hay* instead of *hace: Hay mucho sol.*

PRÁCTICA COMUNICATIVA

Condiciones meteorológicas. Asocia la situación de la columna de la izquierda con la descripción más lógica de la derecha. Compara tus respuestas con tu compañero/a y dile qué te gusta o no te gusta de cada condición meteorológica.

1. _e_ Las calles están blancas.

2. _c_ Las personas llevan impermeable y paraguas.

3. _d_ La casa es un horno y vamos a ir a la playa.

4. _b_ Los árboles se mueven (*move*) mucho.

5. _a_ Vamos a celebrar mi cumpleaños en el parque porque el clima está perfecto.

6. _f_ El cielo (*sky*) está cubierto (*overcast*) y parece que va a llover.

a. Hace muy buen tiempo.

b. Hace mucho viento.

c. Está lloviendo.

d. Hace mucho calor.

e. Está nevando.

f. Está nublado.

En directo

To thank a friend for calling:

Mil gracias por llamar. ¡Fue un gusto escucharte! *Thanks so much for calling. It was a pleasure to hear your voice!*

Gracias por llamar. ¡Qué placer escucharte! *Thanks for calling. What a pleasure to hear from you!*

 Click on the icon to listen to a conversation with these expressions.

7-7

¿Qué tiempo hace? Tu amigo/a te llama por teléfono desde otra ciudad. Pregúntale qué tiempo hace allí y averigua cuáles son sus planes. Tu amigo/a debe hacerte preguntas a ti también.

Modelo

¡Qué sorpresa! ¿Dónde estás?

Estoy en…

¿Qué tiempo hace allí?

Hace…

7-8

El tiempo y las actividades.

PRIMERA FASE. Túrnense para explicar qué hacen o qué les gusta hacer a estas personas en las siguientes condiciones.

1. Cuando llueve yo…
2. Cuando hace mucho calor me gusta…
3. A veces cuando nieva…
4. Mis amigos y yo… cuando hace mal tiempo.
5. En invierno…
6. Los estudiantes… cuando hace buen tiempo.
7. Cuando está nublado…
8. Hoy hace viento pero…

SEGUNDA FASE. Preparen un breve diálogo que incluya al menos (*at least*) una pregunta, tres expresiones de tiempo y un deporte.

Modelo

Hola, Carmen. ¿Vamos a la playa esta tarde? Hace mucho calor.

Sí, pero en la televisión dicen que esta tarde va a llover.

Está nublado pero pienso que no va a llover.

Bueno, pues vamos. Es mejor jugar al vóleibol cuando está nublado.

7-9

Las temperaturas.

PRIMERA FASE. Escojan una ciudad del mapa de Uruguay y túrnense para completar la conversación.

Modelo

¿Qué temperatura hace en... ?

...grados. Su equivalente en Fahrenheit es... .

¿Y qué tiempo hace allí?

...¿Y qué temperatura hace en... ?

SEGUNDA FASE. Preparen un pronóstico del tiempo (*weather report*) de su región. Indiquen la temperatura de tres ciudades, el tiempo que hace hoy y el tiempo que va a hacer mañana. Después compártanlo con la clase.

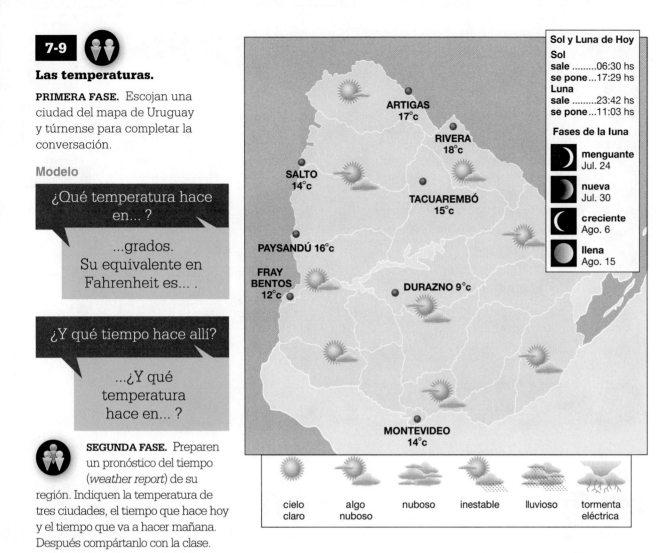

Sol y Luna de Hoy

Sol
sale ....06:30 hs
se pone ...17:29 hs

Luna
sale ....23:42 hs
se pone ...11:03 hs

Fases de la luna

menguante Jul. 24
nueva Jul. 30
creciente Ago. 6
llena Ago. 15

ARTIGAS 17°c
RIVERA 18°c
SALTO 14°c
TACUAREMBÓ 15°c
PAYSANDÚ 16°c
FRAY BENTOS 12°c
DURAZNO 9°c
MONTEVIDEO 14°c

cielo claro | algo nuboso | nuboso | inestable | lluvioso | tormenta eléctrica

Suggestion for 7-9
Have students tell how they describe the weather at the following Celsius temperatures: *0° C (hace mucho frío); 0-10° C (hace frío); 20° C (hace fresco); 30° C (hace calor); 40° C (hace mucho calor).*

You may wish to introduce vocabulary related to moon phases: *menguante, nueva, creciente, llena* by showing the box on the right of map. Both *estar* and *ser* may be used to refer to these phases: *Hoy hay luna llena. La luna está menguante.* Encourage students to prepare for the *Segunda fase* by discussing weather in their area: *¿Cuál es la temperatura máxima aquí en el verano? ¿Y la temperatura mínima en el invierno?* Then give students time to prepare their weather reports and present them to the class as if they were on television.

Cultura

In Hispanic countries the Celsius system is used. To convert degrees Fahrenheit to the Celsius system, subtract 32, multiply by 5, and divide by 9.

$86°F - 32 = 54$

$54 \times 5 = 270$

$270/9 = 30°C$

Compara: ¿Qué temperatura hace ahora en tu ciudad? ¿Cambia mucho el clima con las estaciones? ¿Cuál es tu estación del año favorita? ¿Por qué? ¿Practicas distintos deportes según la época del año? ¿Cuáles?

¿Qué pasó ayer?

Go to the *Capítulo 7* [folder] online to complete the Learning Module for *Vocabulario en contexto: ¿Qué pasó ayer?*

PLAN DE ESTUDIO

◎ LEARN
- Interactive presentation: *¿Qué pasó ayer?*
- Vocabulary tutorials
- *Entrevistas* video

APPLY ◎
- Activities
- *Entrevistas* video activities

PRÁCTICA COMUNICATIVA

7-10

¿Qué significa? Hazle preguntas a tu compañero/a para ver si sabe las respuestas.

Modelo  un grupo de jugadores

¿Cómo se llama un grupo de jugadores?

Equipo.

ganar
gol
partido
árbitro
campeona

1. la jugadora número 1 en un deporte
2. una persona que mantiene el orden en un partido
3. tener más puntos al terminar un juego
4. un juego entre dos equipos o individuos
5. punto en un partido de fútbol

7-11

Otra conversación. Con tu compañero/a lee la conversación entre Rigoberta y Ivana. Después cambien la conversación para hablar de cómo fue su día ayer.

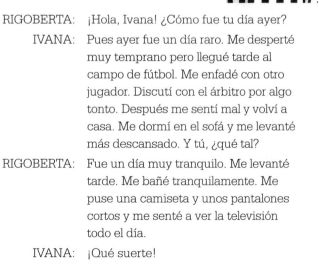

RIGOBERTA: ¡Hola, Ivana! ¿Cómo fue tu día ayer?

IVANA: Pues ayer fue un día raro. Me desperté muy temprano pero llegué tarde al campo de fútbol. Me enfadé con otro jugador. Discutí con el árbitro por algo tonto. Después me sentí mal y volví a casa. Me dormí en el sofá y me levanté más descansado. Y tú, ¿qué tal?

RIGOBERTA: Fue un día muy tranquilo. Me levanté tarde. Me bañé tranquilamente. Me puse una camiseta y unos pantalones cortos y me senté a ver la televisión todo el día.

IVANA: ¡Qué suerte!

Cultura

Hispanic sports fans generally do not boo opposing teams or particular players. Instead they whistle to show their displeasure. This behavior may occur at a soccer game, boxing match, or other popular sports events.

Compara En tu comunidad, ¿cómo demuestran descontento los hinchas con los jugadores o con un partido? ¿Alguna vez viste una escena un poco violenta durante o después de un partido? ¿Qué ocurrió? ¿Qué hiciste tú?

Suggestions for 7-12
Explain that formulating questions is an important skill to acquire. In this activity students formulate questions in the past tense, using regular verbs only. They will learn the past tense of some irregular verbs in *Gramática en contexto*.

Suggestions
Listening activities provide many learning opportunities when done in the classroom and they can be used to enhance communication. You may, for example, play the audio once and ask students to communicate in pairs about what they have understood.

Audioscript for 7-13
Anunciador:
Y ahora el pronóstico del tiempo para las capitales hispanas. Montevideo: El día está muy nublado. No llueve, pero hace mucho frío. La temperatura es de 14 grados centígrados. Es un buen día para ponerse un suéter de lana y una chaqueta. Buenos Aires: Está lloviendo. La temperatura es de 10 grados centígrados. Esta noche va a hacer mucho frío. Póngase un impermeable y no olvide su paraguas. ¡Lo va a necesitar! Caracas: Hace mucho sol y no hace ni frío ni calor. La temperatura es de 20 grados centígrados y esta tarde va a ser de unos 22 grados. Un día ideal para pasear por la ciudad. Ciudad de México: El sol está muy fuerte y hace mucho calor. La temperatura es de 42 grados centígrados. Un día perfecto para quedarse en casa.

7-12

¿Las actividades de ayer?

PRIMERA FASE. Háganse preguntas para obtener la siguiente información sobre sus actividades de ayer.

Modelo
> ¿A qué hora te despertaste el domingo?
>
> Me desperté a las once.

1. hora de despertarse y de levantarse
2. desayuno que tomó
3. número de horas de estudio
4. deporte(s) que practicó y por cuánto tiempo
5. hora de acostarse

SEGUNDA FASE. Comparen sus actividades.

1. ¿Quién de ustedes se levantó más temprano?
2. ¿Quién tomó un desayuno más nutritivo?
3. ¿Quién estudió más?
4. ¿Quién practicó deportes por más tiempo?
5. ¿Quién se acostó más tarde?

7-13

El clima en Hispanoamérica.

PRIMERA FASE. Write down the information you might hear in a weather forecast in your area in each season. Remember to include temperatures. Then ask your partner what weather conditions he/she listed and if you agree

primavera _____ otoño _____

verano _____ invierno _____

Modelo
> ¿Qué tiempo tienes para... ?
> ¿Qué temperatura hace?
>
> Tengo...

 **SEGUNDA FASE.** Focus on the general idea of what you hear. As you listen, indicate (✓) whether each forecast predicts good or bad weather.

	Buen tiempo	Mal tiempo
Montevideo		X
Buenos Aires		X
Caracas	X	
Ciudad de México		X

Online prep for students
Students will have completed the Learning Module for Preterit of reflexive verbs online before class. This includes the Interactive presentation plus corresponding Apply activities. See content online and Instructor's Resources for Supplementary Activities.

Note
Reflexive verbs were presented and practiced in *Capítulo 4* and appeared in *Vocabulario en contexto* of this chapter. You may wish to review the present and model the past tense as follows: *Siempre me levanto temprano, pero hoy no me levanté muy temprano porque no sonó el reloj despertador. Me desperté 30 minutos tarde. Y tú, ¿a qué hora te despertaste esta mañana? Y ¿a qué hora te levantas normalmente? ¿Te levantaste temprano o tarde hoy?*

Standard 4.1
Students demonstrate an understanding of the nature of language through comparisons of the language studied and their own. Draw students' attention to this difference between English and Spanish: When the meaning is clear from the context, Spanish uses the definite article to refer to parts of the body and to clothing (e.g., *Me lavo **el** pelo, Alicia se quitó **la** sudadera*) in contrast to English, which uses possessive adjectives (e.g., **my** hair, **her** sweatshirt).

Gramática en contexto

Talking about the past, personal preferences, and descriptions

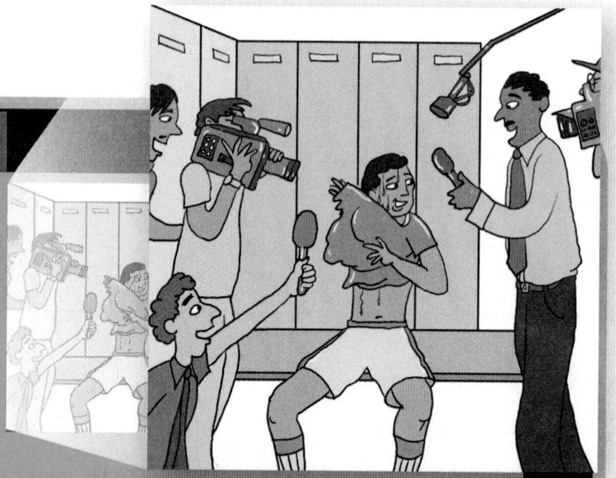

Talking about the past:
Preterit of reflexive verbs

Go to the *Capítulo 7* **folder** online to complete the Learning Module for *Gramática en contexto:* Preterit of reflexive verbs and pronouns.

PLAN DE ESTUDIO

LEARN
- Interactive presentation: Preterit of reflexive verbs
- Grammar tutorials

APPLY
- Activities
- Extra Practice

PRÁCTICA COMUNICATIVA

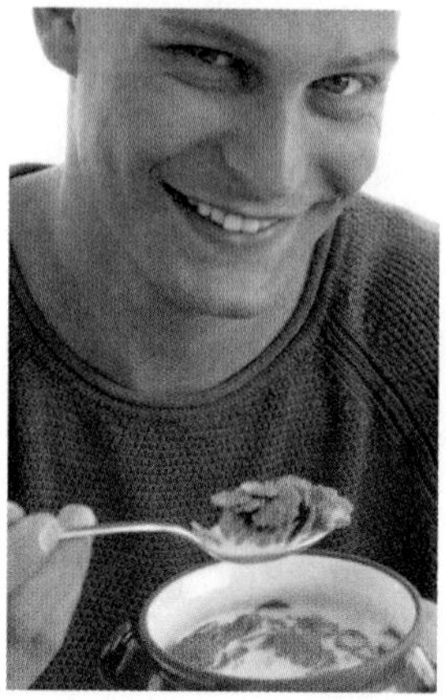

7-14

¿Cómo fue tu día ayer? Pon estas actividades en el orden más lógico y compara tus respuestas con las de tu compañero/a. ¿Tienen el mismo orden? Presenten sus diferencias a otro grupo.

__6__ Me preparé para un examen.
__9__ Me dormí.
__2__ Me levanté.
__5__ Me fui a la universidad.
__8__ Me acosté.
__1__ Me desperté temprano.
__4__ Me senté a desayunar.
__3__ Me bañé.
__7__ Al final del día, me sentí cansado/a.

7-15 ¿Cómo reaccionan?

PRIMERA FASE. Cuando tienen un partido importante, ¿hacen actividades semejantes o diferentes? ¿Reaccionan bien o mal?

1. Yo me despierto…

2. A veces yo me enfado si…

3. Nuestro entrenador se queja cuando nosotros…

4. Cuando cometo un error en la cancha, ellos…

5. Cuando esperamos el comienzo de un partido importante, nosotros siempre…

6. Cuando jugamos muy bien, nosotros…

7. Después de un partido difícil, siempre…

Modelo

> Yo me acuesto temprano la noche anterior.

> Yo no. Yo me acuesto a la hora de siempre.

SEGUNDA FASE. Comparen la información de la *Primera fase* con la de otra pareja. ¿Son semejantes o diferentes sus actividades? ¿Reaccionan igual o de una manera diferente?

Modelo

> Juan y yo nos despertamos muy temprano el día de un partido importante. ¿Y ustedes?

> Yo me despierto temprano también, pero Susana se levanta tarde. Dice que no está nerviosa antes de los partidos.

7-16

Mis actividades. Prepara una lista de por lo menos tres actividades físicas que hiciste (*did*) ayer para cuidar tu salud. Compara tus respuestas con las de tu compañero/a.

Expansion for 7-15
This activity is designed so that students can refresh their knowledge of reflexive constructions in the present tense before using them in the preterit. After they have done the activity, you may wish to reframe the sentences in the past and have students complete them using the preterit.

Suggestions for 7-16
Have students tell the class what they did. You may direct discussion to see who did the most for their health. You may also ask students to offer recommendations to their classmates.

Note
As mentioned in *Vocabulario en contexto*, the forms *hizo* and *hicieron* appear in the direction lines of activities, but students do not have to produce the preterit of *hacer* until it is presented later in this chapter.

Expansion for 7-17
You may wish to increase the amount of student talk by inviting students to use their imaginations to interpret the situations in original and amusing ways.

7-17

¿Qué les ocurrió? Lean las siguientes situaciones y digan lo que probablemente hicieron (*did*) estas personas después. Usen los verbos de la caja. Luego, comparen sus opiniones con las de sus compañeros.

afeitarse	bañarse
despertarse	enfadarse
lavarse	maquillarse
mirarse	peinarse
perfumarse	probarse
quitarse	secarse

Modelo

66 Bernardo se despertó cuando sonó el despertador. 99

Luego se levantó lentamente. En tu opinión, ¿qué pasó después?

Probablemente se afeitó.

1. Teresa se miró en el espejo.
2. Juan y Tomás entraron en el vestuario (*locker room*) del gimnasio después del partido.
3. Marisa y Erica salieron de una tienda deportiva.
4. Ramón salió de la ducha.
5. Marta no está contenta. Habló con la capitana del equipo de unos temas personales y luego la capitana les contó todo a otras jugadoras.
6. Pablo llegó tardeal estadio.

Suggestion for 7-18
Personalize by asking athletes in the class what they normally do to prepare for a game and what they did for their last important match or game.

7-18

El campeonato. El mes pasado ustedes representaron a su universidad en un campeonato de tenis en Montevideo. Digan lo que hicieron (*what you did*)...

1. para prepararse físicamente.
2. para prepararse mentalmente.
3. para cumplir (*to fulfill*) con las responsabilidades académicas.

Loreta se levantó con el pie izquierdo (*got up on the wrong side of the bed*). Observen las siguientes escenas. Túrnense y cuenten lo que ocurrió. Usen su imaginación y los verbos de la lista u otros, si es necesario.

acostarse	ducharse	explicar	practicar
despertarse	enfadarse	golpear (*to knock*)	sentarse
disculparse	enojarse	levantarse	sonar

Situaciones

1

ROLE A. You are the star player for your university's soccer team. You spend a lot of your free time promoting sports and physical activity for children in your community. A reporter for a local TV station interviews you for a special feature on student athletes. Answer the reporter's questions as fully as possible. Remember that you are considered a role model for young athletes.

ROLE B. You are a television reporter. Today you are interviewing the star soccer player for the university team who is also a role model for young athletes in the community. After introducing yourself and greeting the athlete, find out a) what school he/she went to; b) when he/she started to play; c) what his/her daily routine is to keep in shape (**estar en forma**); and d) what sports he/she practiced yesterday.

2

ROLE A. You are visiting a friend who is preparing for a competition at a training camp (**centro de entrenamiento**). Ask a) how many athletes are there; b) what time the athletes went to bed last night; c) what time they got up today; d) when they started practice today; e) what they ate for breakfast and where they ate; and d) if these activities are similar to his/her usual routine.

ROLE B. A friend is visiting you today at the training camp (**centro de entrenamiento**) where you are preparing for a competition. Answer your friend's questions and add any information of interest.

Suggestions for 7-19
You may wish to present some of the verbs listed after the directions for this activity: *enojarse, disculparse, golpear, recriminar*. Ask students to name the characters and tell what each scene shows. You may ask them to use their imagination to explain the what, why, how of each event. Guide them through the scenes by asking questions: Scene #1: *¿A qué hora salió el sol? ¿Sonó el reloj despertador?* Scene #2: *La entrenadora, ¿se levantó antes que Loreta? ¿Cómo llegó la entrenadora al cuarto de… ? ¿Quién abrió la puerta?* Scene #3: *¿Por qué se levantó tarde… ? ¿Qué excusa le dio… a la entrenadora? ¿Por qué se acostó tarde… ?* Scene #4: *¿A qué hora llegó la tenista a la cancha?*

Tech tip for *Situaciones*
You may want to assign partners and have pairs create a mini-skit using the video-posting feature, *MediaShare*, online.

Talking about the past:
Preterit of *-er* and *-ir* verbs whose stem ends in a vowel

Go to the *Capítulo 7* [folder] online to complete the Learning Module for *Gramática en contexto:* Preterit of *-er* and *-ir* verbs whose stem ends in a vowel.

PLAN DE ESTUDIO

⊚ LEARN
- Interactive presentation: Preterit of *-er* and *-ir* verbs whose stem ends in a vowel
- Grammar tutorials

APPLY ⊚
- Activities
- Extra Practice

PRÁCTICA COMUNICATIVA

7-20

¿Cómo se enteraron (*found out*)? Dile a tu compañero/a cuándo y cómo te enteraste de las siguientes noticias. ¿Lo leíste, lo oíste o lo miraste?

Modelo

 el equipo ganador del *Super Bowl*

Lo miré en la televisión. Y tu?

Yo lo leí en Internet.

1. el equipo ganador de la última serie mundial de béisbol
2. los resultados de las últimas elecciones presidenciales
3. la muerte de Michael Jackson
4. la tragedia de los mineros chilenos en 2010
5. tu admisión a esta universidad

7-21

La semana pasada. PRIMERA
FASE. Mira la lista de actividades
e indica en cuáles participaste la
semana pasada. Añade detalles
sobre cada actividad.

> concluir un proyecto
> importante para la clase de...
>
> ir a la biblioteca para...
>
> leer el blog de...
>
> mirar una película con...
>
> oír música de...
>
> contribuir a la organización sin
> fines de lucro (*non-profit* ...)

SEGUNDA FASE. En grupos de tres
o cuatro, comparen sus respuestas
para ver quién hizo más
actividades la semana pasada.

Situaciones

Suggestion for *Situación 1*
Before students do the first
Situación, you may want to
suggest that they do some
research online about the
role/history of Hispanics in
professional sports in the U.S.

1

ROLE A. You are the star player
for your university's soccer team.
You spend a lot of your free time
promoting sports and physical activity
for children in your community. A
journalism student interviews you for
a special feature on student athletes.
Answer his/her questions as fully as
possible. Remember that you are
considered a role model for young
athletes.

ROLE B. You are a
journalism student
and for one of your
classes you are
interviewing the
star soccer player
for the university
team who is also
a role model for
young athletes in
the community.

2

ROLE A. Call a friend to
invite him/her to go to a
sports event with you.
Mention a) what the event is;
b) that you read about it in
the newspaper; and c) that
you want to see the city's
new stadium (**estadio**).

ROLE B. Your friend calls to
invite you to a sports event.
Respond to the invitation with
questions and comments.
Then decide if you want to go
and either accept or decline
the invitation.

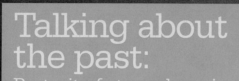

Talking about the past:
Preterit of stem-changing -*ir* verbs

Go to the *Capítulo 7* online to complete the Learning Module for *Gramática en contexto:* Preterit of stem-changing -*ir* verbs.

PLAN DE ESTUDIO

◎ LEARN
- Interactive presentation: Preterit of stem-changing -*ir* verbs
- Grammar tutorials

APPLY ◎
- Activities
- Extra Practice

PRÁCTICA COMUNICATIVA

7-22

La carrera de un campeón. Un famoso deportista recibió muchas medallas durante su carrera. ¿Cómo crees que lo logró (*accomplished*)? Comparen sus opiniones utilizando las siguientes acciones.

Modelo

 se divirtió...

> Yo creo que no se divirtió mucho durante su carrera. Y tú, ¿que crees?

> Yo creo que se divirtió porque le gusta mucho entrenar.

1. durmió...
2. repitió...
3. pidió...
4. se sintió...
5. siguió una dieta especial de...

7-23

Momentos cruciales. Piensa en un momento crucial en tu vida y
compártelo con tu compañero/a. Él/Ella te va a hacer preguntas para
saber más detalles de esta experiencia.

Modelo

Mi momento crucial fue cuando
ganamos la final de baloncesto.

¿Qué pasó? ¿Cómo te sentiste?
¿Con qué número te vestiste? ¿Qué
tipo de entrenamiento seguiste?...

7-24

Celebrando la victoria. Uno de los equipos de su universidad ganó un campeonato importante y ustedes hicieron una fiesta en su honor. Explíquenle a otra pareja los siguientes detalles de la fiesta. Usen los verbos de la lista.

despedirse	pedir	repetir	servir
divertirse	reír	sentirse	vestirse

1. hora y lugar de la fiesta
2. número de personas que asistieron y cómo se vistieron para la fiesta
3. tipo de cooperación que ustedes pidieron para los gastos de la fiesta
4. cómo se divirtieron en la fiesta
5. comida y bebida que sirvieron en la fiesta y tipo de música que escucharon
6. reconocimiento (*recognition*) que les dieron a los jugadores
7. sentimientos de los jugadores durante la fiesta
8. a qué hora se despidieron y se fueron de la fiesta los invitados

Situaciones

1

ROLE A. You had to work late last night and missed an important basketball game at your school. Call a friend who went to the game. After greeting your friend, a) explain why you did not go; b) ask questions about the game; c) answer your friend's questions; and d) accept your friend's invitation to go to another game next Saturday.

ROLE B. A friend calls to find out about last night's basketball game. Answer your friend's questions and then a) say that there is another game on Saturday; b) find out if your friend is free that evening; and c) if free, invite him/her to go with you.

2

ROLE A. You read in today's newspaper that your favorite football (**fútbol americano**) player was interviewed on TV last night. Call your friend, who watched the interview, to find out a) on which channel (**canal**) he/she watched the interview; b) the time of the interview; c) who interviewed (**entrevistar**) the football player; and d) what they talked about.

ROLE B. Your friend calls to get the details of a TV interview of his/her favorite football (**fútbol americano**) player. Answer your friend's questions in as much detail as possible.

Emphasizing or clarifying information:
Pronouns after prepositions

Go to the *Capítulo 7* **folder** online to complete the Learning Module for *Gramática en contexto:* Pronouns after prepositions.

PLAN DE ESTUDIO

◎ LEARN
- Interactive presentation: Pronouns after prepositions
- Grammar tutorials

APPLY ◎
- Activities
- Extra Practice

PRÁCTICA COMUNICATIVA

7-25

Un amigo preguntón. A Rosario le encanta el tenis y tiene un amigo que le hace muchas preguntas. Túrnense para hacer el papel de Rosario y su amigo preguntón.

1. ¿Con quién vas a ir al partido de tenis, Rosario?
2. Rosario, ¿para quién es esta raqueta de tenis?
3. ¿Pueden mis amigos ir a la cancha con nosotros?
4. Después del partido de ayer encontramos una sudadera. ¿De quién es?
5. ¿De quién van a recibir el trofeo los ganadores?

7-26

¿Con quién va? PRIMERA FASE. Completen la siguiente conversación, usando pronombres.

JULIA: Yo salgo ahora para el teatro. ¿Vienes conmigo?

CELIA: No, no puedo ir _____ . Tengo que trabajar hasta muy tarde.

JULIA: ¡Cuánto lo siento! Entonces, ¿vas a salir después con Roberto?

CELIA: Sí, voy a ir con _____ más tarde.

JULIA: ¡Ah, claro! No puedes salir sin _____ . Tú eres su mejor amiga.

CELIA: Sí, somos muy buenos amigos. Entonces, ¿con quién vas a ir al teatro?

JULIA: Pues mi hermana está aquí, y voy a ir con _____ .

SEGUNDA FASE. Lean de nuevo la conversación entre Julia y Celia y cambien la conversación para hablar de sus propios planes.

 7-27

Haciendo planes. Escoge una opción y luego pregúntale a tu compañero/a.

Modelo   ❝ ir al cine/teatro ❞

¿Cuándo puedes ir al cine conmigo?

Puedo ir contigo el sábado.

1. estudiar español/historia/ biología
2. ir al parque/al partido de béisbol/al concierto
3. jugar al golf/al tenis/al vóleibol

Situaciones

1

ROLE A. One of your friends is a basketball player. He gave you two tickets for today's game, but you have no transportation. Call a friend who has a car. After greeting him/her a) explain how you got the tickets for the game; b) invite your friend to go with you; and c) explain that you have no transportation.

ROLE B. A friend calls you to invite you to today's basketball game. After exchanging greetings, a) thank your friend for the invitation; b) respond that you would be delighted to go with him/her; c) say that you can pick him/her up in your car; and d) agree on a time and place.

2

ROLE A. Your friend calls to chat and tells you that he/ she went to a surprise party (**una fiesta sorpresa**) last weekend. Ask a) who gave the party; b) who it was for; c) who your friend went with; and d) what happened at the party.

ROLE B. You call a friend to chat. Talk about the surprise party (**fiesta sorpresa**) you went to last weekend. Answer your friend's questions about the party in as much detail as possible.

Talking about the past:
Some irregular preterits

Go to the *Capítulo 7* [folder] online to complete the Learning Module for *Gramática en contexto*: Some irregular preterits.

PLAN DE ESTUDIO

◎ LEARN
- Interactive presentation: Some irregular preterits
- Grammar tutorials

APPLY ◎
- Activities
- Extra Practice

PRÁCTICA COMUNICATIVA

7-28

¿Qué hiciste?

PRIMERA FASE. De la siguiente lista de quehaceres (*chores*), solo pudiste hacer dos o tres. Marca (✓) los que hiciste y los que no pudiste hacer.

		SÍ	NO
1.	lavar la ropa	___	___
2.	comprar los zapatos de tenis	___	___
3.	probarse el uniforme nuevo	___	___
4.	conocer al nuevo entrenador	___	___
5.	mirar el video del último partido	___	___
6.	comentar las estrategias del próximo partido	___	___

¿Cuál es tu deporte favorito?   **229**

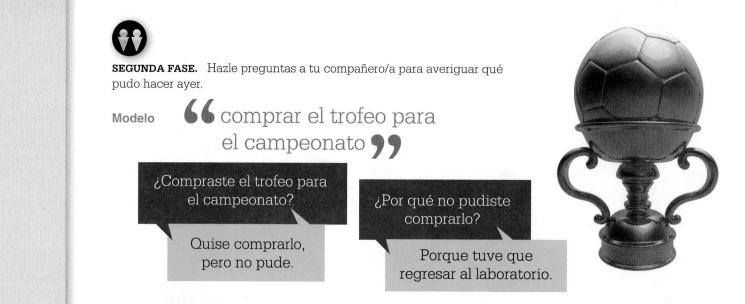

SEGUNDA FASE. Hazle preguntas a tu compañero/a para averiguar qué pudo hacer ayer.

Modelo   " comprar el trofeo para el campeonato "

¿Compraste el trofeo para el campeonato?

¿Por qué no pudiste comprarlo?

Quise comprarlo, pero no pude.

Porque tuve que regresar al laboratorio.

7-29

¿Qué ocurrió? Miren los dibujos. Túrnense y expliquen con detalle todo lo que le ocurrió a Javier el día de su cumpleaños. Después cuéntale a tu compañero/a lo que hiciste tú el día de tu cumpleaños.

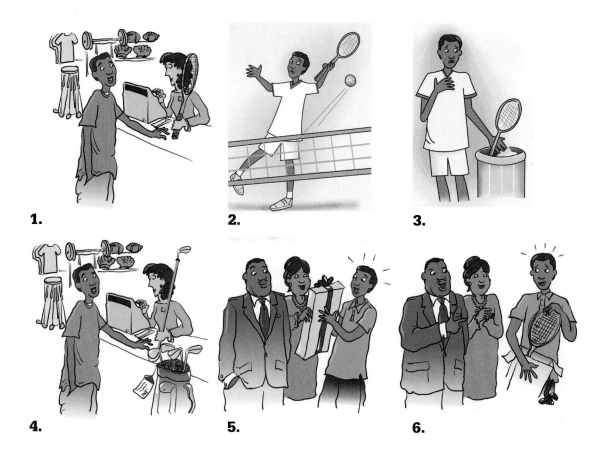

1.   2.   3.

4.   5.   6.

En directo

To express interest and to ask for details:

¡No me digas! ¿Qué pasó? *You don't say! What happened?*

¿Y qué más pasó? *And what else happened?*

¡Cuenta, cuenta! *Tell me more!*

 Click on the icon to listen to a conversation with these expressions.

7-30 👥

Unos días de descanso. Tu compañero/a estuvo unos días en Argentina (o Chile o Uruguay). Pregúntale para saber más de su viaje.

1. lugares adonde fue
2. tiempo que estuvo allí
3. cosas interesantes que hizo
4. los lugares que le gustaron más
5. si pudo hablar español y con quién(es)

LENGUA   Hace, meaning *ago*

- To indicate the time that has passed since an action was completed, use **hace** + *length of time* + **que** + *preterit verb.*

  Hace dos meses **que** fui a la Copa Mundial. *I went to the World Cup two months* **ago.**

  Hace una hora **que** empezó el partido. *The game started an hour* **ago.**

- When **hace** + **length of time** ends the sentence, omit **que.**

  Fui a la Copa Mundial **hace** dos meses.

  El partido empezó **hace** una hora.

 ## Situaciones

1

ROLE A. Congratulations! You entered a contest (**concurso**) and won an all-expenses-paid trip to attend the World Cup. Tell your classmate that you won the contest and that you went to the World Cup. Answer all of his/her questions in detail.

ROLE B. Your classmate won a contest and tells you about it. Ask a) how he/she found out about the contest; b) how long he/she was away; c) how many games he/she attended; d) with whom he/she went; and e) details about the last game.

2

ROLE A. Imagine that yesterday you went to a sports event and had the opportunity to meet your favorite sports star. Explain to a friend a) where you went; b) what happened and where; c) what you did when you saw this person; d) what he/she said to you; and e) what happened after that?

ROLE B. Your friend tells you that he/she met a very famous sports star yesterday. Ask about what happened and what they talked about.

Suggestion for 7-30
Students can consult the *Enfoque cultural* section in this chapter for information on these countries, or they can make up details of their trip.

Audioscript for *En directo*
Belkis: *Ay, Sara. Ayer conocí al amor de mi vida.*
Sara: *¡No me digas! ¿Qué pasó?*
Belkis: *Estaba en un café en el centro cuando lo vi. Me miró y enseguida ¡vino a saludarme!*
Sara: *¿Y qué más pasó?*
Belkis: *Me sentí tan nerviosa.*
Sara: *¡Cuenta, cuenta!*
Belkis: *Por fin se me pasaron los nervios y le toqué la cabeza y el pelo y las orejas. ¡Qué perrito tan cariñoso!*
Sara: *¡¿Cómo?!*

Suggestions for *Lengua* box
Hace meaning *ago*. To clarify the concept, ask *¿Qué hora es?* Students reply *Es/Son la(s)…* Then ask *¿Cuándo empezó esta clase?* Then say *La clase empezó hace… minutos.* Write the formula *pretérito + hace + (minutos, horas,* etc.) on the board and give other examples. Then repeat the process with the second formulation: *hace + (minutos, horas,* etc.) *+ que + pretérito.*

You may write on the board several years and actions: *1990–llegar a San Antonio; 1992–empezar a estudiar; 1996–casarse; 2000–tener el primer hijo.* Then create a story and ask questions: *¿Cuándo llegó a San Antonio? Ah, hace… años que llegó a San Antonio. ¿Y cuántos años hace que empezó a estudiar? ¿Cuántos años hace que se casó? ¿Cuántos años hace que tuvo su primer hijo?* Personalize and encourage students to tell their partners about their experiences.

Tech tip for *Situaciones*
Remind students that they can click on the microphone icon outside of class to connect with a partner online and do the activity.

Listening activities provide many learning opportunities when done in the classroom and can be used to enhance communication. Instructors are also encouraged to guide students' attention to certain passages, and to vary the ways in which the listening activity is presented.

Audioscript for *Escucha*
Reportero: *Nicolás, bienvenido al Programa de Deportes. Sabemos que acabas de regresar de Bariloche, donde te entrenaste por algún tiempo.*
Nicolás: *Sí, efectivamente. Estuve dos meses esquiando, junio y julio. Me encantó el lugar. Me gustó mucho Cerro Catedral; es un lugar maravilloso, con 65 kilómetros de pistas para esquiar. La ciudad de Bariloche es fantástica y la gente es muy amable.*
Reportero: *¿Fue tu primera visita a Bariloche?*
Nicolás: *No. En mi infancia fui con mis padres varias veces.*
Reportero: *¿Y las pistas? ¿Estuvieron bien?*
Nicolás: *Sí, estuvieron maravillosas, porque la primera semana de junio nevó mucho, unos 30 centímetros de nieve y pude esquiar muy bien. Al final llovió dos días y no pude esquiar mucho. Por eso regresé a Buenos Aires. Pero me entrené y me siento muy bien.*
Reportero: *¡Qué bien! Y, dime, ¿a qué distancia está Cerro Catedral de Bariloche?*
Nicolás: *Está muy cerca, a solo 20 kilómetros.*
Reportero: *¿Y cuándo regresas a Bariloche?*
Nicolás: *El próximo año. Voy a ir con unos amigos que quieren prepararse allí también.*
Reportero: *Muy bien y buena suerte en la próxima competencia.*
Nicolás: *Muchas gracias.*

Unidos

ESCUCHA

 **7-31** [Presentational]

Preparación. Vas a escuchar una conversación entre un reportero y Nicolás, un esquiador argentino que habla sobre su viaje a Bariloche, Argentina. Antes de escuchar la conversación, escribe sobre el tiempo que hizo durante su estadía en Bariloche. Después escribe una opinión sobre la gente del lugar que Nicolás probablemente va a conocer.

ESTRATEGIA

Differentiate fact from opinion

When you listen or watch the news or a talk show, you need to distinguish facts from opinions. Facts are provable pieces of information based on statistics, data, and other verifiable evidence. Opinions are personal points of view that combine attitudes and beliefs with factual information.

7-32 [Interpretive]

Escucha. Listen to the conversation and write down in Spanish three pieces of factual information and three opinions Nicolás offered about the place and/or the people.

Información concreta: Cerro Catedral tiene 65 kilómetros de pistas para esquiar; nevó unos 30 centímetros de nieve; llovió dos días; Cerro Catedral está a 20 kilómetros de Bariloche.
Opinión personal: Me gustó mucho Cerro Catedral; Cerro Catedral es un lugar maravilloso; la ciudad es fantástica; la gente es muy amable.

Comprueba
I was able to...

____ listen for specific information.

____ take good notes while listening.

____ distinguish facts from opinions.

 **7-33** [Interpersonal]

Un paso más. Pregúntale a tu compañero/a para averigüar la siguiente información.

1. un deporte que practica y dónde lo practica
2. el tiempo que hace cuando lo practica
3. su atleta favorito/a en ese deporte y por qué

AUTOEVALUACIÓN

☐ I feel confident that I was able to understand what I heard.

☐ I need more listening practice.

STUDY PLAN

▶ Good job! Move on to the next section, *Habla*.

▶ Go to the *Unidos* [folder] online for *Escucha* practice.

HABLA

7-34  [Interpretive]

Preparación. Investiguen en Internet la siguiente información sobre un deporte que se practica en Argentina, Uruguay o Chile.

1. el nombre del deporte

2. dos o tres datos históricos sobre el deporte: cuándo empezó a practicarse; dónde empezó; algo interesante sobre los comienzos (*origin*) del deporte

3. una persona argentina o uruguaya famosa en la historia de este deporte: nombre, fecha y lugar de nacimiento; datos sobre su carrera deportiva

---

7-35  [Presentational]

Habla. Hagan una breve presentación sobre el deporte y el/la deportista que investigaron.

Comprueba

In our preparation and presentation…

____ I spoke in Spanish as much as my partners.

____ I took good notes and contributed useful information.

____ My part of the presentation was clear and easy to understand.

7-36 [Interpersonal]

Un paso más. De las presentaciones en clase, elijan un deporte y un/a deportista y preparen preguntas para hacer a otros compañeros/as. Incluyan la información indicada en las fichas (*note cards*) siguientes.

Deporte	Deportista
Nombre:	Nombre y nacionalidad:
Dónde y cuándo empezó a practicarse:	Fecha de nacimiento:
Dónde se practica ahora:	Campeonatos que ganó:
Su popularidad:	Su reputación nacional e internacional:

AUTOEVALUACIÓN

☐ I feel confident that I communicated successfully.

☐ I need more speaking practice.

STUDY PLAN

▶ Good job! Move on to the next section, *Lee*.

▶ Go to the *Unidos* folder online for *Habla* practice.

ESTRATEGIA

Focus on key information to report what was said

In *Capítulo 6* you practiced taking notes to understand and remember something you heard. Here you will take the next step: turning your notes into a brief report to present to the class. Follow these steps: 1) Decide what aspects of the topic you want to report on; 2) then listen for and take notes on those aspects; and 3) organize your notes for your presentation.

En directo

To discuss ideas while working in a group:

¿Qué te/le/les parece esto?
What do you think about this?
¿Qué te/le/les parece si decimos/organizamos… ?
How about if we say/organize … ?
¿Por qué no lees/hablas/miras… ?
Why don't you read/say/look at … ?

To propose a new idea:

¡Oigan, tengo una idea!
Listen, I have an idea.
Miren, tengo una propuesta.
Look, I have a suggestion.

🔊 Click on the icon to listen to a conversation with these expressions.

En directo

To maintain the interest of listeners:

Hay hechos/datos interesantes sobre…
La información que tenemos sobre… es increíble.
¡Imagínense! Ganó el primer puesto en…
Este/a deportista juega al… como nadie.

🔊 Click on the icon to listen to a conversation with these expressions.

Suggestions for 7-35
Guide students in dividing equitably among members of each group the tasks of preparing and presenting. Remind students that the goal is a clear, comprehensible presentation in their own words, since classmates will take notes and prepare a brief report on what they have heard.

To encourage classmates to participate as active listeners, have them write at least two follow-up questions or comments for the presenters, and encourage them to ask for clarification when necessary.

Audioscript for *En directo*
Luis: *Pienso que debemos hacer algo para animar a nuestro equipo. ¿Qué les parece esto? Hacemos un afiche para cada jugador.*
Héctor: *Me parece bien, pero ¿qué les parece si organizamos un baile para obtener fondos? Necesitan nuevos uniformes.*
Olivia: *¡Me encanta esa idea! ¿Por qué no hablas con John? Él es muy buen DeeJay.*
Andrea: *¡Oigan, tengo una idea! Vamos a hacer las dos cosas. Yo ayudo a Luis con los afiches y Olivia y Héctor organizan el baile.*

Audioscript for *En directo*
Profesora Lynch: *Chicos, hay datos interesantes sobre la alimentación y el éxito en los deportes. La información que tenemos sobre la importancia de la buena nutrición es increíble.*
Chris: *La profesora tiene razón. Mi prima se convirtió en una campeona cuando decidió comer cosas más saludables y eliminar comida basura. Ahora practica karate como nadie. ¡Imagínense! Ganó el primer puesto en su clase después de entrenar por solo dos meses.*

Suggestion for 7-36
To enable students to give their brief reports (no more than 1 minute long), you may wish to have several simultaneous presentations to different small groups, or you may ask 2 or 3 students to give reports at the beginning or end of several future class sessions.

LEE

7-37 Interpersonal

Preparación.

PRIMERA FASE. Mira el texto "Los deportes: Una pasión uruguaya".
Lee el título y examina las fotos. Busca nombres de lugares y deportes
conocidos. Luego responde a las preguntas.

1. Después de examinar el texto, selecciona el posible tema.
   a. los lugares en Uruguay dónde se practican los deportes
   b. los atletas más famosos de Uruguay
   c. el amor de los uruguayos por los deportes

2. Marca (✓) las ideas que vas a encontrar en el texto.
   a. _____ los deportes más populares de Uruguay
   b. _✓_ el origen de los deportes de Uruguay
   c. _____ los lugares donde se practican algunos deportes en Uruguay
   d. _✓_ los campeonatos que ganaron los equipos de fútbol uruguayo
   e. _____ los deportes favoritos de los uruguayos en comparación con
      los de otros países latinoamericanos

SEGUNDA FASE. Háganse preguntas y compartan la información
que recogieron con otra pareja.

1. ¿Te gustan los deportes individuales o prefieres los de equipo?
   ¿Por qué?

2. ¿Sabes esquiar? ¿Esquías en la nieve o en el agua? ¿Esquías bien
   o regular?

3. ¿Qué tipos de surf conoces? ¿Has oído hablar (*Have you heard about*)
   del surf en la arena? ¿Qué sabes acerca de ese deporte?

Estrategia

Predict and guess content

You may enhance your
comprehension of a text by
predicting and guessing its content
before you start to read. Begin by
brainstorming the information you
are likely to find in the text and
identifying the text format.

Suggestion for 7-37
As a warm-up, review and
reinforce some key words in
the activity by asking *¿Con
qué palabras asocian ustedes
los siguientes deportes, con
agua, nieve o arena?* (Write
words on the board.) 1. *el
esquí;* 2. *la natación;* 3. *el
vóleibol en la playa;* 4. *el surf.*
   You may also have
students brainstorm popular
sports in the U.S. For each
sport, ask students where it is
practiced, what equipment or
clothing is needed, and what
weather conditions favor its
practice.

7-38 Interpretive

Lee. Lee el artículo y haz lo siguiente:

1. Indica dos razones que explican la popularidad del fútbol
   en Uruguay.

2. Nombra tres deportes de equipo, dos individuales y uno que
   no requiere una pelota.

3. Explica por qué Punta del Este es un lugar ideal para practicar
   el surf acuático.

Comprueba

I was able to...

_____ **use my knowledge of sports
to anticipate the content of
the reading.**

_____ **distinguish between facts and
opinions.**

_____ **understand most of the
information in the text.**

Los deportes: Una pasión uruguaya

Standard 1.2
Students understand and interpret written and spoken language on a variety of topics. In this section students read a text about the passion for sports in Uruguay, which is followed by comprehension and production activities. Both types of activities help students build their analytical skills and their overall comprehension of written Spanish.

Uruguay es un país pequeño donde los deportes forman una parte integral de la vida de la mayor parte de sus habitantes.

Entre las grandes pasiones nacionales está el fútbol. Desde su infancia, muchos uruguayos acompañan fielmente a sus equipos. En varias ocasiones, la selección nacional uruguaya ganó títulos y campeonatos importantes.

Pero el fútbol no es la única pasión de los uruguayos. El básquetbol, el ciclismo, el fútbol de salón, el rugby, el boxeo y la pelota de mano son otros deportes muy populares.

Las hermosas y privilegiadas playas del Uruguay también favorecen los deportes acuáticos, como el surf, que cuenta con un gran número de aficionados. En 1993 se formó la Unión de Surf del Uruguay (USU). Ese mismo año, el país envió a sus representantes a competir internacionalmente en el Primer Campeonato Panamericano de Surf en Isla de Margarita, Venezuela. Hoy en día la USU promueve el surf, arbitra las competencias clasificatorias a nivel nacional, apoya a los competidores nacionales, representa a Uruguay en competencias internacionales y compite en los Juegos Olímpicos.

Uno de los lugares favoritos para practicar el surf es Punta del Este. Ubicada al sureste del Uruguay, a 140 kilómetros de Montevideo, Punta del Este es una hermosa península de enormes playas, con arenas finas y gruesas, rocas y un entorno de bosques y médanos[1].

Precisamente en estos médanos nació, en el siglo pasado, una variante del surf que está despertando grandes polémicas en el país: el surf en la arena o *sandsurf*. Los brasileños inventaron este deporte en los años ochenta para no aburrirse cuando no había olas. La agradable temperatura de las playas uruguayas, la escasez de olas y la formación arenosa de algunas playas aumentaron considerablemente el número de personas que practican el surf en la arena. Por ejemplo, los médanos de Valizas son los más grandes de Sudamérica y los terceros más grandes del mundo, algunos con 30 metros de altura y una longitud de bajada[2] de aproximadamente 125 metros. Sin embargo, las autoridades uruguayas están controlando e incluso prohibiendo la práctica de este deporte por el posible deterioro ecológico que ocasiona. La prohibición del surf en la arena no va a detener el espíritu activo de los uruguayos quienes seguro que van a buscar o inventar otras opciones para entretenerse.

[1]*dunes* [2]*slope*

7-39 Presentational

Un paso más. Seleccionen algún deporte. Preparen una ficha sobre ese deporte sin mencionar el nombre, y luego intercambien su ficha con la de otro grupo. Traten de adivinar el deporte de sus compañeros.

1. Lugar donde se practica

2. Deporte individual o en grupo
(número de personas en el equipo)

3. En qué clima o estación se practica

4. Un jugador famoso/una jugadora famosa del deporte

5. Otra información relevante

AUTOEVALUACIÓN

☐ I feel confident I understood the reading and was able to use the information.

☐ I need more reading practice.

STUDY PLAN

▷ Good job! Move on to the next section, *Escribe*.

▷ Go to the *Unidos* folder online for *Lee* practice.

ESCRIBE

Preparación. Entrevista a tres compañeros/as sobre los siguientes temas:

1. Las ventajas o desventajas de hacer ejercicio físico durante la infancia (*childhood*).

2. Ventajas o desventajas de unos deportes sobre otros.

3. Deportes y actividades físicas que practicaron de niños.

4. Deportes que practican ahora.

ESTRATEGIA

Use supporting details

Supporting details are facts and examples that follow the topic sentence and make up the body of a paragraph. They should support the main idea of the paragraph and be placed in a logical order. You should then write a closing sentence that summarizes your main point.

En directo

To express facts:

Los expertos afirman/dicen/
aseguran que…
La investigación indica que…
Los estudios muestran que…

To express an opinión:

A mí me parece que…

 Click on the icon to listen to a conversation with these expressions.

7-41 Interpretive

Escribe. Escribe un artículo sobre el papel del ejercicio en la salud de los niños. Usa la información de **7-40** para escribir tu artículo. Incluye lo siguiente:

1. Los beneficios del ejercicio físico para los niños.

2. Tipos de actividad física que son divertidos y beneficiosos para los niños.

3. Estrategias para aumentar la actividad física.

Comprueba

I was able to…

____ **present my main idea clearly, using relevant vocabulary.**

____ **use facts and examples to develop my main ideas.**

____ **provide the supporting details in a logical order.**

7-42 Presentational

Un paso más. Presenta tu proyecto a la clase. Tus compañeros van a hacerte preguntas.

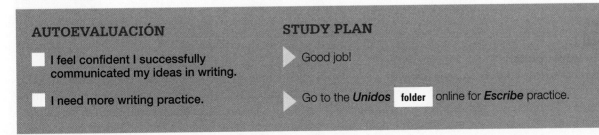

AUTOEVALUACIÓN

☐ I feel confident I successfully communicated my ideas in writing.

☐ I need more writing practice.

STUDY PLAN

▶ Good job!

▶ Go to the *Unidos* folder online for *Escribe* practice.

Audioscript for *En directo*
Doctor Valle: *Los expertos afirman que es más importante comer bien que hacer ejercicio. Sin embargo, la investigación que terminé indica que ambos son igual de importantes.*
Delia: *A mí me parece que depende de la persona. A algunas personas les hace falta más ejercicio mientras que a otros les conviene más tener una dieta equilibrada.*

Suggestion for 7-42
Before presenting their projects to the class, have students check the following. You may write these ideas on the board: 1. *La organización y la cantidad de información;* 2. *El vocabulario y las estructuras que utilizaste; las expresiones para presentar hechos u opiniones;* y 3. *La división de párrafos, la ortografía y los acentos.*

ENFOQUE *cultural*

Note for *La Plaza de Mayo*
The *Plaza de Mayo* is the focal point of the Monserrat barrio in central Buenos Aires. Home to major landmarks such as the *Casa Rosada*, the Metropolitan Cathedral of Buenos Aires and the May Pyramid, the Plaza is a top destination for tourists. In addition, the square invokes many memories for the people of Argentina, of both difficult and prosperous times in their country's history.

Note for *La Paloma*
La Paloma is a small seaside city located in the department of Rocha in southeastern Uruguay. The lighthouse, named the *Faro de Cabo de Santa María,* dates back to 1874. Visitors can climb to the very top of the lighthouse and take in extraordinary views of the sea. In the winter, there's even a good chance of spotting some whales.

Note for *Punta Arenas*
Punta Arenas is the largest and oldest city of Patagonia at the Strait of Magellan. Interestingly, it was first established as a small penal colony. However, given its strategic location in the Antarctic Peninsula, its importance grew during specific times in history such as the Gold Rush. Today, Punta Arenas draws numerous tourists, many of whom use the city as a starting point to their tours of Antarctica.
Integrated Performance Assessment: Three Modes of Communication

Presentational: See activities 7-5, 7-9, 7-14, 7-31, 7-35, 7-39, 7-42, and 7-43.

Interpretive: See activities 7-1, 7-3, 7-4, 7-5, 7-6, 7-8, 7-9, 7-10, 7-11, 7-13, 7-14, 7-15, 7-18, 7-19, 7-20, 7-21, 7-24, 7-26, 7-28, 7-29, 7-30, 7-32, 7-34, 7-38, and 7-41

ARGENTINA

La Casa Rosada, sede del gobierno argentino, está situada en frente de la Plaza de Mayo.

URUGUAY

El Faro de La Paloma, de 42 metros de altura, guía a las embarcaciones.

CHILE

Una calle en Punta Arenas, Chile, con vista al mar y Tierra del Fuego

El ganado y el pescado en la vida de Argentina, Uruguay y Chile

Go to the *Enfoque Cultural* 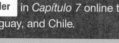 in *Capítulo 7* online to learn more about Argentina, Uruguay, and Chile.

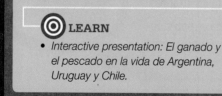

PLAN DE ESTUDIO

LEARN
- *Interactive presentation: El ganado y el pescado en la vida de Argentina, Uruguay y Chile.*

APPLY
- Activities

PRÁCTICA COMUNICATIVA

7-43

Usa la información. Prepara un afiche para comparar tres de las regiones ganaderas más importantes del continente americano: Texas, los Llanos de Colombia y Venezuela, y la Pampa argentina. Alternativamente, puedes hacer el afiche comparando las industrias pesqueras de Chile y Perú. Busca información en Internet y explica tres características de cada una de las regiones. Incluye una foto de cada una de las regiones y escribe una explicación breve para cada una de ellas. Después presenta tu afiche en clase.

En este capítulo...

Comprueba lo que sabes

Go to the *Comprueba lo que sabes* folder online to review what you have learned in this chapter. Practice with the following:

| Vocabulary Flashcards | Games | Oral Practice | Practice Test/ Study Plan | Video en contexto |

Vocabulario

Los deportes
el baloncesto/el básquetbol
el béisbol
el ciclismo
el esquí
el fútbol
el golf
el tenis
el vóleibol

El equipo deportivo
el balón/la pelota
el bate
el cesto/la cesta
el gol
los palos
la raqueta
la red

Los eventos
el campeonato
la carrera
el juego/el partido

Los lugares
el campo
la cancha
la pista

Las personas
el árbitro
el campeón/la campeona
el/la ciclista
el entrenador/la entrenadora
el equipo
el jugador/la jugadora
el/la tenista

La naturaleza
la atmósfera
el lago

El tiempo
está despejado
está nublado
hace buen/mal tiempo
hace calor
hace fresco
hace sol
el hielo
la lluvia
la nieve
el viento

Las descripciones
contaminado/a
contrario/a
mundial

Verbos
aprovechar
congelar(se)
discutir
durar
enfadarse
esquiar
ganar
ir(se)
jugar (ue) a los bolos
llover (ue)
meter un gol
nevar (ie)
patinar
perder (ie)
pitar
recorrer
traducir (zc)

Palabras y expresiones útiles
cada
conmigo
contigo
el penalti

Otros verbos reflexivos
arrepentirse (ie, i)
atreverse
disculparse
divertirse (ie, i)
enfadarse
quejarse
sentirse (ie, i)

Otros verbos irregulares
despedirse (i, i)
morir (ue, u)
pedir (i, i)
reír
repetir (i, i)
seguir (i, i)
servir (i, i)
vestirse (i, i)

Notas

Introduction to chapter
Introduce holidays and celebrations, the chapter theme, and ask questions to recycle content from the previous chapter. Related questions: *¿Cuándo es tu cumpleaños? ¿Cómo lo celebras? ¿Te enfadas si tus amigos no te felicitan? ¿Cómo lo celebraste el año pasado? ¿Qué te regalaron tus amigos o familiares? ¿Qué otras fechas celebras?*

Integrated Performance Assessment: Three Modes of Communication

Presentational: See activities 8-7, 8-30, 8-33, 8-38, 8-40 and 8-42.

Interpretive: See activities 8-1, 8-2, 8-3, 8-4, 8-7, 8-8, 8-9, 8-10, 8-12, 8-13, 8-14, 8-15, 8-19, 8-21, 8-23, 8-25, 8-26, 8-28, 8-31, 8-35, 8-37, and 8-41.

Interpersonal: See activities 8-1, 8-2, 8-3, 8-4, 8-5, 8-6, 8-7, 8-8, 8-9, 8-10, 8-11, 8-12, 8-13, 8-14, 8-15, 8-16, 8-17, 8-18, 8-19, 8-20, 8-21, 8-22, 8-23, 8-24, 8-25, 8-26, 8-27, 8-28, 8-29, 8-32, 8-34, 8-36, 8-39, and all *Situaciones*

8

¿Cuáles son tus tradiciones?

Learning OBJECTIVES

You will:

- learn vocabulary related to holidays, traditions, and celebrations
- learn the forms of the imperfect and its use
- distinguish between the imperfect and preterit
- use comparative and superlative expressions
- connect new information about Mexico to what you already know

Learning OUTCOMES

You will be able to:

- discuss situations and celebrations
- describe conditions and express ongoing actions in the past
- tell stories about past events
- compare people and things
- talk about a Mexican celebration

CULTURA INTERACTIVA
MÉXICO

Una banda de mariachis

Tijuana
La Paz
Chihuahua
Monterrey

ESTADOS UNIDOS

Río Grande

Golfo de California

Golfo de México

MÉXICO

Zacatecas

Las ruinas prehispánicas de Teotihuacán

Cancún
Mérida

Las ruinas de Tulum

OCÉANO PACÍFICO

El Zócalo en Ciudad de México
Guadalajara
Morelia
Ciudad de México
Puebla
Oaxaca

Bahía de Campeche

BELICE
GUATEMALA

El mole poblano, una de las especialidades de la comida mexicana

La pintora mexicana Frida Kahlo pintó este cuadro en 1932. Su título es *Autorretrato entre México y Estados Unidos*.

¿Cuánto sabes?

Completa las siguientes oraciones.

1. Los mariachis son…
   bandas de música mexicana.
2. El Zócalo está en…
   Ciudad de México.
3. La playa de Cancún está en…
   el golfo de México.
4. Un plato típico de la comida mexicana es…
   el mole poblano.
5. Frida Kahlo es…
   una pintora mexicana.
6. En Teotihuacaán y Tulum se encuentran…
   ruinas prehispánicas.

Cultura en línea

To learn more about México and the chapter theme, go to the *Cultura en línea* folder in the *Unidos* online component to view the *Vistas culturales* video and take a virtual art tour.

Tech tip for map
Brainstorm with students the information they may already know about Mexico. Project the map and ask: *¿Qué países tienen frontera con México? ¿Qué ciudades americanas están cerca de la frontera mexicana? ¿Cuál es la capital de México? ¿Qué otras ciudades mexicanas conocen? ¿Qué comida tradicional mexicana les gusta? ¿Qué tradiciones de México conocen?* Point out the pre-Columbian pyramid of Teotihuacán on the map, which is called *la Pirámide del Sol,* and relate it to Frida Kahlo's painting.

Note for art
Autorretrato entre México y Estados Unidos was painted by Frida Kahlo in 1932 during her stay in the U.S. Dressed in pink, she is at the center of a self-portrait that contrasts traditional culture and modernity: Mexico is represented in warm colors, whereas the U.S. abounds in buildings, industries, and electric gadgets depicted in grays and blues. The inscription on this pedestal says "*Carmen* (Frida's baptismal name) *Rivera pintó su retrato en el año 1932.*"

Tech tip for art
Project text image of the painting and ask questions to elicit vocabulary: *¿Cómo es Frida Kahlo? ¿Qué lleva? ¿De qué color es su vestido?* Recycle colors by asking students to describe the flags. Ask about the ruins and pre-Columbian figures on the Mexican side: *¿Qué edificio es este probablemente? ¿Qué representa esta figura?* (The feminine figure represents fertility.) Point out the skull on the ground and ask what they know about *el Día de los Muertos.* Explain that *sol* and *luna* are symbols from the Aztec religion. (The blood from the sun's mouth is a reminder of Aztec sacrifices.) Ask students to describe what they see on the U.S. side (*fábrica, humo, contaminación, aparatos eléctricos*).

Online prep for students
Students will have completed the Learning Module for *Las fiestas y las tradiciones* online before coming to class. This includes the Interactive presentation plus corresponding Apply activities. See content online. You will find additional in-class activities in the Supplementary Activities folder in Instructor's Resources.

Warm-up
Have students provide as much information as possible about holidays that are celebrated in both the U.S. and the Hispanic world.

Tech tip for *Las fiestas y las tradiciones*
Project the images from the online Learning Module in class and ask questions as a warm-up. Provide additional information.

• Locate on a map the province of Huelva (southwestern Spain), where *El Rocío* takes place. Explain that many worshippers arrive in wagons, on horseback, or on foot; that is, *hacen el camino,* from various regions in Spain to attend the festival.

* Point out that Christianity's Holy Week (*Semana Santa*) is the week from Palm Sunday to Easter Sunday. The photograph shows *una hermandad,* a religious brotherhood in Guatemala, whose members wear traditional clothing and carry religious icons mounted on heavy wooden floats as an act of religious devotion, walking on beautiful carpets of flowers, seeds, and tinted sawdust.

Suggestion
Point out similarities and differences of special days in both cultures: April Fool's Day/*el Día de los Inocentes, 28 de diciembre;* Friday the 13th/*martes 13.*

Vocabulario en contexto

Las fiestas y las tradiciones

Go to the *Capítulo 8* [folder] online to complete the Learning Module for *Vocabulario en contexto: Las fiestas y las tradiciones.*

PLAN DE ESTUDIO

◎ LEARN
• Interactive presentation: *Las fiestas y las tradiciones*
• Vocabulary tutorials
• Pronunciation

APPLY ◎
• Activities
• Pronunciation activities

PRÁCTICA COMUNICATIVA

8-1 👥

Definiciones. Asocia el nombre de la festividad en la columna de la izquierda con su descripción en la columna de la derecha. Compara tus respuestas con las de tu compañero/a y dile a cuáles de ellas te gustaría (*would like*) asistir y por qué.

1. __e__ San Fermín

2. __a__ La Diablada

3. __f__ El Rocío

4. __b__ Carnaval

5. __c__ El Día de los Muertos

6. __d__ Semana Santa

a. Se celebra durante el carnaval de Oruro en Bolivia. Muchas personas bailan en las calles disfrazadas de demonios.

b. Muchas personas se disfrazan y bailan en comparsas por las calles.

c. Todos van al cementerio a hacer ofrendas a los seres queridos que están muertos.

d. Hay procesiones por las calles y en Antigua, Guatemala, se hacen unas alfombras de aserrín, flores y semillas.

e. Los jóvenes corren por las calles delante de los toros.

f. Es una fiesta en el sur de España. La gente va en carretas hasta una ermita.

Cultura

El Día de Acción de Gracias (*Thanksgiving*) no se celebra en los países hispanos y tampoco es tradicional el Día de las Brujas (*Halloween*), aunque empieza a celebrarse en algunas ciudades de Hispanoamérica y de España. Por otro lado, debido a la importancia e influencia de la religión católica en los países hispanos, algunas fiestas católicas se consideran también fiestas oficiales y son días feriados. Pero lo más importante es la gran diversidad de fiestas locales. Muchas personas trabajan todo el año para garantizar el éxito de estas celebraciones en las que la gente baila y se divierte durante días enteros.

Compara: ¿Hay fiestas religiosas en tu comunidad? ¿Son fiestas oficiales? ¿Cómo se celebran? ¿Hay feriados religiosos y seculares? ¿Cuáles son?

Imágenes. Escojan cada uno/a una de las siguientes fotos y descríbansela detalladamente contestando las siguientes preguntas.

1. ¿Qué están haciendo las personas en las fotos?
2. ¿Qué ropa llevan estas personas? ¿Qué colores hay en las fotos?
3. ¿Qué objetos hay en las fotos? ¿Para qué sirven?
4. ¿Piensan que la festividad de la foto es religiosa? ¿Por qué?
5. Según ustedes, ¿es la festividad divertida? ¿Por qué?

Note for *Cultura*
Beginning with this chapter, cultural notes are given in Spanish.

Alternate for 8-2
This may be done as a research activity. You may assign students different festivals, have them bring the images they find to class and do the following: 1. Locate the festival on a map. 2. Talk about the purpose of the festival and when it is celebrated. 3. Describe what people do there. 4. Give their opinion about the activities associated with the festival. Other festivals that you may assign include: *la Guelaguetza* (Oaxaca, Mexico); *las Fallas* (Valencia, Spain); *el Carnaval de Barranquilla* (Colombia); *la Fiesta de la Fruta y de las Flores* (Ambato, Ecuador); *el Festival de la Vendimia* (Perú, Chile, Argentina); *el Festival de la Pollera* (Panamá); *el Festival de la Frutilla* (Chile).

Standard 4.2
Students demonstrate understanding of the concept of culture through comparisons of the cultures studied and their own. The photos of festivals in this section, especially of Carnaval, and students' mental images of Mardi Gras in New Orleans provide the opportunity to compare how this event is celebrated in Latin America and the U.S. Students who observe Lent will be able to explain to their classmates the timing of Carnaval/Mardi Gras and the contrast between the secular and the religious character of Carnaval/Mardi Gras and Lent.

8-3

Contextos. Hablen sobre las ideas, sentimientos o costumbres que les evocan las siguientes palabras.

Modelo **" el carnaval "**

> La palabra carnaval me hace pensar en música, baile y alegría

> Pues a mí, en carrozas y mucha gente en la calle.

1. los cementerios
2. los toros
3. las flores
4. los disfraces
5. el baile
6. la música
7. los fuegos artificiales
8. las campanas (*bells*)
9. los colores
10. las banderas

Otras celebraciones

Go to the *Capítulo 8* **folder** online to complete the Learning Module for *Vocabulario en contexto: Otras celebraciones.*

diciembre 24

PLAN DE ESTUDIO

◎ LEARN
- Interactive presentation: *Otras celebraciones*
- Vocabulary tutorials

APPLY
- Activities

Online prep for students
Students will have completed the Learning Module for *Otras celebraciones* online. Additional in-class activities are available for download in the Supplementary Activities folder.

Note
Pascuas can refer to both Christmas and Easter: *la Pascua Florida* refers to Easter, *las Pascuas Navideñas* refers to Christmas.

In many countries, on New Year's Eve people eat 12 grapes at the stroke of midnight to ensure good fortune in the New Year.

September 16 is Mexico's Independence Day. Remind students that the date of Independence Day varies from country to country, and have them research the date in several Latin American countries.

Suggestion
Talk about one Hispanic holiday in detail. Mention that *el Día de los Muertos* in Mexico is on November 1 and 2, All Saints' Day and All Souls' Day, respectively. Families go to cemeteries to decorate the graves of departed loved ones with flowers. Stores sell candy skulls and fanciful skeletons; bakeries make *pan de muerto*. Souls of the departed are believed to return to visit their families on this occasion. Many families place altars, called *ofrendas,* in their homes, on which they place candles and the favorite food and drink of their loved ones.

Suggestion for 8-4
As a preview, compare holiday traditions, using comparatives/superlatives: *¿Qué costumbre es la más/ menos importante de tu familia? ¿Por qué tiene más/ menos importancia ese día?* For the *Segunda fase,* ask students to talk among themselves in groups of 3 or 4 and then share the information with the class.

PRÁCTICA COMUNICATIVA

8-4

Asociaciones.

PRIMERA FASE. Asocia las fechas con los días festivos. Compara tus respuestas con las de tu compañero/a.

1. __h__ el 25 de diciembre
2. __g__ el 2 de noviembre
3. __f__ el 6 de enero
4. __a__ el 4 de julio
5. __c__ el 24 de diciembre
6. __d__ el 31 de diciembre
7. __e__ el 14 de febrero
8. __b__ el 31 de octubre

a. el Día de la Independencia de Estados Unidos

b. el Día de las Brujas

c. la Nochebuena

d. la Nochevieja/el Fin de Año

e. el Día de los Enamorados/del Amor y la Amistad

f. el Día de los Reyes Magos

g. el Día de los Muertos

h. la Navidad

SEGUNDA FASE. Comenten entre ustedes las respuestas a las siguientes preguntas.

1. ¿Cuál(es) de las fiestas de *Primera fase* celebra cada uno/a de ustedes?

2. ¿Cuál es la fiesta favorita de la mayoría de las personas del grupo, y por qué?

3. ¿En cuál de estas fiestas reciben regalos? ¿Qué tipo de regalos?

4. ¿En cuál de estas fiestas hay una comida especial?

Cultura

En muchos países hispanos, los niños reciben regalos de Papá Noel o del Niño Dios el día de Navidad. Sin embargo, la Nochebuena se considera el día más importante. Muchos católicos van a la iglesia a la medianoche para asistir a la Misa del Gallo (*midnight mass*). El 6 de enero, día de la Epifanía, se celebra la llegada de los Reyes Magos con sus regalos para el Niño Jesús. La noche del 5 de enero, muchos niños se acuestan esperando la visita de los tres reyes que llegan montados en sus camellos con regalos para ellos.

Compara: En tu cultura, ¿existen celebraciones en las que se hacen regalos? ¿Hay alguna tradición especial para los niños? ¿Hay celebraciones infantiles que no son religiosas? ¿En qué se inspira esta celebración?

Suggestions for 8-5
Talk about parades with which students are familiar and ask questions. Encourage students to look for additional information. Some people mistakenly connect this date to Mexico's independence from Spain, which took place in 1810 and is celebrated on September 16. *Cinco de Mayo* is a festival about patriotism and unity, and it is celebrated on a larger scale by Mexicans and Mexican Americans in the U.S. Model the activity with a proficient student, if you wish.

El Cinco de Mayo es una fiesta que celebra la victoria de México contra Francia en la Batalla de Puebla en 1862. Ese día hay desfiles y los mexicanos visten sus trajes típicos.

8-5

Festivales o desfiles.

Piensa en algunos festivales o desfiles importantes y completa el cuadro siguiente. Tu compañero/a va a hacerte preguntas sobre ellos.

FESTIVAL O DESFILE	FECHA	LUGAR	DESCRIPCIÓN	OPINIÓN

Modelo

¿En qué fiesta o desfile importante estás pensando?

En el Cinco de Mayo.

¿Dónde lo celebran?

En México y en algunas ciudades de Estados Unidos, como Austin, Texas.

LENGUA The words **fiesta, festividad,** and **festival** are often used interchangeably. **Fiesta** may mean a holiday or a party or celebration. **Festividad** normally refers to a public festivity or a holiday. **Festival** often involves a series of events or celebrations of a public nature. Another term for holiday is **día festivo. Día feriado** is a legal holiday.

8-6 👥

Unos días festivos.

Hablen sobre cómo celebran ustedes estas fechas.

1. la Nochevieja/el Fin de Año
2. el Día de las Brujas
3. el Día de Acción de Gracias
4. el Día de la Independencia
5. el Año Nuevo
6. el Día de la Madre

Modelo **" tu cumpleaños "**

> ¿Cómo celebras tu cumpleaños?

> Lo celebro con mi familia y mis amigos. Recibo regalos y mi madre prepara mi comida favorita con pastel de chocolate de postre. Después escuchamos música, conversamos y a veces bailamos.

La Diablada en Bolivia

8-7 👥

Una celebración importante.

PRIMERA FASE. Escojan una celebración importante del mundo hispano (Carnaval, Semana Santa, Año Nuevo, Las Posadas, La Diablada, Día de la Independencia, etc.) y, si necesitan, busquen información en Internet sobre los siguientes aspectos:

1. el lugar donde se celebra
2. la época del año
3. las actividades
4. los vestidos o disfraces
5. la comida

👥 **SEGUNDA FASE.** Preparen una presentación de 1 o 2 minutos sobre la celebración que escogieron y preséntenla a la clase.

¿Cuáles son tus tradiciones? **247**

Alternate for 8-6
Preview the imperfect by asking students yes/no questions regarding holiday celebrations as children: *De niño/a, ¿celebrabas el Día de las Brujas? ¿Comías mucho el Día de Acción de Gracias? ¿Te gustaba recibir regalos el día de Navidad? ¿Recibías juguetes? ¿Dinero? ¿Ropa?*

Follow-up for 8-6
¿Qué día festivo te gusta más? ¿Por qué? ¿A quién no le gustan los días festivos? ¿Por qué?

Suggestion for 8-7
Assign students to do brief, structured presentations about celebrations they are familiar with, such as Kwanzaa, Hanukkah, Christmas, Ramadan, and Eid.

Alternate for 8-7
Recycle the preterit by asking students to describe their last birthday, what they did last New Year's Eve, and so on: *¿Qué hiciste el día de tu cumpleaños el año pasado? ¿Celebró la Navidad tu familia? ¿Fuiste a una fiesta para la Nochevieja?*

Suggestion
If students have already researched different festivals as suggested as an alternative to **8-2**, they can either do more research on those celebrations or choose others to research for **8-7**.

Las invitaciones

Go to the *Capítulo 8* **folder** online to complete the Learning Module for *Vocabulario en contexto: Las invitaciones.*

PLAN DE ESTUDIO

◎ LEARN
- Interactive presentation: *Las invitaciones*
- Vocabulary tutorials
- *Entrevistas* video

APPLY ◎
- Activities
- *Entrevistas* video activities

PRÁCTICA COMUNICATIVA

8-8

Una invitación.

Con un compañero/a lee la conversación entre Luisa y Arturo. Después invita a tu compañero/a a cenar, a ir al teatro o a un partido importante. Después, tu compañero/a va a invitarte a ti.

> LUISA: Hola, Arturo, ¿cómo estás?
> ARTURO: Bien, Luisa, ¿y tú?
> LUISA: Estupendamente. Mira, me gustaría invitarte a cenar el sábado para hablar de tu viaje a México.
> ARTURO: Mañana no puedo porque tengo un partido de fútbol.
> LUISA: ¡Qué lástima! ¿Y el domingo?
> ARTURO: El domingo está bien. Si quieres, podemos vernos antes para dar un paseo.
> LUISA: ¡Qué buena idea! Nos vemos en la plaza a las seis.
> ARTURO: Hasta el domingo.

En directo

To accept an invitation:
Gracias. Me encanta la idea.
Con mucho gusto.
Encantado/a.
Será un placer. *It will be a pleasure.*

To decline an invitation:
Me gustaría ir, pero…
¡Qué lástima/pena! Ese día tengo que…
No puedo, tengo un compromiso. *I can't, I have a prior engagement.*

 Click on the icon to listen to a conversation with these expressions.

8-9

Una invitación de boda.

Lean la invitación de boda y
la de la recepción, y contesten
las preguntas. Luego preparen
una lista con las diferencias
que encuentran entre estas
invitaciones y las de su país.

1. ¿Cómo se llaman los padres de
   la novia? ¿Y los del novio?
2. ¿Cómo se llaman los novios?
3. ¿Qué día es la boda?
4. ¿A qué hora es?
5. ¿En qué país se celebra
   esta boda?
6. ¿Adónde van a ir los invitados
   después de la ceremonia?

Agradecemos su presencia
después de la ceremonia religiosa
en el Club de Golf Chapultepec
Av. Conscripto Nº 425, Lomas
Hipódromo

R.S.V.P.
529-99-43
520-16-85

Personal

Pedro Martín Salda
Juana Montoya de Martín

Eduardo Calderón Solís
Elisa Noriega de Calderón

participan el matrimonio de sus hijos

Estelita
y
Alberto

y tienen el honor de invitarle a la ceremonia
religiosa que se celebrará el viernes 9 de febrero,
a las diecinueve treinta horas en el Convento de
San Joaquín, Santa Cruz Cocalco Nº 15,
Legaria, dignándose impartir la
bendición nupcial
el R.P. José Ortuno S.J.
Ciudad de México

Suggestion
You may want to describe
the roles of *el padrino* and *la
madrina* in Roman Catholic
weddings and baptisms.

Follow-up for 8-9
Discuss other events students
have attended. You may wish
to point out the abbreviations:
R.P. = *reverendo padre* and
S.J. = *Sociedad de Jesús.*

Cultura

Los mariachis son grupos musicales de México que
cantan y tocan violines, guitarras, guitarrones (guitarras
grandes), trompetas y vihuelas (otro tipo de guitarra).
Muchos creen que la palabra *mariachi* viene del francés
mariage, que significa *boda.* En la época colonial, el novio
contrataba estas bandas para festejar a la novia la noche
de la boda y, aún hoy en día, los grupos de mariachis
participan en muchas bodas mexicanas. Otros opinan
que el término *mariachi* proviene de una palabra indígena
que designa la plataforma donde se paraban los músicos
para tocar.

Compara: ¿Qué tipo de música se escucha en las bodas
en tu cultura? ¿Normalmente hay bandas de música o
DJ? ¿Quiénes contratan a una banda o a un DJ, la gente
modesta o la gente acomodada?

8-10

Una ocasión memorable.

Lean la invitación y contesten las preguntas.

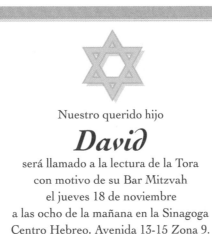

Nuestro querido hijo

David

será llamado a la lectura de la Tora
con motivo de su Bar Mitzvah
el jueves 18 de noviembre
a las ocho de la mañana en la Sinagoga
Centro Hebreo, Avenida 13-15 Zona 9.

Nos sentiremos muy honrados en compartir
con ustedes tan memorable ocasión
y será un placer recibirles en el desayuno
que seguidamente ofreceremos en el
salón de fiestas de la sinagoga.

David y Ruth Bauman
Fax: (502) 238-2042
Ciudad de Guatemala, Guatemala

1. ¿Cuál es el motivo de la celebración?
2. ¿Qué día es la celebración? ¿A qué hora?
3. ¿Hay otra actividad, además de la celebración religiosa?
4. ¿Quiénes son David y Ruth Bauman?
5. ¿En qué país tiene lugar esta celebración?
6. ¿Conoces a alguien que celebró su Bar Mitzvah o Bat Mitzvah últimamente? Cuéntale a tu compañero/a cómo fue esta celebración.

8-11

Una fiesta especial.

PRIMERA FASE. Piensa en una celebración o fiesta en la que participaste recientemente y describe la fiesta a tu compañero/a. Ten en cuenta las preguntas siguientes.

1. ¿Cuál es el nombre de la fiesta?
2. ¿Dónde se celebró? ¿Cuántos invitados asistieron?
3. ¿Cuándo fue la fiesta? ¿A qué hora empezó? ¿Cuánto tiempo duró?
4. Describe la comida que sirvieron.
5. ¿Cómo se divirtió la gente? ¿Qué música tocaron?

SEGUNDA FASE. Ahora compara tu fiesta con la de tu compañero/a y busquen algunas diferencias entre las dos fiestas.

8-12

La fiesta.

PRIMERA FASE. You will listen to four short dialogues about different holidays celebrated in the Hispanic world. Tell your partner one or two things you know about each holiday listed below.

 SEGUNDA FASE. Identify each holiday below according to the corresponding conversation you hear and write the appropriate number next to it. Check answers with a classmate.

___3___ el Día del Amor y la Amistad/Día de los Enamorados   ___4___ el Día de los Reyes Magos

___2___ el Día de los Muertos   ___1___ el Día de las Brujas

Gramática en contexto

Talking about ongoing actions in the past and making comparisons

Expressing ongoing actions and describing in the past:
The imperfect

Go to the *Capítulo 8* [folder] online to complete the Learning Module for *Gramática en contexto:* The imperfect.

PLAN DE ESTUDIO

◎ **LEARN**
- Interactive presentation: The imperfect
- Grammar tutorials

APPLY
- Activities
- Extra Practice

PRÁCTICA COMUNICATIVA

8-13 👥

Cuando yo tenía cinco años.

Marca (✓) las actividades que hacías cuando tenías cinco años y añade una más. Compara tus respuestas con las de tu compañero/a. ¿Cuántas actividades tienen en común?

1. _____ Jugaba en el parque con mi perro.
2. _____ Invitaba a mis amigos a dormir en mi casa.
3. _____ Salía con mis padres los fines de semana.
4. _____ Iba a la playa en el verano.
5. _____ Veía televisión hasta muy tarde.
6. _____ Celebraba el Año Nuevo con mis amigos.
7. _____ Participaba en las fiestas de mi escuela.
8. …

Online prep for students
Students will have completed the Learning Module for the imperfect online. This includes the Interactive presentation and all corresponding Apply activities. See Instructor's Resources for Supplementary Activities.

Tech Tip for *Gramática en contexto*
Project the illustrations from the online Learning Module for *Piénsalo* and ask students: *¿Cómo era la vida cuando la abuela era joven? Según la abuela, la música era mejor porque tenía más melodía y era más suave y romántica. Ella cree que hoy no hay música, que hay solo ruido.* Ask questions to check understanding.

Suggestions
Give examples of some uses of the imperfect: what you used to do while in college, descriptions of places or people, including their ages. You may wish to write some verb forms on the board and use visuals. Ask yes/no and either/or questions with the imperfect.

Suggestions
Bring photos to class or assign students to bring in photos and ask: *¿Qué hacía/hacías/hacían cuando tomaron esta foto?* to preview imperfect/preterit contrast. Allow students to guess what was happening in the photos before you tell them.

Note
Compare time expressions such as *mientras, a veces, siempre, generalmente,* and *frecuentemente* to those related to the preterit: *ayer, una vez, la semana pasada, de repente.*

Note
Point out that the *yo, él, ella, usted* forms of the imperfect are identical.

Suggestion
Present the preterit form *hubo* and explain to students that it is most often used in recounting sudden events, e.g., *hubo un accidente, hubo un tornado.*

Suggestion for 8-14
Students should add to the chart an additional activity that they used to do very often and one they did infrequently.

Follow-up for 8-14
Find out which activities the whole class enjoyed most and least.

8-14

En mi escuela secundaria.

PRIMERA FASE. Marca (✓) la frecuencia con que tus amigos/as y tú hacían estas actividades. Compara tus respuestas con las de tu compañero/a.

Modelo ❝decorar los salones de clase❞

Frecuentemente decorábamos los salones de clase.

Pues nosotros los decorábamos solo a veces.

SEGUNDA FASE. Hablen de los siguientes temas.

1. Tradicionalmente, ¿cómo celebraban y animaban al equipo de su escuela?

2. ¿Cuáles eran las actividades favoritas de cada uno/a ustedes?

ACTIVIDADES	SIEMPRE	FRECUENTEMENTE	A VECES	NUNCA
jugar videojuegos				
organizar reuniones para animar al equipo de la escuela (*pep rallies*)				
ir a los partidos de fútbol y otros deportes				
asistir a conciertos y obras de teatro				
participar en un equipo, en la banda, etc.				
otra actividad				

Follow-up for 8-15
Have students share their descriptions with the class.

Follow-up for 8-16
Ask students to describe their childhood memories of grandparents, parents, or other relatives. Starting with a phrase like *Cuando era niño/a, mi abuelo/a vivía/era…* , etc., anchors the descriptions in the past (imperfect), rather than in the present.

Variation for 8-16
Give students names of famous people and ask for descriptions, using verbs such as *era, vivía, se dedicaba a, pintaba,* and *escribía* (Frida Kahlo, William Shakespeare, Simón Bolívar, George Washington).

8-15

Se fue la luz. (*There was a blackout.*)

El sábado pasado los señores Herrera organizaron una fiesta en su casa. Durante la fiesta hubo un apagón en su barrio. Según el dibujo, describan lo que hacían las personas cuando se fue la luz. ¿Te pasó algo similar alguna vez? Cuéntaselo a tu compañero/a.

8-16

Mi casa.

Descríbele a tu compañero/a la casa o apartamento donde vivías cuando eras niño/a. Después, tu compañero/a debe hacer lo mismo.

8-17

Las fiestas infantiles.

Comenten cómo eran las fiestas de cumpleaños cuando ustedes eran pequeños/as. Hablen de los siguientes aspectos y añadan uno más.

1. lugar de la celebración
2. horas (comienzo y final)
3. dos o tres actividades que hacían
4. personas que participaban
5. comida y bebida que servían
6. ropa que llevaban
7. . . .

Suggestion for 8-17
Ask students what holiday or other event was celebrated most in their families. Have them talk about that holiday with their partner.

En directo

To talk about how things used to be:

Entonces...

Por aquel entonces...

En aquellos tiempos...

En esos años...

 Click on the icon to listen to a conversation with these expressions.

8-18

Antes y ahora.

Explícale a tu compañero/a cómo era tu vida antes de la universidad y cómo es ahora con respecto a los siguientes temas. Háganse preguntas.

1. tus relaciones familiares
2. tus relaciones sociales
3. tus estudios
4. tu tiempo libre
5. tus amigos
6. tus vacaciones

Modelo

"Antes yo vivía con mis padres pero ahora no los veo mucho porque mi universidad está en otro estado. ¿Y tú?"

Suggestion for 8-18
Each group may choose the era they want to compare with today (e.g., ancient/colonial times, the 1960s). After they discuss the various topics, groups should share their opinions with the class.

Audioscript for *En directo*
Stephen: *Abuelo, cuando eras niño, ¿cuál era tu celebración favorita?*
Abuelo: *Mi'jo, por aquel entonces se celebraban muchas fiestas y me divertía en todas. Sin embargo, mi favorita era el desfile que hacíamos todos los años en honor a la Virgen de Guadalupe. Toda la gente del pueblo participaba. Preparábamos carrozas; había desfiles, comida rica y orquestas que tocaban música festiva. En aquellos tiempos yo era muy buen bailarín y formaba parte de las comparsas. Eran unos tiempos maravillosos.*

Situaciones

1

ROLE A. You meet someone at a party, and the two of you are hitting it off. Your new friend asks you questions about yourself; answer with lots of detail.

ROLE B. You really connect with someone you meet at a party, and you want to find out more about him/her. Ask: a) what his/her family life and hometown were like when he/she was younger; b) the type of music he/she used to listen to; c) the books he/she used to read; and d) the holidays he/she celebrated most.

2

ROLE A. You are an exchange student from Mexico and want to find out about your American host brother's/sister's weekend and summer activities when he/she was in high school. Ask: a) what activites there were for high school students in the community, b) what he/she generally did with friends on the weekends; and c) what he/she usually did in the summer.

ROLE B. You are the American host brother/sister of an exchange student from Mexico (your classmate). Answer his/her questions about your weekend and summer activities when you were in high school. Provide lots of detail to give your guest a good idea of your activities and of life in your community.

Narrating in the past:
The preterit and the imperfect

Go to the *Capítulo 8* **folder** online to complete the Learning Module for *Gramática en contexto:* The preterit and the imperfect.

PLAN DE ESTUDIO

◎ LEARN
- Interactive presentation: The preterit and the imperfect
- Grammar tutorials

APPLY ◎
- Activities
- Extra Practice

PRÁCTICA COMUNICATIVA

8-19

¡Qué día más malo!

Ayer iba a ser un día especial para Pedro, pero sus planes terminaron mal. Marca (✓) las tres cosas más graves que le ocurrieron a Pedro según tu opinión y añade una más. Compara tus respuestas con las de tu compañero/a.

1. ____ Mientras se bañaba por la mañana, se cayó.

2. ____ Mientras desayunaba tranquilamente, el teléfono sonó y no pudo terminar de comer.

3. ____ Iba a la tienda para comprarle un anillo a su novia cuando alguien le robó el dinero.

4. ____ Mientras llamaba por teléfono a un restaurante para reservar una mesa, el restaurante se incendió.

5. ____ Iba a proponerle matrimonio a su novia cuando su ex novia lo llamó por teléfono.

6. ____ Mientras preparaba una cena deliciosa para celebrar el cumpleaños de su novia, el perro se comió el pastel.

7. . . .

Online prep for students
Students will have completed the Learning Module for the preterit and the imperfect online. Additional in-class activities are available for download in the Supplementary Activities folder online.

Suggestion
Retell the story of *Cenicienta* from the *Piénsalo* activity online and explain how the events move the story forward in time, and that the background information gives interesting and important details to flesh out the story, but does not advance the action. Ask students to identify the preterit and imperfect forms they recall from the story and help them see that the preterit recounts the events and the imperfect gives information about context and characters.

Suggestion
Create a brief narration to exemplify the use of both tenses or use the following: *Juan y su hermano Carlos fueron a Sonora, México, para pasar el verano con la familia de su padre. Sus tíos tenían una casita en la playa. El lugar era muy bonito. Las playas eran tranquilas y no había muchos turistas. Todos los días se levantaban a las ocho más o menos, desayunaban y se iban a pescar y a conversar con sus primos. Por la tarde, nadaban o hacían buceo y se reunían con sus amigos mexicanos. Pasaron las últimas dos semanas en la ciudad de Hermosillo. En Hermosillo salían por las noches y bailaban mucho en los clubes. Su último día fue muy triste para todos. Almorzaron con sus tíos y sus primos y después todos los llevaron al aeropuerto. Fue un verano maravilloso para estos chicos.*

Suggestion for 8-19
You may wish to have students share their responses with another pair. Alternatively, you may have the whole class compare their responses and defend their choices.

Suggestion for 8-20
Recycle *sentirse* in the context of a situation or story. Example: Say how you reacted to hearing bad/good news: *Cuando escuché la noticia del accidente me sentí muy mal. Fue un accidente terrible y no pude dormir esa noche.* Then say how you were feeling later. *Por la mañana todavía me sentía mal y llamé a mi mejor amiga.*

Note
You may want to point out that *ver* uses the same preterit endings as other *-er* verbs but the *yo* and *usted/él/ella* forms do not have an accent mark.

Suggestion for 8-21
Before doing this activity you may ask pairs to take turns writing descriptions and actions for each photo. Then have them work together on a detailed narration.

8-20

La última vez.

Túrnense para preguntarse cuándo fue la última vez que cada uno /a de ustedes hizo estas actividades y cómo se sentía mientras las hacía.

Modelo

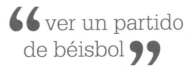

❝ ver un partido de béisbol ❞

1. participar en un campeonato
2. ganar un premio
3. estar en un desfile
4. disfrazarse
5. bailar en un carnaval
6. …

> ¿Cuándo fue la última vez que viste un partido de béisbol?

> Vi un partido de béisbol la semana pasada.

> ¿Y cómo te sentías mientras veías el partido?

> Estaba aburrido/a, porque no me gusta mucho el béisbol.

8-21

¿Qué les pasó?

Miren las fotos y expliquen lo que hacían estas personas y lo que les pasó. Describan con detalle la situación.

Modelo

❝ Meriel: caminar por el mercado, ver pulseras, discutir precio, empezar a llover **❞**

> Meriel caminaba por el mercado cuando vio unas pulseras.

> Y discutía el precio cuando empezó a llover.

1. María: caminar, ladrón (*thief*), robar el bolso, hablar por teléfono, parar.

2. Luisito: jugar con su hermana, caerse, hacerse daño (*hurt himself*), llorar (*to cry*), ayudar

3. Ángela: ir de viaje, caminar por el aeropuerto, abrirse la maleta, salirse la ropa

8-22

Un evento inolvidable.

Cuéntale a tu compañero/a algo inesperado que te ocurrió el año pasado.
Indica qué pasó, dónde y cuándo. Describe la escena con detalles.

Situaciones

1

ROLE A. Tell your friend about a surprise party you attended recently.

ROLE B. Your friend went to a surprise party and is going to tell you about it. Ask: a) where the party took place; b) who went to the party; c) what people did; and d) how your friend reacted to the surprise.

2

ROLE A. You have just come back from a vacation. Tell your classmate about a particular place you visited. Explain what it was like and what you did there.

ROLE B. Your classmate has just returned from a vacation. Ask about a particular place he/she visited while there. Find out a) what the place looked liked; b) what he/she did there; and c) what special event he/she can tell you about.

Warm-up for 8-22
Model this activity by describing an event and an unexpected occurrence, using visuals or gestures to facilitate comprehension: *El sábado pasado fui a una boda. La novia llevaba un velo muy largo. Después de la ceremonia fuimos a un hotel para el banquete. Todos estábamos muy contentos y bailábamos mientras la orquesta tocaba. Una pareja se movía mucho mientras bailaba y tropezó con la mesa donde estaban el pastel de boda y los platos de postre. ¡Total que el pastel se cayó al piso! La madre de la novia corrió hacia donde estaba el pastel y también se cayó. Los novios fueron adonde estaba la señora, pero esta se levantó y dijo que estaba bien. La orquesta empezó a tocar y la fiesta continuó, pero sin pastel. Fue una boda inolvidable.*

Follow-up for 8-22
After each student in the pair finishes narrating, the other should ask questions to obtain more information about the event.

Tech tip for *Situaciones*
Students may want to practice on line with a partner. Remind them that they can click on the microphone icon to link to the page online that explains how students can connect with a partner online to do the activity.

Suggestion for *Situaciones*
Remind students that this is theater, and that they may have to put themselves in an unfamiliar role when presenting *Situaciones*.

Online prep for students
Students will have completed the Learning Module for Comparisons of inequality. See Instructor's Resources for Supplementary Activities.

Note
The structure of comparisons in Spanish is similar to that of English. Students will find this grammar point easier than many others in *Unidos*. You may wish to focus on the irregular comparatives (see next page), as well as on high-frequency comparisons, such as *A + verb + mejor que B* and *Me gusta más + infinitive + que + infinitive*.

Comparing people and things:

Comparisons of inequality

Go to the *Capítulo 8* **folder** online to complete the Learning Module for *Gramática en contexto:* Comparisons of inequality.

Número de días del Carnaval de la Primavera	3	2
	2011	2012
Asistencia del público	25.390	18.864
Mujeres	6.000	2.000
Hombres	4.000	5.000
Niños	25.000	27.000
presupuesto (Budget)	150.000.,000	180.000.,

PLAN DE ESTUDIO

◎ **LEARN**
- Interactive presentation: Comparisons of inequality
- Grammar tutorials

APPLY ◎
- Activities
- Extra Practice

PRÁCTICA COMUNICATIVA

8-23

Comparación de dos desfiles.

PRIMERA FASE. Lee la siguiente información sobre dos desfiles mexicanos. Completa las frases con **más que, menos que, más de** o **menos de,** según la información en la tabla. Compara tus respuestas con las de tu compañero/a.

	VERACRUZ	**MÉRIDA**
habitantes	568.313	717.175
promedio (*average*) de público que participa	15.000 personas	13.000 personas
número de bandas	9	7
número de policías	220	185

1. Mérida tiene __más__ habitantes __que__ Veracruz.
2. __Más__ personas asisten al desfile de Veracruz __que__ al desfile de Mérida.
3. Los dos desfiles tienen __más__ __de__ cinco bandas.
4. Mérida gasta __menos__ dinero en seguridad (*security*) __que__ Veracruz.
5. __Más__ __de__ medio millón de personas viven en Veracruz.
6. Probablemente el público de Mérida es __menos__ entusiasta __que__ el de Veracruz.

Suggestions for 8-23
Point to the location of Veracruz and Mérida on a map. Students will read in the *Cultura* box that Mérida was chosen as *la Capital Americana de la Cultura* in 2000 by the *Organización Capital Americana de la Cultura,* an organization of Latin American nations that selects one city each year for this designation. Recycle weather expressions by asking students to guess what the weather is like in these cities. Ask them to compare the weather in Veracruz and Mérida with that of their own city: *En invierno, ¿hace más o menos frío en Mérida que en tu ciudad? ¿Dónde hace menos humedad, en tu ciudad o en Veracruz? ¿Dónde es peor el clima durante el período de huracanes, en Veracruz o en tu ciudad?*

SEGUNDA FASE. La banda de tu universidad piensa participar en uno de estos desfiles, pero no puede gastar mucho dinero. Con un compañero/a decidan a qué desfile debe asistir y expliquen por qué.

COSTO POR PERSONA	DESFILE DE VERACRUZ	DESFILE DE MÉRIDA
transporte	5.824,50 pesos	6.552,60 pesos
hotel por día	880,50 pesos	915,25 pesos
comidas por día	450,00 pesos	348,00 pesos

Cultura

La moneda mexicana es el peso. Tanto en los billetes como en las monedas de metal está el escudo nacional, que tiene un águila parada sobre un nopal (un tipo de cacto) que está devorando a una serpiente.

Compara: ¿Sabes cuál es la tasa de cambio (*exchange rate*) entre el peso mexicano y el dólar estadounidense? ¿Qué imágenes hay en los billetes de tu país? ¿Y en monedas?

¿Qué importancia histórica y simbólica tienen esas imágenes?

Cultura

Veracruz y Mérida son dos ciudades mexicanas importantes. Veracruz, que está a 400 kilómetros (250 millas) al sureste de la Ciudad de México, fue fundada por el conquistador Hernán Cortés en 1519. Por su puerto, que es el más importante del país, Veracruz es conocida como *la puerta al mundo*.

Mérida es la ciudad principal del estado de Yucatán, en el sureste del país. Está a más de 1.550 kilómetros (965 millas) de la capital. En 2000 Mérida fue nombrada *la Capital Americana de la Cultura* a causa de su alta calidad de vida y su extraordinario desarrollo en las artes.

Compara: ¿Cuáles son las ciudades más turísticas de tu país? ¿Por qué? ¿Dónde están los puertos más importantes? ¿Hay ciudades que han recibido nombres o títulos especiales en tu país? ¿Cuáles?

Suggestion for 8-23
Segunda fase
You may wish to check (or ask students to check) the exchange rate between the American dollar and the Mexican *peso* so students have a better understanding of costs per person.

Suggestion
You may wish to tell students that the coat of arms that appears on Mexican coins and bills is the national symbol that also appears on the flag. The coat of arms was inspired by the Aztec legend about the founding of Tenochtitlán. According to the legend, the war god Huitzilopochtli had commanded the Aztec people to build their capital at the spot where they found an eagle perched on a prickly pear cactus (*nopal*) growing on a rock submerged in a lake. The eagle would have a snake trapped in its mouth that it had just caught. After 200 years of wandering, they found the promised sign on a small island in the swampy Lake Texcoco. Here they founded their new capital, Tenochtitlán, which was later known as Mexico City.

La Calavera (*skull*) Catrina.

Los mexicanos celebran el Día de los Muertos con imágenes como estas. Compárenlas según los siguientes criterios.

1. el tamaño
2. los colores
3. el estilo
4. lo que más te gusta de una de ellas

Personas famosas.

PRIMERA FASE. Comparen a Eva Longoria con Christina Aguilera según los siguientes criterios.

1. su aspecto físico
2. su edad
3. el tipo de trabajo que hacen
4. el dinero o popularidad que tienen

SEGUNDA FASE. Escoge a una de estas famosas y compárate con ella. Tu compañero/a te va a decir si está de acuerdo o no.

Situaciones

1

ROLE A. You and your classmate are preparing a party in honor of your teacher, who is leaving the university at the end of the year. You prefer to have it on campus rather than at a local restaurant. Try to persuade your classmate by explaining the advantages with respect to: a) expenses (**gastos**); b) stress (**estrés**); c) work involved; and d) possible problems. Try to reach an agreement.

ROLE B. You and a classmate are planning a surprise party in honor of your teacher, who is leaving the university at the end of the year. You prefer to have it at a local restaurant than in a location on campus. Give your opinion in regard to: a) expenses (**gastos**); b) stress (**estrés**); c) work involved; and d) possible problems. Try to reach an agreement.

2

ROLE A. You are a student government representative presenting a proposal to the dean to change the graduation ceremony. Compare the ceremony at your school with one at a rival institution. Say that the other ceremony is better because it is smaller, better organized, less expensive, and usually has better music and speeches (**discursos**).

ROLE B. You are the dean. A student government representative is proposing changes in the graduation ceremony. Listen to the presentation and ask questions to compare the advantages of both types of ceremonies.

Comparing people and things:
Comparisons of equality

Go to the *Capítulo 8* **folder** online to complete the Learning Module for *Gramática en contexto:* Comparisons of equality.

PLAN DE ESTUDIO

◎ LEARN
- Interactive presentation: Comparisons of equality
- Grammar tutorials

APPLY ◎
- Activities
- Extra Practice

PRÁCTICA COMUNICATIVA

8-26

Unos estudiantes afortunados.

PRIMERA FASE. Lean algunos datos personales sobre cuatro estudiantes e indiquen si las afirmaciones a continuación son ciertas (**C**) o falsas (**F**). Si son falsas (**F**), corrijan la información.

	PEDRO	VILMA	MARTA	RICARDO
hermanos	2	3	3	2
clases	5	5	4	6
dinero para gastos personales cada mes	5.000 pesos	8.500 pesos	5.000 pesos	8.500 pesos
películas en DVD	200	180	180	215
viajes a otros países	3	8	3	8

Vilma Pedro Marta Ricardo

1. __F__ Pedro tiene **tantos** hermanos **como** Vilma.
2. __F__ Vilma tomó **tantas** clases este semestre **como** Ricardo.
3. __C__ La familia de Marta es **tan** grande **como** la familia de Vilma.
4. __C__ Cada mes, Ricardo recibe **tanto** dinero de sus padres **como** Vilma.
5. __F__ Pedro viaja **tanto como** Ricardo.

SEGUNDA FASE. Escoge uno de los estudiantes de la *Primera fase* y dile a tu compañero/a las cosas que tienes en común con él/ella.

8-27

Opiniones.

PRIMERA FASE. Selecciona a dos personas famosas, dos festividades en tu cultura y dos programas cómicos de la televisión.

SEGUNDA FASE. Ahora, expresen su opinión sobre ellos y compárenlos.

Modelo

> Tom Cruise es tan buen actor como Johnny Depp.

> No, desde mi punto de vista Johnny Depp es mejor actor que Tom Cruise.

Situaciones

Suggestion for *Situaciones*
Additional situations are available in the Instructor's Resource folder.

1

ROLE A. You are reminiscing about Independence Day celebrations when you were a child. Tell your classmate that you think that a) in the past Americans were more patriotic (**patrióticos**); b) the celebrations were less expensive; and c) the celebrations were more family oriented (**se celebraban en familia**) than today.

ROLE B. Your classmate argues that today's Independence Day celebrations are less family oriented than in the past. You disagree. State that a) today Americans are just as patriotic as they were in the past; b) people used to spend less money because they made less money; and c) today families celebrate Independence Day together as much as in the past.

2

ROLE A. Your next-door neighbors are three students, two of whom are identical twins (**gemelos/as**). Even though you have lived there for a year, you cannot tell them apart. When you run into the third roommate on campus, you mention all the ways in which the twins seem absolutely alike to you. Ask your neighbor's help in telling them apart.

ROLE B. You and your long-time friends, who are identical twins (**gemelos/as**), share an apartment. When your neighbor asks you for help in telling them apart, describe a) two ways in which they are exactly alike in appearance, abilities, and preferences; and b) two ways in which they are different that help you tell them apart.

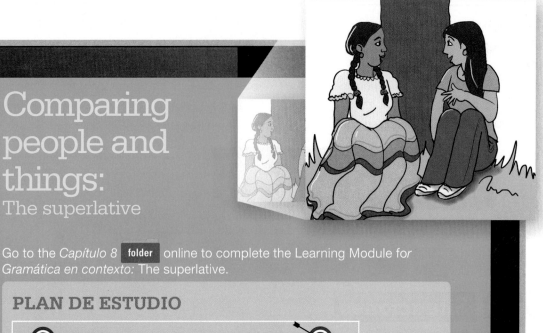

Comparing people and things:
The superlative

Go to the *Capítulo 8* **folder** online to complete the Learning Module for *Gramática en contexto:* The superlative.

PLAN DE ESTUDIO

◎ LEARN
- Interactive presentation: The superlative
- Grammar tutorials

APPLY ◎
- Activities
- Extra Practice

PRÁCTICA COMUNICATIVA

8-28

Estadísticas demográficas. **PRIMERA FASE.** Lee la información de la tabla siguiente e indica a qué país de la columna B se refiere cada oración de la columna A. Compara tus respuestas con las de tu compañero/a.

	MÉXICO	GUATEMALA	ESTADOS UNIDOS
Población (aprox.) del país	114.975.406 habitantes	14.388.929 habitantes	313.847.465 habitantes
Población de la capital	México, D.F.: 8.836.045	Ciudad de Guatemala: 1.110.100	Washington, DC: 601.723
Número de lenguas indígenas	62	23	aprox. 150
Religión predominante	76.5% son católicos (aprox. 88.000.000)	49% son católicos (aprox. 7.058.000)	51.3% son protestantes (aprox. 161.004.000)
Número de estados o departamentos	32 estados	22 departamentos	50 estados

Columna A	Columna B
1. __c__ Este país tiene **el mayor número** de habitantes.	**a.** México
2. __a__ La capital de este país es **la más** grande.	**b.** Guatemala
3. __c__ Es el país donde existe **el mayor** número de lenguas indígenas.	**c.** Estados Unidos
4. __b__ Este es el país con **menos** lenguas indígenas.	
5. __c__ Este país tiene **el menor** porcentaje de personas que profesan el catolicismo.	
6. __c__ Este país tiene **el mayor** número de gobiernos estatales o departamentales.	

SEGUNDA FASE. Escoge otro país sin decir su nombre y menciona tres cosas en las que se distingue de los demás países. Tu compañero/a tiene que adivinar qué país es.

8-29

¿En qué pueblo o ciudad?

Respondan a las siguientes preguntas y, luego, comparen sus respuestas con las de otra pareja. ¿Están de acuerdo o tienen opiniones diferentes?

¿En qué pueblo o ciudad de su país…

1. sirven la mejor comida étnica?

2. se come la comida más picante (*spicy*)?

3. se vende el café cubano más fuerte?

4. celebran las mejores fiestas de Año Nuevo?

5. hay el mayor número de desfiles hermosos?

6. tocan la mejor música folclórica estadounidense?

Tech tip for *Situaciones*
You may want to assign partners and have pairs create a mini-skit using the video-posting feature, MediaShare, online.

 # Situaciones

1

ROLE A. You and your friend are talking about movies. Ask him/her opinion about: a) the best American film and why; b) the best actor/actress in Hollywood; and c) the worst film of the year. Also ask your friend who his/her favorite director is.

ROLE B. You and your friend are talking about movies. Answer your friend's questions about the best/worst American films and actors. Respond to your friend's question about your favorite director.

2

ROLE A. You took a trip for spring break and had a great time. Tell your classmate the five most interesting places you saw or activities you did. Provide details about at least one place or activity.

ROLE B. Ask several questions about your classmate's spring break trip to learn about his/her interesting and enjoyable activities. Then say where you went during spring break, and share the favorite parts of your trip.

ESCUCHA

8-30 [Presentational]

Preparación. Es el 22 de diciembre y dos amigos conversan sobre las celebraciones del fin de año. Antes de escuchar su conversación, describe en un párrafo cómo celebras tú el fin de año.

ESTRATEGIA

Draw conclusions based on what you know

Understanding what someone says involves using the context and the information the speaker provides to draw conclusions that go beyond literal comprehension. This process is called inferencing, or making inferences. For example, if you are driving with a friend and get lost, you may say, "There is a gas station up there on the right." Your friend will probably infer that you want to stop to ask for directions.

Integrated Performance Assessment (IPA)

The activities in each Unidos section correspond to the three modes of communication as indicated by the tag next to each activity.

Warm-up for 8-31
As a prelistening activity, have students work in groups of 4 and narrate what they did last year to celebrate their favorite holiday.

Audioscript for 8-31
Daniel: *Estoy encantado de poder pasar las Navidades contigo y tu familia aquí en México.*
Sandra: *Y te tenemos muchas sorpresas. Esta noche empiezan las Posadas.*
Daniel: *¿Y qué es eso?*
Sandra: *Aquí en México empezamos a celebrar la Navidad nueve días antes y nos reunimos un grupo de familiares y personas cercanas y pedimos posada.*
Daniel: *¿Piden posada?*
Sandra: *Sí, un lugar para pasar la noche, igual que hicieron José y María cuando llegaron a Belén. Vamos a casa de un pariente o alguien conocido, cantamos canciones típicas de Navidad y pedimos posada. Los parientes o amigos responden que no podemos entrar. Nosotros seguimos pidiendo posada hasta que nos dejan entrar. Entonces empieza la fiesta, y al final se rompe una piñata con regalos y dulces.*
Daniel: *Parece ser divertido.*
Sandra: *Sí, es muy divertido. Hacemos esto todas las noches durante nueve días. Y ustedes, ¿qué hacen en Navidad?*
Daniel: *En casa nos reunimos la noche de Nochebuena. Viene toda la familia e intercambiamos regalos.*
Sandra: *Bueno, esta Navidad va a ser muy diferente para ti, pero te va a gustar mucho.*

8-31  [Interpretive]

Escucha. First, read the statements below, and then listen as two friends talk about a Mexican holiday. After listening, mark (✓) the statements that provide information you can infer from what you heard.

1. ____ Daniel es mexicano.

2. ____ Sandra es una persona muy tímida.

3. ✓ Sandra no es estadounidense.

4. ____ Daniel está triste porque no va a celebrar la Navidad con su familia.

5. ____ Pedir posada es una costumbre en la que participa solamente la familia.

6. ✓ Daniel no conoce algunas costumbres mexicanas.

Comprueba
I was able to…

____ **make inferences based upon what I heard.**

____ **use contextual and factual information to draw conclusions.**

8-32  [Interpersonal]

Un paso más. Comparte tus respuestas a estas preguntas con tu compañero/a.

1. ¿Qué fiesta o tradición religiosa te gustaría celebrar en un país hispano? ¿Por qué?

2. ¿Celebras esa fiesta en tu ciudad o país? ¿Cómo se celebra?

3. ¿Qué fiesta o tradición celebras con tus amigos?

AUTOEVALUACIÓN

☐ I feel confident that I was able to understand what I heard.

☐ I need more listening practice.

STUDY PLAN

▶ Good job! Move on to the next section, *Habla.*

▶ Go to the *Unidos* [folder] online for *Escucha* practice.

You may want to give students some examples of open-ended questions that encourage the other person to talk, such as *¿Podrías hablar de los deportes que practicabas de niño/a?* This type of question elicits long and more detailed responses than direct, close-ended questions like *¿Qué deportes practicabas cuando eras niño/a?*

Suggestion for 8-33
Have students work in small groups helping each other prepare open-ended initial and follow-up questions for their interviews.

Audioscript for *En directo*
Ernesto: *Profesora, me gustaría saber en qué países de América Latina se celebra la Navidad. ¿Me podría hablar sobre ello?*
Profesora: *En verdad, la Navidad se celebra por toda América Latina pero las tradiciones varían. Es decir, la gente celebra este día de diferentes formas; tienen diferentes costumbres.*
Ernesto: *¡Qué interesante! ¿Qué más me puede decir sobre estas tradiciones?*

Suggestions for 8-35
To keep identities of the interviewees hidden, pairs can type their reports, referring to each other as *Persona A* and *Persona B*. You may wish to use your course management system to post the reports and have students try to figure out the identity of the pairs as homework and then compare notes in class.
    You may wish to have students read aloud the anonymous reports (randomly handed out), and the class together guesses the identities of the pairs.

HABLA

8-33  [Presentational]

Preparación. Escriban una pregunta de seguimiento (*follow-up*) para cada una de las siguientes afirmaciones. Luego, compártanlas con la clase.

1. Cuando yo tenía doce años practicaba muchos deportes.

2. En mi familia celebrábamos fiestas.

3. Algunas costumbres familiares me gustaban y otras no.

8-34  [Interpersonal]

Habla. Entrevista a tu compañero/a sobre su infancia y adolescencia. Hazle preguntas para iniciar temas y obtener más información. Toma notas de sus respuestas.

Comprueba

In my conversation…

___ I asked both topic-opening questions and follow-up questions.

___ I took effective notes.

8-35 [Interpretive]

Un paso más. Escriban un breve informe comparativo sobre los siguientes aspectos de la infancia y adolescencia de cada uno/a de ustedes. Otros compañeros van a leer su informe y tratar de averiguar quiénes son ustedes. Mantengan su identidad en secreto.

1. Durante la infancia/adolescencia…

2. Con respecto a los deportes/las fiestas…

3. La persona A y la persona B tuvieron una niñez/adolescencia semejante/diferente porque…

Modelo   ALMAS GEMELAS

    ❝ Somos dos almas gemelas. Tanto mi compañero/a como yo nacimos en… ❞

MUNDOS APARTES

    ❝ Somos dos mundos apartes. Mi compañero/a nació en… Yo nací en… ❞

AUTOEVALUACIÓN

☐ I feel confident that I communicated successfully.

☐ I need more speaking practice.

STUDY PLAN

▶ Good job! Move on to the next section, **Lee.**

▶ Go to the **Unidos** folder online for **Habla** practice.

ESTRATEGIA

Conduct an interview

To conduct an interview, you need to ask two types of questions: a) questions to open up a topic; and b) follow-up questions to get additional information. Questions that can be answered with **Sí** or **No** are not likely to elicit much information, unless you follow up with **¿Por qué?** Listen carefully to what your interviewee says so that you can ask relevant follow-up questions.

En directo

To ask someone to talk about a topic:

¿Me podrías hablar sobre… ?
Can you talk to me more about … ?

¿Qué me puede decir usted sobre/de… ?
What can you tell me about … ?

Me gustaría saber…
I would like to know …

To ask someone to expand on a topic:

¿Podrías hablar más sobre… ?

¿Qué más me puedes decir sobre… ?

To show empathy when responding:

¡Oh! ¡Qué lástima! ¡Cuánto lo siento!
How sad! I'm so sorry.

To share someone's happiness:

¡Qué fabuloso/bueno!
How fabulous/great!

¡Cuánto me alegro!
I'm so happy to hear that!

To express interest in what someone said:

¡Qué interesante!
How interesting!

 Click on the icon to listen to a conversation with these expressions.

LEE

Preparación. Las creencias sobre la muerte varían de una cultura a otra. Indica si las siguientes creencias y prácticas se asocian con la cultura egipcia (**E**), con alguna cultura indígena americana (**I**) o con ambas (**A**). Intercambien la información y compárenla con su propia cultura.

1. __A__ Creían que había vida después de la muerte.

2. __A__ Construían pirámides para honrar a los muertos.

3. __I__ Vestían a los muertos con ropa funeraria especial.

4. __A__ Ponían una máscara sobre la cara del muerto.

5. __A__ Enterraban (*They buried*) al muerto en las pirámides, en tumbas o sepulcros, de acuerdo al estatus social de la persona muerta.

6. __A__ La familia de la persona muerta depositaba joyas y objetos de valor en la tumba o pirámide.

7. __I__ Rociaban (*They sprayed*) el cadáver con un polvo de color rojo para simbolizar el renacimiento (*rebirth*).

ESTRATEGIA

Make inferences

Understanding a written text, like listening to a speaker, involves both comprehending the words literally and using information provided to make inferences. To make inferences when you read, use your background knowledge, understanding of context, and active thinking skills, as well as your ability to understand the printed words.

8-37 [Interpretive]

Lee. Determina si las siguientes afirmaciones representan información explícita (**E**) o si son inferencias (**I**) basadas en el contenido del texto. Si es una inferencia, indica la oración o las oraciones en el texto en que se basa(n).

1. __E__ Los expertos no saben de dónde vinieron los mayas.

2. __I__ Los mayas crearon una gran civilización.

3. __I__ Las comunidades mayas tenían autoridades que los gobernaban.

4. __I__ Como los egipcios, los mayas construyeron edificios magníficos para honrar la memoria de personas de alto estatus en su comunidad.

5. __E__ Los mayas, como otros grupos indígenas, pensaban que la vida continuaba después de la muerte.

6. __E__ Para los mayas, el tipo de muerte determinaba el destino de una persona.

7. __I__ No todos los mayas iban al mismo destino después de la muerte.

8. __E__ La comida, el agua y los amuletos ayudaban al espíritu del muerto a llegar a su destino final.

Comprueba

I was able to…

____ use literal as well as implied information to make inferences.

____ differentiate between explicit facts and information provided indirectly.

Suggestion for 8-37
To check that students understand the content of the reading, you might suggest they use the information from it as a basis for comparison with other cultures they may know about, such as Native American culture.

Creencias y costumbres mayas sobre la muerte

El origen de los mayas es incierto. Sin embargo, se sabe que esta civilización ocupó y se desarrolló[1] en los actuales territorios de Guatemala, México, Belice, Honduras y El Salvador. Durante su período de mayor esplendor, los mayas construyeron ciudades y pirámides, donde enterraban a sus gobernantes y los veneraban después de muertos.

Los mayas compartían con otras culturas mesoamericanas algunas creencias y costumbres. Entre otras cosas, creían en la vida después de la muerte y en la interacción entre el mundo humano y el mundo espiritual. Creían que el destino de una persona después de la muerte dependía de la forma en que moría y no de su conducta mientras vivía. Las tumbas y los vestuarios funerarios confirman que los mayas creían que el espíritu se prolongaba más allá de la muerte. La mayoría de los muertos iba a Xibalbá, un lugar en el mundo de abajo.

Para llegar a Xibalbá había que superar numerosos peligros. El espíritu debía comer bien y cuidarse. Por eso, los mayas dejaban en la tumba una vestimenta funeraria. También colocaban comida, agua y amuletos protectores, de acuerdo con el estatus social del muerto.

Los mayas rociaban el cadáver con un polvo rojo que simbolizaba el renacimiento. También lo adornaban con joyas, collares, pulseras y anillos de jade, hueso[2] o concha[3] y un cinturón ceremonial. En muchas tumbas ponían una máscara sobre la cara del muerto para ocultar su identidad. En la boca le ponían una cuenta[4] de jade, símbolo de lo precioso y lo perenne, para preservar su espíritu inmortal.

Algunas de estas creencias y costumbres todavía se conservan, con ciertas variaciones, en algunas comunidades de Guatemala, México y El Salvador.

[1]*developed* [2]*bone* [3]*shell* [4]*bead*

8-38 · Presentational

Un paso más.

Escribe un párrafo e indica qué objetos probablemente ponían los mayas en la tumba o pirámide de un gobernante con las siguientes características:

- Era físicamente activo.
- Le gustaba mucho el arte.
- Estudiaba astronomía.
- Le fascinaba la guerra.
- Tenía ocho hijas, todas muy bellas.

AUTOEVALUACIÓN

☐ I feel confident that I understood the reading and was able to use the information.

☐ I need more reading practice.

STUDY PLAN

▶ Good job! Move on to the next section, *Escribe.*

▶ Go to the *Unidos* folder online for *Lee* practice.

ESCRIBE

8-39 Interpersonal

Preparación. Vas a narrar una historia personal, real o imaginaria. Habla con tu compañero/a para determinar lo siguiente:

1. ¿Cuál es el objetivo de tu narración?
2. ¿Cuántos protagonistas hay? ¿Qué características físicas y de personalidad tienen?
3. ¿Cómo vas a organizar los hechos? ¿En orden cronológico?
4. ¿Qué información vas a presentar en la introducción? ¿Cuál va a ser el conflicto?
5. Escribe una lista de verbos que te ayuden a describir el ambiente (*setting*) y otros que narren la acción. Intercambien sus listas y háganse sugerencias.

8-40 Presentational

Escribe. Usa la información de **8-39** y escribe tu narración.

Comprueba

I was able to…

___ successfully develop a story, including the characters and the events.

___ recount the order of events chronologically.

8-41 Interpretive

Un paso más.

Intercambia tu narración con un/a compañero/a. Mientras leen escriban tres preguntas para hacerle a su compañero/a sobre los personajes, el conflicto o la resolución.

ESTRATEGIA

Select and sequence details to write effective narratives

A successful narrative is characterized by a logical, clear, and believable sequence of events, and a good description of setting and characters.

Structure your narration as follows:

- Introduce the characters, describe the setting, and begin the action.
- Present the unfolding of the action. Describe the characters and the tensions caused by their actions or by the events around them.
- Either resolve the actions/ tensions, or leave the ending unresolved so your reader can imagine what happens.

En directo

To indicate chronological order:

Primero,…

Después,…/Después de (un tiempo),…

Luego,…

Más tarde,…

Finalmente,…/Por fin,…

 Click on the icon to listen to a conversation with these expressions.

Audioscript for *En directo*
Mario: *¡Felicidades, Pati! El carnaval internacional fue increíble.*
Pati: *Gracias, Mario. La verdad es que nos divertimos mucho.*
Mario: *Dime, ¿cómo fueron los preparativos?*
Pati: *Bueno, primero todos los participantes nos reunimos y hablamos del plan. Después, quedamos todos los martes a la una de la tarde para practicar. Luego, el día antes del carnaval, decoramos las carrozas. Por fin, llegó el día del carnaval y ¡todo nos fue perfectamente bien!*

MÉXICO

El Museo Nacional de Antropología, situado dentro del Bosque de Chapultepec en México, D.F., exhibe la mayor colección de piezas arqueológicas de la cultura precolombina. Aquí hay una réplica del templo maya de Hochob dentro de los jardines del museo.

La ciudad de San Miguel de Allende es reconocida por la UNESCO como Patrimonio de la Humanidad por sus contribuciones tanto culturales como arquitectónicas.

Cultura y tradiciones mexicanas

Go to the *Enfoque cultural* [folder] in *Capítulo 8* online to learn more about México.

◎ **LEARN**
- Interactive presentation *Cultura y tradiciones mexicanas*

◎ **APPLY**
- Activities

En 2011 las Naciones Unidas declaró a Mérida "Ciudad de la Paz" por la excelente calidad de vida y seguridad que ofrece a sus habitantes. Festivales como este se celebran semanalmente en las calles del centro.

PRÁCTICA COMUNICATIVA

8-42

Usa la información. Fuiste a México y asististe a una de las siguientes celebraciones.

a. el Cinco de Mayo

b. el Día de los Muertos

c. la Danza del Venado

d. el Día de la Virgen de Guadalupe

Escríbele un correo electrónico a tu profesor/a y cuéntale cuál de las celebraciones viste y dónde la viste. Incluye al menos cuatro datos sobre esta celebración. Visita Internet si necesitas más información.

En este capítulo...

Comprueba lo que sabes

Go to the *Comprueba lo que sabes* folder online to review what you have learned in this chapter. Practice with the following:

| Vocabulary Flashcards | Games | Oral Practice | Practice Test / Study Plan | Video en contexto |

Vocabulario

Las fiestas y las celebraciones
la alegría
el aserrín
el carnaval
la carreta
la carroza
la celebración
la comparsa
la corrida (de toros)
la costumbre
el desfile
el día feriado
el día festivo
el festival
la festividad, la fiesta
la invitación
el preparativo
la procesión
la semilla
el toro
la tradición

Las personas
el antepasado
la gente
el rey/la reina

La música
la melodía
la orquesta
el ruido

Los lugares
el camino
el cementerio
la iglesia
el teatro

El tiempo
antes
el comienzo
entonces
hoy en día
mientras

Las descripciones
adornado/a
animado/a
difunto/a, muerto/a
maravilloso/a
suave
último/a

Verbos
acompañar
comenzar (ie)
dar un paseo
disfrazarse (c)
divertirse (ie, i)
encerrar (ie)
invitar
mantener (g, ie)
quedar
recordar (ue)
reunirse

Otras celebraciones
el Año Nuevo
el Día de Acción de Gracias
el Día de las Brujas
el Día de los Enamorados/ del Amor y la Amistad
el Día de la Independencia de México
el Día de la Madre
el Día del Padre
la Navidad
la Nochebuena
la Nochevieja
la Pascua

Expresiones de tiempo
a veces
frecuentemente
generalmente
mientras
siempre

Comparaciones
más bueno/a / mejor
más de...
más grande / mayor
más joven / menor
más malo/a / peor
más pequeño/a / menor
más... que
más viejo/a / mayor
mejor que
menos de...
menos... que
peor que
tan... como
tanto como
tanto/a... como
tantos/as... como

Notas

Introduction to chapter
Introduce the chapter theme about what people do for a living and ask questions to recycle content from the previous chapter. Related questions: *¿Cuáles son algunos días feriados en que normalmente no trabaja la gente? Sin embargo, hay gente que por profesión siempre está trabajando. ¿Pueden nombrar algunas de estas profesiones? ¿Qué otras profesiones saben decir en español? ¿Te gustaría llevar traje de chaqueta todos los días para ir a trabajar? ¿Cómo te gustaría vestir para ir a trabajar? ¿Trabajaste el verano pasado? ¿Qué trabajo tenías? ¿Qué hacías en tu trabajo?*

Integrated Performance Assessment: Three Modes of Communication

Presentational: See activities **9-17, 9-26, 9-31, 9-343, 9-36, and 9-38.**

Interpretive: See Activities **9-1, 9-2, 9-3, 9-4, 9-6, 9-7, 9-8, 9-9, 9-10, 9-12, 9-13, 9-14, 9-15, 9-16, 9-18, 9-19, 9-20, 9-21, 9-22, 9-23, 9-24, 9-25, 9-27, 9-29, 9-33, and 9-35.**

Interpersonal: See activities **9-1, 9-2, 9-3, 9-4, 9-5, 9-6, 9-7, 9-8, 9-9, 9-10, 9-11, 9-12, 9-13, 9-14, 9-15, 9-16, 9-17, 9-18, 9-19, 9-20, 9-21, 9-22, 9-23, 9-24, 9-25, 9-28, 9-30, 9-32, 9-37,** and all *Situaciones.*

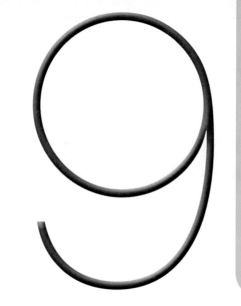

¿Dónde trabajas?

Learning OBJECTIVES

You will:

- use new vocabulary related to the workplace and professions

- use pronouns for direct and indirect objects

- distinguish the meaning of verbs like *conocer, poder,* and *querer* in the preterit and imperfect

- form commands to give instructions to a group and to a person you address as *usted*

- connect new information about history and work in Guatemala with what you already know

Learning OUTCOMES

You will be able to:

- talk about careers and employment

- avoid repetition

- describe past events in more detail

- give instructions and suggestions

- compare demographic and economic changes in Guatemala and in the United States

GUATEMALA

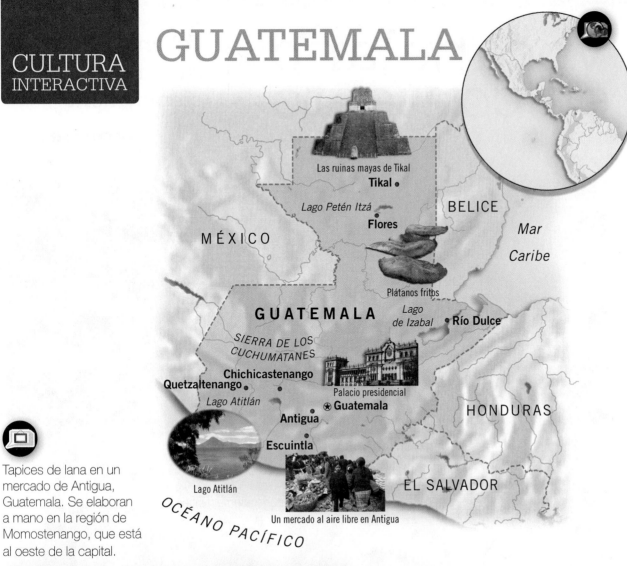

Las ruinas mayas de Tikal

Tikal •

Lago Petén Itzá

Flores

MÉXICO

BELICE

Mar
Caribe

Plátanos fritos

GUATEMALA

Lago
de Izabal   • Río Dulce

SIERRA DE LOS
CUCHUMATANES

Chichicastenango

Quetzaltenango •

Palacio presidencial

Lago Atitlán

⊛ Guatemala

Antigua

HONDURAS

Escuintla

Lago Atitlán

EL SALVADOR

Un mercado al aire libre en Antigua

OCÉANO PACÍFICO

Tapices de lana en un mercado de Antigua, Guatemala. Se elaboran a mano en la región de Momostenango, que está al oeste de la capital.

¿Cuánto sabes?

Piensa en lo que sabes de Guatemala y contesta las siguientes preguntas.

1. ¿Cuál es la capital de Guatemala? Guatemala

2. ¿Cómo se llama el océano que está al oeste del país? Océano Pacífico

3. ¿Qué países están al este de Guatemala? Belice , Honduras y El Salvador

4. ¿Qué civilización fue muy importante en Guatemala? la maya

5. ¿Cuáles son los lagos más importantes de Guatemala? Lago Izabal, Lago Atitlán y Lago Petén Itzá

6. ¿Qué comida es típica de este país? los plátanos fritos

Cultura en línea
To learn more about Guatemala and the chapter theme, go to the *Cultura en línea* folder in the *Unidos* online component to view *Vistas culturales* video and take a virtual art tour.

Tech tip for *Cultura en línea*
You can assign the *Vistas culturales* videos for homework or view them in class.

Tech tip for map
Brainstorm with students information about Guatemala. Ask: *¿Cómo se llaman los habitantes de Guatemala?* Project the map, draw students' attention to Antigua, and have them guess the meaning. (Antigua was formerly the capital of Guatemala.) Ask which major civilization existed in Guatemala before the Spaniards arrived. Call their attention to the names of some cities and ask them to guess what languages are probably spoken in Guatemala.

Use photos to explain that indigenous and *mestizo* people are the majority and that many Guatemalans do not speak Spanish as their first language. Mention Rigoberta Menchú, Nobel Peace Prize winner, and Miguel Ángel Asturias, winner of the Nobel Prize in Literature. Mention two major natural disasters that have affected the country: Hurricane Mitch in 1998; an earthquake in 1976 that killed 23,000 people. Explain that these disasters and political instability have forced many Guatemalans to flee the country in search of better living conditions.

Note for *Tapices*
Handicrafts are an important source of income in Guatemala. Textiles, wood carvings, jewelry, baskets, ceramics, bags, and other forms of folk art are made by indigenous artisans. Mostly women and children are involved in the selling of these items, mainly in local markets. In recent years cooperatives organized by women give artisans greater control over the marketing and exportation of their goods.

Suggestions for *Tapices*
Recycle vocabulary of handicrafts studied in *Capítulo 6.* Ask them to describe what they see in the photo: *¿Qué es esto? ¿Para qué sirve? ¿Qué formas tiene? ¿Qué colores?*

Vocabulario en contexto

Talking about careers and employment

El trabajo

Go to the *Capítulo 9* [folder] online to complete the Learning Module for *Vocabulario en contexto: El trabajo.*

PLAN DE ESTUDIO

◎ LEARN
- Interactive presentation: *El trabajo*
- Vocabulary tutorials
- Pronunciation

APPLY ◎
- Activities
- Pronunciation activities

PRÁCTICA COMUNICATIVA

9-1

¿A qué se dedican? ¿Las siguientes afirmaciones son ciertas (**C**) o falsas (**F**)? Compara tus respuestas con las de tu compañero/a. Si hay respuestas falsas, corrijan la información. Después dile a tu compañero/a qué profesión quieres tener y por qué.

1. __C__ Los peleteros hacen zapatos, bolsas y chaquetas.

2. __F__ Los ceramistas trabajan con el hierro.

3. __C__ Los herreros trabajan los metales.

4. __F__ Los carpinteros hacen los trabajos del campo.

5. __C__ Los joyeros trabajan la plata y el oro para hacer pulseras y collares, por ejemplo.

6. __C__ Los agricultores plantan y cosechan productos para el consumo de la población.

> **LENGUA** The suffix **-ero/-era** is often used in Spanish to designate trades and professions, e.g., **camarero/a** (*server*), **plomero/a** (*plumber*), **peluquero/a** (*hairdresser*). Another common suffix is **-ista,** e.g., **electricista** (*electrician*); **contratista** (*contractor*).

Las tiendas. Túrnense e indiquen adónde van y con quién hablan para conseguir lo siguiente. Después añadan una más.

Modelo

Si necesitas comprar fruta.

Voy a la frutería y hablo con el frutero.

1. Si necesitas pescado para preparar un ceviche. pescadería, pescadero/a

2. Si necesitas arreglar (*repair*) tus sandalias. zapatería, zapatero/a

3. Si vas a regalarle un reloj a tu padre para su cumpleaños. joyería, joyero/a

4. Si necesitas pan para la cena. panadería, panadero/a

5. Si quieres regalarle un libro a tu hermana. librería, librero/a

6. Si quieres adornar la casa con flores. floristería, dependiente/a

7. Si quieres/necesitas...

9-3

Descripciones. Mira los cuadros siguientes y escoge uno para describírselo a tu compañero/a. Describe las escenas con el mayor detalle posible. Tengan en cuenta las siguientes ideas:

1. lugar donde están estas personas
2. rasgos físicos
3. edad aproximada
4. ropa que llevan
5. lo que están haciendo
6. lo que están pensando algunas de las personas en la escena
7. cómo se sienten

Suggestion for 9-2
Students have already learned how to form the names of stores by adding the ending -*ía: zapatería, mueblería, librería*, etc. In this activity they may recycle names of stores and figure out the terms for people who work there by adding the ending -*ero*/ -*era* instead. You may explain that this rule does not always apply. For example, *florero* means vase, and the shop where flowers are sold is called *floristería*. In some cases students may have to use the general term *dependiente: El dependiente de la floristería me dice que las rosas están baratas.*

Suggestion for 9-3
You may wish to model the type of description you are looking for by projecting a different painting and leading the class in a description of it.

Standard 2.2
Students demonstrate an understanding of the relationship between the products and perspectives of the culture studied.
    The paintings by Pedro Rafael González Chavajay depict aspects of the work life of the Mayan people of Guatemala. Have students say as much about the paintings as they can. What do the work, facial expressions, and objects depicted in the paintings say about Mayan culture?

Los oficios y las profesiones

Go to the *Capítulo 9* folder online to complete the Learning Module for *Vocabulario en contexto: Los oficios y las profesiones.*

PLAN DE ESTUDIO

◎ **LEARN**
- Interactive presentation: *Los oficios y las profesiones*
- Vocabulary tutorials

APPLY ◎
- Activities

PRÁCTICA COMUNICATIVA

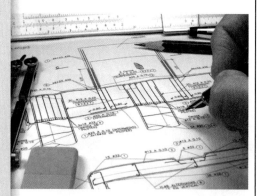

EN OTRAS PALABRAS
In Spain the words for **contador**, **chofer**, and **plomero** are **contable**, **chófer**, and **fontanero**.

9-4 👥

¿Qué profesión tienen? PRIMERA FASE Lean las siguientes descripciones y digan qué profesión u oficio deben tener las personas con estas características.

abogado/a	artista	mecánico/a	plomero/a
actor/actriz	ingeniero/a	médico/a	psicólogo/a

1. A Pablo le gusta observar y analizar el comportamiento (*behavior*) de las personas. psicólogo

2. Los hermanos Pedraza siempre resuelven los problemas del auto de su padre. Lo examinan y lo reparan a la perfección. mecánicos

3. Eva y Ana tienen facilidad para resolver los problemas de otras personas y la habilidad de exponer oralmente ante una corte. abogadas

4. A Jaime le fascina desarmar (*disassemble*) aparatos electrónicos para estudiar cómo funcionan. ingeniero

5. Daniela es una chica muy sensible y una gran observadora. Le fascina expresar sus sentimientos y experiencias de manera artística. actriz/artista

6. Adela siempre lee libros sobre anatomía. Ella sabe el nombre de cada parte del cuerpo humano. médica

SEGUNDA FASE. Piensa en tu ocupación o profesión ideal. Tu compañero/a te va a hacer preguntas para adivinar la ocupación o profesión en que estás pensando.

9-5

Las profesiones y la personalidad.

PRIMERA FASE. Digan cómo deben ser estos/as profesionales. Seleccionen las palabras de la lista para describirlos/las.

autoritario	detallista	perezoso
calculador	estudioso	responsable
cuidadoso	guapo	romántico
dedicado	inteligente	serio
delgado	irónico	simpático
descuidado	paciente	valiente

1. un médico/una médica
2. un actor/una actriz
3. un hombre/una mujer de negocios
4. un peluquero/una peluquera
5. un locutor/una locutora

6. un ama/amo de casa
7. un ejecutivo/una ejecutiva
8. un mecánico/una mecánica
9. un cocinero/una cocinera
10. un abogado/una abogada

Modelo **"un bombero"**

Debe ser valiente, serio y responsable.

Sí, y no debe ser descuidado (*careless*).

 SEGUNDA FASE. Intercambien ideas sobre lo siguiente.

1. ¿Conoces a algún/alguna… (*nombre de la profesión*)? ¿Cómo se llama? ¿Dónde trabaja?
2. ¿Qué características personales o especiales, en tu opinión, lo/la ayudan en su profesión?

Cultura

Un cambio social importante en los países hispanos en las últimas décadas es la entrada masiva de las mujeres al mercado laboral. Sin embargo, aún existen desigualdades. Por ejemplo, los salarios de las mujeres son en muchos casos más bajos que los de los hombres.

Algunos países, como Perú y Chile, tienen Ministerios de la Mujer para proteger y atender las necesidades de las mujeres.

Compara: ¿En tu país, ganan las mujeres tanto como los hombres por el mismo trabajo? Si no lo sabes, averígualo. ¿Existe una agencia similar al Ministerio de la Mujer en tu país? Si no, ¿cómo se protegen los derechos de las mujeres?

Warm-up for 9-5
Recycle previously taught occupations and comparative expressions by having students compare occupations: *¿Un peluquero gana tanto dinero como un médico? ¿Es mejor ser ingeniero o actor?¿Por qué? ¿Un profesor trabaja más o menos que un médico?*

Suggestion for 9-5
Add additional occupations that are cognates: *el/la astronauta, el/la mecánico/a, el/la dentista, el/la piloto, el/la recepcionista, el secretario/la secretaria, el veterinario/la veterinaria.*
    Point out that both forms *la juez* and *la jueza* are accepted in Spanish.
    Inform students that *el amo de casa* has come into usage in Spanish, as has *house husband* in English.

Note for 9-6
Answers may vary but likely answers are included in column 2. Column 3 answers will depend on the students' answers to column 2.

9-6

Asociaciones. Asocien una o más profesiones con los siguientes lugares de trabajo. Túrnense y digan lo que hacen estas personas.

LUGAR	PROFESIÓN	¿QUÉ HACE?
1. el hospital	enfermero/a, médico/a	Atiende a los pacientes.
2. el restaurante	chef, camarero/a	
3. la clase	profesor/a	
4. la estación de radio	locutor/a, ingeniero/a	
5. la tienda de ropa	dependiente/a, vendedor/a	
6. el consultorio médico	médico/a	
7. la peluquería	peluquero/a	

Suggestions for 9-7
In groups of 3, have students brainstorm at least 3 advantages and 3 disadvantages of specific jobs. Model the activity: *¿Cuáles son las ventajas y desventajas de los siguientes trabajos: médico, enfermero, profesor, piloto?* Introduce the words *estrés* and *peligro* to talk about disadvantages. Have them switch roles so that all can practice identifying and describing. Alternatively, you may want to do only the identification part of the activity.

9-7

¿Cuál es la profesión? Identifiquen la ocupación o profesión. Uno/a de ustedes debe decir dos ventajas y el otro/la otra, una desventaja.

Modelo 66 Trabaja en una biblioteca. 99

Es un bibliotecario.

Dos ventajas de ser bibliotecario son estar en contacto con muchos libros y trabajar en un lugar tranquilo.

Una desventaja es la falta de ejercicio físico.

	PROFESIÓN	2 VENTAJAS	1 DESVENTAJA
1. Escribe artículos para el periódico.	periodista		
2. Presenta programas de televisión.	locutor/a		
3. Traduce simultáneamente.	intérprete		
4. Mantiene el orden público.	policía		
5. Apaga incendios.	bombero/a		
6. Defiende o acusa a personas delante de un juez/una jueza.	abogado/a		

Buscando trabajo

Go to the *Capítulo 9* folder online to complete the Learning Module for *Vocabulario en contexto: Buscando trabajo.*

PLAN DE ESTUDIO

LEARN
- Interactive presentation: *Buscando trabajo*
- Vocabulary tutorials
- *Entrevistas* video

APPLY
- Activities
- *Entrevistas* video activities

Online prep for students
Students will have completed the Learning Module for *Buscando trabajo* online. See content online. Additional in-class activities are available for download in the Supplementary Activities folder online.

PRÁCTICA COMUNICATIVA

9-8

Otra conversación. Con un compañero/a lee la conversación entre la Sra. Fuentes y el Sr. López. Después cambien la conversación para hablar de un puesto de trabajo que le interesa a uno/a de ustedes.

SRA. FUENTES:	Buenos días, Sr. López. Soy Ana Fuentes.
SR. LÓPEZ:	Mucho gusto, señora.
SRA. FUENTES:	Usted solicitó el puesto de intérprete, ¿verdad?
SR. LÓPEZ:	Sí, señora.
SRA. FUENTES:	Veo que está enseñando en la universidad. ¿Por qué quiere dejar su puesto?
SR. LÓPEZ:	Pues porque me gustaría trabajar en una compañía internacional. Hablo muchas lenguas.
SRA. FUENTES:	En su solicitud, veo que desea un sueldo de 60.000 quetzales al mes. Pero el sueldo que ofrecemos es de 30.000 quetzales.
SR. LÓPEZ:	Bueno, gracias pero tengo que pensarlo.

Suggestion for 9-8
Encourage students to make the following changes: the job being offered, languages spoken, and salary (using currencies of other countries). If possible, check the current exchange rate of the quetzal, the currency of Guatemala. This salary translates to approximately $3,000 U.S. per month.

Cultura

The **quetzal** (GQT) is the national currency of Guatemala. The exchange rate is about 7.85 GQT to $1 US The word **quetzal** comes from the Nahuatl language and it refers to the strikingly colored bird that is the symbol of Guatemala.

Compara: ¿Conoces algún símbolo que se usa en la moneda de tu país? ¿Qué significa?

Note
Founded in 1880, *El Diario de Centro América* is one of the main newspapers in Guatemala.

Follow-up for 9-9
Have students go through this process in small groups, step by step, as though they were seeking jobs, either imaginary or taken from classified ads.

9-9

¿En qué orden? Cuando alguien busca un trabajo, normalmente ¿en qué orden ocurren las siguientes actividades? Ordénalas de 1 a 8. Después compara tus respuestas con las de tu compañero/a y dile si haces las mismas cosas y en el mismo orden.

_1_ Leo los anuncios del periódico *El Diario de Centro América*.

_4_ Me llaman de la Compañía Rosell para una entrevista.

_7_ Les contesto que no, que se cerró el almacén.

_3_ Con un clic del ratón, envío mis materiales a la Compañía Rosell.

_5_ Voy a la compañía para la entrevista.

_6_ Me preguntan si me despidieron (*fired*) del trabajo anterior.

_2_ Lleno la solicitud en línea para la Compañía Rosell y subo (*upload*) mi currículum.

_8_ Me ofrecen el puesto de vendedor/a.

9-10

El arte de entrevistarse.

PRIMERA FASE. Escoge el anuncio que te parece más interesante y solicita ese puesto. Tu compañero/a, en el papel de jefe/a de personal, debe entrevistarte y tomar notas para obtener la siguiente información. Luego cambien de papel.

1. nombre de la persona que solicita el puesto

2. estudios

3. lenguas que habla

4. lugar donde trabaja y responsabilidades

5. experiencia anterior

6. razones para querer trabajar en esta compañía

INSTITUTO DE CIRUGÍA PLÁSTICA: CLÍNICA CÁRDENAS

Necesita enfermera

Prótesis:
implantes faciales (Botox, silicona)
liposucción papada
abdomen
muslos

Informes:
Clínica Centro, Zona 10
Tel: (502) 2534147

Llamar a secretaria: Marta

 Hotel VILLA ANTIGUA

Necesita

RECEPCIONISTA
• Experiencia
• Bilingüe español-inglés

CAMARERA
• Mín. 2 años de experiencia
• Disponible trabajar por las mañanas y tardes

Dirigirse al Hotel VILLA ANTIGUA
Jefe de Personal
9a. Calle Poniente, Carretera a
Ciudad Vieja, Antigua, Guatemala
Teléfono: +(502) 78323956 ó +(502) 78323955

EMPRESA EXPORTADORA DE ARTESANÍAS

Requiere

CONTADOR

Requisitos:
• Experiencia mínima de 5 años
• Graduado del Colegio de Contadores Públicos
• Para cita llamar al Sr. López al (502) 2764532

EMPRESA MINERA

Requiere
3 Ingenieros de sistemas

REQUISITOS:

1. Mayor de 25 años
2. Experiencia en minas de cobre
3. Flexibilidad horaria (incluidos fines de semana)

OFRECEMOS:

1. Ingreso superior a 20.000 quetzales
2. Capacitación profesional
3. Bonos de participación

Interesados enviar currículum a: Minas de Guatemala S.A.

Oficina de Personal
Diagonal 19, 29-78, Zona 11
Ciudad de Guatemala, Guatemala
Teléfono: (502) 2762147
Fax: (502) 2763482

 SEGUNDA FASE. Ahora informa al presidente de la empresa (otro/a compañero/a) sobre las calificaciones del candidato/ de la candidata que acabas de entrevistar.

Warm-up for 9-10
Model the activity with one of your stronger students, projecting the image of a job ad as the starting point. Encourage students to answer giving as much information as possible.

Expansion for 9-10
Primera fase
7. fecha en que puede empezar a trabajar; 8. sueldo que desea ganar; 9. habilidades especiales.

Suggestion for 9-10
Segunda fase
Remind students that they will be reporting on an interview that already took place, so they will need to use the preterit or imperfect. You may model this phase for them as follows: *Yo entrevisté a X. X estudió contabilidad en la Universidad… y se graduó en el año…*, etc.

9-11

¿Comportamiento apropiado? Preparen una lista de cinco acciones que se deben hacer antes de una entrevista y cinco que no se deben hacer durante una entrevista. Después comparen su lista con la de otros compañeros/otras compañeras.

LO QUE SE DEBE HACER ANTES DE UNA ENTREVISTA	LO QUE NO SE DEBE HACER DURANTE UNA ENTREVISTA

9-12

Mi profesión.

PRIMERA FASE. You will listen to Julieta Odriozola talk about her profession. Before listening, one of you will write down the names of four professions that have traditionally been associated with women. The other will write down four professions traditionally associated with men. Share your answers.

 SEGUNDA FASE. Pay attention to the general idea of what is said. As you listen mark (✓) the appropriate ending to each statement. Check answers with a classmate.

1. Julieta Odriozola es…

_____ artista.

_____ política.

✓ _____ periodista.

2. Julieta tiene un horario…

_____ de 9 a 5.

✓ _____ variable.

_____ de lunes a sábado.

3. Julieta hace casi todo su trabajo en…

_____ su auto.

_____ su casa.

✓ _____ diferentes lugares.

4. Julieta trabaja con…

_____ artistas jóvenes.

✓ _____ personas importantes.

_____ empleados de la comunidad.

Gramática en contexto

Avoiding repetition, talking about the past, and giving instructions

Online prep for students
Students will have completed the Learning Module for Review of direct and indirect object online. This includes the Interactive presentation and all corresponding Apply activities. You will find online content and additional in-class activities in the Supplementary Activities folder in Instructor's Resources.

Suggestion
This section reviews direct and indirect objects and pronouns, presented in *Capítulos 5* and *6*, in anticipation of the introduction of the double object pronoun structure in the next section. Help students focus their attention on the pronouns and their referents.

Avoiding repetition:
Review of direct and indirect object pronouns

Go to the *Capítulo 9* [folder] online to complete the Learning Module for *Gramática en contexto:* Review of direct and indirect object pronouns.

PLAN DE ESTUDIO

◎ LEARN
- Interactive presentation: Review of direct and indirect object pronouns
- Grammar tutorials

APPLY ◎
- Activities
- Extra Practice

PRÁCTICA COMUNICATIVA

9-13 **Los preparativos para la evaluación.**

PRIMERA FASE. Trabajas en la oficina de una arquitecta y mañana empieza la evaluación anual. Indica si la arquitecta (**A**) o el asistente administrativo (**AA**) está haciendo estos trabajos.

1. _____ Está terminando el último informe.

2. _____ Está firmando el contrato.

3. _____ Está sacando las fotocopias.

4. _____ Está organizando el horario.

 SEGUNDA FASE. Túrnense y comparen sus respuestas siguiendo el modelo.

Modelo

¿Quién está examinando el contrato?

La arquitecta está examinándolo.

Suggestion for 9-13
Remind students about the need for a written accent on the present participle when a pronoun is attached.

9-14

El jefe ideal.

PRIMERA FASE. Hablen entre ustedes sobre lo que hace (o no hace) por sus empleados un jefe/una jefa ideal.

Modelo

❝darles las gracias por la calidad de su trabajo❞

❝*Les da las gracias por la calidad de su trabajo.*❞

1. sugerir estrategias de trabajo eficientes
2. mandar correos electrónicos durante el fin de semana
3. ofrecer ayuda para resolver conflictos
4. subir el salario
5. dar un mes de vacaciones
6. hacer trabajar horas extras sin recompensa

SEGUNDA FASE. Ahora túrnense para hacerse preguntas sobre lo que ustedes van a hacer por sus empleados cuando sean jefes de una empresa.

Modelo

¿Vas a darles las gracias a tus empleados?

Sí, les voy a escribir una carta de reconocimiento todos los años.

Situaciones

1

ROLE A. You meet with a career counselor (**consejero/a vocacional**) for tips on how to look for a job. Explain the type of job you are looking for and answer the counselor's questions about your past experience. Ask the counselor questions of your own.

ROLE B. You are a career counselor (**consejero/a vocacional**) who is meeting with a new client. After listening to the client, ask whether he/she a) prepared a résumé; b) looked for job ads (and where); c) applied for a job (which one); and d) prepared questions to ask in an interview. Be ready to answer the client's questions.

2

ROLE A. Role A. You have come back from a trip to Guatemala and have brought with you the following items that you bought at an outdoor market: blouses, tapestries, and jewelry.

With your classmate, decide who in your class will be the recipients of your gifts.

ROLE B. One of your classmates has come back from a trip to Guatemala, and he/she has a few gifts to distribute among your classmates. Help him/her decide for whom each gift is most appropriate.

Suggestion for *Situaciones*
For the first *Situación*, have students prepare in advance 2 ads about one of the following marketing areas: *ropa, maquillaje, computadoras*. Have them use their ads when they do the activity.

For both *Situaciones*, encourage students to use object pronouns whenever possible.

Avoiding repetition:

Use of direct and indirect object pronouns together

Go to the *Capítulo 9* **folder** online to complete the Learning Module for *Gramática en contexto:* Use of direct and indirect object pronouns together.

PLAN DE ESTUDIO

◎ **LEARN**
- Interactive presentation: Use of direct and indirect object pronouns together
- Grammar tutorials

◎ **APPLY**
- Activities
- Extra Practice

PRÁCTICA COMUNICATIVA

9-15

¿Qué hizo el supervisor?
Eres el dueño/la dueña de una compañía. Habla con tu nuevo empleado/nueva empleada (tu compañero/a) para saber si el supervisor le explicó cómo funciona su departamento.

Modelo

"darle el manual de la compañía"

¿Le dio el manual de la compañía?

Sí, me lo dio.

1. explicarle la campaña de publicidad
2. mostrarle los anuncios
3. traerle las revistas
4. pedirle un documento que faltaba
5. dejarle las fotos
6. describirle los modelos que se necesitan

9-16

¿Qué haces?

PRIMERA FASE. La imparcialidad, la amabilidad y la confidencialidad son fundamentales en el trabajo. Lee las siguientes situaciones y selecciona lo que harías (*would do*) en cada una.

1. Un cliente te pide el teléfono de la oficina del presidente de la compañía.

   a. ____ Se lo das. **b.** ____ No se lo das.

2. Alguien quiere leer un documento confidencial.

   a. ____ Se lo muestras. **b.** ____ No se lo muestras.

3. La nueva jefa de personal viene a una reunión de su departamento. Alguien tiene que presentarla a los empleados.

   a. ____ Se la presentas. **b.** ____ No se la presentas.

4. Una empleada nueva te dice que quiere dos semanas de vacaciones después de trabajar solo tres meses.

   a. ____ Se las das. **b.** ____ Decides no dárselas.

SEGUNDA FASE. ¿Estás de acuerdo con tu compañero/a? ¿Por qué?

Modelo

66 Un cliente te pide información personal sobre las finanzas de otro cliente. Los dos clientes son hermanos. 99

No se la doy porque no le gustaría al segundo cliente.

Yo se la doy porque los dos clientes son hermanos.

9-17

¡El cliente siempre tiene razón!

PRIMERA FASE. Cada uno de ustedes comió recientemente en un restaurante. Comparen su experiencia.

1. ¿Cuándo te sirvieron el agua?
2. ¿Te trajeron pan?
3. ¿Te dijo el camarero cuáles eran los platos especiales del día?
4. ¿Te describió los platos?
5. ¿Te ofreció postres y café?
6. ¿Aceptaron tu tarjeta de crédito?

SEGUNDA FASE. Presenten a la clase un breve resumen del servicio en sus respectivos restaurantes.

Suggestion for 9-16
Segunda fase
If students have chosen the same response as their partners in the *Primera fase*, encourage them to come up with different justifications.

Suggestions for 9-17 *Primera fase*
Have students start the activity by explaining to their partners to which recent restaurant experience (where, when, with whom) they will be referring in the *Primera fase*. Students can alternate asking and answering the questions. You may also wish to remind students that the questions and answers refer to the group with whom they ate (*les, nos*), not just to themselves.

Suggestion for 9-17 *Segunda fase*
You may use students' summaries as the basis for conducting a discussion on the service at restaurants that students frequent.

Tech tip for *Situaciones*
You may want to assign partners and have pairs create a mini-skit using the video-posting feature, MediaShare, online.

Situaciones

1

ROLE A. You have gone to Guatemala on a service–learning trip, and you are going to produce a video to document the project. Unfortunately, you left your camera (**videocámara**) at home. Luckily, you have a friend from home who is studying in Guatemala for the semester and probably has the equipment you need. Call your friend and a) explain what happened; b) ask your friend if he/she has a video camera and, if so, if you can borrow it; and c) make arrangements to pick it up.

ROLE B. You are studying in Guatemala for the semester. Out of the blue a friend from home texts you to ask for a favor. When you talk on the phone and hear what your friend needs, a) ask questions to find out more about your friend's service–learning project, b) agree to lend him/her your video camera; and c) make arrangements to meet with your friend.

2

ROLE A. It is the end of the semester, and you just finished the paper for one of your classes. You have to catch a plane, so you ask your friend to turn in (**entregar**) the paper for you. The professor is waiting in her office to receive the papers by the deadline. You call your friend from the airport to ask a) if he/she gave the paper directly to the professor; b) at what time he/she turned it in; and c) what the professor said to him/her.

ROLE B. A friend asks you to turn in his/her paper because he/she has to leave for the airport. Your friend is nervous about turning in the paper before the deadline. When your friend calls you from the airport, answer all of his/her questions.

Talking about the past:
More on the imperfect and the preterit

Go to the *Capítulo 9* [folder] online to complete the Learning Module for *Gramática en contexto:* More on the imperfect and preterit.

PLAN DE ESTUDIO

◎ LEARN
- Interactive presentation: More on the imperfect and the preterit
- Grammar tutorials

APPLY ◎
- Activities
- Extra Practice

PRÁCTICA COMUNICATIVA

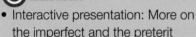

Una oficina muy ocupada.
Ustedes visitaron la oficina que aparece en la siguiente escena. Túrnense para preguntar qué estaban haciendo las personas cuando cada uno/a de ustedes llegó.

Modelo

¿Qué estaba haciendo Alicia cuando llegaste a la oficina?

Estaba conversando con un cliente.

Online prep for students
Students will have completed the Learning Module for More on the imperfect and the preterit online. See content online. Additional in-class activities are available for download in the Supplementary Activities folder online.

Suggestion for More on the imperfect and the preterit
You may want to project the dialogue from *Piénsalo* in the online Learning Module and explain to students that the statements the verbs in bold refer to background activities for the narrative event (*el asalto*).
Students can invent other background information to describe the scene in the bank (i.e., what was going on) when the robbery started. Point out to students that the imperfect is used to establish the context for an event or series of events that will be narrated.

Suggestion for More on the imperfect and the preterit
You may wish to use the interview of the witness to the bank robbery in *Piénsalo* to show students additional uses of *iba a* + infinitive and the preterit of *poder, querer,* and *saber.*

Suggestions
Contrast the use of preterit and imperfect by giving examples: *El año pasado ustedes no estaban en mi clase de español. Yo no los conocía. Yo los conocí en... cuando vinieron a mi clase. Yo no sabía entonces si eran después de tener una o dos clases con ustedes supe que eran buenos.*

9-19

Una explicación lógica. Ayer ustedes tuvieron una reunión en su compañía para mostrarles unos productos nuevos a unas empresas extranjeras. Den una explicación lógica de todo lo que salió mal.

Modelo ❝ La secretaria no contestaba el teléfono. ❞

Estaba buscando un intérprete para la reunión.

No, estaba buscando un salón más grande.

1. Varios empleados llegaron tarde.

2. El técnico no pudo conseguir el proyector que se necesitaba para la presentación.

3. Los periodistas no podían comprender lo que decía un director extranjero.

4. No les sirvieron café ni refrescos a los invitados.

5. Uno de los vendedores no quiso mostrar los productos nuevos.

6. No se pusieron anuncios en los periódicos.

9-20

¡A usar la imaginación! Estas descripciones indican lo que estaban haciendo varias personas ayer. Identifiquen cuál era el oficio o profesión de ellos y qué iban a hacer después.

Modelo ❝ Esta persona llevaba un traje espacial, guantes, botas muy grandes y un plástico transparente frente a los ojos para poder ver. ❞

Era un astronauta.

Iba a caminar en la Luna.

1. Un señor tenía un secador en la mano y le arreglaba el pelo a una señora que estaba sentada enfrente de él.

2. Unos señores iban en un camión rojo con una sirena. El camión iba muy rápido y los autos le daban paso (*yielded*).

3. Una joven que llevaba un vestido similar a los que se llevaban en la época de Cleopatra hablaba frente a una cámara. Estaba muy maquillada y tenía una línea negra alrededor de los ojos.

4. Un señor estudiaba los planos de un edificio y decía que ciertas cosas no estaban bien.

¡Malas sorpresas! Lean las siguientes situaciones y digan cuáles eran probablemente los planes de estas personas.

Modelo « Martín está enfadado porque su bicicleta se descompuso (*broke*). »

Martín no pudo ir al parque con sus amigos.

Él quiso arreglar su bicicleta, pero. . .

1. Lorena está molesta porque la fotocopiadora de la oficina no funciona.

2. Fuiste a tu restaurante favorito, pero el restaurante estaba cerrado.

3. El jefe de producción llamó a una reunión urgente ayer. Anoche comenzó a nevar y muchos empleados no llegaron a su trabajo porque los caminos estaban en malas condiciones.

4. Al carro de Marta y Francisco se le acabó (*ran out of*) la gasolina cerca de la playa. Tuvieron que dejarlo en la carretera.

5. Esteban tenía una entrevista con el jefe de personal a las nueve pero no llegó a tiempo.

Situaciones

Suggestion for *Situaciones*
Remind students that this is theatre, and that they may have to put themselves in an unfamiliar role when presenting *Situaciones*.

1

ROLE A. One of your employees did not come to an important meeting, so you call him/her to your office. Greet your employee and ask why he/she was not present. After listening to the explanation, say that a) this is the second time this happened; and b) he/she has to attend all meetings in the future.

ROLE B. You were expected to attend an important meeting at work, but you could not make it. After greeting your boss, apologize and explain the circumstances. As you were driving to work, your spouse called to say that a) there was a fire in the kitchen; b) the firefighters were there; and c) the children were fine but scared. Explain that you had to go home.

2

ROLE A. You work for the catering service at your university. While you were working at a large party at the home of the university president, the deck (**terraza**) of the house collapsed (**colapsar**), resulting in several injured people (**heridos**). A reporter for the school newspaper interviews you about the accident.

ROLE B. You are a reporter for your school newspaper, and you are investigating an accident that took place at a party at the home of the university president. Ask the student worker (your classmate) approximately how many guests and servers were on the deck (**terraza**) when it collapsed (**colapsar**); b) what the guests were doing at the time of the incident; and c) what the witness was doing when the deck collapsed.

Giving instructions or suggestions:
Formal commands

Go to the *Capítulo 9* folder online to complete the Learning Module for *Gramática en contexto:* Formal commands.

PLAN DE ESTUDIO

◎ LEARN
- Interactive presentation: Formal commands
- Grammar tutorials

APPLY ◎
- Activities
- Extra Practice

PRÁCTICA COMUNICATIVA

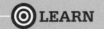

Muñecos quitapenas (*Worry dolls*) de Chichicastenango

9-22

Instrucciones a un/a estudiante. No asististe a clase durante la semana dedicada a Guatemala y quieres ponerte al día. ¿Cómo crees que va a responderte tu profesor/a? Compara tus respuestas con las de tu compañero/a y añade una pregunta más.

Modelo

¿Estudio el capítulo 9?

Sí, estúdielo.

1. ¿Contesto las preguntas sobre los lugares turísticos en Guatemala?
2. ¿Miro los DVD de bailes folclóricos de Guatemala?
3. ¿Aprendo sobre la cultura de Guatemala en línea?
4. ¿Hago la tarea sobre las culturas indígenas de Guatemala?
5. ¿Leo el artículo sobre Rigoberta Menchú?
6. ¿...?

Cultura

En Guatemala, los niños se dirigen normalmente a sus padres y a otras personas mayores con la forma **usted.** El uso de **tú** y de **usted** varía mucho en el mundo hispano, pero en general la forma **tú** es más común para comunicarse con los padres.

Compara: No todas las lenguas tienen el equivalente de las formas **tú** y **usted.** ¿Cómo se dirige la gente a otras personas en tu cultura para marcar el respeto?

9-23

En el hospital. Un enfermero/ Una enfermera entra en la habitación y le hace las siguientes preguntas al/a la paciente. Túrnense para hacer los papeles de enfermero/a y paciente, y añadan una pregunta más.

Modelo

> ¿Le abro las cortinas?

> Sí, ábramelas, por favor. Quisiera leer.

1. ¿Le pongo la televisión?
2. ¿Le traigo un jugo?
3. ¿Le pongo otra almohada?
4. ¿Me llevo estas flores?
5. ¿Le traigo el teléfono?
6. ¿…?

9-24

Mandatos del entrenador de un equipo. Preparen una lista de sugerencias que el entrenador/la entrenadora puede darles a los miembros de su equipo para lograr los objetivos siguientes. Comparen su lista con la de otra pareja.

Modelo

> **"** para mantenerse en buen estado físico **"**

> Practiquen todos los días.

> No se acuesten tarde.

1. para tener mejor rendimiento (*performance*)
2. para prepararse mentalmente para un partido difícil
3. para evitar problemas con el árbitro
4. para dormir bien cuando tienen mucho estrés
5. para ser buenos alumnos y buenos deportistas también

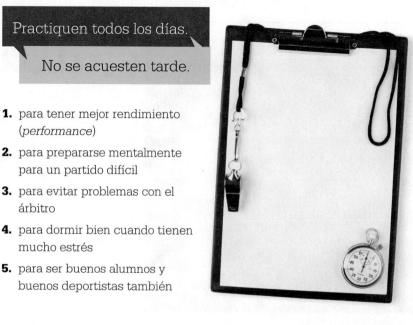

Suggestion for 9-23
Model the use of pronouns with negative commands. You may wish to direct students to respond negatively to some of the situations.

9-25

¿Qué deben hacer estas personas? Busquen una solución a los siguientes problemas y díganle a cada persona lo que debe hacer.

Modelo   El Sr. Álvarez dice: **"No estoy contento en mi trabajo."**

Sr. Álvarez, busque otro trabajo inmediatamente.

Hable con su jefe y explíquele la situación.

1. La Sra. Jiménez dice: "Necesito más vendedores en mi compañía".

2. El Sr. Jiménez se queja (*complains*): "Tengo que terminar un informe económico pero mi computadora no funciona".

3. Unos hombres de negocios van a ir a Ciudad de Guatemala, pero no saben hablar español.

4. La Sra. Peña tuvo un accidente serio con su auto; el chofer que provocó el accidente no quiere darle la información que ella necesita para informar a su seguro.

5. La Sra. Hurtado entra en su apartamento y ve que hay agua en el piso de la cocina.

6. La Sra. Fernández quiere ir al Festival Folclórico Nacional de Cobán, pero el Sr. Fernández no se siente bien.

Cultura

En la ciudad de Cobán, en el centro de Guatemala, se celebra anualmente la Fiesta Nacional Indígena de Guatemala (un festival folclórico). Incluye un certamen (*contest*) de belleza para mujeres indígenas de Guatemala. Participan aproximadamente 100 señoritas que expresan sus ideales en su idioma materno y en español. La ganadora es coronada con el título de *Rabin Ajau*, que significa Hija del Rey en Q'eqchi', un idioma maya.

Compara: ¿Conoces algún certamen de belleza en tu país? ¿Es para cierto grupo de personas (como el certamen de belleza indígena de Guatemala), o es para todos? ¿Qué opinión tienes sobre los concursos de belleza en general?

Situaciones

Suggestion for *Situaciones*
Additional situations are available in the Instructor's Resource folder.

1

ROLE A. Tell your neighbor that you are leaving for three days for job interviews. Ask if your neighbor can do a few things for you. After he/she agrees, tell him/her to a) feed (**dar de comer a**) the cat and play with her every day; b) water the plants; c) pick up the mail (**correspondencia**); and d) any other things that you may need. Thank him/her for helping you out.

ROLE B. Your neighbor tells you that he/she is going to be away. Agree to help him/her out. After you find out what you will have to do, a) ask whom you should call if there is an emergency (**emergencia**); and b) get the telephone number of the vet (**veterinario/a**).

2

ROLE A. You are going to participate for the first time in a study abroad in Guatemala. You meet with your advisor to ask for some tips on how to make the most of the experience. Ask about: a) recommendations to prepare for traveling; b) ideas for places to visit; and c) ideas on how to improve your Spanish quickly.

ROLE B. You are a university advisor. A student who is participating for the first time in a study abroad in Guatemala wants some advice. Answer his/her questions and give him/her the following recommendations: a) read about Guatemalan culture before the trip; b) don't take a lot of clothes; c) use a debit card rather than carry cash; and d) make Guatemalan friends rather than spend time with other Americans.

Unidos

ESCUCHA

9-26 [Presentational]

Preparación. En la siguiente conversación, dos amigas hablan sobre las ventajas y desventajas de su trabajo. Antes de escuchar, escribe el nombre de una profesión relacionada con los negocios y otra con la salud. Luego, escribe una ventaja y una desventaja para cada una de las profesiones. Comparte tus notas con la clase.

ESTRATEGIA

Use contextual guessing

When you have a conversation in a second language, it is common not to understand everything the other person says. You can figure out the overall message by using contextual cues; that is, by paying attention to the topic or to the words that precede or follow what you did not understand.

PROFESIÓN	VENTAJA	DESVENTAJA

9-27 [Interpretive]

Escucha. Read the words in the left column and then listen to the conversation between Estela and Susana. State the probable meaning of each word in English based on the contextual cues you heard in the conversation. Finally, write down the cue words that helped you understand.

ESCUCHÉ...	POSIBLE SIGNIFICADO	ADIVINÉ EL SIGNIFICADO PORQUE...
1. neuróloga	neurologist	neuralgias, nervios (cognados); dolores de cabeza
2. primordial	prime, fundamental	de primera importancia
3. guardias	to be on duty	una vez a la semana, quedarse en el hospital 24 horas

Comprueba

I was able to...

____ **comprehend the overall meaning by focusing on what I understood.**

____ **use context to figure out the meaning of unknown words.**

9-28 [Interpersonal]

Un paso más. Comparte con tu compañero/a las respuestas a las siguientes preguntas.

1. ¿Cuáles son las ventajas y desventajas de la profesión que te gusta más?

2. En general, ¿qué profesión u ocupación te parece menos estresante?

3. ¿Qué profesión u ocupación da más satisfacciones personales? ¿Por qué?

AUTOEVALUACIÓN

☐ I feel confident that I was able to understand what I heard.

☐ I need more listening practice.

STUDY PLAN

▶ Good job! Move on to the next section, *Habla.*

▶ Go to the *Unidos* [folder] online for *Escucha* practice.

HABLA

9-29  Interpretive

Preparación. Lee los siguientes anuncios con ofertas de trabajo. Escoge un anuncio y prepara una lista con los requisitos que cumples (*meet*).

JEFE DE SERVICIO
necesita importante empresa
MANUFACTURERA DE PLÁSTICOS

Nos urge un buen diseñador gráfico
Requisitos: Conoce al 100% PhotoShop
y Freehand. Maneja ambiente Mac y
PC. De preferencia estudiante
de diseño en la U, con ideas frescas.
Dispuesto a trabajar bajo presión.
Ofrecemos: Salario a convenir.
Capacitación constante. Desarrollo
dentro de la organización. Horario
flexible. Seguro de vida y médico.
Interesados, enviar curriculum y
fotografía reciente, especificando
pretensiones de sueldo, a Casilla 2568,
Correo Guatemala, zona 1, Guatemala

INSTITUTO PRIVADO

necesita
DIRECTOR/A
Lugar de residencia, Región de los Lagos

Empresa de Hotelería necesita
Director/a

Requisitos: Estudios universitarios avanzados. Experiencia
mínima de 1 a 2 años en ventas directas, preferiblemente en el
área de servicios. Edad 26 a 32 años. Excelente presentación.
Poseer vehículo propio. Buenas relaciones interpersonales.

Ofrecemos: Salario a convenir según experiencia, gasolina,
comisiones sobre ventas. Excelente ambiente de trabajo.
Oportunidades de crecimiento.

Sueldo compatible con calificaciones

Interesados, enviar currículum a
gruporecursoshumanos@hotmail.com

BANCO AZTECA
necesita
10 CONTADORES AUDITORES
Lugar de trabajo ideal: Viña del Mar

- Título universitario
- Mínimo dos años de experiencia
- Flexibilidad horaria
- Deseo de viajar a otras regiones del país
- Capacidad de organización y trabajo

Sueldo atractivo

Interesados, enviar currículum, con fotografía a:
Bco. Azteca, 7 Av. 19-28, zona 5

9-30 Interpersonal

Habla. Escojan un papel. Uno/a es el jefe/la jefa de personal de una compañía representada en los anuncios y los otros dos son personas que solicitan el mismo trabajo en esa compañía.

Jefe/a de personal: Entrevista separadamente a dos personas que están interesadas en el mismo puesto. Pregúntales sobre su experiencia, sus estudios, sus preferencias de sueldo, etc., y decide cuál es la persona indicada para el puesto.

Personas que buscan trabajo: Cada uno de ustedes debe escoger un trabajo. Respondan a las preguntas del jefe/de la jefa de personal y háganle preguntas para saber más acerca del puesto.

Comprueba

In my conversation…

____ **I asked questions relevant to the position.**

____ **I provided answers relevant to the questions asked.**

____ **I supported my questions and answers with appropriate information.**

ESTRATEGIA

Gather information strategically to express a decision

When you speak to convey a decision, you need to present your decision and the reasons behind it in an organized and convincing way. Lay out your facts and arguments logically (in your mind or in written notes) before you start to speak.

En directo

To welcome someone to your office:

Pase/Adelante, por favor./ Tenga la amabilidad de pasar. *Please come in.*

Por favor, tome asiento. *Please have a seat.*

Siéntese aquí, por favor. *Sit here, please.*

To put someone at ease:

Por favor, póngase cómodo/a. *Please make yourself comfortable.*

To say good-bye at the end of an interview:

Fue un placer conocerlo/la. *It was a pleasure to meet you.*

 Click on the icon to listen to a conversation with these expressions.

Note for 9-29
In *Preparación* students will interpret the information in some job ads to find some requirements that they may meet to apply for the jobs and to prepare for the interpersonal activity that follows. In *Un paso más* students will present a report to the class informing about the results of the job interviews.

Audioscript for *En directo*
Mateo: *Buenas tardes, Sra. Durán. Soy Mateo Williams.*
Sra. Durán: *Buenas tardes, Sr. Williams. Adelante, por favor. Siéntese aquí.*
Mateo: *Gracias. Aquí le entrego una copia de mi currículum.*
Sra. Durán: *Muchas gracias. Por favor, póngase cómodo.*
Mateo: *Gracias. [brief pause, allowing Sra. Durán to quickly scan his resume] Como puede ver, tengo mucha experiencia en ventas y mi especialidad son los aparatos electrónicos.*
Sra. Durán: *Sí, ya veo. También sé que usted tiene muy buena reputación como vendedor, que trata muy bien a sus clientes. Para nuestra empresa, el trato de nuestros clientes es lo más importante.*
Mateo: *¡Cómo no! Hacen falta buenos productos como los que produce su compañía. Sin embargo, es igual de importante hacerse sentir bien a los clientes.*
Sra. Durán: *De acuerdo. Bueno, Sr. Williams, ahora tengo que entrevistar a otro candidato. Fue un placer conocerlo.*
Mateo: *Igualmente Muchísimas gracias.*

Suggestions for 9-30
To do the interpersonal activity you will need to organize students into groups of 3: one *jefe/a de personal* and 2 *personas que buscan trabajo*. In the preceding activity, students selected 1 job ad from the 4 ads presented; the 2 job seekers in this activity should be applying for the same job.

Cultura

La manera de expresar la dirección de un negocio o un domicilio en Ciudad de Guatemala puede confundir a los extranjeros. Por ejemplo, "7 Av. 11-38, zona 9" significa que la casa está en la avenida 7, entre las calles 11 y 12 en la zona 9, y el número de la casa es 38. Las zonas tienen la misma función que los códigos postales (*zip codes*) en Estados Unidos.

Decir la zona es importante, porque los números de las avenidas (que van del norte al sur) y de las calles (que van del este al oeste) se repiten en cada zona.

Compara: ¿Cómo está dividida tu ciudad? ¿Conoces el nombre de algunas zonas? ¿Se incluye el nombre de la zona en la dirección postal?

9-31  [Presentational]

Un paso más. Los jefes de personal y las personas que buscaban trabajo deben informar a la clase sobre lo siguiente.

Informe de las personas que buscaban trabajo:

1. ¿Qué puesto buscabas? ¿Qué requisitos cumples?
2. ¿Qué aspecto de la oferta de trabajo te pareció más atractivo?
3. ¿Crees que vas a recibir la oferta de trabajo? ¿Por qué?

Informe de los jefes de personal:

1. ¿Qué puesto ofrecía tu compañía en el anuncio?
2. ¿Qué cualidades debía tener el candidato/la candidata que buscaba trabajo en tu compañía?
3. ¿A qué candidato/a(s) vas a contratar? ¿Por qué?

AUTOEVALUACIÓN

☐ I feel confident that I communicated successfully.

☐ I need more speaking practice.

STUDY PLAN

▶ Good job! Move on to the next section, *Lee.*

▶ Go to the *Unidos* [folder] online for *Habla* practice.

LEE

9-32 [Interpersonal]

Preparación. Lee el título y los subtítulos del texto en la página siguiente y mira la foto. Basándote en esta información y en lo que sabes sobre la inmigración, anota unas ideas para compartir con tu compañero/a.

1. ¿Son frecuentes los matrimonios interculturales? ¿Conoces alguno? ¿Qué ventajas o desventajas piensas que tienen estas parejas?

2. ¿Cuáles son las nuevas tendencias demográficas en Estados Unidos? ¿Qué grupos de inmigrantes son los más numerosos?

3. Según tú, ¿cómo puede afectar la emigración a la economía de los países?

ESTRATEGIA

Organize textual information into categories

To understand what you are reading, you need to focus on what is being conveyed by the text. By *focus* we mean organizing the information into meaningful categories, which helps you connect the information to what you already know. As you read, focus on the main point of each section. Use the subtitles to help you anticipate the content.

9-33 [Interpretive]

Lee. Indica a qué categoría pertenecen las siguientes afirmaciones, según el contenido del artículo: información personal sobre una familia (**P**), información general sobre los inmigrantes guatemaltecos en Estados Unidos (**EU**) o información sobre Guatemala (**G**).

1. _____ Viven en comunidades donde el grupo predominante son los mexicanos.

2. _____ Se conocieron en un club de baile.

3. _____ Reciben dinero de sus familiares que viven en el extranjero.

4. _____ El dinero que viene del exterior estimula la economía.

5. _____ Hay más hombres que mujeres.

6. _____ Trabaja de obrero y mantiene a su familia en Los Ángeles.

Comprueba

I was able to…

_____ use the subtitles to anticipate and reflect on the content.

_____ organize the content into general categories.

_____ identify the main ideas in the text.

Note for 9-32
In *Preparación* students exchange ideas to activate background knowledge and help them focus on the topic of the reading and its different subtopics. In *Lee*, students will learn about a specific group of immigrants in the United States from personal, demographic, and economic perspectives. In *Un paso más* they present in a brief paragraph some of the ideas that they have learned through discussion and reading.

Standard 5.1
Students use the language both within and beyond the school setting. Mexicans and Guatemalans are only two groups of the growing Hispanic population of the U.S. You may wish to encourage students to talk about and perhaps do some research on how their career plans could be expanded and enhanced by having sufficient proficiency in Spanish to use it in their chosen professions.

Note
Other cities with a high concentration of Guatemalans include Phoenix, Houston, Chicago, Miami, Washington, DC, and New York.

Note
Families in Guatemala use 50% of the money they receive from family members in the United States for basic needs such as food and clothing. The other 50% goes for living and health expenses, products for the home, and savings.

LOS GUATEMALTECOS EN ESTADOS UNIDOS

Matrimonios entre guatemaltecos y mexicanos

Gustavo Rivera conoció a Marta Rodríguez en un club hispano de Los Ángeles y la invitó a bailar. Marta, que era de Ciudad de México, se dio cuenta que Gustavo hablaba español con un acento diferente y que usaba unas palabras diferentes también. Después de un rato, ella le preguntó: "¿De dónde eres, Gustavo?". "Soy de Guatemala", dijo él. Después de esa noche, los dos empezaron a conversar por teléfono y a salir juntos. Pasaron dos años y Gustavo y Marta se casaron; ahora tienen tres hijos.

Esta familia representa una tendencia demográfica en Los Ángeles y en otras ciudades del suroeste: más inmigrantes guatemaltecos y mexicanos se casan entre sí y tienen hijos, creando familias hispanas mixtas que tienen conexiones con tres países al mismo tiempo. Esa mezcla es ahora tan común que dio lugar al nombre de "guatemexicoestadounidenses" para describir a esas familias.

Nuevas tendencias demográficas

Hay varias razones que explican esta tendencia demográfica. Primero, el número de personas de ascendencia guatemalteca en Estados Unidos está creciendo. Según la Organización Internacional para las Migraciones (OIM), en 2008 había 1.3 millones de guatemaltecos en Estados Unidos. La mayoría son jóvenes, entre 15 y 44 años, y hay muchos más hombres (72%) que mujeres (28%). Por esta razón, muchos guatemaltecos en Estados Unidos se casan con mujeres no guatemaltecas.

Segundo, cuando los inmigrantes guatemaltecos nuevos buscan vivienda en comunidades hispanas establecidas, conocen a muchos mexicanos, porque son el grupo hispano más grande del país. La constante interacción entre hombres guatemaltecos y mujeres mexicanas da como resultado más matrimonios entre los dos grupos.

Impacto económico en Guatemala

Gustavo Rivera es un inmigrante guatemalteco típico. Como el 88% de los guatemaltecos que viven en Estados Unidos, se mantiene activo económicamente, trabaja en una fábrica. Como el 33% de los guatemaltecos en Estados Unidos, vive en Los Ángeles. Y como el 93% de los emigrantes guatemaltecos, mantiene contacto con su familia en Guatemala. Llama a sus padres todas las semanas y les envía remesas todos los meses. Según la OIM, más de 600.000 familias en Guatemala reciben remesas de familiares que viven en el extranjero.

9-34 Presentational

Un paso más. En un párrafo resume las ideas más interesantes del artículo y compártelo con la clase.

Suggestion for 9-34
You can assign this as a pair activity. Have student pairs work together and then present to the class.

AUTOEVALUACIÓN

☐ I feel confident I understood the reading and was able to summarize the information.

☐ I need more reading practice.

STUDY PLAN

▶ Good job! Move on to the next section, *Escribe*.

▶ Go to the *Unidos* 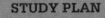 online for *Lee* practice.

ESCRIBE

9-35 Interpretive

Preparación. Lee el siguiente anuncio de trabajo en Internet y prepara una lista de datos sobre tu experiencia y tus talentos para solicitar el puesto.

Descripción:

Se necesita estudiante para cuidar niños guatemaltecos durante el verano. Imprescindible inglés nativo y saber preparar comidas ligeras.

El trabajo es en Estados Unidos

Detalles generales:
Oferta por: **Empresa Ofertas**
Correo electrónico: empresaoferta@gmail.com

Detalles del anuncio
Número: 13800
Número de visitas: 354
La oferta vence: dentro de 196 días
Fecha: 2012.06.19

9-36 Presentational

Escribe. Escribe un correo electrónico solicitando el trabajo. En un mensaje breve, organizado y convincente, preséntate y explica cómo tu experiencia, tu conocimiento y tus talentos son perfectos para el puesto.

9-37  Interpersonal

Un paso más. Comparte tu correo electrónico con tu compañero/a para que te dé su opinión.

ESTRATEGIA

Focus on purpose, content, and audience

To get the job that is right for you, consider the following when responding to an ad in any language:

- Your purpose: What kind of job do you want?

- Your response: What academic degree do you need for the job? What general abilities and job-specific skills should you possess?

- Your audience: What experience does the employer require? What personality characteristics will you need to be considered a serious candidate?

Comprueba
I was able to…

___ **appropriately address the potential employer.**

___ **convincingly describe my qualifications for the position.**

AUTOEVALUACIÓN

☐ I feel confident that I successfully communicated my ideas in writing.

☐ I need more writing practice.

STUDY PLAN

▶ Good job!

▶ Go to the *Unidos* folder online for *Escribe* practice.

ENFOQUE *cultural*

Note for *Museo Nacional de Arqueología y Etnología*
Located at Finca La Aurora in Guatemala City, the National Museum of Archeology and Ethnology contains the most important and complete collection of Maya artifacts in all of Guatemala. Its exhibits include indigenous textiles, a room dedicated to Maya technology, and an impressive collection of jade pieces.

Note for *Biotopo del Quetzal*
The Quetzal Biotope is administered by the University of San Carlos's Center for Conservation Studies. While only a small portion of this vast reserve is open to the public, visitors have plenty to take in as they cover the biotope's two trails. Rich vegetation, waterfalls and, with some luck, the quetzal itself await visitors from around the world.

Note for *La marimba*
There are conflicting ideas about the origins of the marimba. Some believe it was first developed by the Mayans. Others contend it originated in Southeast Asia while others credit West African slaves for its creation. Today, there are different variations on the instrument both in terms of its size and in terms of the materials used to make it. However, the traditional marimba is made from the hormigo tree, which grows only in the forests of Guatemala.

El Museo Nacional de Arqueología y Etnología en la Ciudad de Guatemala contiene una colección masiva de artefactos mayas.

El Biotopo Mario Dary Rivera está situado en Cobán. También conocido como el Biotopo del Quetzal, esta reserva natural contiene cavernas y cataratas.

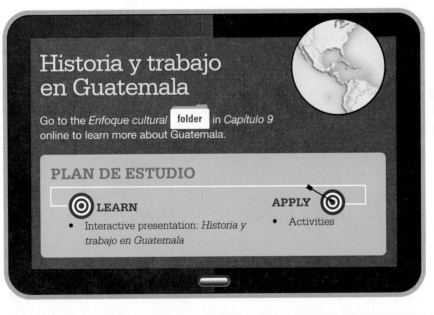

Historia y trabajo en Guatemala

Go to the *Enfoque cultural* [folder] in *Capítulo 9* online to learn more about Guatemala.

PLAN DE ESTUDIO

◎ **LEARN**
- Interactive presentation: *Historia y trabajo en Guatemala*

◎ **APPLY**
- Activities

La marimba es el instrumento nacional de Guatemala que, junto con el quetzal y otros símbolos nacionales, une al pueblo guatemalteco. El Monumento a la Marimba, homenaje a los compositores de música de marimba como también al instrumento, se encuentra en Quetzaltenango.

PRÁCTICA COMUNICATIVA

9-38

Usa la información. Escribe un correo electrónico para contestar a un anuncio de trabajo en Guatemala. Incluye lo siguiente:

1. qué trabajo solicitas
2. dónde trabajas actualmente y por cuánto tiempo
3. qué experiencia tienes en ese tipo de trabajo
4. cuándo puedes empezar a trabajar

En este capítulo...

Comprueba lo que sabes

Go to the *Comprueba lo que sabes* folder online to review what you have learned in this chapter. Practice with the following:

Vocabulary Flashcards | Games | Oral Practice | Practice Test/Study Plan | Video en contexto

Vocabulario

Las profesiones, oficios y ocupaciones
el/la abogado/a
el actor/la actriz
el/la agricultor/a
el ama/o de casa
el/la arquitecto/a
el/la artesano/a
el/la bibliotecario/a
el/la bombero/a
el/la cajero/a
el/la carpintero/a
el/la ceramista
el/la chef
el/la chofer
el/la científico/a
el/la contador/a
el/la contratista
el/la ejecutivo/a
el/la electricista
el/la empleado/a
el/la enfermero/a
el/la gerente (de ventas)
el herrero

el hombre/la mujer de negocios
el/la ingeniero/a
el/la intérprete
el jefe/la jefa
el/la joyero/a
el/la juez/a
el/la locutor/a
el/la médico/a
el/la obrero/a
el/la peletero/a
el/la peluquero/a
el/la periodista
el/la plomero/a
el/la policía
el/la (p)sicólogo/a
el/la técnico/a
el/la vendedor/a

Los lugares
el banco
el campo
la compañía/la empresa
el consultorio
la peluquería
el taller

El trabajo
la agricultura
el anuncio
el cliente/la clienta
el currículum
la entrevista
la especialidad
la experiencia
el incendio
la madera
el puesto
la solicitud
el sueldo
la vacante
las ventas

Verbos
apagar
cosechar
dejar
elaborar
emigrar

enviar
esperar
llenar
mandar
ofrecer (zc)
sobrevivir
solicitar

Palabras y expresiones útiles
actualmente
¡Cómo no!
en realidad/realmente
lo importante
por cierto
propio/a
la señal
sin embargo

Notas

Introduction to chapter
Introduce the chapter theme about food, cooking, and healthy eating. Ask questions to recycle content from the previous chapter. Related questions: *¿Sabes cocinar? ¿Quién en tu familia cocina mejor? ¿Qué tipo de comida te gusta más? ¿La comida italiana/china/india? ¿Conoces la comida de algunos países hispanos? ¿Cuáles? ¿Qué platos conoces? En general, ¿comes bien o necesitas mejorar tu dieta con más frutas y vegetales? ¿Eres vegetariano/a? ¿Cómo es tu dieta?*

Integrated Performance Assessment: Three Modes of Communication

Presentational: See activities **10-6**, **10-7**, **10-17**, **10-23**, **10-24**, **10-27**, **10-29**, **10-34**, **10-37**, **10-39**, and **10-41**.

Interpretive: See activities **10-1**, **10-2**, **10-3**, **10-4**, **10-5**, **10-11**, **10-12**, **10-13**, **10-14**, **10-16**, **10-19**, **10-20**, **10-21**, **10-22**, **10-23**, **10-25**, **10-26**, **10-28**, **10-30**, **10-32**, **10-36**, and **10-38**

Interpersonal: See activities **10-1**, **10-2**, **10-3**, **10-4**, **10-5**, **10-6**, **10-7**, **10-8**, **10-9**, **10-10**, **10-11**, **10-12**, **10-13**, **10-14**, **10-15**, **10-16**, **10-17**, **10-18**, **10-19**, **10-20**, **10-21**, **10-22**, **10-23**, **10-24**, **10-25**, **10-26**, **10-27**, **10-28**, **10-31**, **10-33**, **10-35**, **10-40**, and all *Situaciones*.

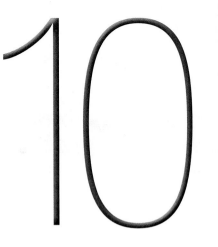

10

¿Cuál es tu comida preferida?

Learning OBJECTIVES

You will:

- learn vocabulary to discuss food and food-related activities
- use *se* + verb
- use the present perfect
- use commands
- learn to form the future tense
- connect new information about the cultural and geographic diversity of Ecuador and its impact on food production to what you already know

Learning OUTCOMES

You will be able to:

- talk about ingredients, recipes, and meals
- state impersonal information
- talk about the recent past
- give instructions in informal settings
- talk about the future
- present information, concepts, and ideas about food and public health in Ecuador and other Latin American countries

ECUADOR

Islas Galápagos

Tortuga de las Galápagos

COLOMBIA

Tulcán

Ibarra
Otavalo

Quito

El distrito histórico
de Quito

Manta

Ambato

Riobamba

Textiles de Ecuador

Región amazónica

Guayaquil • Milagro

ECUADOR

Isla
Puna

Cuenca

La reserva amazónica
de Kapawi

Golfo de
Guayaquil

Machala

Loja

OCÉANO PACÍFICO

CORDILLERA DE LOS ANDES

PERÚ

Cataratas de Los Andes

Este cuadro del siglo XVIII presenta a un indígena yumbo cerca de Quito, Ecuador. Junto a él hay árboles y frutas típicas de su país.

Cultura en línea
To learn more about Ecuador and the chapter theme, go to the *Cultura en línea* folder in the *Unidos* online component to view *Vistas culturales* video and take a virtual art tour.

¿Cuánto sabes?

Mira el mapa y las fotos, y contesta las siguientes preguntas sobre Ecuador.

1. ¿Qué países tienen frontera (*border*) con Ecuador?
   Colombia y Perú

2. ¿Cuál es la capital de Ecuador?
   Quito

3. ¿Qué producto de artesanía se elabora en Ecuador? textiles

4. ¿Qué islas famosas pertenecen a Ecuador? islas Galápagos

5. ¿Qué animal es una especie protegida de Ecuador? la tortuga

Vocabulario en contexto

Talking about ingredients, recipes, and meals

Los productos y las recetas

Go to the *Capítulo 10* **folder** online to complete the Learning Module for *Vocabulario en contexto: Los productos y las recetas.*

PLAN DE ESTUDIO

◎ **LEARN**
- Interactive presentation: *Los productos y las recetas*
- Vocabulary tutorials
- Pronounciation

◎ **APPLY**
- Activities
- Pronounciation activities

PRÁCTICA COMUNICATIVA

10-1

Parejas. Asocia las fotos con las descripciones siguientes. Después, escribe tu propia leyenda (*caption*) para una de las fotos y compártela con tu compañero/a.

1. __d__ Las ovejas son animales de los que se aprovechan la carne y la lana.
2. __b__ Estos pasteles son dulces típicos de Ecuador.
3. __a__ En Ecuador se cultivan muchos plátanos.
4. __e__ En el mercado de Zumbahua se encuentran los productos que se usan en las muchas recetas de la comida de Ecuador.
5. __c__ El pescado y los mariscos son muy importantes en la dieta de los países hispanos.

a.

b.

c.

d.

e.

10-2

Una receta ecuatoriana. Lean la siguiente receta y clasifiquen sus ingredientes según las siguientes categorías. Después dile a tu compañero/a cuál es tu comida favorita y por qué.

1. carnes o pescados: pescado crudo, camarones, almejas

2. vegetales: cebolla, tomate, pimiento

3. condimentos: culantro/cilantro, perejil, ajo, aceite, achiote, sal, pimienta, comino

4. frutas: coco

> **LENGUA** These are some useful words that appear in the recipe: **almejas** (*clams*), **perejil** (*parsley*), **paiteña** (*a type of onion*), **diente de ajo** (*clove of garlic*), **picado** (*chopped*), and **comino** (*cumin*). Other cooking expressions include **picar** (*chop*), **pelar** (*peel*), **machacar** (*crush*), **tapar** (*cover*), **agregar/añadir** (*add*), **taza** (*cup*), and **cucharada** (*spoonful*).

Pescado Encocado

Ingredientes:
1 coco
1 libra de camarones
2 libras de pescado crudo

Refrito:
1 cebolla paiteña finamente picada
¼ taza de cebolla blanca finamente picada
1 pimiento picado
4 cucharadas de cilantro picado
4 cucharadas de perejil picado
2 dientes de ajo machacados
4 cucharadas de aceite
1 un tomate grande rojo, pelado y picado
un poquito de achiote
sal, pimienta, comino al gusto

Elaboración:
Haga un refrito con los ingredientes. Agréguele una libra de camarones crudos, pelados y limpios y dos libras de pescado crudo, cortado en trozos. Refríalos durante un rato y luego agregue la mitad de la leche del coco. Tape la olla y deje cocinar durante 20 ó 30 minutos. Después, añada la otra mitad de la leche del coco. Sirva inmediatamente, acompañado de arroz blanco y plátano verde asado.

10-3

Cómo hacer una pizza casera (*home*). Ordenen cronológicamente los pasos para preparar una pizza. ¿Falta algún ingrediente para preparar su pizza favorita? Inclúyanlo y preséntenlo a la clase.

_1_ Se compran los ingredientes para la pizza.

_2_ Se calienta el horno a 350° F.

_4_ Se echa un poco de aceite (*oil*) antes de poner la masa en la bandeja de horno.

_6_ Se agregan el queso (*cheese*), algún tipo de carne, vegetales y especias.

_5_ Se pone la salsa de tomate.

_3_ Se trabaja bien la masa y se extiende para formar un círculo.

_7_ Se hornea por unos 20–25 minutos.

Note for 10-2
Explain that *refrito* refers to the fried or sautéed ingredients of the dish to which the other ingredients will be added.

Suggestions for 10-3
Explain that the structure *se* + *verb* is often used in recipes and will be studied in *Gramática en contexto* in this chapter. Encourage student pairs to add another ingredient to the recipe using this structure and present all the steps to the class. You may also want to introduce pizza ingredients: *la masa* (dough), *salchicha* (sausage), *queso* (cheese).

Follow-up for 10-3
To preview the structure *se* + *verb* ask questions such as: *Típicamente, ¿qué se bebe con la pizza? ¿Se come algo más con la pizza? ¿Se trae la pizza a casa o se come en un restaurante?*

En el supermercado

Go to the *Capítulo 10* folder online to complete the Learning Module for *Vocabulario en contexto: En el supermercado*.

PLAN DE ESTUDIO

◎ LEARN
- Interactive presentation: *En el supermercado*
- Vocabulary tutorials

APPLY ◎
- Activities

PRÁCTICA COMUNICATIVA

10-4 👥

Asociaciones. Asocien cada explicación con la palabra adecuada y comenten si les gustan o no estos alimentos.

1. __d__ Se toma mucho en el verano, cuando hace calor.
2. __e__ Se pone en la ensalada.
3. __b__ Se usan para hacer vino.
4. __a__ Se come en el desayuno con huevos fritos.
5. __f__ Se prepara para el Día de Acción de Gracias.
6. __c__ Se usa para preparar la ensalada de atún o de pollo.

a. el jamón
b. las uvas
c. la mayonesa
d. el helado
e. el aderezo
f. el pavo

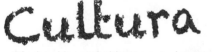

Cultura

Muchos hispanohablantes que viven en Estados Unidos mantienen las tradiciones y costumbres de su país natal (*native*) con respecto a las comidas. Estas tradiciones y costumbres, que varían mucho de un país a otro, se reflejan en las recetas, maneras de cocinar y aun en las horas diferentes de comer. Hay productos como los frijoles, el arroz, los chiles, los plátanos y el maíz, que constituyen la base de la dieta de muchos países de Hispanoamérica y que se encuentran en casi todos los supermercados de Estados Unidos.

Compara: ¿Qué tradiciones relacionadas con la comida tiene tu familia? ¿Qué productos o platos asocias con estas tradiciones?

10-5

Dietas diferentes.

PRIMERA FASE. Completen la tabla con las comidas o productos adecuados para estas dietas.

DIETA	SE DEBE COMER	NO SE DEBE COMER
vegetariana		
para diabéticos		
para desarrollar los músculos		
para bajar de peso (*lose weight*)		

SEGUNDA FASE. Completen las siguientes ideas con sus recomendaciones para cada una de estas personas. Digan por qué.

1. Laura, que es vegetariana…
2. Mi padre, que es diabético,…
3. Luis, que levanta pesas (*weights*),…
4. Joaquín y Amalia quieren bajar de peso. Por lo tanto…

10-6

¿Qué necesitamos?

PRIMERA FASE. Ustedes son estudiantes de intercambio en Ecuador y quieren preparar una cena para su familia ecuatoriana. Describan el menú y hagan una lista de los ingredientes que necesitan.

 SEGUNDA FASE. Compartan su menú con otra pareja.

10-7

Los estudiantes y la comida.

PRIMERA FASE. Respondan a las siguientes preguntas.

1. ¿Qué comieron hoy?
2. ¿Cuándo y dónde comieron?
3. ¿Cuánto gastaron en comida?

SEGUNDA FASE. Hagan una lista de recomendaciones para una dieta estudiantil más saludable (*healthier*) y compártanla con el resto de la clase.

En directo

To give some general advice:

Deben + *infinitive* (comer/beber/etc.)…

Para bajar de peso/comer saludable, recomendamos + *noun* (las verduras, el agua, etc.)

Para obtener calcio/proteínas/fibra es bueno + *infinitive* (comer/beber/etc.)

Click on the icon to listen to a conversation with these expressions.

Note for 10-5
Students did a similar activity in *Capítulo 3*. This is an opportunity to recycle *deber + infinitive* and to expand nutrition-related vocabulary.

Note for 10-5 *Segunda fase*
Provide a model response so that students know not to use the *se* from the column headers in their responses: *Laura, que es vegetariana, no debe comer…*

Follow-up for 10-5
Present additional vocabulary related to nutrition: *vitaminas, calcio, fibra, proteínas, sin aditivos, calorías, grasa, colesterol.* Discuss preparation methods: *crudo, asado, al horno, hervido, al vapor.* Discuss the pros and cons of vegetarianism.

Suggestion for 10-6
Have students list the types of food that they consider typically American. Ask what food or dishes they would like to share with people from other cultures and why.

Suggestions for 10-7
Have students describe meals during a typical day at home or when they are away at school. Have them prepare a list of what they buy and eat in a typical week.

Audioscript for *En directo*
Dra. Duarte: *Bienvenidos al programa* Tu Salud. *Estoy aquí para contestar sus preguntas sobre la salud y la comida. Adelante con la primera pregunta.*
Male 1: *He subido mucho de peso recientemente y quiero perder al menos 5 libras. ¿Qué recomendaciones me puede dar?*
Dra. Duarte: *Para bajar de peso, debe comer muchas verduras y frutas y también debe beber mucha agua. Claro, también es importante hacer ejercicio.*
Female 2: *Mi médica me dijo que debía consumir comidas con calcio. ¿Qué comidas me recomienda?*
Dra. Duarte: *Para obtener calcio, es bueno comer no solo productos lácteos sino también verduras como la espinaca, frijoles blancos y pescado como el salmón.*

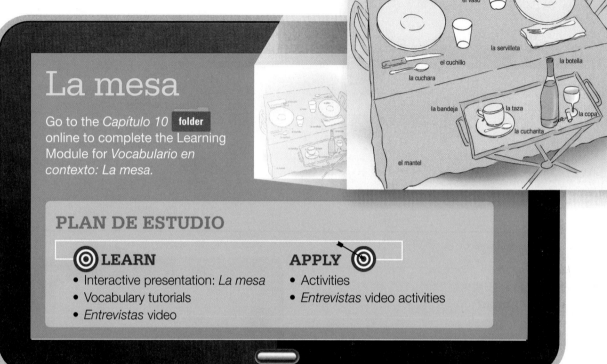

La mesa

Go to the *Capítulo 10* [folder] online to complete the Learning Module for *Vocabulario en contexto: La mesa.*

PLAN DE ESTUDIO

◎ **LEARN**
- Interactive presentation: *La mesa*
- Vocabulary tutorials
- *Entrevistas* video

APPLY ◎
- Activities
- *Entrevistas* video activities

PRÁCTICA COMUNICATIVA

 10-8

El camarero nuevo. Ustedes son camareros en un restaurante pero uno/a de ustedes es nuevo/a. El/la experto/a debe decirle a la persona nueva dónde debe poner cada cosa de acuerdo con la foto. Después cambien de papel.

Modelo

Pon el cuchillo a la derecha del plato.

Muy bien. ¿Y dónde pongo la copa?

10-9

Los preparativos. Ustedes deben organizar una fiesta formal para el aniversario de boda de sus mejores amigos. Primero, preparen un presupuesto (*budget*), una lista de invitados, un menú y una lista de compras. Luego divídanse el trabajo y den instrucciones al otro/a la otra sobre lo siguiente:

1. la decoración del salón   **3.** la comida y las bebidas   **5.** el lugar, la hora, el día

2. el tipo de entretenimiento   **4.** los invitados   **6.** …

10-10

Una cena. Estuviste muy ocupado/a ayer porque tuviste invitados a cenar. Dile a tu compañero/a todas las cosas que hiciste. Él/Ella te va a preguntar dónde hiciste las compras, a quién invitaste, qué serviste y si lo pasaste bien. Después cambien de papel.

En directo

To express that you had a good time:

Lo pasé muy bien./Lo pasamos muy bien.

Fue estupendo.

Estuvo muy divertido.

 Click on the icon to listen to a conversation with these expressions.

10-11

Una cena perfecta.

PRIMERA FASE. You will listen to a married couple talk about their plans for their dinner party tonight. Before you listen, make a list of four ingredients that you will need in order to prepare a salad and an entrée. Share your answers with a classmate.

 SEGUNDA FASE. Now listen to the conversation. As you listen, mark (✓) the appropriate ending to each statement.

1. Rodolfo es…

　✓ un buen cocinero.

　＿ muy perezoso.

　＿ vegetariano.

2. Manuela va a…

　＿ cocinar ceviche.

　✓ poner la mesa.

　＿ llamar a los invitados.

3. Rodolfo va a comprar…

　✓ pescado y maíz.

　＿ limón y camarones.

　＿ espinacas y aguacates.

4. Manuela tiene…

　＿ todos los ingredientes.

　＿ muchos vegetales y frutas.

　✓ casi todos los ingredientes.

Cultura

La comida de los países hispanoamericanos es muy variada. En Ecuador, al igual que en Perú, el ceviche de pescado o de camarón es muy popular. Otro plato muy popular es la fritada, un combinado de diversas carnes con plátano (*plantain*) maduro, plátano tostado y maíz. Y entre los postres, además de la pastelería, es muy sabroso el dulce de higos (*candied figs*).

Dulce de higos

Compara: ¿Qué productos son populares en la comida de tu país o región? ¿Qué platos se preparan con estos productos? ¿Hay postres especiales que se consumen generalmente en tu región? ¿Se comen en una época especial?

Audioscript for *En directo*
Jimena: *Alex, ¿cómo lo pasaron Ricky y tú en la fiesta anoche?*
Alex: *Lo pasamos muy bien. Fue estupendo compartir con tantos amigos.*
Jimena: *Y, ¿qué tal el DJ? ¿Tocó música buena?*
Alex: *¡Sí! Tocó música buenísima. Estuvimos bailando toda la noche. Estuvo muy divertido.*

Audioscript for 10-11
Manuela: *Rodolfo, esta noche tenemos invitados. Como ellos son americanos, quiero que prepares un ceviche de pescado al estilo del Hotel Colón de Quito. ¿Qué te parece?*
Rodolfo: *Lo que tú digas, Manuela. Tú sabes que a mí me gusta cocinar y, según tú, soy un cocinero excelente. Dime, ¿tenemos todos los ingredientes para el ceviche?*
Manuela: *Sí, creo que tenemos todo. Solo hay que comprar el pescado porque en casa tenemos todo lo demás: cebollas, tomates, limón, lechuga.*
Rodolfo: *¿Tenemos maíz?*
Manuela: *¡Ay! No, no tenemos. ¿Puedes comprar maíz, por favor?*
Rodolfo: *Muy bien. Entonces tú pones la mesa y yo hago todo lo demás.*
Manuela: *¡Estupendo!*
Rodolfo: *Bueno, me voy al supermercado. Si se te ocurre otra cosa me llamas al celular.*
Manuela: *Gracias, Rodolfo.*

Gramática en contexto

Talking about the recent past and the future and giving instructions

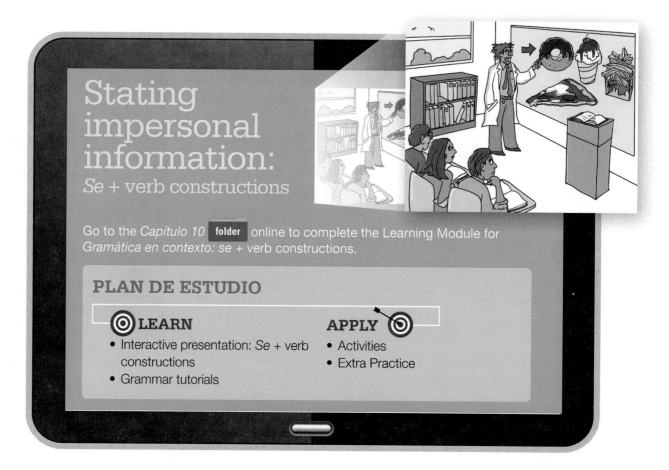

Stating impersonal information:
Se + verb constructions

Go to the *Capítulo 10* **folder** online to complete the Learning Module for *Gramática en contexto: se* + verb constructions.

PLAN DE ESTUDIO

◎ **LEARN**
- Interactive presentation: *Se* + verb constructions
- Grammar tutorials

APPLY ◎
- Activities
- Extra Practice

PRÁCTICA COMUNICATIVA

Se ven lobos marinos en las playas de las islas Galápagos.

 10-12

Asociaciones.

PRIMERA FASE. Asocia las actividades con los lugares donde ocurren. Compara tus repuestas con las de tu compañero/a.

1. __c__ Se cambian cheques en…   **a.** un almacén o tienda.
2. __a__ Se vende ropa en…   **b.** un restaurante.
3. __d__ Se toma el sol y se nada en…   **c.** un banco.
4. __b__ Se sirven comidas en…   **d.** una playa.

SEGUNDA FASE. Piensa en un edificio o lugar público que te gusta mucho y dile a tu compañero/a qué se hace allí.

Modelo 66 *Me gusta mucho la zona peatonal (pedestrian area) de mi ciudad. Allí se camina mucho y en el verano se escucha la música de conjuntos locales.* 99

El supermercado y las tiendas del barrio. Indica (✓) los productos y/o servicios que se encuentran solo en los supermercados y los que se encuentran en las tiendas de tu barrio. Compara tus respuestas con las de tu compañero/a. Después dile a tu compañero/a qué productos compras con más frecuencia.

PRODUCTOS/ SERVICIOS	SUPERMERCADO SOLAMENTE	SUPERMERCADO Y TIENDA DEL BARRIO
productos lácteos		✓
carnes orgánicas	✓	
frutas de América del Sur	✓	
detergente para lavadoras		✓
alimentos enlatados (*canned*)		✓
pescado fresco	✓	
DVD para alquilar		✓

EN OTRAS PALABRAS

The concept of *convenience stores* is expressed differently depending on the country. In Mexico they are **tiendas de conveniencia,** translated directly from English. In Costa Rica the term **tiendas de gasolinera** is used. **La tienda de la esquina o del barrio** is frequently used in several Spanish-speaking countries to refer to the small or medium-sized stores located in residential neighborhoods. The convenience stores open 24/7 in Spain are called **tiendas de 24 horas.**

Follow-up for 10-13
You may expand this activity as follows: *Marca las cuatro cosas y/o servicios que consideras más esenciales en los supermercados hoy en día y compara tus resultados con los de tu compañero/a. Después, en grupos pequeños, escojan las cuatro cosas y/o servicios que obtuvieron más votos y comenten entre todos por qué se necesitan. Comparen sus resultados con los de otros grupos.*

10-14

Recetas creativas.

PRIMERA FASE. Lean estas recetas originales. Luego, intercambien opiniones sobre cuáles les gustaría probar y cuáles no. Digan por qué.

1. Plátano derretido (*melted*): Se corta un plátano en rebanadas (*slices*) no muy finas. Se echa azúcar. Se calienta en el microondas por uno o dos minutos.

2. Batido de tarta de manzana (*apple pie smoothie*): Se ponen en la licuadora (*blender*): media taza de jugo de manzana, tres cucharadas de helado de vainilla y media cucharadita de canela (*cinnamon*). Se bate por un minuto.

3. Hamburguesa y salsa con queso (*nacho cheese sauce*): Se calienta la parrilla. Se pone la hamburguesa en la parrilla. Se pone la salsa con queso en el panecillo y se calienta. Se pone la hamburguesa en el panecillo.

4. Ensalada de pollo: Se abre una bolsa de lechuga prelavada. Se cortan en rebanadas dos pechugas de pollo (*chicken breasts*) cocidas, y se corta media libra de queso en cubos pequeños. Se combinan los ingredientes en una fuente (*bowl*). Se agrega un aliño de vinagre balsámico.

SEGUNDA FASE. Escriban y, si es posible, preparen juntos una receta para compartir con la clase.

10-15

¿Cómo se prepara este plato?

PRIMERA FASE. Tu compañero/a y tú quieren darle una sorpresa a otra persona y deciden prepararle su plato favorito. Primero, seleccionen uno de estos platos a la derecha.

espaguetis a la boloñesa

tacos al carbón

Luego, escriban en cada caja una lista de los ingredientes que se necesitan para hacer este plato.

CARNES	VERDURAS/ VEGETALES	ESPECIAS	OTROS

SEGUNDA FASE. Tú sabes cocinar, pero tu amigo/a no. Responde a sus preguntas mientras preparan el plato. Los siguientes verbos pueden ser útiles.

asar	dorar (*brown*)	rallar (*grate*)
cocinar	hervir	(so)freír
cortar	hornear	tostar

Modelo

Vamos a preparar pollo asado. ¿Qué se hace con el pollo?

Primero se lava bien el pollo. Luego se ponen sal y pimienta.

¿Y después?

Se asa en el horno por dos horas y se dora.

En directo

To propose an idea:

Tengo una idea.

¿Qué te parece esto?

Se me ocurrió una idea.

To agree with someone's idea:

Me parece perfecto.

Suena muy bien.

¡Qué buena idea!

Click on the icon to listen to a conversation with these expressions.

Audioscript for *En directo*
Marta: *¡Se me ocurrió una idea!*
Rubén: *Ah, ¿sí? Dime…*
Marta: *¿Qué te parece esto? Sabes que el Profesor O'Donnell se muda a Cuenca este mes y que es el mejor profesor del mundo.*
Rubén: *Es cierto. Nos ha enseñado tantas cosas importantes.*
Marta: *¿Por qué no le hacemos una fiesta de despedida en el centro estudiantil? Todos podemos contribuir con comida y refrescos.*
Rubén: *¡Me parece perfecto! ¡Qué buena idea!*

Situaciones

1

ROLE A. You are an international student who has just arrived in town. A student has offered to help with your orientation. You are not familiar with shopping in the United States, so you ask a) where one buys personal items like vitamins and toothpaste (**pasta de dientes**); b) where on campus one can find a decent meal; c) where one goes to buy fresh fruit; and d) where one can get good American pizza. Ask follow-up questions to be sure you understand the answers.

ROLE B. You have offered to show a new international student around campus. Answer his/her questions about where one goes to buy different things. Offer several options, and be prepared to answer your new friend's questions.

2

ROLE A. You have just moved into your own apartment, and you are living away from home for the first time. You have never done your own food shopping and are not sure how to go about it. Ask a friend for help and ask questions so he/she will expand on the explanation.

ROLE B. A friend has just told you that he/she does not know how to go food shopping. Explain the process step by step, starting with the shopping list (**se hace una lista…**). Provide additional explanation or clarification in response to your friend's questions.

Tech tip for *Situaciones*
Students may want to practice online with a partner. Remind them that they can click on the microphone icon to connect with a partner online.

Talking about the recent past:
Present perfect and participles used as adjectives

Go to the *Capítulo 10* folder online to complete the Learning Module for *Gramática en contexto:* Present perfect and participles used as adjectives.

PLAN DE ESTUDIO

◎ **LEARN**
- Interactive presentation: Present perfect and participles used as adjectives
- Grammar tutorials

APPLY
- Activities
- Extra Practice

PRÁCTICA COMUNICATIVA

10-16

Lo que no he hecho. Tu compañero/a y tú deben decir las cosas de cada lista que no han hecho. Después, comparen sus respuestas con las de otros estudiantes.

1. Yo nunca he estado en…
   a. Paraguay.
   b. Guatemala.
   c. Ecuador.

2. Yo nunca he visto…
   a. las islas Galápagos.
   b. un volcán activo.
   c. un huracán.

3. Yo nunca he comido…
   a. aguacate.
   b. un postre con leche de coco.
   c. langosta.

4. Yo nunca he roto…
   a. una taza.
   b. una vaso.
   c. un plato.

Hispanos famosos.

PRIMERA FASE. Piensen en un hispano famoso/una hispana famosa y preparen una lista de cinco cosas que creen que ha hecho para tener éxito (*to be successful*). Después compartan su lista con la de otra pareja.

Modelo

Cameron Díaz es una actriz famosa.

Ha protagonizado más de treinta películas...

SEGUNDA FASE. Digan tres cosas que ustedes han hecho que los/las ha ayudado a tener éxito en su vida personal, académica o profesional.

Una cena importante. Ustedes van a preparar una cena para su profesor/a de español. Háganse preguntas para ver qué preparativos ha hecho cada uno/a para la cena.

Modelo **" comprar la carne "**

¿Has comprado la carne?

No, no la he comprado todavía.

1. leer las recetas
2. cortar los vegetales
3. hacer el postre
4. decidir la música
5. poner la mesa
6. decorar el lugar de la cena
7. ...

Justo ahora. Digan qué acaban de hacer estas personas. Den la mayor información posible.

Modelo **" Maricarmen y sus amigos ya no tienen hambre. "**

Acaban de comer toda la comida.

Dejaron la nevera vacía.

1. Juan y Ramiro salen del estadio.
2. Pedro y Alina salen de una tienda donde se alquilan películas.
3. Mercedes y Paula traen palomitas de maíz (*popcorn*) para todo el grupo.
4. Un hombre sale corriendo de un banco.
5. Jorge y Rubén salen de un supermercado.
6. Frente a todos sus amigos, Rubén le da una sorpresa a su novia.

¿Qué acaba de pasar?

Preparation for 10-17
One class before doing activity **10-17**, prepare students by brainstorming with them the names of famous Hispanics in various fields: film, music, fiction, sports, science, journalism, etc. Assign pairs to gather information about a person of their choice ahead of time.

Suggestion for 10-18
Have students brainstorm 5 or more steps that are involved in preparing a meal. Then have them share their ideas with the whole class. Encourage them to produce both negative and affirmative responses.

Warm-up for 10-19
Practice by having students list 5 things that they have just done. Or ask questions: *¿Tienes hambre? (No, acabo de comer.) ¿Tienes sueño? ¿Quieres bailar? ¿Quieres nadar? ¿Tienes sed?*

10-20

¿Qué ha pasado? Después de unas horas de haber limpiado y ordenado su apartamento, ustedes encuentran todo muy desordenado. Túrnense para describirle al/a la policía lo que han hecho hoy para ordenar el apartamento y lo que ven ahora.

Modelo **" las ventanas (cerrar, abrir) "**

¿Qué ha pasado con las ventanas?

Las he cerrado esta mañana…

pero ahora están abiertas.

1. el espejo (usar, romper)
2. la cama (tender, desordenar)
3. el televisor (apagar, encender)
4. las camisas (colgar, tirar al piso)
5. la puerta del apartamento (cerrar, abrir)
6. la comida en el refrigerador (cubrir, descubrir [to uncover])

Situaciones

1

ROLE A. You are a journalism student and need to interview the new chef of the student cafeteria. Ask about a) other restaurants where he/she has worked; b) some examples of dishes he/she has developed; and c) changes he/she has already made in the cafeteria.

ROLE B. You are the new chef of the student cafeteria. A journalism student is interviewing you. Answer his/her questions, adding as many details as possible.

2

ROLE A. You are a high school counselor at school. Call one of the students with attendance and academic problems to your office. Explain that the teachers have just told you that a) he/she has not attended classes for four days; b) he/she has not done homework for two weeks. Say that the teachers are worried and ask him/her questions to determine the problem.

ROLE B. You are a high school student. You have been acting strangely, and the school counselor calls you in. Answer his/her questions with detail.

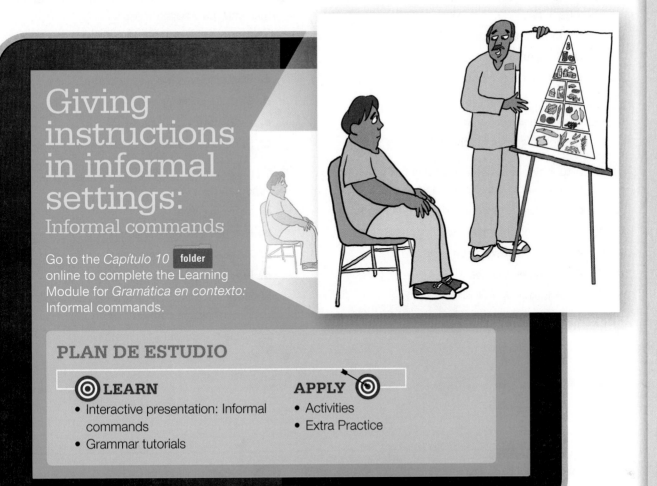

Giving instructions in informal settings:
Informal commands

Go to the *Capítulo 10* [folder] online to complete the Learning Module for *Gramática en contexto*: Informal commands.

PLAN DE ESTUDIO

◎ **LEARN**
- Interactive presentation: Informal commands
- Grammar tutorials

◎ **APPLY**
- Activities
- Extra Practice

Online prep for students
Students will have completed the Learning Module for Informal commands online. See Instructor's Resources for Supplementary Activities.

Suggestions
Write the *tú* form of some verbs (*cocinas, bebes, escribes*) on the board and erase the final *-s*. Do TPR using informal commands. Model several *tú* commands, going from the negative to the affirmative (*no leas/lee; no llames/llama*). Then give the negative and have students supply the affirmative, and vice versa.

PRÁCTICA COMUNICATIVA

 👥

Consejos. Escoge los consejos más adecuados, según cada situación. Compara tus respuestas con las de tu compañero/a y después añade otra situación. Tu compañero/a te va a dar un consejo.

1. Tu compañero/a comió demasiado en una fiesta de cumpleaños y ahora le duele mucho el estómago.

   a. Come más para recuperarte.

   b. Llama al médico.

   c. Ve a la farmacia y compra medicamentos.

   d. Camina una hora esta tarde.

   e. Practica deportes para olvidarte del dolor de estómago.

   f. No te acuestes.

Follow-up for 10-21
Have students write down 5 questions they would ask if they needed advice regarding a healthy diet: *¿Cuánto líquido debo beber todos los días? ¿Debo tomar desayuno o comer algo rápido antes de almorzar?* Then have them exchange roles asking and giving advice using a *tú* command. Ask if classmates agree with the advice given; if not, they should provide their own advice.

2. Tu hermana está enferma. Está congestionada y tiene fiebre.

  a. Toma sopa de pollo.

  b. Come una hamburguesa.

  c. No duermas mucho.

  d. Bebe jugos y agua.

  e. No bebas vino ni cerveza.

  f. No consumas mucha cafeína.

3. A tu amiga le fascina la comida basura (*junk food*), por eso, subió diez libras en un mes.

  a. Ve a los restaurantes de comida rápida.

  b. Bebe muchas gaseosas.

  c. Come en casa, no en restaurantes.

  d. No tomes alcohol.

  e. Evita los batidos de McDonald's.

  f. No pidas ensaladas.

4. Tu mamá quiere alimentarse mejor para tener más energía y bajar de peso.

  a. Evita la grasa.

  b. Toma muchos helados.

  c. Come huevos moderadamente.

  d. Compra papas fritas.

  e. Acuéstate y descansa.

  f. Si no tienes energía, consume mucha cafeína.

5. Tu mejor amigo quiere preparar una cena espectacular para su novia.

  a. Compra pizza.

  b. Haz un plato sofisticado.

  c. No te olvides de comprar un buen vino.

  d. Prepara la mesa el día anterior.

  e. No le pongas chile picante al plato. Ella detesta la comida picante.

  f. Ponle mucha sal a la comida.

6. . . .

10-22

Una cura de reposo. Tu amigo/a estuvo muy enfermo/a y su médico le recomendó pasar dos semanas de descanso en las Termas de Papallacta en Ecuador. Como tú has visitado este lugar, dile a tu amigo/a qué puede hacer allí. Después cambien de papel.

1. disfrutar del sol
2. respirar aire puro y descansar
3. no hacer tarea
4. tomar fotos y hacer videos
5. probar un plato típico ecuatoriano
6. salir por las noches y conversar con las personas del lugar
7. tomar baños termales a diario
8. asistir a un concierto de música andina

Modelo   **"disfrutar de la tranquilidad"**

Disfruta de la tranquilidad y no escuches música en tu iPod.

Y ¿qué más puedo hacer?

Las Termas de Papallacta

Suggestion for 10-22
You may have students do some research on the Internet before doing this activity.

10-23

Buenos hábitos alimenticios.

PRIMERA FASE. Ustedes están preocupados por los hábitos de comida de uno/a de sus amigos/as. Lean lo que esta persona come y bebe en un día típico e identifiquen los problemas que tiene.

Todos los días se levanta al mediodía. Tan pronto se levanta, toma varias tazas de café. Una hora más tarde, come tres huevos fritos con tocino y tostadas. Toma dos tazas de café cubano con bastante azúcar. Luego lee el periódico en su dormitorio, mira televisión y come chocolate mientras habla por teléfono con sus amigos. Por la tarde, llama por teléfono al restaurante de la esquina, pide una hamburguesa con papas fritas y toma unas cervezas. Después, duerme una siesta larga. Por la noche, tiene problemas para dormir, por eso, toma un batido.

SEGUNDA FASE. Hagan una lista con cinco recomendaciones o instrucciones que su amigo/a debe seguir. Comparen su lista con las de otros grupos.

Warm-up for 10-23
Give examples of healthful and unhealthful foods. Students respond: *(No) es/ son sano/as* or *(No) es/ son bueno/a(s): la leche, las naranjas, la mantequilla, el chocolate, la pasta en grandes cantidades, la carne de res todos los días, el queso en pequeñas cantidades, una copa de vino por día.*

You may have students do some Internet research before doing this activity.

Expansion for 10-24
You may wish to have pairs of students prepare different dishes, or expand the presentation modes to include live presentations, PowerPoint presentations of recipe preparation done outside of class (for students who are particularly interested in cooking), and/or posters.

Cocina paso a paso (step by step).

PRIMERA FASE. Escojan una receta para un plato que se consume en su país y escriban una lista de los ingredientes.

 SEGUNDA FASE. Presenten la preparación a la clase. Sigan los siguientes pasos: a) describan el plato; b) presenten sus ingredientes; y c) expliquen cómo se prepara.

Situaciones

1

ROLE A. You are not feeling well, so you call your friend to ask for the recipe to make chicken soup. Take notes as your friend gives you the recipe. Ask questions as necessary.

ROLE B. Your friend is not feeling well and calls to ask for the recipe for chicken soup. Tell him/her to a) buy skinless chicken (**pollo sin piel**); b) wash and cut garlic, onions, carrots, and celery (**apio**); c) sauté (**saltear**) the chicken and vegetables with a little olive oil; and d) add water, salt, and pepper and cook for 30 minutes.

2

ROLE A. To improve your health, you call your friend who is studying to be a nutritionist. Explain what you generally eat for breakfast, lunch, and dinner. Ask questions and answer the nutritionist's questions.

ROLE B. You are studying to be a nutritionist and a friend calls you for help with eating habits. Ask what he/she eats for breakfast, lunch, and dinner. Advise him/her a) to eat fruits, vegetables, fish, and chicken; b) not to drink soft drinks or alcohol; c) to consume foods with lots of fiber; and d) to do physical activity daily. Answer your friend's questions.

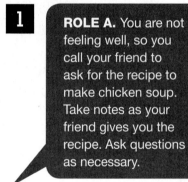

Talking about the future:
The future tense

Go to the *Capítulo 10* [folder] online to complete the Learning Module for *Gramática en contexto:* The future tense.

PLAN DE ESTUDIO

◎ **LEARN**
- Interactive presentation: The future tense
- Grammar tutorials

◎ **APPLY**
- Activities
- Extra Practice

PRÁCTICA COMUNICATIVA

 10-25

¿Qué lugares de Ecuador visitarán estas personas?
Completa las oraciones de la izquierda con la acción en la columna de la derecha. Añade un lugar que te interesa y dile a tu compañero/a lo que harás o adónde irás.

1. A Carlos y Eugenia les gusta comer bien. __b__ al restaurante especializado en la cocina de Guayaquil.

2. A doña Lourdes y a su hija les fascinan la zoología y la botánica. __d__ un viaje juntas a las islas Galápagos para ver la gran variedad de especies animales.

3. Don Jorge y yo __c__ el mercado indígena de Cuenca para comprar artesanía ecuatoriana.

4. A ti te gusta disfrutar del aire libre, ver la arquitectura colonial y las montañas. __a__ por la Plaza San Blas en Quito.

5. A mí. _____ . . .

a. caminarás
b. irán
c. visitaremos
d. harán

Basílica del Voto Nacional, Quito

Suggestion
Tell the story shown in a sequence of pictures. For example: *La semana próxima Rafael va a ir en un viaje de negocios a Ecuador. Estará dos días en Quito, donde tendrá varias reuniones de negocios. Su secretaria le hará una reservación en un hotel que le recomendaron unos clientes. Visitará algunas plantaciones de banano en la costa del Pacífico. Al regresar a Estados Unidos, se pondrá en contacto con algunas compañías para importar bananas de Ecuador.*

Note
The *ir a + infinitive* construction is commonly used to express future action; allow students to answer using either construction.

Suggestion
Have students think of a dish they will cook together, whose step-by-step preparation they will describe to the class. Their classmates will guess the name of the dish.
Model the activity: *Prepararemos un plato cubano. Necesitaremos arroz, carne, aceite, sal y especias. Yo comenzaré. Pondré aceite en una olla/cazuela. Mary pondrá el arroz en la olla y lo dorará. Yo freiré la carne, pero antes Jorge pondrá especias,* and so forth. Students will finally guess the name of the dish.

Suggestion
To give students further practice with irregular verbs, have them finish the idea using the verbs *tener, hacer,* or *poder.*

1. *Es la última semana de clase. Los estudiantes… (tener)*
2. *Mario y Ernesto irán de vacaciones juntos. Ellos… (poder)*

Cultura

Ecuador tiene muchos parques nacionales y reservas ecológicas cuyo propósito es conservar la riqueza natural de las cuatro regiones del país: las islas Galápagos, la costa, la sierra y la selva amazónica. En las reservas se encuentran muchas especies de flora y fauna. Para los visitantes, hay muchas maneras de explorar las reservas y gozar de la naturaleza.

Compara: ¿Hay reservas naturales en tu país? ¿Dónde están? ¿Qué se conserva? ¿Alguna vez has visitado alguno de estos lugares? ¿Qué se puede hacer allí?

10-26

Intercambio: Un viaje a Guayaquil.

PRIMERA FASE. Ramiro va a Guayaquil a visitar a su familia. Háganse preguntas y contesten según la agenda que Ramiro preparó.

Modelo

¿Qué hará Ramiro el miércoles por la noche?

Cenará con unos amigos.

¿Cuándo irá al cine con los primos?

Irán al cine el martes.

LUNES	MARTES	MIÉRCOLES	JUEVES	VIERNES
salir para Guayaquil	visitar el Parque de las Iguanas	salir de compras al Mercado Artesanal	viajar al Parque Nacional Cajas	empacar las maletas
cenar con los tíos	visitar a otros familiares	ir a un museo	caminar en la reserva, sacar fotos	almorzar con toda la familia
acostarse temprano	ir al cine con los primos	cenar con unos amigos	dormir en el parque	regresar a Estados Unidos

SEGUNDA FASE. Hagan una lista de cinco actividades que Ramiro probablemente hará al regresar a Estados Unidos. Expliquen por qué.

10-27

Planes de fiesta.

PRIMERA FASE. Sus amigos José y Silvia se casaron durante sus vacaciones en Ecuador. Regresarán a Estados Unidos en dos semanas y ustedes organizarán una fiesta para celebrar su matrimonio. Planifiquen la fiesta considerando lo siguiente: número de invitados, lugar de la fiesta, menú que ofrecerán (comida y bebida), música, baile y otras actividades en la fiesta.

 SEGUNDA FASE. Compartan sus planes con otra pareja. Hagan una lista de tres semejanzas y tres diferencias entre las dos fiestas.

10-28

¿Qué recomendaciones seguirá? Maricela sufre de estrés, insomnio y anemia. Por eso les pide sugerencias a su mejor amiga y a su nutricionista. Discutan qué recomendaciones probablemente seguirá Maricela y expliquen por qué.

Follow-up for 10-28
You may wish to have students discuss what Maricela will do and what she probably won't do, and why.

RECOMENDACIONES DE LA NUTRICIONISTA	RECOMENDACIONES DE SU MEJOR AMIGA
1. Coma en pequeñas cantidades por lo menos cuatro veces al día.	**1.** Come cuando quieras. Si subes de peso puedes seguir una dieta.
2. No consuma cafeína para tener energía. Consuma proteínas.	**2.** Para tener energía, come mucho chocolate y, luego, haz ejercicio.
3. Consuma calcio. Beba leche y coma espinacas.	**3.** Toma helado todos los días porque la leche tiene mucho calcio.
4. Para eliminar la tensión y relajarse, haga yoga.	**4.** Escucha música suave y no contestes el teléfono de la oficina.
5. Compre verduras y carnes orgánicas en supermercados especializados en productos naturales.	**5.** Pide ensalada con pollo en los restaurantes de comida rápida y un refresco de dieta.

Situaciones

1

ROLE A. You are organizing a picnic and some of the guests are vegetarians. Call your nutritionist friend (your classmate) to discuss what food to serve. Say that a) you will prepare vegetarian and non-vegetarian food; b) for the vegetarians, you will make salads and a Spanish tortilla; c) for the meat eaters, you will serve a chicken salad and hamburgers; and d) you will serve beer, soft drinks, and juice. Ask your friend for advice.

ROLE B. A friend is calling to ask for advice regarding the menu for a picnic that will include both vegetarian and non-vegetarian guests. Give your friend feedback on the proposed menu and offer additional advice.

2

ROLE A. You and a friend are concerned about people's quality of life and the food they eat. Tell your friend that you think in ten years from now people will eat a) more healthful foods; b) fewer fats and sugars; and c) less junk food (**comida basura**). Add that you think food will be more expensive but of better quality and that people will live longer because they will be healthier.

ROLE B. You don't agree with your friend's opinions about what people will eat ten years from now. In your view, a) people will continue to eat unhealthful food; b) people will continue to eat fats and sugar; c) children will have more opportunities to eat junk food (**comida basura**) because parents will be very busy; d) food will cost less, so people will eat more; and e) people will die younger but happier.

ESCUCHA

10-29  [Presentational]

Preparación. Escucharás una lista de productos que compraron Andrea, Carolina, Roberto y Darío. Antes de escuchar, prepara una lista de productos que compras regularmente y otra de aquellos que solo compras en ocasiones especiales. Compártela con la clase.

10-30 [Interpretive]

Escucha. Andrea, Carolina, Roberto, and Darío have each offered to contribute a dish for their friend Óscar's birthday party. Each has bought some kind of vegetable, meat, or seafood to prepare his/her dish. As you listen, mark (✓) the foods that each of them bought. Note that not all the items purchased are listed below.

ESTRATEGIA

Record relevant detail

Note-taking is a useful strategy for recording what you hear. To take useful notes, sort out and prioritize the information as you listen, writing down what is relevant to your purpose for listening.

Comprueba

I was able to…

____ distinguish between key and secondary information.

____ listen for and make note of relevant details.

ANDREA	CAROLINA	ROBERTO	DARÍO
____ sal	✓ ajos	____ mermelada	____ huevos
✓ pollo	____ cerdo	____ pepinos	____ ajos
✓ carne molida	✓ espinacas	✓ pimienta	____ fruta
____ azúcar	____ jamón	____ aceite	✓ jamón
✓ zanahorias	____ langosta	____ pavo	✓ aderezo
✓ aguacates	✓ maíz	✓ aguacates	✓ pimientos verdes
✓ camarones	✓ pollo	____ zanahorias	____ pasta

10-31 [Interpersonal]

Un paso más. Túrnense para hacerse las siguientes preguntas.

1. ¿Cuál es tu plato favorito?

2. ¿Qué productos o ingredientes necesitas para prepararlo?

3. ¿Con quién compartes generalmente tu plato favorito? ¿Por qué?

4. ¿Qué dice esta persona cuando preparas este plato?

LENGUA **Pimienta** refers to the spice (*ground pepper*) and **pimiento** refers to the vegetable. Therefore, **pimienta roja** is the red (*cayenne*) pepper that one sprinkles on pizza, and **pimiento rojo** is a red bell pepper. The word for hot, spicy peppers is **chile** or **ají,** as in **chile habanero, chile jalapeño,** and so forth.

AUTOEVALUACIÓN

☐ I feel confident that I was able to identify the relevant information.

☐ I need more listening practice.

STUDY PLAN

▶ Good job! Move on to the next section, *Habla.*

▶ Go to the *Unidos* | folder | online for *Escucha* practice.

Integrated Performance Assessment (IPA)

The activities in each *Unidos* section correspond to the three modes of communication as indicated by the tag next to each activity.

Audioscript for 10-30
Andrea decidió cocinar dos platos esta vez, paella y una ensalada de papas. Como tenía pescado para la paella en casa, decidió comprar pollo y camarones. Para la ensalada de papas compró zanahorias y papas. También compró aguacates para decorar la ensalada.

Carolina iba a comprar aguacates y tomates para preparar guacamole, pero decidió comprar ajos, cebollas, espinacas, maíz y pollo para hacer una tortilla de verduras y pollo asado.

Roberto pensó que era una buena idea llevar uno de los platos favoritos de Óscar. Por eso compró langosta, sal, pimienta y aguacates.

Darío estaba enfermo y no pudo ir al supermercado. Su hermana hizo las compras para él. Ella compró jamón, papas, aderezo y pimientos verdes.

Todos compraron carne molida.

Suggestion for 10-32
Primera fase
Model for students ways
to state and defend their
classifications and their points
of view.

HABLA

10-32

Preparación. ⏵Interpretive

PRIMERA FASE. Marca cuáles de los siguientes alimentos son más saludables (+) o menos saludables (–).

___ los camarones	___ las espinacas	___ el jamón	___ el pollo
___ la carne de res	___ la fruta	___ las legumbres	___ el queso
___ la cerveza	___ las galletas	___ el pan blanco	___ los refrescos
___ los dulces	___ el helado	___ las papas	___ el vino

Suggestion for 10-32
Segunda fase
Answers will vary according
to students' beliefs about food
and health. Model for students
ways to state and defend
their classifications and their
points of view. Encourage
them to present and support
their points of view, and to
persuade their group mates.

SEGUNDA FASE. Escribe en la tabla los productos o alimentos de la *Primera fase* que en general producen los siguientes efectos. Explica por qué.

ENGORDAN	NO ENGORDAN	DAN ENERGÍA	AUMENTAN EL COLESTEROL

ESTRATEGIA

Give and defend reasons for a decision

When you make a decision that you wish to communicate effectively to others, it is important to a) state your decision clearly; b) present and explain your reasons logically; and c) urge your listeners to consider your point of view.

10-33 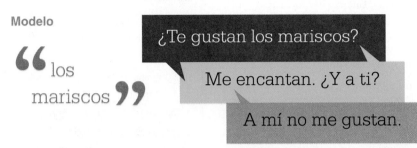 [Interpersonal]

Habla. Entrevista a por lo menos tres compañeros/as para averiguar las preferencias de comida en las siguientes categorías. ¿Qué comida les gusta más y cuál les gusta menos?

Modelo

"los mariscos"

¿Te gustan los mariscos?

Me encantan. ¿Y a ti?

A mí no me gustan.

ALIMENTO	ENCANTAR	GUSTAR MUCHO	GUSTAR	NO GUSTAR
la fruta				
las verduras				
la carne				
los mariscos				
los productos lácteos				
los pasteles				

En directo

To influence someone's decision:

Es mejor/menos dañino (*harmful*) + *infinitive*…

¿No te/le(s) parece más saludable + *infinitive*…?

¿Qué te/le(s) parece si + *indicative*… ?

 Click on the icon to listen to a conversation with these expressions.

Comprueba

In my conversation…

____ I expressed my decision clearly.

____ I explained my reasons logically.

____ I encouraged my listener to consider my point of view.

10-34  [Presentational]

Un paso más. Preparen un informe comparando los resultados obtenidos en **10-33** sobre las categorías de alimentos que se consumen más en la clase. Usen las siguientes preguntas como guía. Después presenten su informe a la clase.

1. ¿Qué tipos de comida se comen más en la clase?

2. En general, ¿tus compañeros se alimentan bien o mal? ¿Por qué?

3. ¿Deben ustedes mejorar su dieta? ¿Qué deben hacer?

AUTOEVALUACIÓN

☐ I feel confident that I communicated successfully.

☐ I need more speaking practice.

STUDY PLAN

▶ Good job! Move on to the next section, *Lee.*

▶ Go to the *Unidos* [folder] online for *Habla* practice.

Note for 10-33
Inform students that they will need to write a report in **10-35** about the results obtained in their interviews. Ask them to walk around the class interviewing at least 5 classmates.

Suggestion for 10-33
Put students in groups of 4 or 6. Ask them to interview each other in pairs and then record their combined results in the group table.

Audioscript for *En directo*
Male Cousin: *Prima, estoy un poco preocupado por ti. Veo que ya no estás comiendo bien. Siempre te veo comiendo dulces y frituras. Sabes bien que es dañino comer estas cosas. ¿Qué pasa?*
Female Cousin: *Es que siempre estoy corriendo de clase en clase. No tengo tiempo para comer bien.*
Male Cousin: *Bueno, acabo de tomar un curso sobre cómo preparar comida saludable en poco tiempo. ¿Qué te parece si te enseño lo que he aprendido?*
Female Cousin: *¡¿De veras?! ¡Eres el primo más bueno del universo!*

Suggestion for 10-35
Encourage students to draw on their general knowledge about food to guess what *fusión culinaria* means. You may draw their attention to the italicized food items in the first paragraph (*California roll, taco pizza*) as examples of *fusión culinaria*, and ask them to figure out what these two items have in common.

LEE

10-35 Interpersonal

Preparación. Lean el título y los subtítulos de la lectura en la página siguiente, miren las fotos y lean sus leyendas. Luego, hablen entre ustedes de lo que esperan encontrar en el artículo guiándose por las preguntas siguientes. Razonen sus respuestas.

1. ¿Qué información esperan encontrar en el artículo?

a. una definición del término *fusión culinaria*

b. recetas para platos de cocina fusión

c. información sobre la influencia china en la cocina de un país

d. información sobre la cocina Tex-Mex

2. Marquen (✓) los elementos que les ayudaron a responder a la pregunta 1.

a. _____ el título y los subtítulos

b. _____ las fotos junto con sus leyendas

3. ¿Qué es la fusión culinaria? Marquen (✓) la definición más lógica.

a. _____ La combinación de la cocina con otras artes, como la decoración de interiores

b. _____ Una cocina que combina la influencia de dos tradiciones culinarias

4. Preparen una lista de comidas Tex-Mex que conozcan. ¿Cuáles les gustan más?

Suggestion for 10-36
You may wish to remind students that dishes that are Americanized versions of other national cuisines are examples of fusion cuisine. You may also ask students to think about when a dish ceases to be considered "fusion" and is seen as native to a particular cuisine. For example, pasta with tomato sauce, considered an Italian dish, actually represents a fusion of influences from China (noodles) and the New World (tomatoes).

10-36 Interpretive

Lee. Según el contenido del artículo, ¿son las siguientes afirmaciones ciertas (**C**) o falsas (**F**)? Si la afirmación es falsa, corrige la información.

1. __C__ El artículo afirma que la cocina fusión se limita a la combinación de influencias asiáticas en la cocina del Oeste.

2. __C__ La cocina peruana incorpora influencias culinarias de muchos países.

3. __F__ La inmigración de muchos chinos a Perú empezó al principio del siglo XX.

4. __C__ El Chifa es un término que se refiere a la cocina chino-peruana.

5. __F__ La cocina Tex-Mex es igual a la cocina mexicana. Hay diferencias.

6. __F__ Se usa menos carne y menos queso en la cocina Tex-Mex que en la cocina mexicana tradicional. Usa más carne y más queso que la cocina mexicana.

7. __C__ Los nachos y las fajitas son invenciones de la cocina Tex-Mex.

8. __C__ El chile con carne que se come en San Antonio, Texas, se prepara con especias similares a las que se usan en Marruecos, en el norte de África.

ESTRATEGIA

Learn new words by analyzing their connections with known words

As you read in a second language, you encounter words that are unfamiliar to you. In some cases, you can skip over a word and still understand the overall meaning of the sentence or paragraph. In other cases, you should focus on the unfamiliar word and guess its meaning. You can figure out the meanings of unfamiliar words and expand your vocabulary by mentally linking them to words you know that are related in meaning or in grammatical form.

Comprueba

I was able to...

_____ **use words I know to guess the meaning of new words.**

_____ **understand the main points of the reading.**

Plato chino-peruano o Chifa

Nachos, un plato popular de la cocina Tex-Mex

La fusión culinaria: una tendencia nueva con una historia larga

La fusión en la cocina contemporánea

Todos hemos comido platos que combinan la cocina de dos países o culturas. El llamado *California roll* es un ejemplo; la *taco pizza* es otro. La fusión culinaria, o cocina fusión ejemplifica la mezcla de ingredientes y estilos culinarios de diferentes culturas en el menú de un restaurante o en un mismo plato. Hoy en día es común encontrar restaurantes en Estados Unidos con nombres como *Roy's Hawaiian Fusion Cuisine* o *Fusion Restaurant and Lounge*. Hay muchas posibles combinaciones, limitadas solamente por la creatividad del chef y los gustos de los clientes.

La fusión en la historia culinaria

A pesar de la creciente popularidad de estas combinaciones gastronómicas, sería un error pensar que la cocina fusión es un fenómeno nuevo. Dos ejemplos de este antiguo fenómeno en las Américas son la cocina chino-peruana y la cocina mexicano-norteamericana, o Tex-Mex.

El Chifa: La cocina fusión de Perú

La cocina peruana es una mezcla de muchas influencias: indígena, española, africana, china y japonesa. El Chifa, o cocina chino-peruana, es el resultado de la mezcla de la comida criolla de Lima con la cocina traída por los inmigrantes chinos desde mediados del siglo XIX.

Los chinos que fueron a Perú se adaptaron a la sociedad y a sus costumbres, pero siempre mantuvieron sus tradiciones culinarias. Con el progreso económico, importaron de China especias y otros productos esenciales para su comida, pero por lo general tenían que cultivar las verduras que necesitaban o sustituirlas por ingredientes locales.

La cultura chino-peruana revolucionó la gastronomía. Algunos platos considerados típicamente peruanos, como el arroz chaufa (preparado con carne picada, cebollitas, pimentón, huevos y salsa de soja) y el tacu-tacu (una tortilla hecha de un puré de frijoles, arroz, ajo, ají y cebolla) reflejan la influencia de la cocina china.

La comida Tex-Mex: La cocina mexicana en Estados Unidos

Un ejemplo de la cocina fusión que se conoce en todas partes de Estados Unidos es la cocina Tex-Mex. Se trata de la fusión del estilo de México y del de Texas. La cocina que conocemos hoy en día como Tex-Mex empezó como una mezcla de la comida del pueblo nativo de Texas y la cocina española. Los indígenas contribuyeron con ingredientes como los frijoles pintos, los nopales (las hojas de un cacto), las cebollas silvestres[1] y el mesquite. La influencia española empezó con la llegada del ganado[2] a la región, traído por los colonizadores al final del siglo XVI. Pero también hay influencias del norte de África. Un grupo de colonizadores de las Islas Canarias y de Marruecos inmigraron en el siglo XVIII a lo que es ahora San Antonio, Texas. De ellos vinieron nuevas especias, cilantro y chiles. El *chili con carne* de San Antonio todavía retiene los sabores de la cocina marroquí.

En los últimos treinta años se ha intentado separar *la cocina mexicana* de *la cocina mexicana americanizada,* o Tex-Mex. La Tex-Mex utiliza más carne y usa las tortillas para envolver mayor variedad de rellenos. Los nachos, los tacos fritos, las chalupas, el chile con queso y el chile con carne son invenciones Tex-Mex que no se encuentran en la cocina mexicana tradicional. La costumbre universal en los restaurantes Tex-Mex de servir las *tortilla chips* con salsa picante como aperitivo tampoco existe en la cocina mexicana tradicional.

[1]*wild*   [2]*cattle*

Suggestion for 10-37
For the presentational part of this activity encourage students to do some research on the Internet and prepare a presentation. As an alternative, they may present about a famous Hispanic chef.

10-37

Un paso más. Presentational

PRIMERA FASE. Hagan una lista de platos en restaurantes que son ejemplos de la cocina fusión. Luego, seleccionen uno de estos platos.

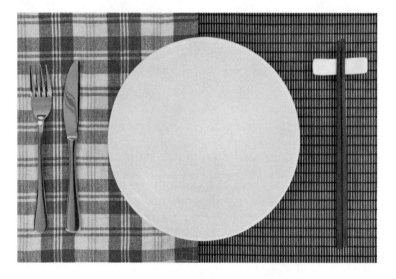

SEGUNDA FASE. Preparen una presentación sobre algún plato de cocina fusión que conocen y sus antecedentes culinarios, y preséntenla a la clase.

Dos ejemplos de cocina fusión

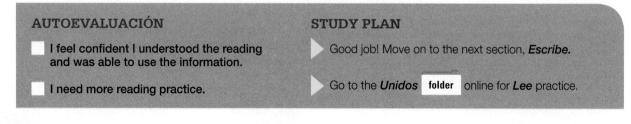

AUTOEVALUACIÓN

☐ I feel confident I understood the reading and was able to use the information.

☐ I need more reading practice.

STUDY PLAN

▶ Good job! Move on to the next section, *Escribe.*

▶ Go to the *Unidos* folder online for *Lee* practice.

ESCRIBE

10-38 Interpretive

Preparación. Lee una vez más el artículo "La fusión culinaria: una tendencia nueva con una historia larga". Identifica las secciones del artículo y pasa tu marcador (*highlighter*) por las ideas centrales de cada sección.

10-39 Presentational

Escribe. Escribe con tus propias palabras un resumen del artículo, usando las ideas principales que marcaste en *Preparación*.

10-40 Interpersonal

Un paso más. Envíale tu resumen a un compañero editor/una compañera editora para que te dé su opinión.

ESTRATEGIA

Summarize information

A good summary maintains the structure of the original text, synthesizes its principal ideas and information, and accurately captures the central meaning of the original. To write a summary:

- Read the text carefully for the main ideas more than once.
- In your own words, write one or two sentences that summarize the main idea of each section you identify in the text.
- Do not inject your own opinion or add anything not in the original text.

Comprueba

I was able to…

____ identify the main ideas in each section of the reading.

____ relay the main ideas in my own words.

____ focus on factual information rather than my opinion.

Suggestion for 10-38
You may suggest students identify concepts they will need to express in their own words in the summary.

Suggestion for 10-39
To help students who may have difficulty expressing themselves, accept summaries that reproduce ideas verbatim as long as they are able to distinguish the main ideas from the secondary ones.

Suggestion for 10-40
Have students check the following:
1. ¿Representa el resumen una síntesis del texto original? ¿El resumen refleja con precisión las ideas expresadas en el texto? ¿Hay detalles innecesarios?
2. ¿Sigue el resumen la estructura del texto original?
3. ¿Hay transiciones claras que muestran las diversas secciones del texto original?
4. ¿Fluyen (Flow) las ideas de una manera clara y natural? ¿Hay que aclarar algunos puntos?
5. ¿El vocabulario y las estructuras son correctas?
6. ¿La ortografía y la acentuación son correctas?

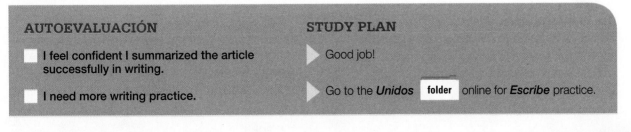

AUTOEVALUACIÓN

☐ I feel confident I summarized the article successfully in writing.

☐ I need more writing practice.

STUDY PLAN

▶ Good job!

▶ Go to the *Unidos* folder online for *Escribe* practice.

ENFOQUE *cultural*

ECUADOR

Note for Manta
The city of Manta is located in the Manabí Province of Ecuador. Its population is modest compared to major cities like Quito and Guayaquil. However, it is ranked third in Ecuador in terms of its economic contribution to the country. One key reason is Manta's leading performance in the fishing industry.

Note for Panama hats
Cuenca is indeed the primary exporter of Panama hats. However, many argue that Montecristi, another city in Ecuador, produces the highest quality Panama. Both cities have an extensive tradition of hat-making, a skill that has been passed down throughout several generations.

Note for *Museo Etnográfico Mitad del Mundo*
The monument is home to the Museo Etnográfico Mitad del Mundo, which is dedicated to the indigenous ethnography of Ecuador. In addition, visitors to Mitad del Mundo can visit its planetarium and enjoy musical and cultural presentations in the central plaza.

Note for *Enfoque cultural*
In this chapter, students are asked to summarize the text online in Spanish, rather than English.

Standard 1.3
Students present information, concepts, and ideas to an audience of listeners or readers on a variety of topics.
Activity **10-41** encourages students to synthesize what they have read in a coherent and informative summary. The instructions suggest a structure, but students take responsibility for organizing their summaries, which may be used as the basis for a written or oral report.

Manta es una ciudad popular entre los turistas nacionales e internacionales por sus playas, su vida nocturna y su festival anual de teatro. También cuenta con el puerto más grande de Ecuador.

Los sombreros de paja toquilla (*Panama hats*) hechos a mano en Cuenca se hicieron famosos durante la construcción del Canal de Panamá. Hoy día a Ecuador se le considera el primer exportador de estos sombreros y el de la mejor calidad.

Ecuador: alimentación y salud pública

Go to the *Enfoque Cultura* [folder] in *Capítulo 10* online to learn more about Ecuador.

LEARN
• Interactive presentation: *Ecuador: alimentación y salud pública*

APPLY
• Activities

El monumento del ecuador se encuentra en la Ciudad Mitad del Mundo. No marca exactamente el paralelo 0° - 0' - 0" sino que está localizado 240 metros al sur del verdadero ecuador. Se dice que si uno pone un pie en el hemisferio norte y el otro en el hemisferio sur, se pesa menos.

PRÁCTICA COMUNICATIVA

10-41

Usa la información. Prepara un afiche sobre el tema de la malnutrición. Ve a Internet si necesitas información sobre este tema y usa algunas de estas preguntas para preparar tu afiche:

• ¿Cómo se comparan entre sí algunos países de América Latina en cuanto a la malnutrición?

• ¿Qué progresos o retrocesos han ocurrido recientemente en cuanto a la malnutrición en América Latina y en otras regiones del mundo? ¿Qué papel juega la malnutrición en el desarrollo económico de los países?

• ¿Por qué es importante la buena nutrición materno-infantil?

• ¿Qué organizaciones están luchando contra la malnutrición a nivel global?

En este capítulo...

Comprueba lo que sabes

Go to the *Comprueba lo que sabes* folder online to review what you have learned in this chapter. Practice with the following:

Flashcards | Games | Oral Practice | Practice Test/Study Plan | Video en contexto

Vocabulario

Las especias y los condimentos
el aceite
el aderezo
el azúcar
las especias
las hierbas
la mayonesa
la mostaza
la pimienta
la sal
la salsa de tomate
la vainilla
el vinagre

Las frutas y las verduras
el aguacate
el ajo
la cebolla
la cereza
las espinacas
la fresa
el limón
el maíz
la manzana
el maracuyá
el melón
la papaya
el pepino
la pera
el pimiento verde
la piña
el plátano/la banana
la toronja/el pomelo
la uva
la zanahoria

El pescado y la carne
las aves
el camarón/la gamba
la carne molida/picada
    de res
el cerdo
la chuleta
el cordero
la costilla
la langosta
los mariscos
la oveja
el pavo

Otros productos
los churros
la crema
el dulce
la galleta
la harina
la leche de coco
las legumbres
las lentejas
la manteca/la mantequilla
la margarina
el pan dulce
el pastel
el queso crema
el yogur

En la mesa
la bandeja
la botella
la copa
la cuchara
la cucharita
el cuchillo
el mantel
el plato
la servilleta
la taza
el tenedor
el vaso

Verbos
agregar/añadir
batir
disfrutar
freír (i)
hervir (ie, i)
probar (ue)
recomendar (ie)

Las descripciones
agrio/a
lácteo/a

Palabras y expresiones útiles
el campesino/la campesina
la receta
todavía
ya

Notas

¿Cómo es tu salud?

Learning OBJECTIVES

You will:

- learn vocabulary related to health, medical care, and the body

- learn forms and some functions of the present subjunctive

- learn to distinguish between *por* and *para*

- connect information about Cuba, the Dominican Republic, and Puerto Rico to what you already know

Learning OUTCOMES

You will be able to:

- discuss health and medical treatments

- express expectations and hopes

- describe emotions, opinions, and wishes

- express goals, purposes, and means

- present information about music and dance traditions in Cuba, the Dominican Republic, and Puerto Rico

CULTURA INTERACTIVA

OCÉANO ATLÁNTICO

El Malecón de la Habana

La Habana
Pinar del Río
Cienfuegos
CUBA
Camagüey
Un mojito cubano
Santiago de Cuba   Guantánamo

Mar Caribe

JAMAICA

REPÚBLICA DOMINICANA

Puerto Plata
Sabana de La Mar   Punta Cana
HAITÍ   Santiago   San Juan   Arecibo   San Juan
Santo   Mayagüez
Domingo   Isla Saona   Ponce
La Catedral de Santo Domingo

El coquí, la rana nativa de Puerto Rico

Isla de Culebra

PUERTO RICO   Isla de Vieques

Paracaidismo em el Isla Saona

El Carnaval de Ponce

CUBA, REPÚBLICA DOMINICANA Y PUERTO RICO

Las divinidades Oxum Xango y Yemaja del pintor cubano Almeri

Cultura en línea

To learn more about Cuba, the Dominican Republic, Puerto Rico, and the chapter theme, go to the *Cultura en línea* folder in the *Unidos* online component to view the *Vistas culturales* video and take a virtual art tour.

¿Cuánto sabes?

Comprueba lo que sabes sobre Cuba, República Dominicana y Puerto Rico contestando las siguientes preguntas.

1. ¿Cómo se llama el mar que rodea estas tres islas? el Mar Caribe

2. ¿Cuál es la capital de Cuba? La Habana

3. ¿Qué país limita por tierra (*land*) con República Dominicana? Haití

4. ¿Qué deporte puede practicarse en Isla Saona? paracaidismo

5. ¿Qué festividad se celebra en Ponce? el Carnaval

6. ¿Cuál es un animal típico de Puerto Rico? el coquí

Vocabulario en contexto

Talking about health, medical care, and the body

Médicos, farmacias y hospitales

Go to the *Capítulo 11* **folder** online to complete the Learning Module for *Vocabulario en contexto: Médicos, farmacias y hospitales*.

PLAN DE ESTUDIO

◎ LEARN
- Interactive presentation: *Médicos, farmacias y hospitales*
- Vocabulary tutorials
- Pronunciation

APPLY ◎
- Activities
- Pronunciation activities

PRÁCTICA COMUNICATIVA

11-1

Definiciones. PRIMERA FASE. Completa las siguientes oraciones con las palabras apropiadas. Compara tus respuestas con las de tu compañero/a.

1. En las _____farmacias_____ se venden medicinas y productos de belleza.

2. El té de manzanilla se recomienda para el _____dolor_____ de estómago.

3. Los/Las _____enfermeros/as_____ ayudan a los médicos en los hospitales y cuidan a los enfermos.

4. Los/Las _____pacientes_____ son las personas que sufren enfermedades.

SEGUNDA FASE. Háganse las siguientes preguntas.

1. ¿Cuándo y para qué vas generalmente a la farmacia?
2. ¿Qué tomas cuando tienes dolor de estómago?
3. ¿Conoces a alguien que tome hierbas medicinales? ¿Para qué enfermedad?

Cultura

Los indígenas del continente americano nos han transmitido muchos conocimientos de medicina natural. Conocían los efectos positivos de las infusiones de hierbas y tenían fórmulas para cerrar las heridas (*wounds*) y curar las úlceras. También trataban fracturas de huesos. Acompañaban muchas de estas prácticas con ceremonias en las que invocaban a sus dioses, pidiéndoles protección y ayuda.

Compara: ¿Qué remedios naturales se usan en tu cultura? ¿Para qué se usan? ¿Recuerdas alguno que se usa hoy en día en tu familia?

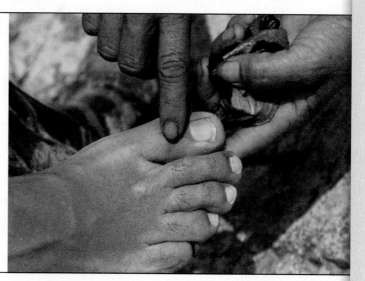

11-2

Conversación.

Háganse las siguientes preguntas para intercambiar información.

1. Cuando necesitas una operación o tienes un accidente, ¿adónde vas? ¿Tienes que pagar o no?
2. ¿Hay muchos hospitales en tu ciudad? ¿Cómo se llama el más importante?
3. Cuando estás enfermo/a y necesitas medicinas, ¿adónde vas a comprarlas? ¿Qué necesitas del médico/de la médica para poder comprarlas?
4. ¿Qué venden en las farmacias de tu país? ¿Por qué venden muchos otros productos, además de medicinas?
5. ¿Usas hierbas medicinales? ¿Para qué las usas? ¿Las usa alguien de tu familia?
6. ¿Te interesa la medicina alternativa? ¿Alguna vez usaste la acupuntura, la homeopatía o alguna otra? ¿Cómo fue tu experiencia?

EN OTRAS PALABRAS

In some Spanish-speaking countries, the word **sanatorio** is used instead of **hospital;** in others, **sanatorio** connotes a hospital that specializes in pulmonary and respiratory diseases. In some countries **clínica** refers to a private hospital. **Hospital** may refer to a government- or church-run facility that may provide free medical care.

11-3

Una emergencia.

PRIMERA FASE. Tu compañero/a y tú están de viaje en República Dominicana y los dos están enfermos por algo que comieron. En su hostal en Santo Domingo, han encontrado este anuncio. Decidan cuál es el número más apropiado para llamar. ¿Necesitan ir a una farmacia, o es mejor ir a una clínica médica? ¿Por qué?

SEGUNDA FASE. En preparación para su consulta médica, preparen las respuestas a las preguntas que les van a hacer.

1. ¿Cuáles son sus síntomas?

2. ¿Cuándo comenzaron a sentirse mal? ¿Cómo se sienten ahora?

3. ¿Saben ustedes qué causó el problema? Explíquenlo.

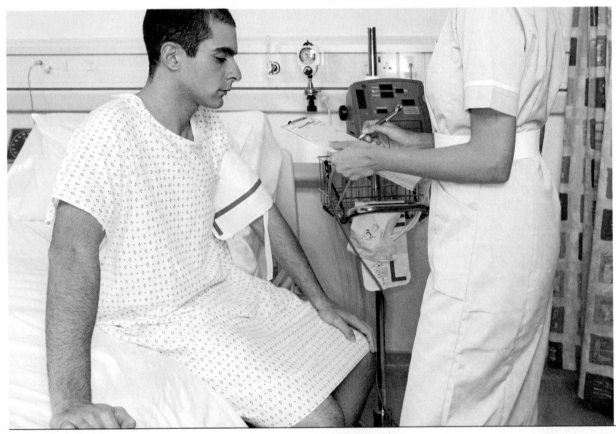

CYBER CENTRO AGUITA

Servicios Médicos

10-2-2001 · **Santo Domingo**

- Badosa Farmacéutica. 563-4230 ·········➤ Medicina Natural
- Centro de Cirugía Plástica Santo Domingo. 686-7863 ···➤ Cirugía
- Clínica Dental. 685-3752 ····················➤ Odontología
- Clínica Dental Dra. Carmen Gómez. 587-3576 ·····➤ Odontología
- Consultores en Psicología y Sexualidad. 548-3690 ···➤ Psicología
- Dr. Rubén Suárez, MD. 538- 2943 ···········➤ Medicina General
- Dr. Eliseo Alonso, DDS. 672-3928 ···········➤ Medicina General
- Farmacia Estrella. 688-4799 ···············➤ Farmacia
- Óptica Central, CxA. 682-9505; 689-1308 ·········➤ Óptica
- Productos Naturales. 686-1576 ····➤ Farmacéuticos - productos
- Sándalo, 672-3287 ·······················➤ Medicina Aromática

Las partes del cuerpo

Go to the *Capítulo 11* **folder** online to complete the Learning Module for *Vocabulario en contexto: Las partes del cuerpo.*

PLAN DE ESTUDIO

◎ LEARN
- Interactive presentation: *Las partes del cuerpo*
- Vocabulary tutorials

APPLY ◎
- Activities

PRÁCTICA COMUNICATIVA

11-4

Asociación.

PRIMERA FASE. Indica en qué parte del cuerpo se ponen estos accesorios y esta ropa.

1. __e__ los calcetines   **a.** la muñeca
2. __f__ los guantes   **b.** la cintura
3. __b__ el cinturón   **c.** las orejas
4. __d__ el collar   **d.** el cuello
5. __c__ los aretes   **e.** los pies
6. __a__ el reloj   **f.** las manos

 SEGUNDA FASE. Digan qué accesorios de la lista en la *Primera fase* no tienen ustedes y mencionen tres que consideren indispensables. Comparen sus respuestas.

Online prep for students
Students will have completed the Learning Module for *Las partes del cuerpo* online. See content online and Instructor's Resources for Supplementary Activities.

Tech tip for *Las partes del cuerpo*
Start by reviewing again the parts of the body that students already know from previous chapters. Then review other body vocabulary by pointing to yourself or projecting the images from the online Learning Module. Personalize and use gestures to facilitate comprehension: *A mí me gusta esquiar, pero tengo problemas con las rodillas. También tengo problemas con este hombro porque el año pasado me caí. Mi amigo Pedro también esquía. Esquía muy bien, pero el sábado pasado se cayó y se fracturó el brazo. El médico dice que no debe mover el brazo porque tiene un hueso fracturado. Pedro está muy aburrido porque no puede esquiar.* Ask questions to check comprehension.

Mention parts of the body and have students point to them. Give commands using parts of the body; recycle *derecho/a* and *izquierdo/a* to make the commands more challenging: *Ponga la mano derecha sobre la cabeza. Ponga la mano izquierda sobre el hombro derecho.* In groups, have students give commands to one another.

Note
You may present additional words such as *lengua, talón, nalgas, piel, costilla, hígado, riñones.*

Expansion for 11-4
You may have students work in groups to come up with additional accessories or clothing items for their classmates to associate with parts of the body.

Suggestion for 11-5
You may wish to turn this activity into a contest similar to Jeopardy, in which you ask *Unen las manos con el cuerpo* and teams of students compete to come up with the question *¿Qué son los brazos?*

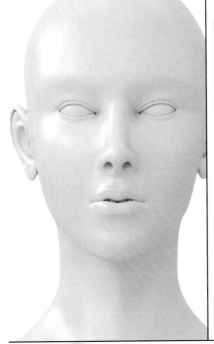

11-5

¿Para qué sirve(n)?

Lean las siguientes definiciones y túrnense para asociarlas con la parte del cuerpo correspondiente. Luego dile a tu compañero/a cuál de estas partes te parece más importante y por qué.

los brazos	la nariz
el cerebro	los ojos
el corazón	las piernas
los dientes	los pulmones
las manos	la sangre

1. _____Los brazos_____ unen las manos con el cuerpo.

2. _____Los ojos_____ permiten que las personas vean.

3. _____Los pulmones_____ toman el oxígeno del aire y lo pasan a la sangre.

4. _____La sangre_____ es un líquido rojo que circula por el cuerpo.

5. _____Las piernas_____ unen el cuerpo con los pies.

6. _____Los dientes_____ se usan para masticar (*chew*) la comida.

7. _____Las manos_____ están al final de los brazos.

8. _____El cerebro_____ le da órdenes al cuerpo.

9. _____El corazón_____ impulsa la sangre por las venas del cuerpo.

10. _____La nariz_____ está entre la frente y la boca.

11-6

Partes del cuerpo.

PRIMERA FASE. Indiquen qué parte(s) del cuerpo se relaciona(n) con cada una de las siguientes situaciones.

SITUACIÓN	PARTE DEL CUERPO
1. A Felipe le gusta escuchar música muy fuerte.	los oídos
2. María se maquilla todos los días.	la cara
3. Necesito ponerme gafas porque veo mal.	los ojos
4. Un futbolista del Real Madrid le pasa la pelota a un compañero de su equipo.	los pies
5. Se necesita mucha agilidad para tocar el violín.	los dedos
6. Esta mujer ha perdido 30 libras. La falda le queda ancha.	la cintura
7. Daniela lleva siempre el mismo collar.	el cuello
8. El té de hierbas es muy bueno para la digestión.	el estómago

SEGUNDA FASE. Ahora inventen dos adivinanzas para hacer asociaciones con partes del cuerpo.

Modelo

Sirven para besar.

los labios

La salud

Go to the *Capítulo 11* **folder** online to complete the Learning Module for *Vocabulario en contexto: La salud.*

PLAN DE ESTUDIO

◎ LEARN
- Interactive presentation: *La salud*
- Vocabulary tutorials
- *Entrevistas* video

APPLY ◎
- Activities
- *Entrevistas* video activities

PRÁCTICA COMUNICATIVA

11-7

La enfermedad de Jorgito.

Indica si las siguientes afirmaciones se refieren a síntomas (**S**) o recomendaciones (**R**). Compara tus respuestas con las de tu compañero/a. Después añade otro síntoma para Jorgito. Tu compañero/a va a darle una recomendación.

1. ___R___ Jorgito tiene que cuidarse.
2. ___S___ Tiene dolor de garganta.
3. ___R___ Debe tomar dos pastillas cada cuatro horas.
4. ___S___ Estornuda y tose mucho.
5. ___R___ Tiene que beber mucho líquido.
6. . . .

11-8

Remedios y consejos.

Elige la mejor recomendación para cada uno de los problemas siguientes. Luego compara tus respuestas con las de tu compañero/a, y piensen en otras dos sugerencias para cada una de estas personas.

1. Esteban tiene una infección en los ojos. Le recomiendo…

   a. nadar en la piscina. **b.** tomar antibióticos. **c.** leer mucho.

2. Valeria tiene fiebre y le duele el cuerpo. Le aconsejo…

   a. descansar y tomar aspirinas. **b.** comer mucho y caminar. **c.** ir a su trabajo.

3. Carmen se torció un tobillo. Le sugiero…

   a. correr todos los días. **b.** tomar clases de baile. **c.** descansar y no caminar.

4. Pablo se fracturó un brazo. Le recomiendo…

   a. jugar al tenis. **b.** no usar el ordenador por una semana. **c.** hacer ejercicio.

Online prep for students
Students will have completed the Learning Module for *La salud* online before class. Additional in-class activities are available for download in the Supplementary Activities folder online.

Suggestion
When presenting *tiene catarro* and *estornuda*, you may want to introduce the Spanish equivalents of "(God) bless you": *¡Salud!* or *¡Jesús!*

Tech tip for *Vocabulario en contexto*
Project the first drawing from the online Learning Module to review the vocabulary. Use gestures: *Jorgito no está bien. Está enfermo. Tiene mala cara y se siente muy mal. Tiene dolor de garganta y tose. Su mamá quiere saber si Jorgito tiene fiebre y le pone el termómetro. Jorgito tiene 39 grados (102° Fahrenheit). Ella está más preocupada ahora y llama a la pediatra.*

Ask yes/no questions to check understanding: *¿La mamá está enferma? ¿Jorgito tiene dolor de espalda? ¿Jorgito tiene dolor de garganta?* Point to yourself and say, *Tengo 37°. ¿Tengo fiebre?* Explain that 37° is normal (98.6°F).

Ask questions to personalize: *¿Cuándo vas al médico/a la médica? ¿Qué haces cuando te duele la garganta? ¿Para qué son los antibióticos?*

Act as if you had various aches and pains, complaining, *Me duele(n)…* Remind students that the structure of the verb *doler* is like that of *gustar* and that it has a vowel change in the stem.

Follow-up for 11-8
Set up other situations, asking pairs to come up with recommendations. Have each pair share its suggestions with the class.

11-9

¿A quién debo llamar?

Explícale a tu compañero/a tus síntomas o lo que necesitas. Él/Ella te va a decir a quién debes llamar según los anuncios. Después añadan una situación más para intercambiar.

1. dolerte la cabeza cuando lees o miras televisión

2. sentirte triste y deprimido/a

3. estar enfermo/a y tener fiebre

4. no poder dormir

5. no poder respirar bien y tener la piel (*skin*) irritada

6. dolerte los dientes cuando comes

7. buscar un médico/una médica para tu sobrino de cinco años

8. …

Modelo

66 necesitar un examen médico para el trabajo 99

Necesito un examen médico para el trabajo.

Debes llamar a la Dra. Corona López.

Dr. Fco. Javier Amador Cumplido
Cirugía y enfermedades de los ojos
86-43-57
Consultorio 204

Dra. Silvia Corona López
Medicina Interna
86-51-49

Dr. Héctor Molina Oviedo
Psiquiatra
86-51-49
Consultorio 402

Dr. Jaime A. Rodríguez Peláez
Pediatra
Niños y Adolescentes
86-17-15

Clínica de Asma y Alergias
Dr. Rubén Shturman
Amsterdam 219-A
2° piso
294-3866
584-0153

DR. RAÚL ELGUEZÁBAL R.
Medicina Familiar y Cirugía
86-34-73 EU.
428-4846
Consultorio 309

Dra. Gabriela Jacobo de Alcaraz
Cirujano Dentista
86-48-44
Consultorio 314

LENGUA Traditionally, law and medicine were professions dominated by men. Therefore, only the masculine form was used in Spanish: **el médico, el abogado.** Now that more women practice these professions, the feminine forms have entered the language. The feminine article is sometimes used before a masculine noun (**la médico, la abogado, la juez**), but it is increasingly common to use the feminine forms of the nouns: **la médica, la abogada, la jueza.**

11-10

En el consultorio. Tienes un catarro terrible y vas a ver a tu médico/a. Dile cómo te sientes y pregúntale qué debes hacer. Tu médico/a (tu compañero/a) te va a dar alguna recomendación y contestar tus preguntas.

Modelo

Me siento... /Tengo...

Creo que...

¿Es bueno...

Es excelente...

11-11

Me duele mucho.

PRIMERA FASE. You will listen to a teenage boy talk to his father about a sports injury. Before you listen, list two symptoms you think he probably has and compare your answers with those of your partner.

 SEGUNDA FASE. Pay attention to the general idea of what is said. As you listen, select the letter that indicates the appropriate ending to each statement.

1. Esteban tiene…

  a. una infección en el dedo.

  b. mucho dolor.

  c. fiebre.

2. El padre de Esteban cree que…

  a. su hijo se ha fracturado el dedo del pie.

  b. Esteban debe acostarse.

  c. es necesario que Esteban ponga hielo en el pie.

3. El padre de Esteban quiere…

  a. que Esteban descanse y se cuide.

  b. llevar a Esteban al hospital.

  c. que Esteban tome una aspirina.

4. El padre de Esteban le dice que…

  a. lo ayuda a caminar para llevarlo al hospital.

  b. decida si prefiere descansar o ir al hospital.

  c. el médico puede verlo esa tarde.

5. Esteban decide…

  a. no escuchar a su padre.

  b. jugar al fútbol al día siguiente.

  c. ir al hospital con su padre.

Suggestions for 11-10
Before this activity, brainstorm with students the most common symptoms of a bad cold. You may also write down a list with recommendations that they may get from the doctor: *tomar vitaminas, especialmente vitamina C, beber ocho vasos de agua todos los días, no salir de casa, descansar y dormir más, tomar un analgésico para el dolor de cabeza,* etc.

Warm-up for 11-11
As a pre-listening activity, have students form groups of 4 to discuss if they or someone they know has ever had an injury or accident and what he/she did to take care of him/herself.

Audioscript for 11-11
Esteban: *Papá, tú sabes, esta mañana cuando jugaba al fútbol, me torcí el pie. Mira qué hinchado está. Me duele mucho.*
Padre: *Esteban, parece que te has fracturado el dedo del pie. Creo que lo mejor será llevarte al médico para que te saquen una radiografía.*
Esteban: *¿Crees que sea necesario? ¿No sería mejor acostarme y descansar? Quizás si tomo una aspirina y me pongo una bolsa de hielo en el pie, me sentiré mejor.*
Padre: *¿Por qué no quieres ir al hospital? Allí te pueden examinar con cuidado.*
Esteban: *Es que… es que quiero jugar al fútbol mañana y no quiero que el médico me diga que no puedo hacerlo.*
Padre: *Es necesario que el médico te diga qué tienes y qué puedes hacer. Ven, te llevo al hospital.*
Esteban: *Bueno, si tú lo dices… ¡Ay! Me duele mucho; no puedo caminar.*
Padre: *Pronto te vas a sentir mejor. Vas a ver. Vamos, déjame ayudarte a caminar, así, poco a poco.*

Note
The characters in this dialogue use the subjunctive (*te cuides/ ponga*) in 2 sentences. You may call students' attention to these verbs and tell them that they will study this form later in the chapter.

Gramática en contexto

Expressing hopes, opinions, and goals

Expressing expectations and hopes:
Introduction to the present subjunctive

Go to the *Capítulo 11* online to complete the Learning Module for *Gramática en contexto*: Introduction to the present subjunctive.

PLAN DE ESTUDIO

◎ LEARN
- Interactive presentation: Introduction to the present subjunctive
- Grammar tutorials

APPLY ◎
- Activities
- Extra Practice

PRÁCTICA COMUNICATIVA

11-12 👥

Comentarios y deseos. Tu compañero/a y tú están hablando de la fiesta de mañana. Pónganse de acuerdo y marquen (✓) lo que esperan y desean que pase en la fiesta. Luego añadan un deseo más.

1. _____ Queremos que la fiesta empiece puntualmente.

2. _____ Ojalá que no sirvan comida.

3. _____ Preferimos que pongan música caribeña, porque queremos bailar salsa y merengue.

4. _____ Esperamos que también asistan estudiantes de odontología (*dentistry*) y de enfermería.

5. _____ Necesitamos que la fiesta termine temprano.

6. _____ Deseamos que nuestros profesores vayan a la fiesta.

7. _____ Queremos que todos recojan la basura después de la fiesta.

8. _____ Ojalá que nos divirtamos.

9. . . .

11-13 👥

Trabajo voluntario en el hospital.

PRIMERA FASE. Unos estudiantes trabajan de voluntarios en el hospital. ¿Qué espera la directora del programa de voluntarios que hagan estos estudiantes? Túrnense para hablar sobre cada escena.

Modelo

> " Elena: llevar flores/ conversar con los pacientes "

La directora espera que Elena les lleve flores a los pacientes.

También espera que Elena converse con los pacientes. Algunos pacientes se sienten muy solos.

1. José y Camila: jugar con los niños/hablar con los padres de los niños/leerles libros infantiles a los niños

2. Marisa: trabajar en la tienda de regalos/hacerles recomendaciones a los clientes/ poner flores frescas en el mostrador de la tienda

3. Sofía y Eduardo: conversar con los familiares de los pacientes/ofrecerles café/darles almohadas si quieren dormir mientras esperan

Suggestion for _Ojalá_
Ask students to list things that they would like to have happen in the future, using _ojalá: Ojalá que yo encuentre un buen trabajo._

Standard 4.1
Students demonstrate understanding of the nature of language through comparisons of the language studied and their own.
Students are aware that many words in English come from Spanish and Mexican influence in the American Southwest: _adobe, canyon, hacienda, lasso, vigilante,_ and many others. The lexical influence of Arabic on Spanish is similarly pervasive. Common words like _aceite, álgebra, azúcar, café, máscara, ojalá, olé,_ and _tarea_ come from Arabic. Explain to students that Arabic-speaking Moors from northern Africa ruled the Iberian peninsula from 711 until 1492, and that their culture is still alive in present-day Spain in architectural style, monuments, place names, and language.

Note
The activities in this section present a sequence that varies from input based to open ended. To maximize the communicative experience in the input-based activities, students are encouraged to share or check their answers with a classmate. When doing this, make sure that they are using the target language.

Suggestion for 11-13
Explain to students that object pronouns are placed immediately before the subjunctive verb form.

Follow-up
After students compare their lists with a partner, those pairs can compare their lists with another pair of students.

SEGUNDA FASE. ¿Qué más esperan los pacientes que hagan los voluntarios en el hospital? Escriban una lista de cuatro cosas más.

Modelo

66 *Los pacientes esperan que los voluntarios les traigan la comida.* 99

11-14

Clínica de Familia.

En una semana se abre una nueva clínica y ustedes están ayudando con los preparativos. En la tabla siguiente, escriban una lista de las cosas que ustedes tienen que hacer y otra de lo que esperan que hagan los empleados.

Modelo

Tenemos que pintar la sala de espera.

Y también tenemos que limpiar los pisos.

Espero que los empleados lleguen a tiempo.

Y yo espero que los carpinteros terminen su trabajo.

LO QUE TENEMOS QUE HACER	LO QUE ESPERAMOS QUE HAGAN
_____	la médica especialista: _____
_____	los enfermeros: _____
_____	la recepcionista: _____
_____	la chofer de la ambulancia: _____
_____	el anestesista: _____
_____	los empleados de limpieza: _____

Normas de conducta en el trabajo.

PRIMERA FASE. Tu amiga Rebeca tiene un trabajo nuevo como recepcionista y te pide consejos sobre qué normas de conducta seguir. Indica (✓) tus recomendaciones y compáralas con las recomendaciones de tu compañero/a.

	SE PROHÍBE	SE PERMITE	SE RECOMIENDA
1. fumar			
2. comer chocolates			
3. hablar por teléfono con amigos			
4. almorzar en la oficina			
5. conversar con los pacientes			
6. llevar vaqueros			

SEGUNDA FASE. Piensen en un trabajo que tienen ahora o que tiene un miembro de su familia. Hagan una lista de las actividades que se prohíben, las que se permiten y las que se recomiendan. ¿Son semejantes o diferentes las normas en sus respectivos lugares de trabajo?

Consejos y sugerencias.

Estás organizando un nuevo programa en Puerto Rico para estudiantes que quieren trabajar en programas de salud. Explícales a dos compañeros/as los aspectos del programa que aún no están resueltos. Ellos te recomendarán qué hacer.

Modelo   " viajar a Puerto Rico "

> Hay varias opciones: podemos viajar a Puerto Rico en grupo, o cada estudiante puede hacer su propia reservación.

> Es mejor que viajen en grupo, así se consigue mejor precio.

> Y también es importante que todos los estudiantes lleguen juntos.

1. empezar clases de español

2. establecer conexiones con las clínicas en la capital

3. buscar alojamiento (*lodging*)

4. escoger actividades de ocio (*free time*)

Warm-up for 11-16
Encourage students to use their imagination. Give details: The program is for students in the health professions (*las profesiones de la salud, como medicina, odontología, enfermería, terapia física, etc.*). Ask for ideas about setting up the program, such as publicity to recruit students, location, programming, living arrangements, etc. Write *Es importante/bueno/mejor que...* on the board and ask for students' suggestions.

Suggestion for 11-16
Put students in groups of 3 for this activity. They can change groups, redoing parts of the activity as needed, to play different roles.

Follow-up for 11-17
You may create groups of 6 and assign 1 research item to each student. Once they exchange the information they have obtained, encourage them to brainstorm what they will need or have to do to prepare for the trip. Recycle vocabulary for clothes and weather expressions. Example: *¿Qué necesitas llevar para protegerte del sol? ¿Qué ropa es más cómoda para caminar mucho?*

Suggestion for *Situaciones*
Remind students that this is theater, and that they may have to put themselves in an unfamiliar role when presenting *Situaciones*.

11-17

Boca Chica, República Dominicana

Excursión a República Dominicana.

PRIMERA FASE. Tu clase está planeando una excursión a la playa Boca Chica en República Dominicana. Escribe una lista de todas las cosas que hay que hacer en cuanto al alojamiento, transporte y equipaje (*luggage*) para preparar la excursión. Después compártela con tu compañero/a.

Modelo

> Es importante reservar los pasajes.

> Sí, y necesitamos comprar unas mochilas.

SEGUNDA FASE. En grupos de tres o cuatro decidan qué quieren que haga cada persona de su grupo. Compartan la información con la clase.

Modelo

> Queremos que David reserve los pasajes.

> Sí, y que Alicia compre unas mochilas.

> Necesitamos que...

Situaciones

1

ROLE A. You are sick today so you will miss the review session for the Spanish midterm. Call a classmate and a) say that you need him/her to take notes for you; b) give him/her advice about what you think is most important to write down; c) say when you want your friend to bring you the notes; and d) thank your friend.

ROLE B. When a friend from your Spanish class calls to ask a favor, say that you will be happy to take notes for him/her. Ask a) when your friend wants you to bring over the notes; b) how your friend is feeling; and c) what the doctor's recommendations are. Say that it is important that your friend rest and that you hope he/she feels better soon.

2

ROLE A. You are allergic to (**ser alérgico/a a**) cats, and you have just come back from spending the weekend with your friend who has two cats. Now you have a headache, your eyes itch (**me pican los ojos**), your lungs hurt, and it is hard to breathe. Call the clinic to a) explain your situation; b) describe your symptoms; and c) ask what the nurse recommends that you do. Ask questions to be sure you understand the recommendations.

ROLE B. You work as a nurse at the clinic, and someone calls for advice about an allergic reaction. Ask about the person's symptoms and offer advice about what he/she should do.

Expressing emotions, opinions, and attitudes:
The subjunctive with expressions of emotion

Go to the *Capítulo 11* **folder** online to complete the Learning Module for *Gramática en contexto:* The subjunctive with expressions of emotion.

PLAN DE ESTUDIO

◎ LEARN
- Interactive presentation: The subjunctive with expressions of emotion
- Grammar tutorials

APPLY ◎
- Activities
- Extra Practice

Online prep for students
Students will have completed the Learning Module for the subjunctive with expressions of emotion online. See content online and Instructor's Resources for Supplementary Activities.

Suggestions
Introduce the verb *molestar*, give examples, and clarify meaning, i.e., that it does not have any sexual connotations. Give examples using expressions of emotion: *Me alegro de que estén todos aquí. A mí me gusta que todos lleguen temprano y practiquen español con sus compañeros. Siento que no tengamos películas en español para hoy.* Ask students to finish the following introductory clauses: *Me alegro de que tú… Siento que tú… No me gusta que tú…*

PRÁCTICA COMUNICATIVA

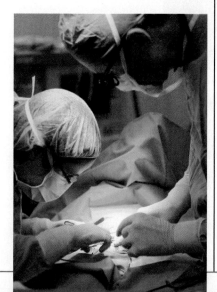

11-18

Estoy enfermo.

Estás enfermo/a. Túrnense y asocien cada comentario sobre su enfermedad con la reacción adecuada. Después añade una preocupación más sobre tu enfermedad y tu compañero/a debe reaccionar a lo que le dices.

1. __b__ Estoy muy enfermo/a.

2. __a__ Mis padres llegan hoy para estar conmigo.

3. __c__ Creo que el doctor Pérez me va a operar.

4. __e__ Dicen que es una operación seria.

5. __d__ No voy a poder participar en el campeonato.

6. . . .

a. Me alegro de que vengan.

b. Siento mucho que estés tan mal.

c. ¡Qué bueno que sea ese el médico!

d. Es una lástima que no puedas jugar.

e. Ojalá que no tengas complicaciones.

Audioscript for *En directo*
Dra. Villa: *Cati, me alegro de que te sientas mejor, pero temo que tengas que continuar con el tratamiento por dos semanas más.*
Cati: *De acuerdo, Doctora. Me duelen mucho las inyecciones, pero espero que me ayuden a curarme pronto.*
Dra. Villa: *Así será. ¡Qué agradable que tengas una actitud tan positiva!*

En directo

To express empathy:

Siento que…

Me alegro de que…

Temo que…

Espero que…

No me gusta que…

¡Qué agradable que…!

 Click on the icon to listen to a conversation with these expressions.

11-19

Una visita.

Estás en la clínica para visitar a tu compañero/a, a quien han operado de la rodilla. Tu compañero/a te cuenta sobre su experiencia en la clínica y cómo se siente. Escoge entre las expresiones de *En directo* para responderle e intercambien papeles.

Modelo

> No me gusta la comida del hospital.

> Siento que la comida no sea buena. ¿Qué te sirven?

> …

1. Me duele bastante la rodilla.
2. Tengo fiebre y dolor de cabeza.
3. Estoy mal del estómago porque las medicinas son muy fuertes.
4. Mis amigos me mandan flores y tarjetas.
5. Detesto estar en cama tanto tiempo.
6. Hay tanto ruido que no puedo dormir.
7. Las enfermeras vienen a verme cada media hora.

11-20

Reacciones.

Túrnense para reaccionar a las actividades que Luisa y Rafael piensan hacer la próxima semana.

Modelo ❝Luisa / no desayunar❞

> Luisa no va a desayunar.

> No me gusta que Luisa no desayune.

> Y yo temo que…

PERSONAS	LUNES	MIÉRCOLES	VIERNES	DOMINGO
Luisa	empezar una dieta	ir al gimnasio	hacer ejercicio en su casa	caminar 2 kilómetros
Rafael	trabajar en el hospital todo el día	salir del hospital temprano para ir al cine	quedarse en su casa	reunirse con sus amigos

11-21 👥

¿Qué me molesta?

PRIMERA FASE. Haz una lista de los hábitos que te molestan de otras personas. Compara tu lista con la de tu compañero/a.

Modelo

❝ *Me molesta que mis amigos lleguen tarde.* ❞

SEGUNDA FASE. En pequeños grupos, comparen sus listas y escojan seis hábitos que les molestan más a todos y digan por qué. Compartan sus resultados con el resto de la clase.

Situaciones

Follow-up for 11-21
Students list what they like others to do and then share their lists with partners.

1

ROLE A. Recently you decided to join an aerobics class (**clase de ejercicios aeróbicos**). You are also following a healthful diet and you feel great. When you run into a friend you have not seen for some time, you try to convince him/her to join you in your exercise class.

ROLE B. You run into a friend whom you have not seen for some time. Say that he/she looks (**verse**) great and ask what he/she is doing. Inquire a) how many times a week he/she goes to aerobics class (**clase de ejercicios aeróbicos**); b) how he/she feels about the class; and c) what he/she likes and doesn't like about his/her new plan for eating better. He/She will try to persuade you to join the program.

Tech tip for *Situaciones*
Students may want to practice online with a partner. Remind them that they can click on the microphone icon to connect with a partner online to do the activity.

2

ROLE A. You have gone to your doctor for a physical examination. Describe your symptoms and your lifestyle (**vida activa, vida sedentaria**). Respond to the doctor's reactions and recommendations with questions and comments.

ROLE B. You are a doctor doing a routine physical examination. As the patient talks, you a) ask pertinent questions; b) express approval or disapproval of the patient's lifestyle; and c) give advice or prescribe medication. Respond to the patient's comments about your recommendations.

Expressing goals, purposes, and means:
Uses of *por* and *para*

Go to the *Capítulo 11* folder online to complete the Learning Module for *Gramática en contexto:* Uses of *por* and *para*.

PLAN DE ESTUDIO

◎ LEARN
- Interactive presentation: Uses of *por* and *para*
- Grammar tutorials

APPLY ◎
- Activities
- Extra Practice

PRÁCTICA COMUNICATIVA

11-22

Un episodio.

PRIMERA FASE. Selecciona la preposición que debe usarse, según el significado entre paréntesis.

1. Salimos **por/para** el consultorio del médico a las nueve de la mañana. (*toward a destination*)

2. Fuimos **por/para** el túnel para llegar más rápido. (*through*)

3. Ana fue a ver al médico **por/para** su dolor de garganta y tos. (*reason or motive*)

4. El médico escribió la receta de un antibiótico **por/para** Ana. (*for whom it is intended*)

5. Yo fui a la farmacia **por/para** el antibiótico. (*object of an errand*)

6. ¿Cuánto pagaste **por/para** el antibiótico? (*exchange or substitution*)

SEGUNDA FASE. Túrnense para hablar del siguiente episodio.

1. ¿Cuándo fue la última vez que fuiste al médico?
2. ¿Por qué fuiste?
3. ¿Qué te recomendó el médico y para qué?
4. ¿Cuánto pagaste por la consulta?
5. ¿Cuánto pagaste por los medicamentos?

11-23

En el laboratorio.

Túrnense para averiguar cuándo estarán listos los resultados del análisis (*test*) de unos pacientes. Consulten la tabla para obtener información.

Modelo

" Alfredo Benítez/2:00 de la tarde "

¿Cuándo va a estar listo el análisis del Sr. Benítez?

Va a estar listo para las dos de la tarde.

PACIENTE	RESULTADOS DEL ANÁLISIS
Hilda Corvalán	11:00 de la mañana
Alfonso González	esta tarde
Jorge Pérez Robles	3:15 de la tarde
Aleida Miranda	mañana por la mañana
César Gómez Villegas	martes
Irene Santa Cruz	…

11-24

Una cura de estrés.

Para curarse del estrés, el médico le recomienda a tu compañero/a que pase quince días de descanso y relajación. Tú le aconsejas que vaya a Puerto Rico. Sugiérele algunas actividades y escoge de la lista el propósito para cada actividad. Después cambien de papel.

Modelo

" ACTIVIDAD: caminar por el Morro
PROPÓSITO: ver la hermosa bahía de San Juan **"**

" *Camina por el Morro para ver la hermosa bahía de San Juan.* **"**

ACTIVIDAD	PROPÓSITO
• participar en el Carnaval de Ponce	• ver las exhibiciones interactivas en el observatorio
• ir al Parque de la Cavernas del Río Camuy	• explorar el sistema de cavernas más grande del hemisferio occidental
• visitar el Radiotelescopio de Arecibo	• bailar en las calles
• explorar el Bosque Nacional El Yunque	• aprender cómo se hace el ron puertorriqueño
• salir a cenar en El Jibarito en el Viejo San Juan	• disfrutar del paisaje, la flora y la fauna
• visitar la Casa Bacardí en Cataño	• comer comida típica puertorriqueña

El Morro, San Juan, Puerto Rico

11-25

Nuestros motivos.

Cuéntense sus planes profesionales para el futuro y túrnense para hacerse preguntas que incluyan lo siguiente: **¿Qué…?, ¿Por qué…?, ¿Para qué…?, ¿Para quién…?,** etc.

Situaciones

1

ROLE A. You hurt your ankle while playing soccer, so you go to the health center at your college or university. Tell the doctor that a) you fell while running to make a goal (**marcar un gol**); b) your ankle is swollen (**hinchado**); and c) you cannot walk. Ask questions and answer your doctor's questions.

ROLE B. A patient comes to see you with a sports injury. After you hear how the injury happened, ask a) what the coach did for him/her and b) how he/she got to the health center. After determining that the ankle is not broken, recommend that the patient a) rest for three or four days; b) take medication (**una pastilla**) for the pain; and c) put ice on his/her ankle to reduce the swelling (**reducir la hinchazón**). Add that because of the injury, he/she should not play soccer for a month.

2

ROLE A. You want to rent a furnished apartment at the beach. You see a promising ad and call the landlord. Explain when you will need the apartment and for how long. Inquire about the rent, furnishings, and the number of rooms.

ROLE B. You are a landlord who is renting an apartment at the beach. A prospective renter calls you. Answer his/her questions and ask how many people will be staying at the apartment. Mention that the rent must be paid by the first of the month. Agree on a date and time to show the property.

Tech tip for *Situaciones*
Some students may want to film themselves and post their interaction using the MediaShare feature online.

Nutricionista: *Como ustedes saben, es necesario mantener una dieta sana y balanceada para evitar enfermedades y mantener un peso ideal. En primer lugar, es necesario hacerse un examen médico anual, alimentarse bien, mantenerse activo, no fumar ni consumir mucho alcohol.*

Fabián: *Pero aquí en la universidad muchos estudiantes toman cerveza para relajarse y divertirse. ¿Qué tiene eso de malo?*

Nutricionista: *En realidad tomar cerveza o alcohol no es malo. Lo importante es la moderación. La sal, por ejemplo, es buena, pero en altas cantidades puede ser dañina.*

Fabiola: *¿Y la carne roja?*

Nutricionista: *Un factor importante es limitar el consumo de grasas animales para evitar el aumento del colesterol en la sangre; el pescado y el pollo tienen menos grasa. Consuman estos últimos con más frecuencia.*

Fabián: *En mi casa mis padres comen muchas frutas y verduras, pero a mí no me gustan mucho.*

Nutricionista: *Es una lástima, porque las frutas y verduras tienen muchos minerales y vitaminas. Además, tienen fibra, y la fibra es buena para la salud.*

Fabiola: *Yo quiero bajar de peso. ¿Qué debo hacer?*

Nutricionista: *Mantén una dieta balanceada y haz ejercicios regularmente, por lo menos veinte minutos, tres veces a la semana. Es preferible bajar de peso poco a poco y cambiar los hábitos de comida y ejercicios. Así se puede mantener el peso ideal, mejorar la salud y la apariencia física.*

Fabiola: *Suena fácil, pero debo tener mucha disciplina.*

Fabián: *Sí, sobre todo los fines de semana cuando se socializa con amigos.*

Nutricionista: *Recuerden, todo con moderación. Buena suerte, y si necesitan más información pueden venir a verme al hospital.*

Unidos

ESCUCHA

11-26 [Presentational]

Preparación. Vas a escuchar una conversación entre un nutricionista y un grupo de estudiantes universitarios hispanos. Antes de escuchar, escribe dos preguntas que los alumnos probablemente le harán al nutricionista y dos sugerencias que les dará el nutricionista. Presenten sus preguntas y sugerencias a la clase, y escriban entre todos una lista.

11-27  [Interpretive]

Escucha. Mark (✓) the statements that best identify the main ideas of what you heard.

1. ___✓___ Consultar al médico una vez por año es importante para evitar enfermedades.

2. _____ El consumo de tomates, lechugas, uvas, naranjas, cerveza y carne de res es recomendable para tener energía.

3. ___✓___ La buena alimentación y el ejercicio tienen un efecto positivo en la salud.

4. _____ Se recomienda comer bastante y hacer muchísimo ejercicio para mantener una vida saludable.

5. _____ Bajar de peso afecta positivamente a la salud y a la apariencia de las personas.

6. ___✓___ La buena salud requiere disciplina.

11-28  [Interpersonal]

Un paso más. Háganse las siguientes preguntas. ¿Tienen los mismos hábitos de salud? Comparen sus puntos de vista.

1. ¿Qué hábitos de comida y actividad física tienes? ¿Son tus hábitos buenos o malos?

2. ¿Crees que eres lo que comes?

3. ¿Qué aspecto de tu vida piensas que puedes cambiar para mejorar tu estado físico?

ESTRATEGIA

Listen for the main idea

You can focus your attention on the main ideas when you listen by following these tips:

1. Rely on knowledge of the topic to make connections.

2. Think about the specific words or concepts you may hear.

3. Pay attention to the introduction and the conclusion, where the main ideas are usually stated.

4. Listen for transitional phrases that signal main ideas, such as **Lo importante es…, Recuerde(n)…, Otro punto importante/central…**

Comprueba

I was able to…

____ **use my knowledge of the topic to anticipate what I would probably hear.**

____ **listen for parts of the conversation where main ideas are about to be presented.**

____ **identify the main ideas.**

AUTOEVALUACIÓN

☐ **I feel confident that I was able to understand what I heard.**

☐ **I need more listening practice.**

STUDY PLAN

▷ Good job! Move on to the next section, *Habla.*

▷ Go to the *Unidos* [folder] online for *Escucha* practice.

HABLA

Preparación. Marca (✓) los hábitos o condiciones que ayudan a prolongar la vida de las personas.

1. _____ hacer ejercicio físico regularmente

2. _____ trabajar poco

3. _____ poner el cuerpo bajo mucho estrés

4. _____ ser vegetariano/a

5. _____ beber vino con el almuerzo o la cena

6. _____ llevar una vida sedentaria

7. _____ tomar remedios de casa para curar el catarro

8. _____ evitar fracturarse los huesos

ESTRATEGIA

Select appropriate phrases to offer opinions

When you are talking with someone, it is natural to offer opinions and evaluations of what the other person has said and to express agreement or disagreement. An effective way to do this is to acknowledge the value of what the other person has said and then express your reaction to it.

11-30 [Interpersonal]

Habla. Entrevista a tu compañero/a sobre los temas siguientes. Reacciona y opina según lo que escuches. Da recomendaciones cuando sea necesario.

1. sus actividades

2. sus hábitos de comida

3. las bebidas que toma cuando salen con sus amigos

En directo

To congratulate or praise someone:

Felicitaciones por + *verb, noun.*

Te felicito. Te cuidas muy bien.

¡Qué bien! Vas a vivir muchos años.

To express happiness at someone's success:

Me alegro de que + *subjunctive.*

¡Qué fabuloso que + *subjunctive*

To introduce a contrasting opinion:

Lo que dices es interesante, pero mi perspectiva es diferente./Yo lo veo diferente.

Entiendo tu punto de vista, pero no estoy de acuerdo contigo.

Click on the icon to listen to a conversation with these expressions.

En directo

To make a general recommendation:

Es importante/bueno/ conveniente/aconsejable + *infinitive.*

To make a recommendation to someone specific:

Es importante que + *name(s)* + *subjunctive.*

 Click on the icon to listen to a conversation with these expressions.

Comprueba

In my conversation, I...

_____ used the correct expressions to praise and encourage.

_____ used the appropriate expressions to acknowledge what the speaker said and then express a different opinion.

_____ used expressions effectively to make recommendations.

11-31 [Presentational]

Un paso más. Usa la información de la entrevista a tu compañero/a para escribir un informe que incluya lo siguiente:

1. Las actividades y hábitos de tu compañero/a.

2. Una comparación con los tuyos.

3. Tu opinión y recomendaciones para tener una vida más saludable.

AUTOEVALUACIÓN

☐ I feel confident that I communicated successfully.

☐ I need more speaking practice.

STUDY PLAN

▶ Good job! Move on to the next section, *Lee.*

▶ Go to the *Unidos* [folder] online for *Habla* practice.

Suggestion for 11-30
Ask students to prepare a questionnaire. Give them some models to ask related questions: *¿Te mantienes activo/a? ¿Comes verduras regularmente? ¿Bebes alcohol? ¿Con qué frecuencia?*

Audioscript for *En directo*
Nurse: *Te felicito, Juan. Estás en perfectas condiciones. Se nota que te cuidas muy bien.*
Patient: *Gracias. Como muy bien y hago ejercicio casi todos los días.*
Nurse: *¡Qué bien! Vas a vivir muchos años.*
Patient: [suddenly becoming very serious] *Entiendo tu punto de vista, pero no estoy de acuerdo contigo. Anoche soñé que estaba muy enfermo. ¡Por eso pienso que me voy a morir muy pronto¡* [pause] *¡Ja, ja! ¡Estoy bromeando!*
Nurse: [chuckling] *Me alegro de que seas una persona alegre. El buen humor también es muy bueno para la salud.*

Suggestion for *En directo*
You may provide students with *enhorabuena* as an additional expression to congratulate someone.

Audioscript for *En directo*
Miriam: *Mamá, el doctor dijo que es aconsejable que dejes de fumar cuanto antes. ¿Por qué sigues fumando?*
Mother: *Hija, es bien difícil parar. Cuando fumo, me siento muy relajada.*
Miriam: *Lo entiendo, pero si no quieres enfermarte, es importante que busques ayuda ya.*

LEE

Suggestion for *Estrategia*
Follow *Estrategia* suggestions
a through *c* and point out to
students what you are doing.
Encourage them to follow *d* as
they read the text.

Suggestion for 11-33
Have students find additional
ideas principales and *ideas
secundarias* in the text. Have
them explain the difference.

11-32 | Interpersonal

Preparación.

PRIMERA FASE. Marca (✓) en la siguiente lista las enfermedades
tropicales que conoces.

1. _____ la viruela (*smallpox*)

2. _____ la tuberculosis

3. _____ el dengue

4. _____ el virus del Nilo

5. _____ la malaria

6. _____ la enfermedad del sueño

SEGUNDA FASE. Habla con tu compañero/a sobre las ideas que
esperan encontrar en el artículo.

ESTRATEGIA

Focus on relevant information

Identifying the relevant information in
a text and disregarding what you think
is irrelevant helps you read faster and
understand more. Techniques that help
you identify what is important include
a) reading the titles and subtitles; b) looking
at the visuals and reading the captions;
c) brainstorming possible content by
using your knowledge of the topic; and
d) comparing those ideas with what you
find as you read.

11-33 | Interpretive

Lee. Según el contenido del artículo en la página siguiente, selecciona
las expresiones de la derecha que se relacionan con los siguientes temas.

TEMAS	EXPRESIONES RELACIONADAS
enfermedades tropicales	las infecciones, la viruela, la tuberculosis, el virus del Nilo
desafíos de las enfermedades para los expertos	la infección, la adaptabilidad, el desarrollo, la evolución, la resistencia
medidas que los gobiernos toman para enfrentar estas enfermedades	campañas, inmunización, reproducción, vacunas, prevención

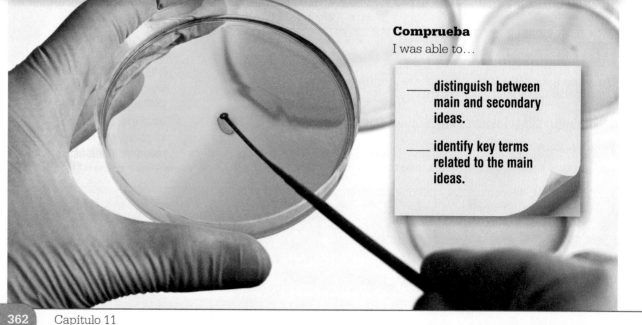

Comprueba
I was able to…

_____ **distinguish between
main and secondary
ideas.**

_____ **identify key terms
related to the main
ideas.**

Las enfermedades
y la globalización

Enfermedades tropicales como el dengue, la viruela, la malaria, la tuberculosis y el virus del Nilo que, según muchos expertos, ya no existían, ahora reaparecen y se extienden por todo el mundo. Las causas de su reaparición son evidentes: cambios en el medio ambiente[1] y el constante movimiento de personas entre los continentes. Los turistas, los trabajadores migratorios y los inmigrantes transportan estos virus e infecciones. De la misma manera, los cambios climáticos facilitan la adaptación de los virus a nuevos ambientes y los hacen resistentes.

Bacterias, parásitos y virus viajeros y resistentes

Un claro ejemplo de la adaptabilidad de estas enfermedades infecciosas es la tuberculosis. Los científicos pensaban que estaba controlada en los países desarrollados. Sin embargo, los hechos nos muestran que esta enfermedad ha evolucionado y ha retornado.

La Organización Mundial de la Salud (OMS) expresa gran preocupación por la malaria. El mosquito que la provoca puede sobrevivir largos viajes interoceánicos. Por eso, hay personas enfermas de malaria en muchas partes del mundo. La malaria es peligrosa si no se detecta a tiempo. Los médicos sin experiencia en este tipo de enfermedades la pueden confundir con la gripe y tratarla con medicamentos inadecuados.

El virus del Nilo constituye otra enfermedad que afecta a los turistas. Se reportaron 3.500 casos de la enfermedad en Estados Unidos en 2007, de los que murieron más de cien personas.

Las enfermedades migratorias

A fines del siglo XX, gracias a una campaña mundial contra la viruela, casi toda la población mundial fue inmunizada contra esta enfermedad. Sin embargo, en Estados Unidos ha sido necesario fabricar vacunas contra la viruela que no se producían desde hacía años.

El dengue es indudablemente la enfermedad más extendida del mundo en los últimos años. Los expertos afirman que es posible que el 40% de la población del mundo contraiga[2] esta mortal fiebre. Geográficamente, el dengue nació en el suroeste de Asia, pero rápidamente pasó al Caribe y Centro y Sudamérica. En los últimos años se han descubierto casos incluso en España.

La malaria aumenta a causa de las inundaciones del río Amazonas.

La lista de enfermedades que surgen de nuevo por la movilidad de la población del mundo actual es larga, pero los fondos mundiales para realizar investigaciones sobre las enfermedades que causan el 90% de las muertes en el mundo son mínimos y limitados. Sin duda, la globalización ha resuelto algunos problemas, pero ha creado otros.

[1]environment   [2]contracts

11-34 **Presentational**

Un paso más. Escribe un párrafo informativo sobre las enfermedades tropicales y las medidas que los gobiernos toman para enfrentarlas, y compártelo con la clase.

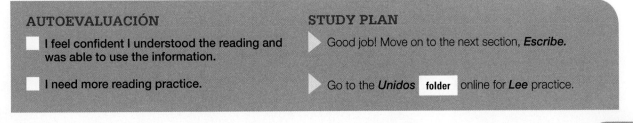

AUTOEVALUACIÓN

☐ I feel confident I understood the reading and was able to use the information.

☐ I need more reading practice.

STUDY PLAN

▶ Good job! Move on to the next section, *Escribe.*

▶ Go to the *Unidos* folder online for *Lee* practice.

ESCRIBE

 Interpretive

Preparación.

PRIMERA FASE. Lee este correo electrónico de uno de tus buenos amigos.

> Hola,
>
> Perdón por no escribirte antes, pero últimamente no me siento bien. No puedo trabajar un día completo y no tengo apetito. No tengo energía para cocinar, así que a veces como solo sopa enlatada. Otras voy a un restaurante de comida rápida. Tomo café constantemente, porque necesito la cafeína para sobrevivir, pero luego no puedo dormir. Mi vida es una pesadilla. Quisiera ver a un médico, pero no tengo dinero. ¿Qué me aconsejas?
>
> Bueno, escríbeme para saber de ti. Te contestaré tan pronto pueda.
>
> Un fuerte abrazo,
>
> Tomás

SEGUNDA FASE. Escribe tres problemas que tiene Tomás y algunas ideas para ayudarlo a resolver cada problema.

PROBLEMAS DE TOMÁS	ALGUNAS POSIBLES SOLUCIONES
1.	1.
2.	2.
3.	3.

ESTRATEGIA

Persuade through suggestions and advice

Well-structured suggestions and advice are important for effective persuasion in writing. Remember to …

- decide whether to address your reader as **tú** or **usted,** based on your relationship (e.g., friend vs. supervisor at work).
- select suggestions that match the nature of your relationship.

En directo

To express concern or sympathy:

Me preocupa (mucho) que…

Siento/Lamento que…

Qué lástima que…

To persuade a friend through suggestions:

Te recomiendo/sugiero/ aconsejo que…

Es importante/necesario/ urgente/mejor que…

Ojalá (que)…

 Click on the icon to listen to a conversation with these expressions.

11-36 [Presentational]

Escribe. Responde al correo electrónico de Tomás. Usa la información de **11-35** y expresa tus sentimientos o preocupación por los problemas. Indícale algunas sugerencias para que los resuelva.

Comprueba

I was able to…

___ use a familiar tone to communicate with a friend.

___ use appropriate expressions to express concern and sympathy.

___ use appropriate suggestions for effective persuasion.

___ use transitions effectively to move from one idea to the next.

En directo

To put ideas together coherently:

Por un lado…
On one hand …

Por otro (lado)…
On the other (hand) …

En primer/segundo lugar…
In the first/second place …

Además…
Besides/In addition/Furthermore …

To contrast ideas:

No obstante… *However …*

Sin embargo… *Nevertheless …*

Click on the icon to listen to a conversation with these expressions.

11-37 [Interpersonal]

Un paso más. Lean los correos electrónicos que cada uno/a le escribió a Tomás y comenten lo siguiente:

1. ¿Qué problemas de Tomás les parecen más serios? ¿Por qué?

2. ¿Qué soluciones le proponen ustedes? ¿Por qué?

AUTOEVALUACIÓN

☐ I feel confident I successfully communicated my ideas in writing.

☐ I need more writing practice

STUDY PLAN

▶ Good job!

▶ Go to the *Unidos* [folder] online for *Escribe* practice.

Suggestion for 11-36
Depending on your group, you may wish to turn this into a paired activity. Weak students may profit from the skills of stronger ones.

Audioscript for *En directo*
Doctor Ayuda: *Queridos radioyentes, les habla el Doctor Ayuda, y tenemos nuestra primera llamada. Alicia, ¿en qué puedo servirla?*
Alicia: *Doctor Ayuda, por un lado, mi médica me dice que estoy muy saludable. Mi presión arterial está muy bien. No tengo dolores. Por otro lado, desde el sábado me siento muy mal. Me duele la cabeza y además, me pica la piel.*
Doctor Ayuda: *Alicia, es posible que necesite volver a su médica. Sin embargo, me pregunto si usted comió algo o está usando algún producto nuevo.*
Alicia: *Pues sí, Doctor. Ahora que lo pienso, empecé a usar una nueva loción el sábado.*
Doctor Ayuda: *¡Ajá! Es posible que usted sea alérgica a esa loción. Le recomiendo que vaya a ver a su dermatólogo.*

Suggestion for 11-37
Ask students to revise their e-mails according to the following:

1 *¿Tiene el correo electrónico una introducción, un cuerpo, un párrafo de cierre y una despedida?*

2 *¿Corregiste la concordancia, la puntuación y la ortografía? ¿Usaste comas, puntos, etc., donde eran necesarios?*

3 *¿Usaste vocabulario apropiado al tema y expresiones de cohesión? ¿Revisaste el tiempo (presente, pasado, futuro) y los modos (indicativo, subjuntivo)?*

ENFOQUE *cultural*

CUBA

En el centro histórico de la capital se encuentra la famosa Plaza de la Catedral de La Habana que fue declarada Patrimonio de la Humanidad por la UNESCO. Cada día se transforma en un mercado de artesanía cubana.

REPÚBLICA DOMINICANA

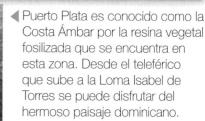

◀ Puerto Plata es conocido como la Costa Ámbar por la resina vegetal fosilizada que se encuentra en esta zona. Desde el teleférico que sube a la Loma Isabel de Torres se puede disfrutar del hermoso paisaje dominicano.

PUERTO RICO

El Viejo San Juan conserva aún su estilo colonial con sus casas pintadas, sus balcones típicos y calles de adoquines (*cobblestones*). Además, cuenta con plazas públicas, iglesias históricas y una abundancia de tiendas y restaurantes.

Cuba, República Dominicana y Puerto Rico: la música y el baile

Go to the *Enfoque cultural* [folder] in *Capítulo 11* online to learn more about this region.

◎ **LEARN**
- Interactive presentation: *Cuba, República Dominicana y Puerto Rico: la música y el baile*

APPLY
- Activities

PRÁCTICA COMUNICATIVA

11-38

Usa la información. Durante los años 50 y 60 muchas estrellas y orquestas de música caribeña se hicieron muy famosas en todo el mundo. Mira o escucha algunos fragmentos de cine latinoamericano de la época y escoge a una de las estrellas. Luego, prepara cinco preguntas que le harías (*would ask*) si este/a artista estuviera vivo/a (*were alive*). Para preparar esta actividad, visita Internet.

En este capítulo...

Comprueba lo que sabes

Go to the *Comprueba lo que sabes* folder online to review what you have learned in this chapter. Practice with the following:

Vocabulary Flashcards	Games	Oral Practice	Practice Test/ Study Plan	Video en contexto

Vocabulario 🔊

El cuerpo humano
la boca
el brazo
el cabello
la cabeza
la cadera
la cara
la ceja
el cerebro
la cintura
el codo
el corazón
el cuello
el dedo
el diente
la espalda
el estómago
la frente
la garganta
el hombro
el hueso
el labio
la mano
la mejilla
la muñeca
el músculo
la nariz

el nervio
el oído
la oreja
el pecho
la pestaña
el pie
la pierna
el pulmón
la rodilla
la sangre
el tobillo
la vena

La salud
el cáncer
el catarro
el dolor
la enfermedad
el enfermo/la enferma
la fiebre
la gripe
la infección
el/la paciente
el síntoma
la tensión/la
    presión (arterial)
la tos

Los proveedores de salud
la clínica/el centro de
    salud/el sanatorio
el farmacéutico/la
    farmacéutica
la farmacia
el gobierno
el hospital

Los tratamientos médicos
el analgésico
el antibiótico
la inyección
la medicina/el
    medicamento
la pastilla
la receta
el remedio
el termómetro

Verbos
alegrarse (de)
caer(se)
cuidar(se) (de)
curar

doler (ue)
enfermarse
estornudar
examinar
fracturar(se)
fumar
molestar(le)
recetar
respirar
sentir (ie, i)
temer
torcer(se) (ue)
toser
tratar

Las descripciones
deprimido/a
enfermo/a
grave
serio/a

Palabras y expresiones útiles
el artículo de belleza
cada... horas
¿Qué te/le(s) pasa?
tener dolor de...
tener mala cara

Notas

12 Buen viaje

Learning OBJECTIVES

You will:

- learn vocabulary related to travel and transportation
- use demonstrative pronouns
- learn affirmative and negative expressions
- use the subjunctive to express doubt
- talk about past events using the preterit and imperfect
- connect new information about Panama and Costa Rica to what you already know

Learning OUTCOMES

You will be able to:

- talk about travel arrangements and preferences
- express possession and clarify what belongs to you and others
- express affirmation and negation
- express doubt and uncertainty
- talk about past travel experiences
- talk about the social and economic impact of the Panama Canal

PANAMÁ Y COSTA RICA

NICARAGUA

COSTA RICA
Volcán Arenal

Puntarenas • **Heredia** • **Puerto Limón**
San ⊛ • **Cartago**
José

Mar Caribe

Canal de Panamá

Isla San Blas

Golfo de Nicoya • **San Isidro**

Golfo de los Mosquitos **Colón** • **Ciudad de Panamá**

PANAMÁ

Cocos para comer

•**David** **Penonomé**•

Isla de Coiba

Puente Centenario

Golfo de Panamá

La Palma

COLOMBIA

OCÉANO PACÍFICO

Una mola tradicional de los kuna, indígenas de isla San Blas en Panamá

¿Cuánto sabes?

Piensa en lo que sabes de Panamá y Costa Rica, y selecciona la terminación correcta para completar las afirmaciones.

1. El Canal de Panamá permite pasar del Mar Caribe al...
   a. Océano Atlántico.
   b. Golfo de Nicoya.
   c. Golfo de Panamá.

2. La capital de Costa Rica es...
   a. San Juan.
   b. San José.
   c. Santo Domingo.

3. Panamá limita al oeste con Costa Rica y al este con...
   a. Colombia.
   b. Nicaragua.
   c. República Dominicana.

4. Los turistas van a las playas de Costa Rica en...
   a. Heredia.
   b. Cartago.
   c. Puntarenas.

Cultura en línea
To learn more about Panamá and Costa Rica and the chapter theme, go to the *Cultura en línea* folder in the *Unidos* online component to view the *Vistas culturales* video and take a virtual art tour.

Tech tip for map
Ask what students know about Costa Rica and Panama. Project the map and ask: *¿Dónde está el Canal de Panamá? ¿Qué océanos conecta? ¿Cuándo se construyó?* (early 1900s) Explain that going from New York to San Francisco using the Panama Canal is only 6,000 miles (9,500 kms), compared to 14,000 miles (20,500 kms) going around Cape Horn. Personalize to introduce the chapter topic: *¿Adónde les gusta ir de vacaciones, a la playa, a la montaña?* Explain that tourism is very important in Costa Rica: *En Costa Rica hay playas muy buenas donde se puede hacer surf. ¿Les gusta el surf? ¿Les gusta visitar lugares exóticos?*

Note for art
The *mola* is part of the traditional clothing of the Kuna, an indigenous people of Panama and Colombia. In Dulegaya, the Kuna language, the word *mola* means "clothing." Typical molas are made in layers of different colors. They are sewn by hand, and some require a great deal of work. Today, the production of molas includes dresses, T-shirts, wall hangings, quilts, and blouses.

Tech tip for art
Project the image of the artwork and ask students to describe the shapes and colors of the mola. Point to Panama's Islands of San Blas on the map and explain that the Kuna now live on a large reservation there. You may explain that San Blas is a tourist destination for cruises (*cruceros*). Producing and selling molas is an important source of income for the Kuna. Ask: *¿Cuánto cuestan las molas, probablemente? ¿De qué depende el precio? ¿Del trabajo? ¿Del tamaño?* Help students make connections with the art of quilting in the U.S.

Vocabulario en contexto

Talking about travel arrangements and modes of travel

Los medios de transporte

Go to the *Capítulo 12* **folder** online to complete the Learning Module for *Vocabulario en contexto: Los medios de transporte.*

PLAN DE ESTUDIO

LEARN
- Interactive presentation: *Los medios de transporte*
- Vocabulary tutorials
- Pronunciation

APPLY
- Activities
- Pronunciation activities

PRÁCTICA COMUNICATIVA

12-1

Asociaciones. Asocia cada palabra con su descripción. Luego, compara tus respuestas con las de tu compañero/a y dile qué medio de transporte prefieres y por qué.

1. __d__ transporte público para viajar por las calles de la ciudad
2. __h__ viaje en un barco grande de pasajeros
3. __a__ persona que sirve la comida en un vuelo
4. __e__ transporte subterráneo
5. __f__ inspección al llegar a otro país
6. __b__ identificación necesaria para viajar al extranjero
7. __g__ pasaje para ir y volver
8. __c__ se viaja en un asiento cómodo y se come bien

a. el/la auxiliar de vuelo
b. pasaporte
c. primera clase
d. autobús
e. metro
f. aduana
g. boleto de ida y vuelta
h. crucero

EN OTRAS PALABRAS
Depending on the region, different words for **autobús** are used: **camión** (Mexico), **ómnibus** (Peru), **bus, guagua** (Puerto Rico, Cuba), **colectivo** (Argentina), **micro** (Chile), **chiva** (Colombia).

SALIDA DEPARTURE	ABORDAR BOARDING	PUERTA GATE	DESTINO DESTINATION
3:30	3:00	1A	SAN JOSÉ
3:50	3:20	4	MANAGUA
4:10	3:40	6	GUATEMALA
4:25	3:55	10	PANAMÁ
4:45	4:15	8	LIMÓN
5:10	4:40	5	MÉXICO D.F.
6:00	5:30	5	KINGSTON

12-2

Salidas y llegadas. Miren los horarios y la puerta de salida de los siguientes vuelos y háganse preguntas.

Modelo

> ¿A qué hora sale el vuelo para San José?

> El avión para San José sale a las tres y media por la puerta 1A.

Suggestion for 12-2
Review the phrases *pasaje/ boleto de ida y vuelta* and *pasaje/boleto de ida*. Project the image of the airport scene from the online Learning Module. Ask where the people are, what they are doing, what luggage they have, and so on.

Suggestions for 12-2
As a warm-up, replay the dialogue from the online Learning Module to practice vocabulary. Ask: *¿Qué prefiere el pasajero, ventanilla o pasillo? ¿Qué necesita? ¿Cuál es su puerta de salida?*

Suggestion for 12-2
Have students role-play the interaction between an airline agent and a traveler who needs to find out the departure time and gate number for a flight.

12-3

Haciendo turismo. Seleccionen uno de los destinos siguientes y planeen un itinerario. Incluyan en su itinerario la información de la lista. Busquen información en Internet si es necesario. Después, presenten su itinerario a la clase.

DESTINOS:	
COSTA RICA	**PANAMÁ**
• Parque Nacional Isla del Coco	• Bocas del Toro
• Reserva Biológica Bosque Nuboso Monteverde	• Comarca Kuna Yala
• Playa Nosara	• Playas de Colón

Itinerario:

1. Destino y por qué lo seleccionaron
2. Fechas de viaje (número de días)
3. Vuelos (aerolíneas), precio de los boletos
4. Alojamiento (hotel, precio)
5. Sus actividades

Online prep for students
Students will have completed the Learning Module for *El alojamiento y las reservaciones* online. See content online and Instructor's Resources for Supplementary Activities.

Tech tip for *Vocabulario en contexto*
Practice phrases for giving directions by projecting a simple map of the university campus. Mention that *plano* is another word for map, often used to refer to a city map or street map. Tell how to get from one place to the other: *Para ir a la biblioteca, salgo de este edificio y sigo derecho hasta la Facultad de Ciencias. Allí doblo a la izquierda y enseguida veo la biblioteca.* Then give directions to other buildings. If students have maps of the campus, they can follow the directions by drawing a dotted line. For additional practice, use a map of your town or city and have students work in pairs, asking and giving directions.

El alojamiento y las reservaciones

Go to the *Capítulo 12* **folder** online to complete the Learning Module for *Vocabulario en contexto: El alojamiento y las reservaciones.*

PLAN DE ESTUDIO

◎ **LEARN**
- Interactive presentation: *El alojamiento y las reservaciones*
- Vocabulary tutorials

APPLY ◎
- Activities

PRÁCTICA COMUNICATIVA

12-4

Estoy perdido/a. Estás en la Ciudad de Panamá y estás perdido/a. Usa el plano siguiente y pregúntale a una persona en la calle (tu compañero/a) cómo ir a ciertos lugares. Tu compañero/a debe explicarte cómo llegar.

ESTÁS EN	DESEAS IR
la Plaza 5 de Mayo	al Palacio Presidencial
la Avenida Ancón y la Avenida A	al Casco Viejo
el Museo de Historia del Canal de Panamá	al Centro Turístico Mi Pueblito

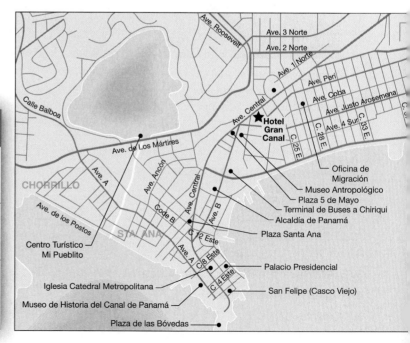

12-5 👥

En el hotel. Túrnense para hacer el papel de recepcionista de hotel y cliente en las siguientes situaciones. Usen el vocabulario y las expresiones de la lista. Después escojan una situación y preséntenla a la clase.

una habitación doble/sencilla	la tarjeta magnética	Quisiera...
la llave	el equipaje	¿Dónde...?
una reservación	la caja fuerte	¿Podría...?

	CLIENTE	RECEPCIONISTA
SITUACIÓN 1	llega al hotel y necesita una habitación	hace muchas preguntas
SITUACIÓN 2	necesita una habitación para él y su colega de trabajo pero no tiene reservación	solo tiene una habitación sencilla
SITUACIÓN 3	quiere reservar una habitación por teléfono	acaba de empezar su nuevo trabajo y no sabe mucho

Suggestion for 12-5
You may provide additional vocabulary: *ascensor, taxista, inscribirse.* A variation: Each group must find lodging in its price range (*casa de huéspedes, albergue, pensión, posada, parador, hotel, hotel de lujo*). Tell students that in lower-price establishments, it is often wise to ask to see the room before deciding to stay there. Remind students of the polite use of *quisiera.* You say rudely *Quiero una habitación;* students correct you, *Quisiera una habitación.*

Cultura

Hoy en día las personas prefieren comunicarse mediante los *chats*, Facebook (u otras redes sociales) o el correo electrónico. En todas las ciudades del mundo hay cibercafés desde donde podemos comunicarnos instantáneamente con los familiares y amigos. Sin embargo, aún existen lugares turísticos donde venden postales para enviar por correo normal, pero esto está desapareciendo cada vez más.

Compara: ¿Cómo prefieres comunicarte con tus amigos cuando estás de vacaciones? ¿Y con tu familia? ¿Hay cibercafés en tu comunidad? Explica cuántos hay y cómo son.

12-6 👥

Un correo electrónico. Estás en Panamá y envías un correo electrónico a tu compañero/a. Cuéntale algunos aspectos especiales de tus experiencias. Después, reacciona al correo electrónico de tu compañero/a y hazle preguntas para obtener más detalles.

1. lugar(es) que visitaste
2. lugar donde te quedaste y el tipo de alojamiento
3. personas que conociste
4. experiencias divertidas que viviste
5. comida nueva que probaste
6. regalos que compraste

Viajando en coche

Go to the *Capítulo 12* **folder** online to complete the Learning Module for *Vocabulario en contexto: Viajando en coche.*

PLAN DE ESTUDIO

◎ **LEARN**
- Interactive presentation: *Viajando en coche*
- Vocabulary tutorials
- *Entrevistas* video

APPLY ◎
- Activities
- *Entrevistas* video activities

PRÁCTICA COMUNICATIVA

12-7

¿Qué es? Digan la palabra que corresponde a las siguientes descripciones. Después, den una descripción de otras partes del coche para ver si otra pareja sabe cómo se llama cada una.

1. Es para poner el equipaje.   el maletero

2. Permite ver bien cuando llueve.   el limpiaparabrisas

3. Son negras y llevan aire por dentro.   las llantas

4. Controla la dirección del coche.   el volante

5. Tiene letras y números, y sirve para identificar el coche.   la placa

6. Le permite al conductor ver los carros que vienen detrás.   el espejo retrovisor

---

12-8

Mi auto favorito. Averigüen qué medio de transporte usa cada uno/a de ustedes con más frecuencia. Después, pregúntense cuál es el auto favorito de cada uno/a y por qué. Cada persona debe dar cuatro razones para explicar su preferencia.

Suggestion for 12-9
This is a good opportunity to review the use of the subjunctive when giving advice (*Capítulo 11*). You may wish to do a quick review of the forms.

12-9

Para evitar accidentes. Escriban un anuncio con recomendaciones para evitar accidentes de tráfico. El anuncio debe tener la siguiente información:

1. un título o eslogan

2. el nombre de la compañía o grupo que patrocina (*sponsors*) el anuncio

3. tres recomendaciones para evitar accidentes

Cultura

Aunque en los países hispanoamericanos se usa mucho el transporte público, el tráfico y la contaminación son problemas serios en las ciudades grandes. Además, cada vez es más difícil encontrar estacionamiento. Por eso se usan mucho las motos y los carros pequeños.

Compara: ¿Qué modos de transporte hay en tu comunidad? ¿Cuáles son más populares entre los jóvenes? ¿Cuáles son más populares entre los mayores? ¿Qué problemas se asocian con el transporte en tu comunidad y tu región?

Warm-up for 12-10
As a pre-listening activity, have students in groups of 4 discuss whether they have traveled abroad and where, what documents they had to get before they traveled, and what problems they had to deal with.

12-10

Antes de viajar.

PRIMERA FASE. You will listen to a man who is checking in at the airport. Before you listen, list two questions you think the airline employee will ask him and the answers that you think the man will provide. Compare your answers with your partner.

SEGUNDA FASE. Now listen to the exchange, and choose the appropriate ending to each statement.

1. El empleado le pide al viajero…
   a. su boleto de ida y vuelta.
   b. su tarjeta de embarque.
   c. su pasaporte y su pasaje.

2. El viajero va a facturar…
   a. tres maletas.
   b. un maletín de mano.
   c. dos maletas.

3. El viajero prefiere un asiento…
   a. al lado de la ventanilla.
   b. en el pasillo.
   c. en la parte posterior del avión.

4. El empleado le puede conseguir un asiento…
   a. de pasillo, el 28C.
   b. en el centro, entre la ventanilla y el pasillo.
   c. en la ventanilla en primera clase.

5. El empleado le dice al pasajero que…
   a. tiene tiempo para llamar por teléfono.
   b. puede llamar desde el avión.
   c. no tiene que pasar por seguridad.

Audioscript for 12-10
Agente: *Buenas tardes, señor. Su pasaje y pasaporte, por favor.*
Viajero: *Buenas tardes. Aquí están.*
Agente: *Muy bien. ¿Cuántas maletas va a facturar?*
Viajero: *Dos. Llevo también un maletín de mano, pero no lo voy a facturar.*
Agente: *Muy bien. Ponga las maletas aquí, por favor. Ahora dígame, ¿prefiere ventanilla, pasillo o en el centro?*
Viajero: *En el pasillo, por favor. Y quisiera uno de los primeros asientos.*
Agente: *Lo siento, pero solo quedan asientos después de la fila 27. Le puedo dar el 28 C.*
Viajero: *Bueno, está bien.*
Agente: *La puerta de salida es la número 8. Aquí tiene su pasaporte y tarjeta de embarque. Ahora, pase por seguridad y luego diríjase a la puerta de salida.*
Viajero: *Gracias, señor. ¿Tengo tiempo para hacer una llamada?*
Agente: *Sí, el avión sale en 45 minutos. No se preocupe. Que tenga un buen viaje.*

Gramática en contexto

Talking about possession, affirmation and negation, and uncertainty

Expressing possession:
Possessive pronouns

Go to the *Capítulo 12* [folder] online to complete the Learning Module for *Gramática en contexto*: Possessive pronouns.

PLAN DE ESTUDIO

◎ LEARN
- Interactive presentation: Possessive pronouns
- Grammar tutorials

APPLY ◎
- Activities
- Extra Practice

PRÁCTICA COMUNICATIVA

12-11

¿De quién(es) son estas cosas? PRIMERA FASE. En la clase de español decidieron hacer un viaje de estudios a Costa Rica. En este momento van a tomar el bus para ir al aeropuerto. Escoge la respuesta correcta para cada una de las preguntas. Compara tus respuestas con las de tu compañero/a.

1. Miguel, ¿es tuya esta mochila?
   - **a.** Sí, es mía.
   - **b.** Sí, es tuya.

2. ¿Son estas maletas de Pedro?
   - **a.** Sí, son suyas.
   - **b.** Sí, son mías.

3. ¿El maletín de color café es de Alicia?
   - **a.** No, es tuya.
   - **b.** No, no es suyo.

4. Este mapa de San José, ¿es tuyo?
   - **a.** Sí, es mía.
   - **b.** Sí, es mío.

5. ¿Son nuestros estos boletos?
   - **a.** Sí, son suyos.
   - **b.** Sí, son suyas.

SEGUNDA FASE. Ve por la clase y pregunta a varios compañeros/as de quién son algunos de los objetos que ves o encuentras.

¿Quién tiene carro?

PRIMERA FASE. Entrevístense para saber quién(es) tiene(n) carro. Hablen de sus carros: marca, modelo, año y color. Tomen apuntes sobre la información.

Modelo

> Mi carro es un Toyota Corolla de 2009. ¿Y el tuyo?

> El mío es un Ford Taurus de 2012.

> Yo no tengo carro, pero uso el de mi hermana.

 SEGUNDA FASE. Combinen la información de todos los grupos y preparen un informe sobre las características más comunes de los carros de los miembros de la clase.

Suggestion for 12-12
Primera fase
You may create a category of cars owned by friends or family members so that students who do not have their own vehicles may talk about them.

12-13

Preparándose para un viaje. Van a hacer un viaje en auto y deben tomar varias decisiones antes de salir. Háganse preguntas para decidir lo que van a hacer y den una razón.

Modelo **" usar mi coche o tu coche "**

> ¿Vamos a usar mi coche o el tuyo?

> Prefiero usar el tuyo porque es más nuevo.

1. llevar tus maletas o las de mi hermano
2. usar mis mapas o tus mapas
3. llevar tu cámara o mi cámara
4. llevar tu portátil o mi portátil
5. usar tu GPS o el de mis padres

Note for 12-13
GPS in Spanish is *Sistema de Posicionamiento Global*. However, people commonly call it GPS [ge-pe-ese].

Recuerdo de vacaciones.
Túrnense para hablar de sus vacaciones favoritas. Busquen aspectos similares y diferentes entre sus experiencias.

1. adónde fueron y con quiénes
2. cómo viajaron al lugar
3. el alojamiento
4. la comida
5. sus diversiones
6. sus actividades culturales

12-15

Objetos perdidos. Durante un viaje en avión tu amigo/a y tú perdieron sus maletas. Vayan a la oficina de reclamaciones y explíquenle a un agente cómo son sus maletas.

Modelo

Mi maleta y la de mi amigo no llegaron.

La mía es...

Sí, la suya es... pero la mía...

Tech tip for *Situaciones*
For the second *Situación*, students may need to prepare ahead of time so they can talk about their ecotourism activities in Costa Rica. They may want to practice online with a partner. Remind them that they can click on the microphone icon to connect with a partner online and do the activity.

Situaciones

1

ROLE A. Yesterday, you lost your wallet (color, size, contents) at a hotel in Panama City. Answer the questions of the employee at the Lost and Found desk. Then show him/her an identification document and thank him/her.

ROLE B. You are a hotel employee who is helping a guest who has lost a wallet. Find out a) the person's name; b) a description of the wallet and its contents; and c) when he/she lost it. Ask for identification to verify ownership, and then return the wallet.

2

ROLE A. On the plane home from an ecotourism trip to Costa Rica, you sit next to a student returning from a similar trip. Ask your seatmate a) why he/she went on an ecotourism trip; b) what national park he/she liked best, and why; c) one thing he/she learned from the trip; and d) whether he/she has plans to return to Costa Rica. Answer your seatmate's questions about your trip.

ROLE B. On the plane home from an ecotourism trip to Costa Rica, you sit next to a student returning from a similar trip. After answering your seatmate's questions, ask him/her similar questions about his/her trip. Comment on how your experience was similar to that of your seatmate.

Expressing affirmation and negation:
Affirmative and negative expressions

Go to the *Capítulo 12* **folder** online to complete the Learning Module for *Gramática en contexto:* Affirmative and negative expressions.

PLAN DE ESTUDIO

◎ **LEARN**
- Interactive presentation: Affirmative and negative expressions
- Grammar tutorials

◎ **APPLY**
- Activities
- Extra Practice

Online prep for students
Students will have completed the Learning Module for Affirmative and negative expressions online. Additional in-class activities are available for download in the Supplementary Activities folder.

Note
Explain that *nunca* and *jamás* may be used interchangeably, although *jamás* is more emphatic. For dramatic emphasis, you may wish to use them together: *Nunca jamás me va a gustar el arte abstracto.*

PRÁCTICA COMUNICATIVA

 12-16

Nada de nada. Asocia cada pregunta con su probable respuesta. Luego, comparen sus respuestas y añadan una pregunta más para hacerle a su compañero/a.

1. ¿Visitaste Panamá alguna vez? e
2. ¿Conoces a alguien en Costa Rica? d
3. ¿Bailas alguno de los bailes típicos de la región? b
4. ¿Sabe alguien quién escribió la novela *Pasiones griegas*? c
5. ¿Conoces alguna canción de Maribel Guardia? a
6. . . .

a. No, ninguna.
b. No, ninguno.
c. Nadie lo sabe.
d. No, a nadie.
e. No, nunca.

Note for 12-16
The author of *Pasiones griegas* is Roberto Ampuero, a Chilean writer based in the U.S. In January 2012 he was appointed the Chilean ambassador to Mexico, and he currently resides in Mexico City.

Follow-up for 12-17
Have students change partners and share the information they have just gathered with the new partner.

¿Con qué frecuencia?

Indica con qué frecuencia participas en cada una de las actividades de la tabla siguiente y di por qué las haces. Después pregúntale a tu compañero/a.

Modelo

66 ver una película en español 99

Veo una película en español todas las semanas porque me gusta escuchar la lengua. ¿Y tú?

Yo nunca veo películas en español porque no me gustan los subtítulos.

ACTIVIDAD	YO	RAZÓN	MI COMPAÑERO/A	RAZÓN
viajar a otro país				
visitar museos				
leer libros de historia				
comprar pasajes de avión en Internet				
usar transporte público				
ir a restaurantes mexicanos				
ver películas extranjeras				

12-18

Una excursión de ecoturismo.
Estás en Costa Rica y vas a hacer una excursión de ecoturismo. Tu compañero/a ya hizo la excursión y piensa que fue un desastre. Él/Ella va a contestar tus preguntas negativamente. Añade una pregunta más.

1. ver tortugas en la playa
2. ver las vistas panorámicas
3. comer un almuerzo típico costarricense
4. dejar entrar a muchas áreas protegidas
5. ...

Modelo

❝ofrecer excursiones❞

¿Ofrecieron excursiones sobre la fauna y la flora?

No, no ofrecieron ninguna excursión.

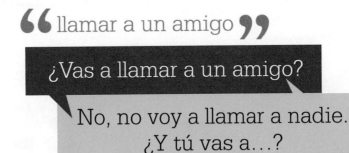

12-19

¡La negatividad es contagiosa!
Después de pasar tus vacaciones con tu amigo negativo/amiga negativa, te sientes influenciado/a y contestas a todo negativamente. Túrnense para preguntarse y añadan alguna actividad más.

Modelo

❝llamar a un amigo❞

¿Vas a llamar a un amigo?

No, no voy a llamar a nadie.
¿Y tú vas a...?

1. visitar Panamá alguna vez en el futuro
2. ver alguna película latinoamericana este fin de semana
3. leer un artículo sobre los siete pueblos indígenas de Panamá
4. invitar a alguien a ver un documental sobre los parques nacionales de Costa Rica
5. ...

Warm-up for 12-18
In this activity, since the partner's visit to the museum already took place, students should use the preterit in their questions and responses. Call attention to the verb forms in the *modelo* and ask some additional questions before students do the activity in pairs. Point out that some questions ask about the partner's experience and others inquire about museum policies.

Suggestion for 12-18
You may wish to have students change roles (asker or responder) midway through the activity or change partners, each time taking a different role.

Warm-up for 12-20
Have students tell you what they want to do: *Quiero aprender unas frases en la lengua kuna.* You agree: *Yo también.* Then have students tell you what they do not want to do: *No quiero ir a la ópera…* You agree: *Yo tampoco.*

Suggestion for 12-20
You may wish to highlight the cultural information in this activity by referring students to the photos in the chapter opener and the *Enfoque cultural* section of this chapter. You may want to explain that *cumbia* is a popular dance style that began as a courtship dance among African slaves on the Caribbean coast of what is now Colombia, and spread throughout South and Central America, mixing African percussion, indigenous Amerindian flutes, and later, European brass and orchestral instruments. Culturally, *cumbia* is most associated with Colombia. Encourage students to search the Internet for videos of *cumbia* music and dancing.

Suggestion for 12-20
Segunda fase
Have students brainstorm ways to respond negatively to others' plans: *Nunca voy a los parques nacionales. No me gusta caminar mucho. No he ido jamás a ningún partido de fútbol.*

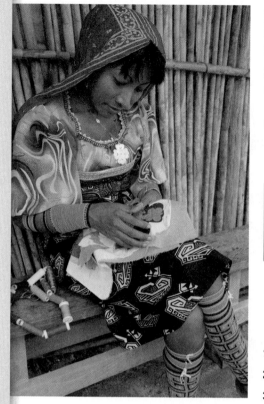

 12-20

Planeando un viaje.

PRIMERA FASE. Quieren hacer un viaje a Panamá para conocer su cultura. Comenten qué van a hacer allí.

Modelo

66 pasar unos días en la capital 99

Quiero pasar unos días en la capital.

Yo también. Es una ciudad interesante.

1. hacer una excursión al canal de Panamá
2. tomar una clase de cumbia, un baile folclórico
3. conocer las comunidades indígenas
4. comprar unos textiles de mola, hechos por artesanos indígenas kuna
5. asistir a un partido de fútbol
6. comer unas empanadas

 SEGUNDA FASE. Conversen sobre dos o tres actividades que quieren hacer en Panamá. Después, reúnanse con otra pareja, explíquenle sus planes y escuchen los planes de sus compañeros/as. Respondan negativamente a los planes de la otra pareja.

1

ROLE A. You are a flight attendant on a flight to Panama City. Ask a passenger if he/she would like to watch the movie. Then respond to his/her complaints and requests by saying that a) there are no blankets but you can bring a pillow; b) there are no magazines in Spanish; and c) they do not have iced coffee because nobody ever asks for it.

ROLE B. You are a passenger on a flight to Panama City. Tell the flight attendant that you can never sleep on planes. Ask if you can have a magazine in Spanish and some iced coffee. It's a long flight, and you are in a bad mood, so respond negatively to whatever the flight attendant says.

2

ROLE A. You call a tourism agency to purchase tickets for an excursion. When the clerk answers, ask a) if sometimes they offer free tickets for students; b) if they have any tickets for Friday or Saturday; and c) whether lunch at a restaurant is included in the price. You may express your annoyance at all the negative answers you receive when you thank the clerk for his/her help.

ROLE B. You work for a tourism agency. A customer calls to ask about tickets for an excursion. Reply that a) they never give free tickets to anyone (not students, not young children); b) there aren't any tickets for the days the customer inquires about; and c) there will be two breaks for snacks (*merienda*), but not a restaurant meal. You are in a bad mood and you let it show during the conversation.

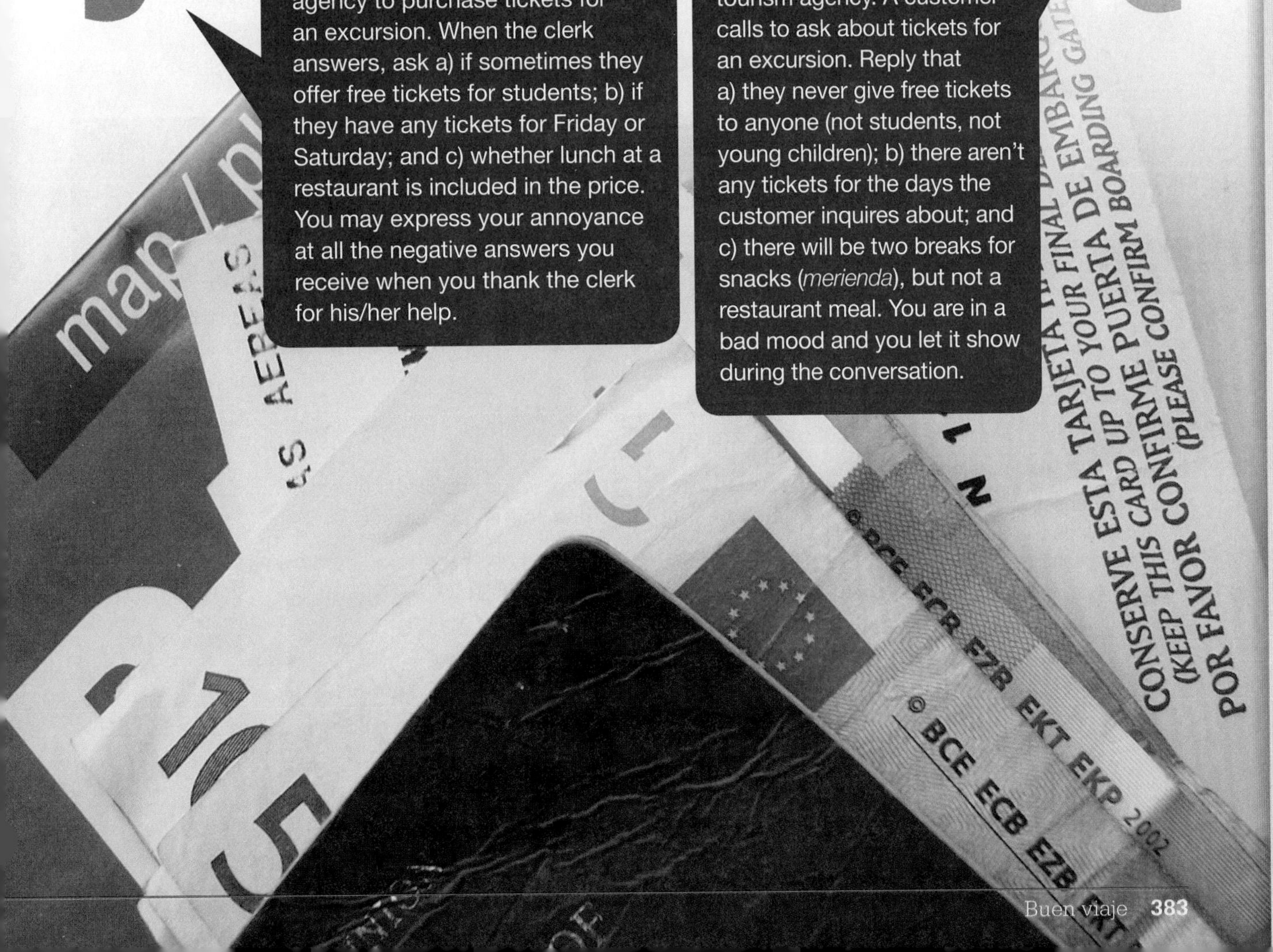

Expressing doubt and uncertainty:
Subjunctive with expressions of doubt

Go to the *Capítulo 12* [folder] online to complete the Learning Module for *Gramática en contexto*: Subjunctive with expressions of doubt.

PLAN DE ESTUDIO

◎ LEARN
- Interactive presentation: Subjunctive with expressions of doubt
- Grammar tutorials

APPLY ◎
- Activities
- Extra Practice

PRÁCTICA COMUNICATIVA

En directo

To report agreement:

Todos creemos/pensamos que…

Nosotros estamos de acuerdo con que…

To report different opinions:

No hay consenso entre nosotros/ellos. Unos piensan que…, otros creen que…

 Click on the icon to listen to a conversation with these expressions.

¿Están de acuerdo?

Lee las siguientes opiniones y marca (✔) si estás de acuerdo o no. Luego, compara tus respuestas con las de tu compañero/a. Explíquense las razones de sus respuestas.

	sí	no
1. Yo creo que los bailes folclóricos son fáciles de aprender.	___	___
2. Yo dudo que el fútbol sea más popular en Estados Unidos que en América Latina.	___	___
3. Creo que los parques nacionales de Costa Rica son muy importantes para la ecología del planeta.	___	___
4. Es posible que viajar en tren sea más costoso que viajar en avión.	___	___
5. Es obvio que el precio de la gasolina en Estados Unidos afecta el turismo.	___	___
6. No creo que los estudiantes hoy viajen a otros países tanto como viajaban los estudiantes hace veinte años.	___	___

12-22

Opiniones. Intercambia opiniones sobre los siguientes temas con tu compañero/a. Después, comparen sus opiniones con las de otros compañeros/otras compañeras y compartan sus conclusiones con la clase.

1. los cruceros

2. ir de camping con la familia

3. los bailes folclóricos

4. ver exposiciones de arte

Modelo

❝ el ecoturismo ❞

> Creo que el ecoturismo es aburrido. Prefiero disfrutar de la vida de noche en las ciudades grandes. Y tú, ¿qué opinas?

> Dudo que las grandes ciudades representen lo mejor de un país. Yo prefiero conocer la diversidad de la naturaleza.

12-23

Un viaje.

PRIMERA FASE. Ustedes ganaron un concurso y su premio es un viaje de una semana a cualquier ciudad del mundo hispano. Escojan una ciudad y hagan una lista de tres cosas que posiblemente ocurran durante la semana y tres cosas que dudan que pasen. Expliquen por qué.

Modelo ❝ Puntarenas, Costa Rica ❞

> Esperamos que algún [costarricense] nos invite a un club porque nos gusta mucho bailar. También es posible que vayamos de excursión al volcán Arenal porque dicen que es muy impresionante.

> Dudamos que llueva, porque hace buen tiempo casi todo el año. No es probable que volvamos otra vez; por eso queremos hacer muchas actividades.

 SEGUNDA FASE. Reúnanse con otra pareja y explíquenle qué ciudad escogieron y por qué. Infórmenle sobre sus expectativas y dudas con respecto a su viaje. Comenten si están de acuerdo con lo que dicen sus compañeros/as.

Suggestion for 12-23
You may wish to assign pairs of students ahead of time, and have them select their city and research their lists of 3 things that will probably happen and 3 things that they doubt will happen.

1

ROLE A. You are showing a friend how to play the game "Two Truths and a Lie" (**"Dos verdades y una mentira"**). State three pieces of information about yourself, two of which are true and one which is not. Comment on your friend's responses. Then change roles and play the game again.

ROLE B. A friend is showing you how to play the game "Two Truths and a Lie" (**"Dos verdades y una mentira"**). Your friend will tell you three pieces of personal information, two of which are true and one that is not. Say which statement you think is true, which is possibly true, and which you doubt is true. Then change roles and play the game again.

2

ROLE A. A friend borrowed your car and brought it back a whole day later than the two of you had agreed, which caused you a lot of inconvenience. Ask your friend for an explanation. Express doubt about at least three reasons your friend gives you. To avoid ongoing conflict with your friend, make sure the situation is resolved.

ROLE B. You borrowed a friend's car, and you brought it back a whole day later than the two of you had agreed, which caused your friend a lot of inconvenience. Now you have to explain yourself. You don't want to tell the real reason, so you make up a detailed story of what happened. Your friend is skeptical, so you have to try hard to be convincing. To avoid ongoing conflict with your friend, make sure the situation is resolved.

Talking about the past:
Review of the preterit and imperfect

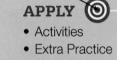

Go to the *Capítulo 12* **folder** online to complete the Learning Module for *Gramática en contexto:* Review of the preterit and imperfect.

PLAN DE ESTUDIO

◎ LEARN
- Interactive presentation: Review of the preterit and imperfect
- Grammar tutorials

APPLY ◎
- Activities
- Extra Practice

Online prep for students
Students will have completed the Learning Module for Review of the preterit and imperfect online. Additional in-class activities are available for download in the Supplementary Activities folder online.

Suggestion
The preterit is presented in *Capítulos 6* and *7,* the imperfect in *Capítulo 8,* and the preterit and imperfect together in *Capítulos 8* and *9.* You may wish to go back to some of the activities that have students use preterit and imperfect together, and have students self-assess their understanding of the differences in their meaning and communicative function in the context of storytelling.

PRÁCTICA COMUNICATIVA

Una erupción del Volcán Arenal, Costa Rica

12-24 👥

Un viaje accidentado. **PRIMERA FASE.** Unos turistas hicieron un viaje al Volcán Arenal. Mientras viajaban, el volcán comenzó a erupcionar. Un turista cuenta la historia. Indica si las siguientes afirmaciones narran los eventos (**E**) o si describen (**D**) el lugar y los personajes. Luego, compara tus respuestas con las de tu compañero/a.

Al acercarnos al área del Volcán Arenal, **nos dimos cuenta** (E) de que todos **miraban** (D) desde la distancia el humo y la lava que **salían** (D) del volcán. El guía turístico nos **indicó** (E) qué hacer. Todos **sabíamos** (D) que acercarnos al volcán no **era** (D) prudente. Después de treinta minutos **llegaron** (E) dos helicópteros y nos **llevaron** (E) a un lugar seguro. Todos **estábamos** (D) aliviados (*relieved*) de estar fuera de peligro. Esa noche, les **contamos** (E) la historia de nuestro escape del volcán a los otros huéspedes del hotel. Después, yo no **podía** (D) dormir. Finalmente **me dormí** (E) , y **me desperté** (E) al día siguiente con ganas de continuar la excursión.

SEGUNDA FASE. Cuéntale a tu compañero/a algún viaje accidentado que hiciste. ¿Qué te pasó? ¿Dónde fue? ¿Cómo ocurrió?

Note for 12-24
The Arenal Volcano, one of the world's 10 most active volcanos, erupted in 1968 after being dormant for more than 400 years, killing 78 people. Since then it has remained constantly active, emitting columns of ash and steam almost every day, as well as occasional explosions and lava flows.

Nuestro viaje a Panamá.

Ustedes viajaron a Panamá durante sus vacaciones y sacaron algunas fotos. Seleccionen una de ellas y presenten un informe breve a la clase. Incluyan la siguiente información. Vayan a Internet si necesitan información sobre este lugar.

1. qué muestra la foto y dónde se encuentra

2. dos o tres actividades que hicieron en este lugar

3. cómo se relaciona la imagen con la cultura panameña

Playa Boca del Toro

Un barco de crucero pasa por las esclusas (*locks*) del Canal de Panamá

Un mercado de Ciudad de Panamá en donde se vende artesanía

Palacio Presidencial
Ciudad de Panamá

Cultura

La construcción del Canal de Panamá, que une el océano Atlántico con el océano Pacífico, hizo realidad un sueño de más de tres siglos. Requirió la participación de varios países y es una de las iniciativas internacionales que más positivamente ha influido en la economía mundial. El Canal de Panamá se inauguró en 1914 y tiene 71 kilómetros de largo.

Compara: ¿Hay un puente, un canal, una carretera, un peaje (*tollbooth*) u otro conector geográfico importante en tu región? ¿Qué impacto tiene en las personas y la industria? ¿Se parece el impacto al que tuvo el Canal de Panamá en en ese país?

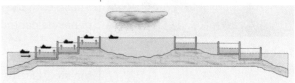

12-26

Un viaje inolvidable.

PRIMERA FASE. Piensa en un viaje emocionante que hiciste en el pasado. Habla con tu compañero/a sobre el viaje e incluye la siguiente información.

1. lo que sabías acerca del lugar antes de visitarlo

2. algo nuevo que descubriste después de llegar

3. lo que esperabas hacer allí

4. dos actividades que hiciste y dos actividades que no hiciste

5. lo que más recuerdas del viaje

 SEGUNDA FASE. Determinen cuál de los dos viajes es el más interesante y por qué. Compártanlo con la clase.

Situaciones

Preparation for *Situación 1*
You may wish to have students do some research on San Blas and the Kuna people.

1

ROLE A. You and a friend just started your trip to the San Blas Islands in Panama, the home of the Kuna people. Call your roommate to say that a) your plane left your city on time; b) the weather between your city and the city where you will take the connecting flight (**vuelo de conexión**) was very bad, so the airline cancelled your flight; and c) you and your friend are at the airport waiting. Finally, d) promise that you will call again soon.

ROLE B. Your roommate and a friend just left for a trip to Panama. After a few hours, your roommate calls you with some bad news. React appropriately and ask pertinent questions. Ask him/her to call you again soon. Wish them a good trip.

2

ROLE A. You just won a trip to the Spanish-speaking country of your choice. Call a friend who has traveled a lot and a) tell him/her the news; b) ask for suggestions about where to go; c) mention how much money you received to spend in the country (**dinero para llevar**); and d) invite her/him to go with you.

ROLE B. Your friend calls with some good news. React appropriately and a) answer his/her questions; b) offer ideas about where to go; and c) accept his/her invitation.

Unidos

ESCUCHA

 12-27  Presentational

Preparación.

Vas a escuchar una conversación telefónica entre una agente de viajes y el Sr. Hernández, quien busca un hotel para él y su familia en San José. Antes de escuchar, escribe tres características que el Sr. Hernández probablemente desea que tenga el hotel y tres preguntas que probablemente le hará la agente. Compártelas con la clase.

12-28 Interpretive

Escucha. As you listen to the conversation between Sr. Hernández and the travel agent, check (✓) the statements that best report what was said.

1. _____ El Sr. Hernández dice que quiere un hotel económico que esté cerca del centro de la ciudad.

2. __✓__ La agente tiene varias posibilidades y le describe tres hoteles para que escoja.

3. __✓__ El Sr. Hernández afirma que prefiere que sus hijos y esposa estén cómodos aunque (*even though*) él tenga que tomar un taxi o manejar mucho.

4. _____ La agente le dice al cliente que su elección no es buena porque el hotel es muy caro y está muy lejos del centro de la ciudad.

12-29  Interpersonal

Un paso más. Háganse las siguientes preguntas.

1. Cuando buscas un hotel, ¿es más importante que sea económico o que sea de lujo (*luxurious*)?

2. ¿Qué servicios o comodidades prefieres que ofrezca un hotel?

3. ¿Cuál es el hotel más cómodo en el que has estado? Explica.

ESTRATEGIA

Use background knowledge to support comprehension

When you listen to a conversation or lecture in Spanish, your personal experience may lead you to expect certain content. To support your comprehension, do the following:

Before you listen...

- brainstorm a list of ideas you expect to hear about the topic.
- read about the topic on the Internet if you are not familiar with it.

As you listen...

- use your prior knowledge to help you understand. For example, when you hear numbers announced at an airport, they probably refer to flight or gate numbers.

Comprueba

I was able to...

_____ **understand the main points of the conversation.**

_____ **use experience and logic to confirm what I understood.**

Habitación doble en el Hotel Grano de Oro, San José, Costa Rica

AUTOEVALUACIÓN

☐ I feel confident that I was able to understand what I heard.

☐ I need more listening practice.

STUDY PLAN

▶ Good job! Move on to the next section, *Habla.*

▶ Go to the *Unidos* [folder] online for *Escucha* practice.

HABLA

12-30 [Interpretive]

Preparación. PRIMERA FASE. Cuando alguien vuelve a casa después de un viaje, sus amigos siempre le dicen: "Cuéntanos de tu viaje. ¿Te pasó algo interesante?" Piensa en tus viajes y elige una experiencia para contarle a tu compañero/a. Usa la tabla siguiente y organiza tus ideas. Puedes usar uno de estos temas.

- perderse en un lugar desconocido
- un artículo perdido
- un error lingüístico o cultural
- un robo
- una situación embarazosa o peligrosa (*dangerous*)
- ponerse enfermo

EVENTOS	DESCRIPCIÓN (Dónde, cuándo, con quiénes y otros detalles)	PARTES IMPORTANTES
1.		
2.		
3.		

12-31 [Interpersonal]

Habla. Usa la tabla anterior y cuéntale tu historia a tu compañero/a. Usa las expresiones de *En directo* para llamar la atención a las partes más importantes de tu historia. Tu compañero/a debe hacerte preguntas.

Comprueba

In my conversation…

_____ I effectively used expressions to spark my listeners' curiosity about what happened next.

_____ I successfully used expressions to relay my emotions during key parts of the story.

_____ I have successfully answered my classmate's questions.

12-32 [Presentational]

Un paso más. Escribe un breve párrafo resumiendo la historia de tu compañero/a. Incluye lo que pasó, dónde y cuándo ocurrieron los eventos, qué sintió el/la narrador/a durante los eventos.

AUTOEVALUACIÓN

☐ I feel confident that I communicated successfully.

☐ I need more speaking practice.

STUDY PLAN

▶ Good job! Move on to the next section, *Lee.*

▶ Go to the *Unidos* [folder] online for *Habla* practice.

ESTRATEGIA

Engage and maintain the interest of your listeners

Conversations among friends often include stories about interesting or unusual experiences or events. When you tell a story, you can keep your listeners engaged in what you are saying by inserting remarks about moments in the story that are particulary funny, surprising, or frightening. These remarks are your way of drawing the attention of your listeners to the main points of your story.

En directo

To draw a listener's attention to the next part of your story:

¿Sabes lo que pasó después?

¡No lo vas a creer!

No puedes imaginar lo que me pasó.

To express emotions about moments in your story:

¡Y esto me sorprendió mucho!
And this surprised me very much!

¡Estaba tan asustado/a!
I was so scared!

Por poco me muero de la risa/ del susto.
I almost died laughing./I almost died, it was so scary.

🔊 Click on the icon to listen to a conversation with these expressions.

Suggestion for *Estrategia*
You may wish to explain that stories about personal experiences are made up of 3 elements: facts about what happened (usually recounted using the preterit); descriptive background information about the setting, the people, etc. (usually told using the imperfect); and evaluation, which consists of comments on the parts of the story that the narrator wants listeners to pay attention to.

Suggestion for 12-31
Have students work in groups of 3 so that each person will have enough time to tell his/ her story. To maximize the oral storytelling focus of the activity, you may wish to limit students to the notes they wrote in *Preparación*.

Audioscript for *En directo*
Frank: *Hola, Jenny. ¿Qué tal? Me contó Lexi que te fue horrible ayer en el aeropuerto.*
Jenny: *¡Fue una pesadilla! Primero, cuando traté de facturar el equipaje, no me dejaron. Aunque iba con prisa, me pararon para revisar mi maleta. Luego confiscaron mi perfume preferido porque el frasco era muy grande. ¡Me va a costar mucho dinero comprar uno nuevo!*
Frank: *Ay, qué lástima, Jenny.*
Jenny: *Y ¿sabes lo que pasó después? ¡No lo vas a creer!*
Frank: *¡¿Qué?!*
Jenny: *Mientras revisaban mi equipaje, el pasajero que estaba detrás de mí se puso a saltar y gritar como un loco, diciendo que estaba cansado de hacer cola. ¡Estaba tan asustada!*
Frank: *No lo creo.*
Jenny: *¡Pues créelo! Rápido llegó la policía y se lo llevaron. ¡Por poco me muero del susto!*

Follow-up for 12-32
You may wish to have students write their stories after telling them orally and receiving feedback from the members of their group.

LEE

12-33  Interpersonal

Preparación.

Hablen entre ustedes de lo siguiente.

1. ¿Prefieren los viajes en avión o por tierra? ¿Por qué?

2. ¿Les gusta organizar su propios viajes o prefieren una agencia? ¿Por qué?

3. ¿Qué problema serio ha tenido cada uno/a de ustedes en un viaje?

4. ¿Han tenido problemas semejantes o diferentes?

ESTRATEGIA

12-34 Interpretive

Lee. PRIMERA FASE. Marca (✓) los problemas que enfrentan los viajeros, según el artículo de la página siguiente.

1. ___✓___ agencias de viajes deshonestas

2. ___✓___ maletas perdidas

3. ___✓___ vuelos cancelados

4. _____ choques de avión

5. ___✓___ robo de las tarjetas de crédito

6. _____ autos alquilados que no funcionan

7. ___✓___ problemas para entrar en otro país

8. _____ enfermedades causadas por la comida

SEGUNDA FASE. Busca en el artículo la siguiente información.

1. Tres problemas que tuvieron Isabel y Mario en sus vacaciones

2. La causa principal de la situación desagradable de Isabel y Mario

3. Recomendaciones para evitar o minimizar problemas

Comprueba

I was able to…

_____ **identify the problems described by the authors.**

_____ **focus on the relationship between different parts of the content to discover key problems, their causes and their possible solutions.**

Vacaciones o pesadilla[1]

Cómo reducir los problemas en los viajes

Isabel y Mario, una pareja norteamericana de origen uruguayo, decidieron celebrar su aniversario de boda en Costa Rica. Para preparar el viaje se pusieron en contacto por Internet con la agencia Viajes Reales. La agencia ofrecía paquetes de excursiones que incluían billete de avión, hotel y coche de alquiler por precios bastante baratos. Las fotos prometían una estancia relajada en un hotel de ambiente exótico al noroeste del país. La variedad de piscinas, la cercanía del mar, la apetecible gastronomía local y los cócteles refrescantes que se veían en lujosas mesitas junto a las hamacas de los afortunados clientes confirmaban que se trataba de un verdadero paraíso.

Isabel y Mario pagaron la cantidad requerida y no dudaron ni un momento de su decisión. Pero al llegar a su destino comprobaron que las fotos no correspondían a la realidad. El hotel no tenía ni vista al mar ni jardines exóticos. Las habitaciones eran pequeñísimas e incómodas y la comida dejaba mucho que desear.

Lamentablemente, esta no es una anécdota aislada entre los viajeros. ¿Quién no ha sufrido alguna vez la pérdida de su equipaje, las incomodidades de un vuelo cancelado, el robo de su pasaporte o sus tarjetas de crédito, los problemas en la aduana por comprar un producto comestible que no se permite pasar?

Sin embargo, algunos de estos problemas se pueden prevenir. La experiencia de los viajes nos enseña a ser prudentes y prever los riesgos. La facilidad que proporciona Internet es conveniente, pero cuando se viaja por primera vez es preferible dirigirse a una agencia local para que los especialistas de viajes nos ayuden a elegir las mejores opciones. Frecuentemente es más caro hacerlo así, pero se puede ahorrar tiempo y evitar sorpresas desagradables. Por otra parte, a veces resulta más barato comprar un seguro de cancelación que arriesgarse a perder, por una razón u otra, el costo de un billete de avión.

Algunos incidentes son naturalmente inevitables, pero otros se pueden prevenir. Por ejemplo, es posible minimizar el riesgo de un robo llevando los pasaportes y papeles importantes en una bolsita colgada del cuello que se oculta debajo de la ropa, o en un bolsillo doble del pantalón. En cuanto a los impedimentos en la aduana, hay que tener en cuenta que las medidas de seguridad son cada vez más estrictas. Ya no se puede subir al avión con líquidos de más de tres onzas y solo se permite viajar con las bebidas y comestibles comprados en las tiendas del aeropuerto.

Por suerte, las vacaciones de Mario e Isabel no fueron un desastre total. La pareja pudo disfrutar del maravilloso país en sus excursiones a Puntarenas, Puerto Limón y los parques naturales cercanos a Orosí. También pudieron celebrar su aniversario en un magnífico restaurante. ¡Qué lástima que la experiencia completa no fuera tan agradable! Como dice un conocido refrán[2]: Más vale prevenir... que lamentar.

[1]*nightmare*   [2]*proverb*

12-35   Presentational

Un paso más.

¿Qué palabras y frases del artículo están asociadas con las siguientes situaciones? Escribe un resumen breve que incorpore tus respuestas a las preguntas.

1. Una agencia quiere hacer publicidad para atraer clientes.

2. Los problemas que tienen algunas personas durante un viaje:
   a. la pérdida de su equipaje
   b. un vuelo cancelado
   c. encuentros con la policía de aduana o seguridad en los aeropuertos

3. Presentar el tema del artículo por medio de un refrán.

AUTOEVALUACIÓN

- ☐ I feel confident I understood the reading and was able to use the information.

- ☐ I need more reading practice.

STUDY PLAN

▶ Good job! Move on to the next section, *Escribe.*

▶ Go to the *Unidos* [folder] online for *Lee* practice.

Suggestion for 12-35
You may wish to bring magazine ads to class so students can identify words and phrases that are intended to highlight problems and solutions. For question 3, you may wish to have students explain the proverb and apply it to situations other than the one presented in the article.

Answers to 12-35
1. *estancia relajada; ambiente exótico; variedad de piscinas; cercanía del mar; apetecible gastronomía local; cócteles refrescantes; lujosas mesitas, paraíso.* 2. a. *han sufrido;* b. *las incomodidades;* c. *los impedimentos (aduana), estrictas (medidas de seguridad).* 3. *Más vale prevenir... que lamentar.*

ESCRIBE

12-36  [Interpretive]

Preparación.

En un concurso, tu amigo/a ganó diez mil dólares para viajar a San José, Costa Rica. Nunca ha hecho un viaje largo, siente mucha ansiedad (*anxiety*) y te pidió ayuda con la planificación de su viaje. Para ayudarle, haz lo siguiente:

1. En Internet, lee uno o dos artículo(s) sobre este lugar.

2. Subraya y toma nota de las ideas y los datos concretos más relevantes y útiles.

3. Decide cuáles son tus consejos principales sobre la planificación del viaje, y selecciona la información que lo sustente (*support*).

4. Organiza la información y las ideas en orden de importancia.

5. Selecciona las palabras adecuadas para lograr (*achieve*) el tono adecuado.

ESTRATEGIA

Use facts to support a point of view

In your academic work, you are often expected to present factual information. Facts are considered objective representations of reality. You are expected to provide reliable data, such as statistics and expert opinions.

Facts also serve as the basis to support a point of view on an issue. For example, a person may be against drinking and driving (personal point of view) because statistics show that drunk driving causes accidents (fact).

Therefore, to support your point of view on a particular issue in an objective manner…

- inform yourself by consulting reliable sources.
- base your statements on the information you gathered.
- acknowledge your information sources.

12-37  [Presentational]

Escribe.

Escríbele un correo electrónico a tu amigo/a y compártelo con la clase. Incluye la información que preparaste. Además, dale buenos consejos para disminuir su ansiedad.

En directo

To present factual information:

Es evidente/un hecho que…

La evidencia/Los expertos afirma(n) que…

El… por ciento de…

No hay duda que…

To give advice:

Es importante/necesario/ aconsejable que…

Te recomiendo/aconsejo que…

¿Por qué no… ?

 Click on the icon to listen to a conversation with these expressions.

Comprueba

I was able to…

____ state my position on the topic.

____ locate and organize key factual information.

____ give advice based on factual information.

____ use the *En directo* expressions to present and support my positions.

Suggestion for 12-37
Depending on your students' level of proficiency and their interests, you may wish to expand the scope of this writing task. You may give them the option of writing a brief essay on a travel-related issue, such as how to prepare for a long trip, how to plan an adventure trip, or how to book trips using the Internet. This may give students the opportunity to research an area of personal interest and to use the information to write a letter and help others.

Audioscript for *En directo*
Carolina: *Pedro, estoy planeando un viaje a la capital, pero no sé si debo tomar el tren o el autobús.*
Pedro: *Ayer leí un artículo en el periódico sobre esto mismo. Los expertos afirman que es mucho más relajante viajar por tren. Según una encuesta, el 75% de las personas prefiere los trenes porque piensan que son más seguros y que sufren menos retrasos que los autobuses. Claro, es importante tomar en cuenta que es más caro viajar por tren.*
Carolina: *Wow, cuánto sabes tú de estas cosas. ¿Por qué no te conviertes en mi agente de viajes? ¡Aunque sea yo tu única clienta!*

 **12-38** 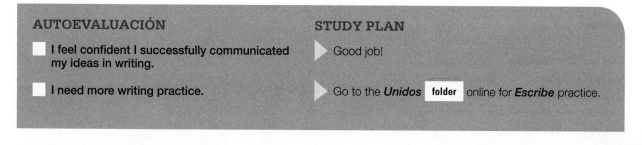 Interpersonal

Un paso más. Comparen sus respectivos correos. ¿Dieron consejos similares o diferentes? ¿Cuáles son los consejos más importantes? Preparen un informe breve para compartir con la clase.

San José, Costa Rica

ENFOQUE *cultural*

PANAMÁ

La pollera es el traje nacional de las mujeres panameñas. Hecha de diferentes materiales como el algodón y la lana, es elaborada muy detalladamente con decoraciones coloridas y minuciosas.

COSTA RICA

Costa Rica ofrece una gran variedad de opciones a quienes buscan la aventura acuática. Entre las actividades más populares están el buceo y la pesca. También se puede hacer rafting y surfing.

Note for *Panamá*
The *pollera* finds its roots in 16th century Spain and typically consists of an off-the-shoulder blouse and a skirt. Both the blouse and skirt have ruffles and both tend to contain either flower- or bird-inspired designs. In addition to the intricate details found on the blouse and skirt, great attention is paid to accessories such as ribbons, chains of gold and highly adorned hair combs.

Note for *Costa Rica*
Costa Rica has become one of the world's favorite destinations for those who are interested in surfing. Be they novices, experts or any level in between, surfers can find a myriad of options. There are various destinations throughout the coast where they can practice the sport, and there are packages available for groups, families, couples and individuals.

Centroamérica:
un puente entre dos océanos

Go to the *Enfoque cultural* [folder] in *Capítulo 12* online to learn more about these countries.

PLAN DE ESTUDIO

◎ **LEARN**

- Interactive presentation: *Centroamérica: un puente entre dos océanos*

◎ **APPLY**

- Activities

PRÁCTICA COMUNICATIVA

12-39

Usa la información. Prepara una presentación oral breve sobre uno de los temas siguientes. Enfócate en el impacto económico y social de los eventos históricos que trates en tu informe.

- Cornelius Vanderbilt
- el Canal de Nicaragua
- el Canal de Panamá
- la ampliación del Canal de Panamá
- la ecología del Canal de Panamá

En este capítulo...

Comprueba lo que sabes

Go to the *Comprueba lo que sabes* folder online to review what you have learned in this chapter. Practice with the following:

| Vocabulary Flashcards | Games | Oral Practice | Practice Test/ Study Plan | Video en contexto |

Vocabulario

Los medios de transporte
el autobús/bus
el avión
el barco
el metro
el tren

En el aeropuerto
la aduana
la aerolínea/línea aérea
el asiento
    de pasillo/ventanilla
la clase turista
el mostrador
la primera clase
la puerta (de salida)
la salid a de
    emergencia
el vuelo

Las personas
el/la agente de viajes
el/la auxiliar de vuelo
el pasajero/la pasajera

Las partes de un coche
el capó
el espejo retrovisor
la guantera
el limpiaparabrisas
la llanta
la luz (las luces)
las luces intermitentes
el maletero/el baúl
el motor
el parabrisas
el parachoques
la placa
el radiador
la rueda
el volante

Los viajes
la agencia de viajes
la autopista
el boleto/el pasaje
la carretera
el crucero
el equipaje
la escala
la maleta

el maletín
el pasaporte
la tarjeta de embarque
el trayecto
la velocidad

En el hotel
el alojamiento
la caja fuerte
la habitación doble/sencilla
la llave
la recepción
la tarjeta magnética

Los lugares
la cuadra
la esquina

Las descripciones
bien/mal aparcado
lleno/a
vacío/a

Verbos
cancelar
descomponerse

doblar
facturar
manejar
perderse (ie)
recorrer
reservar
revisar
viajar
volar (ue)

Palabras y expresiones útiles
el cajero automático
de ida y vuelta
hacer cola
la licencia de conducir
la multa
seguir (i) derecho
una vez

Pronombres posesivos
mío(s) / mía(s)
tuyo(s) / tuya(s)
suyo(s) / suya(s)
nuestro(s) / nuestra(s)
vuestro(s) / vuestra(s)

Notas

Verb Charts

Regular Verbs: Simple Tenses

Infinitive Present Participle Past Participle	Indicative					Subjunctive		Imperative
	Present	Imperfect	Preterit	Future	Conditional	Present	Imperfect	Commands
hablar hablando hablado	hablo hablas habla hablamos habláis hablan	hablaba hablabas hablaba hablábamos hablabais hablaban	hablé hablaste habló hablamos hablasteis hablaron	hablaré hablarás hablará hablaremos hablaréis hablarán	hablaría hablarías hablaría hablaríamos hablaríais hablarían	hable hables hable hablemos habléis hablen	hablara hablaras hablara habláramos hablarais hablaran	habla (tú), no hables hable (usted) hablemos hablad (vosotros), no habléis hablen (Uds.)
comer comiendo comido	como comes come comemos coméis comen	comía comías comía comíamos comíais comían	comí comiste comió comimos comisteis comieron	comeré comerás comerá comeremos comeréis comerán	comería comerías comería comeríamos comeríais comerían	coma comas coma comamos comáis coman	comiera comieras comiera comiéramos comierais comieran	come (tú), no comas coma (usted) comamos comed (vosotros), no comáis coman (Uds.)
vivir viviendo vivido	vivo vives vive vivimos vivís viven	vivía vivías vivía vivíamos vivíais vivían	viví viviste vivió vivimos vivisteis vivieron	viviré vivirás vivirá viviremos viviréis vivirán	viviría vivirías viviría viviríamos viviríais vivirían	viva vivas viva vivamos viváis vivan	viviera vivieras viviera viviéramos vivierais vivieran	vive (tú), no vivas viva (usted) vivamos vivid (vosotros), no viváis vivan (Uds.)

Regular Verbs: Perfect Tenses

Indicative										Subjunctive			
Present Perfect		Past Perfect		Preterit Perfect		Future Perfect		Conditional Perfect		Present Perfect		Past Perfect	
he has ha hemos habéis han	hablado comido vivido	había habías había habíamos habíais habían	hablado comido vivido	hube hubiste hubo hubimos hubisteis hubieron	hablado comido vivido	habré habrás habrá habremos habréis habrán	hablado comido vivido	habría habrías habría habríamos habríais habrían	hablado comido vivido	haya hayas haya hayamos hayáis hayan	hablado comido vivido	hubiera hubieras hubiera hubiéramos hubierais hubieran	hablado comido vivido

Irregular Verbs

Infinitive Present Participle Past Participle	Indicative					Subjunctive		Imperative
	Present	Imperfect	Preterit	Future	Conditional	Present	Imperfect	Commands

andar
andando
andado
	ando
	andas
	anda
	andamos
	andáis
	andan
		andaba
		andabas
		andaba
		andábamos
		andabais
		andaban
			anduve
			anduviste
			anduvo
			anduvimos
			anduvisteis
			anduvieron
				andaré
				andarás
				andará
				andaremos
				andaréis
				andarán
					andaría
					andarías
					andaría
					andaríamos
					andaríais
					andarían
						ande
						andes
						ande
						andemos
						andéis
						anden
							anduviera
							anduvieras
							anduviera
							anduviéramos
							anduvierais
							anduvieran
								anda (tú),
								  no andes
								ande (usted)
								andemos
								andad (vosotros),
								  no andéis
								anden (Uds.)

caer
cayendo
caído
	caigo
	caes
	cae
	caemos
	caéis
	caen
		caía
		caías
		caía
		caíamos
		caíais
		caían
			caí
			caíste
			cayó
			caímos
			caísteis
			cayeron
				caeré
				caerás
				caerá
				caeremos
				caeréis
				caerán
					caería
					caerías
					caería
					caeríamos
					caeríais
					caerían
						caiga
						caigas
						caiga
						caigamos
						caigáis
						caigan
							cayera
							cayeras
							cayera
							cayéramos
							cayerais
							cayeran
								cae (tú),
								  no caigas
								caiga (usted)
								caigamos
								caed (vosotros),
								  no caigáis
								caigan (Uds.)

dar dando dado	doy das da damos dais dan	daba dabas daba dábamos dabais daban	di diste dio dimos disteis dieron	daré darás dará daremos daréis darán	daría darías daría daríamos daríais darían	dé des dé demos deis den	diera dieras diera diéramos dierais dieran	da (tú), no des dé (usted) demos dad (vosotros), no deis den (Uds.)

decir
diciendo
dicho
	digo
	dices
	dice
	decimos
	decís
	dicen
		decía
		decías
		decía
		decíamos
		decíais
		decían
			dije
			dijiste
			dijo
			dijimos
			dijisteis
			dijeron
				diré
				dirás
				dirá
				diremos
				diréis
				dirán
					diría
					dirías
					diría
					diríamos
					diríais
					dirían
						diga
						digas
						diga
						digamos
						digáis
						digan
							dijera
							dijeras
							dijera
							dijéramos
							dijerais
							dijeran
								di (tú),
								  no digas
								diga (usted)
								digamos
								decid (vosotros),
								  no digáis
								digan (Uds.)

estar
estando
estado
	estoy
	estás
	está
	estamos
	estáis
	están
		estaba
		estabas
		estaba
		estábamos
		estabais
		estaban
			estuve
			estuviste
			estuvo
			estuvimos
			estuvisteis
			estuvieron
				estaré
				estarás
				estará
				estaremos
				estaréis
				estarán
					estaría
					estarías
					estaría
					estaríamos
					estaríais
					estarían
						esté
						estés
						esté
						estemos
						estéis
						estén
							estuviera
							estuvieras
							estuviera
							estuviéramos
							estuvierais
							estuvieran
								está (tú),
								  no estés
								esté (usted)
								estemos
								estad (vosotros),
								  no estéis
								estén (Uds.)

haber habiendo habido	he has ha hemos habéis han	había habías había habíamos habíais habían	hube hubiste hubo hubimos hubisteis hubieron	habré habrás habrá habremos habréis habrán	habría habrías habría habríamos habríais habrían	haya hayas haya hayamos hayáis hayan	hubiera hubieras hubiera hubiéramos hubierais hubieran	

hacer
haciendo
hecho
	hago
	haces
	hace
	hacemos
	hacéis
	hacen
		hacía
		hacías
		hacía
		hacíamos
		hacíais
		hacían
			hice
			hiciste
			hizo
			hicimos
			hicisteis
			hicieron
				haré
				harás
				hará
				haremos
				haréis
				harán
					haría
					harías
					haría
					haríamos
					haríais
					harían
						haga
						hagas
						haga
						hagamos
						hagáis
						hagan
							hiciera
							hicieras
							hiciera
							hiciéramos
							hicierais
							hicieran
								haz (tú),
								  no hagas
								haga (usted)
								hagamos
								haced (vosotros),
								  no hagáis
								hagan (Uds.)

Irregular Verbs (*continued*)

Infinitive Present Participle Past Participle	Indicative					Subjunctive		Imperative
	Present	Imperfect	Preterit	Future	Conditional	Present	Imperfect	Commands
ir yendo ido	voy vas va vamos vais van	iba ibas iba íbamos ibais iban	fui fuiste fue fuimos fuisteis fueron	iré irás irá iremos iréis irán	iría irías iría iríamos iríais irían	vaya vayas vaya vayamos vayáis vayan	fuera fueras fuera fuéramos fuerais fueran	ve (tú), no vayas vaya (usted) vamos, no vayamos id (vosotros), no vayáis vayan (Uds.)
oír oyendo oído	oigo oyes oye oímos oís oyen	oía oías oía oíamos oíais oían	oí oíste oyó oímos oísteis oyeron	oiré oirás oirá oiremos oiréis oirán	oiría oirías oiría oiríamos oiríais oirían	oiga oigas oiga oigamos oigáis oigan	oyera oyeras oyera oyéramos oyerais oyeran	oye (tú), no oigas oiga (usted) oigamos oíd (vosotros), no oigáis oigan (Uds.)
poder pudiendo podido	puedo puedes puede podemos podéis pueden	podía podías podía podíamos podíais podían	pude pudiste pudo pudimos pudisteis pudieron	podré podrás podrá podremos podréis podrán	podría podrías podría podríamos podríais podrían	pueda puedas pueda podamos podáis puedan	pudiera pudieras pudiera pudiéramos pudierais pudieran	
poner poniendo puesto	pongo pones pone ponemos ponéis ponen	ponía ponías ponía poníamos poníais ponían	puse pusiste puso pusimos pusisteis pusieron	pondré pondrás pondrá pondremos pondréis pondrán	pondría pondrías pondría pondríamos pondríais pondrían	ponga pongas ponga pongamos pongáis pongan	pusiera pusieras pusiera pusiéramos pusierais pusieran	pon (tú), no pongas ponga (usted) pongamos poned (vosotros), no pongáis pongan (Uds.)
querer queriendo querido	quiero quieres quiere queremos queréis quieren	quería querías quería queríamos queríais querían	quise quisiste quiso quisimos quisisteis quisieron	querré querrás querrá querremos querréis querrán	querría querrías querría querríamos querríais querrían	quiera quieras quiera queramos queráis quieran	quisiera quisieras quisiera quisiéramos quisierais quisieran	quiere (tú), no quieras quiera (usted) queramos quered (vosotros), no queráis quieran (Uds.)
saber sabiendo sabido	sé sabes sabe sabemos sabéis saben	sabía sabías sabía sabíamos sabíais sabían	supe supiste supo supimos supisteis supieron	sabré sabrás sabrá sabremos sabréis sabrán	sabría sabrías sabría sabríamos sabríais sabrían	sepa sepas sepa sepamos sepáis sepan	supiera supieras supiera supiéramos supierais supieran	sabe (tú), no sepas sepa (usted) sepamos sabed (vosotros), no sepáis sepan (Uds.)

Irregular Verbs (*continued*)

Infinitive Present Participle Past Participle	Indicative					Subjunctive		Imperative
	Present	Imperfect	Preterit	Future	Conditional	Present	Imperfect	Commands
salir saliendo salido	salgo sales sale salimos salís salen	salía salías salía salíamos salíais salían	salí saliste salió salimos salisteis salieron	saldré saldrás saldrá saldremos saldréis saldrán	saldría saldrías saldría saldríamos saldríais saldrían	salga salgas salga salgamos salgáis salgan	saliera salieras saliera saliéramos salierais salieran	sal (tú), no salgas salga (usted) salgamos salid (vosotros), no salgáis salgan (Uds.)
ser siendo sido	soy eres es somos sois son	era eras era éramos erais eran	fui fuiste fue fuimos fuisteis fueron	seré serás será seremos seréis serán	sería serías sería seríamos seríais serían	sea seas sea seamos seáis sean	fuera fueras fuera fuéramos fuerais fueran	sé (tú), no seas sea (usted) seamos sed (vosotros), no seáis sean (Uds.)
tener teniendo tenido	tengo tienes tiene tenemos tenéis tienen	tenía tenías tenía teníamos teníais tenían	tuve tuviste tuvo tuvimos tuvisteis tuvieron	tendré tendrás tendrá tendremos tendréis tendrán	tendría tendrías tendría tendríamos tendríais tendrían	tenga tengas tenga tengamos tengáis tengan	tuviera tuvieras tuviera tuviéramos tuvierais tuvieran	ten (tú), no tengas tenga (usted) tengamos tened (vosotros), no tengáis tengan (Uds.)
traer trayendo traído	traigo traes trae traemos traéis traen	traía traías traía traíamos traíais traían	traje trajiste trajo trajimos trajisteis trajeron	traeré traerás traerá traeremos traeréis traerán	traería traerías traería traeríamos traeríais traerían	traiga traigas traiga traigamos traigáis traigan	trajera trajeras trajera trajéramos trajerais trajeran	trae (tú), no traigas traiga (usted) traigamos traed (vosotros), no traigáis traigan (Uds.)
venir viniendo venido	vengo vienes viene venimos venís vienen	venía venías venía veníamos veníais venían	vine viniste vino vinimos vinisteis vinieron	vendré vendrás vendrá vendremos vendréis vendrán	vendría vendrías vendría vendríamos vendríais vendrían	venga vengas venga vengamos vengáis vengan	viniera vinieras viniera viniéramos vinierais vinieran	ven (tú), no vengas venga (usted) vengamos venid (vosotros), no vengáis vengan (Uds.)
ver viendo visto	veo ves ve vemos veis ven	veía veías veía veíamos veíais veían	vi viste vio vimos visteis vieron	veré verás verá veremos veréis verán	vería verías vería veríamos veríais verían	vea veas vea veamos veáis vean	viera vieras viera viéramos vierais vieran	ve (tú), no veas vea (usted) veamos ved (vosotros), no veáis vean (Uds.)

Stem-Changing and Orthographic-Changing Verbs

Infinitive Present Participle Past Participle	Indicative					Subjunctive		Imperative
	Present	Imperfect	Preterit	Future	Conditional	Present	Imperfect	Commands
almorzar (ue) (c) almorzando almorzado	almuerzo almuerzas almuerza almorzamos almorzáis almuerzan	almorzaba almorzabas almorzaba almorzábamos almorzabais almorzaban	almorcé almorzaste almorzó almorzamos almorzasteis almorzaron	almorzaré almorzarás almorzará almorzaremos almorzaréis almorzarán	almorzaría almorzarías almorzaría almorzaríamos almorzaríais almorzarían	almuerce almuerces almuerce almorcemos almorcéis almuercen	almorzara almorzaras almorzara almorzáramos almorzarais almorzaran	almuerza (tú), no almuerces almuerce (usted) almorcemos almorzad (vosotros), no almorcéis almuercen (Uds.)
buscar (qu) buscando buscado	busco buscas busca buscamos buscáis buscan	buscaba buscabas buscaba buscábamos buscabais buscaban	busqué buscaste buscó buscamos buscasteis buscaron	buscaré buscarás buscará buscaremos buscaréis buscarán	buscaría buscarías buscaría buscaríamos buscaríais buscarían	busque busques busque busquemos busquéis busquen	buscara buscaras buscara buscáramos buscarais buscaran	busca (tú), no busques busque (usted) busquemos buscad (vosotros), no busquéis busquen (Uds.)
corregir (i, i) (j) corrigiendo corregido	corrijo corriges corrige corregimos corregís corrigen	corregía corregías corregía corregíamos corregíais corregían	corregí corregiste corrigió corregimos corregisteis corrigieron	corregiré corregirás corregirá corregiremos corregiréis corregirán	corregiría corregirías corregiría corregiríamos corregiríais corregirían	corrija corrijas corrija corrijamos corrijáis corrijan	corrigiera corrigieras corrigiera corrigiéramos corrigierais corrigieran	corrige (tú), no corrijas corrija (usted) corrijamos corregid (vosotros), no corrijáis corrijan (Uds.)
dormir (ue, u) durmiendo dormido	duermo duermes duerme dormimos dormís duermen	dormía dormías dormía dormíamos dormíais dormían	dormí dormiste durmió dormimos dormisteis durmieron	dormiré dormirás dormirá dormiremos dormiréis dormirán	dormiría dormirías dormiría dormiríamos dormiríais dormirían	duerma duermas duerma durmamos durmáis duerman	durmiera durmieras durmiera durmiéramos durmierais durmieran	duerme (tú), no duermas duerma (usted) durmamos dormid (vosotros), no durmáis duerman (Uds.)
incluir (y) incluyendo incluido	incluyo incluyes incluye incluimos incluís incluyen	incluía incluías incluía incluíamos incluíais incluían	incluí incluiste incluyó incluimos incluisteis incluyeron	incluiré incluirás incluirá incluiremos incluiréis incluirán	incluiría incluirías incluiría incluiríamos incluiríais incluirían	incluya incluyas incluya incluyamos incluyáis incluyan	incluyera incluyeras incluyera incluyéramos incluyerais incluyeran	incluye (tú), no incluyas incluya (usted) incluyamos incluid (vosotros), no incluyáis incluyan (Uds.)

Stem-Changing and Orthographic-Changing Verbs (*continued*)

Infinitive Present Participle Past Participle	Indicative					Subjunctive		Imperative
	Present	Imperfect	Preterit	Future	Conditional	Present	Imperfect	Commands
llegar (gu) llegando llegado	llego llegas llega llegamos llegáis llegan	llegaba llegabas llegaba llegábamos llegabais llegaban	llegué llegaste llegó llegamos llegasteis llegaron	llegaré llegarás llegará llegaremos llegaréis llegarán	llegaría llegarías llegaría llegaríamos llegaríais llegarían	llegue llegues llegue lleguemos lleguéis lleguen	llegara llegaras llegara llegáramos llegarais llegaran	llega (tú), no llegues llegue (usted) lleguemos llegad (vosotros), no lleguéis lleguen (Uds.)
pedir (i, i) pidiendo pedido	pido pides pide pedimos pedís piden	pedía pedías pedía pedíamos pedíais pedían	pedí pediste pidió pedimos pedisteis pidieron	pediré pedirás pedirá pediremos pediréis pedirán	pediría pedirías pediría pediríamos pediríais pedirían	pida pidas pida pidamos pidáis pidan	pidiera pidieras pidiera pidiéramos pidierais pidieran	pide (tú), no pidas pida (usted) pidamos pedid (vosotros), no pidáis pidan (Uds.)
pensar (ie) pensando pensado	pienso piensas piensa pensamos pensáis piensan	pensaba pensabas pensaba pensábamos pensabais pensaban	pensé pensaste pensó pensamos pensasteis pensaron	pensaré pensarás pensará pensaremos pensaréis pensarán	pensaría pensarías pensaría pensaríamos pensaríais pensarían	piense pienses piense pensemos penséis piensen	pensara pensaras pensara pensáramos pensarais pensaran	piensa (tú), no pienses piense (usted) pensemos pensad (vosotros), no penséis piensen (Uds.)
producir (zc) (j) produciendo producido	produzco produces produce producimos producís producen	producía producías producía producíamos producíais producían	produje produjiste produjo produjimos produjisteis produjeron	produciré producirás producirá produciremos produciréis producirán	produciría producirías produciría produciríamos produciríais producirían	produzca produzcas produzca produzcamos produzcáis produzcan	produjera produjeras produjera produjéramos produjerais produjeran	produce (tú), no produzcas produzca (usted) produzcamos producid (vosotros), no produzcáis produzcan (Uds.)
reír (i, i) riendo reído	río ríes ríe reímos reís ríen	reía reías reía reíamos reíais reían	reí reíste rió reímos reísteis rieron	reiré reirás reirá reiremos reiréis reirán	reiría reirías reiría reiríamos reiríais reirían	ría rías ría riamos riáis rían	riera rieras riera riéramos rierais rieran	ríe (tú), no rías ría (usted) riamos reíd (vosotros), no riáis rían (Uds.)
seguir (i, i) (ga) siguiendo seguido	sigo sigues sigue seguimos seguís siguen	seguía seguías seguía seguíamos seguíais seguían	seguí seguiste siguió seguimos seguisteis siguieron	seguiré seguirás seguirá seguiremos seguiréis seguirán	seguiría seguirías seguiría seguiríamos seguiríais seguirían	siga sigas siga sigamos sigáis sigan	siguiera siguieras siguiera siguiéramos siguierais siguieran	sigue (tú), no sigas siga (usted) sigamos seguid (vosotros), no sigáis sigan (Uds.)

Stem-Changing and Orthographic-Changing Verbs (*continued*)

Infinitive Present Participle Past Participle	Indicative					Subjunctive		Imperative
	Present	Imperfect	Preterit	Future	Conditional	Present	Imperfect	Commands
sentir (ie, i) sintiendo sentido	siento sientes siente sentimos sentís sienten	sentía sentías sentía sentíamos sentíais sentían	sentí sentiste sintió sentimos sentisteis sintieron	sentiré sentirás sentirá sentiremos sentiréis sentirán	sentiría sentirías sentiría sentiríamos sentiríais sentirían	sienta sientas sienta sintamos sintáis sientan	sintiera sintieras sintiera sintiéramos sintierais sintieran	siente (tú), no sientas sienta (usted) sintamos sentid (vosotros), no sintáis sientan (Uds.)
volver (ue) volviendo vuelto	vuelvo vuelves vuelve volvemos volvéis vuelven	volvía volvías volvía volvíamos volvíais volvían	volví volviste volvió volvimos volvisteis volvieron	volveré volverás volverá volveremos volveréis volverán	volvería volverías volvería volveríamos volveríais volverían	vuelva vuelvas vuelva volvamos volváis vuelvan	volviera volvieras volviera volviéramos volvierais volvieran	vuelve (tú), no vuelvas vuelva (usted) volvamos volved (vosotros), no volváis vuelvan (Uds.)

Spanish-English Glossary

This vocabulary includes all words and expressions presented in the text, except for proper nouns spelled the same in English and Spanish, diminutives with a literal meaning, typical expressions of the Hispanic countries presented in the *Enfoque cultural,* and cardinal numbers (found on page 14). Cognates and words easily recognized because of the context are not included either.

The number following each entry corresponds to the **capítulo** in which the word was first introduced.

A

a *at, to* P
a la derecha *to the right* 2r
a la izquierda *to the left* 2r
a veces *at times* 12r
el/la abogado/a *lawyer* 9
abrazos y besos *hugs and kisses* 4r
el abrigo *coat* 6
abril *April* Pr
la abuela *grandmother* 4
el abuelo *grandfather* 4
aburrido/a *boring; bored* 6r
aburrirse *to get bored* 8r
el accesorio *accessory* 5
el aceite *oil* 4r, 10, 10r
acompañar *to accompany* 8
aconsejar *to advise* 5r
acostar(se) (ue) *to put to bed; to go to bed* 4
el actor/la actriz *actor/actress* 9
actualmente *now, at present* 9
además *besides/in addition/ furthermore* 11r
el aderezo *salad dressing* 10
adiós *good-bye* Pr
adivinar *to guess* 6r
¿Adónde? *Where (to)?* 3
el adoquín *cobblestone* 11r
adornado/a *decorated* 8
la aduana *customs* 12
la aerolínea/línea aérea *airline* 12
el aeropuerto *airport* 12
afeitar(se) *to shave; to shave (oneself)* 4
el afiche *poster* 4r
las afueras *outskirts* 5
la agencia de viajes *travel agency* 12
el/la agente de viajes *travel agent* 12
agosto *August* Pr
agradable *nice* 2
agregar *to add* 10
el/la agricultor/a *farmer* 9

la agricultura *farming, agriculture* 9
agrio/a *sour* 10
el agua *water* 3
el aguacate *avocado* 10
el/la ahijado/a *godchild* 4
ahorrar *to save* 6r
el aire acondicionado *air conditioning* 5
el ají *hot, hot pepper* 10r
el ajo *garlic* 10
al *to the (contraction of* a + el*)* 3
al aire libre *open air, outdoors* 2r, 3
al lado (de) *next to* P
al menos *at least* 7r
alegrarse (de) *to be glad (about)* 11
alegre *happy, glad* 2
la alegría *joy* 8
alemán/alemana *German* 2
la alfombra *carpet, rug* 5
algo *something, anything* 12r
alguien *someone, anyone* 12r
algún/alguno(s)/alguna(s) *some, any, several* 12r
alguna vez *sometime, ever* 12r
algunas veces *sometimes* 12r
el almacén *department store; warehouse* 6
la almeja *clam* 10r
la almohada *pillow* 5
almorzar (ue) *to have lunch* 4
el almuerzo *lunch* 3
el alojamiento *lodging* 11r, 12
alquilar *to rent* 3
el alquiler *rent* 5
alto/a *tall* 2
amarillo/a *yellow* 2
el ambiente *setting* 8r
ambos/as *both* 4r
el/la amigo/a *friend* P
el/la amo/a de casa *homemaker* 9
añadir *to add* 10
anaranjado/a *orange* 2
ancho/a *wide* 6

¡Anda, anímate! *Come on, cheer up!* 3r
el anillo *ring* 6
animado/a *lively* 8
animar *to encourage* 7r
el año *year* P
el año pasado *last year* 6r
anoche *last night* 6r
anteanoche *the night before last* 6r
anteayer *day before yesterday* 6r
el/la antepasado/a *ancestor* 8
antes *before* 8
el antibiótico *antibiotic* 11
antipático/a *unpleasant* 2
el anuncio *ad, advertisement* 2r, 9
apagar *to extinguish, turn off* 9
la apariencia *physical appearance* 2r
el apartamento *apartment* 5
el apio *celery* 10r
aprovechar *to take advantage* 7
aquel/aquella *that (over there)* 5r
aquellos/aquellas *those (over there)* 5r
el árbitro *umpire, referee* 7
el árbol *tree* 7
el arete *earring* 6
argentino/a *Argentinian* 2
el armario *closet, armoire* 5
el/la arquitecto/a *architect* 9
la arquitectura *architecture* 5
el arroz *rice* 3
la artesanía *handicrafts* 6
el/la artesano/a *craftsman/woman; craftsperson* 9
el artículo de belleza *beauty item* 11
el aserrín *sawdust* 8
el asiento *seat* 12
el asiento de pasillo *aisle seat* 12
el asiento de ventanilla *window seat* 12
la aspiradora *vacuum cleaner* 5
la atmósfera *atmosphere* 7

atrever se [atreverse] (a) *to dare to* 7r
el auto *car* 2
el autobús/bus *bus* 12
la autopista *freeway* 12
el/la auxiliar de vuelo *flight attendant* 12
averiguar *to find out* 5r
las aves *poultry, fowl* 10
el avión *plane* 12
ayer *yesterday* 6r
ayudar *to help* 3r, 5
el azúcar *sugar* 10
azul *blue* 2

B

bajar de peso *to lose weight* 3r, 10r
bajo/a *short (height)* 2
el balón *ball* 7
el baloncesto *basketball* 7
la banana *banana, plantain* 10
bañar(se) *to bathe; to take a bath* 4
el banco *bank* 9
la bandeja *tray* 10
la bañera *bathtub* 5
el baño *bathroom* 5
barato/a *inexpensive, cheap* 6
la barbacoa *barbecue pit; barbecue (event)* 5
el barco *ship/boat* 12
barrer *to sweep* 5
el barrio *neighborhood* 5
el básquetbol *basketball* 7
bastante *rather* P; *enough* 3r
la basura *garbage, trash* 5
la bata *robe* 6
el bate *bat* 7
el batido *shake* 3r
batir *to beat* 10
el baúl *trunk* 12
el bautizo *baptism, christening* 4
beber *to drink* 1
la bebida *drink* 3
el béisbol *baseball* 7
el/la bibliotecario/a *librarian* 9
bien *well* P
bien/mal aparcado *legally/illegally parked* 12
bilingüe *bilingual* 2
el billete *ticket bill (paper money)* 3r
la billetera *wallet* 6
el bistec *steak* 3
blanco/a *white* 2
la blusa *blouse* 6
la boca *mouth* 11
la boda *wedding* 3
el boleto *ticket* 12
el bolígrafo *ballpoint pen* P
boliviano/a *Bolivian* 2

la bolsa/el bolso *purse* 6
el/la bombero/a *firefighter* 9
bonito/a *pretty* 2
el borrador *eraser* P
la bota *boot* 6
la botella *bottle* 10
la botella para refrescos *soft drink bottle* 5r
el brazo *arm* 6r, 11
la broma *joke* 10r
bromear *to joke* 3r
buenas tardes *good afternoon* P
buenas noches *good evening, good night* P
bueno/a *good (character); well (health); physically attractive* 6r
buenos días *good morning* P
la bufanda *scarf* 6
la butaca *armchair* 5

C

el cabello *hair* 11
la cabeza *head* 6r, 11
cada *each* 7
cada... horas *every ... hours* 11
la cadera *hip* 11
caer(se) *to fall* 11
el café *coffee; coffee shop* 3
la caja de objetos perdidos *lost-and-found box* 6r
la caja fuerte *safe, lockbox* 12
el cajero automático *ATM* 12
el/la cajero/a *cashier* 9
la calavera *skull* 8r
los calcetines *socks* 6
la calculadora *calculator* P
la calefacción *heating* 5
caliente *hot* 3
callado/a *quiet* 2
la calle *street* 5
los calzoncillos *boxer shorts, briefs* 6
la cama *bed* 5
la Cámara de Representantes *House of Representatives* 3r
el/la camarero/a *server* 9/*server, waiter/waitress (restaurant)* 3, 9
el camarón *shrimp* 10
cambiar *to change, exchange* 6
el cambio *change* 2r
el camino *road; path* 8
la camisa *shirt* 6
la camiseta *T-shirt* 6
el camisón *nightgown* 6
el campeón/la campeona *champion* 7
el campeonato *championship; tournament* 7, 7r
el/la campesino/a *peasant* 10
el campo *field* 7; *countryside* 9

canadiense *Canadian* 2
el canal *channel* 7r
cancelar *to cancel* 12
el cáncer *cancer* 11
la cancha *court; golf course* 7
la canción *song* 3
la canela *cinnamon* 10r
cansado/a *tired* 2
cantar *to sing* 3
el capó *hood* 12
la cara *face* 11
el cargador del móvil/celular *cell phone charger* 5r
el cariño *affection* 4r
el carnaval *carnival* 8
la carne *meat* 10
la carne de res *beef* 10
la carne molida/picada *ground meat* 10
caro/a *expensive* 6
el/la carpintero/a *carpenter* 9
la carrera *race* 7; *career* 9
la carreta *cart, wagon* 8
la carretera *highway* 12
el carro *car* 2
la carroza *float (in a parade)* 8
casado/a *married* 2
casar(se) *to get married* 4, 5r
casero/a *homemade* 10r
el catarro *cold* 11
la cebolla *onion* 10
la ceja *eyebrow* 11
la celebración *celebration* 3
celebrar *to celebrate* 3
el cementerio *cemetery* 8
la cena *dinner, supper* 3
cenar *to have dinner* 3
Cenicienta *Cinderella* 3r
el centro *downtown; center* 5
el centro comercial *shopping center* 6
el centro de entrenamiento *training camp* 7r
el centro de salud *clinic* 11
el/la ceramista *potter* 9
cerca (de) *close to, near* 3, 5; *close* 5r
el cerdo *pork* 10
el cereal *cereal* 3
el cerebro *brain* 11
la cereza *cherry* 10
cerrar (ie) *to close* 4
el certamen *contest* 9r
la cerveza *beer* 3
el césped *lawn* 5; *grass* 5r
el cesto *wastebasket* P
el cesto/la cesta *basket, hoop* 7
el ceviche *dish of marinated raw fish and seafood* 3
las chanclas *flip-flops* 9r
chao *good-bye* Pr
la chaqueta *jacket* 6

el/la chef *chef* 9
el/la chico/a *boy/girl* P
el chile *hot, spicy pepper* 10r
chileno/a *Chilean* 2
la chimenea *fireplace* 5
el/la chofer *driver* 9
la chuleta *chop* 10
los churros *fried dough* 10
el ciclismo *cycling* 7
el/la ciclista *cyclist* 7
el cielo *sky* 7r
el/la científico/a *scientist* 9
el cine *movies* 3
la cintura *waist* 11
el cinturón *belt* 6
el/la cirujano/a *surgeon* 11r
la ciudad *city* 3
¡Claro! *Of course!* 3, 4r
la clase de ejercicios aeróbicos *aerobics class* 11r
la clase turista *tourist class* 12
el cliente/la clienta *client* 9
la clínica *clinic* 11
el coche *car* 2
la cocina *kitchen* 5
cocinar *to cook* 5
el/la cocinero/a *cook* 5r
el código postal *zip code* 9r
el codo *elbow* 11
colapsar *to collapse* 9r
el collar *necklace* 6
colombiano/a *Colombian* 2
el color *color* 2
el comedor *dining room* 5
comenzar (ie) *to begin* 8
la comida *food; meal; dinner, supper* 3
la comida basura *junk food* 10r
la comida rápida *fast food* 3r
el comienzo *beginning* 7r, 8
el comino *cumin* 10r
¿Cómo es? *What is he/she/it like?* P
¿Cómo está? *How are you? (formal)* P
¿Cómo estás? *How are you? (familiar, informal)* P
¡Cómo no! *Of course!* 9
¿Cómo se dice... en español? *How do you say... in Spanish?* Pr
¿Cómo se llama usted? *What's your name? (formal)* P
¿Cómo te llamas? *What's your name? (familiar, informal)* P
la cómoda *dresser* 5
cómodo/a *comfortable,* 5
la comodidad *comfort* 5r
el/la compañero/a *roommate* 2r
la compañía *company* 9
la comparsa *group dressed in similar costumes* 8
compartir *to share* 4r

el comportamiento *behavior* 9r
las compras *shopping* 6
la computadora *computer* P
la computadora portátil *laptop* P
la comunicación *communication* 3
con mucho cariño *affectionately; with much love* 4r
con permiso *pardon me, excuse me* Pr
¿Con quién hablo? *Who is this?* 5r
la concha *shell* 8r
el concurso *contest* 5r, 7r
el condimento *seasoning* 10
la conferencia *lecture* 2r
congelar(se) *to freeze* 7
conmigo *with me* 7
conocer *to meet* 3r
el/la consejero/a *counselor* 4r
el/la consejero/a vocacional *career counselor* 9r
el consejo *advice* 5r
la consola de videojuegos *games console* 5r
construir *to build* 7r
el consultorio *office (of doctor, dentist, etc.)* 9
el/la contador/a *accountant* 9
contaminado/a *polluted, contaminated* 7
contar (ue) *to count* 3r, 6r
contar eventos *to tell the events* 8r
contento/a *happy, glad* 2
contigo *with you (familiar)* 7
contraer *to contract* 11r
contrario/a *opposing* 7
el/la contratista *contractor* 9
conversador/a *talkative* 2
la copa *(stemmed) glass* 10
el corazón *heart* 11
la corbata *tie* 6
el cordero *lamb* 10
la corrida (de toros) *bullfight* 4r, 8
cortar *to cut; to mow (lawn)* 5
la cortina *curtain* 5
corto/a *short (length)* 2
la cosa *thing* 6
cosechar *to harvest* 9
costar (ue) *to cost* 4
costarricense *Costa Rican* 2
la costilla *rib* 7r, 10
la costumbre *custom* 8
crecer *to grow* 5r
creer *to believe* 5
la crema *cream* 10
el crucero *cruise* 12
el cuaderno *notebook* P
la cuadra *city block* 12
el cuadro *picture; painting* 5
¡Cuánto me alegro! *I am so happy for you!; I'm so happy to hear that!* 4r, 8r

la Cuaresma *Lent* 4r, 8r
el cuarto *bedroom; room* 2r, 5
cubano/a *Cuban* 2
cubierto *overcast (sky)* 7r
la cuchara *spoon* 10
la cucharada *spoonful* 10r
la cucharita *teaspoon* 10
el cuchillo *knife* 10
el cuello *neck* 11
el cuero *leather* 6
el cuerpo (humano) *body* 6r; *human body* 11
cuidar(se) (de) *to take care of* 11
el cumpleaños *birthday* 3
cumplir *to fulfill (goals)* 7r; *to meet* 9r
curar *to cure* 11
el currículum *résumé* 9

D

dar *to give; to hand over* 6
dar información de fondo *to give background information* 8r
dar un paseo *to take a walk* 8
de *of, from* 2
de acuerdo con *according to* 4r
de ida y vuelta *round trip* 12
de moda *in style* 6r
de nada *you're welcome* Pr
¿De quién? *Whose?* 2
debajo (de) *under* P
débil *weak* 2
decir (g, i) *to say, tell* 4
el dedo *finger* 11
dejar *to leave* 9
del *of the (contraction of de + el)* 2
delante *in front* 2r
delgado/a *thin* 2
los deportes *sports* 7
deprimido/a *depressed* 11
derecha *right* 4
derretido/a *melted* 10r
desarmar *to disassemble, to take apart* 9r
desarrollar *to develop* 8r
desayunar *to have breakfast* 4
el desayuno *breakfast* 3
descansar *to rest* 3
descomponerse *to break down* 12
la descripción *description* 2
descubrir *to uncover, discover* 10r
descuidado/a *careless* 9r
desear *to wish, want* 2
el desempleo *unemployment* 5r
Deseo hablar con... [nombre de persona]. *I would like to speak with ... [person's name].* 5r
el desfile *parade* 8
despedir (i) *to fire* 9r

despedirse (i) *to say goodbye* 7r
despertar(se) (ie) *to wake (someone up); to wake up* 4
después *after, later* 3
la desventaja *disadvantage* 5
detener (g, ie) *to stop* 9r
detrás (de) *behind* P, 2r
el día *day* P
el Día de Acción de Gracias *Thanksgiving* 8
el Día de las Brujas *Halloween* 8r
el día feriado *legal holiday* 8
el día festivo *holiday* 8
el dibujo *drawing* 5r
diciembre *December* P
el diente *tooth* 11
el diente de ajo *clove of garlic* 10r
el/la difunto/a *dead* 8
el dinero *money* 6
el discurso *speech* 8r
discutir *to argue, discuss* 7
disfrazarse *to wear a costume* 8
disfrutar *to enjoy* 5r, 10
la distribución *layout* 5r
las diversiones *leisure activities* 3
divertido/a *funny, amusing* 2
divertirse (ie) *to have a good time* 8
divorciado/a *divorced* 4
doblar *to fold* 5; *to turn* 12
doler (ue) *to hurt, ache* 11
el dolor *pain* 11
el domingo *Sunday* P
dominicano/a *Dominican* 2
¿Dónde está... ? *Where is ... ?* P
dorar *to brown* 10r
dormir (ue) una siesta *to take a nap* 4
dormir(se) (ue) *to sleep; to fall asleep* 4
la ducha *shower* 5
duchar(se) *to give a shower to; to take a shower* 4
el dulce *candy, sweets* 10
el dulce de higos *candied figs* 10r
durante *during* 3
durar *to last* 7
el DVD *DVD; DVD player* P

E

ecuatoriano/a *Ecuadorian* 2
la edad *age* 4r
el edificio *building* 2r, 5
el/la ejecutivo/a *executive* 9
él *he* P
elaborar *to produce* 9
el/la electricista *electrician* 9
los electrodomésticos *appliances* 5
elegir (i) *to choose* 5r
ella *she* P
emigrar *to emigrate* 9

empezar (ie) *to begin, start* 4
el/la empleado/a *employee* 9
la empresa *company* 9
en *in* P
en cambio *on the other hand* 4r
En contraste... *In contrast ...* 4r
en efectivo *in cash* 6
en medio *in the middle* 2r
En primer/segundo lugar... *In the first/second place ...* 11r
¿En qué página? *On what page?* Pr
¿En qué puedo ayudarle(s)? *How can/ may I help you?* 5r
¿En qué puedo servirle(s)? *How can/ may I help you?* 6
en realidad/realmente *in fact, really, actually* 9
Encantado/a. *Pleased/nice to meet you.* P
encantar *to delight; to love* 6
encerrar (ie) *to lock up, shut in* 8
encontrar (ue) *to find* 6
enero *January* P
enfadarse *to get angry* 7
enfermarse *to become sick* 11
la enfermedad *illness* 11
el/la enfermero/a *nurse* 9
enfermo/a *sick* 3r, 11
el/la enfermo/a *person who is sick* 11
enfrente (de) *in front of* P
enlatado/a *canned* 10r
enojado/a *angry* 2
la ensalada *salad* 3
enseguida *immediately* 6
entender (ie) *to understand* 4
enterar *to find out* 7r
enterrar *to bury* 8r
entonces *then* 8
entrar (en) *to go in, enter* 6
entre *between, among* P
entregar *to deliver; to turn in* 5r, 9r
el entrenador/la entrenadora *coach* 7
la entrevista *interview* 9
entrevistar *to interview* 4r, 7r
enviar *to send* 9
el equipaje *luggage* 11r, 12
el equipo *team* 2r; *equipment* 7
el equipo deportivo *sports equipment* 7
eres *you are (familiar)* P
la ermita *hermitage* 8r
es *you are (formal), he/she is* P
la escala *stopover* 12
la escalera *stairs* 5
el escaparate *store window* 6
la esclusa *lock (of a canal)* 12r
escoger *to choose* 4r
el escritorio *desk* P
ese/esa *that (adj.)* P

esos/esas *those* 5r
los espaguetis *spaghetti* 3
la espalda *back* 11
español/española *Spanish* 2
la especialidad *specialty* 9
las especias *spices* 10
el espejo *mirror* 5
el espejo retrovisor *rearview mirror* 12
esperar *to wait for* 9
las espinacas *spinach* 10
la esposa *wife* 4
el esposo *husband* 4
el esquí *skiing; ski* 7
esquiar *to ski* 7
la esquina *corner* 12
está *he/she is, you are (formal)* P
está despejado *it's clear* 7
está lloviendo *it is raining* Pr
está nublado *it's cloudy* 7
¿Está... [nombre de persona], por favor? *Is ... [person's name] there, please?* 5r
¡Estaba tan asustado/a! *I was so scared!* 12r
el estadio *stadium* 7r
el estado de ánimo *mood* 5r
el estado libre asociado *commonwealth* 2r
estadounidense *U.S. citizen* 2
estar de moda *to be fashionable* 6
estás *you are (familiar)* P
la estatura mediana *average, medium (height)* 2
este/esta *this* 5
el estilo *style* 5
el estómago *stomach* 11
estornudar *to sneeze* 11
estos/estas *these* 5
estrecho/a *narrow, tight* 6
el estrés *stress* 8r
el/la estudiante *student* P
la estufa *stove* 5
¡Estupendo! *fabulous, great* 3
el evento *event* 7
examinar *to examine* 11
la experiencia *experience* 9
explicar *to explain* 6r
la expresión *expression* 2

F

fabuloso/a *fabulous, great* 3
facturar *to check in (luggage)* 12
la falda *skirt* 6
la falta *lack of* 2r, 4r
la familia *family* 4
el/la farmacéutico/a *pharmacist* 11
la farmacia *pharmacy* 11

fascinar *to fascinate, to be pleasing to* 6; *to like a lot; to love* 6r

febrero *February* P

felicidades *congratulations* 3

feo/a *ugly* 2

el festival *festival* 8

la festividad *festivity; holiday; celebration* 8

la ficha *note card* 7r

la fiebre *fever* 11

la fiesta *party* 3; *festivity; holiday; celebration* 8

la fiesta sorpresa *surprise party* 7r

la fiesta *holiday* 8

fijarse *to focus* 4r

¡Fíjate qué noticia! *How about that!* 3r

la flor *flower* 2

la foto(grafía) *photo(graph)* 4

fracturar(se) *to fracture, break* 11

francés/francesa *French* 2

el fregadero *kitchen sink* 5

freír (i) *to fry* 10

la frente *forehead* 11

la fresa *strawberry* 10

el frijol *bean* 3

frío/a *cold* 3

frito/a *fried* 3

la frontera *border* 10r

la fruta *fruit* 3, 10

Fue un placer conocerlo/la. *It was a pleasure to meet you.* 9r

la fuente *bowl* 10r

fuerte *strong* 2

fumar *to smoke* 11

el fútbol *soccer* 3r, 7

el fútbol americano *football* 7

G

las gafas de sol *sunglasses* 6

la galleta *cookie* 10

la gamba *shrimp* 10

ganar *to win* 3r, 7

la ganga *bargain* 6

el garaje *garage* 5

la garganta *throat* 11

gastar *to spend* 6

el gasto *expense* 8r

el/la gemelo/a *twin* 4

la gente *people* 8

el/la gerente (de ventas) *(sales) manager* 9

el gobierno *government* 11

el gol *goal* 7

el golf *golf* 7

golpear *to knock* 7r

gordo/a *fat* 2

la gorra *cap* 6

gracias *thanks, thank you* P

la grasa *fat* 10

grave *serious (situation); seriously ill* 6r, 11

la gripe *flu* 11

gris *gray* 2

el guante *glove* 6

la guantera *glove compartment* 12

guapo/a *good-looking, handsome* 2

guatemalteco/a *Guatemalan* 2

el/la guía *guide* 6r

la guitarra *guitar* 3

gustar *to be pleasing to, to like* 6

H

la habitación *bedroom* 5

la habitación doble/sencilla *double room; single room* 12

hace buen tiempo *the weather is good* Pr

hace buen/mal tiempo *it's good/bad weather* 7

hace calor *it's hot* 7

hace fresco *it's cool* 7

hace mal tiempo *the weather is bad* Pr

hace sol *it is sunny* Pr, 7

hace un día/mes/año (que) *it has been a day/month/year since* 6r

hacer la cama *to make the bed* 3

hacer cola *to stand in line* 12

hacer preguntas *to ask questions* 4r

hacerse daño *to hurt oneself* 8r

la hamburguesa *hamburger* 3

la harina *flour* 10

hasta luego *see you later* P

hasta mañana *see you tomorrow* P

hasta pronto *see you soon* P

hay *there is, there are* P

el hecho *fact* 6r

el helado *ice cream* 3

herida *wound* 11r

el/la herido/a *injured person* 9r

la hermana *sister* 4

la hermanastra *stepsister* 4

el hermanastro *stepbrother* 4

el hermano *brother* 4

el herrero *blacksmith; ironworker* 9

hervir (ie, i) *to boil* 10

el hielo *ice* 7

la hierba *herb* 10

la hija *daughter* 4

el hijo *son* 4

el/la hijo/a único/a *only child* 4

hinchado/a *swollen* 11r

hispano/a *Hispanic* 2

el hogar *home* 4r

la hoja *leaf* 5

hola *hi, hello* P

el hombre *man* 3

el hombre/la mujer de negocios *businessman/woman* 9

el hombro *shoulder* 11

hondureño/a *Honduran* 2

el (horno) microondas *microwave (oven)* 5

el hospital *hospital* 11

el hotel *hotel* 12

hoy *today* P

hoy en día *nowadays* 8

el hueso *bone* 11

el huevo *egg* 3

I

la iglesia *church* 8

igualmente *likewise* P

el impermeable *raincoat* 6

la impresora *printer* 5r

el incendio *fire* 9

independizarse *become independent* 5r

la infancia *childhood* 7r

la infección *infection* 11

el informe *report* 4r

el/la ingeniero/a *engineer* 9

el inodoro *toilet* 5

intercambiar *to exchange* 4r

interesar *to interest* 6

el/la intérprete *interpreter* 9

la invitación *invitation* 8

invitar *to invite* 8

la inyección *injection* 11

ir de compras *to go shopping* 6

ir(se) *to go away, leave* 7

la izquierda *left* 4

J

el jabón *soap* 5

jamás *never, (not) ever* 12r

el jamón *ham* 3

japonés/japonesa *Japanese* 2

el jardín *garden* 5

los jeans *jeans* 6

el/la jefe/a *boss* 9

joven *young* 2

el/la joven *young man/woman* 3

la joya *piece of jewelry* 6

el/la joyero/a *jeweller* 9

el juego *game* 7

el jueves *Thursday* P

el juez/la jueza *judge* 9

el jugador/la jugadora *player* 7

jugar (ue) *to play (a game, sport)* 4

jugar (ue) a los bolos *to bowl* 7

el jugo *juice* 3

el juguete *toy* 6

julio *July* P

junio *June* P
juntos/as *together* 4

L

la *you (formal, singular), her, it (feminine)* 5
la ocupación *occupation* 9
el labio *lip* 11
lácteo/a *dairy (product)* 10
el ladrón/la ladrona *thief* 8r
el lago *lake* 7
la lámpara *lamp* 5
la langosta *lobster* 10
lanzar *to throw* 7r
el lápiz *pencil* P
largo/a *long* 2
las *you (formal and familiar plural), them (feminine)* 5
el lavabo *bathroom sink* 5
la lavadora *washer* 5
la lavandería *laundry room; dry cleaner* 5, 6r
el lavaplatos *dishwasher* 5
lavar(se) *to wash (oneself)* 4
le *to/for you (formal), him, her, it* 6
le gusta(n) *you (formal) like; he/she likes* 2
la leche *milk* 3
la leche de coco *coconut milk* 10
la lechuga *lettuce* 3
las legumbres *legumes* 10
lejos (de) *far (from)* 4r, 5
las lentejas *lentils* 10
los lentes de contacto *contact lenses* 2
les *to/for you (plural), them* 6
levantar pesas *to lift weights* 10r
levantar(se) *to raise; to get up* 4
levantarse con el pie izquierdo *to get up on the wrong side of the bed* 7r
el libro *book* P
la licencia de conducir *driver's license* 12
la licuadora *blender* 10r
el limón *lemon* 10
el limpiaparabrisas *windshield wiper* 12
limpiar *to clean* 5
limpio/a *clean* 5
la lista de compras *shopping list* 10r
listo/a *clever* 6; *smart; ready* 2
el llano *prairie* 4r
la llanta *tire* 12
la llave *key* 12
llenar *to fill (out)* 9
lleno/a *full* 12
llevar *to take* 4r; *to wear, to take* 6

llorar *to cry* 8r
llover (ue) *to rain* 7
llueve *it is raining* Pr
la lluvia *rain* 7
lo *you (formal, singular), him, it (masculine)* 5
lo importante *the important thing* 9
lo siento *I'm sorry (to hear that)* Pr
el/la locutor/a *radio announcer* 9
lograr *to accomplish* 7r; *to achieve* 12r
la longitud de bajada *slope* 7r
los *you (formal and familiar, plural), them (masculine)* 5r
las luces intermitentes *flashing lights* 12
luego *after, later* 3
el lugar *place* 3
la luna de miel *honeymoon* 4r
el lunes *Monday* P
la luz (las luces) *light(s)* 12

M

machacar *to crush* 10r
la madera *wood* 2r, 9
la madrastra *stepmother* 4
la madre *mother* 4
la madrina *godmother* 4
magnífico/a *great* 6
el maíz *corn* 10
mal *bad* P
la maleta *suitcase* 12
el maletero *trunk* 12
el maletín *briefcase* 12
malo/a *bad (character); ill* 6r
la mamá *mom* 4
mañana *tomorrow* P
la mañana *morning* P
mandar *to send* 9
el mandato *command* 9r
manejar *to drive* 12
la mano *hand* 6r, 11
la manta *blanket* 5
la manteca *butter* 10
el mantel *tablecloth* 10
mantener (g, ie) *to maintain* 8
la mantequilla *butter* 10
la manzana *apple* 10
la manzanilla *chamomile* 11r
el mapa *map* P
maquillar(se) *to put makeup on (someone); to put makeup on (oneself)* 4
el mar *sea* 3
el maracuyá *passion fruit* 10
maravilloso/a *marvelous* 8
el marcador *marker* P; *highlighter* 5
la margarina *margarine* 10

los mariscos *shellfish* 10
marrón *brown* 2
marroquí *Moroccan* 2
el martes *Tuesday* P
marzo *March* P
Más alto, por favor. *Louder, please.* Pr
más bueno/a *better* 8r
Más despacio, por favor. *More slowly, please.* Pr
más grande *bigger* 8r
más joven *younger* 8r
más malo/a *worse* 8r
más o menos *more or less* P
la masa *dough* 10r
masticar *to chew* 11r
mayo *May* P
la mayonesa *mayonnaise* 10
mayor *old* 2; *the oldest* 4; *bigger; older* 8r
me *to/for me* 6r
me gusta(n) *I like* 2
Me gustaría... *I would like ...* 6
Me llamo... *My name is ...* P
¿Me podrías hablar sobre...? *Can you talk to me more about ...?* 8r
los médanos *dunes* 7r
la media hermana *half-sister* 4
las medias *stockings, socks* 6
el medicamento *medicine* 11
la medicina *medicine; medication* 11
el/la médico/a *medical doctor* 9
el medio ambiente *environment* 11r
el medio hermano *half-brother* 4
los medios de transporte *means of transportation* 12
la mejilla *cheek* 11
mejor (que) *better (than)* 4r, 8
mejorar *to improve* 4r
la melodía *melody* 8
el melón *melon* 10
menor *the youngest* 4; *smaller; younger* 8r
la mentira *lie* 7r
el mercado *market* 6
la merienda *snack* 12r
el mes *month* P
la mesa *table* P, 10
meter un gol *to score a goal* 7
el metro *subway* 12
mexicano/a *Mexican* 2
mi(s) *my* P
mientras *while* 3, 8
el miércoles *Wednesday* P
mío(s)/mía(s) *mine* 12
Miren, tengo una propuesta. *Look, I have a suggestion.* 7r
la Misa del Gallo *Midnight Mass* 8r

la mochila *backpack* P
molestar(le) *to bother; to be bothered by* 11
morado/a *purple* 2
moreno/a *brunette* 2
morir (ue) *to die* 6r
la mostaza *mustard* 10
el mostrador *counter* 12
mostrar (ue) *to show* 6
el motor *motor* 12
mover (ue) *to move* 7r
mucho (*adv.*) *much, a lot* 2
Mucho gusto. *Pleased/nice to meet you.* P
mucho/a (*adj.*) *many* 2
mudarse *to move* 5r
los muebles *furniture* 5
muerto/a *dead (atmosphere)* 6r; *deceased* 6r; *dead* 8
la mujer *woman* 3
la multa *ticket or fine* 12
mundial *world, worldwide* 7
la muñeca *wrist* 11; *doll* 12r
el/la muñeco/a quitapenas *worry doll* 9r
el músculo *muscle* 11
la música *music* 3, 8
muy *very* P

N

la nacionalidad *nationality* 2
nada *nothing* 12r
nadar *to swim* 3
nadie *no one, nobody* 12r
la naranja *orange* 3
la nariz *nose* 6r, 11
natal *native* 10r
la naturaleza *nature* 7
negro/a *black* 2
el nervio *nerve* 11
nervioso/a *nervous* 2
nevar (ie) *to snow* 7
ni... ni *neither ... nor* 12r
nicaragüense *Nicaraguan* 2
el nido *nest* 5r
la nieta *granddaughter* 4
el nieto *grandson* 4
la nieve *snow* 7
nigeriano/a *Nigerian* 2
la niñera *babysitter* 4r
ningún/ninguno/ninguna *no, not any, none* 12r
el/la niño/a *child* 4
No comprendo. *I do not understand.* Pr
no me diga(s) *really* 4r
no obstante *however* 11r
No sé. *I do not know.* Pr

nos *us* 5; *to/for us* 6r
la noticia *news item* 4
la novia *fiancée; girlfriend* 4
noviembre *November* P
el novio *fiancé; boyfriend* 4
nuestro(s)/nuestra(s) *ours* 12r
nuevo/a *new* 2
nunca *never, (not) ever* 12r

O

o... o *either ... or* 12r
el/la obrero/a *worker* 9
el ocio *free time* 11r
octubre *October* Pr
ocupado/a *busy* 4
odiar *to hate* 8r
la odontología *dentistry* 11r
los oficios *trades* 9
ofrecer (zc) *to offer* 9
¡Oh! ¡Qué lástima! ¡Cuánto lo siento! *How sad! I'm so sorry.* 8r
el oído *inner ear* 11
¡Oigan, tengo una idea! *Listen, I have an idea!* 7r
oír hablar (de) *to hear about* 7r
ojalá que *I/we hope [that]* 11r
el ojo *eye* 2
la oración *sentence* 4r
ordenado/a *tidy* 5
ordenar *to straighten up* 5
la oreja *ear* 6r, 11
organizado/a *organized* 4r
el oro *gold* 2r, 6
la orquesta *orchestra* 8
os *you (familiar plural, Spain)* 5r; *to/for you (familiar)* 6r
oscuro/a *dark* 2
otra vez *again* Pr
otro/a *other, another* 3
la oveja *sheep* 10

P

el/la paciente *patient* 11
el padrastro *stepfather* 4
el padre *father* 4
los padres *parents* 4
el padrino *godfather* 4
pagar *to pay (for)* 6
el país *country, nation* 3
la paiteña *a type of onion* 10r
la palabra *word* 2
las palomitas de maíz *popcorn* 10r
los palos *golf clubs* 7
el pan *bread* 3
el pan dulce *bun; small cake* 10
el pan tostado *toast* 3
la panadería *bakery* 6r

panameño/a *Panamanian* 2
la pantalla *screen* P
los pantalones *pants* 6
los pantalones cortos *shorts* 6
las pantimedias *pantyhose* 6
el pañuelo *handkerchief* 6
la papa *potato* 3
el papá *dad* 4
las papas fritas *French fries* 3
la papaya *papaya* 10
el parabrisas *windshield* 12
el parachoques *bumper* 12
el paraguas *umbrella* 6
paraguayo/a *Paraguayan* 2
parecer *to seem* 6, 6r
la pareja *couple* 4r
el parentesco *kinship* 4r
el/la pariente *relative* 4
el parque de entretenimiento *amusement park* 3r
las partes de un coche *parts of a car* 12
el partido *game* 7
el pasaje *ticket* 12
el/la pasajero/a *passenger* 12
el pasaporte *passport* 12
pasar *to spend (time)* 4
pasar la aspiradora *to vacuum* 5
pasarlo bien *to have a good time* 3r
pase/adelante por favor *please come in* 9r
pasear *to take a walk, stroll* 4
el pasillo *corridor, hall* 5
el paso *step* 5r
la pasta de dientes *toothpaste* 10r
el pastel *cake* 5r; *pastry* 10
la pastilla *pill* 11
la pata *foot (animal)* 2r
patinar *to skate* 7
patrocinar *to sponsor* 12r
el pavo *turkey* 10
el peaje *tollbooth* 12r
el pecho *chest* 11
la pechuga de pollo *chicken breast* 10r
el pediatra *pediatrician* 11r
pedir (i) *to ask for; to order* 4
peinar(se) *to comb (someone's hair); to comb (one's hair)* 4
pelar *to peel* 10r
pelear *to argue* 4r
el/la peletero/a *furrier* 9
la película *film* 3
peligroso/a *dangerous* 12r
pelirrojo/a *redhead* 2
el pelo *hair* 2
la pelota *ball* 7
la peluquería *beauty salon, barbershop* 9

el/la peluquero/a *hairdresser* 9
el penalti *penalty (in sports)* 7
pensar (ie) + infinitive *to think* 4; *to plan to + verb* 4
pensar en *to think about* 3r
peor *worse* 8r
el pepino *cucumber* 10
la pera *pear* 10
perder (ie) *to lose* 6r, 7
perderse (ie) *to get lost* 12
perdón *pardon me, excuse me* P
el perejil *parsley* 10r
perezoso/a *lazy* 2
el periódico *newspaper* 3
el/la periodista *journalist* 9
la personalidad *personality* 2r
las personas *people* 3
peruano/a *Peruvian* 2
la pesadilla *nightmare* 12r
el pescado *fish* 3, 10
la pestaña *eyelash* 11
picado/a *chopped* 10r
picante *spicy* 8r
picar *to chop* 10r
picar(se) *to itch* 11r
el pie *foot (human)* 2r, 6r, 11
la piel *skin* 11r
la pierna *leg* 2r, 6r, 11
la pimienta *pepper* 10; *pepper (spice)* 10r
el pimiento (verde) *(green) pepper* 10
la piña *pineapple* 10
la piscina *swimming pool* 5
el piso *floor; apartment* 5
la pista *slope; court; track* 7
pitar *to whistle* 7
el/la piyama *pajamas* 6
la pizarra *chalkboard* P
la placa *license plate* 12
planchar *to iron* 5
la planta baja *first floor, ground floor* 5
la plata *silver* 6
el plátano *banana, plantain* 10
el plato *dish, plate* 5, 10
el/la plomero/a *plumber* 9
pobre *poor* 2
poder (ue) *to be able to, can* 4
¿Podría mostrarme...? *Could you show me ...?* 5r
¿Podría ver...? *Could I see ...?* 5r
polaco/a *Polish* 2
el/la policía *police officer* 9
el pollo *chicken* 3
el pollo sin piel *skinless chicken* 10r
el pomelo *grapefruit* 10
poner (g) *to put* 3r
poner la mesa *to set the table* 3

poner(se) *to put on* 6
poner(se) (g) la ropa *to put one's clothes on* 4
por cierto *by the way* 9
por favor *please* P
Por favor, póngase cómodo/a. *Please make yourself comfortable.* 9r
Por favor, tome asiento. *Please have a seat.* 9r
Por otro lado... *On the other hand ...* 4r, 11r
Por poco me muero de la risa. *I almost died laughing.* 12r
Por poco me muero del susto. *I almost died, it was so scary.* 12r
¿Por qué no lees/hablas/miras... ? *Why don't you read/say/look at ... ?* 7r
por un lado *on the one hand* 4r, 11r
portugués/portuguesa *Portuguese* 2
el precio *price* 6
precioso/a *beautiful* 6
preferir (ie) *to prefer* 4
el premio *award* 6r
la prenda de vestir *article of clothing* 6r
preparar *to prepare* 5
el preparativo *preparation* 8
presente *here* Pr
la presión (arterial) *(blood) pressure* 11
el presupuesto *budget* 10r
la primera clase *first class* 12
el/la primo/a *cousin* 4
probar (ue) *to try; to taste* 10
probarse (ue) *to try on* 6
el problema *problem* 4r
la procesión *procession* 8
el producto *product* 10
la profesión *profession* 9
el/la profesor/a *professor, teacher* P
el programa de verano *summer program* 4r
el promedio *average* 8r
promocionar *to advertise* 6r
el pronóstico del tiempo *weather report* 7r
propio/a *own* 9
el propósito *purpose* 4r
el proveedor de salud *healthcare provider* 11
próximo *next* 2r, 5r
el/la (p)sicólogo/a *psychologist* 9
el/la psiquiatra *psychiatrist* 11r
el pueblo *village* 5
la puerta *door* P
la puerta (de salida) *gate* 12
puertorriqueño/a *Puerto Rican* 2
el puesto *position* 9

el pulmón *lung* 11
la pulsera *bracelet* 6
el pupitre *student desk* P

Q

¡Qué bien/bueno! *That's great!* 4r
¿Qué desea? *What would you like? (lit., What do you desire?)* 5r
¡Qué divertido! *How funny!* 3r
¡Qué fabuloso/bueno! *How fabulous/ great!* 8r
¡Qué increíble! *Incredible!* 4r
¡Qué interesante! *How interesting!* 8r
¡Qué lata! *What a nuisance!* 3r
¡Qué lío! *What a mess!* 3r
¿Qué me puede decir usted sobre/ de... ? *What can you tell me about ... ?* 8r
¿Qué tal? *What's up? What's new? (informal)* P
¿Qué te parece? *What do you think?* 3
¿Qué te/le(s) pasa? *What's wrong (with you/her/him them)?* 11
¿Qué te/le/les parece esto? *What do you think about this?* 7r
¿Qué te/le/les parece si decimos/ organizamos... ? *How about if we say/organize ... ?* 7r
quedar *to arrange to meet* 8; *to fit; to be left over* 6; *to have something left* 6r
los quehaceres *chores* 7r
quejarse *to complain* 9r
querer (ie) *to want* 4
Querido/a... , *Dear ... ,* 4r
el queso *cheese* 3, 10
el queso crema *cream cheese* 10
¿Quién es... ? *Who is ... ?* P
Quisiera... *I would like ...* 5r, 6
quitar(se) *to take away; to take off* 4

R

el radiador *radiator* 12
el/la radio *radio* 5
la Radio Pública Nacional *NPR* 3r
el/la radiólogo/a *radiologist* 11r
rallar *to grate* 10r
rápido/a *fast* 3
la raqueta *racquet* 7
la razón *reason* 4r
real *royal* 4r
la rebaja *sale* 6
rebajado/a *marked down* 6
la rebanada *slice* 10r
la recepción *front desk* 12
la receta *recipe* 10; *prescription* 11
recetar *to prescribe* 11

rechazar *to decline (invitation)* 3r
recoger *to pick up* 3r, 5
recomendar (ie) *to recommend* 10
el reconocimiento *recognition* 7r
recordar (ue) *to remember* 8
recorrer *to travel, to cover (distance)* 7, 12
el recuerdo *souvenir* 6r
la red *net* 7
reducir *to reduce* 11r
el refresco *soda; soft drink* 3
el refrigerador *refrigerator* 5
regalar *to give (a present)* 6
el regalo *gift* 3r; *present* 6
regar (ie) *to water* 5
regatear *to haggle* 6r
regular *fair* P
reír(se) (ie) *to laugh* 7r
el reloj *clock* P
el remedio *remedy, medicine* 11
el renacimiento *rebirth* 8r
el rendimiento *performance* 9r
repetir (i) *to repeat* 7r
reservar *to make a reservation* 12
resolver (ue) *to resolve* 4r
respirar *to breathe* 4r, 11
la respuesta *answer* 4r
el restaurante *restaurant* 3
la reunión *meeting, gathering* 3
reunirse *to get together* 8
revisar *to inspect* 12
la revista *magazine* 3
el rey/la reina *king/queen* 8
el riachuelo *creek* 4r
rico/a *delicious (food)* 6r; *rich, wealthy* 2,6r
el robo *robbery* 10r
rociar *to spray* 8r
la rodilla *knee* 11
rojo/a *red* 2
la ropa *clothes* 6
la ropa interior *underwear* 6
rosa *pink* 2
rosado/a *pink* 2
roto/a *torn; with holes* 6r
el rotulador *marker* P
rubio/a *blond* 2
la rueda *wheel* 12
la rueda de prensa *press conference* 6r
el ruido *noise* 5r, 8
las ruinas *ruins* 5

S

el sábado *Saturday* P
la sábana *sheet* 5
sacar *to take out* 5
el saco *blazer, jacket* 6

la sal *salt* 10
la sala *living room* 5
la salida de emergencia *emergency exit* 12
la salsa con queso *nacho cheese sauce* 10r
la salsa de tomate *tomato sauce* 10
saltear *sauté* 10r
la salud *health* 11
saludable *healthful* 2r
salvadoreño/a *Salvadoran* 2
el sanatorio *clinic* 11
las sandalias *sandals* 6
el sándwich *sandwich* 3
la sangre *blood* 11
la secadora *dryer* 5
secar(se) *to dry (oneself)* 4
seco/a *dry* 5
seguir (i) *to follow* 4, 7; *to go on* 4 7
seguir (i) derecho *to go straight* 12
según *according to* 4r
la seguridad *security* 8r
la semana *week* P
la semilla *seed* 8
la señal *signal* 9
el/la senderista *hiker* 4r
el señor (Sr.) *Mr.* P
la señora (Sra.) *Ms., Mrs.* P
la señorita (Srta.) *Ms., Miss* P
sentarse (ie) *to sit down* 4
el sentimiento *emotion* 11r; *feeling* 3r
sentir(se) (ie) *to feel* 4, 7r, 11
septiembre *September* Pr
ser *to be* 2
ser alérgico/a a *to be allergic to* 11r
serio/a *serious* 11
la servilleta *napkin* 10
servir (i) *to serve* 4, 7r
si *if* 3
sí *yes* P
sí mismo/a *himself/herself* 6r
siempre *always* 12r
Siéntese aquí, por favor. *Sit here, please.* 9r
la silla *chair* P
simpático/a *nice, charming* 2
sin embargo *nevertheless* 9, 11r
sin fines de lucro *nonprofit* 7r
el síntoma *symptom* 11
sobre *on, above* P
sobrevivir *to survive* 9
la sobrina *niece* 4
el sobrino *nephew* 4
el sofá *sofa* 5
solicitar *to apply (for)* 9
la solicitud *application* 9
soltero/a *single* 2; *unmarried* 5r

el sombrero *hat* 6
la sopa *soup* 3
la sorpresa *surprise* 4r
el sostén *bra* 6
sostener (g, ie) *to support* 12r
el sótano *basement* 5r
soy *I am* P
su(s) *his/her/their* P, 2
suave *soft* 8
subir *to upload* 9r
subir de peso *to gain weight* 3r
subrayar *to underline* 4r
sucio/a *dirty* 3r, 5, 5r
la sudadera *sweatshirt; running suit* 6
el sueldo *salary, wages* 9
el suéter *sweater* 6
el supermercado *supermarket* 6
suyo(s)/suya(s) *his / hers / yours (formal) / theirs* 12r

T

la talla *size (clothes)* 6
el taller *workshop* 9
también *also, too* 12r
tampoco *neither, not* 12r
tan... como *as ... as* 8r
tanto/a... como *as much ... as* 8r
tantos/as... como *as many ... as* 8r
tapar *to cover* 10r
tarde *late* 4
la tarjeta de crédito *credit card* 6
la tarjeta de embarque *boarding pass* 12
la tarjeta magnética *key card* 12
la tarta de manzana *apple pie* 10
la tasa de cambio *exchange rate* 8r
la taza *cup* 10, 10r
te *you (familiar, singular)* 5r; *to/for you (familiar)* 6r
el té *tea* 3
te gusta(n) *you (familiar) like* 2
Te recuerdo con cariño, *I remember you (familiar) with affection,* 4r
el teatro *theater* 8
el/la técnico/a *technician* 9
la tela *fabric* 2r
el teléfono *telephone* 3
el televisor *television set* P
el tema *topic* 4r
temer *to fear* 11
temprano *early* 4
tender (ie) *to hang (clothes)* 5
el tenedor *fork* 10
tener (g, ie) *to have* 4
tener calor *to be hot* 5
tener cuidado *to be careful* 5

tener dolor de... *to have a(n) ... ache* 11
tener éxito *to be successful* 10r
tener frío *to be cold* 5
tener hambre *to be hungry* 5
tener mala cara *to look terrible* 11
tener miedo *to be afraid* 5
tener prisa *to be in a hurry/rush* 5
tener razón *to be right* 5, 6r; *to be correct* 5
tener sueño *to be sleepy* 5
tener suerte *to be lucky* 5
Tenga la amabilidad de pasar. *Please come in.* 9r
Tengo... años. *I am ... years old.* 2
el tenis *tennis* 7
el/la tenista *tennis player* 7
la tensión (arterial) *(blood) pressure* 11
el tercio *third* 9r
el termómetro *thermometer* 11
la terraza *terrace* 5; *deck* 9r
la tía *aunt* 4
el tiempo *weather* 7; *time* 8
el tiempo libre *free time* 3
la tienda *store* 6
la tienda de 24 horas *convenience store* 10r
la tienda de conveniencia *convenience store* 10r
la tienda de la esquina *convenience store* 10r
la tierra *land* 11r
el tío *uncle* 4
típico/a *typical* 3
la tiza *chalk* P
la toalla *towel* 5
el tobillo *ankle* 11
tocar (un instrumento) *to play (an instrument)* 3
todavía *still, yet* 10
todo *everything* 12r
todos los días *every day* 3r
todos/as *everybody* 2, 12r; *all* 12r
tomar el sol *to sunbathe* 3
el tomate *tomato* 3
tonto/a *silly, foolish* 2
torcer(se) (ue) *to twist* 11
el torneo *tournament* 7r
el toro *bull* 8
la toronja *grapefruit* 10
la tos *cough* 11
toser *to cough* 11
la tostada *toast* 3
trabajador/a *hardworking* 2
el trabajo *work* 5, 9

la tradición *tradition* 8
traducir *to translate* 7, 7r
el traje *suit* 6
el traje de baño *bathing suit* 6
el traje de chaqueta *suit* 6
el traje pantalón *pantsuit* 6
el tratamiento médico *medical treatment* 11
tratar *to try* 5r; *to treat* 11
el trayecto *route* 12
trazar *to trace* 3r
el tren *train* 12
triste *sad* 2
tú *you (familiar)* P
tu(s) *your (familiar)* P
túrnense *take turns* P
tuyo(s)/tuya(s) *yours (fam.)* 12r

U

último/a *last* 8
un poco *a little* 4
un/una *a, an* P
la uña de gato *cat's claw* 11r
una semana atrás *a week ago* 6r
una vez *once* 12
uruguayo/a *Uruguayan* 2
usar *to use* 2
usted *you (formal)* P
útil *useful* 2
la uva *grape* 10

V

las vacaciones *vacation* 3, 4r
vacante *opening* 9
vacío/a *empty* 12
la vainilla *vanilla* 10
valer *to be worth* 6
los vaqueros *jeans* 6
el vaso *glass* 3r, 10
el/la vecino/a *neighbor* 5r
el vegetal *vegetable* 3
la velocidad *speed* 12
la vena *vein* 11
el/la vendedor/a *salesman, saleswoman* 9
vender *to sell* 6
venezolano/a *Venezuelan* 2
¡Venga, anímate! *Come on, cheer up!* 3r
venir (g, ie) *to come* 4
la ventaja *advantage* 5
la ventana *window* P
las ventas *sales* 9
el ventilador *fan* 5
ver *to look* 6r, 11r

la verdad *truth* 7r
verde *green; unripe* 2, 6r
la verdura *vegetable* 3. 10
el vestido *dress* 6
vestir(se) (i) *to dress* 4; *to get dressed* 4, 7r
el vestuario *locker room* 7r
viajar *to travel* 3r, 12
viaje *trip* 3r, 12
la vida *life* 2r
la vida activa *active lifestyle* 11r
la vida sedentaria *sedentary lifestyle* 11r
la videocámara *camera* 9r
el vidrio *glass* 2r
viejo/a *old* 2
el viento *wind* 7
el viernes *Friday* Pr
el vinagre *vinegar* 10
el vino *wine* 3
la viruela *smallpox* 11r
visitar *to visit* 4
la vista *view* 5
la vivienda *housing* 5
vivo/a *lively (personality)* 6r; *alive* 4r, 6r, 11r
el volante *steering wheel* 12
volar (ue) *to fly* 3r, 12
el vóleibol *volleyball* 7
volver (ue) *to return* 4
el vuelo *flight* 12
el vuelo de conexión *connecting flight* 12r
vuestro(s)/vuestra(s) *your/s (fam. pl. Spain)* 12r

Y

y *and* P
¡Y esto me sorprendió mucho! *And this surprised me very much!* 12r
ya *already* 10
ya que *since* 5r
yo *I* P
el yogur *yogurt* 10

Z

la zanahoria *carrot* 10
las zapatillas de deporte *tennis shoes* 6
las zapatillas *slippers* 6
el zapato *shoe* 6
los zapatos de tacón *high-heeled shoes* 6
la zona *area* 5

English-Spanish Glossary

A

a little un poco
a lot mucho (*adv.*)
a week ago una semana atrás
a, an un/una
accessory el accesorio
to accompany acompañar
to accomplish lograr
according to de acuerdo con; según
accountant el/la contador/a
to ache doler (ue)
to achieve lograr
active lifestyle la vida activa
actor el actor
actress la actriz
actually en realidad, realmente
ad, advertisement el anuncio
to add agregar; añadir
advantage la ventaja
to advertise promocionar
advice el consejo
to advise aconsejar
aerobics class la clase de ejercicios aeróbicos
affection el cariño
affectionately con cariño
after después; luego
again otra vez
age la edad
agriculture la agricultura
air conditioning el aire acondicionado
airline la aerolínea/línea aérea
airport el aeropuerto
aisle seat el asiento de pasillo
alive vivo/a
all todos/as
already ya
also también
always siempre
among entre
amusement park el parque de entretenimiento
amusing divertido/a
ancestor el/la antepasado/a
and y

And this surprised me very much! ¡Y esto me sorprendió mucho!
angry enojado/a
ankle el tobillo
another otro/a
answer la respuesta
antibiotic el antibiótico
any algún/alguno(s)/alguna(s)
anyone alguien
anything algo
apartment el apartamento; el piso
apple la manzana
apple pie la tarta de manzana
appliances los electrodomésticos
application la solicitud
to apply (for) solicitar
April abril
architect el/la arquitecto/a
architecture la arquitectura
area la zona
Argentinian argentino/a
to argue discutir; pelear
arm el brazo
armchair la butaca
armoire el armario
to arrange to meet quedar
article of clothing la prenda de vestir
as ... as tan... como
to ask for pedir (i)
to ask questions hacer preguntas; preguntar
as many ... as tantos/as... como
as much ... as tanto/a... como
at a
at least al menos
at present actualmente
at times a veces
ATM el cajero automático
atmosphere la atmósfera
August agosto
aunt la tía
average el promedio
average, medium (height) la estatura mediana
avocado el aguacate
award el premio

B

babysitter la niñera
back la espalda
backpack la mochila
bad mal; malo/a
bakery la panadería
ball el balón; la pelota
ballpoint pen el bolígrafo
banana la banana; el plátano
bank el banco
baptism el bautizo
barbecue (event; pit) la barbacoa
barbershop la peluquería
bargain la ganga
baseball el béisbol
basement el sótano
basket (hoop) el cesto/la cesta
basketball el baloncesto; el básquetbol
bat el bate
to bathe bañar(se)
bathing suit el traje de baño
bathroom el baño
bathroom sink el lavabo
bathtub la bañera
to be ser
to be able to poder (ue)
to be afraid tener miedo
to be allergic to ser alérgico/a a
to be bothered by molestar(le)
to be careful tener cuidado
to be cold tener frío
to be correct tener razón
to be fashionable estar de moda
to be glad (about) alegrarse (de)
to be hot tener calor
to be hungry tener hambre
to be in a hurry/rush tener prisa
to be left over quedar
to be lucky tener suerte
to be pleasing to gustar
to be right tener razón
to be sleepy tener sueño
to be successful tener éxito
to be worth valer
to beat batir
to become sick enfermarse
to begin comenzar (ie); empezar (ie)

to believe creer
black negro/a
blacksmith el herrero
blanket la manta
blazer el saco
blender la licuadora
blond rubio/a
blood la sangre
(blood) pressure la presión (arterial)
blouse la blusa
blue azul
boarding pass la tarjeta de embarque
boat el barco
body (human) el cuerpo (humano)
to boil hervir (ie, i)
Bolivian boliviano/a
bone el hueso
book el libro
boot la bota
border la frontera
bored, boring aburrido/a
boss el/la jefe/a
both ambos/as
to bother molestar(le)
bottle la botella
bowl la fuente
to bowl jugar (ue) a los bolos
boxer shorts los calzoncillos
boy el/la chico/a
boyfriend el novio
bra el sostén
bracelet la pulsera
brain el cerebro
bread el pan
to break fracturar(se); romper
to break down descomponerse
to breathe respirar
briefcase el maletín
briefs los calzoncillos
brother el hermano
brown marrón
to brown dorar
brunette moreno/a
budget el presupuesto
to build construir
building el edificio
bull el toro
bullfight la corrida (de toros)
bumper el parachoques
bun el pan dulce
to bury enterrar
bus el autobús/bus
businessman/woman el hombre/la mujer de negocios
busy ocupado/a
butter la manteca; la mantequilla
by the way por cierto

C

cake el pastel
calculator la calculadora
camera la videocámara
can poder (ue)
Can you talk to me more about … ? ¿Me podrías hablar sobre… ?
Canadian canadiense
to cancel cancelar
cancer el cáncer
candied figs el dulce de higos
candy el dulce
canned enlatado/a
cap la gorra
car el auto; el carro; el coche
career counselor el/la consejero/a vocacional
careless descuidado
carnival el carnaval
carpenter el/la carpintero/a
carpet la alfombra
carrot la zanahoria
cart la carreta
cashier el/la cajero/a
cat's claw la uña de gato
to celebrate celebrar
celebration la celebración; la festividad; la fiesta
celery el apio
cell phone charger el cargador del móvil/celular
cemetery el cementerio
cereal el cereal
chair la silla
chalk la tiza
chalkboard la pizarra
chamomile la manzanilla
champion el campeón/la campeona
championship el campeonato
change el cambio
to change cambiar
channel el canal
charming simpático/a
cheap barato/a
to check (luggage) facturar
cheek la mejilla
cheese el queso
chef el/la chef
cherry la cereza
chest el pecho
to chew masticar
chicken el pollo
chicken breast la pechuga de pollo
child el/la niño/a
childhood la infancia
Chilean chileno/a
to choose elegir (i); escoger
chop la chuleta

to chop picar
chopped picado/a
chores los quehaceres
christening el bautizo
church la iglesia
Cinderella Cenicienta
cinnamon la canela
city la ciudad
city block la cuadra
clam la almeja
clean limpio/a
to clean limpiar
clever listo/a
client el cliente/la clienta
clinic la clínica; el sanatorio
clock el reloj
to close cerrar (ie)
close (to) cerca (de)
closet el armario
clothes la ropa
clove of garlic el diente de ajo
coach el entrenador/la entrenadora
coat el abrigo
cobblestone el adoquín
coconut milk la leche de coco
coffee el café
cold el catarro; frío/a (adj.)
to collapse colapsar
Colombian colombiano/a
color el color
to comb (someone's hair) peinar(se)
to come venir (g, ie)
Come on, cheer up! ¡Anda, anímate!; ¡Venga, anímate!
comfort comodidad
comfortable cómodo/a
command el mandato
commonwealth el estado libre asociado
communication la comunicación
company la compañía; la empresa
to complain quejarse
computer la computadora
congratulations felicidades
Congress la Cámara de Representantes
connecting flight el vuelo de conexión
contact lenses los lentes de contacto
contaminated contaminado/a
contest el certamen; el concurso
to contract contraer
contractor el/la contratista
convenience store la tienda de 24 horas; la tienda de conveniencia; la tienda de la esquina
cook el/la cocinero/a
to cook cocinar

cookie la galleta
corn el maíz
corner la esquina
corridor el pasillo
to cost costar (ue)
Costa Rican costarricense
cough la tos
to cough toser
Could I see ...? ¿Podría ver…?
Could you show me ...? ¿Podría
    mostrarme…?
counselor el/la consejero/a
to count contar
counter el mostrador
country el país
countryside el campo
couple la pareja
court la cancha; la pista
cousin el/la primo/a
to cover tapar
to cover (distance) recorrer
cream la crema
cream cheese el queso crema
credit card la tarjeta de crédito
creek el riachuelo
cruise el crucero
to crush machacar
to cry llorar
cucumber el pepino
cumin el comino
cup la taza
to cure curar
curtain la cortina
custom la costumbre
customs la aduana
to cut cortar
cycling el ciclismo
cyclist el/la ciclista

D

dad el papá
dairy (product) (producto) lácteo/a
dangerous peligroso/a
to dare to atreverse (a)
dark oscuro/a
daughter la hija
day el día
day before yesterday anteayer
dead difunto/a; muerto/a
Dear ... , Querido/a… ,
December diciembre
deck la terraza
to decline (an invitation) rechazar
decorated adornado/a
delicious (food) rico/a
to delight encantar
to deliver entregar
dentistry la odontología

department store el almacén
depressed deprimido/a
description la descripción
desk el escritorio
to develop desarrollar
to die morir (ue)
dining room el comedor
dinner la cena; la comida
dirty sucio/a
disadvantage la desventaja
to disassemble desarmar
dish el plato
dishwasher el lavaplatos
divorced divorciado/a
doll la muñeca
Dominican dominicano/a
door la puerta
double/single room la habitación
    doble/sencilla
dough la masa
downtown, center el centro
drawing el dibujo
dress el vestido
to dress; to get dressed
    vestir(se) (i)
dresser la cómoda
drink la bebida
to drive manejar
driver el/la chofer
driver's license la licencia de
    conducir
dry seco/a
to dry (oneself) secar(se)
dry cleaners la lavandería
dryer la secadora
dunes los médanos
during durante
DVD; DVD player el DVD

E

each cada
ear la oreja; el oído
early temprano
earring el arete
eastern occidental
Ecuadorian ecuatoriano/a
egg el huevo
either ... or o… o
elbow el codo
electrician el/la electricista
emergency exit la salida de
    emergencia
to emigrate emigrar
emotion el sentimiento; la emoción
employee el/la empleado/a
empty vacío/a
to encourage animar
engineer el/la ingeniero/a

to enjoy disfrutar
enough bastante
to enter entrar (en)
environment el medio ambiente
equipment el equipo
eraser el borrador
event el evento
ever alguna vez
every ... hours cada… horas
every day todos los días
everybody todo el mundo; todos/as
everything todo
to examine examinar
to exchange intercambiar
excuse me con permiso; perdón
executive el/la ejecutivo/a
expense el gasto
expensive caro/a
experience la experiencia
expression la expresión
to explain explicar
to extinguish, turn off apagar
eye el ojo
eyebrow la ceja
eyelash la pestaña

F

fabric la tela
fabulous estupendo/a; fabuloso/a
face la cara
fact el hecho
fair regular
to fall caer(se)
family la familia
fan el ventilador
far (from) lejos (de)
farmer el/la agricultor/a
farming la agricultura
to fascinate fascinar
fast rápido/a; rápidamente
fast food la comida rápida
fat la grasa; gordo/a (adj.)
father el padre
to fear temer; tener miedo
February febrero
to feel sentir(se) (ie)
feeling el sentimiento
festival el festival
festivity la festividad; la fiesta
fever la fiebre
fiancé el novio
fiancée la novia
field el campo
to fill (out) llenar (rellenar)
film la película
to find encontrar (ue)
to find out averiguar; enterarse
finger el dedo

fire el incendio; el fuego
to fire despedir
firefighter el/la bombero/a
fireplace la chimenea
first class la primera clase
first floor la planta baja
fish el pescado
to fit quedar
flashing lights las luces intermitentes
flight el vuelo
flight attendant el/la auxiliar de vuelo
flip-flops las chanclas
float (in a parade) la carroza
floor el piso
flour la harina
flower la flor
flu la gripe
to fly volar (ue)
to focus fijarse
to fold doblar
to follow seguir (i)
food la comida
foolish tonto/a
foot la pata (*animal*); el pie (*human*)
football el fútbol americano
forehead la frente
fork el tenedor
fowl las aves
to fracture fracturar(se)
free time el ocio; el tiempo libre
freeway la autopista
to freeze congelar(se)
French francés/francesa
French fries las papas fritas
Friday el viernes
fried frito/a
fried dough los churros
friend el/la amigo/a
from de
front desk la recepción
fruit la fruta
to fry freír (i)
to fulfill cumplir
full lleno/a
funny divertido/a
furniture los muebles
furrier el/la peletero/a
furthermore además

G

to gain weight subir de peso
game el juego; el partido
games console la consola de videojuegos
garage el garaje

garbage la basura
garden el jardín
garlic el ajo
gate (airport) la puerta de salida
gathering la reunión
German alemán/alemana
to get angry enfadarse
to get bored aburrirse
to get lost perderse (ie)
to get married casarse
to get together reunirse
to get up levantar(se)
to get up on the wrong side of the bed levantarse con el pie izquierdo
to give dar
to give (a present) regalar
to give background information dar información de fondo
to go ir
to go away irse
to go in entrar (en)
to go on seguir (i)
to go shopping ir de compras
to go straight seguir (i) derecho
to go to bed acostarse (ue)
golf clubs los palos
golf course la cancha
good (character) bueno/a
good afternoon buenas tardes
good evening buenas noches
good morning buenos días
good night buenas noches
good-bye adiós; chao
good-looking guapo/a
government el gobierno
granddaughter la nieta
grandfather el abuelo
grandmother la abuela
grandson el nieto
grape la uva
grapefruit el pomelo; la toronja
grass el césped
to grate rallar
gray gris
great fabuloso/a; magnífico/a
green verde
(green) pepper el pimiento (verde)
ground floor la planta baja
ground meat la carne molida; la carne picada
to grow crecer
Guatemalan guatemalteco/a
to guess adivinar
guide (book) la guía
guide (person) el/la guía
guitar la guitarra

H

to haggle regatear
hair el cabello; el pelo
hairdresser el/la peluquero/a
half-brother el medio hermano
half-sister la media hermana
hall el pasillo
Halloween el Día de las Brujas
ham el jamón
hamburger la hamburguesa
hand la mano
to hand in dar; entregar
handicrafts la artesanía
handkerchief el pañuelo
handsome guapo/a
to hang (clothes) tender (ie)
happy alegre; contento/a
hardworking trabajador/a
to harvest cosechar
hat el sombrero
to hate odiar
to have tener (g, ie)
to have a good time divertirse (ie) pasarlo bien
to have a(n) ... ache tener dolor de…
to have breakfast desayunar
to have dinner cenar
to have lunch almorzar (ue)
to have something left quedar
healthful saludable
to hear about oír hablar de
heart el corazón
heating la calefacción
hello hola
to help ayudar
herb la hierba
here presente
hermitage la ermita
hi hola
high-heeled shoes los zapatos de tacón
highlighter el marcador; el rotulador
highway la carretera
hiker el/la senderista
himself/herself sí mismo/a
hip la cadera
his/her/their su(s)
his/hers/yours (formal)/theirs suyo(s)/suya(s)
Hispanic hispano/a
holiday la festividad; el día festivo; la fiesta; el dia feriado
home el hogar
homemade casero/a
homemaker el amo/a de casa
Honduran hondureño/a

honeymoon la luna de miel
hood (of a car) el capó
hospital el hospital
hot caliente (*temperature*); picante (*spicy*)
hot pepper el ají; el chile
hotel el hotel
housewife el ama de casa
housing la vivienda
How about if we say/organize … ? ¿Qué te/le/les parece si decimos/organizamos… ?
How about that! ¡Fíjate qué noticia!
How are you? ¿Cómo está? (formal); ¿Cómo estás? (informal)
How can/may I help you? ¿En qué puedo ayudarle(s)/servirle(s)?
How do you say… in Spanish? ¿Cómo se dice… en español?
How fabulous/great! ¡Qué fabuloso/bueno!
How funny! ¡Qué divertido!
How interesting! ¡Qué interesante!
How sad! I'm so sorry. ¡Oh! ¡Qué lástima! ¡Cuánto lo siento!
however no obstante
hugs and kisses abrazos y besos
to hurt doler (ue)
to hurt oneself hacerse daño

I

I yo
I almost died laughing. Por poco me muero de risa.
I almost died; it was so scary. Por poco me muero del susto.
I am soy
I am … years old. Tengo… años.
I am so happy for you!; I'm so happy to hear that! ¡Cuánto me alegro!
I do not know. No sé.
I do not understand. No comprendo.
I like me gusta(n)
I remember you (*familiar*) with affection, Te recuerdo con cariño,
I was so scared! ¡Estaba tan asustado/a!
I would like … Me gustaría… ; Quisiera…
I would like to speak with … [person's name]. Quisiera/Me gustaría hablar con… [nombre de persona].
I/we hope [that] ojalá que
ice el hielo
ice cream el helado
if si

ill malo/a
illness la enfermedad
I'm sorry (to hear that) lo siento
immediately enseguida
to improve mejorar
in en
In addition Además…
in cash en efectivo
in contrast en contraste
in fact en realidad/realmente
in front (of) delante (de); enfrente (de)
to inspect revisar
in style de moda
In the first/second place … En primer/segundo lugar…
in the middle en medio
Incredible! ¡Qué increíble!
inexpensive barato/a
infection la infección
injection la inyección
injured person el/la herido/a
inner ear oído
to interest interesar
interpreter el/la intérprete
interview la entrevista
to interview entrevistar
invitation la invitación
to invite invitar
to iron planchar
ironworker el herrero
Is … [person's name] there, please? ¿Está… [nombre de persona], por favor?
it has been a day/month/year since hace un día/mes/año (que)
it is raining está lloviendo; llueve
it is sunny hace sol
it was a pleasure to meet you fue un placer conocerlo/la
it's clear está despejado
it's cloudy está nublado
it's cool hace fresco
it's good/bad weather hace buen/mal tiempo
it's hot hace calor

J

jacket el saco; la chaqueta
January enero
Japanese japonés/japonesa
jeans los jeans; los vaqueros
jeweller el/la joyero/a
jewelry la joya
joke la broma; el chiste
to joke bromear
journalist el/la periodista
joy la alegría
judge el juez/la jueza

juice el jugo
July julio
June junio
junk food la comida basura

K

key la llave
key card la tarjeta magnética
king el rey
kinship el parentesco
kitchen la cocina
kitchen sink el fregadero
knee la rodilla
knife el cuchillo
to knock golpear

L

lack of la falta de
lake el lago
lamb el cordero
lamp la lámpara
land la tierra
laptop la computadora portátil
last último/a
to last durar
last night anoche
last year el año pasado
late tarde
later después; luego
to laugh reír(se) (i)
laundry room la lavandería
lawn el césped
lawyer el/la abogado/a
layout la distribución
lazy perezoso/a
leaf la hoja
leather el cuero
to leave dejar; ir(se)
lecture la conferencia
left la izquierda
leg la pierna
legal holiday el día feriado
legally/illegally parked bien/mal aparcado
legumes las legumbres
leisure activities las diversiones
lemon el limón
Lent la Cuaresma
lentils las lentejas
lettuce la lechuga
librarian el/la bibliotecario/a
license plate la placa
lie la mentira
life la vida
to lift weights levantar pesas
light(s) la luz (las luces)
to like gustar

likewise igualmente
lip el labio
Listen, I have an idea! ¡Oigan, tengo una idea!
lively animado/a; vivo/a
living room la sala
lobster la langosta
to lock up encerrar (ie)
lock (of a canal) la esclusa
locker room el vestuario
lodging el alojamiento
long largo/a
to look ver
to look at mirar
to look for buscar
to look terrible tener mala cara
to lose perder (ie)
to lose weight bajar de peso
Louder, please. Más alto, por favor.
to love encantar
luggage el equipaje
lunch el almuerzo
lung el pulmón

M

magazine la revista
to maintain mantener (g, ie)
to make a reservation reservar
to make the bed hacer la cama
map el mapa
March marzo
margarine la margarina
marinated raw fish and seafood el ceviche
marked down rebajado/a
marker el marcador; el rotulador
market el mercado
married casado/a
marvelous maravilloso/a
May mayo
mayonnaise la mayonesa
meal la comida
means of transportation los medios de transporte
meat la carne
medical doctor el/la médico/a
medical treatment el tratamiento médico
medicine el medicamento; la medicina; el remedio
to meet conocer (make someone's acquaintance); encontrarse con (get together with someone)
meeting la reunión
melody la melodía
melon el melón
melted derretido/a
Mexican mexicano/a

microwave (oven) el (horno) microondas
Midnight Mass la Misa del Gallo
milk la leche
mine mío(s)/mía(s)
mirror el espejo
mom la mamá
Monday el lunes
money el dinero
month el mes
mood el estado de ánimo
more or less más o menos
More slowly, please. Más despacio, por favor.
morning la mañana
Moroccan marroquí
mother la madre
motor el motor
mouth la boca
to move mover (ue); mudarse (change residence)
movies el cine
to mow (lawn) cortar
Mr. el señor (Sr.)
Ms., Miss la señorita (Srta.)
Ms., Mrs. la señora (Sra.)
much mucho (adv.); mucho/a (adj.)
muscle el músculo
music la música
mustard la mostaza
my mi(s)
My name is ... Me llamo…

N

nacho cheese sauce la salsa con queso
napkin la servilleta
narrow estrecho/a
nation el país; la nación
nationality la nacionalidad
native (country) natal
nature la naturaleza
near cerca (de)
neck el cuello
necklace el collar
neighbor el/la vecino/a
neighborhood el barrio
neither tampoco
neither ... nor ni… ni
nephew el sobrino
nerve el nervio
nervous nervioso/a
nest el nido
net la red
never jamás; nunca
nevertheless sin embargo
new nuevo/a
news la noticia; (news item); las noticias (news broadcast)
newspaper el periódico

next (to) al lado (de); próximo/a (adj.)
Nicaraguan nicaragüense
nice agradable; simpático/a
niece la sobrina
Nigerian nigeriano/a
nightgown el camisón
nightmare la pesadilla
no ningún/ninguno/ninguna
no one nadie
nobody nadie
noise el ruido
none ningún/ninguno/ninguna
nonprofit sin fines de lucro
nose la nariz
not tampoco
not any ningún/ninguno/ninguna
(not) ever jamás; nunca
note card la ficha
notebook el cuaderno
nothing nada
November noviembre
now actualmente; ahora
nowadays hoy en día
NPR la Radio Pública Nacional
nurse el/la enfermero/a

O

occupation la ocupación
October octubre
of de
Of course! ¡Claro!; ¡Cómo no!
of the (contraction of de + el) del
to offer ofrecer (zc)
office (of doctor, dentist, etc.) el consultorio
oil el aceite
old mayor; viejo/a
on the one hand por un lado
on the other hand en cambio; por otro lado
On what page? ¿En qué página?
on, above sobre
once una vez
onion la cebolla
only child el/la hijo/a único/a
open air al aire libre
opening el vacante
opposing contrario/a
orange anaranjado/a; la naranja
orchestra la orquesta
to order pedir (i)
organized organizado/a
other otro/a
ours nuestro(s)/nuestra(s)
outdoors al aire libre
outskirts las afueras
overcast (sky) cubierto
own propio/a

P

pain el dolor
painting el cuadro
pajamas la piyama
Panamanian panameño/a
pants los pantalones
pantsuit el traje pantalón
pantyhose las pantimedias
papaya la papaya
parade el desfile
Paraguayan paraguayo/a
pardon me con permiso;
    perdón
parents los padres
parsley el perejil
parts of a car las partes de un
    coche/carro
party la fiesta
passenger el/la pasajero/a
passion fruit el maracuyá
passport el pasaporte
pastry el pastel
path el camino
patient paciente; el/la paciente
to pay (for) pagar
pear la pera
peasant el/la campesino/a
pediatrician el/la pediatra
to peel pelar
penalty (in sports) el penalti
pencil el lápiz
people la gente; las personas
pepper el pimiento (*vegetable*); la
    pimienta (*spice*)
performance el rendimiento
personality la personalidad
Peruvian peruano/a
pharmacist el/la farmacéutico/a
pharmacy la farmacia
photo(graph) la foto(grafía)
physical appearance la
    apariencia
physically attractive bueno/a
    (*slang*)
to pick up recoger (j)
picture el cuadro
pill la pastilla
pillow la almohada
pineapple la piña
pink rosa; rosado/a
place el lugar
to plan to + verb pensar (ie)
    + *infinitive*
plane el avión
plantain el plátano
plate el plato
to play (a game, sport) jugar
    (ue)

to play (an instrument) tocar (un
    instrumento)
please por favor
Please come in. Pase/Adelante,
    por favor.; Tenga la amabilidad de
    pasar.
Please have a seat. Por favor, tome
    asiento.
**Please make yourself
    comfortable.** Por favor, póngase
    cómodo/a.
pleased/nice to meet you
    encantado/a; mucho gusto
plumber el/la plomero/a
policeman/woman el/la policía
Polish polaco/a
polluted contaminado/a
poor pobre
popcorn las palomitas de maíz
pork el cerdo
Portuguese portugués/portuguesa
position el puesto
poster el afiche
potato la papa
potter el/la ceramista
poultry las aves
prairie el llano
to prefer preferir (ie)
to prepare preparar
to prescribe recetar
prescription la receta
present el regalo
press conference la rueda de
    prensa
pretty bonito/a
price el precio
printer la impresora
problem el problema
procession la procesión
to produce elaborar; producir
product el producto
profession la profesión
professor el/la profesor/a
psychiatrist el/la psiquiatra
psychologist el/la (p)sicólogo/a
Puerto Rican puertorriqueño/a
purple morado/a
purpose el propósito
purse la bolsa/el bolso
**to put makeup on
    (oneself)** maquillar(se)
to put on poner(se)
to put one's clothes on poner(se) (g)
    la ropa
to put to bed acostar (ue)

Q

queen la reina

R

racquet la raqueta
radiator el radiador
radio el/la radio
radio announcer el/la locutor/a
radiologist el/la radiólogo/a
rain la lluvia
to rain llover (ue)
raincoat el impermeable
to raise levantar
rather bastante
ready listo/a
really en realidad; realmente
Really! ¡No me diga(s)!
to recommend recomendar (ie)
rearview mirror el espejo retrovisor
reason la razón
recipe la receta
recognition el reconocimiento
red rojo/a
redhead pelirrojo/a
to reduce reducir
referee el árbitro
refrigerator el refrigerador
relative el/la pariente
remedy el remedio
to remember recordar (ue)
rent el alquiler
to rent alquilar
to repeat repetir (i)
to resolve resolver (ue)
to rest descansar
restaurant el restaurante
résumé el currículum
to return volver (ue)
rib la costilla
rice el arroz
rich, wealthy rico/a
right la derecha
ring el anillo
road el camino
robbery el robo
robe la bata
roommate el/la compañero/a
round trip de ida y vuelta
route el trayecto
royal real
rug la alfombra
ruins las ruinas
running suit la sudadera

S

sad triste
safe la caja fuerte
salad la ensalada
salad dressing el aderezo
salary el sueldo

sale la rebaja
sales las ventas
(sales) manager el/la gerente (de ventas)
salesman, saleswoman el/la vendedor/a
salt la sal
Salvadoran salvadoreño/a
sandals las sandalias
sandwich el sándwich
Saturday el sábado
sauté saltear
to save ahorrar
sawdust el aserrín
to say decir (g, i)
to say goodbye despedirse (i)
scientist el/la científico/a
to score a goal meter un gol
screen la pantalla
sea el mar
seasoning el condimento
seat el asiento
security la seguridad
sedentary lifestyle la vida sedentaria
see you later hasta luego
see you soon hasta pronto
see you tomorrow hasta mañana
seed la semilla
to seem parecer
to sell vender
to send enviar; mandar
sentence la oración
September septiembre
serious serio/a
serious (situation) grave
seriously ill grave
to serve servir (i)
server el/la camarero/a
to set the table poner la mesa
setting el ambiente
several algunos/as
shake el batido
to share compartir
to shave (oneself) afeitar(se)
sheep la oveja
sheet la sábana
shell la concha
shellfish los mariscos
ship el barco
shirt la camisa
shoe el zapato
shopping las compras
shopping center el centro comercial
shopping list la lista de compras
short (height) bajo/a
short (length) corto/a
shorts los pantalones cortos

shoulder el hombro
to show mostrar (ue)
shower la ducha
shrimp el camarón; la gamba
to shut in encerrar (ie)
sick enfermo/a
sick person el/la enfermo/a
signal la señal
silly tonto/a
silver la plata
since ya que
single soltero/a
to sing cantar
sister la hermana
to sit down sentarse (ie)
Sit here, please. Siéntese aquí, por favor.
size (clothes) la talla
to skate patinar
to ski esquiar
skiing el esquí
skin la piel
skinless chicken el pollo sin piel
skirt la falda
skull la calavera
sky el cielo
to sleep (to fall asleep) dormir(se) (ue)
slice la rebanada
slippers las zapatillas
slope la longitud de bajada; la pista
smaller más pequeño/a; menor
smallpox la viruela
smart listo/a
to smoke fumar
snack la merienda
to sneeze estornudar
snow la nieve
to snow nevar (ie)
soap el jabón
soccer el fútbol
socks los calcetines; las medias
soda el refresco
sofa el sofá
soft suave
soft drink el refresco
soft drink bottle la botella para refrescos
some algunos/as
someone alguien
something algo
sometime alguna vez
sometimes algunas veces
son el hijo
song la canción
soup la sopa
sour agrio/a
souvenir el recuerdo
spaghetti los espaguetis

Spanish español/española
specialty la especialidad
speech el discurso
speed la velocidad
to spend gastar
to spend (time) pasar
spicy picante
spinach las espinacas
to sponsor patrocinar
spoon la cuchara
spoonful la cucharada
sports los deportes
sports equipment el equipo deportivo
to spray rociar
stadium el estadio
to stand in line hacer cola
stairs la escalera
start empezar (ie); comenzar (ie)
steak la carne de res; el bistec
steering wheel el volante
step el paso
stepbrother el hermanastro
stepfather el padrastro
stepmother la madrastra
stepsister la hermanastra
still todavía
stockings las medias
stomach el estómago
to stop detener
stopover la escala
store la tienda
store window el escaparate
stove la estufa
strawberry la fresa
street la calle
stress el estrés
strong fuerte
student el/la estudiante
student desk el pupitre
style el estilo
subway el metro
sugar el azúcar
suit el traje; el traje de chaqueta
suitcase la maleta
summer program el programa de verano
to sunbathe tomar el sol
Sunday el domingo
sunglasses las gafas de sol
supermarket el supermercado
supper la cena; la comida
to support sostener
surgeon el/la cirujano/a
surprise la sorpresa
surprise party la fiesta sorpresa
to survive sobrevivir
sweater el suéter
sweatshirt la sudadera

to sweep barrer
to swim nadar
swimming pool la piscina
swollen hinchado/a
symptom el síntoma

T

table la mesa
tablecloth el mantel
to/for me me
to/for us nos
to/for you (familiar) os; te
to/for you (formal), him, her, it le
to/for you (formal), them les
to take a shower ducharse
to take a walk dar un paseo; pasear
to take advantage aprovechar
to take away quitar
to take care of cuidar(se) (de)
to take off quitarse
to take out sacar
to take turns turnarse
to taste probar (ue)
to tell decir (g, i)
terrace la terraza
thanks, thank you gracias
Thanksgiving el Día de Acción de
    Gracias
that (*adj.*) ese/esa
that (over there) aquel/aquella
That's great! ¡Qué bien/bueno!
to the left a la izquierda
to the right a la derecha
the weather is bad hace mal tiempo
the weather is good hace buen
    tiempo
theater el teatro
then entonces
there is, there are hay
thermometer el termómetro
these estos/estas
thief el ladrón/la ladrona
thin delgado/a
thing la cosa
to think pensar (ie) + *infinitive*
to think about pensar (ie) en
this este/esta
those esos/esas
those (over there) aquellos/
    aquellas
throat la garganta
to throw lanzar
Thursday el jueves
ticket el billete; el boleto; la multa; el
    pasaje
tidy ordenado/a
tie la corbata
tight estrecho/a; apretado/a

time el tiempo; la hora
tire la llanta
tired cansado/a
to a
toast el pan tostado; la tostada
today hoy
together juntos/as
toilet el inodoro
tollbooth el peaje
tomato el tomate
tomato sauce la salsa de tomate
tomorrow mañana
too también
tooth el diente
toothpaste la pasta de dientes
topic el tema
torn roto/a
tourist class la clase turista
tournament el campeonato; el
    torneo
towel la toalla
toy el juguete
to trace trazar
track la pista
trades los oficios
tradition la tradición
train el tren
training camp el centro de
    entrenamiento
to translate traducir
trash la basura
to travel recorrer; viajar
travel agency la agencia de
    viajes
travel agent el/la agente de
    viajes
tray la bandeja
to treat tratar
tree el árbol
trip viaje
to try probar (ue); tratar
to try on probarse (ue)
truth la verdad
T-shirt la camiseta
Tuesday el martes
turkey el pavo
to turn doblar
to turn in entregar
to twist torcer(se) (ue)
typical típico/a

U

U.S. citizen estadounidense
ugly feo/a
umbrella el paraguas
umpire el árbitro
uncle el tío
to uncover descubrir

under debajo (de)
to underline subrayar
to understand entender (ie)
underwear la ropa interior
unemployment el desempleo
unmarried soltero/a
unpleasant antipático/a
to upload subir
unripe verde
Uruguayan uruguayo/a
us nos
to use usar
useful útil

V

vacation las vacaciones
to vacuum pasar la aspiradora
vacuum cleaner la aspiradora
vanilla la vainilla
vegetable el vegetal; la verdura
vein la vena
Venezuelan venezolano/a
very muy
view la vista
village el pueblo
vinegar el vinagre
to visit visitar
volleyball el vóleibol

W

wages el sueldo
wagon la carreta
waist la cintura
to wait for esperar
waiter/waitress (restaurant) el/la
    camarero/a
to wake (someone up) despertar (ie)
to wake up despertarse (ie)
wallet la billetera
to want desear; querer (ie)
warehouse el almacén
to wash (oneself) lavar(se)
washer la lavadora
wastebasket el cesto
water el agua
to water regar (ie)
weak débil
to wear llevar
to wear a costume disfrazarse
weather report el pronóstico del
    tiempo
wedding la boda
Wednesday el miércoles
week la semana
well bien
well (health) bueno/a
What a mess! ¡Qué lío!

What a nuisance! ¡Qué lata!

What can you tell me about … ? ¿Qué me puede decir usted sobre/de… ?

What do you think about this? ¿Qué te/le/les parece esto?

What do you think? ¿Qué te/le/les parece?

What is he/she/it like? ¿Cómo es?

What would you like? (*lit.*, **What do you desire?**) ¿Qué desea?

What's up? What's new? (informal) ¿Qué tal?

What's wrong (with you/them)? ¿Qué te/le(s) pasa?

What's your name? (familiar, informal) ¿Cómo te llamas?

What's your name? (formal) ¿Cómo se llama usted?

wheel la rueda

where (to)? ¿adónde?

Where is … ? ¿Dónde está… ?

while mientras

to whistle pitar

white blanco/a

Who is … ? ¿Quién es… ?

Who is this? ¿Con quién hablo?

Whose? ¿De quién?

Why don't you read/say/look at … ? ¿Por qué no lees/hablas/miras… ?

wide ancho/a

wife la esposa

to win ganar

wind el viento

window la ventana

window seat el asiento de ventanilla

windshield el parabrisas

windshield wiper el limpiaparabrisas

wine el vino

to wish desear

with me conmigo

with much love con mucho cariño

with you (familiar) contigo

woman la mujer

wood la madera

word la palabra

work el trabajo

worker el/la obrero/a

workshop el taller

world, worldwide mundial

worry doll el muñeco/la muñeca quitapenas

worse más malo/a; peor

wound la herida

wrist la muñeca

Y

year el año

yellow amarillo/a

yes sí

yesterday ayer

yet todavía

yogurt el yogur

you (familiar plural, Spain) os

you (familiar) tú

you (familiar) like te gusta(n)

you (familiar, singular) te

you (formal and familiar plural), them (feminine) las

you (formal and familiar, plural), them (masculine) los

you (formal) usted

you (formal) like; he/she likes le gusta(n)

you (formal, singular), her, it (feminine) la

you (formal, singular), him, it (masculine) lo

you are (familiar) eres; estás

you are (formal), he/she is es

young joven

young man/woman el/la joven

younger; youngest más joven; menor

your (familiar) tu(s)

your(s) (familiar plural, Spain) vuestro(s)/vuestra(s)

you're welcome de nada

yours (familiar) tuyo(s)/tuya(s)

Z

zip code el código postal

Communicative Functions and Learning Strategies Index

Note: This index shows chapter numbers rather than page numbers. "P" refers to the Preliminary chapter.

Photo Credits

Common Art

tablet computer: popcic/Shutterstock; **yellow memo note:** kanate/Shutterstock; **newspaper:** Milos Luzanin/Shutterstock.

Front Matter

p. xiv: ImageryMajestic/Shutterstock; **p. xxvi:** William Perugini/Shutterstock; **p. xxvii:** © Silvano Rebai/Fotolia; **p. xxviii (top):** Monkey Business Images/Shutterstock; **(bottom):** © Michael Flippo/Fotolia; **p. xxix:** max blain © Shutterstock; **p. xxx (top):** David Mercado/Sygma/CORBIS; **(bottom):** Skyline/ Shutterstock; **p. xxxi:** © J.Enrique Molina/Alamy; **p. xxxii (top):** anat_tikker/ Fotolia; **(bottom):** Jose Luis Stephens/Alamy; **p. xxxiii:** © Jose Angel Murillo / Alamy; **p. xxxiv:** William Perugini/Shutterstock; **p. xxxv (tl):** Elizabeth Guzman; **(tr):** Judith E. Liskin-Gasparro; **(b):** Paloma Lapuerta.

Capítulo Preliminar

p. 3: Jeff Greenberg / Alamy; **p. 5:** © michaeljung/Fotolia; **p. 6 (top):** Ian O'Leary/ Getty Images Inc. - Stone Allstock; **(bottom):** © paulo Jorge cruz/Fotolia; **p. 7:** Poznyakov/ Shutterstock; **p. 9 (top):** © priganica/Fotolia; **(bottom):** Kim Reinick/Shutterstock; **p. 11:** © xy/ Fotolia; **p. 14 (top):** © pedrosala/Fotolia; **(bottom):** © Silvano Rebai /Fotolia; **p. 17 (top):** © chokniti/Fotolia; **(bottom):** © Photoroller/ Fotolia; **p. 18 (top):** © Scanrail /Fotolia; **(bottom):** © adimas/Fotolia; **p. 19 (top):** © Brad Pict /Fotolia; **(bottom):** Alex Havret © Dorling Kindersley; **p. 20:** © Faraways/Fotolia.

Online Component

O-2 (tl): Ian O'Leary/Getty Images Inc. - Stone Allstock; **(tr):** Tony Souter © Dorling Kindersley; **(bl):** EdBockStock © Shutterstock; **O-3:** © Dorling Kindersley; **O-8:** © diego cervo/ Fotolia; **O-9:** © pedrosala/Fotolia; **O-13:** © robootb/Fotolia; **O-14:** © Scanrail /Fotolia; **O-15:** © Petr Vaclavek/Fotolia; **O-16 (tl):** © Faraways/Fotolia; **(tr):** Paul Bricknell © Dorling Kindersley; **(c):** © Barone Rosso/Fotolia; **(bl):** © Dorling Kindersley; **(br):** © Dorling Kindersley; **O-17:** © Silkstock/Fotolia.

Capítulo 1

p. 23 (top, clockwise from top): Dorota Jarymowicz and Mariusz Jarymowicz © Dorling Kindersley; Pilar Echevarria/Shutterstock; age fotostock/Robert Harding; Matt Trommer/ Shutterstock; Rafael Ramirez Lee/Shutterstock; **(bottom):** Album / Prisma/Newscom; **p. 24:** Andresr/Shutterstock; **p. 25 (left):** © lansbricae/ Fotolia; **(right):** © Volker Z/Fotolia; **p. 26:** Jenkedco/Shutterstock; **p. 27:** © Roman Sigaev/ Fotolia; **p. 30:** © santiago pais /Fotolia; **p. 31 (top):** © Andres Rodriguez/Fotolia; **(bottom):** Tim Draper © Rough Guides/Dorling Kindersley; **p. 33:** © WavebreakmediaMicro/Fotolia; **p. 35:** Richard Nowitz/National Geographic Stock; **p. 37 (top):** JHershPhoto/Shutterstock;

(bottom): Rough Guides/Dorling Kindersley; **p. 40:** © MIMOHE/Fotolia; **p. 43 (top):** © Spencer Grant / PhotoEdit; **(bottom):** © auremar/Fotolia; **p. 44:** © Gabriel Blaj; **p. 48:** © Miguel Castaño/Fotolia; **p. 49:** Dmitriy Shironosov/Shutterstock; **p. 50 (top):** Linda Whitwam © Dorling Kindersley; **(cl):** EFE/Juan Carlos Hidalgo/Newscom; **(cr):** Max Alexander © Dorling Kindersley.

Online Component

O-18 (t): Andresr/Shutterstock; **(b):** © goodluz/ Fotolia, **O-19:** Jenkedco/Shutterstock; **O-21 (top):** Lucian Coman/Shutterstock; **(bottom):** © Gina Sanders/Fotolia; **O-25:** © Aaron Amat/ Fotolia, **O-30:** © Prod. Numérik/Fotolia; **O-31:** © Spencer Grant / PhotoEdit; **O-32:** f9photos/ Shutterstock; **O-33 (tl):** © Paco Ayala/Fotolia; **(tr):** © STEPHANE - FOTODECLIC / age fotostock / SuperStock; **(b):** ASSOCIATED PRESS; **O-34:** © Miguel Castaño/Fotolia.

Capítulo 2

p. 53 (top, clockwise from top): © ZUMA Wire Service / Alamy; © Hola Images / Alamy; Robin Holden Sr - Holden Photography/Shutterstock; April Turner/Shutterstock; Graça Victoria/ Shutterstock; © Photos 12 / Alamy; **(bottom):** © Images.com / Alamy; **p. 54:** © Andres Rodriguez/Fotolia; **p. 55 (top):** Greg Roden/ Rough Guides/Dorling Kindersley Ltd.; **(bottom):** © AVAVA/Fotolia; **p. 57 (center, left to right):** Wallenrock/Shutterstock; Dallas Events Inc/Shutterstock; © michaeljung/Fotolia; Yuri Arcurs/Shutterstock; **(bottom):** © WONG SZE FEI/Fotolia; **p. 58:** Elizabeth Guzman; **p. 60:** © berc/Fotolia; **p. 61:** JinYoung Lee/Shutterstock; **p. 62:** © WavebreakmediaMicro/Fotolia; **p. 63 (left to right):** Michael Germana / SSI Photo / Landov; Jack Vartoogian/Front Row Photos; REUTERS/Steve Nesius /Landov; ASSOCIATED PRESS; **p. 64 (top):** ASSOCIATED PRESS; **(bottom):** William Perugini/Shutterstock; **p. 65 (top):** michaeljung/Shutterstock; **(bottom):** © Gino Santa Maria/Fotolia; **p. 66:** © sdecoret/ Fotolia; **p. 69:** dwphotos/Shutterstock; **p. 70:** Andresr/Shutterstock; **p. 71 (top):** ARENA Crea-tive/Shutterstock; **(center):** © ArchMen/Fotolia; **(bottom):** © Andres Rodriguez/Fotolia; **p. 72:** Jaimie Duplass/Shutterstock; **p. 73:** © Andres Rodriguez/Fotolia; **p. 74 (top):** © Andres Rodriguez/; **(center):** Skyline/Shutterstock; **p. 75:** AISPIX by Image Source/Shutterstock; **p. 76 (top):** © Alliance Images / Alamy; **(bottom):** © Monkey Business/Fotolia; **p. 77:** © Scanrail/Fotolia, **p. 78:** Andresr/Shutterstock; **p. 79:** Leonidovich/Shutterstock; **p. 80 (tl):** Alessandra Santarelli / Jeoff Davis © Dorling Kindersley; **(tr):** © Alfonso Vicente / Alamy; **(cr):** Robert Holmes © Dorling Kindersley.

Online Component

O-35 (tl): © Andres Rodriguez/Fotolia; **(tr):** © Samuel Borges/Fotolia; **(bl):** Mel Lindstrom/ Creative Eye/MIRA.com; **O-36 (tl):** © CS Productions/Fotolia; **(tr):** Andresr/Shutterstock; **(b):** EDHAR/Shutterstock; **O-39 (left to right):**

Elizabeth Guzman; © Paloma Lapuerta; Judy Liskin-Gasparro; **O-42:** ASSOCIATED PRESS; **O-46:** Andresr/Shutterstock; **O-48:** © Andres Rodriguez/Fotolia; **O-50 (tl):** © Yaroslav/Fotolia; **(tr):** Library of Congress; **(bl):** Kendal Larson; **(br):** © michal812/Fotolia.

Capítulo 3

p. 83 (top, top to bottom): Suzanne Porter/ Dorling Kindersley Ltd.; Mike VON BERGEN/ Shutterstock; colacat/Shutterstock; Chris Howey/ Shutterstock; Paul Clarke/Shutterstock; **(bottom):** © Mireille Vautier / Alamy; **(frame):** Studio DMM Photography, Designs & Art/Shutterstock; **p. 84:** Copyright Todd Powell/ Mira.com; **p. 85:** Nik Wheeler/Dorling Kindersley; **p. 86 (left):** Luis Santos/Shutterstock; **(right):** Giuseppe_R/ Shutterstock; **p. 87 (t):** Robert Kneschke/ Shutterstock; **(bottom):** © Pixel Embargo/ Fotolia; **p. 88:** © Comugnero Silvana/Fotolia; **p. 89:** © Adalberto Rios Szalay/Sexto Sol/Value-line/Getty Punchstock RF Images Inc.; **p. 90:** © rebecca abel/Fotolia; **p. 91 (left):** © John Van Hasselt/Sygma/Corbis; **(right):** © Tim Draper © Rough Guides; **p. 93:** Netfalls - Remy Musser © Shutterstock; **p. 94:** © James Thew/Shutterstock; **p. 96 (bottom, left to right):** Stone Allstock/ Getty; National Geographic Stock; Victor Engle-bert; © Jeff Greenberg / Alamy; **p. 97:** ostill/Shut-terstock; **p. 98:** © Elenathewise/Fotolia; **p. 104:** © ZUMA Wire Service / Alamy; **p. 105 (top):** © robert lerich/Fotolia; **(bottom):** Neale Cousland/ Shutterstock; **p. 109:** © robert lerich/Fotolia; **p. 112:** Christian Vinces/Shutterstock; **p. 113:** © iPics /Fotolia; **p. 114: (tl):** Linda Whitwam © Dorling Kindersley; **(tr):** Dorling Kindersley © Jamie Marshall; **(bottom):** steve estvanik/ Shutterstock.

Online Component

O-52 (tr): Nik Wheeler/Dorling Kindersley; **(tl):** Copyright Todd Powell/ Mira.com; **(bl):** © moodboard / Alamy; **(br):** © Bob Daemmrich / PhotoEdit; **O-53 (left):** Luis Santos/Shutterstock; **(right):** Giuseppe_R/Shutterstock; **O-54:** © Adalberto Rios Szalay/Sexto Sol/Valueline/ Getty Punchstock RF Images Inc.; **O-58:** jocic/ Shutterstock; **O-60:** Kitch Bain/Shutterstock; **O-64:** Christian Draghici/Shutterstock; **O-67 (top):** Suzanne Porter/Dorling Kindersley Ltd.; **(bottom):** Edyta Pawlowska © Shutterstock; **O-68:** Tomasz Pado © Shutterstock.

Capítulo 4

p. 117 (top, clockwise from top): Amra Pasic/ Shutterstock; louhan/iStock; Coast-to-Coast/ iStock; Galyna Andrushko/Shutterstock; ARCHIVO EL TIEMPO/El Tiempo de Colombia/ Newscom; **(bottom):** Fernando Botero, "En familia" (The Family). © Fernando Botero, courtesy of Marlborough Gallery, New York; **(frame):** © rprongjai/Fotolia; **p. 118 (top):** Paloma Lapuerta; **(bottom):** © Monkey Business; **p. 119 (top):** Monkey Business Images/Shutterstock; **p. 120 (top):** © White House Photo / Alamy;

(bottom): © FotoLuminate/Fotolia; **p. 121:** © Lucky Dragon USA/Fotolia; **p. 122:** © M.studio/Fotolia; **p. 123 (left):** © dennisjacobsen/Fotolia; **(right):** © WavebreakmediaMicro/Fotolia; **p. 125:** © Doruk Sikman/Fotolia; © Dimitar Marinov/Fotolia; **p. 126 (top):** © A.Pavlov/Fotolia; **(bottom):** © Monkey Business; **p. 129 (left):** gary yim/Shutterstock; **(right):** Helen Kattai/Shutterstock; **p. 131 (top):** Ivanushka/iStock; **(bottom):** absolut/Shutterstock; **p. 132 (top):** szefei/Shutterstock; **(bottom):** Robert Kneschke/Shutterstock; **p. 134:** AVAVA/Shutterstock; **p. 136:** © Giuseppe_R/Fotolia; **p. 137:** Blaz Kure/Shutterstock; **p. 138:** © OMKAR A.V/Fotolia; **p. 139:** © Orange Line Media; **p. 141 (left):** Golden Pixels LLC © Shutterstock; **(right):** Bill Aron/PhotoEdit; **p. 142:** © Andres Rodriguez/Fotolia; **p. 143:** ra2 studio/Shutterstock;. **p. 144 (tl):** max blain © Shutterstock; **(tc):** © Dr. Ö / Fotolia; **(tr):** RODRIGO ARANGUA/AFP/Getty Images/Newscom.

Online Component

O-69 (t): Paloma Lapuerta; **(bl):** Tony Freeman/PhotoEdit; **(br):** Michael Newman/PhotoEdit; **O-77:** Ivanushka/iStock; **O-83:** HERMANN BREHM/Nature Picture Library; **O-84:** Helen Kattai/Shutterstock.

Capítulo 5

p. 147 (top, left to right): thumb/Shutterstock; Valentyn Volkov/Shutterstock; Tatiana Popova/Shutterstock; fotoon/iStock; digi_guru/iStock; mammamaart/iStock; © Eli Coory/Fotolia; **(bottom):** © Danita Delimont / Alamy; **p. 148 (top):** Nik Wheeler/ Alamy; **(bottom):** Vorm in Beeld/Shutterstock; **p. 149 (top):** © perros19; **(bottom):** Kochneva Tetyana/ Shutterstock; **p. 150:** © Photoroller/Fotolia; **p. 152:** © Natalia Danecker/Fotolia; **p. 154:** Africa Studio/ Shutterstock; **p. 155 (top):** © Ljupco Smokovski /Fotolia; **(bottom):** rj lerich/Shutterstock; **p. 158 (left to right):** nouseforname/Shutterstock; Bruce Ayres/Getty Images Inc. - Stone Allstock; Associated Press; **p. 159:** © A.Pavlov/Fotolia; **p. 161:** © Rafal Kuczowicz/Fotolia; **p. 162 (top):** Tony Freeman/PhotoEdit Inc.; **(bottom):** © MP2/Fotolia; **p. 164:** © Monkey Business/Fotolia; **p. 165:** © Enigmatico/Fotolia; **p. 167:** © cameraman/Fotolia; **p. 168:** © Mat Hayward/Fotolia; **p. 169:** Jaroslaw Kubak/Shutterstock; **p. 171:** © rangizzz/Fotolia; **p. 173:** © Kablonk Micro/Fotolia; **p. 174 (top):** iQoncept/Shutterstock; **(bottom):** Monkey Business Images/ Shutterstock; **p. 176 (tl):** © John Mitchell / Alamy; **(tr):** © foodstock / Alamy; **(cr):** © Mireille Vautier / Alamy.

Online Component

O-85: Nik Wheeler/ Alamy; **O-86:** © alexandre zveiger; **O-89:** Sergey Mironov/ Shutterstock; **O-90:** irabel8/ Shutterstock; b © cynoclub/Fotolia; **O-93 (l):** Tony Freeman/PhotoEdit Inc.; **(c):** © CandyBox Images/Fotolia; **(r):** © erwinova/Fotolia; **O-95:** © Gabriel Blaj/Fotolia; **O-98 (tl):** Associated Press; **(c):** Bettmann/CORBIS; **(b):** ASSOCIATED PRESS.

Capítulo 6

p. 179 (top, left to right): Kimberly White/Reuters/CORBIS; © Gastromedia / Alamy; Jose Enrique Molina/AGE Fotostock America, Inc.; Malcolm Schuyl/Alamy; Mark Cosslett/National Geographic Image Collection; **(bottom):** Simon Bolivar (1783-1830) (chromolitho) by Artist Unknown (pre 20th century). Private Collection / Archives Charmet / Bridgeman Art Library.; **(frame):** © flik47/Fotolia; **p. 180:** Ulrike Welsch/PhotoEdit; **p. 181 (top):** © Morten Heiselberg/Fotolia; **(bottom):** Dorling Kindersley; **p. 182:** snie-girova mariia/Shutterstock; **p. 183:** Africa Studio/Shutterstock; **p. 184 (center):** © Dmitriy Shironosov/Shutterstock; **(bottom):** © Dorling Kindersley; **p. 186:** glamour/Shutterstock; **p. 187:** © pablocalvog/Fotolia; **p. 188:** urfin/Shutterstock; **p. 189:** Tropper2000/Shutterstock; **p. 191 (left to right):** © JKaczka Digital Imaging/Fotolia; HereBeDragons/iStock; Yann Arthus-Bertrand/Bettmann/CORBIS; Juan Silva/Getty Images Inc. - Image Bank; **p. 192:** © T.Tulic/Fotolia; © tashka2000/Fotolia; **p. 193:** © tashka2000/Fotolia; p. 194 © Sergey Andrianov/Fotolia; **p. 195 (c):** MIKE NELSON/EPA/Newscom; **(bl):** PETER WEST - ACE PICTURES/Newscom; **(br):** Splash News/Newscom; p. 196 (left): © Gordana Sermek/Fotolia; (right): © Monika 3 Steps Ahead/Fotolia; p. 197: © Monkey Business/Fotolia; **p. 198 (left, clockwise from top):** Kurhan/ Shutterstock; Conrado/ Shutterstock; Monkey Business Images/Shutterstock; **(right, clockwise from top):** LUIS GENE/AFP/Getty Images; Rob Rich/Newscom; JD3 WENN Photos/Newscom; **p. 199:** © Jürgen Fälchle/Fotolia; **p. 200:** Demetrio Carrasco © Dorling Kindersley; **p. 201 (top):** ETIENjones/Shutterstock; **(bottom):** ancroft/Shutterstock; **p. 203:** Christina Richards/Shutterstock; **(inset):** Digital Genetics/Shutterstock; **p. 204 (tl):** © Ariwasabi/Fotolia; **(br):** © Ariwasabi/Fotolia; **p. 205:** kaarsten/Shutterstock; **p. 206 (tl):** Alexander Chaikin/Shutterstock; **(tr):** Guy Shapira/Shutterstock; **(br):** Jesus Bauza/Shutterstock.

Online Component

O-100 (tl): Rob Crandall/Stock Connection/Glow Images; **(tr):** Ulrike Welsch/PhotoEdit; **(b):** Jeff Greenberg/PhotoEdit; **O-101:** Africa Studio/Shutterstock; **O-103:** crystalfoto/Shutterstock; **O-107:** Fotocrisis/Shutterstock; **O-110:** Kovalchuk Oleksandr/Shutterstock; **O-113:** John Kasawa/Shutterstock; **O-118 (tl):** Michael Stokes/Shutterstock; **(bl):** ASSOCIATED PRESS; **(br):** Javier Galeano / AP Wide World.

Capítulo 7

p. 209 (top, clockwise from top): eye ubiquitous/Robert Harding Picture Library Ltd; Greg Roden/Rough Guides/Dorling Kindersley; © Klaus Heidemann/Fotolia; Nigel Hicks © Dorling Kindersley; Galina Barskaya/Shutterstock; **(bottom):** © SuperStock / Alamy; **(frame):** Studio DMM Photography, Designs & Art/Shutterstock; **p. 210 (top):** Marcos Brindicci/Reuters/Corbis; **(bottom):** Thomas Anderson/Newscom; **p. 211 (top):** Odua Images/Shutterstock; **(bottom):** © Michael Flippo/Fotolia; **p. 212 (left to right):** © David Edsam / Alamy; Adrees Latif /Reuters / CORBIS; © PCN Photography / Alamy; **p. 214:** © Michael Flippo/Fotolia; **p. 215:** © vladischern/Fotolia; **p. 216:** © Innovated Captures/Fotolia; **p. 217 (top):** © photocreo/Fotolia; **(bl):** © jeffrey van daele/Fotolia; **(br):** © Pixelstudio/Fotolia; **p. 218:** © Imagery Majestic/Fotolia; **p. 219:** © yanlev/Fotolia; **p. 220 (top):** © Image Source IS2/Fotolia; **(center):** Alexander Chaikin/Shutterstock; **(bottom):** mama_mia/Shutterstock; **p. 222:** © Monkey Business/Fotolia; **p. 223:** mangostock/Shutterstock; **p. 224:** © Maridav/Fotolia; **p. 225:** © .shock /Fotolia; **p. 226:** bikeriderlondon/Shutterstock; **p. 227:** PHILETDOM /Fotolia; **p. 228:** © bodo011/Fotolia; **p. 229:** © solovyova/Fotolia; **p. 230:** Allgusak/Shutterstock; **p. 232 (top):** © rruss/Fotolia; **(center):** © Sveta/Fotolia; **(bottom):** © Rob Bouwman/Fotolia; **p. 234:** © fimg/Fotolia; **p. 235 (left to right):** kycstudio/iStock; Eddie Lawrence © Dorling Kindersley; MoniqueRodriguez/iStock; **p. 236 (top):** © István Hájas/Fotolia; **(center):** © István Hájas/Fotolia; **(bottom):** © István Hájas/Fotolia; **p. 237 (top):** © pressmaster/Fotolia; **(center):** valzan/Shutterstock; **p. 238 (tl):** Greg Roden/Rough Guides/Dorling Kindersley; **(tr):** © Leonardo Tumonis/Fotolia; **(br):** Nigel Hicks © Dorling Kindersley.

Online Component

O-120 (top): Marcos Brindicci/Reuters/Corbis; **(center):** Bill Bachmann/PhotoEdit; **(bottom):** © Daily Mail/Rex / Alamy; **O-125:** © karandaev/Fotolia; **O-126:** © auremar/Fotolia; **O-128:** © ChrisP/Fotolia; **O-130:** .shock/Shutterstock; **O-132:** © Elnur/Fotolia; **O-135 (tl):** © Stuart Cohen/The Image Works; **(tr):** © Dmitry Pichugin/Fotolia; **(b):** Nigel Hicks © Dorling Kindersley.

Capítulo 8

p. 241 (top, top to bottom): Ken Welsh/AGE Fotostock America, Inc.; stevenallan/iStock; trekholidays/iStock; Kinetic Imagery/Shutterstock; Nathalie Speliers Ufermann/Shutterstock; **(bottom):** Frida Kahlo, "Self-Portrait at the Border Between Mexico and the United States". 1932. Museo Nacional de Arte Moderno, © 2001 Banco de Mexico Diego Rivera & Frida Kahlo Museums Trust/Artists Rights Society (ARS), NY. Av. Cinco de Mayo No. 2, Col. Centro, Del. Cuauhtemoc 06059, Mexico, D.F. Reproduction authorized by the Instituto Nacional de Bellas Artes y Literatura. © Christie's Images / CORBIS All Rights Reserved; **(frame):** Studio DMM Photography, Designs & Art/Shutterstock; **p. 242:** Superstock/Art Life Images; **p. 243 (top):** Tony Souter © Dorling Kindersley; **(center):** David Mercado/Sygma/CORBIS; **(bl):** © Fabienne Fossez / Alamy; **(br):** © Jerome Dancette/Fotolia; **p. 244:** Demetrio Carrasco © Dorling Kindersley; **p. 246 (top):** Anneka; **(bottom):** © David Yong-Wolff / PhotoEdit; **p. 247 (top):** Sandra van der Steen/Shutterstock; **(bottom):** Eduardo Rivero/Shutterstock; **p. 248:** © diego cervo/Fotolia; **p. 249:** Demetrio Carrasco © Dorling Kindersley; **p. 250:** Tomislav Forgo/Shutterstock, **p. 251:** © Monkey Business/Fotolia; **p. 253:** © auremar/Fotolia; **p. 254:** oliveromg/Shutterstock; **p. 255:** Annette Shaff/Shutterstock; **p. 256:** La Vieja Sirena/Shutterstock; **p. 257 (left to right):** Dmitri-Maruta/Shutterstock; Juriah Mosin/Shutterstock; Anetlanda/Shutterstock; **p. 258:** © chicagophot/Fotolia; **p. 259 (top):** ©2008 Popescu Mario-Cezar. All rights reserved.; **(bottom):** © ALCE/Fotolia, **p. 260 (top, left to right):** © John Mitchell / Alamy; © Fernando Martínez/Fotolia; **(bottom, left to right):** © epa european press-photo agency b.v. / Alamy; PETER KNEFFEL/EPA/Newscom; **p. 261:** Stephen Coburn/Shutterstock; **p. 262:** © Andres Rodriguez/Fotolia; **p. 265:** Clara Gonzalez/Shutterstock; **p. 266:** Deklofenak/Shutterstock; **p. 267:** © lunamarina/Fotolia; **p. 268:** © Monkey Business/Fotolia; **p. 270 (tr):** Mireille Vautier/Alamy; **(cl):** Holbox/Shutterstock; **(b):** jupeart/Shutterstock; **p. 271:** Alberto Zornetta/Shutterstock; **p. 272 (tl):** Peter Wilson © Dorling Kindersley; **(tr):** © Bryan Busovicki/Fotolia; **(br):** Dan Bannister © Rough Guides.

Online Component

O-137 (tr): © Paul Conklin / PhotoEdit; **(tl):** Superstock/Art Life Images; **(b):** David Mercado/Sygma/CORBIS; **O-138 (tl):** © Jerome

Dancette/Fotolia; **(tr):** Fabienne Fossez/Alamy; **(b):** Larry Mangino/The Image Works; **O-140:** © diego cervo/Fotolia; **O-142:** Monkey Business Images/Shutterstock; **O-143:** YanLev/Shutterstock; **O-149:** © MNStudio/Fotolia; **O-152 (top):** Anne Lewis/Alamy; **(bottom):** © Danny Lehman / Bettmann / CORBIS; **(b):** Franck Boston/Fotolia.

Capítulo 9

p. 275 (top, clockwise from top): kschrei/Shutterstock; Linda Whitwam © Dorling Kindersley; © robert lerich/Fotolia; Tim Draper/Rough Guides/Dorling Kindersley; Kim Seidl/Shutterstock; **(bottom):** © Jamie Marshall; **p. 276:** Pedro Rafael Gonzales Chavajay, "Los Baneros Mayas (Maya Banana Workers", 2001, 11" x 9". Arte Maya Tz'utuhil; **p. 277 (top):** Lynn Watson © Shutterstock; **(bottom, left to right):** Pedro Rafael Gonzales Chavajay, "Los Baneros Mayas (Maya Banana Workers), 2001, 11" x 9". Arte Maya Tz'utuhil; Pedro Rafael Gonzales Chavajay, "Los Baneros Mayas (Maya Banana Workers", 2001, 11" x 9". Arte Maya Tz'utuhil; Pedro Rafael Gonzales Chavajay, "Los Baneros Mayas (Maya Banana Workers", 2001, 11" x 9". Arte Maya Tz'utuhil; **p. 278 (top):** © Alan Bolesta/Index Stock Imagery/Getty; **(bottom):** FERNANDO BLANCO CALZADA © Shutterstock; **p. 279 (top):** T-Design/Shutterstock; (bottom) © Andres Rodriguez/Fotolia; **p. 280:** Monkey Business Images © Shutterstock; **p. 281:** Liudmila P. Sundikova © Shutterstock; **p. 282 (top):** © Dave Rock/Shutterstock; **(bottom):** © WavebreakmediaMicro/Fotolia; **p. 283:** wavebreakmedia/Shutterstock; **p. 284:** © snowwhiteimages/Fotolia; **p. 286:** nokhoog © Shutterstock; **p. 287:** Raymond Gregory/Shutterstock; **p. 288:** © Andres Rodriguez/Fotolia; **p. 289 (top):** corepics © Shutterstock; **(bottom):** MSPhotographic/Shutterstock; **p. 290:** MO:SES/Shutterstock; **p. 292:** © Lasse Kristensen/Fotolia; **p. 293:** © Dmytro Titov/Fotolia; **p. 294:** Dorling Kindersley © Jamie Marshall; **p. 295 (top):** Rough Guides Dorling Kindersley; **(bottom):** © rangizzz/Fotolia; **p. 296 (top):** Yuri Arcurs/Shutterstock; **(bottom):** © Tibor Bognar / Alamy; **p. 297 (left):** © ulucceylani/Fotolia; **(right):** © rvlsoft/Fotolia; **p. 298:** © goodluz/Fotolia; **p. 300:** © Robert Harding Picture Library Ltd / Alamy; **p. 301:** dwphotos/Shutterstock; **p. 302:** A. Ramey/PhotoEdit; **p. 304 (tl):** Rough Guides Dorling Kindersley; **(tr):** © J.Enrique Molina / Alamy; **(br):** Rough Guides Dorling Kindersley.

Online Component

O-155 (tl): Pedro Rafael Gonzales Chavajay, "Los Baneros Mayas (Maya Banana Workers", 2001, 11" x 9". Arte Maya Tz'utuhil; **(tr):** Pedro Rafael Gonzales Chavajay, "Los Baneros Mayas (Maya Banana Workers", 2001, 11" x 9". Arte Maya Tz'utuhil; **(bl):** Pedro Rafael Gonzales Chavajay, "Los Baneros Mayas (Maya Banana Workers", 2001, 11" x 9". Arte Maya Tz'utuhil; **(br):** Pedro Rafael Gonzales Chavajay, "Los Baneros Mayas (Maya Banana Workers", 2001, 11" x 9". Arte Maya Tz'utuhil; **O-156 (top):** © Science Photo Library / Alamy; **(cl):** © Alan Bolesta/Index Stock Imagery/Getty; **(c):** Rob Crandall/The Image Works; **(cr):** Ed Lallo; **(bl):** Tsian © Shutterstock; **(bc):** © Mugs/Fotolia; **(br):** wavebreakmedia ltd/Shutterstock; **O-159:** Liudmila P. Sundikova © Shutterstock; **O-171 (tl):** Daniel Loncarevic © Shutterstock; **(bl):** © Tomas Hajek/Fotolia; **O-172:** Richard Lord Enterprises.

Capítulo 10

p. 307 (top, clockwise from top): Rob Reichenfeld © Dorling Kindersley; © Jennifer Elizabeth/Fotolia; © Steve100/Fotolia; © Andrew Linscott / Alamy; © Jennifer Elizabeth/Fotolia; **(bottom):** Museo de America, Madrid, Spain/The Bridgeman Art Library; **p. 308 (top and center):** © Owen Franken / CORBIS; **(bottom, left to right):** © Janice Hazeldine / Alamy; David R. Frazier Photolibrary, Inc.; Lee Peterson; © Jeremy Horner/CORBIS; **p. 309 (tr):** Wendy Slocum/Shutterstock; **(cr):** kearia/ Shutterstock; **(cl):** Comugnero Silvana/ Fotolia; **(b):** L_amica/Shutterstock; **p. 311:** © Oleg Zhukov/Fotolia; **p. 312:** © Mihai Simonia/Fotolia; **p. 313 (top):** © AZP Worldwide/Fotolia; **(bottom):** © Photofollies/Fotolia; **p. 314:** Lucia Pitter/Shutterstock; **p. 315 (top):** lindilu/ Shutterstock; **(center):** Fedorov Oleksiy/ Shutterstock; **(bottom):** Skyline/Shutterstock; **p. 316 (top):** © Gordan Gledec/Fotolia; **(bl):** © lily/Fotolia; **(br):** © paul_brighton/Fotolia; **p. 318:** Vulkanette © Shutterstock; **p. 319 (top):** © Allstar Picture Library / Alamy; **(bottom):** © Renee Jansoa/Fotolia; **p. 320:** © Sergey Peterman/Fotolia; **p. 321:** © MSPhotographic/Fotolia; **p. 322:** Olga Danylenko/ Shutterstock; **p. 323:** © John Mitchell / Alamy; **p. 324:** © redav/Fotolia; **p. 325:** Greg Roden © Rough Guides; **p. 326 (top):** Greg Roden © Rough Guides; **(bottom):** Arun Roisri © Shutterstock; **p. 327 (top):** auremar/ Fotolia; **(bottom):** Maridav/ Fotolia; **p. 328:** berna namoglu/ Shutterstock; **p. 329:** © SOMATUSCANI /Fotolia; **p. 330 (top):** Nitr/ Shutterstock; **(bottom):** © viperagp/Fotolia; **p. 332:** Ildi Papp / Shutterstock; **p. 333 (left):** Christian Vinces/Shutterstock; **(right):** © julenochek/Fotolia; **p. 334 (top):** Elena Rostunova/ Fotolia; **(bl):** ep stock/ Fotolia; **(br):** MAErtek/ Fotolia; **p. 335:** pressmaster/ Fotolia; **p. 336 (tl):** © kertis/Fotolia; **(tr):** © laurent33/Fotolia; **(br):** © robert lerich/Fotolia.

Online Component

O-174 (top): © Owen Franken / CORBIS; **(center):** © Janice Hazeldine / Alamy; **(bottom):** David R. Frazier Photolibrary, Inc.; **O-175 (top):** Lee Peterson; **(bottom):** © Jeremy Horner/CORBIS; **O-176:** Gleb Semenjuk/ Fotolia; **p. 181 (top):** kevers/ Fotolia; **(bottom):** valery121283/Fotolia; **O-184:** © Jake Hellbach/Fotolia; **O-187:** Andrzej Tokarski/ Fotolia; **O-189:** Alexander Raths/ Fotolia; **O-190:** belahoche/ Fotolia; **O-191 (top):** Mark Conlin / Alamy; **(bottom):** Jean-Leo Dugast/Corbis; **O-192:** Getty Images.

Capítulo 11

p. 339 (top, left to right): Alex James Bramwell/ Shutterstock; osov/ Shutterstock; Elias H. Debbas II/ Shutterstock; Rob Huntley/ Shutterstock; Joseph/ Shutterstock; Nicholas Pitt/Alamy; **(center):** Mireille Vautie/ Alamy; **p. 340 (top):** Andresr/Shutterstock; **(bottom):** millaf/ Fotolia; **p. 341 (top):** António Duarte/ Fotolia; **(center):** © chiakto/Fotolia; **(bottom):** JJAVA/ Fotolia; **p. 342:** Image Source IS2/ Fotolia; **p. 343 (left):** Luis Carlos Jiménez/ Fotolia; **(right):** johny007pan/ Fotolia; **p. 344 (top):** martanfoto/ Fotolia; **(bottom):** U.P.images/ Fotolia; **p. 345:** Warren Goldswain/ Fotolia; **p. 347:** © lenets_tan/Fotolia; **p. 348:** cstyle/ Fotolia; **p. 349:** Anterovium/ Fotolia; **p. 350:** Kimberly Reinick/ Fotolia; **p. 351(top):** diego cervo/ Fotolia; **(bottom):** Alx/ Fotolia; **p. 352:** Hemis/

Alamy; **p. 353:** Franck Boston/ Fotolia; **p. 354 (top):** Paul Moore/ Fotolia; **(bottom):** William Shaw/ Dorling Kindersley; **p. 355:** Viorel Sima/ Fotolia; **p. 356 (top):** Linda Whitwam/ Dorling Kindersley; **(bottom):** lenets_tan/ Fotolia; **p. 357 (top):** anat_tikker/ Fotolia; **(bottom):** Alexander Raths/ Fotolia; **p. 358:** jeff gynane/ Fotolia; **p. 359:** © Ljupco Smokovski/Fotolia; **p. 360:** Kimberly Reinick/ Fotolia; **p. 361:** James Thew/ Fotolia; **p. 362:** angellodeco/ Fotolia; **p. 363:** BrazilPhotos.com / Alamy; **p. 364:** pablocalvog/ Fotolia; **p. 365:** © rangizzz/Fotolia; **p. 366 (left):** Tony Souter/ Dorling Kindersley; **(center):** Dorling Kindersley/ Lucio Rossi; **(right):** ARENA Creative/ Shutterstock.

Online Component

O-193 (tr): Demetrio Carrasco/ Dorling Kindersley; **(cl):** Andresr/ Shutterstock; **(cr):** Nigel Hicks/ Dorling Kindersley; **(bl):** Dorothy Alexander/ Alamy; **O-199:** duckman76/ Fotolia; **O-201:** drhanson/ Fotolia; **O-202 (top):** Linda Whitwam/ Dorling Kindersley; **(bottom):** Galina Barskaya/ Fotolia; **O-204:** wolfelarry/ Fotolia; **O-205 (top):** Julio Etchart/ Alamy; **(bottom):** Dorling Kindersley/ Lucio Rossi; **O-206:** ASSOCIATED PRESS.

Capítulo 12

p. 369 (top, left to right): Brandon Holmes/ Shutterstock; Jon Spaull/ Dorling Kindersley; Jim Lipschutz/ Shutterstock; rj lerich/ Shutterstock; Marcus/ Fotolia; **(bottom):** Kevin Schafer / Alamy; **p. 370:** Jose Luis Stephens/ Alamy; **p. 371 (top):** Andres Rodriguez/ Fotolia; (bottom): Natalia Bratslavsky/ Shutterstock; **p. 372:** Tracy Kahn/ Corbis Super RF / Alamy; **p. 373 (top):** Frank Gärtner/ Fotolia; **(center):** Andriy Petrenko/ Fotolia; **(bottom):** Joao Virissimo/ Shutterstock; **p. 374:** aberenyi/ Fotolia; **p. 375 (top):** Misha/ Fotolia; **(center):** Dixon Hamby/ Alamy; **(bottom):** michaeljung/ Fotolia; **p. 376:** fotomatrix/ Fotolia; **p. 377:** Maridav/ Fotolia; **p. 378:** swisshippo/ Fotolia; **p. 379 (top):** kebox/ Fotolia; **(bottom):** platynus/ Fotolia; **p. 380 (top):** fergregory/ Fotolia; **(bottom):** Igor Dutina/ Fotolia; **p. 381 (top):** Jgz/ Fotolia; **(bottom):** Serghei Velusceac/ Fotolia; **p. 382 (top):** James Brunker/ Dorling Kindersley; **(bottom):** Matthias Koch/ Fotolia; **p. 383:** TheThirdMan/ Fotolia; **p. 384:** Michael Fritzen/ Fotolia; **p. 385 (top):** amelie/ Fotolia; **(bottom):** Kzenon/ Fotolia; **p. 386:** Andres Rodriguez/ Fotolia; **p. 387 (top):** Allen Furmanski/ Shutterstock; **(bottom):** beboy/ Shutterstock; **p. 388 (tl):** sorincolac/ Fotolia; **(tr):** Luis M. Seco/ Shutterstock; **(cl):** Six Drive/ Fotolia; **(cr):** rj lerich/ Shutterstock; **(b):** Chris Forsey/ Dorling Kindersley; **p. 389:** Jgz/ Fotolia; **p. 390:** Michele Molinari/ Alamy; **p. 392:** Csaba Peterdi/ Fotolia; **p. 395:** Radius Images/ Alamy; **p. 396 (left):** © Jose Angel Murillo / Alamy; **(right):** Jon Spaull © Dorling Kindersley.

Online Component

O-209 (tl): Jose Luis Stephens/ Alamy; **(tr):** Prisma Archivo/ Alamy; **(b):** formiktopus/ Shutterstock; **O-211:** Igor Mojzes/ Fotolia; **O-212:** Tracy Kahn/ Corbis Super RF / Alamy; **O-216:** kebox/ Fotolia; **O-220:** bepsphoto/ Fotolia; **O-221:** Allen Furmanski/ Shutterstock; **O-223:** Courtesy Everett Collection/ Alamy.

Index

Note: This index shows chapter numbers rather than page numbers. "P" refers to the Preliminary chapter.

R

recoger
- imperative, 9
- present subjunctive, 11

reflexive pronouns, 4, 7

reflexive verbs, 4, 7
- preterit, 6

regalar, 6

reír, 7

repetir
- imperative, 9
- present indicative, 4

romper, 7, 10

S

saber
- future, 10
- imperative, 9
- past tenses, 9
- present indicative, 3
- present subjunctive, 11
- preterit, 7
- uses of, 7

sacar
- imperative, 9
- present subjunctive, 11
- preterit, 6

salir, 3
- future, 10
- imperative, 10
- present subjunctive, 11

schools, 1

se constructions, 10

seguir
- imperative, 9
- present indicative, 4
- present subjunctive, 11

sentir(se), 7

ser
- with adjectives, 2
- imperative, 9, 10
- imperfect, 8
- present indicative, P, 2
- present subjunctive, 11
- preterit, 6
- uses of, 2, 6

servir, 4
- preterit, 7

sin, 7

sobre, 7

stem-changing verbs
- **e** to **i,** 4
- **e** to **ie,** 4
- **o** to **ue,** 4
- present indicative, 4
- present participles of, 5
- preterit, 6, 7

street names, P

subir, 10

subjunctive. *See also* present subjunctive

with expressions of doubt, 12
with expressions of emotion, 11
indicative compared, 12

suffixes, 8

superlative, 8

T

tener
- expressions with, 5
- future, 10
- imperative, 10
- present indicative, 4
- present subjunctive, 11
- preterit, 7

tener que + infinitive, 4

time, P, 2
- expressions that denote, P, 1, 3, 6, 8
- **hace,** 4, 7

titles, 1

traducir, 7

traer, 3
- present subjunctive, 11
- preterit, 7

tu, P

tú, P, 2

V

vender, 6

venir
- future, 10
- imperative, 10
- present indicative, 4
- present subjunctive, 11
- preterit, 7

ver, 10
- imperfect, 8
- present indicative, 1
- present subjunctive, 11

verb forms. *See* **-ar** verbs; **-er** verbs; **-ir** verbs; irregular verbs; reciprocal verbs; reflexive verbs; *See specific verbs*; spelling-change verbs; stem-changing verbs

vestir(se), 4

vivir
- future, 10
- imperfect, 8
- present indicative, 1
- present subjunctive, 11
- preterit, 6

vocabulary
- academic life, 1
- accessories, 6
- airport, 12
- appliances, 5
- car travel, 12
- celebrations, 8
- chores, 5
- classroom, P
- clothing, 6
- communication, 3
- computers, 1
- courses, 1
- drinks, 3
- electronics, 5
- entertainment, 3
- family, 4
- food, 1, 3, 10
- friends, 2
- fruit, 10
- furnishings, 5
- furniture, 5
- health, 11
- holidays, 8
- home life, 5
- household activities, 5
- housing, 5
- kitchen, 5
- leisure activities, 3
- lodging, 12
- meat, 10
- medical care, 11
- music, 8
- nature, 7
- occupations, 9
- parts of the body, 2, 6, 11
- professions, 9, 11
- recipes, 10
- restaurants, 3
- schools, 1
- seafood, 10
- seasonings, 10
- seasons, 6, 7
- shopping, 6
- spices, 10
- sports, 7
- students, 1
- table settings, 10
- trades, 9
- traditions, 8
- transportation, 12
- travel, 12
- universities, 1
- vegetables, 10
- weather, 7
- work, 9
- workplaces, 9

volver, 10
- present indicative, 4
- present subjunctive, 11
- preterit, 6

W

weather, P, 7
- expressions that denote, 8

week, days of, P

Y

y, 2, 81

ESTADOS

UNIDOS

Golfo de
México

Mexicali
Tijuana
Nogales
Ciudad
Juárez

Río Bravo del Norte

Río Grande

Nuevo Laredo

Monterrey

SIERRA MADRE OCCIDENTAL

SIERRA MADRE ORIENTAL

Golfo de California

Baja California

MÉXICO

Guadalajara

Comala

México, D.F.
✪

Veracruz

Mérida

*Península
de
Yucatán*

Taxco

Palenque
Belice
✪ Belmopan
BELICE

Acapulco

Oaxaca

Tikal

Copán

GUATEMALA

Quetzaltenango

Ciudad de Guatemala ✪

Volcán Izalco ▲ ✪ San
Salvador

**EL
SALVADOR**

OCÉANO

PACÍFICO

✪	Capital
•	Otras ciudades
▲	Volcán
⁙	Ruinas

*Islas
Galápagos
(Ec.)*

México, América Central y el Caribe

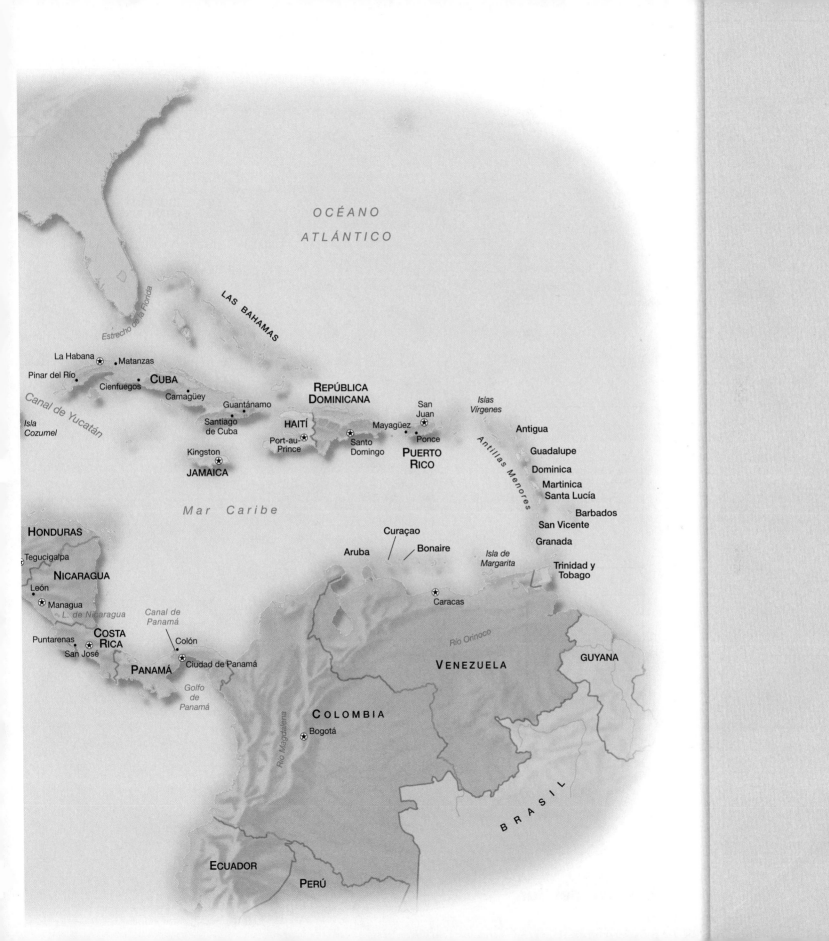

OCÉANO
ATLÁNTICO

LAS BAHAMAS

Estrecho de la Florida

La Habana ⊛ • Matanzas
Pinar del Río •
Cienfuegos • • **CUBA**
Camagüey •
Canal de Yucatán
Guantánamo •
Isla
Cozumel
Santiago
de Cuba •
Kingston ⊛
JAMAICA

**REPÚBLICA
DOMINICANA**

HAITÍ
Port-au- ⊛
Prince
Santo
Domingo

San
Juan
Mayagüez • ⊛
• Ponce
**PUERTO
RICO**

Islas
Vírgenes

Antigua

Guadalupe

Dominica

Martinica
Santa Lucía

Antillas Menores

Barbados
San Vicente

Granada

Mar Caribe

Curaçao
Aruba
Bonaire

Isla de
Margarita

Trinidad y
Tobago

HONDURAS
• Tegucigalpa

NICARAGUA
León •
⊛ • Managua
L. de Nicaragua

Canal de
Panamá

Puntarenas • **COSTA
RICA** ⊛
San José •
Colón •
PANAMÁ
⊛
Ciudad de Panamá

Golfo
de
Panamá

Caracas ⊛

Río Orinoco

VENEZUELA

GUYANA

Río Magdalena

COLOMBIA
⊛ Bogotá

BRASIL

ECUADOR

PERÚ

América del Sur